CW01091581

Book in Honor of Augustus
(*Liber ad Honorem Augusti*)

MEDIEVAL AND RENAISSANCE
TEXTS AND STUDIES
VOLUME 398

Book in Honor of Augustus

(*Liber ad Honorem Augusti*)

by

Pietro da Eboli

With English translation by

Gwenyth Hood

ACMRS

(Arizona Center for Medieval and Renaissance Studies)
Tempe, Arizona
2012

Published by ACMRS (Arizona Center for Medieval and Renaissance Studies)
Tempe, Arizona
© 2012 Arizona Board of Regents for Arizona State University.

Library of Congress Cataloging-in-Publication Data

Petrus, de Ebulo, fl. 1196.
  Book in honor of Augustus = (Liber ad honorem Augusti) / by Pietro da Eboli;
with English translation by Gwenyth Hood.
    pages. cm. -- (Medieval and renaissance texts and studies ; volume 398)
  Text in Latin and English.
  ISBN 978-0-86698-446-1 (alkaline paper)
  1. Henry VI, Holy Roman Emperor, 1165-1197--Poetry. 2. Constance,
Empress, consort of Henry VI, Holy Roman Emperor, 1154-1198--Poetry.
I. Hood, Gwenyth. II. Petrus, de Ebulo, fl. 1196. Liber ad honorem Augusti.
English. 2011. III. Petrus, de Ebulo, fl. 1196. Liber ad honorem Augusti. Latin.
2011. IV. Title. V. Title: Liber ad honorem Augusti. VI. Series: Medieval &
Renaissance Texts & Studies (Series) ; v. 398.
  PA8395.P4L513 2011
  871'.03--dc23
                                                          2011047952

Illustrations:
The illustrations througout this translation are reproduced from Petrus de Ebulo,
Liber ad honorem Augusti, sive de rebus Siculis, Burgerbibliothek Bern Cod. 120.II
with which the copyright remains.

∞
This book is made to last. It is set in Adobe Caslon Pro,
smyth-sewn and printed on acid-free paper to library specifications.
Printed in the United States of America

TABLE OF CONTENTS

Introduction:
The Story and its Interest

In 1746, Samuel Engel published, at Basel, an illustrated Latin poem with a long title: *Petri d'Ebulo Carmen de Motibus Siculis, et rebus inter Henricum VI Romano-rum Imperatorem et Tancredum seculo XII gestis* (*Peter of Eboli's Song of the Sicilian Troubles, and of the Deeds Done Between Henry VI, Emperor of the Romans, and Tancred, in the Twelfth Century*). His edition was based on a manuscript owned by the Bürgerbibliothek of Bern, of which he was director.[1] We now know that this manuscript is the only surviving copy of this twelfth-century work, prob-ably produced under the direct supervision of the poet, who gives his name in a colophon. He wrote the book, he says, "in honor of Augustus," that is, in honor of the Holy Roman Emperor, Henry VI of Hohenstaufen, whose conquest of the Norman kingdom of Sicily is celebrated in the work. From this colophon is drawn the title by which the poem is generally known today, *Liber ad honorem Augusti (Book in Honor of Augustus)*. This title was first used in Eduard Winkel-mann's 1874 edition.[2] Several more editions followed, notably those of Ettore Rota (1904)[3] and G. B. Siragusa (1906).[4] In 1994, Theo Kölzer, Marlis Stähli, and others brought out their near-facsimile edition with a German translation by Gereon Becht-Jördens, while Francesco De Rosa published his full-sized facsim-ile edition in 2001.[5] Previous to Winkelmann, Giuseppe Del Re had published

---

[1] Marlis Stähli, "Petrus de Ebulos 'Unvollendete'—Eine Handschrift mit Rätseln," in *Petrus de Ebulo: Liber ad Honorem Augusti, sive de rebus Siculis: Codex 120 II der Bürger-bibliothek Bern*, ed. Theo Kölzer, eadem et al. (Sigmaringen: Jan Thorbecke, 1994), 247–274, here 270.

[2] Eduard Winkelmann, ed., *Des Magisters Petrus de Ebulo liber ad honorem Augusti* (Leipzig: Duncker u. Humblot, 1874).

[3] Ettore Rota, ed., *Petri Ansolini de Ebulo de rebus Siculis carmen*. RIS n.s. 31/1. (Cit-tà di Castello: Lapis, 1904).

[4] G. B. Siragusa, *Liber ad Honorem Augusti di Pietro da Eboli, secondo il Cod. 120 della Biblioteca Civica di Berna: Testo con una tavola illustrativa* (Rome: Istituto Storico Italiana, 1906). Unless otherwise stated, citations of Siragusa are citations to this edition.

[5] Francesco De Rosa, *Pietro da Eboli: Liber ad Honorem Augusti* [facsimile] (Cassino: F. Ciolfi, 2001).

an edition[6] (in 1845), along with an Italian translation by Emmanuele Rocco, using Engel's original title. These editions and their readers testify to the perennial fascination inspired by the poem. The fascination springs from many sources. Though the events it recounts are contained within the space of a few short years, those were significant years, and the events had wide-ranging implications for history and literature.

Pietro's poem, vivid in places, highly allusive and symbolic in others, is intriguing for its own sake. The fifty-three pages of miniatures, too, give a wealth of images, some as the eye would have seen them in the twelfth century, others rather general or symbolic but still offering insight about the way the twelfth-century mind perceived the world and its people. Pictures include people in their characteristic dress—the empress and emperor, kings, queens, nobles, knights, ladies, notaries, physicians and attendants, messengers, midwives, and servants. They document court ceremonies, overland journeys, voyages, battles, councils, parleys, conspiracies, and trials. Amateur and professional historians study them for what they have to say about the clothing, armor, and heraldry of the time. Up until now, however, no translation of the whole work has been made available to readers of English. This translation is an attempt to remedy this lack.

Modern historians would say that the story begins with a crisis. King William II, Norman king of Sicily, dies childless in 1189. William, though he has left no written testament, has previously recognized his paternal aunt, Constance, and her husband, Henry VI of Hohenstaufen, as his legitimate successors. His nobles and officials had been required to swear loyalty to them as such. Accordingly, upon his death, many nobles and clerics send messengers to Henry and Constance, inviting them to claim their new realm. However, a faction led by William's vice-chancellor, the notary Matthew (now traditionally called "Matthew of Ajello," after the county Tancred conferred on one of his sons),[7] decides to elect another king in preference to Henry, and chooses Tancred, count of Lecce. Tancred is an illegitimate grandson of Roger II, William II's grandfather. At this time, Tancred already has two sons, besides some daughters, by his countess, Sibylla. Matthew, the vice-chancellor, instructs him to bring the boys when he comes to receive his crown (ll. 144–145), setting before the eyes of the

---

[6] Giuseppe Del Re, *De Tumulti Avvenuti in Sicilia e de' Fatti Operati nel XII Secolo tra Arrigo VI, Imperatore de' Romani e Tancredi: Carme di Pietro d'Eboli*, in *Cronisti e Scrittori Sincroni della Dominazione Normanna nel Regno di Puglia e Sicilia*, vol. 1 (Naples: Giannini, 1845), 401–53.

[7] This family had no surname in the modern sense. However, the brother of Nicholas, Richard, was made the count of Ajello by Tancred. Therefore, scholars took to applying the designation "of Ajello" to each known member of the family, starting with Matthew, the father of Nicholas and Richard, although they are not named that way in contemporary sources. Because the name is convenient and well established in the scholarship, I also use it here and in the biographical sketches.

people not only their king but the next generation of the dynasty. Henry and Constance, on the other hand, are still childless after nearly four years of marriage, though Pietro withholds mention of this point until it is remedied with the birth of the future Frederick II, at the time of Henry's successful conquest in 1194 (ll. 1363–1396).

Childless or not, Henry of Hohenstaufen does not choose to suffer Tancred's usurpation in silence. Though delayed at first by his father's crusade and then the latter's death (which Pietro describes briefly but gloriously), Henry soon receives his imperial coronation at Rome (in April 1191) and immediately sets out to win Sicily. He besieges Naples, but Tancred resorts to bribery to slow down the action of Henry's supposed allies (ll. 355, 497–513). Meanwhile, an epidemic strikes the German forces, obliging Henry, himself so ill that his life is in danger, to raise the siege suddenly and retreat northward (ll. 514–521). Seizing the opportunity, Archbishop Nicholas of nearby Salerno, son of Tancred's original king-maker Matthew (once William II's vice-chancellor, but now Tancred's chancellor), instigates the citizens to attack the empress at Salerno, before she can rejoin her husband. Unable to persuade the Salernitans to withdraw, Constance surrenders herself to a certain noble, Elias of Gesualdo, kinsman both to herself and Tancred, who arrives at this point. Before departing, she requires the citizens to swear that her soldiers may depart safely (ll. 687–692). She is taken aboard a ship and brought to Messina and to Tancred, with whom she has a chilly interview in which each reproaches the other.

Meanwhile, in the ensuing days and weeks, Henry's commanders in nearby Capua and the surrounding region fight with desperate courage against attacks from Tancred's brother-in-law, Count Richard of Acerra, as they wait to hear what has become of the emperor and empress.

As for Constance, Tancred at first sends her to Palermo and Queen Sibylla, who complains that the responsibility is too dangerous and troublesome. Tancred then instructs her to put the whole matter into the hands of Matthew "of Ajello," his chancellor, who recommends that the empress be sent to the isolated fortress of San Salvatore near Naples (in modern times called the Castel dell'Ovo). This is done, but Constance is soon released at the demand of Pope Celestine III, who tells Tancred that the emperor's great anger should be feared, that he is already angry, and that Constance's pacifying influence is needed (ll. 861–1038).

Then (late December 1192), King Richard of England, who had become Tancred's ally on his way to the crusade, suffers shipwreck while returning from it. Sneaking across the emperor's realms in disguise, he is captured and handed over to Henry. Before the Imperial senate [*cesareum . . . senatum*] (more usually called the Diet of the German princes), Henry greets him as the murderer of a kinsman, and also points out that during Richard's recent visit to Sicily, he had first threatened Tancred and then received a great deal of money from him, supposedly as the dowry owed to his sister (Joanna Plantagenet, daughter of Henry II of England and widow of William II of Sicily). King Richard spiritedly denies the murder charge (which relates to Conrad of Montferrat) and offers to defend himself in single combat against any champion willing to accuse him. As for the other matters, he admits his fault and throws himself on Henry's mercy. At this, the emperor decides to let him go free; Pietro insists that ransom was not Henry's motive, while implying that a thousand talents [*mille talenta*] was nevertheless paid (ll. 1047–1088).

Soon Henry undertakes his second expedition against the kingdom of Sicily. Unfortunately, at this point in the narrative, pages start to go missing. Somewhere in the lacunae, Tancred dies, presumably a natural death, as do his eldest son Roger and his invaluable chancellor Matthew, although these points are not mentioned in the surviving portions of the poem. Salerno is sacked, although the poem shows only the prelude and the aftermath (ll. 1151–1187). In the surviving verses, Tancred's widow, Sibylla, is left to face Henry VI's invasion, with her three daughters and her minor son, who has been crowned William III. As the emperor approaches Palermo, its citizens send an embassy to invite his peaceful entrance (ll. 1227–1256). Sibylla, realizing that her situation is hopeless, approaches Henry and begs pardon for herself and her son, which the emperor grants (ll. 1257–1303). He then takes triumphant possession of the palace.

However, neither Archbishop Nicholas nor Sibylla is content. They plot to kill the emperor. Unfortunately the verses which presumably describe their plans have been lost. Illustrations make it clear that a monkish informer reveals the secret and brings or helps the emperor obtain a secret letter in which the names of all the conspirators are written. Everyone involved is arrested, including (as the illustrations clearly show) Tancred's minor son, the former King William III. But showing characteristic clemency, as the poet explains, Henry does nothing worse than hold them as prisoners (ll. 1329–1362).

Then news comes that the empress Constance has given birth to a son. Pietro joyously celebrates the boy's name, Frederick Roger, drawn from the child's two grandfathers. He predicts future peace, prosperity, and glory for the boy and the empire he will rule, in terms that recall biblical prophecy and classical mythology (ll. 1363–1428).

The rest of the poem celebrates Henry VI's achievements and his government. Pietro creates a mythological setting in which Henry is nursed and educated by *Sapientia*, Divine Wisdom herself, assisted by the Virtues and the Liberal Arts, to become the most accomplished of princes (ll. 1539–1640). The proud nurse, Wisdom, speaks the last lines of the poem. She claims Henry as a protégé and son, handing over the defeated figures of Tancred and his role model Andronicus, the murderous Byzantine emperor, to her rival, fickle Fortune. In allegorical terms, she celebrates the glories of Henry's Sicilian palace and court (ll. 1643–1674).

But perhaps more to the point, in a rhyming acrostic near the end of the work, the poet predicts that Henry will win Jerusalem again for Christendom, restore the Roman Empire to its ancient boundaries, and return for a long peaceful reign in Italy (ll. 1463–1470). How could the poet have conferred more glory upon the emperor?

Modern readers (and perhaps medieval ones as well) may wonder whether Henry VI of Hohenstaufen was worthy of such honor. Readers also may wonder whether a discerning literary and historical audience can spare any admiration or sympathy for an author who could portray Henry VI as worthy of such honor, when outside the *Liber* this monarch has a very bad name. To be sure, other important figures in the poem, notably Empress Constance and her son Frederick II, are better liked, but even audiences sympathetic to them may be uneasy to see them praised in such a context.

Nevertheless, the poem is of unquestionable historical value, made so by the relative scarcity of chronicles and documents from this time. Pietro writes vividly about events of which few accounts have survived; of some he may have been an eyewitness, and for others he draws on good information. Though he writes with a strong imperial line, he may preserve some facts and perspectives which otherwise have no witness. While his biases force us to question his reliability on many points, the same is true of most other sources from the period. Among other things, the poem illustrates strikingly how much importance some contemporaries attached to the concept of the Roman Empire, and how closely that empire was linked to the idea of the crusade and the recovery of Jerusalem. This is indeed a reflection of the importance of these matters in the history of the period, and is mirrored in the lives of the main characters of the poem, particularly that of Henry VI, who died while preparing for another crusade, and of his son, whose claims on the Roman Empire and participation or non-participation in crusades was an invariable theme in his conflicts with the papacy, which were to dominate his career.

Thus Pietro's biases themselves are of historical value in that they express an attitude which others might have shared in his time, and the literary form in which he chooses to write helps make the appeal of his viewpoint vivid for modern readers. That is why the question of literary value is not easy to separate from the historical one. Pietro was, after all, a twelfth-century Latin poet, writing a generation or so before the Italian vernacular began to flower as a literary language. His subject matter—a poem clearly intended to glorify an emperor, his family, and his government, and to solidify popular support for him and for the Holy Roman Empire—is one that could well have employed a vernacular high style, of the sort that Dante would later devise for his *Commedia*, joining the dignity of the Latin, with its sacred associations as well as its weight of learning, to the popular appeal of common speech. Pietro did not try to craft such a vernacular, but chose Latin, still the language of scholars and also (perhaps a point of some significance) a language shared, if not always fluently, by most nobles and clerics in the multi-lingual and multicultural court of Henry VI. Nevertheless, Pietro's focus on emotionally affecting scenes and bracing rhetoric, along with his decision to supplement the text with copious pictures, does show an attempt to reach a wider audience. Though the poem is spotty, some passages are genuinely moving, especially the sequence involving the siege of Naples, and the attack upon the Empress Constance at Salerno, where the poet may well have been an eyewitness, or might have drawn on eyewitness testimony.

After this introduction follows a fuller discussion of the issues surrounding the author and his background, the history of the manuscript, the historical background and aftermath of the story, the literary value of the poem, and the format of the translation.

A. The Author and His Background

The colophon (fol. 147v, discussed in more detail in the translation and commentary) contains the most specific information we have about the author's identity. In its entirety, it reads:

> I, Master Peter of Eboli, servant of the Emperor and faithful, composed this book in honor of Augustus. Give me, Lord, a sign of your favor, so that the Tancredines may see me and be confounded. May my Lord and my God provide me with some reward, he who is and will be blessed throughout the ages. Amen. Amen, amen, amen.

> Ego magister Petrus de Ebulo, servus imperatoris et fidelis, hunc librum ad honorem Augusti composui. Fac mecum, Domine, signum in bonum, ut videant me Tancridini et confundantur. In aliquo beneficio michi provideat Dominus meus et Deus meus, qui est et erit benedictus in secula. Amen. Amen, amen, amen.

Apart from his name, what does he tell us about himself? He calls himself "master," very likely meaning that he has an advanced academic degree of some kind. Some scholars believe that he studied medicine, because the work shows him to be fairly sophisticated, for his times, in his medical understanding, and also because one of the miniatures (fol. 103r) apparently depicts him as a youth, perhaps a medical student, listening with respectful bearing to the famous physician Urso as the latter explains the cause of Tancred's dwarfish stature. In the introduction to his edition, Siragusa says that the title "Magister" or "Master," which Pietro bore, was given especially to physicians, and that the ease with which the poet employs medical ideas and technical jargon, throughout *De Balneis* and in various scenes in the *Liber* (for example, ll. 470–489 and captions on fols. 109r and 110r), also suggests a medical background. Though aware that popes and church councils discouraged clerics from devoting themselves to medical studies, Siragusa points out that the practice continued anyway. Near-contemporaries of Pietro who were clerics with medical training included Romuald, archbishop of Salerno (author of a contemporary chronicle), and Matthew, archbishop of

Capua, whom Pietro calls "the Hippocratic Capuan" (*Capuanus ypocraticus*) in fol. 108r, cap. 8. Lesser-known figures include a Master Pietro Saraceno who is "doctor in physic and canon" (*doctor in phisica et canonicus*), a Master Tomasso Saraceno described as "cleric and Salernitan doctor in physic" (*clericus et Salernitanus doctor in phisica*), and "a Sergio and a Giovanni, both clerics and physicians, and a Romualdo who is both a deacon and a physician." However, Siragusa affirms only that Pietro had likely studied medicine. He doubts that he actually practiced as a physician, and especially that he was a physician at the medical school of Salerno. After all, the medical school disapproved of the baths of Pozzuoli which Pietro chose to celebrate.[8]

Other scholars, drawing on later documents about the dispute over the poet's inheritance, in which a judge with the same name is mentioned,[9] suggest that he had learned jurisprudence.[10] However, as Theo Kölzer points out, there is no reason to assume that the author had an academic degree at all, since *Magister* was used loosely at the time for those who had mastered their crafts or professions.[11]

This "Master Peter" also provides an illustration of himself presenting his book to the emperor through the mediation of the chancellor Conrad, bishop of Hildesheim (fol. 139r). Here he wears brown robes and is tonsured like a monk or priest. In yet another miniature (fol. 140r), which depicts the poet calling on Wisdom [*Sapientia*] to guide his verses, his garments suggest a certain prestige. As Siragusa writes:

---

[8] Siragusa, *Liber*, xvi–xvii.

[9] Jean Marie D'Amato, "Prolegomena to a Critical Edition of the Illustrated Medieval Poem *De Balneis Terre Laboris* by Peter of Eboli (Petrus de Ebulo)" (Ph.D. diss., Johns Hopkins University, 1975), 51.

[10] Another Fredrican document, in 1244, orders the son of a certain former judge (*quondam iudex*) called *Petrus de Ebulo* in Latin (and presumably "Pietro da Eboli" in Italian) to cease holding this property and return it to the archbishopric. The documents do not specifically mention the poet or *versificator* to whom the mill was once granted by Henry VI, and *Pietro* was a rather common name. To complicate matters, as D'Amato points out, there actually was a "*Petrus de Ebulo Iudex*" who is "noted in Svevian [Hohenstaufen-era] documents until 1225, when the poet . . . would have been dead" ("Prolegomena" 52). All the same, individuals seizing church property would presumably have some pretext beyond mere greed, and D'Amato states, "It seems unlikely that the sons of anyone other than *Petrus versificator* would have laid claim to the property." She suggests that the poet may actually have been a judge. Siragusa (*Liber*, xv) and De Rosa (*Pietro*, chap. 1) assume that the *iudex* in question was not the poet himself but a relative taking advantage of the confused and violent times to seize the mill. He then tried to leave the property to his sons.

[11] Theo Kölzer, "Autor and Abfassungzeit des Werkes," in *Petrus de Ebulo*, ed. idem et al., 11–13, here 11.

[T]he long tunic ornamented by a band near the lower hem, which seems to be embroidered, and the mantle closed with a buckle [*fibula*] near the left shoulder, similar to those which persons of ecclesiastical authority wear in these miniatures, such as the chancellor in the one before this [fol. 139r], the archdeacon of Salerno in illustration 18 [fol. 112r], and the "*domini curie* [lords of the court]" in illustration 3 [fol. 97r], etc, would lead us to suppose that he was invested with some such dignity.[12]

"Master Peter" also tells us where he comes from: the town of Eboli, near Salerno, which is in the region of Italy called *Campania* and *Terra Laboris* in Latin and *Terra di Lavoro* in modern Italian. This was also known, in ancient times, as the *campi phlegrei* (fields of fire) due to the persistent volcanic activity there.[13] Identifying his home town helped earn Pietro da Eboli (as he is called in his native Italian) belated recognition as the author of another poem, this one about the healing powers of the mineral baths nearby. The work, sometimes titled *De balneis Puteolanis* (*On the Baths of Puteoli*) and sometimes *Nomina et virtutes balneorum Terra Laboris* (*The Names and Powers of the Baths of Terra Laboris*), exists in many versions and has been translated into several languages. In the illuminated versions, the oldest of which dates back perhaps to 1260,[14] the general format is very similar to that of the *Liber*; each page of Latin elegiac verse faces a page of miniatures depicting what is described in the text, sometimes adding insight and details. In both works, the author reveals that he comes from Eboli and praises his native town.[15] All these things and more were pointed out by Huillard-Bréholles in 1852.[16] That Pietro, whatever his claims to learning, authored both *Liber ad*

---

[12] *Liber*, xiii. Translation mine.

[13] D'Amato, "Prolegomena," 3–4, 6. Actually, as D'Amato states in the last passage cited, the name "*campi phlegrei*" was first applied to "the plain in the peninsula of Pallene in Macedonian Chalcedice, site of the battle between the gods and the giants." Thus, the name implies the volcanic activity that reminded "the ancients" of this mythological warfare, and finding another volcanic site, they associated it with similar events. The Italian *campi phlegrei*, as D'Amato explains, include "the volcanic area between Posillipo in the northwest section of Naples up to Cumae, including the islands of Nisida, Procida, and Ischia."

[14] D'Amato, "Prolegomena," 58.

[15] D'Amato, "Prolegomena," 48, 51.

[16] J. L. A. Huillard-Bréholles, "Notice sur le véritable auteur du poème *De balneis Puteolanis*, et sur une traduction française inédite du même poème," *Mémoires et dissertations sur les antiquités nationales étrangères* 21 (1852): 334–53. To be sure, Salvatore De Renzi afterwards stated that he had made the same discovery and had written an article about it already when Huillard-Bréholles preceded him into print; see Salvatore De Renzi, *Storia documentata della scuola medica di Salerno*, 2nd ed. (Naples: Nobile, 1857), 410–11. Also Siragusa, *Liber ad honorem*, xix.

honorem and *De Balneis* is now the scholarly consensus.[17]

The addition of a second work to our author's credit adds piquancy to our curiosity about his career, but also creates a controversy about his dates, since while there is no reason to believe that the author of *Liber ad honorem Augusti* outlived the reign of Henry VI, there is widespread, though not universal, belief that *De Balneis* was dedicated to the latter's son, Frederick II, or at least that its author enjoyed Frederick's patronage. Indeed it is clear that Frederick II knew about the baths of Pozzuoli, because he went there for healing when a serious illness forced him to postpone his departure for his own crusade in 1227, as Richard of San Germano explains in his chronicle.[18] However, he could have learned of them through many intermediaries, whether Pietro's book was dedicated directly to him or to his father.[19] Apart from that, the main evidence suggesting that Pietro survived to the time of Frederick's majority comes from the dedication verses to *De Balneis*, the very passage which pointed to Pietro da Eboli as an author in the first place. However, it centers largely on the interpretation of a debatable passage.

A.1. *De Balneis* and the Poet's Imperial Patron: Which Emperor?

Like the dedication verses in *Liber ad honorem* (ll. 1445–1470), the *De Balneis* has dedication verses which clearly address an emperor. But which emperor? The verses run as follows:

> Take up, Sun of the world, this little book which I present to you.
> It comes to you, its master, the third of three.
> The first holds patrial[20] triumphs in civil Mars.
> The second holds the wonderful deeds of Frederick.

---

[17] See Silvia Maddalo, *Il De Balneis Puteolanis di Pietro da Eboli* (Città del Vaticano: Biblioteca Apostolica Vaticana, 2003), 22. Illustrated with miniatures from several manuscripts of *De Balneis*, this work also includes the dedication miniature from the *Liber* (fol. 139r) as an image of the poet who wrote about the famous baths.

[18] Richard of San Germano, *Ryccardi de Sancto Germano Chronica Priora*, in *Ignoti Monachi Cisterciensis S. Mariae De Ferraria Chronica et Ryccardi de Sancto Germano Chronica Priora*, ed. Augustus Gaudenzi (Naples: Giannini, 1888), 127.

[19] D'Amato ("Prolegomena," 60) points out that in the correspondence (of uncertain date) between Frederick II and Michael Scot, neither mentions the baths in Terra Laboris and both mention baths elsewhere.

[20] Here *patrios* is rendered with the neologism '*patrial*' merely to preserve the ambiguity. A readable translation would no doubt employ some such word as *paternal, ancestral,* or *national*, depending on the context. I translate the word as "ancestral" in *Liber* l. 309, and "paternal" in ll. 741–742, although in both places the word still undoubtedly has the secondary meaning "pertaining to the homeland."

This third restores with the Euboean[21] waters
  Matters whose localities, powers, and names were almost in their graves.
Behold, I have written three books for Caesar's praise;
  Very firm is the word that stands in the mouth of three.
If it please you, Caesar, read the annals of your ancient forefathers;
  With Augustus, no poet was poor.
Remember, Caesar, your bard from Eboli,
  So that he might write the deeds of your son.

Suscipe, Sol mundi, tibi quem presento libellum
  De tribus ad dominum tertius iste venit.
Primus habet patrios civili marte triumphos.
  Mira Federici gesta secondus habet.
Tam loca quam vires quam nomina pene sepulta
  Tertius Euboycis iste reformat aquis.
Cesaris ad laudem tres scripsimus ecce libellos:
  Firmius est verbum quod stat in ore trium.
Si placet, annales veterum lege, Cesar, avorum;
  Pauper in Augusto nemo poeta fuit.
Ebolei vatis, Cesar, reminiscere vestri,
  Ut possit nati scribere facta tui. [22]

Among other key points, Pietro here claims to have written a total of three books for "Caesar." The first book, concerning "*patrios civili marte triumphos*" (line 469), is surely the *Liber ad honorem Augusti*. Since the Roman god Mars signifies warfare, "civil Mars" clearly means "civil war," which is the subject of *Liber ad honorem*, as Pietro announces on the opening page, fol. 95r, where Lucan appears as one of his models, displaying the first line of his masterpiece *De bello civili* (*The Civil War*).[23] Pietro's second book, concerning "the wonderful deeds of Frederick," is apparently lost. Scholars dispute whether Henry's father, Frederick Barbarossa, or his son, Frederick II, is the "Frederick" meant. The poem itself has not been found.

Obviously *De Balneis* itself, the poem containing these dedication verses, is the third and last work dedicated to "Caesar." That only one "Caesar" is addressed seems the most natural interpretation, barring some clear indication otherwise. However, scholars (including Huillard-Bréholles in the article originally identifying Pietro as the author of *De Balneis*)[24] find such an indication in the

[21] The region of the baths had been a colony of Euboea in antiquity.

[22] ll. 467–478 in Jean D'Amato's forthcoming critical edition. These lines also appear in Siragusa, *Liber*, xix-xx; De Rosa, *Liber*, chap. 2; D'Amato, "Prolegomena," 47; Huillard-Bréholles, "Notice sur le véritable auteur du poème *De balneis Puteolanis*," 338.

[23] Lucan [Marcus Annaeus Lucanus], *The Civil War* [*De bello civili*; *Pharsalia*], trans. J. D. Duff (New York: Putnam, 1928).

[24] "Notice sur le véritable auteur du poème *De balneis Puteolanis*," 338.

word *patrios*, in the third line. (In my translation here, this is rendered by the neologism *patrial* so as to preserve its ambiguity.) The adjective *patrius* clearly could mean "paternal," and if it does, the line in question suggests that Pietro's first work celebrates the triumphs of the father of the "Caesar" currently addressed. In that case, *De Balneis* could well be dedicated to Frederick II, son of Henry VI to whom the *Liber* is clearly dedicated. If the poem is dedicated to Frederick II, the poet must have survived at least until 1212, when young Frederick, after being elected emperor with the consent of the Pope, could be addressed that way without offense.[25]

However, to read *patrius* as "paternal" does not exclude other possibilities. After all, in the *Liber*, Pietro makes it clear that Henry VI must claim Sicily in order to vindicate the rights of his own father and ancestors as well as those of his consort (ll. 306–333). His victory would be, in a sense, a "paternal" triumph, even if Henry himself was the instrument by which it was accomplished. Besides, the adjective *patrius* can also mean "ancestral" in a larger sense. Certainly Henry's triumph in Sicily would be a triumph for his ancestors.

Moreover, the Latin noun *patria*, which means *fatherland* or *homeland*, also yields an adjective in Latin, *patrius –a –um*, which means "pertaining to the homeland or fatherland."[26] With this definition, the disputed line would mean, "Triumphs in the homeland during civil strife." For Pietro, "the homeland" clearly meant Rome, or rather, Rome and the Italian territories originally at the heart of the Roman Empire. Henry's triumph was surely a triumph for that em-

---

[25] At that time Frederick, not yet eighteen, and the father of an infant son to whom the dedicatory verses might allude, started north to meet the pope. On the way, he came to Gaeta, in the *Terra Laboris* region, where he was forced to delay about a month "in March-April" (D'Amato, "Prolegomena," 57). "[H]ostile Pisan vessels" waited off the coast to seize him on behalf of his Welf rival, as Thomas Curtis Van Cleve relates in *The Emperor Frederick II of Hohenstaufen* (Oxford: Clarendon Press, 1981), 81. This is the time when some scholars believe that Pietro sought out the young emperor and presented *De Balneis* to him. (See C. M. Kauffmann, *The Baths of Pozzuoli* [Oxford: Bruno Cassirer, 1959], 11–12.) To be sure, the young emperor-elect was not the most suitable audience at this time for a poem on this subject, but if Pietro had already written a version of it, he had nothing to lose by presenting it to his sovereign. Also, his being the author of *Liber ad honorem Augusti*, with its enthusiastic prognostications for Frederick, would have guaranteed him a welcome. However, if Pietro did not meet Frederick in Gaeta then, it would have been difficult to catch up with his patron until much later. Frederick did not return to his Sicilian kingdom until 1220, when as we have seen, it is clear that the poet was already dead.

[26] I am indebted to Jean D'Amato for suggesting this reading here. In her dissertation, D'Amato argues ("Prolegomena," 56–58) in favor of a reading suggested by Block, that the original word here was actually *partos* instead of *patrios*. However, in her current work, as she told me in an e-mail sent 27 May, 2006, she has come to prefer the *patrios* reading, with, however, the interpretation relating to *patria*.

pire.[27] When the word is read this way, Henry VI must be the emperor addressed in *De Balneis*.

Apart from Huillard-Bréholles, a number of scholars, including Siragusa,[28] have believed that Frederick II is the emperor to whom *De Balneis* was dedicated. Among recent scholars, Silvia Maddalo also endorses this view, giving the poet's dates as "ca. 1160–ca. 1120."[29] Kölzer avoids complete commitment, saying that *De Balneis* is "presumably"[30] dedicated to Frederick II. Jean D'Amato, however, observes in her dissertation, "[I]t is curious that the poet (if he ever had worked under Frederick) is never mentioned as being alive in the vast corpus of Frederican documents."[31]

The poet was not entirely unknown to Frederick II, however, because documentary evidence from the latter's reign make mention of a mill granted to Pietro by Henry VI and in turn bequeathed by Pietro to the archbishopric of Salerno. The date of the original donation is not clear, but in 1220 or 1221[32] Frederick II confirmed it among the properties of the archdiocese, describing it in these words:

> We confirm . . . . the mill of Albiscenda, located in Eboli, which Master Peter, versifier, received and held with right of inheritance, from our father the Lord Henry, emperor of the Romans of illustrious memory, and which at the end of his life the same Master Peter both gave and bequeathed to the holy church of Salerno.

---

[27] The chronicler Otto of Freising, bk. 2, chap. 30, shows that Rome and the surrounding territories could be regarded as the "homeland" of citizens of the Roman Empire when he puts the word in the mouth of Frederick Barbarossa, who, before his imperial coronation in 1155, addresses envoys from Rome: "*Quomodo patriam et precipue imperii mei sedem usque ad periculum capitis non defenderem . . .?*" This is the text as given in *Ottonis et Rahewini Gesta Frederici I imperatoris*, ed. B. de Simpson (Hanover and Leipzig: Hahn, 1912), 138–39. In Otto of Freising and Rahewin, *The Deeds of Frederick Barbarossa*, trans. Charles Christopher Mierow, with Richard Emery (New York: Columbia University Press, 1953; repr. New York: Norton, 1966), the passage is translated with the words, "How could I fail to defend the fatherland, and especially the seat of my empire, even at the risk of my life. . . ?" (148). Indeed, "*patrios . . . triumphos,*" in the context of the *Liber*, could pick up resonances of *paternal, ancestral,* and *patriotic* at the same time, Henry being the instrument by which victory for forefathers and the fatherland (simultaneously) is brought about.

[28] Siragusa, *Liber*, xvi.

[29] Maddalo, *Il De Balneis Puteolanis di Pietro da Eboli*, 23.

[30] Kölzer, "Autor," 13; "*wohl.*"

[31] "Prolegomena," 55–56. On this page, D'Amato also enumerates the authors lining up in support of the respective emperors, father and son. For Frederick II, there are [M. A.] Huillard-Bréholles, R[obert] Ries, and others; favoring Henry VI there are P[aul] Block, Ettore Rota, and Mario Pelaez.

[32] See D'Amato, "Prolegomena," 70, nn. 31–32.

Confirmamus. . . . molendinum de Albiscenda in Ebulo consistens, quod magister Petrus versificator a clare memorie domino Henrico imperatore Romanorum patre nostro iure hereditario habuit, tenuit et in fine vite sue idem magister Petrus illud sancte Salernitane ecclesie donavit pariter et legavit.[33]

Another document, or the summary of one from the episcopal archives, shows that "by July, 1220, the mill had passed into the hands of the Episcopate of Salerno, indicating that Peter was already dead."[34] The date of the "versifier's" death is not given in either document. Moreover, the date at which the privilege was confirmed has everything to do with Frederick II's career and nothing much to do with the poet's. For at this time Frederick II, having gained his German kingdom and received his imperial coronation at Rome, returned to his kingdom of Sicily and attempted to recover the "domain" lands and privileges which had been squandered during the times of usurpation and the ensuing war. In pursuit of this, he issued a decree called "*de resignandis privilegiis*," which "declared to be null and void all grants, gifts, donations, privileges, confirmation of titles and the like of the last thirty years," that is, since the time of William II's death and Tancred's usurpation. Everyone who claimed to hold such things should bring them "and table them in the imperial chancery," where they would be confirmed or not at the discretion of the current emperor.[35] Thus, no matter when our poet died, his bequest would have fallen within the period of disturbed rule. In fact, the document in question confirms not only the grants of that period but all the gifts given from the time of Robert Guiscard onward. Thus, although the document does indicate that Pietro was dead by 1220 or 1221, it does not pinpoint the day, month, or even the year of his death, which might have happened quite some time before.

Indeed, a supposed epitaph, published by G. Augelluzi, one of the scholarly pioneers who searched for information about Pietro, states that the poet predeceased Henry VI. Reportedly transcribed from an inscription on Pietro's grave in Eboli and preserved among the papers of an Ebolitan, the Primicerio Pisciotta, the epitaph reads in its entirety:

HERE REST THE COLD ASHES
   OF THE GREAT BARD PETER OF EBOLI,
WHO, MASTER AND GOVERNOR FOR HENRY THE EMPEROR;
   WRITING MANY PAGES FOR HIM,
     SUDDENLY DIED.

---

[33] J. L. A. Huillard-Bréholles, *Historia Diplomatica Frederici Secundi Sive Constitutiones, Privilegia, Mandata, Instrumenta quae supersunt istius imperatoris et filiorum ejus* (Paris: Plon, 1852–1861, repr. Turin: Bottega D'Erasmo, 1964), 2:111.

[34] D'Amato, "Prolegomena," 50; 70, n. 30–31; see also Siragusa, *Liber*, ix, n. 1.

[35] Ernst Kantorowicz, *Frederick the Second*, trans. E. O. Lorimer (New York: Richard R. Smith, 1931), 112. See also Van Cleve, *Emperor Frederick*, 139–43.

NOT WITHOUT LAMENTATION, THE MOURNFUL EBOLITAN
CITIZENS, HAVING LAID HIM BENEATH THIS STONE,
TOOK CARE THAT THE FAMOUS MAN SHOULD BE HONORED.

CINERES HIC QVIESCVNT FRIGIDAE
MAGNI VATIS PETRI DE EBVLO
QVI MAGISTER AC HENRICI IMPERATORIS RECTOR
MVLTAS PRO EO PAGINAS SCRIBENS
REPENTE OBVIT.
NON SINE LVCTV MOERENTES EBOLITANI
CIVES SUB HOC LAPIDE SVBLATVM
INSIGNEM VIRVM HONESTARI CVRAVERVNT.[36]

However, since neither the inscription itself nor the grave from which it came are currently extant, the epitaph is held in great suspicion.[37]

Apart from the suspect epitaph and absence of reference to a living poet during Frederick's reign, Pietro's very choice of the archbishopric of Salerno as the beneficiary for his bequest suggests an earlier date of death. For Pietro supported the Hohenstaufen, while Archbishop Nicholas of Ajello, the incumbent at the time of the confirming document, did not. In the *Liber*, Nicholas is the target of Pietro's invective. First, Pietro implies that Nicholas was behind the Salernitan uprising against Frederick's mother, the empress Constance, as a result of which she was captured and sent as a prisoner to Tancred. In this context, Pietro has the Empress (line 601) call him a serpent, "born from the Hydra" (*natus ab ydra*), the Hydra being Nicholas's father, Matthew, who engineered Tancred's rise to power. As far as Pietro is concerned, the whole family is serpentine.

Later, after Henry's victory, the poet shows Nicholas as the leader of a conspiracy which aimed to murder Henry VI and to replace Tancred's son on the throne. Here Pietro calls Nicholas "Archbishop Caiaphas" (*Caypha Presul*) (line 1338), likening his intent to murder the emperor to an attempt upon the life of

---

[36] D'Amato, "Prolegomena," 51. Del Re, *De Tumulti*, 441. Rota, *Petri Ansolini*, XXIV. De Rosa, *Liber ad Honorem*, chap. 1.

[37] Del Re, *De Tumulti*, 403, 441, states in editorial comments that in "form and Latinity" (*sua forma e latinità*) the poem belongs to a later time. He gives no specific details. Rota states (*Petri Ansolini*, xxiv) that the primicerio himself might well have composed the poem after reading Engel's edition of the *Liber*. This opinion De Rosa accepts and passes on in the introduction to his facsimile edition, chap. 1, n. 17. D'Amato, on the other hand, in "Prolegomena," 71, n. 33, points out that such epitaphs have a history in the region. She suggests that this one could be genuine. Rota, in dismissing the inscription, puts stress on "several historical errors" [*parecchi errori storici*], but the only error he specifies is the placement of the poet's death before that of Henry VI. Apparently Rota (*Petri Ansolini*, xx) assumed that Pietro had died fairly close to the dates on which the documents mentioning his bequests were written, that is, around 1220; at any rate, he does not propose alternate possibilities for the poet's death.

Christ himself. As a result of this, Nicholas spent the rest of Henry VI's reign as a prisoner in Germany, and though he was released during Frederick's minority, some years passed before he regained control of his archbishopric. Available evidence suggests that the final reconciliation between Hohenstaufen and archbishop was tenuous at best.

Though time can change many minds, still, it does seem strange that Pietro would put his property at the disposal of a bishop whom he thought a wicked and treacherous man. On the other hand, if Pietro predeceased Henry VI, or if he died in the earliest years of Frederick II's minority, there is no mystery to explain. While Nicholas remained a prisoner in Germany, the archdiocese of Salerno was under the control of the party represented by Iohannes Princeps, toward whom Pietro directs praises in the *Liber*. There is no difficulty in explaining why a poet who wears the robes of a cleric would bequeath property to the church when the church was in the hands of pastors whom he respected.[38]

It may also seem strange the a poet who wrote so vivaciously during the reign of Henry VI should fall so completely silent afterwards, at least on political matters. Perhaps, then, it is true that both *Liber* and *De Balneis*, and one other lost poem, were all finished or nearly finished during the life of Henry VI.[39]

---

[38] Given Pietro's pro-Hohenstaufen sympathies and the Hohenstaufens' ongoing trouble with the archdiocese of Salerno, it is not astonishing that even after Frederick II's confirmation of the grants in 1221, Pietro's mill at Albiscenda somehow became alienated from the archbishopric's possessions. Perhaps, if the claimant shared his kinsman's hostility toward the archbishop Nicholas, he might have believed that he was doing as Pietro would have wished.

[39] Other documents mentioning men named Peter or *Petrus* in Eboli have been brought forward by scholars as possible information about the poet, but none have won wide acceptance. Rota called the poet "*Petrus Ansolinus de Ebulo*" in his 1904 edition because of documents relating to a certain "*Magister Petrus*" who donated property in Eboli to the convent of *Santa Maria di Monte Vergine* at a date when the *versificator* might also have been alive. Rota (xx) thought that the "*Magister Petrus Ansolinus*" of these documents was the same as the "*versificator*" because he bears the title "Magister" and no other and because the kind and location of his donations are similar to those of the *versificator*, whom he apparently did not outlive, since there is no evidence of him after 1219. Siragusa, rejecting Rota's version of the poet's name, does not discount all possibility that these documents may refer to him. He insists, however, that the identification is not quite definite and even if it were, *Ansolinus* might not be a cognomen. In the Latin, *Petrus* and *Ansolinus* are both in the genitive case: "*Magistri Petri Ansolini*." Although this might mean "of Pietro Ansolino," it could also mean "of Pietro, son of Ansolino," since use of the genitive was a common way to indicate fathers and sons. If Ansolinus had been the poet's cognomen, Siragusa argues, he would have put it in his colophon, or at least it would have been in the other document that mentions him as the *versificator* who received property from Henry VI (xii).

Another document sometimes brought into the discussion involves a family dispute in 1239, concerning sons illegitimately begotten by a certain "Petrus de Ebulo" who

A.2. Composition:
Scribes, Illustrators, and Revision Hands

The 1674 surviving lines of the poem are divided into three books, the first (and longest) running from 1 to 1118, the second from 1119 to 1470, and the third from 1471 to 1674. The first two books are narrative in intent, while the third is largely an allegorical panegyric, celebrating Henry VI in mythological terms as an ideal ruler.

The poet seems to have changed his principle of organization while he was composing his work; close studies of the manuscript, especially Stähli's "Eine Handschrift mit Rätseln," support the hypothesis that the poet did not at first divide his work into "books," only into short sections (one per page), each called a "particula." This is an unusual name for a unit of division, but another twelfth-century poet connected with the Hohenstaufen court, Godfrey of Viterbo, also uses it.[40] Pietro's numbers and titles still appear as far as Particula XXIV, but cease before the end of Book I. Because some headings, numbers, and titles were lost even on the early pages, it is quite possible that some later ones were also lost, through wear and tear, or through the cutting off of the margins when, at an unknown date, the manuscript pages were trimmed so as to be bound with pages belonging to another book (see below). However, Marlis Stähli concluded, probably correctly, that Pietro himself abandoned the *particula* pattern when he adopted a *liber* or book pattern, more compatible with his epic models.[41] Hence, the last pages of Book I lack *particula* divisions, and there are no divisions of this kind at all in Books II and III. However, Rota, whose 1904 edition proved influential, devised *particula* titles for each verse page which lacked one. These were passed on with minor adaptations by Kölzer and Stähli in their 1994 edition, bracketed to show that they do not belong to the manuscript. I also pass them on with bracketing.[42]

Siragusa suspected, and Kölzer and Stähli confirmed in the detailed scholarship accompanying their edition, that Pietro's manuscript was produced in two stages, each associated with different scribes and artists. Where verse is concerned, Books I and II, extending as far as line 1470, belong to the first stage of production, while only the relatively short third book (ll. 1471–1674) belongs to the second. Thus, as Stähli explains and demonstrates with photographic

---

later legitimized them by marrying their mother, Marocta. Their paternal uncles, however, will not accept their legitimate status and continue to harass them. Siragusa (xiii) points out that the "Petrus de Ebulo" who is the father in this case is called "a citizen of Naples," and is not called "Magister," although one of his brothers, also named "Petrus," does receive that title; however, these events took place after the author of the *Liber* was dead (xiii-xiv).

[40] Becht-Jördens, "Der Dichter und sein Text," 289.

[41] Stähli, "Eine Handschrift," 248–49.

[42] De Rosa, however, in his more recent edition, omits these invented headings.

samples,[43] one professional scribe set down most of the first two books, while another scribe, with a hand perhaps even more skilled, set down most of Book III. However, the poet's colophon is written in a much rougher hand, and the same hand appears throughout the manuscript, in corrections and in later additions. This "revision hand," which also wrote the captions on the illustration pages throughout the work as well as the incipits and explicits for Books II and III,[44] is widely regarded as the poet's own hand.[45] This cannot be definitely confirmed, since no samples of Pietro's handwriting are independently known.[46] To be sure, the rough revision-hand could have belonged to another hired scribe. However, it makes sense that the author would be a literate man with a hand not quite as polished as the professionals'. The poet's presumed revisions attract interest and excite commentary because of what they imply about his intentions and the political circumstances under which he wrote. Noteworthy examples of such passages include ll. 609–620 on 115v, discussing Tancredine violence against Pietro's native town of Eboli; ll. 743–772, which cover fol. 120v in its entirety, where Tancred expresses fears about a future from which his eldest son has suddenly disappeared; and ll. 1429–1444 on what is left of 144v (half missing), in which Conrad the chancellor, the poet's patron, declares the need for justice, reconciliation, and unity of purpose among Henry VI's followers after his conquest of Sicily.

The illustrations in the manuscript likewise belong to two stages; to be sure, as Fuchs, Mrusek, and Oltrogge explain,[47] some illustrations created during the second stage have found their way into Book II (which belongs to the first stage as far as the original script is concerned) and may have replaced some previous miniatures there. The dedication miniature, for example, belongs to the second stage, but now appears at the end of Book II, illustrating its last verse-page. Its verso contains the opening lines to Book III. Two other second-stage miniatures in Book II involve the chancellor Conrad (144r and 145r), and apparently illustrate passages which have gone missing. The writing on both versos is also the poet's "revision hand."[48]

Originally, a team of two artists, one perhaps a pupil of the other, illustrated the first two books, using relatively inexpensive paints.[49] For the second stage, another artist took over, using more expensive materials, including vermilion paint and gold leaf, to illustrate the third book, and add some illustrations to the

---

[43] Stähli, "Eine Handschrift," 261–62.

[44] Stähli, "Eine Handschrift," 263.

[45] Examples: Siragusa, *Liber*, viii, lxxxiii. Kölzer, "Autor," 12

[46] Stähli, "Eine Handschrift," 262.

[47] Robert Fuchs, Ralf Mrusek, and Doris Oltrogge, "Die Entstehung der Handschrift: Materialien und Maltechnik," in *Petrus de Ebulo: Liber ad Honorem Augusti*, ed. Kölzer, Stähli et al., 275–92.

[48] Stähli, "Eine Handschrift," 262.

[49] Stähli, "Eine Handschrift," 266.

second book, perhaps partly replacing what was already there. In addition, this artist or someone else touched up the illustrations in the first two books with the more expensive paints (especially gold and vermilion) to make the whole look equally luxurious.[50]

A variety of other changes were made to earlier illustrations. Some were intended to vilify Tancred further, especially the alteration of his face from a three-quarter view in the miniatures on 99r, 101r and 102r to the less sympathetic profile, and the smudging of his face with black "soot-ink" (*Russtusche*) in the first of these.[51] Some were meant to glorify Henry VI more. On fol. 107r, a vivid though allegorized depiction of Frederick Barbarossa's death was painted over, probably at the second stage. Originally it was a three-level illustration showing Frederick Barbarossa, at the top, departing on his crusade, and his son at the bottom, departing on his. The middle picture, however, which was partly uncovered in modern times, showed Frederick Barbarossa dead through drowning, while his soul, in the form of a swaddled child, was raised to heaven by an angel. After the picture was completed, it was painted over with a solid blue background, ornamented with a formal pattern, probably because the depiction of his father's death might seem a "bad omen" for Henry VI's crusade, scheduled to depart in September of 1197 and prominent in the emperor's mind when the work was undergoing final revisions.[52]

In one place only, fol. 121r, still in Book I, a fourth artist appears. Siragusa did not scruple to say that his miniature was clearly "inferior" to the others.[53] However, Fuchs, Mrusek, and Oltrogge shrink from making this aesthetic judgment, while Stähli suggests rather that the miniature's strange qualities may serve an expressive purpose, to hint at the approaching deaths of Tancred and his brother-in-law Richard of Acerra.[54] Be that as it may, the miniature was drawn over a previous illustration which had been erased, and it illustrates a verse-page in the author's own hand, replacing an erased passage. This shows that it belongs to a later stage in the manuscript's production, perhaps the last one.[55]

---

[50] Fuchs, Mrusek, and Oltrogge, "Die Entstehung," 283–84.

[51] Fuchs, Mrusek, and Oltrogge, "Die Entstehung," 278.

[52] Fuchs, Mrusek, and Oltrogge, "Die Entstehung," 282.

[53] *Liber*, 134, n. 4.

[54] Stähli, "Eine Handschrift," 251–52.

[55] The easiest assumption would be that the picture was done at the last minute, when the poet needed to finish the manuscript and could not get any of the previous artists to work for him. In desperation, he might have done the picture himself, or if completely incompetent, perhaps he would have hired an inferior artist. This theory, of course, presumes the aesthetic judgment that this illustration really is inferior to the rest. The scholars of the Kölzer and Stähli edition avoid such a judgment and hold out the possibility that the picture might have been drawn after "stage one" and before what they label "stage two." If Pietro had thought the picture inferior, no doubt he would have

Siragusa and the scholars of the Kölzer and Stähli edition, especially Fuchs, Mrusek, and Oltrogge, suggest a motive for the revisions of the second stage: after composing the original version, comprising Books I and II in their original form, Pietro acquired Conrad of Querfurt, the emperor's chancellor, as a patron, and added the changes at his direction and with his financial help. The scholars of the Kölzer and Stähli edition all observe that the empress Constance, quite prominent in the first two books, both in narrative and in pictures, disappears from the last, and is neither mentioned nor pictured in Book III. [56] Perhaps, they suggest, Constance had been the poet's patron for Books I and II. Or perhaps the poet, working independently, hoped to gain her patronage, but gained Conrad's instead, and made changes in the manuscript to suit him. The relative modesty of the materials in the original version makes the second hypothesis more likely. Also, such an "abrupt change" in patron would be "almost monstrous."[57] But it is easy to imagine that Pietro, as an independent poet of modest means, wrote the earlier and longer portions of the *Liber* before acquiring any patron from the royal court, and that with the financial help of the chancellor Conrad he might quickly have transformed his manuscript, with some additions, into the revised, more lavishly decorated version now in the library at Bern. Pietro's other two books might have followed in quick succession, perhaps based on drafts already begun.

The *Liber* in its current form was obviously completed after the birth of Frederick II (26 December 1194), which the poet joyously celebrates. The poem also records that the newborn child was committed to the care of the duchess of Spoleto before the 1195 Easter court at Bari, which the empress attended.[58] Also, in a passage immediately following the account of his birth, young Frederick is the recipient of a magnificent fish, gift of a proud Iberian fisherman (ll. 1397–1428). Through his tutor or guardian, he issues instructions that it be divided into three pieces, of which he keeps two for himself, sending the third to his father. There being no clear date for this incident, scholars are driven to wonder how old the infant must have been to make any sense at all of the maritime delicacy. Siragusa reports that Engel and Rocco, in their notes on this passage, assume that the child in this scene must be imagined as more than a year old, which would bring the poem to the end of 1195 at the earliest, with 1196 as a more realistic estimate. Siragusa mistrusted so imprecise a measure, but he did observe that this period overlaps with time when Conrad of Querfurt, Pietro's much-depicted patron, was acting as imperial chancellor in Italy and in the region of Campania, "between the summer of 1195 and the autumn of 1196,"

---

arranged to replace it during the second stage, but if he supposed that it was as good as the rest, he might have left it.

[56] Siragusa, *Liber*, lxxxvi. Stähli, "Eine Handschrift," 249. Fuchs, Mrusek, and Oltrogge, "Die Entstehung der Handschrift," 283.

[57] "abrupter Wechseln . . . nahezu ungeheuerlich": Stähli, "Eine Handschrift," 256.

[58] Kölzer, "Autor," 12.

providing an opportunity for Pietro to become acquainted with him and gain his patronage.[59] Conrad first became chancellor in March 1195,[60] but in this capacity he soon followed Henry VI back to Germany, only to return in 1196 with instructions to destroy the fortifications of Naples. In 1196, too, he wrote a long letter to "the provost at his German cathedral" at Hildesheim,[61] describing his journey and making many mythological and literary references to the places he was passing through. Among other things, he mentions the mineral baths at Baiae, where ancient statues of bathers supposedly remained, with the figures of the bathers pointing to the parts of their bodies which could be healed by the powers of the waters.[62] Kauffmann points out that this might be "the very subject of the *De Balneis* illustrations," particularly for the baths at Trituli.[63] This could be an indication that he had by this time become acquainted with Pietro, and the latter, having completed the first version of the *Liber*, may have been thinking about, or have already begun, work on *De Balneis*. Perhaps some public presentations for court entertainment had won Conrad's interest. Perhaps, too, Pietro might already have written versions of his second poem about Frederick Barbarossa. Pietro's passages in the *Liber* praising Henry's father suggest that he was eager to treat this subject (ll. 314–333; 1581–1606). Conrad might also have suggested or directed some of Pietro's revisions to the *Liber*. Perhaps he warned Pietro that a match was being contemplated between the emperor's brother Philip and Tancred's widowed daughter-in-law, Irene Angelina, which may have prompted him to remove passages about Irene's first husband, Roger, and Tancred's Byzantine alliance, where the hastily revised miniature on fol. 121r now appears in the manuscript. The poem mentions Philip's interest in Irene (line 1292) but does not describe their wedding, solemnized in May 1197. By that time, to be sure, the kingdom of Sicily was convulsed by fresh conspiracies and resultant bloodshed which are also unmentioned in the *Liber* and incompatible with its reconciling tone. There is no need to assume that Pietro was revising the *Liber* up until the moment of his death, but still, the evidence is consistent with his having predeceased the emperor, perhaps dying unexpectedly, without a long illness.

It is true that some scholars point to the many corrections and revisions in the *Liber* and ask whether such a book, in such an imperfect form, would have been presented to the Holy Roman Emperor. Was it not, perhaps, a draft, from which a better copy would be made? Fuchs, Mrusek, and Oltrogge present arguments for both sides.[64] Both sides sound convincing. The materials and produc-

---

[59] Siragusa, *Liber*, lxxxiv, lxxxiii.

[60] Kölzer, "Autor," 13.

[61] Evelyn Jamison, *Admiral Eugenius of Sicily* (London: British Academy, 1957), 149.

[62] Arnold of Lübeck, *Chronica Slavorum*, ed. G. H. Pertz, MGH 21 (Hanover: Hahn, 1869)192–96; (bk. 5, chap. 19).

[63] Kauffmann, *The Baths of Pozzuoli*, 57–59.

[64] "Entstehung," 263.

tion costs seem too much for a mere draft, while the errors and corrections seem excessive for an imperial copy. But against those who argue that the manuscript may never have been presented to Henry VI (perhaps the emperor died first?) we have, as Kölzer points out,[65] the unambiguous evidence from the Fredrican documents that Henry VI gave his *versificator* a mill. As a compromise between the views, Siragusa suggests that the poem was indeed presented, but Pietro then took it back for further work.[66] Henry VI did not necessarily need to wait for the finished copy before he rewarded the poet, nor do we know that the mill was a reward for only one poem. The emperor might well have known that several works were in progress. D'Amato, calling attention to a previous argument by Block,[67] points out that the poet sounds ungrateful in *De Balneis* if he suggests that he is a pauper after an emperor had already given him a mill. She writes, "A more probable explanation is that the mill was Henry's bequest for all three works dedicated to him."[68]

B. History of the Completed Manuscript

Whether Pietro da Eboli predeceased Henry VI or survived him, we can be confident that interest in the *Liber ad honorem Augusti* would have crashed to a halt at the time of the emperor's death in September 1197, for a number of reasons. Not only was its main subject, Henry VI, dead, but for the previous nine months or so (depending on the interpretation of fragmentary and contradictory sources) the kingdom of Sicily had been wracked by rebellions and conspiracies, and the emperor, exasperated by continued resistance and treachery, threw off all pretense at mildness and ordered grisly executions clearly meant to terrify his remaining enemies into submission or flight. Nowadays he is remembered for little else. After his death, the widowed Empress Constance, attempting to re-establish order in her hereditary kingdom, also had to face the fact that the Holy Roman Empire was elective, not hereditary. A disputed election in Germany soon turned into a civil war, and the Hohenstaufen faction rejected the child Frederick as its imperial candidate, choosing Henry's brother, Philip of Swabia, to oppose the rival Otto of Brunswick, scion of the rival Welf family, who had powerful support from England, being the grandson of Eleanor of Aquitaine and Henry II of England. Unsurprisingly, Constance chose to renounce her son's imperial heritage in order to gain the pope's support for his rights to the kingdom of Sicily. She dismissed her husband's imperial officials and had little reason to value a poem which declared that the kingdom of Sicily rightfully belonged to the Holy

---

[65] "Autor," 12.
[66] *Liber,* lxvi.
[67] Paul Block, *Zur Kritik des Petrus de Ebulo* (Prenzlau: Visconti, 1883) 2:2–5.
[68] "Prolegomena," 59.

Roman Empire. It is still possible that she might have treasured the book as a record of her past, especially the passages celebrating the birth of her son. In any case, she survived Henry VI little more than a year, and it is not to be expected that the four-year-old Frederick could yet have taken much interest in the book. Perhaps it sat neglected and undisturbed upon some shelf in Palermo until he was old enough to enjoy it. The truth is that we have no evidence that he ever saw it. Nevertheless, a copy survived: the opulent, though flawed, manuscript apparently produced by the poet himself. So what happened to the *Liber* and how did it end up at the Bürgerbibliothek Bern? Scholars still work to interpret the few known facts.

B. 1. The Manuscript at Bern

When Siragusa produced his edition, the manuscript of the *Liber ad honorem Augusti* was bound in a codex with other works, the whole being designated as ms. 120 of the Bongarsiana collection at the Bürgerbibliothek Bern.[69] Since then, it has been separated and given its own binding in a manuscript designated Codex 120 II, while its companion texts are in Cod. 120 I.[70] However, the *Liber* was originally an independent work, and its pages, somewhat larger than those of its companions, had to be trimmed when the works were bound together.[71] Then folio numbers were added to the composite manuscript; since the *Liber* came last, these numbers run from 95r to 147r.

The texts once bound with the *Liber* provide clues about its past. As Siragusa describes it, the composite ms. 120 began with a page covered with verses on both sides, largely about "the Passion of Jesus Christ," most of them from Prudentius. Then follows the *Chronica Adonis adbreviata*, with two continuations written "in several hands of the 11th century," from fol. 2r to fol. 58v.[72] Next, covering only about half of 58v, comes an interrupted excerpt in a 12th-century hand, titled *Qualiter Tiberius Cesar Ierosolimam Volusianum ad Iesum direxit* [How Tiberius Caesar sent Volusianus to Jesus at Jerusalem], which is taken from the apocryphal gospel of Nicodemus, also called *Acta Pilati* [The Acts of Pilate]. There followed a history of Rome by Sextus Aurelius Victor, going from Octavius Caesar [Augustus] to Theodosius (fols. 59r–74r), followed by a list of Roman emperors, "from Augustus to Henry III of Germany" (fols. 74v–76r). Next comes *Excerptum de gestis Romanorum pontificum* [*Excerpt of the Deeds of the Roman Pontiffs*] by Abbo of Fleury (fols. 76r–93r). The text goes as far as Gregory

---

[69] Siragusa, *Liber*, liv.

[70] Stähli, "Eine Handschrift," 248.

[71] Siragusa, *Liber*, xiv–xv.

[72] Siragusa, *Liber*, lv. One of the continuations is apparently unique to the codex at Bern, and can be found published in *Chronica Adonis: Continuatio II ex codice Bernensi a 897–1031*, ed. G. H. Pertz, MGH 2 (Hanover: Hahn, 1829), 326.

II, and it is followed by a list of later popes as far as Sylvester II (fols. 76r–93r). There follows a blank page (fol. 94), and then *Liber ad honorem Augusti*, from fol. 95r to fol. 147r. Siragusa concludes that the *Liber*'s companions were copied in a French monastery, probably of Fleury (as marginal notations suggest), but were later given to another monastery, that of St-Maximin-sur-Loire. Likewise, the Old French comments written on fol. 140r of the *Liber* suggest that this manuscript was in France by the thirteenth century, and that is where it was bound with the other texts in a single codex.[73]

B.2. Pietro da Eboli and William of Brittany

But how did the *Liber* reach a French monastery? We have only one piece of evidence which does not come from a physical examination of the manuscript itself. Siragusa notes that Pietro da Eboli's' verses were known and imitated by William of Brittany, whose poem *Philipis*, about the French king Philip Augustus (contemporary and ally of Henry VI and later of Frederick II), was composed between the years 1220 and 1225.[74] In fact, William of Brittany apparently takes a line from Pietro's poem, narrating King Richard's journey in disguise across imperial lands: *Quid prodest versare dapes, servire culine?* (What is the use of turning dishes and serving in the kitchen?)[75] Despite many differences—after all, the actions of King Richard, rival and antagonist of Philip Augustus, are far more central to *Philipis* than to the *Liber*—William's account parallels Pietro's in other ways. Thus Richard's activities in Sicily are of concern in both, but more detailed in *Philipis*, since Philip Augustus was present too. Richard's trial before Henry VI is also given in both, more detailed in the *Philipis*. In both accounts, the Lionheart offers to clear himself by fighting a duel. In Pietro's poem, the most dangerous charge against King Richard is murder, presumably for complicity in the death of Conrad of Montferrat, whose claim on the kingdom of Jerusalem Richard had long refused to accept. Although William also mentions Conrad's assassination, that event is important merely as a sample of what Richard might do; in William's poem, Henry then goes on to accuse Richard of attempting to betray Henry's "brother" and ally, Philip Augustus, to "the Parthians"—that is, to the Moslems. Perhaps the *Liber* hints at this obscurely in the suggestion that Richard will go on to shed more blood if released (line 1057). Naturally, William

---

[73] Siragusa, *Liber*, lv–lvi, lix–lxi.

[74] Siragusa, *Liber*, lxii. Also William of Brittany, *Ex Willelmus Brittonis operibus*, ed. A. Molinier, A. Pannenborg, and G. Waitz, MGH 26 (Hanover: Hahn, 1882), 295–389, here 300.

[75] *Philipis* 4.343; *Liber ad honorem* l. 1049. The editors (A. Molinier, A. Pannenborg, and G. Waitz) of the selections from *Philipis* in the MGH edition also point out the line from Pietro da Eboli (333, n. 7). One might argue that the two poems draw upon a common source, but thus far this source has not turned up.

of Brittany emphasizes Richard's status as a vassal of Philip, and alludes to their quarrel over lands in France (including those which were the dowry of Philip's sister Alais, whom Richard had jilted on the eve of the crusade):

> Indeed you wished to hand over your lord, the friend of our father,
> our brother, to the Parthians,
> so that France would mourn its broken strength
> and not reclaim what you unjustly hold (ll. 388–391).

> Immo tuum dominum, nostri genitoris amicum
> Et fratrem nostrum, voluisti tradere Parthis,
> Ut mutilata suo lugeret Francia cornu,
> Ne sua que retines iniuste iura reclamet.

Both poems call Richard's good faith as a crusader into question. However, while in the *Liber* Henry only hints darkly that Richard did not really try to recover Jerusalem, in *Philipis* the emperor openly accuses him of making peace with Saladin in exchange for gifts, to the disadvantage of Christendom:

> Also, lately in Syria, fingering the gifts of Saladin,
> you sold the Christians to the enemies of Christ's cross,
> for you willingly handed over Gaza, Joppa and Ascalon
> To destruction without arms or battle.
> (Book 4, ll. 382–385).

> Nuper et in Syria, Saladini exenia palpans
> Christicolas Christi crucis hostibus exposuisti,
> Dum Gazam, Ioppen Ascalonemque sine armis
> Et sine conflictu subverti sponte tulisti.

Nevertheless, the *Philipis*, like the *Liber*, emphasizes Richard's courage in offering to prove his innocence through single combat:

> From his lion's heart he broke forth with this declaration:
> "Let him come forth in the midst, he who accuses me of treason.
> Let him make his accusations, let him come armed and fight a duel
> Against me, if he can convict me on these things.
> Courage has not so far deserted me that anyone can defeat me,
> When I rely on my right and my accustomed strength.
> Let it be so although [my royal] right would prevent it:
> Lest the Law should be refused me, I do not beg off even death."
> (See commentary on fols. 128v–129r, ll. 1047–1088).

> Corde leonino vocem prorupit in istam:
> "Prodeat in medium, qui me de proditione
> Arguat, armatus veniat subeatque duellum

Me contra, si me super hoc convincere possit.
Non tamen usque adeo virtus michi deficit, ut me
Fidentem de iure meo solitoque vigore
Vincere quis possit; fiat quod iure cavetur,
Lex michi ni parcat, mortem non deprecor ultra." [76]
(Book 4, ll. 395–402)

Certainly the line which William shares with Pietro suggests that the former had seen or heard at least an excerpt of the poem. Elsewhere he seems ill-informed about the Hauteville family; he describes Constance as William's sister (4.78), and Tancred as William's uncle (4.80). However, the manuscript of *Liber* would not necessarily have corrected these errors, for while Pietro may know the precise relationships, he does not explain them clearly in the surviving portions of the narrative.[77]

As Siragusa reconstructs the manuscript's history, it was given to Henry VI, but Pietro took it back to correct it.[78] Therefore Conrad the Chancellor, his patron, had it in his possession after Henry VI's death, and valued it because of its flattering depiction of him. He, or someone to whom he gave it, eventually passed it on to William of Brittany, chaplain of the French king Philip Augustus, with whom the German adherents to the Hohenstaufen family were friendly. Through William of Brittany it reached a French monastery whose collection was eventually acquired by Jacques Bongars (1554–1612), the "French humanist, scholar and diplomat"[79] whose collection ultimately reached the Bürgerbibliothek Bern. Bongars may have acquired the composite codex as the Bürgerbibliothek originally owned it, or, as Stähli suggests, he may have bound the manuscripts together himself. The Celestines of Sens (in Burgundy) placed their mark of ownership on fols. 95r and 146v,[80] but no similar mark appears on the companion works.

---

[76] Here "ni" could mean either "ne" ("lest") or "nisi" ("unless"). My translation follows the "ne" reading: Richard waives his royal exemption from trial by combat in order to take advantage of the legal right to defend himself, at the risk of death; his scrupulous captor might prefer to spare him the combat but leave the intolerable calumny unrefuted. The "nisi" reading would suggest that Richard does not wish to escape death except by lawful means. I think Richard Lionheart won the day by seeming heroic rather than legalistic.

[77] He never mentions William I, son of Roger II, who was the father of William II and half-brother of Constance. He states that Henry VI is King Roger's son-in-law (line 44), but later he implies that Constance is William II's sister (line 82). He makes it clear that Tancred is reputedly a bastard of the royal line (line 220) but does not name his father or father's relationship to William II.

[78] *Liber*, lxi–lxvi.

[79] Stähli, "Eine Handschrift," 268.

[80] Stähli, "Eine Handschrift," 266.

Much remains uncertain about the history of the manuscript. Instead of seeing the original, William of Brittany could have worked with a copy or partial copy of the poem, as Stähli suggests.[81] If indeed William of Brittany did see the original, it might have reached him at a later time, when young Frederick II sought and gained the help of Philip Augustus against Otto the Welf. The mutual troubles of the Hohenstaufen and of Philip Augustus with the Plantagenets of England would have been very much to the point, as would the legitimate claims of young Frederick II to the Holy Roman Empire. Of course, there are many other routes which could have brought the *Liber* from the Hohenstaufen court to the monastery which apparently housed it for many decades until it came into the hands of Bongars. However, none is, at this time, clearly illuminated by hard evidence.

B. 3. Lacunae in the Text

A total of four and a half leaves, or eight pages and two halves, are thought to be missing, involving an unknown number of lines. These are briefly mentioned in the commentary on those parts of the manuscript. Still, it seems fitting to place a summary here. Kölzer and Stähli identify the losses as follows:

(1, 2). The illustrations corresponding to verses 1151–1176 are missing, but a fragment apparently remains, now designated 131a in the Codex;[82] this should have followed 131v and preceded 132r. On the reverse of that page, the verses illustrated by the miniatures on fol. 132r are also missing. The general subject matter of this missing leaf is the siege and sack of Salerno.[83]

(3, 4). The illustrations corresponding to verses 1301–1328 are missing. They would have followed 135v and preceded 136r. On the verso, the lines illustrated by the miniatures on 136r would have appeared, but are missing. They should have narrated Sibylla's successful petition for pardon from Henry VI, the latter's triumphal entry into Palermo, and the beginning of the conspiracy by the pardoned but ungrateful Tancredines. No fragment survives.[84]

(5, 6) The miniatures illustrating verses 1397–1428 are missing. Presumably, they should contain a picture of little Frederick Roger dividing a splendid fish under the supervision of his "master" or guardian. This would follow the current 138v and precede the current 144r. Likewise, the verses illustrated by the badly mutilated miniatures in fol. 144r are missing. Presumably they contained

---

[81] Stähli, "Eine Handschrift," 266.

[82] Stähli, "Eine Handschrift," 254

[83] Siragusa identifies the same loss, *Liber*, lxxxi–lxxxii.

[84] Siragusa identifies the same loss, *Liber*, lxxxi–lxxxii.

a description of the emperor's court. Rota suggests that perhaps the birth of the imperial heir is announced here.[85]

144r is a badly mutilated page; nearly half is missing.

(7, 8) The miniatures illustrating verses 1606–1639 are missing. Presumably they would show the Emperor Henry with the Liberal Arts. The picture-page would follow fol. 143v in the current format and precede 146r. The verses illustrating 146r are missing. The subject is an allegory expressing the relation between Wisdom, the Virtues, and Fortune.[86]

C. Historical Background and Aftermath

The *Liber* needs to be read in its historical context for full appreciation, and although much is supplied in the commentary accompanying the translation, readers will probably desire more illumination about the background and aftermath, especially since many passages in the poem do allude to previous events or foreshadow later ones. Here, therefore, is a somewhat detailed sketch of the events leading up to and then succeeding those of the *Liber* itself.

C. 1. The Holy Roman Empire and the
Kingdom of Sicily

It was no mere dynastic accident[87] that, at the time of the death of William II of Sicily, Henry VI, King of the Romans, was married to Sicily's heiress. The marriage was made purposely, with full awareness that Henry might inherit the Norman kingdom of Sicily because of it. The *Liber* recounts (ll. 43–44, 118–119) that William II had required his nobles to swear that they would recognize Constance and her husband as his successors, and this is confirmed by many other chronicles, including those of Richard of San Germano (63–64); *Annales Casinenses* (codices 4 and 5 for 1190),[88] and Roger of Hoveden.[89] Yet Henry (and our poet) did not believe that the Empire's claim to Sicily was based entirely upon Constance's rights. Sicily had, of course, originally been part of the Roman Em-

---

[85] Siragusa identifies the same loss, *Liber*, xliv. The number advances from 138 to 144 because the leaves were bound out of order when the numbers were added.

[86] Siragusa identifies the same loss, *Liber*, lxxxi–lxxxii. Again the gap in number is caused by the incorrect ordering of the leaves when numbers were added.

[87] Hubert Houben, for example, uses this phrase in *Roger II of Sicily*, tr. Graham A. Loud and Diane Milburn (New York: Cambridge University Press, 2002), 7. By "accident," he means "the childless death of Roger II's grandson, William II," but the implication that Constance's succession was not foreseen, at least to some extent, is faulty.

[88] *Annales Casinenses*, ed. G. H. Pertz, MGH 19 (Hanover: Hahn, 1866), 314.

[89] Roger of Hoveden, *Gesta Heinrici II et Richardi I*, ed. G. Waitz, MGH 27 (Hanover: Hahn, 1885), 129.

pire, as Pietro points out, even while confirming Constance's hereditary rights (ll. 306–333).

In fact, the negotiations which resulted in the marriage between Frederick Barbarossa's son and King Roger's daughter marked an amicable phase in a long, bitter struggle between the Germans and Normans. Byzantine emperors also entered the fray. So did the papacy, sometimes playing one side against the other, and sometimes making claims of its own. All of these players — eastern emperor, western emperor, king of Sicily, and pope — make their appearance in Pietro's *Liber*. It helps to understand that all these potentates had, for some centuries, been laying claim to the classical Roman Empire.

More specifically, all laid claim to the Roman Empire as it existed under Constantine, the first emperor to embrace Christianity, who then made it a lawful religion in the Empire in 313. At this time, Rome still ruled most of the known world; Augustus Caesar defined his empire as the lands bordering "on the West, the Atlantic Ocean, the Rhine and Danube on the north, Euphrates on the east, and towards the south, the sandy deserts of Arabia and Africa."[90] Obviously, this included the island of Sicily and the southern Italian regions of Apulia, Calabria, and Terra di Lavoro which were later to compose the Norman kingdom of Sicily.

But Constantine, the first Christian emperor, moved his capital to the town by the Bosphorus then called Byzantium, which he rebuilt and named Constantinople, after himself. His successors became strangers to Rome and to the Latin language, for Greek, already widely cultivated among the educated throughout the empire, naturally came to predominate in the new capital. And if Italian affairs commanded less attention than before, events in what are now modern France, Spain, and Germany became still more remote from the emperor's thoughts.

Since the church owed its legal position to the conversion of the Roman emperors and needed support from them to retain it, some Byzantine churchmen claimed that church leadership changed capitals along with their emperor.[91] The bishops of Rome (the popes) claimed on the contrary that their primacy was derived from the Apostle Peter. Naturally, with emperors absent from Rome, popes became even more prominent in Italy as populace and potentate appealed to them in all kinds of troubles. Popes contended and negotiated with the Lombard princes who overran Italy. They encouraged and made alliances with the Christian rulers of Gaul, first the Merovingian dynasty and then the

---

[90] Edward Gibbon, *The Decline and Fall of the Roman Empire* (London, 1776–1788; Everyman's Library Edition, 1910; repr. New York: Random House, 1993), 3 vols., 1:5; chap. 1. Gibbon here is citing Tacitus, *Annals* 1.2; and Dio Cassius, 50.56.

[91] Romilly Jenkins, *Byzantium: The Imperial Centuries, AD 610–1071* (London: Weidenfeld and Sons, 1966; repr. New York: Random House, 1969), 176; Anna Comnena, *Alexiad*, trans. E.R.A. Sewter (New York: Penguin Books, 1969), 62; Bk. 1, ch. 13.

Carolingians. When scions of the latter dynasty rose to defend western Christendom against Moslem conquest, the papacy conferred imperial rank upon it, establishing the western or Holy Roman empire. Or that is the view the papacy came to emphasize increasingly in the twelfth and thirteenth centuries. In the seventh and eighth centuries, the popes were in too much peril, and their need for military help and protection too obvious, for them to be making realistic claims of sovereignty over powerful western rulers.

For soon after Mohammed's death in 632, Moslem rulers conquered Roman Egypt and North Africa. In 638, Jerusalem fell to Caliph Omar, Mohammed's second successor.[92] By the early 700s, Moslem rulers had conquered most of Spain and began encroachments into France. However, in 732, the Carolingian Charles Martel ("Charles the Hammer") defeated the Moslem Abd ar-Rahman decisively in a battle "between Tours and Poitiers," and this marked the end of Moslem advances into France.[93] Sicily, however, fell to Moslem conquest in the mid-800s, along with stretches of territory in Calabria.[94] Spain remained mostly in the possession of various Moslem rulers until after the time of our poet. However, as the Carolingians gained great prestige, Christendom came to see them as champions.

At time of his great victory, Charles Martel was not king of France but only "Mayor of the Palace," the highest official of the Merovingian king, actually performing most of the royal responsibilities. However, in 751, Charles Martel's son and successor, Pepin, appealed to Pope Zacharias, asking whether the man who performed all the responsibilities of kingship should be king or not. The pope declared in favor of the man who performed the duties. At the news of this decision, Pepin deposed the Merovingian king Childeric III. Thus the precedent was established that incompetent rulers might be deposed and replaced with competent ones, and that popes (or perhaps others with spiritual discernment), had the authority, and perhaps the responsibility, to declare when this was necessary.[95]

Pope Leo III took this authority even further when he crowned Pepin's son Charles as emperor at Rome in the year 800.[96] Popes later claimed the first Christian emperor had given them legal jurisdiction over Italy through the so-

---

[92] Steven Runciman, *A History of the Crusades,* 3 vols., (New York: Cambridge University Press, 1951–1954), 1:3; Ch. 1.

[93] Edward Gibbon, *The Decline and Fall of the Roman Empire,* Vol. 5, New Edition, with notes by Rev. H. H. Milman (New York: Collier, 1899), 290; Ch. LII.

[94] G. A. Loud, *The Age of Robert Guiscard* (New York: Pearson, 2000), 15–16, 54–56.

[95] Otto of Freising, *Two Cities,* bk. 5, chaps. 9, 22. Edward Peters, *The Shadow King: Rex Inutilis in Medieval Law and Literature, 751–1327* (New Haven: Yale University Press, 1970), 34.

[96] R. Winston, *Charlemagne* (New York: Vintage, 1954), 345; Ch. 17.

called "Donation of Constantine," afterwards recognized as a forgery.[97] At the time, Charlemagne probably believed that his imperial status included the responsibility to govern the church, as in the Byzantine model, and Leo III apparently acknowledged this by prostrating himself before the newly crowned emperor.[98] Indeed, popes depended on pious western emperors to ensure their security in office and to champion them against local tyrants and usurpers. Sometimes emperors took it upon themselves to depose corrupt claimants to the papacy, clearing the way for new elections, as Henry III the Salian did, supporting the elevation of Leo IX to the papacy in 1049.[99] It is this relationship between Holy Roman Empire and Pope that Pietro da Eboli seems to envision when he describes the sword given to Henry VI at his coronation as "doubly powerful, defender of the Church and the World" because "here it rules the Church, and there corrects the earth" (ll. 282–283). However, by Pietro's time the papacy had ceased to depend much on western emperors. This was partly because the Normans had come to southern Italy in the eleventh century and altered the political dynamic.

C. 2. Robert Guiscard and the Norman Conquest of Sicily

It began with Norman adventurers and mercenaries coming to southern Italy, first to serve local Lombard princes and then to challenge their power. The most famous and (ultimately) successful of these Normans were sons of Tancred of Hauteville, a poor Norman *vavassor* with a territory in Normandy too small to satisfy the many sons he had by his two successive wives. Hence these youths, when old enough, went to Italy for careers as mercenaries. Robert Guiscard, the elder son by the second wife (Fressende), significantly increased his power by marrying Sichelgaita, sister of Gisulf II, the Lombard prince of Salerno, whom Robert later ejected from that territory. Subsequently, as duke of Apulia, Robert made Salerno his capital.[100]

The growing power of the Normans displeased Pope Leo IX, who, although more or less appointed by the German Emperor Henry III, is usually regarded as a "reformer," that is, one who was concerned with improving the independence, integrity, dignity, and effectiveness of the papacy. Still, Leo believed that pious emperors should help the church, and he hoped that Henry III and even the Byzantine emperor, influenced by his many appeals to the "donation of Constantine,"

[97] Jenkins, *Byzantium*, 351–52.

[98] Jenkins, *Byzantium*, 109.

[99] See Otto of Freising, *Two Cities,* 395; Bk 6, Ch. 32. Otto reports that Leo later insisted on canonical election. See also Karl Hampe, *Germany Under the Salian and Hohenstaufen Emperors,* trans. Ralph Bennett (Totowa, NJ: Rowman and Littlefield, 1973), 51.

[100] Loud, *Age of Robert Guiscard,* 139–41.

would aid his struggle.[101] Leo was unable to muster as much power as he hoped, but trusted to battle anyway, and at Civitate, in 1053, he suffered defeat and then capture by the Normans.[102]

Before the battle, the Normans had proposed that they would "hold all their conquered lands as a papal fief and . . . pay tribute for them"[103] if the pope would agree to peace. In his captivity, Leo IX accepted their solution. As prisoner he was held at Benevento;[104] they released him only a little before his death in 1054.[105] Nevertheless, his agreement with the Normans, of whom Robert Guiscard soon became the leader, was kept by his successors, who, despite some misgivings, found the alliance useful. In 1059, Pope Nicholas II formally accepted Robert Guiscard's homage as "Duke of Apulia and Calabria, and in future, with the help of both [God and St Peter], of Sicily."[106]

C. 3. Roger, Great[107] Count of Sicily, Legate of the Holy See

Implementing the plans he and the pope had made, Robert Guiscard, with the help of his younger brother Roger, conquered Sicily from the Moslems, a project well underway by January 1072 when the Hauteville brothers took Palermo, and completed when Noto surrendered to Roger in 1091.[108] Ultimately, Roger received Sicily as his share in the conquest. Because he undertook responsibilities for re-establishing Christianity and ecclesiastical institutions in a land where they had been seriously disturbed or even uprooted under Moslem rule, and for overseeing efforts to convert the Moslem population to Christianity, Roger received from the pope, as his descendants claimed, the status of "perpetual legate

---

[101] Hampe, *Germany Under the Salian and Hohenstaufen Emperors*, 53.

[102] Ferdinand Chalandon, *Histoire de la Domination Normande en Italie et en Sicilie*, 2 vols. (Paris: 1907; repr. New York: Burt Franklin, 1960), 1:135–42. All citations are from the reprinted edition, unless otherwise specified. See also Loud, *Age of Robert Guiscard*, 110–20.

[103] Hampe, *Germany Under the Salian and Hohenstaufen Emperors*, 54. Loud, *Age of Robert Guiscard*, 118–120.

[104] M. Walsh, *An Illustrated History of the Popes* (New York: Bonanza Books, 1980), 101.

[105] Hampe, *Germany Under the Salian and Hohenstaufen Emperors*, 54.

[106] Loud, *Age of Robert Guiscard*, 129–30.

[107] Houben, *Roger II*, 23, points out that Roger I was not styled *magnus comes* ("great count") until after his death, in the documents of his son, Roger II. The title might really mean "elder," to distinguish father from son, instead of being a comment on the vastness of Roger's comital territory. However that may be, Roger I is now traditionally called the "great count."

[108] Loud, *Age of Robert Guiscard*, 158–61, 172–72.

of the Holy See,"[109] giving him more rights over the church in his realms than popes currently conceded to Holy Roman emperors. Throughout the years when he established his power and built the church in Sicily, Roger probably understood his status in that light; hence he was angry and imprisoned the bishop of Troina when Urban II appointed the latter as a legate. The quarrel was soon resolved and the pope "granted a bull to the count [Roger], and to his heirs," in which he "pledged not to appoint legates to his lands without his prior consent" and also permitted him to act as a legate himself when he saw fit. [110] This "legateship" was claimed by all of Roger I's successors after him, until Tancred gave it up in 1192 with the Concordat of Gravina, in return for recognition as king of Sicily. [111] Though Emperor Henry VI would try to reclaim this legateship as part of Constance's rightful inheritance, death cut short his attempt. Constance herself, granddaughter of Roger I, was obliged to accept the diminished rights of her kingdom as a price for Innocent III's consent to the succession of her infant son. [112]

---

[109] Philip Schaff, *History of the Christian Church* (New York: Scribners, 1910), 5:15; chap. 1, sec. 7.

[110] Loud, *Age of Robert Guiscard*, 231–32.

[111] John Julius Norwich, *The Kingdom in the Sun* (London: Longman, 1970), 379–80. Also Chalandon, *Histoire*, 2: 464–67. Chalandon, within this passage (2:465–67) sums up the alterations that the Concordat of Gravina made to the 1156 Treaty of Benevento, between William I and Hadrian IV (translation mine):

1. The right of appeal to the court of Rome is introduced into Sicily; up until then the appeal could not take place except on the request of the king.

2. Tancred abandoned the right that his predecessors had reserved to admit into Sicily only those papal legates requested by the king himself. Henceforth, the pope had the right to send a legate to Sicily every five years, or even more often if the need was felt or if the king requested it.

3. Concerning the legates sent to Apulia and Calabria, the clause prescribing that they not abuse the goods of the church is omitted.

4. Likewise suppressed is the clause which forbids the legates to hold a council in any city where the king or his heirs is residing.

5. Similarly, Tancred loses the right to annul elections which do not suit him; in the future he will have to make his opposition known to Rome and it will be the pope who will reject the candidates who are to be set aside.

[112] *The Deeds of Pope Innocent III: By an Anonymous Author*, trans. James M. Powell (Washington, DC: Catholic University of America Press, 2004), 20; chap. 21. However, Graham A. Loud, "The Papacy and the Rulers of Southern Italy," in *The Society of Norman Italy*, ed. idem and A. Metcalfe (Boston: Brill, 2002), 151–84, here 182, emphasizes a tactful change of wording meant to soften the diminution of royal authority, without, however, actually giving the Sicilian king the right to exclude candidates unacceptable to him if the pope preferred them.

C. 4. Norman Sicily Among Two Roman Empires and Papal Policy

Meanwhile, as a trusted ally of the pope, and with his territories in southern Italy growing larger mostly at the expense of Lombards and Byzantines, Robert Guiscard found himself approached by envoys of the Byzantine emperor, Michael VII, seeking a marriage alliance. Some time after 1074, Guiscard agreed to send one of his daughters, later called Helena, to Constantinople, to be educated as the future bride for Michael's son Constantine.[113] Instead, however, of bringing east and west together, this match became a cause of war when Michael VII was overthrown by Nicephorus Botaniates, who was in turn (and very shortly afterwards) overthrown by Alexius I Comnenus. Robert Guiscard, in the spirit of a dynastic alliance, invaded Byzantine territory on behalf of his deposed ally, accompanied by an impostor claiming to be the deposed emperor himself. But Michael VII, as Anna Comnena, daughter of Alexius I, proclaims, did not truly regret his crown and prospered in his second career as a bishop.[114] His son was treated very kindly by Alexius I Comnenus and was promised Anna Comnena herself as his bride. Guiscard's daughter Helena was, of course, thrust aside.

How all this would have ended is unclear, for in the midst of his invasion, Guiscard learned that Pope Gregory VII was besieged at Rome by the armies of Henry IV of Germany, another episode in the so-called investiture controversy, but one which the Byzantine emperor did his best to encourage, or so says his daughter.[115] Fulfilling his obligations to the papacy, Robert Guiscard turned back from Constantinople. The German emperor withdrew from Rome, which was then sacked by Guiscard's armies. The pope, knowing himself to be hated in his ravaged capital, accompanied the victorious Norman to Salerno, where he found himself in the care and company of Bishop Alfano, the poet, scholar, and physician. Despite all the comfort the latter could give him, Gregory soon died (25 May 1085) declaring to those who gathered around him, "I have loved righteousness and hated iniquity; therefore I die in exile."[116] Alfano and Robert Guiscard also died within the year.[117]

Thus the kingdom of Sicily, under the control of the Normans, came to enjoy a relationship to the papacy analogous to the one held by the Holy Roman Empire, though less dignified in theory. Sometimes popes called upon the Normans

---

[113] Chalandon, *Histoire*, 1:264.

[114] Anna Comnena, *Alexiad*, bk. 1, chap. 12.

[115] Anna Comnena, *Alexiad*, bk. 3, chap. 10.

[116] *Dilexi justitiam et odi iniquitatem: propterea morior in exilio* (alluding to Psalm 44:8). See Herbert Edward John Cowdrey, *Pope Gregory VII, 1073–1085* (New York: Oxford University Press, 1998), 680. Also Schaff, *History of the Christian Church*, 5:38; sec. 18.

[117] Generoso Crisci and Angelo Campagna, *Salerno Sacra* (Salerno: Edizioni della Curia Archivescovile, 1962), 48.

for help and support; sometimes popes attempted to drive them from their realms and supplant them. When quarreling with the emperor, popes would seek help from the Normans; quarreling with the Normans, they sought help from western and eastern emperors. Not that these were their only resources. Of course, popes appealed to the consciences of their opponents and of their families, which led to complex entanglements. For example, Gregory VII's successors, prosecuting their quarrel with Emperor Henry IV, stirred up his sons against him. The younger became more famous in the end, as Henry V, but Conrad, the elder, showed him the way. Against his father's will and at the instigation of Matilda of Tuscany, Conrad had himself crowned king of Lombardy in 1093, although those lands and that title belonged to the empire. Later, in 1095, at the Council of Piacenza, Conrad swore his loyalty to Pope Urban II, who in recompense arranged a marriage between him and a daughter of Roger I, the Great Count of Sicily.[118] All this has been mostly forgotten by history, since Conrad died without issue in 1101, and his young queen, Maximilla, did not remarry but lived quietly until at least 1138 in the territories governed by her brother, Roger II.[119]

Henry V profited from his father's troubles by supplanting him with help from the papacy; then he fought for imperial rights more fiercely than his father had. In 1111, as he besieged Pope Paschal II at Rome, the latter waited in vain for help from Guiscard's heir, but Roger Borsa, mortally ill, died 22 February of that year, succeeded by his minor son, William.[120] Paschal accepted hard terms which the cardinals refused to ratify, drawing fresh imperial persecution. At length, in 1122, with Pope Calixtus II reigning, the Concordat of Worms was concluded, a "compromise" concerning the respective claims of the pope and the emperor to choose and claim the loyalty of the bishops who controlled massive amounts of territory in Germany. The papacy gained "right of investiture by the delivery of the ring" which signified the bishop's office; however, the emperors were left with considerable power to supervise elections, to intervene in case of irregularities, and to decide disputes.[121]

C. 5. Lothar of Supplingburg, Founder of the Welf Imperial Claim

After Henry's childless death in 1125, the German princes, weary of his wars, passed over his nephews by his sister Agnes to choose Lothar of Supplingburg, scion of another family, for their next emperor. The papacy found him friendly to their interests and even gained his support against the Normans of Sicily. For the

---

[118] Hampe, *Germany Under the Salian and Hohenstaufen Emperors*, 97.

[119] Walter Holtzmann, "Maximilla Regina, soror Rogerii Regis," *Deutsches Archiv für Erforschung des Mittelalters* 19 (1964): 148–67, here 154. Also Houben, *Roger II*, 23.

[120] Chalandon, *Histoire*, 1:313.

[121] Schaff, *History of the Christian Church*, 5:45; sec. 21.

Great Count Roger had died in 1101, leaving two sons, of whom only the younger, Roger II, survived to maturity. This second Roger became a skilled ruler and talented politician who increased his already extensive domains at the expense of Robert Guiscard's descendants. Not that he robbed them directly. Robert Guiscard, on his death in 1085, had bequeathed most of his territory to his second son Roger Borsa, born to the Lombard princess Segelgaita. This displeased his eldest son Bohemund, born to his first wife, the Norman Alberada. Astutely, their uncle Roger I declared for Roger Borsa, the less energetic and warlike of the two, and gained concessions in return.[122] Bohemund turned his eyes toward foreign realms and joined the first crusade, in which enterprise he won a princedom in Antioch, along with much admiring and hostile notice by the contemporary chroniclers, including Anna Comnena.[123] A granddaughter of his later married the Byzantine Manuel III and bore a son, Alexius, whom our poet mentions as a victim of the Emperor Andronicus (ll. 158–162).

Meanwhile, William, duke of Apulia (Robert Guiscard's grandson), died without issue in 1127, and Roger II claimed his dukedom of Apulia,[124] the event mentioned in the first line of the *Liber*. After some hostilities, Pope Honorius II officially recognized these acquisitions in 1128.[125] Honorius died in 1130, however, and there followed a disputed papal election from which two claimants emerged, calling themselves Innocent II and Anacletus II, respectively. Roger II supported Anacletus II, who soon gave permission for him to be crowned king of Sicily. Innocent II, however, with the help of Bernard of Clairvaux, ultimately gained the support of the king of France and of Lothar of Supplingburg, the Holy Roman emperor. Lothar of Supplingburg invaded southern Italy to enforce the pope's rights. However, battles and epidemics thinned his army, so that he ultimately withdrew and died in 1137.[126]

Lothar had no sons, but he did have a daughter, Gertrude, and a son-in-law, Henry the Proud[127] who expected to succeed him as emperor.[128] Nevertheless, the monarchy was elective, and the rival dynasty ultimately regained the kingship in the person of Conrad III of Hohenstaufen, nephew of Henry VI. Conrad's imperial coronation, though often negotiated and planned, was, for various

---

[122] Loud, *Age of Robert Guiscard*, 257–58, emphasizes that the chroniclers of the time overstate Roger Borsa's incompetence. Much of his weakness resulted from his status as the younger half-brother of a displaced legitimate son.

[123] For example, *Alexiad*, bk. 10, chap. 11.

[124] Chalandon, *Histoire*, 1:328; chap. 15. Houben, *Roger II*, 40–41.

[125] Norwich, *The Kingdom in the Sun*, 5. Also Houben, *Roger II*, 46–47.

[126] Hampe, *Germany Under the Salian and Hohenstaufen Emperors*, 136; Karl Jordan, *Henry the Lion*, trans. P. S. Falla (Oxford: Clarendon Press, 1986), 18–19. Norwich, *The Kingdom in the Sun*, 35–56.

[127] See Genealogical Table 4.

[128] Jordan, *Henry the Lion*, 7.

reasons, never carried out.[129] Meanwhile, Henry the Proud remained in a strong position as duke of Saxony and of Bavaria. He passed his claim to the empire on to his descendants.

C. 6. King Roger's Dynasty Reconciled with the Popes

Then, in 1138, Pope Anacletus II died. His rival, Pope Innocent II, gathered armies of his own and attacked Roger of Sicily, perhaps encouraged because Roger had seemed timid and unwarlike during Lothar's invasion. Roger, however, was bolder this time, and after his attempts to negotiate were spurned, he attacked Innocent's forces and captured him. Captive, Innocent soon came to terms through the Treaty of Mignano in 1139. As one scholar puts it,

> [H]e had to confirm all the concessions Roger had extorted from the antipope. For the grant of Apulia and Calabria as fiefs to Roger's two sons was only a face-saving sham, and so was the drafting skill of the curia when it made no mention of Anacletus's privilege and traced the recognition of the Sicilian kingdom back to Honorius II.[130]

Thereafter King Roger avoided open war with the papacy until his own death in 1154. He was succeeded by William I, his only surviving son by Elvira of Castile. William had already been Roger's co-ruler since 1152. He faced warfare, serially and at times almost simultaneously, from the pope, the Byzantine emperor Manuel I, and the German king, Conrad III of Hohenstaufen,[131] who was Manuel's brother-in-law.

C. 7. The Future King Tancred's Participation in the Coup against William I

However, William I was victorious against the invaders of his realms. His costliest warfare was with his own Sicilian nobles, who repeatedly rose against him, by themselves and in combination with foreign allies. In 1161, there was a palace

---

[129] Hampe, *Germany Under the Salian and Hohenstaufen Emperors*, 138–39; 150.

[130] Hampe, *Germany Under the Salian and Hohenstaufen Emperors*, 141. Also, Houben (*Roger II*, 71) remarks, "To avoid mentioning the anti-pope Anacletus, the bull of investiture alleged, quite untruthfully, that Honorius II had promoted the duke to be King of Sicily."

[131] Conrad III died without an imperial coronation at Rome, and therefore he is customarily called "king," not "emperor." For some compressed information about the somewhat fluid relationship between the titles *rex Romanorum* and *Romanorum imperator*, see Robert Benson, "Political *Renovatio*: Two Models from Roman Antiquity," in *Renaissance and Renewal in the Twelfth Century*, ed. idem and Giles Constable (Cambridge, MA: Harvard University Press, 1982), 339–86, here 373.

coup in which prisoners, suddenly freed from the palace dungeons, seized him and took him prisoner. Tancred, the later usurper, was among them. To save his life, William offered to abdicate, and the rebels held him in prison while they proclaimed his nine-year-old son Roger as king and paraded him through the city. After three days, however, the people of the city rose on the king's behalf. The rebels released the king in exchange for permission to depart safely, but the nine-year-old Roger was accidentally struck by an arrow and died of the wound. [132]

In short, William's reign was troubled, and his most vivid chronicler, Hugo Falcandus, describes him in such scathing terms that historically he is known by the epithet *il Malo* (the Bad). Historians debate whether he deserved it, more than his father or son. Assessments of his character will inevitably affect estimates of Tancred's character.

C. 8. Frederick Barbarossa, William II, and Pope Alexander III: Conflict and Reconciliation

When William I of Sicily died in 1166, his son William II was a boy of about twelve, for whom his mother, Margaret of Navarre, was to be regent. This is the "beautiful" king whose death in the early lines of the *Liber* leads to lamentations and a disputed succession (ll. 35–109). William II's youthful reign was troubled by the threat of invasion by the German emperor Frederick Barbarossa, but Manuel I Comnenus, the eastern emperor, having made peace with William I, renewed the alliance with his son. He even negotiated a marriage between William and his elder daughter, though nothing came of it except bitterness and insult when, years later, Manuel finally promised but did not send the bride. Manuel, hoping to restore some rights of the eastern empire in Italy, also posed as the protector of Pope Alexander III, whose election to the papacy was disputed by a rival, antipope Victor IV, supported by Frederick Barbarossa. To be sure, Victor IV remained entrenched at Rome, while Alexander III had to flee. Later, after Victor's death, Alexander returned, with Byzantine and Sicilian support, only to suffer an invasion from Barbarossa, who took Rome and enthroned another antipope, Paschal III. Though pestilence (in a familiar pattern) forced the emperor to withdraw, Paschal remained in control of Rome until he died in 1168.

Nevertheless, Pope Alexander III survived and gained support in Christendom, while Barbarossa's next antipopes, elected by the increasingly small and iso-

---

[132] Hugo Falcandus, *La Historia o Liber de regno Sicilie e la Epistola ad Petrum Panormitane Eclesie Thesaurarium di Ugo Falcando*, ed. G[ian] B[attista] Siragusa (Rome: Istituto Storico Italiano, 1897), 62; English translation: *The History of the Tyrants of Sicily*, ed. and trans. Graham Loud and Thomas Wiedemann (New York: Manchester University Press, 1998), 113–14. The accidental killer of young Roger may be the "Darius" mentioned in *Liber* l. 609; see his biographical sketch.

lated imperialist faction among the cardinals, lost ground. Frederick Barbarossa eventually withdrew his support from the last of them and sought peace with the pope and with William of Sicily. Soon, indeed, he was offering one of his daughters in marriage to William II, who, however, refused out of respect for the pope. In any case, the daughter in question soon died, according to the chronicler, Romuald of Salerno.[133] Eventually, through the Peace of Venice, negotiated with the help of William II of Sicily, Frederick Barbarossa was reconciled to Pope Alexander III, who returned to Rome in 1177, supported by Barbarossa's soldiers against the unruly populace.[134]

C. 9. Pope Lucius, the Crusade, and the Match Between Henry and Constance

A few years later, Frederick Barbarossa once more proposed a dynastic alliance with William's family, but this time the wedded partners were to be his son and heir, Henry VI, already elected king of the Romans, and Constance, William's paternal aunt and presumed successor. This time, William did not refuse, and if Pietro is to be believed, Pope Lucius III encouraged or possibly even proposed the match, for he writes (line 22), "*Lucius in nuptu pronuba causa fuit*" (Lucius played matchmaker for their nuptials). For Lucius's involvement, Pietro seems to be the only witness, and his accuracy here has been widely doubted, largely because later popes, particularly Frederick II's contemporaries Innocent III, Gregory IX, and Innocent IV, made it clear that they regarded the permanent union between the Holy Roman Empire and the kingdom of Sicily as something the papacy simply could not tolerate. Thus, after the collision between Frederick II and the papacy in the thirteenth century, it became difficult for scholars to believe popes had ever felt differently. Even McGinn, putting forward evidence that Lucius may indeed have supported the match, is moved to comment that Lucius was "naïve."[135]

To be sure, the events just now reviewed do not suggest that popes had, by this time, rejected on principle the idea that the Roman Empire should regain its ancient territories. On the contrary, the papacy deplored the suffering that resulted from weak and unstable governments, which is why various popes advised kings and encouraged emperors to extend their claims. Munz accepts Pietro's ac-

---

[133] *Chronicon Romualdi II Archiepiscopi Salernitani*, ed. C. A. Garufi, RIS 7.1 (Città di Castello: Lapi, 1909–1935), 265–66. This is also discussed by Erwin Assmann, "Friedrich Barbarossas Kinder," *Deutsches Archiv für Erforshung des Mittelalters* 33 (1977): 435–72, here 448.

[134] Chalandon, *Histoire*, 2:384; Peter Munz, *Frederick Barbarossa: A Study in Medieval Politics* (Ithaca: Cornell University Press, 1969), 363.

[135] Bernard McGinn, *The Calabrian Abbot: Joachim of Fiore in the History of Western Thought* (New York: Macmillan, 1985), 11.

count of Lucius's attitude and points out that in the autumn of 1184, when the marriage was being negotiated, the pope had once more been driven from Rome by local quarrels. Under these conditions, Barbarossa, upon whose military support he relied, had been unable to help him because his own position in central Italy had deteriorated. Seeing peace and stability in the vicinity of Rome as a positive good, Lucius proposed the alliance with the Norman Sicilians and the match between Henry and Constance.[136] No doubt Lucius also hoped the match would pave the way for a more successful crusade, one of the matters most at issue at the Verona conference.

For as Barbarossa negotiated with Lucius, the situation in the Middle East was deteriorating fast. In 1144, the county of Edessa had fallen to the Turkish Zengi, and the second crusade, led by Louis VII of France and Conrad III of Hohenstaufen, had failed to recover it and had also accomplished little else. In 1174 King Amalric of Jerusalem died, leaving as his heir Baldwin IV, the so-called "leper king." This youth was remarkably responsible and energetic, but clearly destined, because of his disease, for an early death without physical descendants. When the end came in March 1185, his designated heir was his eight-year-old nephew, Baldwin V, whose mother (Sibylla) and stepfather (Guy of Lusignan) the leper king had not trusted with the regency. But a few months before his death, the leper king had sent the Latin patriarch Heraclius and "the Grand Masters of the Temple and Hospital" to the West, to stir up interest in a crusade.[137] In November 1184 they reached the Council of Verona and related their message to Pope Lucius III and to Frederick Barbarossa, warning them that the kingdom of Jerusalem would soon fall unless it received significant help from the Christian West. Concerned and accommodating, Barbarossa offered to speak about the matter with his princes and to set out himself after the following Christmas.[138]

C. 10. Andronicus, Isaac Angelus, and William II's Attack on Constantinople

However, another crisis, not wholly unrelated, was brewing at the same time in the eastern empire. In 1176, the Emperor Manuel suffered a serious defeat at the hands of the Turks at Myriocephalum.[139] In 1180, he died, leaving as his successor a son perhaps eleven or twelve years of age, and a young widow whose Latin origin (she was a princess of Antioch, one of the crusader states, and a descendant of Robert Guiscard) made her unpopular in the city. Taking advantage of this, a wily cousin of the emperor, Andronicus Comnenus, made common

---

[136] Munz, *Frederick Barbarossa*, 367; chap. 8.

[137] Runciman, *A History of the Crusades*, 2:440–45.

[138] Theodor Toeche, *Kaiser Heinrich VI.* (Leipzig: Duncker u. Humblot, 1867), 37.

[139] Runciman, *A History of the Crusades*, 2:214.

cause with the angry populace and seized power in Constantinople. Their first act was a great massacre of Latins in April 1182, to which Pietro alludes in ll. 1644–1646.[140] Soon Manuel's widow and both his children were murdered and Andronicus was sole eastern emperor.

At some point, William II of Sicily decided to invade Constantinople, to remove Andronicus from power and replace him with a friendly emperor. Another of Manuel's kinsmen, called Alexius the Cupbearer, had sought refuge at his court and William had promised him support, though he reportedly also protected a youth who claimed to be the murdered boy-emperor himself, Alexius II.[141] Eustathios of Thessaloniki[142] declares that William II actually meant to take the throne of Constantinople for himself instead of either alleged claimant, but the basis for his judgment is unclear, though Norwich, whose opinion of William II is quite low, accepts it.[143] Norwich and Chalandon[144] also assume that William's alliance with Frederick Barbarossa was mainly intended to ensure the security of the kingdom of Sicily while his military resources were engaged in this enterprise. However, as help from Constantinople was essential to any successful crusade, the common concern for the Holy Land sufficiently explains the alliance. Andronicus had shown himself both hostile and treacherous to the Latins. Pope Lucius and those who heeded the leper-king's appeal all wanted him removed. Constance's betrothal to Henry of Hohenstaufen was announced at Augsburg, and then as Toeche reconstructs the matter in his biography of Henry VI, negotiations continued at Verona.[145]

All parties to the marriage between Henry and Constance probably had some doubts whether the union would produce children and whether those children would inherit the crown of Sicily. Constance would be nearly thirty-two years old when the wedding was solemnized, her bridegroom about twenty-one. William, childless and about the same age as Constance, had married Joanna

---

[140] For a more detailed account, see Charles Brand, *Byzantium Confronts the West 1180–1204* (Cambridge, MA: Harvard University Press, 1968), 41–42.

[141] The pseudo-Alexius is mentioned both by Eustathios, the Byzantine chronicler, in *The Capture of Thessaloniki*, trans., notes and comm. John R. Melville-Jones (Canbarra: Australian Association for Byzantine Studies, 1988), chap. 51; and by the Arab traveler Ibn Jubayr in *The Travels of Ibn Jubayr*, trans. R. J. C. Broadhurst (London: Jonathan Cape, 1952), 354; "The Month of Shawwal." Most writers who deal with William's invasion mention this child, including Brand, *Byzantium Confronts the West*, 161, and Norwich, *Kingdom in the Sun*, 332–33. In Appendix 2 of his edition of Eustathios's work, Melville-Jones points out that there were rumors about five such pretenders, and some of them, particularly "the 'Alexios Komnenos' who appeared in France shortly afterwards" (236), might be the same one who had been in Sicily.

[142] *The Capture of Thessaloniki*, 63; chap. 51.

[143] *Kingdom in the Sun*, 333.

[144] *Histoire*, 2:386.

[145] Toeche, *Kaiser Heinrich VI*, 38.

Plantagenet, then eleven years old, in 1177. In 1185, there was plenty of reason for hope (if age were the only issue) that she would yet bear children. However, we can only guess what William knew about his own health. As Pietro is careful to state (ll. 39–44), he required his nobles to swear that they would recognize Constance and her husband as the rulers of Sicily should he die childless; other chronicles say the same.[146]

William II's cousin, Tancred of Lecce (the future king), was the commander of the naval forces sent to attack Constantinople. Richard of Acerra, often mentioned by Pietro as Tancred's brother-in-law, went with the land forces. The Sicilians famously captured the city of Thessalonica. But before they reached Constantinople itself, the people of the capital rose against their tyrant and chose a new emperor, Isaac Angelus. With the change of government the tide turned against William's forces, though chroniclers report that Isaac's generals used treachery, attacking while a truce was still in force and capturing many Norman soldiers. These later starved to death when Isaac put them in prison without making provision to feed them.[147]

Meanwhile, in Italy, the amiable Lucius III had died, and the next popes were not pleased with the Sicilian-Hohenstaufen alliance. The wedding between Constance and Henry VI was celebrated, it is true, with special magnificence at Milan, on 27 January 1186. Frederick Barbarossa made the occasion even more spectacular by adding some coronations. He himself was crowned king of Burgundy, Constance was crowned queen of Germany, and Henry was crowned king of Lombardy by the patriarch of Aquileia. This offended the new pope, Urban III, who, as bishop of Milan, believed that the coronation of the king of Lombardy was his prerogative. Even more, according to Toeche, the new pope was angered that Barbarossa had accomplished the next best thing to an imperial coronation for his son in his father's lifetime, and without any help from the papacy.[148] Byzantine emperors made a regular practice of crowning their heirs as co-rulers, and the great western emperors Charlemagne and Otto I had managed to do so too.[149] Lucius III, it seems, had been willing to perform this ceremony at Frederick's request, but the cardinals had refused to consent, alleging that it was an unheard-of thing to have two living emperors at once. So Frederick made a grand display with coronations for which he did not need papal consent.

In retaliation, Urban intervened provocatively in a disputed German archiepiscopal election, consecrating the candidate whom the emperor did not favor despite a previous promise to the contrary. In no mood to submit, Frederick

---

[146] Richard of San Germano, *Chronica*, 63–64. *Annales Casinenses*, cod. 4 and 5 for 1190. Hoveden, *Gesta*, 129.

[147] Niketas Choniates, *O City of Byzantium: Annals of Niketas Choniates*, trans. Harry J. Magoulias (Detroit: Wayne State University Press, 1984), 199–200.

[148] *Kaiser Heinrich VI*, 56.

[149] Hampe, *Germany Under the Salian and Hohenstaufen Emperors*, 210.

barred the pope's choice from his archdiocese and consolidated his own power in Lombardy at the pope's expense. Meanwhile, he instructed his son to take firm control of central Italy, including the disputed territory of Tuscany, which, generations before, the Countess Matilda had attempted to bequeath to the Holy See in the eleventh century.[150] Urban tried to stir up rebellion against Barbarossa among the German bishops, but it fell apart when Barbarossa returned to Germany. There, a council of German princes backed the emperor and protested the pope's actions.

Embittered, Urban III considered excommunicating Frederick Barbarossa, but death prevented him. Meanwhile, dreadful news came from the Holy Land. For early in July 1187, at the disastrous battle called "Horns of Hattin," Saladin defeated the army of the Latin Kingdom of Jerusalem, under Guy of Lusignan (stepfather of young Baldwin V, who had died in the meantime). Those who were not slain were captured; the Holy Cross or True Cross of Christ's crucifixion was said to be among the booty, and was, according to Moslem sources, "fixed upside down on a lance and carried into Damascus" by a Qādī.[151] Pietro does not mention this insult but states (ll. 1034–1036) that the capture of the True Cross, more than anything else, stirred up crusading zeal in the Christian world. But meanwhile, Saladin, measured and calculating in severity and leniency, ordered the summary slaughter of the Templars and Hospitallers, after making them a *pro forma* offer to convert to Islam, which few accepted. With his own sword, he killed a certain nobleman, Reynald of Chatillon, against whom he had a particular grudge. Otherwise, the Christian nobles were held for ransom, while the poor were sold into slavery.[152] He quickly followed up his military success, taking stronghold after stronghold. Jerusalem, too, soon (2 October 1187) surrendered on terms which permitted most Latin inhabitants to ransom themselves and depart.[153] The crusader kingdom faced imminent destruction.

Now Pope Urban's successors gave the crisis in the Holy Land their primary attention. All the greatest Christian princes pledged their help. William II of Sicily promised the resources of the kingdom of Sicily and patched up a peace with the Byzantine emperor.[154] The date of the treaty is not known, but it must have been concluded by 1189, because the events which unfolded after William's

---

[150] Jordan, *Henry the Lion*, 19.

[151] Malcolm Cameron Lyons and D. E. P. Jackson, *Saladin: The Politics of Holy War* (New York, Cambridge University Press, 1983), 265.

[152] Runciman, *A History of the Crusades*, 2: 259–60. Lyons and Jackson, *Saladin*, 264–66. Supposedly Saladin offered Reynald the chance to concert to Islam, and he refused. Other prisoners, including Guy de Lusignan, were ransomed, released, or enslaved without being required to convert.

[153] Lyons and Jackson, *Saladin*, 274–77.

[154] Brand, *Byzantium Confronts the West*, 174.

death show that Richard of Acerra, commander of the land forces who had been captured by the Byzantines, was back in Italy by then.[155]

C. 11. The Third Crusade Begins

Some individual crusaders set out for the Holy Land immediately after the battle of Hattin. However, monarchs leading armies took longer to prepare. Of these, Frederick Barbarossa was ready first, and he set out in May 1189, taking with him his second son, Frederick of Swabia. He had also laid careful plans by negotiations with rulers and tribes along his proposed route, to avoid disasters like those which had befallen his uncle Conrad III on the previous crusade, which Frederick had accompanied. Despite his precautions, Barbarossa was soon embroiled in quarrels with Isaac Angelus, who, after promising safe passage and the provision of supplies, instead arranged ambushes and resistance. It seems he had made an agreement with Saladin, who had been hospitable to the Angelus family during their years of exile under Andronicus, to hold back the crusaders as much as he could.[156] Therefore, in November, Frederick wrote to ask his son Henry for naval support with which to take Constantinople, an action which would have anticipated the results of the fourth crusade by more than a decade. Pietro alludes to this conflict when he writes of "Isaac's lying promise and feigned alliance" (*Ysaac mentita fides et fictile fedus*) (line 1591).

Isaac Angelus, it is true, was eventually induced to honor his original promise and ferry the Germans across the straits near Gallipoli.[157] Barbarossa fought and won a battle against the Turks before he drowned in the river Salef, on 10 June 1190.[158]

However, William II of Sicily died on 18 November 1189, while Barbarossa was still encamped on the near side of Gallipoli, frustrated by Isaac's machinations. Henry VI was soon weighing the problems of supporting his father's great project, governing the imperial realms in Germany and northern Italy, and

---

[155] Chalandon (*Histoire*, 2:414–15), dealing masterfully with uninformative or disingenuous chroniclers, observes that while Niketas Choniates, in his *Annales*, says that William II gave up Durazzo because of the expense of the occupation (200), and while the *Annales Ceccanenses* (ed. G. H. Pertz, MGH 19 [Hanover: Hahn, 1866], 287), claim for the year 1185 that Isaac Angelus released his Sicilian prisoners when he learned that they had been treacherously seized during a truce, neither account is plausible. He thinks it more likely that the two sovereigns made a treaty, with William yielding Durazzo and Isaac releasing his prisoners.

[156] Charles Brand, "The Byzantines and Saladin, 1185–1192," *Speculum* 37 (1962): 167–73.

[157] Niketas Choniates, *Annales*, 226.

[158] *The Chronicle of the Third Crusade: Itinerarium Peregrinorum et Gesta Regis Ricardi*, trans. Helen Nicholson (Burlington, VT: Ashgate, 1997), 64–66; Bk. 1, chap. 24. Munz, *Frederick Barbarossa*, 395.

taking possession of his consort's kingdom of Sicily at the same time. Meanwhile, Sicily mourned their king and fretted about the uncertain future, while in Palermo, Matthew of Ajello and others decided that, despite any previous agreements and oaths, they would prefer a Sicilian noble to the German Henry. So the stage is set for the actions in Pietro's *Liber ad honorem Augusti*.

C. 12. The Struggle for Sicilian Succession

From this point on, the *Liber* and its commentary give a more detailed account of most events than this introduction can do. Of course, Pietro selected his information carefully and may have changed his account as he was writing. More fell out later along with missing pages. Also, the *Liber* stops about two and a half years short of the end of Henry's reign. And people with no knowledge beyond Pietro's poem would not be prepared to hear the epilogue because so much of it follows from matters not discussed in the surviving portions of the poem.

The surviving poem gives no details (beyond brisk allusions) about Tancred's alliance with the Byzantine emperor, and the marriage between Tancred's son Roger and Irene, the daughter of Isaac Angelus. The poet also ignores Tancred's military campaigns in 1193, when the king took the field personally, until illness apparently obliged him to withdraw to Palermo. Yet more significant to the long-term picture, Pietro suppresses indications of papal opposition to Hohenstaufen imperial ambitions. Misleadingly, he implies that Henry VI had consistent papal support; at any rate, he describes helpful papal actions in detail and alludes most obscurely to unhelpful ones (for example, ll. 768, 991; see commentary). Not only is he the only witness to Lucius III's role as a matchmaker (see C.9 above), but he also recounts that Celestine III crowned the emperor and empress and later induced Tancred to release Constance when she was his prisoner, so that she might "pacify her husband" (*pacificare virum*) (1038). Other chronicles report Celestine's involvement here,[159] but in the wider context, by "pacify," the pope evidently means that Constance might persuade Henry to accept Tancred's position.

The surviving poem does not state that afterwards, with the Concordat of Gravina in 1192, Celestine officially recognized Tancred as king of Sicily,[160] receiving in return Tancred's surrender of the Sicilian king's rights as "legate of the Holy See" (see C.3 above). Recognition by the pope undoubtedly strengthened Tancred's position. Perhaps it also helped him gain his alliance with the Byzantine emperor, who soon sent his daughter Irene to Sicily as a bride for Tancred's son Roger. Not much, however, is known about this marriage; no chronicle,

---

[159] Godfrey of Viterbo, *Gesta Heinrici VI*, ed. G. H. Pertz, MGH 22 (Hanover: Hahn, 1872), 334–38, here 336. Richard of San Germano, *Chronica*, 65. *Annales Ceccanenses*, 292. *Annales Casinenses*, 316. More details are given in the biographical sketch for Constance of Hauteville.

[160] Jamison, *Admiral Eugenius*, 94; Chalandon, *Histoire*, 2:464–67.

Latin or Greek, discusses details of the negotiations between Tancred and Isaac or explains what each monarch expected from the alliance. But since Irene Angelina later fell into the hands of the Hohenstaufen, we cannot doubt that she actually reached Sicily. Young Roger, though he was declared his father's co-ruler about this time, apparently neither led armies nor took any other actions of which an account has survived. He predeceased his father by several weeks.

C. 13. The Welfs and the English

Pietro also omits mention of Henry's significant opposition in Germany, which also shaped subsequent events. For example, after Henry abandoned the siege of Naples in 1192, he was kept occupied in Germany with a scandal related to the murder of a cleric, Albert, brother of the duke of Brabant, in a disputed episcopal election at Liège,[161] and by serious insurrections among his Welf opponents. These descendents of Henry the Proud and Gertrude, the daughter of Lothar of Supplingburg (see C. 5 above), come into the *Liber* only as distant allusions, the background to vague accusations that Tancred has bribed Henry's friends away before the siege of Naples (ll. 490, 512), and to the account of Henry's dealings with the captive King Richard I of England (ll. 1047–1088).

Lothar's son-in-law, Henry the Proud, did not long survive him, but he left a ten-year-old son, later called Henry the Lion, to carry on his struggle. The conflict lasted throughout the reign of Conrad III of Hohenstaufen, wearying Germany. This, ironically, helped the election of Frederick Barbarossa in 1152. Not only did the dying Conrad III designate his nephew Frederick as his successor, passing over his minor son, but also Frederick's mother Judith was a sister of Henry the Proud.[162] It was hoped that he could end strife between the two families. In fact, Frederick Barbarossa was at first friendly with Henry the Lion, supporting his ambitions in his northern territories and enabling him to become an even more extraordinarily wealthy and powerful prince.[163] However, the Lion's aggressive policies alienated other princes and nobles, while his failure to cooperate with Barbarossa's imperial projects eventually cooled his cousin's friendship. At length, responding to many complaints, Barbarossa initiated legal proceedings against the Lion, which the latter failed to take very seriously. When, after extensive notification and warnings, Henry neglected to appear and answer the charges, a council of princes deprived him of both his duchies, Saxony and

---

[161] Hampe, *Germany Under the Salian and Hohenstaufen Emperors*, 222; chap. 14; see also Thomas Curtis Van Cleve, *Markward of Anweiler and the Sicilian Regency* (Princeton: Princeton University Press, 1937), 6.

[162] Otto of Freising and Rahewin, *The Deeds of Frederick Barbarossa*, bk. 2, chap. 2; see also Mierow's n. 2, on page 49.

[163] Munz, *Frederick Barbarossa*, 261–66; 338–47.

Bavaria. These territories were divided and given to others.[164] To be effective, of course, the judicial sentence had to be followed by successful military action against Henry, and it was. The Lion, overwhelmed, approached Frederick in the November of 1181 and submitted.[165] He was still a wealthy man, since the decree only applied to his duchies insofar as they were fiefs held from the emperor, and had no bearing on other extensive properties, called "allodial," which Henry still possessed directly. However, he presumably risked losing these too if he continued in his rebellion.[166] Frederick banished him for three years, with the stipulation that he could return after that only if the emperor specifically gave permission. As for his possessions, he was "permitted to retain only certain of his hereditary estates situated around Braunschweig [Brunswick] and Lüneburg."[167]

Though exiled, the Welf was hardly destitute. Fifteen years before, in 1164 or 1165, Henry had become betrothed to Matilda, daughter of Henry II of England, a marriage which finally took place in 1168.[168] Now the English king interceded with Barbarossa on behalf of his son-in-law. With persistence and good timing, the Plantagenet gained some concessions. Advised to send envoys to Barbarossa during the Verona negotiations of 1184, he obtained the removal of the Lion's banishment.[169] As part of the bargain, Henry II supposedly agreed to a marriage between his son Richard and one of Barbarossa's daughters, but

---

[164] Munz, *Frederick Barbarossa*, 353–54.

[165] Munz, *Frederick Barbarossa*, 358.

[166] Munz indicates that the choice of procedure, somewhat unusual and not well defined by precedent, limited the possible penalties. A "tribal court" could "outlaw Henry and deprive him of all his property," but Henry had engaged in machinations which prevented the "tribal court" from convening and judging his case. The "feudal court" which Frederick ultimately used was not subject to the same kind of tampering but could only make judgments regarding fiefs. This was, however, acceptable to Barbarossa because "his plan was merely to put an end to Henry's extraordinary power in Saxony. He had no personal animosity against him, and no real grounds for wishing to make him a pauper" (351). Jordan, *Henry the Lion*, 169–70, gives a somewhat different account, stating that even though Henry failed to appear when summoned, the proceedings under "customary law (*Landrecht*)" had concluded with "a ban (*Acht*)" by 1179, before Frederick Barbarossa "instituted a suit under feudal court" which resulted in Henry's being deprived of "his two duchies and all imperial fiefs" at Würzburg, 13 January 1180.

[167] Munz, *Frederick Barbarossa*, 358. Jordan, *Henry the Lion*, 178, states that after his submission, Henry "regained his wide allodial estates in Saxony."

[168] Jordan, *Henry the Lion*, 144–47. (Originally, this marriage was negotiated as part of a bargain in which another daughter of the English king was promised to Frederick Barbarossa's short-lived firstborn son; hence Barbarossa had no reason to be offended by it.)

[169] Toeche, *Kaiser Heinrich VI*, 39.

the maiden died before the marriage could take place.[170] The English king was also asked to influence his other son-in-law, William II of Sicily, to agree to the match between Constance and Henry, king of the Romans.[171] Still, Frederick Barbarossa would never consent to restore the Lion's duchies to him.

The Lion's obvious discontent with this situation made some sort of resolution necessary before Barbarossa departed on his crusade. The emperor offered the Welf three choices: he must renounce all ambition to regain his previous rank, or he must accompany the emperor on the crusade at the emperor's own expense and receive back his original rank on his return, or else he must agree to a three-year banishment for himself and his son Henry. The Lion chose banishment and went to England.[172] But after the emperor's departure, Henry the younger returned to Germany and his father soon followed. Therefore, Henry VI was obliged to undertake a military expedition against them in the winter of 1189–1190, but because he had much other business to deal with, he soon agreed to a peace and allowed Henry the Lion to remain on his lands while his eldest son, also called Henry, would follow the emperor to Italy, and Lothar, the second son, would be a hostage.[173] In the midst of all this war, peace, and pledging of hostages, the younger Henry managed to join his uncle King Richard as the latter moved about his domains in France, preparing to set out from Marseilles for his crusade; this fact is known because the younger Henry, called Henry of Brunswick, witnessed a document of his uncle's at La Réolle, 3 February 1190.[174]

---

[170] The main source on the arrangements for this marriage is Roger of Hoveden, *Gesta*, 106–8. Also Assmann examines these negotiations and their context in "Friedrich Barbarossas Kinder," 451–52. The maiden who was supposed to marry Richard the Lionheart is one for whom Assmann was unable to recover a name, since her grave has not been found, and the names of Barbarossa's daughters appear only at their graves, even though contemporary chronicles often report marriage negotiations about them and sometimes record their deaths. Assmann speculates that Richard's intended bride may have accompanied Barbarossa on his Italian journey around this time, and that she might be buried in one of the Northern Italian Cathedrals or cloisters (457 and n. 95). Jordan, *Henry the Lion*, 184, identifies this princess with Barbarossa's daughter Agnes, who died that year about the same time as her mother, Empress Beatrix. Assmann, however, believes that the evidence, though tenuous, suggests that marriage negotiations were progressing simultaneously for two daughters of different ages, and Agnes cannot have been both.

[171] Chalandon, *Histoire*, 2:388.

[172] Toeche, *Kaiser Heinrich VI*, 122. Jordan, *Henry the Lion*, 188, observes that the chronicler Arnold of Lübeck is the main source for this story and doubts his precision while accepting the general concept.

[173] Toeche, *Kaiser Heinrich VI*, 125–26. Jordan, *Henry the Lion*, 190.

[174] Toeche, *Kaiser Heinrich VI*, 157. Jordan, *Henry the Lion*, 191.

Still, the younger Henry accompanied the emperor on his Italian expedition. When fever broke out among the imperial soldiers, the young Welf deserted and went to Naples, where he remained a while, supporting the besiegers against the Germans. Then he traveled to Marseilles on a Neapolitan ship,[175] having previously obtained from Pope Celestine a privilege exempting him from excommunication except at the direct command of the pope; this would prevent German churchmen from imposing spiritual penalties on him for breaking the treaty with the Hohenstaufen.[176] Henry VI openly declared Henry of Brunswick an outlaw at Pentecost at Worms.[177]

Given this context, when Richard I of England left the Holy Land after his own crusade in 1193 and was found journeying in disguise across imperial territory, Henry VI inevitably had the darkest of suspicions. Since the Welfs were currently in rebellion against him, Henry of Hohenstaufen naturally assumed that Richard meant to join forces with them. Richard, however, somehow blundered into Austria and was captured by Duke Leopold,[178] whom he had insulted and belittled in the Holy Land, denying him a share in the booty although he and many other crusaders had suffered for the taking of Acre long before French or English forces arrived.[179] Duke Leopold handed his royal prisoner over to the emperor. Henry VI has been much vilified for this episode. The best-known result of it was that Henry eventually released Richard in return for a large ransom. However, as Gillingham, among others, explains clearly in his biography of Richard, Henry VI was not at first sure that any amount of money would compensate him for Richard's release. What he wanted from his captive was not merely money but the rectification of an unfavorable political situation, complicated and perhaps even created by Richard's machinations with his Welf relations. In short, Richard would need to reconcile the latter with Henry VI. The negotiations for this purpose stalled several times but were at length helped by

---

[175] Toeche, *Kaiser Heinrich VI*, 198. That Henry the Lion's sons were hostages and that Henry of Brunswick deserted the emperor's camp during the siege of Naples, and then went by way of Marseilles back to Saxony, is told in *Continuationes Weingartenses*, ed. G. H. Pertz, MGH 21 (Hanover: Hahn, 1869), 478.

[176] Toeche, *Kaiser Heinrich VI*, 199. Jordan, *Henry the Lion*, 193.

[177] Toeche, *Kaiser Heinrich VI*, 210. Jordan, *Henry the Lion*, 194.

[178] Leopold V; see Hereford Brooke George, *Genealogical Tables Illustrative of Modern History*, 2nd ed. (Oxford: Clarendon Press, 1875), Table XIII. Also Louis Leger, *A History of Austro-Hungary from the Earliest Times to the Year 1889*, tr. Mrs. Birkbeck Hill (London: Rivington's Waterloo Place, 1889), 131. Leopold V was a son of Henry Jasomirgott, who had contended with Richard's Welf relations for his dukedom of Bavaria. In settling the matter, Frederick Barbarossa had restored the duchy to Henry the Lion and made Henry Jasomirgott's Austrian territories into a dukedom. See genealogical Table 2 in this volume.

[179] John Gillingham, *The Life and Times of Richard I* (London: Weidenfeld and Nicolson, 1973), 115–17.

a runaway marriage between young Henry of Brunswick and Agnes of Hohenstaufen, a cousin of the emperor. (She was the daughter and heiress of Conrad, count palatine of the Rhine, half-brother of Frederick Barbarossa.) The bride's mother helped the young couple to fulfill in secret a promise to marry which had been made long before; Arnold of Lübeck discusses the match at some length.[180] The emperor was bitterly angry, all the more so because he had just promised his cousin to his ally Philip Augustus.[181] Still, the bride's father mediated, until at length the emperor relented. Now allied to the Hohenstaufen family and promised a rich heritage, Henry the Lion's son gave up his belligerence and sense of grievance. Tensions eased, and definite arrangements were made for King Richard's ransom and release, a bargain completed on 4 February 1194.[182] The money he paid helped finance Henry's second Sicilian expedition, now well underway.

C. 14. Tancred's Last Battles

Of course, the situation in Italy did not stand still while all this was going on. Henry's commanders tried to hold his position in Italy, which the *Liber* covers to some extent. When Henry returned to Germany, he had left Conrad of Lützelhard in control of Capua, a strategic city, while Diepold of Vohburg (or Schweinspeunt) held the strategic fortress of Rocca D'Arce. The *Liber* describes how Tancred's brother-in-law attacked Capua, and how, after a heroic defense, Conrad negotiated the right to leave the city with his arms and his surviving men (ll. 773–860). Diepold retained control of Rocca D'Arce, but as Richard of Acerra recovered much of the surrounding region for Tancred, he was obliged to sustain his armies through plunder of the surrounding territory (*Liber*, ll. 1089–1181). The deacon Adenulf (not named in the poem) had remained in charge of Monte Cassino while its abbot, Roffredo, accompanied the emperor to Germany. Adenulf cooperated with Diepold in arranging for the people of the surrounding region to give hostages and supplies to the imperial armies in exchange for relative peace.[183] Naturally, this drew threats from Count Richard of Acerra against the abbey itself, but the deacon held firm.

---

[180] Bk. 5, chap. 20. See also Jordan, *Henry the Lion*, 196; C. von Reisinger, *Tankred von Lecce* (Köln: Böhlau, 1992), 177; Kölzer, "Die Staufer im Süden," in *Petrus de Ebulo: Liber ad Honorem Augusti*, ed. idem et al., 15–31.

[181] Philip Augustus had at this time declared null and void his marriage to the Danish princess Ingeborg. The French church went along with this, but the bride did not, nor did the pope. Conflict and complications resulting from this continued for years, and Philip Augustus eventually recognized Ingeborg as queen without actually treating her as a wife.

[182] Gillingham, *The Life and Times of Richard I*, 188.

[183] *Annales Casinenses*, 316. (The story is told in codices 4 and 5, for the year 1192.)

Outside the Sicilian kingdom, Conrad of Urslingen remained firmly in control of the duchy of Spoleto, able to lend some support to those within the borders and to help communication with Germany. Berthold of Künsberg, who is perhaps to be identified with Pietro's Rombanldus (line 757), was sent to join him in 1192, bringing with him Abbot Roffredo. The latter played a mysterious role in Constance's release, which was not nearly so straightforward a matter as Pietro describes it (ll. 1009–1046). Berthold himself, with the help of Diepold of Schweinspeunt and Conrad of Lützelhard, made such significant territorial gains that Tancred actually took the field against him and crossed into Apulia. Pietro implies, on the contrary, that Tancred was too cowardly to do this (ll. 743–772), bribery being his preferred method. It is clear, however, that he also understood warfare well enough. He may have avoided direct clashes with Henry's major commanders; Richard of San Germano reports that when Tancred was about to meet Berthold on Monte Fusculo, he suddenly decided that such a victory would give him no great honor and drew back.[184] He did capture the fortress of St. Agatha and the castle of Savignano, after which triumphs he put many German captives to death (*extremo supplicio*).[185] Meanwhile, the imperialists attacked Monte Rodone, where Berthold himself was killed by a stone thrown from the walls. Conrad of Lützelhard took command and captured the city, although many had deserted the imperial army and its impetus was stalled.[186] Tancred, however, declined to challenge Diepold even in this weakened form. He besieged Caserta but withdrew when its Count William approached. His next chosen target, Aversa, surrendered to him and gave hostages. Then, recognizing how crucial Monte Cassino was in the campaign, Tancred approached Abbot Roffredo at Teano and tried offers and threats upon him, including messages from the pope, but nothing worked and illness soon forced the king to withdraw.[187] His son Roger died in December 1193, in circumstances unexplained in any source. Tancred himself died 20 February 1194,[188] of grief at the loss of his son, at least according to Innocent III's anonymous chronicler,[189] leaving a minor son, William III, as his successor.

---

[184] *Chronica*, 67.

[185] *Annales Casinenses*, 317.

[186] Kölzer, "Die Staufer im Süden," 25.

[187] *Annales Casinenses*, 317. For the strategic significance of this monastery, see Herbert Bloch, *Monte Cassino in the Middle Ages*, 3 vols. (Cambridge, MA: Harvard University Press, 1988), esp. vol. 1.

[188] Jamison, *Admiral Eugenius*, 101.

[189] *The Deeds of Pope Innocent III*, 18; chap. 20.

C. 15. Conquest and Conspiracies

Meanwhile, Henry VI had made detailed plans and assembled a glorious army, backed by naval forces from both Genoa and Pisa. Salerno was sacked, and elsewhere the former Tancredines either fled or joined the emperor. Realizing that her cause was hopeless, Queen Sibylla asked for peace, and Henry VI granted her fairly generous terms. He agreed that she could keep the county of Lecce, which Tancred had held, and added that he would confer on her son the princedom of Taranto, which had not previously belonged to Tancred's family. However, shortly after Henry's triumphant coronation as king of Sicily, he arrested Sibylla and her family, along with the archbishop Nicholas of Salerno and many others, accusing them of a conspiracy against his life. As Pietro leaves the story, the convicted conspirators are prisoners in Apulia, but we know that subsequently they were sent as prisoners to Germany, where some were later blinded and perhaps mutilated in other ways. From contemporary chronicles it is easy to get the impression that Henry's reign in Sicily is one long bloodbath, beginning at his coronation. This is because chronicles often telescoped events, no doubt because many of the stories took years to arrive and were then told retrospectively by witnesses who remembered causal connections but did not know exact dates. However, Henry's biographer, Theodor Toeche, established by painstaking work, comparing chronicles with other documents, that Henry VI ordered no executions or mutilations immediately upon the discovery of the 1194 conspiracy. Instead, a large group of prisoners, including the former queen Sibylla and her family, were sent to Germany and held under relatively mild conditions there. Sibylla and her daughters were brought to the convent of Hohenburg, while most of the others were kept together at Trifels, which had also served as a prison for Richard I.[190] Later, however, exasperated by more trouble in Sicily, the emperor sent more instructions concerning these prisoners who had, until then, been kept in the Rhine region (*in confinia Rheni*), ordering that "certain ones should be blinded, and certain ones imprisoned separately from each other" (*missa legatione quosdam exoculari, quosdam incarcerari ab invicem separatos precepit*).[191] There is still dispute about what events precipitated this harsher treatment and which prisoners received the worst of it, and whether the former boy-king, Tancred's son William, was among them. Most scholars on the subject feel compelled to measure these deeds against their own standards of justice, and find them wanting, even in Toeche's mitigated version. Henry seems, as Chalandon points out, to have punished his prisoners for offenses they could not have been involved in, a point on which Norwich echoes him.[192] When Henry is measured against other potentates of his time and afterwards, he may not prove the worst of them. As is plain

---

[190] Jamison, *Admiral Eugenius*, 125–26.

[191] *Continuationes Weingartenses*, 477, cod. 2.

[192] Chalandon, *Histoire*, 2:490. Norwich, *Kingdom in the Sun*, 387.

from the narrative up until now, the taking and holding of hostages for the good behavior of their families and connections was the custom of the times, and if the prisoners of 1194 were regarded *de facto* as hostages as well as wrongdoers, their treatment would not have seemed completely arbitrary. To carry out a sentence, passed previously but suspended for a while, on a prisoner actually proven guilty of treason, would seem more just than to mistreat entirely innocent hostages.

Pietro seems to know nothing about the grisly executions which were to end Henry VI's reign. Yet his rather obscure words about the prisoners of 1194 may contain a hint of what was to happen. He writes, "*In condempnatos meritum sententia tardat, / Quo datur ut vinctos Apula dampnet humus,*" (Against the condemned, the sentence holds back its full weight / By which it is granted that Apulian soil might doom the prisoners) (ll. 1357–1386). Falcandus, describing the minority of William II, records that one sentence passed by the royal justiciars put the defendant at "the king's mercy for limbs and body" (*de membris et corpore regis misericordie subiacere*);[193] in fact, the defendant, Richard of Mandra, was put in prison and later set free by a rebellion, though the castellan tried to kill him to prevent his escape.[194] Another source records that the prisoner was about to be blinded when rescued.[195] Perhaps something similar happened with the conspirators of 1194. Putting them at the "king's mercy for limbs and body" might be the least severe sentence which could possibly express the gravity of what they had attempted, though perhaps specific sentences would have been recommended. Rather like Stephen du Perche in Falcandus's account, the emperor held them prisoner but did nothing further at the time, perhaps hoping that the imprisonment would be enough to restrain further rebellions, and that at some future time when everything was peaceful they could be pardoned altogether. If there were further rebellions, however, their kinsmen and allies would intrigue for their release, and when freed they would be dangerous enemies. Though at first glance it may seem that the prisoners in Germany were quite remote from such a risk, we have already seen that the emperor had enemies there too, and his German enemies had already formed alliances with his Sicilian opponents. Hence, in carrying out the long postponed punishments on his imprisoned enemies, the emperor would have minimized the harm they could later cause; of course, while such justifications would satisfy his allies, they would not prevent outrage and anguish among his enemies.

Of course, another question about the incident is whether the conspiracy happened at all. Jamison asserts that the initial mild treatment of the conspirators of 1194 is evidence that they were innocent. In her view, Henry VI trumped

---

[193] *La Historia,* 141. *History of the Tyrants,* trans. Loud and Wiedemann, 194.

[194] *History of the Tyrants,* trans. Loud and Wiedemann, 207.

[195] *Ignoti Monachi Cisterciensis S. Mariae De Ferraria Chronica,* in *Ignoti Monachi Cisterciensis S. Mariae De Ferraria Chronica et Ryccardi de Sancto Germano Chrionica Priora,* ed. Augustus Gaudenzi (Naples: Giannini, 1888), 30.

up the conspiracy as an excuse to annul the excessively generous bargain he had made with Sibylla, or at least seized on a minor conspiracy to allege the involvement of many other people.[196] She explains that Henry needed to offer generous terms in order to draw Sibylla from her fortified castle, but he could not afford to keep the bargain because it left her and her son too free, with her brother, Count Richard of Acerra, at large in Apulia. The idea sounds plausible, but is based more on speculative interpretation of scant evidence than on known facts. After all, the precise terms of Henry's agreement with Sibylla have not come down to us. The most detailed information we have about it is in *The Deeds of Pope Innocent III* (29–31). Innocent's anonymous biographer reports that after Henry's death, and during the minority of Frederick II, the pope, being the young king's guardian, decided to support the claim of Tancred's daughter Alberia to the princedom of Taranto. This was all on the strength of Henry VI's promise to Tancred's son William, whose claim Alberia supposedly inherited. However, the account suggests that the agreement had been in the form of an oath given in public; there is no mention of any written document, nor of any attempt on Innocent's part to obtain such a document. Also, the account indicates that the pope did not consult Henry VI's former ministers or those of Constance (that is, the governing council of *familiares* in Palermo), to learn whether they remembered the oath or understood it differently than did Alberia's new husband, who petitioned him. Rather, the pope announces his decision and his reasoning but invites the *familiares* to require further guarantees for Walter's good behavior if they think it necessary. In explaining his decision, he stresses the fact that Henry VI had promised the princedom to young William III, who, like his sister, was then a minor and could not be blamed for any conspiracies in which his elders might have been involved.

All this says nothing about clauses in the agreement which obliged the emperor to permit Sibylla, while her brother was still in open rebellion, to take her son and her three daughters away from his supervision to live as they pleased on their lands. For evidence of such an agreement, Jamison cites Pietro himself, line 1302: *"Ad Lichium veniam poscit itura suum."* In my translation, I render this "She asks pardon, meaning to return to her Lecce." One could bring it closer to Jamison's interpretation by rendering it, plausibly, as "She asks the favor of [being allowed to] return to her Lecce." Even so, this hardly sounds like the language of a treaty, and the passage suggests no time limit. Other chronicles do nothing to clarify the matter. Some tell the story with considerable sympathy for Sibylla's family, but they give few details about the terms which led the former queen to summon her children away from their stronghold in Caltabellotta. One of the most detailed accounts comes from the *Annales Cassinenses*, which say:[197]

---

[196] Jamison, *Admiral Eugenius*, 118–46
[197] *Annales Casinenses*, 317; codices 4 and 5 for the year 1194.

William, the new little king, having left the palace to his mother, took refuge in a fortified castle which is called Caltabellotta. Seeing this, the people of Palermo summon the emperor. But he, having sent envoys ahead and made a treaty with the queen about giving to her the county of Lecce and to her son the principality of Taranto, hastens on, entering Palermo magnificently, and is received into the palace. Not much later, the same little king, laying down his fortune with his crown, comes to his feet.

Wilelmus novus regulus dimisso palatio matri, recipit se in castrum munitum quod dicitur Calatabillotta. Quo viso populus Panormitanus imperatorem vocat. At ille praemissis nuntiis et foedere facto cum regina de dando sibi comitatu licii et filio principatu Tarenti, properat, et magnifice Panormum ingrediens in palatio recipitur, nec multo post idem regulus fortunam cum corona deponens, ad pedes eius venit.

All in all, it seems most likely that Henry's oath was a promise to accept Sibylla and her children as loyal subjects and to grant them the lands repeatedly mentioned, Lecce and Taranto. No doubt it was understood that many other points needed to be worked out, including the continued rebellion of Sibylla's brother. Henry would hardly consider himself obliged to let her leave court with her children until these things were settled. Absent inflexible terms of the kind Jamison describes, Henry had no motive to trump up charges against Tancred's family. As long as Sibylla began by keeping her side of the bargain, he had plenty of time to attach her family to his cause or to maneuver them into positions of impotence and insignificance. Meanwhile, it was in his interest to receive the kingdom as little damaged as possible, so that more resources could be devoted to his crusade. Sibylla's supporters, on the other hand, needed to act fast, before the Sicilians completely transferred their loyalty to their new rulers. In short, reasons can be found to believe Henry VI's (or Pietro's) version of the events.

Though what remained of Henry's reign was short, it was full of activity. After the birth of his son, Henry started working to arrange for the infant's succession to the empire and the kingdom of Sicily at the same time. This involved many complications, since the empire was elective and the kingdom, though hereditary, was in theory the papacy's feudal possession. Henry negotiated a preliminary agreement whereby the German princes agreed to make the empire hereditary, as long as the pope consented. The pope, of course, denied consent, and Henry had to content himself with the election of his infant son as "king of the Romans"[198] in the traditional fashion. Henry hoped also to settle the long dispute between empire and papacy about the lands of the Countess Matilda of Tuscany, and apparently intended to offer generous financial terms, but these, too, the pope rejected.[199] In fact, Celestine III excommunicated the emperor's

---

[198] Van Cleve, *Emperor Frederick II of Hohenstaufen*, 20–23.

[199] Hampe, *Germany Under the Salian and Hohenstaufen Emperors*, 227.

brother, Philip of Swabia (whom the emperor had made duke of Tuscany), because of his attempts to govern there.[200]

Also, he imposed a special tax to finance his crusade.[201] This undoubtedly caused some discontent and distress in the kingdom. Henry also declared Tancred's acts invalid and demanded that all his grants be surrendered for confirmation, which is not surprising, nor is it surprising that he re-granted many of Tancred's gifts to nobles who had come over to his side.[202] He had powerful reasons to reject some of Tancred's precedents (particularly his abandonment of the special status of the Sicilian church), but no reason to spurn the service or damage the prosperity of those he now trusted to follow him. Nevertheless, serious opposition to him once more took shape toward the end of 1196, and Sibylla's brother, Richard of Acerra, attempted some major action, perhaps in alliance with Count Roger of Molise. Both were defeated, but the latter negotiated permission from the vassal charged with subduing him, Conrad of Lützelhard, to depart from his lands and the kingdom of Sicily peacefully. Richard of Acerra, however, was captured by Diepold of Schweinspeunt and handed over to the emperor, who executed him in grisly fashion. Also, Henry sent instructions to Germany for some of the prisoners there to be treated more severely.[203]

Then, in the spring of 1197, there was another conspiracy against his life. Chronicles say and some scholars, including Van Cleve, believe that "both the Pope and Empress appear to have had a part."[204] Evidently the rebels had chosen one of their number to marry Constance and become the next king. Toeche also expresses belief that Constance had turned against her husband and even against her infant son; he seems to regard this as something of an extenuating circumstance for the vicious retaliations and gruesome executions Henry then ordered.[205]

The conspirators, having raised an army, intended to surprise and kill the emperor while he was hunting. However, warning reached him in time and he took refuge in Messina, whose citizens supported him, giving him cause to thank them (on 11 May) for their loyalty.[206] At once Markward of Anweiler and Henry of Kalden came to his help, along with some of the crusaders already gathered near the port city, preparing for their departure.[207] But their enemies were not easily overcome. Some of their forces took refuge in Catania, since the bishop of

---

[200] *Deeds of Pope Innocent III*, 20–21.

[201] Jamison, *Admiral Eugenius*, 154.

[202] Jamison, *Admiral Eugenius*, 115

[203] Jamison, *Admiral Eugenius*, 153–55.

[204] *The Emperor Frederick II of Hohenstaufen*, 23.

[205] *Kaiser Heinrich VI*, 453–57, 582–83.

[206] Peter Csendes, *Heinrich VI.* (Darmstadt: Wissenschaftliche Buchgesellschaft, 1993), 191 and n. 4.

[207] Van Cleve, *The Emperor Frederick II of Hohenstaufen*, 23–24.

that city was one of their leaders. Catania was attacked and burned. The rest fled to Enna (also called Castrogiovanni), which was soon taken.

It is often asserted, and may even be true, that at this time Henry executed more people, and with more cruelty, than his predecessors had at any one time in Sicily. For example, Norwich writes that Henry's last months were "more violent than anything known under the Normans."[208] But complaints are not lacking about previous Norman rulers,[209] who after all wrested these lands from Lombard, Greek, and Moslem rulers, imposing in the end a kingdom where only scattered jurisdictions had ruled before. They did not do this by using mild and gentle methods all the time. Precise statistics are hard to come by.

Certainly the ringleaders of this conspiracy were cruelly executed. Their leader, supposedly the pretender who meant to marry Constance, had a crown nailed to his head. Jamison convincingly identifies this man as Jordan Lupin, one of the Lupin brothers. Many histories and fictions about Frederick II mention this execution, saying that the empress Constance was ordered by her imperial husband to watch it, because he dared not punish her in any other way for her disloyalty. There are, however, other ways to understand his orders.

Toeche asserts that Henry VI and Frederick II both suppressed knowledge of Constance's guilt.[210] Csendes, however, points out[211] that most of the details about this last conspiracy come from the German chroniclers, and their accusations against Constance are partly a result of their mistrust of their emperor's foreign consort. The emperor himself left no clear sign that he suspected Constance. In fact, one of the provisions of the "testament" which he supposedly dictated to Markward of Anweiler in his last days was that Constance should rule Sicily for life if she should outlive both himself and their son.[212]

By September 1197, Henry VI was too ill to depart on his long-planned crusade. Some of his chief officials set out ahead of him, including his chancellor

---

[208] *Kingdom in the Sun*, 387.

[209] Houben, *Roger II*, 1–7.

[210] *Kaiser Heinrich VI*, 583.

[211] Csendes, *Heinrich VI.*, 191.

[212] Henry's supposed "Testament," discussed in *The Deeds of Innocent III*, in Van Cleve's *Markward of Anweiler*, and to a lesser extent in the latter's *Emperor Frederick II*, is something of a historical puzzle. The document was seized from Markward's captured baggage after he lost the battle of Monreale, and part of it published by Innocent's anonymous chronicler (*Deeds of Pope Innocent III*, 34–35; chap. 26), the only context from which any of it is known. As Van Cleve convincingly describes it, it was not a last will or testament in the usual sense, but "a body of instructions for the guidance of his executor in his negotiations with the Pope" (*Emperor*, 38; *Markward*, 67) and David Abulafia concurs in *Frederick II* (Oxford: Oxford University Press, 1988), 90. See Introduction C.17 below.

Conrad of Querfurt and his marshal, Henry of Kalden.[213] They expected him to follow soon, but instead of recovering, he grew worse. On 26 September 1197 he died at Messina,[214] and Constance was with him in his last moments (*Deeds of Pope Innocent II*, 19).[215]

C. 16. Constance After Henry's Death

As she surely foresaw, Constance and her son were caught in a whirlwind of reaction after Henry's death. But whether she knew it or not, she had little more than a year to live, and during that time much needed to be done to create a stable situation for her son's upbringing. As is reported in all the biographies of Frederick II, she soon dismissed the Germans from her kingdom. Kantorowicz, in his famous biography *Frederick the Second*, attributes this to her "hatred of Germans" and states that it was "the first act of her reign" to "banish" Markward of Anweiler, along with "all other German notables" (15) in her kingdom. Van Cleve, in *Emperor Frederick II*, interprets Constance similarly (36), though with less flamboyant words, while admitting that details are uncertain. The empress's near-contemporaries were indeed vague about timing and motive. As Richard of San Germano describes the event in his chronicle, Constance summoned her German officials and made them swear to go beyond the borders of her kingdom and to stay away unless she specifically summoned them back. Her stated objective was to preserve the peace. Markward obeyed her, evidently in leisurely fashion. Given safe-conduct (*securitate*) by Count Peter of Celano, he left his castellans in charge in his county of Molise, so clearly he had not actually been deprived of his fief, though he apparently handed over some territory (Vairano) to the count in exchange for his protection. Then he crossed into the March of Ancona.[216]

Perhaps Constance's fears of violent upheaval were not idle. In her childhood and youth, she had lived through and surely heard about massacres on at

---

[213] Eduard Winkelmann, *Philipp von Schwaben und Otto IV von Braunschweig*, 2 vols. (Leipzig: Verlag von Duncker und Humblot, 1873–1878), 60.

[214] Assmann, "Friedrich Barbarossas Kinder," 459.

[215] Conventionally, during the twelfth century one would naturally expect a dying man's family to gather around him, including his wife. Thus what is surprising about the *Gesta*'s report is not the empress's presence, but the author's specific mention of it in what is otherwise not a detailed account of Constance's life. What did it mean to him, and to Pope Innocent III, that she was there? Perhaps Henry's "testament" in Markward's possession was on their minds; if she were with him when he died, she would surely have some notion whether such a thing were being prepared and what was in it. Her failure to say anything about it suggests its invalidity—or does it? If there is truth in Roger of Hoveden's allegations (*Chronica*, ed. G. Waitz, MGH 27 [Hanover: Hahn, 1885], 177), that Henry died excommunicated and Constance had trouble getting permission for a proper burial, her knowledge of his state of mind at death might perhaps have been an issue.

[216] Richard of San Germano, *Chronica Priora*, 68.

least two occasions (both described by the chronicler Falcandus). During the coup of 1161, an angry mob had risen to murder every "Saracen" or Moslem they could catch, until the threatened population withdrew to a more defensible location.[217] In 1169 the people of Messina rose, enraged by the arrogant behavior of the French entourage surrounding Stephen du Perche, and murdered all the Frenchmen they could find.[218] A similar scene might have occurred in Palermo except that Stephen agreed to leave the kingdom. Perhaps, after all, Constance knew something about the potential for conflict to break out between discordant linguistic and ethnic groups. Even Kantorowicz observes that German crusaders returning by way of Sicily after the emperor's death "were surprised and plundered by the excited Sicilians."[219]

Constance's situation was made more difficult by the death of Celestine III and the election of a new pope, Innocent III, who was more vehemently hostile to the Hohenstaufens than Celestine had been. He also had grander plans to improve the position of the papacy with territorial powers and claims. And if Celestine III was a fraction less than absolutely certain that a union between the kingdom of Sicily and the Holy Roman Empire would be an unmitigated disaster, Innocent had no such doubts. His actions suggest that he thought the safest way to avoid the possibility was to remove Hohenstaufen rulers from both realms.

Nevertheless Constance, having fetched her son from the care of the duchess of Spoleto in Foligno (where he had remained since shortly after his birth), persuaded Innocent III to acknowledge young Frederick as king of Sicily, to consent to his crowning, and to become his guardian. Of course, as Abulafia points out, "Innocent, as overlord of a minor, Frederick, hardly needed to be appointed his guardian; it was his feudal duty, as suzerain of the king of Sicily, to protect his ward once Frederick's parents were both dead."[220] Hence, it must be understood, Constance's purpose here was actually to gain Innocent's recognition, by arranging terms good enough that he dare not refuse them in the hopes of getting a more favorable position some other way. For this she had to renounce Frederick's imperial election and even to give up the special rights of the Sicilian church, putting herself and her son on the same footing the usurper Tancred had negotiated for himself.[221] Innocent III's biographer asserts that she was reluctant to do this, but Innocent firmly insisted that he would not grant her son these hereditary rights of the Norman Sicilian kingdom, so at last she gave her

---

[217] *History of the Tyrants*, trans. Loud and Wiedemann, 109–10.

[218] *History of the Tyrants*, trans. Loud and Wiedemann, 205–6.

[219] *Frederick the Second*, 15.

[220] Abulafia, *Frederick II*, 93.

[221] Van Cleve, *Emperor Frederick II of Hohenstaufen*, 36. J. L. A. Huillard-Bréholles, *Historia Diplomatica*, 1:8 and 1:10–11.

envoys permission to make such an agreement. However, she died before the final treaty reached her.[222]

C. 17. Frederick II as the Pope's Ward

Thus began Frederick II's chaotic minority, described in all his biographies, but in most detail by Van Cleve. Innocent III found that the government ministers, or *familiares*, whom Constance had appointed, were uncooperative, though she cannot be blamed for thwarting him deliberately there. The chief of them, Walter of Palear, bishop of Troia, was one whom Innocent himself had imposed on Constance, although she had distrusted him and tried to dismiss him.[223] Innocent wished, more for the sake of the papacy than the good of the kingdom, to get rid of Henry's German followers, not only the ones based in Sicily, but also those who held imperial lands in central Italy. Some, like Conrad of Urslingen, duke of Spoleto, departed peacefully, but others fought back. Diepold of Vohburg (or Schweinspeunt), who had refused Constance's orders to depart, remained entrenched in Apulia, while Markward of Anweiler initially departed but crossed back into the kingdom after the empress's death, attempting, as he claimed, to carry out the instructions in Henry VI's so-called "testament," which had been entrusted to him.

Meanwhile, in Germany, there had been a disputed imperial election. Philip of Swabia had at first positioned himself to represent the rights of his young nephew, "to assume the guardianship in accordance with German law, which recognized this as a right and duty of the nearest agnate."[224] But when it became clear that a rival faction had formed around Otto the Welf, encouraged by King Richard of England and by the pope, Philip realized that their machinations could not be defeated by an absent child. Therefore, he allowed himself to be elected as emperor, which happened on 8 March 1198.[225] Philip still kept an eye on Sicily, and communicated with Markward of Anweiler. While Philip certainly had not forgotten the Roman Empire's ancient claim to Sicily, the treaty between Barbarossa and William II, as well as Philip's own kinship with young Frederick, obliged him to respect the Norman kingdom as an independent entity. Also, the boy was still Philip's most likely successor as emperor, since as yet he had neither sons nor sons-in-law.

Philip of Swabia's alliance with Markward only made Pope Innocent more anxious to drive the Germans out. To help in this undertaking, he was even willing to admit into the kingdom a new son-in-law of Tancred, Walter of Brienne. Walter, who had just married Tancred's daughter Alberia, appealed to Pope

---

[222] *Deeds of Pope Innocent III*, 20.

[223] *Deeds of Pope Innocent III*, 22; chap. 22.

[224] Van Cleve, *Emperor Frederick II of Hohenstaufen*, 29.

[225] Van Cleve, *Emperor Frederick II of Hohenstaufen*, 51.

Innocent to restore his wife's inheritance to her; that is, to grant her the county of
Lecce and the princedom of Taranto, which Henry VI had, in 1194, promised to
Alberia's brother William, now dead (see above). Innocent accepted the claim as
valid, and chroniclers such as Thomas Tuscus and Giovanni Villani indicate that
popes continued to look with favor upon Alberia and her family after the death
of her first husband.[226] Frederick II's biographers ask what the pope's thoughts
and motives could have been when he proposed to put the heir of the usurper
in a position of power over his own ward. Pope Innocent's own biographer ac-
knowledged that he realized young Frederick might mistrust him and that the
Sicilian *familiares* might literally "be scandalized" (*scandalizarentur*)[227] by this
action, despite the oaths he had made Walter swear. Nevertheless, he evidently
did not expect as much resistance as he actually received from the *familiares*.
They refused to accept Tancred's heir as a trustworthy associate and even allied
themselves with the Germans against him. When the pope's marshal, James, de-
feated Markward in a battle at Monreale, they did not provide resources to pay
his army, so that he was forced to withdraw.[228] Quarrels between Innocent and
the *familiares* took bizarre forms at times. According to Innocent's biographer,
the boy-king's chancellor wrote a letter to the pope as if from the young king,
complaining that his hereditary enemy had been summoned into the kingdom.
Innocent wrote a letter in reply, ostensibly addressed to the young king but actu-
ally intended for the *familiares*, assuring the young king that Tancred's son-in-
law was more his friend than Markward, who wished to kill him and usurp his
throne. He added that the king's current *familiares* were more dangerous to him
than Walter of Brienne. Still, he urged the young king to forgive them if they
repented. In this letter, the pope puts Tancred on an equal footing with Con-
stance, calling them both "of illustrious memory," but extending no such cour-
tesy to Henry VI (40–45). Whether the *familiares* actually showed the letter to
their six-year-old ward at the time is uncertain, but probably he read it eventu-
ally. The pope's championship of Walter of Brienne was still a bitter point with
him in later years. For example, in 1246, after Innocent IV had proclaimed his
deposition, Frederick still thought this action from the past worth mentioning
among all his other troubles: "[Pope Innocent] sent the Count of Brienne, who,

---

[226] Thomas Tuscus, *Gesta imperatorum et pontificum*, ed. Ernesto Ehrenfeuchter,
MGH 22 (Hanover: Hahn, 1872), 490–528, here 499. The same material appears in the
chronicle of Giovanni Villani, *Selections from the Chronicle of Villani*, trans. Rose E. Selfe,
ed. Philip H. Wicksteed (London: Archibald Constable, 1906), bk. 4, chap. 20.

[227] *Deeds of Pope Innocent III*, 29, chap. 25 (Powell's translation). The original Latin
can be found in David Richard Gress-Wright, ed., "The *Gesta Innocentii III*: Text, Intro-
duction and Commentary" (Ph.D. diss., Bryn Mawr College, 1981), 27. Among scan-
dalized biographers, the most vehement is perhaps Van Cleve, *Emperor Frederick II of
Hohenstaufen* (42–43).

[228] Van Cleve, *Emperor Frederick II of Hohenstaufen*, 45.

as the son-in-law of Tancred the usurping king, was thirsting for our death and blood, into the kingdom under the pretense of being our protector" (*Comitem de Brenna, qui velut gener Tancredi regis intrusi mortem nostram et sanguinem sitebat, sub defensionis nostrae specie misit in regnum*).[229]

Walter of Brienne came to claim his inheritance and enjoyed some success. Reacting to this, Markward suddenly seized the palace at Palermo and the young king. A surviving letter tells how, when Markward came upon the boy-king in his hiding place to seize him, the child first struggled, then tore his clothes and "his own flesh" in outrage at his own helplessness. As Van Cleve points out, the contemporary observer, "Reginald of Capua," inteprets his reaction as "the proud disdain of Mount Sinai when touched by a beast of prey," though the modern history sees it as the "conduct . . . of a high-spirited boy confronted with something he had been taught to fear."[230] Markward, however, did not harm the boy, though the author of Innocent's *Gesta* claims that he was restrained only by the fear that Walter of Brienne would claim the throne if young Frederick should die, thus becoming a worse obstruction to Markward's aims.[231]

Markward soon died, but another warlord took his place as the king's "guardian." Pope Innocent finally managed to regain custody of him in 1206, with the help of Diepold of Schweinspeunt.[232]

As he reached the age of majority in 1209, Frederick married (through the pope's arrangement) Constance of Aragon, whose dowry was supposed to bring him resources he needed to put the kingdom into order. Unfortunately, a sudden epidemic killed Constance's brother and many of the knights he had brought with him, before he could help.[233]

C. 18. Frederick II Becomes Emperor

At this time, Innocent's interventions in Germany seemed to bear fruit. It is true that the candidate he backed, Otto the Welf, lost most of his support when Richard of England died in 1199. After that, Otto fared so badly that Innocent became reconciled to Philip of Swabia and agreed to perform his imperial coronation. Evidently they made an agreement whereby one of Philip's daughters was to marry a nephew of the pope, to settle some questions about the Countess Matilda's land.[234] Thus, ironically, the pope attempted to check the dynastic

---

[229] Huillard-Bréholles, *Historia Diplomatica*, 6:389; see also T. L Kington, *The History of Frederick the Second: From Chronicles and Documents Published Within the Last Ten Years* (London: Macmillan, 1852), 2:383.

[230] Van Cleve, *Emperor Frederick II of Hohenstaufen*, 46–47.

[231] *Deeds of Pope Innocent III*, 47; chap. 35.

[232] Van Cleve, *Emperor Frederick II of Hohenstaufen*, 53–54.

[233] Van Cleve, *Emperor Frederick II of Hohenstaufen*, 66–67.

[234] Hampe, *Germany Under the Salian and Hohenstaufen Emperors*, 242.

ambitions of secular princes through dynastic alliances of his own. But suddenly Philip was murdered by Otto of Wittelsbach, a disappointed suitor of one of his daughters.

No doubt with relief, Innocent III threw his support back to Otto the Welf, crowning him in 1209 after requiring him to promise that he would respect the territories of the Roman church, including the duchy of Spoleto and the marquisate of Tuscany, and that he would leave the kingdom of Sicily in peace. However, Otto of Brunswick began to break these promises almost as soon as he was crowned. He gave Spoleto to a German of his choice, Diepold of Vohburg (or Schweinspeunt), and set about conquering Sicily.

Dismayed, Pope Innocent wrote to Philip Augustus of France, admitting that the king had warned him well about Otto's character, and asking for his help.[235] Philip Augustus, on bad terms both with Otto and with the latter's uncle, King John of England, went to work willingly. Soon the German supporters of the Hohenstaufen elected Frederick II once more and sent envoys to Sicily to persuade the youth to accept. Innocent III excommunicated Otto and declared for Frederick, who was, however, obliged to promise to give up Sicily to his newborn son Henry, while he himself rode off to claim the empire. In 1214, countering these blows, Otto the Welf attacked Philip Augustus of France in concert with King John of England. Defeated at the battle of Bouvines, Otto returned home in disgrace. He died in 1218.

C. 19. Frederick II's Crusade, Later Career, and Death

Frederick II's long and complex reign as emperor then began. About this, many books, in various genres, from different perspectives, and with differing levels of seriousness, have been written. They cannot be summarized here. But since, if Pietro is telling the truth, Frederick was born only because, for a short time, the pope, the emperor, and the king of Sicily all agreed that a crusade was of paramount importance, it seems right to break off this account after summing up Frederick II's relationship to crusades. The plans for a crusade called him into existence by making his parents' marriage possible; he participated famously in a crusade at the midpoint of his life; and toward the end of his reign, after Pope Innocent IV pronounced his deposition, a crusade was preached against him.

All the time Frederick was winning his empire in the north, the pope continued to direct crusades. Frederick himself took a crusader's vows on 24 July 1215, the day he was crowned at Aachen.[236] Years passed, however, before he was able to go on this expedition. By the time he did, his first consort had died, and he married, in 1225, Isabella of Brienne, heiress of the kingdom of Jerusalem.[237]

---

[235] Van Cleve, *Emperor Frederick II of Hohenstaufen*, 71.

[236] Van Cleve, *Emperor Frederick II of Hohenstaufen*, 96.

[237] Van Cleve, *Emperor Frederick II of Hohenstaufen*, 163.

Then, in 1227, he actually sailed, but an epidemic struck his army. His companion, the landgrave of Thuringia, died aboard ship, and Frederick himself, seriously ill, turned back. He sent to Pope Gregory IX explaining the reason for the new delay, but the latter refused to believe him and proclaimed the sentence of excommunication against him, thus carrying out a formal threat which his predecessor, Honorius, had made against those who had not by this date fulfilled their crusading vows.

Frederick visited the famous baths of Pozzuoli, subject of Pietro's other surviving poem, during his convalescence and then made new plans to sail. He repeatedly appealed to Gregory to remove the excommunication, but the pope refused, seeing the opportunity to demand Frederick's submission on many other issues as the price for his absolution.[238] Instead of submitting, Frederick II departed on his crusade, still under the sentence of excommunication.

In response, the pope invaded Frederick's Sicilian kingdom and sent envoys to prevent the Templars, Hospitallers, and barons of the crusader kingdom from cooperating with Frederick's actions in the Holy Land. Nevertheless, Frederick accomplished what no crusading army had done since 1187: he gained Jerusalem for Christendom. This was also what Pietro had imagined for his father in the *Liber* (ll. 1463–1472). Frederick II did not do it through warfare, however, but by negotiation. To be sure, his status and aims as a crusader were a major point of the negotiations. He made it clear to Sultan al-Kamil, with whom, as king of Sicily, he had long enjoyed friendly diplomatic relations, that he would prefer to gain the lands peacefully but would ultimately be obliged to fight for them if they were not given. Al-Kamil, troubled by indigenous rivals, eventually decided to oblige him, yielding Jerusalem and some essential adjacent territories and cities. The pope and his allies had, predictably, nothing good to say about the treaty; some claimed that crusaders were not allowed to fortify the regained territories, but accounts vary and no copy has survived to clarify the point.[239] Frederick obviously could not hold out for a better deal. He raced home to drive the papal occupation forces out of Sicily.

Pope Gregory was, for the time, obliged to make peace with him, a peace which did not last. Further quarrels and another breach came later, and Gregory's successor Innocent IV pronounced Frederick's deposition. As Frederick attempted reconciliation toward the end of his life, he offered, among other things, to go to the Holy Land permanently and work for the restoration of the kingdom there. However, Innocent IV rejected these terms and had a crusade preached against him.[240] This spiritual backing for earthly warfare had an effect, of course, but not a speedy one where Frederick was concerned. He died in 1250, still actually in possession of his kingdom, after making a confession in accordance

---

[238] Van Cleve, *Emperor Frederick II of Hohenstaufen*, 196–98.

[239] Van Cleve, *Emperor Frederick II of Hohenstaufen*, 216–22.

[240] Van Cleve, *Emperor Frederick II of Hohenstaufen*, 485, 495, 503.

with Christian rites and receiving absolution from Berard, the archbishop of Palermo, who had always been loyal to him. The popes still worked to dispossess his dynasty, however, and instigated Charles of Anjou to conquer the kingdom of Sicily. Successful in this undertaking, King Charles eventually executed the last Hohenstaufen claimant to the throne, Frederick's grandson Conradin, who was also grandson of John of Brienne and heir to the kingdom of Jerusalem. The destruction of the Hohenstaufen dynasty, and the realistic end of the dream of Constantine's empire, did not result, as Popes Innocent III and IV had hoped, with an independent papacy securely in control of Rome and central Italy. Instead it paved the way for the Avignon papacy and the great schism.

In the kingdom of Jerusalem, the treaty with al-Kamil was kept and Jerusalem remained in Christian hands until the attack, in 1244, by the Khorezmians or Kwarismians.[241] After that, Jerusalem was never again recovered by the crusader kingdom. The kingdom itself fell in 1271 with its last stronghold, Acre.[242]

D. Form and Literary Value

Marlis Stähli, in the Kölzer and Stähli edition of the *Liber*, reviews the theory, which she reports is widespread, that Pietro's choice of form was influenced by the liturgical Exultet Rolls much used in southern Italy at this time.[243] These rolls, consisting of sheets of parchment stitched together so that pictures alternate with text, would be unrolled vertically during the service for blessing the Paschal Candle, so that for each part of the sequence, the script would face the reader, while the pictures would face the congregation.[244] This would help a congregation follow a liturgy whose language it could only partly understand. Though Pietro's works are, of course, bound in a codex, they do make use of the same close association between picture and text, perhaps for the same reason: the audience was somewhat familiar with Latin, but not always enough to understand the words easily. Therefore pictures gave the audience more to enjoy and helped convey the story.

---

[241] Van Cleve, *Emperor Frederick II of Hohenstaufen*, 473; Runciman, *History of the Crusades*, 3:224.

[242] Runciman, *History of the Crusades*, 3:420.

[243] Stähli, "Unvollendete," 257.

[244] Michelle P. Brown, *Illuminated Manuscripts: A Guide to Technical Terms* (Los Angeles: Getty Publications, 1994), 108. However, see also Thomas Forrest Kelly, *The Exultet in Southern Italy* (New York: Oxford University Press, 1996). Kelly points out (200–8) that, due to distance and poor lighting, congregations would not have been able to see the *Exultet* illustrations in detail. Thus their rich ornamentation was mostly intended to increase the status of the bishops who owned them.

In the manuscript which has come down to us, the pictures and the text were clearly designed to complement one another. The first page of the manuscript is actually a picture-page, showing three poets with unrolled scrolls, each bearing, as a caption or legend, the first line of that poet's work. The poem itself begins on the back of that page, facing a page of illustrations as the book opens. This pattern continues throughout the manuscript: as Siragusa (lxvii) points out, the book is designed so that when it is opened at any given place, there will be text on the left and miniatures illustrating it on the right. The illustrations are accompanied by captions or legends which often add details or clarifications not in the verse.

There indeed are some passages where the poet must have assumed that the reader would look at the pictures first, before reading the verse, to get a sense of the meaning. For example, this is true in the complementary verses and pictures on fol. 112v (ll. 490–513) and 113r. Lines 493–505 are usually interpreted as a dialogue between Tancred's brother-in-law, Count Richard of Acerra, and Tancred's key supporter, Archbishop Nicholas of Salerno. Then, in ll. 506–513, the poet himself interrupts, with a denunciation of the archbishop. There is nothing in the verse passage to indicate the beginning or ending of the speeches, or the change of speakers; no quotation marks, of course, and no expressions such as *ait* or *inquit* to mark dialogue. However, this section or "*particula*" does have a title, "*Exeundi prohibitio*" (The Prohibition of Sorties), and a caption on the illustration page explains it further: "*Recedente Augusto a obsidione Neapolim, comes Riccardus et Nicolaus presul Salerni prohibent ne populus extra muros atemptet exire*" (Augustus having drawn back from the siege at Naples, Count Richard and Nicholas, the archbishop of Salerno, forbid the people to attempt to go out from the walls). Nicholas and Richard are depicted in the miniatures, each identified with a caption, in a context which shows that they are making an announcement that will affect their city. Presumably, with the situation briefly sketched in this fashion, the poet expected his audience to understand which lines of the dialogue belonged to which speaker. Perhaps he even envisioned public readings in which the mannerisms of the different speakers would be dramatized. Through the pictorial form, the poet sought to reach beyond the scholarly audience which could most easily understand Latin.

Poets not much later than he, even in the court of Frederick II, whose birth he celebrates, would help create the Italian vernacular as a literary language. Pietro did not do so in this poem, perhaps because he lacked the ambition, or perhaps because (in accordance with his vision of a revived Roman Empire) he wished to write in the ancient language of the empire, which was also the language of the church, and which was held in common (to some degree) by all the nobles and courtiers of varied backgrounds who followed the Hohenstaufen court, whether of German, Northern Italian, Sicilian, Greek, or other origin. Did he imagine that the language would revive along with the empire? We cannot know.

Committed to the ancient language and some of its conventions, Pietro tries in other ways to reach out to a wider audience. His choice of subject matter was, of course, appealing in itself, at least to a courtly audience. As the poem's German translator, Becht-Jördens, points out, the *Liber* belongs to an epic tradition dating from antiquity. Pietro announces this link to the epic tradition in his first miniature, presenting as his models the three great Latin epic poets, Virgil, Lucan, and Ovid, each pictured with a scroll containing the first line of his epic masterpiece.[245] Through these three writers, to be sure, Pietro is establishing a connection with their many medieval imitators in various genres. Siragusa (xxxiii–xxxiv) offers the opinion that, out of all his three announced models, Pietro might be thoroughly familiar only with Ovid, and that lines in the poem which appear to echo these models may actually echo later classical and medieval poets, including Venantius Fortunatus and Ermoldus Nigellus, who imitate the poetic craft of the same masters while also drawing on biblical and Christian motifs. Yet some knowledge of the original must be presumed; Pietro's homage to Lucan is such that he adopts a line from *De Bello Civili* (1.15) as his own, one which implies that the Roman Empire needs peace within itself in order to expand its borders (see commentary on line 1419).

Perhaps because his theme is a revived Roman Empire, Pietro, like the classical authors whom he announces as his models, writes most of his poem in quantitative meter, rather than the rhyming accentual verse which had become popular in medieval Latin by his time. He does, however, use rhyme in his acrostic on the emperor's name (ll. 1463–1470), showing that he was familiar with this form. Siragusa indeed suggests (xxxii) that the accentual form (developed in contemporary poetry in the vernacular European languages, as well as medieval Latin) was more natural to him than the quantitative form which he chose to adopt, and this accounts for some of his metrical irregularities. This problem was surely endemic in most Latin poets of his time.

Becht-Jördens points out that Pietro is a "hyperclassicist" who avoids licenses involving elision and the treatment of long and short syllables which classical poets sometimes allowed.[246] Janet Martin notes that this was a general tendency among what she describes as "the modernists who emerged in the twelfth century," who preferred a "polished, exaggeratedly 'correct' line that opposes itself both to recent medieval developments and to the ancient *auctores*."[247] However, instead of the dactylic hexameter of the classical epic, Pietro chose elegiac cou-

---

[245] Gereon Becht-Jördens, "Der Dichter und sein Text," in *Petrus de Ebulo*, ed. Kölzer and Stähli, 287–92, here 287. The manuscript as it currently survives has two lines of poetry on each scroll, but Siragusa (*Liber*, 119) and Becht-Jördens ("Der Dichter," 287) both point out that the second lines were added later.

[246] Becht-Jördens, "Der Dichter und sein Text," 289.

[247] Janet Martin, "Classicism and Style in Latin Literature," in *Renaissance and Renewal in the Twelfth Century*, ed. Benson and Constable, 537–68, here 563.

plets or distichs, that is, paired verses in which one line of hexameter is followed by a line of pentameter.[248] This was, as Becht-Jördens points out, the meter used by Ovid in all his works besides the *Metamorphoses*.

In other ways Pietro showed himself open to innovation even as he wrote in an ancient form. However, Becht-Jördens also observes here that Pietro digresses from the ideal of classical unity of form. He does, after all, incorporate the acrostic into his work, which spells out the emperor's name, HENRICUS (ll. 1463–1472) and is in hexameter rather than elegiac meter. These lines are preceded by a brief prose passage, introducing and explaining them. Becht-Jördens suggests that Pietro may have intended to add yet more variation to the unfinished poem, and that he drew this idea of mixed and varied forms from the late antique period.[249]

His pictorial emphasis is, of course, another way in which Pietro sought to adapt his ancient forms to the needs of a new time and a new audience. Also, his brief sections or *particulae*, into which most of Book I is divided, are well adapted to the presentation of brief, loosely connected episodes, easier for his audience to follow than an intricate interlocking narrative. Later, to be sure, as noted above (A.2), he abandoned that approach and adopted a division into books as more appropriate to an epic.[250]

Pietro also strove to make the poem vivid, moving, and memorable for his audience. Of course, it helped that he wrote of so recent and important a conflict. Simply to describe the events would awake some interest, but the poet must also be artful. Becht-Jördens analyzes the variety of rhetorical devices Pietro uses: enough, without doubt, to impress the sophisticated Latin readers of that time, who were trained to expect and respond to such techniques. Becht-Jördens does point out that among those rhetorical figures which involve repetition, Pietro makes especially frequent and elaborate use of anaphora, as for example in ll. 1407–1428, where *vive* is repeated eleven times at the beginnings of lines or phrases.[251] Such devices may have enabled an audience to make the most of their understanding of the literary language, and to maximize the emotional impact of each understood word. For similar reasons, Pietro may also have favored wordplay, sometimes with coinages, because such devices would enable him to build on the impact of verbal associations by repeating them in a variety of forms and contexts to produce a pleasing mixture of the familiar and unfamiliar. Striking

---

[248] Although in English "couplets" usually rhyme, the classical Latin distich does not. So to avoid confusion, I write "distich" rather than "couplet," in this discussion, even though the latter usage could be technically correct.

[249] Becht-Jördens, "Der Dichter und sein Text," 289. A model of the mixed form with which Pietro and his audience were undoubtedly familiar would have been the sixth-century *De Consolatione Philosophiae* of Boethius, which also mixes prose and verse.

[250] Becht-Jördens, "Der Dichter und sein Text," 289.

[251] Becht-Jördens, "Der Dichter und sein Text," 290.

examples include his multiple plays on the names of Popes Lucius and Celestine in ll. 22- 29 (*Lucius . . . Lucidus . . . .luceat; Celestinus. . . . Celicus. . . celestiat*). He coins a word to describe the political advocacy of Archbishop Walter of Palermo: *gualterizatur* or "Walterize" (line 102*).* He uses the word "Augustus" in varied forms to bind together the imperial party, identifying Henry VI primarily as "Augustus" (starting in line 21, if we omit the title, derived from the colophon) and Constance as "Augusta" (l. 723). Henry's imperial forebears, as ancestors and role models to imitate, are "Augustuses" (*Augustos,* l. 330). Henry's knights (l. 755) and the empress's prayers (the title of Particula XXII) gain this august quality through the adjective *augustalis.* However, Pietro varies this and also rewards those who have learned their Roman history, with many references to Henry as "Caesar" (line 198, etc.), and assigns Constance another name appropriate to the Julian family (*Julia,* l. 729). Because the emperor is likened to Jove (line 82, etc.), extension of the trope allows the poet to associate the empress with Juno (430) and the emperor's commanders on land and sea to Mars (l. 1562) and Neptune (l. 1561). In contrast, Tancred's supporters, with dreary monotony, are mostly "Tancredines" (11r, cap. 5; line 437, etc.).

Inevitably, scholars of equal learning will perceive aspects of the poem differently. Siragusa notes that there are, in the whole work, ten metrically incomplete verses which seem, however, to be "complete in meaning"; these are ll. 6, 199, 255, 572, 620, 644, 676, 844, 910, and 1400.[252] He is content to accept these as an anomaly or a feature of the work's unfinished nature, but Becht-Jördens suggests that these incomplete verses are a Vergilian device for structure and emphasis.[253]

Clearly, then, our poet reaches backwards to Rome's greatness to revive classical form, but also prepares innovations for his intended audience in the new era of the empire's imagined revival. The literary challenges which he took upon himself were considerable, perhaps insurmountable. Yet the results are not to be despised. Though the *Liber* will never be judged in the top ranks of world literary masterpieces, it holds an honored place among those works of art which reward study by illuminating and bringing to life the historical periods in which they were written. As for the literary pleasure which the poem affords its readers, Siragusa, in his edition, sums it up in a balanced manner:

> Only those who are acquainted with many poetic compositions of the Middle Ages, and especially of the eleventh and twelfth centuries, will be able to arrive at the opinion that this Ebolitan, despite his defects, which are not trivial, is one of the better ones. The image is often very vivid in the mind

---

[252] *Liber,* xxvii.
[253] Becht-Jördens, "Der Dichter und sein Text," 289.

of the poet; easily and freely the word, the phrase, and the verse gush out from his spring.[254]

Also Siragusa acknowledges that Pietro, probably constrained by the wish to praise the emperor and vilify his enemies, does produce too many "obscure passages, difficult and limping." However, he asserts that when free of these concerns, Pietro produces passages of "true poetry" especially in his "lyrical flights, similes, and descriptions" (xxxvi). I concur with that assessment.

E. Format of Translation, and Textual Notes

The text from Siragusa's edition (both for the poem itself and the captions to the accompanying miniatures) is the basis of my translation, but I place the miniatures and my account of them next to the verses they illustrate, as do the modern editions of Kölzer and Stähli (Thorbecke) and De Rosa (Ciolfi). When, after line 1505, Siragusa's line numbers are consistently one less than those of these more recent editions (because he chooses not to number the phrase "Sol Augustorum," taking it to be a heading rather than an incomplete hexameter), I follow the recent editions, since I presume that this will be more convenient to my readers.

Siragusa, unlike the other editors, leaves space between lines of the poem when he believes that such space was left intentionally in the manuscript. One marker of such an intention is a paragraph mark, which I represent as "¶" in the text. I make no mention of those marks in my notes, although Siragusa mentions them in his. Otherwise, I follow Siragusa in passing along his reasons for leaving blank spaces.

Since the Bern Codex 120 II is the only surviving manuscript of *Liber ad honorem Augusti*, one might suppose that there would be few variant readings for a translator to contend with. However, there are lacunae in the manuscript, as well as blurred and smudged passages which editors interpret differently. There are obscure words, and differences in spelling which some editors regard as errors in need of correction and some do not. Also, the scribes who wrote the original text made use of abbreviations that were, in some cases, clearer to them than to later scholars, who expand them differently. In addition, there are marginalia and corrections made by later hands to which editors assign differing levels of interest and value.

For the purposes of this translation, however, I do not aspire to produce a full critical edition. For the underlying text, I use Siragusa's carefully produced

---

[254] "Solo chi conosce parecci componimenti poetici del medio evo, e specialmente dei secoli XI e XII, potrà convenire nella sentenza che questo dell'Ebolitano, malgrado i suoi non lievi difetti, sia uno dei migliori. L'immagine è viva assai spesso nella mente del poeta; facili e liberi sgorgano sovente della sua vena la parola, la frase, il verso" (xxxii).

edition of 1906, which he based on a study of the previous editions and a close examination of the manuscript itself, as well as on his impressive erudition and detailed knowledge of the history of the period, its poetry and its chronicles, not to mention his considerable classical learning. However, he cannot always be followed; on some snarled passages, I find myself in agreement with a reading which he did not adopt, and which later editions did adopt (sometimes in common with earlier editions). Also, while Siragusa's insistence on examining the precise spellings of the words in the Codex has led him to recover some splendid readings, such as *exparta* (line 1363) and *Fredericiades* (line 1596) — De Rosa follows him in the latter but not the former — it sometimes goes beyond what is useful in a text intended to accompany a translation, as in his rendering of *victis* for *vittis* (line 422) and *pluplicat* (line 1330) for *publicat* (or Kölzer and Stähli *puplicat*). When I choose a non-Siragusan reading, I identify it briefly in textual notes at the bottom of sections of verses or captions. For those readings only, I list the variants in the other editions.[255] Otherwise, I do not list the variants in the textual notes, but in my commentary and Additional Notes, I will identify and comment on variants only if I am aware that they would result in a significantly different translation, or if I believe the discussion might interest my readers.

Abbreviations (for purpose of textual notes) are as follows: S= Siragusa, KS = Kölzer and Stähli; Pre-S= all editions previous to Siragusa. Non-S= all editions but Siragusa. E=Engel, W= Winkelmann. Codex, Del Re, De Rosa, and Gravier[256] are not abbreviated.

I do not follow Siragusa's punctuation of the Latin text consistently, though more often than not I follow his interpretation of sentence structure. However, instead of Italian conventions for quotation marks, I use those of American English. I capitalize the beginnings of sentences and some proper names in places where Siragusa does not, and occasionally I add or remove commas, question marks, quotation marks, and exclamation points to tone down obvious clashes with my translation. These changes are not tracked by the few, brief textual notes, but are sometimes touched upon in my commentary and in the Additional Notes, where I mention points on which I am aware of being influenced by earlier editions and scholars. In the Commentary with the text, I focus on interpretation necessary to illuminate the poem. In the Additional Notes which follow, I explore some more detailed points for interested readers, and matters for which there simply is not space in the commentary.

---

[255] My information on the variants in editions previous to Siragusa's is drawn from Siragusa's edition, except where the 1904 edition of Ettore Rota is concerned. Siragusa evidently did not have the opportunity to consult the latter, so I have examined it separately.

[256] Joannes Gravier, ed., *Petri d'Ebulo Carmen de Motibus Siculis et rebus inter Henricum VI Romanorum Imperatorem et Tancredum seculo XII gestis*, 2nd ed. (Neapoli, 1777).

Pietro's changing concept of literary structure (see A.2 above) creates some additional problems. The finished work is divided into three "books," the first one much longer than the second and third. The first book is also divided into sections that he called *Particulae* (or, in medieval Latin, *Particule*), each numbered, but that method of structuring the poem eventually disappears. Book I begins with headings and numbers for eighteen *particule*; then, for a while, numbers disappear (probably because of damage to the manuscript) though titles continue. Then, once more for *Particule* XXII–XXIV, complete headings and numbers appear. After that, both headings and numbers disappear. Some of them may have been cut off accidentally, as they were in the earlier sections, but since none appear again, and the beginnings of Books II and III are marked by headings without further subdivision, it seems likely, as Marlis Stähli suggests persuasively,[257] that in fact the poet had abandoned the division into *particule* at some point. Rota, however, for the sake of consistency, inserted numbers for the *particule* and headings of his own devising. Though this is convenient for the reader, another problem arises when we consider that apparently four and a half leaves are missing, each of which would have contained illustrations on its recto and poetry on the verso. That is, four *particule* would be missing, and to assign consecutive numbers to the remaining ones creates a misleading impression. Faced with the absence of headings in the latter part of the poem, Siragusa and De Rosa simply left them out. In the Kölzer and Stähli edition, however, Becht-Jördens follows Rota, whose edition he uses as the basis of his translation. Sometimes he changes the headings, in one case substantively (see Additional Notes on Section 51, fol. 143v). For the reader's convenience, I have provided and translated the headings of Rota in angle brackets and also those of Kölzer and Stähli where they differ. However, I have added my own section numbers in SMALL CAPS, along with brief comments, taking into account the pages we know are missing.

The Codex of *Liber ad honorem Augusti* itself has numbers marked on it, visible in the facsimile manuscript, on upper right hand side, front (recto) only. The numbers, running from 95 to 147, are not original to the manuscript, but were added while the work was bound with several other texts in the manuscript at Bern. Because, however, these numbers have been associated with the miniatures since the manuscript has been studied, they are a valuable cross-reference for scholars. Therefore, I also supply this number at the top of the center column for each section of verse and each illustration, distinguishing between the recto and verso; thus "fol. 106v" means "the verso of the page numbered 106 in the Codex." Toward the end of the work, these numbers will not proceed consecutively, because in the process of rebinding or before (perhaps when some of the pages were damaged and lost), the sequence of the last few pages became confused. I present

---

[257] "Eine Handschrift," 248–49.

them in the order which Siragusa, like the modern editors Kölzer and Stähli, and De Rosa, believed was correct.

In my discussion of the miniatures, translations of Siragusa's summary of the contents appear in italics above each panel of "legends" or captions, followed by his by his remarks about the lines and page illustrated and (where applicable) on the corresponding illustrations in the Engel and Del Re editions. (In a few places, my notes, in parenthesis, about missing pages, interrupt or replace his account.) There follows the panel of captions and my translation; then my commentary. At the end, Siragusa's page numbers appear in parentheses, followed by those of Kölzer and Stähli (abbreviated "KS"). De Rosa's facsimile edition has no page numbers, but it is easy enough to locate passages by use of line numbers, and illustrations by the numbers from the codex.[258] After line 1505, when my line numbers follow the KS and De Rosa editions and Siragusa's is consistently one less, I indicate Siragusa's line numbers as well as his page numbers.

---

[258] Siragusa denotes recto and verso by "A" and "B," but to avoid confusion, I translate them as "r" and "v" both on the Italian side and the English. KS references indicate the KS edition, commentary, and notes; photographic reproductions from the codex are adjacent to these pages.

LIBER AD HONOREM AUGUSTI

BOOK IN HONOR OF AUGUSTUS

by

Pietro da Eboli

English Translation and Commentary by

Gwenyth Hood

Translation:
Italics: Translation of Siragusa's summary of the illustrations
SMALL CAPS: missing pages, fol. x1–fol. x4.

Commentary:
S: page in Siragusa's edition
KS: page in Kölzer and Stähli edition.

95r *Virgil, Lucan, Ovid. Contains three figures representing the above-mentioned three
poets, each carrying an inscription with two hexameters.*

. . . .

Virgilius	1	Virgil
Arma Virumque cano Troie qui primus ab horis.		Arms and the man I sing, who first, from the borders of Troy. . .
Felix qui potuit rerum cognoscere causas		Happy is the man who can know the causes of things.
Lucanus	2	Lucan
Bella per Emathios plus quam civilia campos.		Wars most uncivil throughout the Emathian fields.
Lucanum queras qui Martis prelia dicet		You seek Lucan, who tells of the battles of Mars. . .
Ovidius.	3	Ovid
In nova fert animus mutatas dicere formas.		It comes to my mind to tell of forms changed to new [bodies].
Munera crede michi capiunt hominesque deosque.		Gifts, believe me, take captive both men and gods.

Commentary and Notes [95r]: Three figures representing poets appear in the faded illustration. Each holds a partly unrolled scroll from which two lines of poetry can be read. However, in each case, only the first selection, the first line of that author's masterpiece (the *Aeneid*, *De Bello Civili*, and the *Metamorphoses*, respectively), was originally on each scroll. The others were added later, perhaps in the thirteenth or fourteenth century (Kölzer, "Bildkommentar," 36). The second line on the scroll of Virgil (Publius Vergilius Maro, BC 70–19), is *Georgics* 2.490. Elsewhere, (ll. 1472; 1513–1533), Pietro alludes to his *Eclogues* 1 and 4. The second verse attributed to Lucan (Marcus Annaeus Lucanus. ca. AD 39–65) is not his at all but comes rather from an epigraph attributed to Cato the Elder, in *Disticha Catonis*, bk. 2, line 4 (Kölzer, "Bildkommentar," 34). The second line given to Ovid (Publius Ovidus Naso, BC 43–AD 17), is from *Ars Amatoria* (3.653). Pietro himself echoes *Remedium Amoris* 5.305 in his l. 893, and possibly *Heroides* 1.97–98 in l.771 (see Additional Notes here).

By placing these classical poets and their verses here, Pietro shows that they are his models and also that he draws some of his themes from them. Like Virgil, he will celebrate the greatness of a Roman hero. Like Lucan, he will deplore a civil war and the destruction it causes. Like Ovid, he will treat of interventions from supernatural powers.

(S 119; KS 35)

95v [Incipit Liber Primus].
Incipit prima primi regis Sicilie particula.

Dux ubi Roggerius, Guiscardi clara propago,   1
    Iam fastidiret nomen habere ducis,   2
Altius aspirat, qui, delegante Calisto,   3
    Ungitur in regem. Rex nova regna facit,   4
Quem fera barbaries timuit, quem Nilus et omnis   5
    Circulus oceani.   6
Rex, ut regna suis subduxit plurima regnis,   7
    Disposuit nomen perpetuare suum;   8
Inclita cui peperit plures Albidia natos,   9
    Occubuit tandem mater et orba suis.   10
Successit viduo post hanc Sibilia lecto.   11
    Infelix, sterilem clausit aborsa diem.   12
Sic erat in fatis ut tercia nuberet uxor,   13
    Per quam Romani cresceret orbis honor.   14
A magnis veniens natalibus orta Beatrix,   15
    Concipit a sole lux paritura diem.   16
Virtutem virtus, docilem proba, casta pudicam,   17
    Formosam peperit pulchra, beata piam;   18
Nascitur in lucem de ventre beata beato,   19
    De Constantini nomine nomen habens;   20
Traditur Augusto coniunx Constantia magno;   21
    Lucius in nuptu pronuba causa fuit;   22
Lucius hos iungit quos Celestinus inungit;   23
    Lucidus hic unit, Celicus ille sacrat.   24
Tertius in sexto digne requiescit uterque,   25
    Sic notat Henricus Sextus utrumque patrem.   26
Nominibus tantis utinam respondeat actus,   27
    Adsint et meritis nomina digna suis!   28
Luceat in sanctis unus, celestiat alter,   29
    A quibus Henricus munera bina capit;   30
Tercius antistes sacrat hanc, et tercius alter   31
    Copulat, et patri tercia nupta tulit.   32
Non licuit quartam patri traducere nuptam,   33
    Nam paritas numeri displicet ipsa Deo.   34

[Here Begins the First Book <Siragusa>]
Here begins the first section, about the first king of Sicily.

When Roger became duke, Guiscard's famous offspring,
  He then disdained to have the name of duke.
He aspires higher, and, Calixtus giving the order,
  He is anointed as king. The king makes new realms;
The savage Berber feared him, the Nile and the whole
  Circle of the ocean.
The king, when he had subjected many realms to his realms,
  Set about to perpetuate his name.
To him famous Elvira bore many children,
  But in the end, the mother lay down in death, bereft of her own.
Then Sibylla succeeded to the widowed bed.
  Unlucky woman, she ended her sterile days in a miscarriage.
And the Fates ruled thus: he should marry a third wife,
  Through whom the honor of the Roman world would increase.
Beatrice, scion coming from great ancestry,
  Was the Light who conceived of the Sun to bring forth day.
Virtue gave birth to virtue: the dutiful to the obedient, the chaste to the modest,
  The lovely to the beautiful, the blessed to the faithful.
She was born into the light, that blessed one, from a blessed womb,
  And she bears a name from the name of Constantine.
Constance is given to the great Augustus as his wife;
  Lucius played matchmaker for their nuptials.
Lucius unites, Celestine anoints them;
  This Lucent one joins them and that Celestial one makes them holy.
This pair of Thirds finds rest in the Sixth;
  Thus does Henry the Sixth signify both fathers.
Oh, may such names correspond to deeds,
  And may their true value accompany them!
May the Lucent one shine among the saints and the Celestial one dwell in
      the heavens,
  Since Henry receives the double gifts from them.
One "third" bishop consecrates her, and the second "third"
  Makes the match. The third bride bore her to her father.
Her father was not permitted to take a fourth bride,
  Since that coupling of numbers displeases God.

Commentary and Notes [95v]: The stage is set for the coming conflict: the struggle of Henry VI of Hohenstaufen (ca. 1165–1197) to establish himself as Holy Roman Emperor and king of Sicily. These lines cover a great sweep of years, from Roger's succession to the dukedom of Apulia in 1127, to Henry's imperial coronation at Rome in 1191. Thus, Pietro's account is misleading for those who look for a detailed history. His purpose is to celebrate Henry's achievements, especially his conquest of Sicily. Of course this conquest, completed in 1194, is, for the poet, merely a prelude to the full revival of the Roman Empire as it stood in the time of the Emperor Constantine. Its most precious accomplishment will be the recovery of Jerusalem from its Moslem conquerors, as Pietro indicates later in his rhymed acrostic (lines 1462–1469). The poet downplays or omits details not contributing to these themes.

Because the Sicilian conflict will be his focus, Pietro begins with Roger II of Hauteville (1095–1154), second Great Count and first King of Sicily. Because the Norman Hauteville family had come to Italy as mercenaries and gained their titles by conquest and strategically extorted grants from the papacy, the German kings, who also claimed the rights of the Roman Emperors, were often in conflict with them. After Roger II's coronation in 1130, three German emperors (Lothar of Supplingburg, Conrad III of Hohenstaufen, and Frederick I Barbarossa) contended with the Normans for their lands. However, after the Peace of Venice in 1177, when Frederick Barbarossa had composed his differences with the papacy, the Norman kingdom, and the Lombard states, he arranged a marriage between his own son, Henry (ca. 1165–1197), and King Roger's daughter, Constance. By the 1190s, when Pietro wrote his poem, the legitimate Hauteville line was extinct except for Constance (ca. 1154–1198). Though Constance's hereditary rights did not, in the end, lead to Henry's peaceful succession, they did give the Hohenstaufen the moral high ground. Thus Pietro begins his poem with Constance's family background, treating Roger with respect. Within thirty-four lines of poetry, Constance is born, grows up, marries, and is crowned empress. Simultaneously, Pietro establishes that she is the legitimate heiress and sole survivor of an impressive dynasty.

Pietro describes Roger as the *propago* or "offspring" of Robert Guiscard (ca. 1015–1085), a name famous in legend. Actually, King Roger (1095–1154) was not Robert Guiscard's son, but his nephew. His father, the first "Great Count" Roger (d. 1101), was Guiscard's younger brother, who fought beside him to win Sicily. Pietro may be using the word *propago* loosely, or he might have accepted legendary accounts, like those told by the chroniclers Thomas Tuscus (497–498) and Giovanni Villani (88; Book IV), which make Roger the son of Guiscard.

In this legend, the saintly Robert Guiscard shows hospitality to a forlorn leper whom he meets while hunting. The leper, who proves to be Christ himself in disguise, rewards Guiscard with the promise of illustrious sons, including future kings of Sicily. Pietro states that Pope Calixtus sent permission for Roger to be crowned king, but the permission actually came from the antipope Anacletus II. Anacletus sent Roger permission to be annointed king by an archbishop of his realm, to be chosen by himself. Probably the archbishop of Palermo performed the ceremony, as Deér speculates in *Dynastic Porphyry Tombs of the Norman Period*, trans. G. A. Gillhoff, Dumbarton Oaks Studies 5 (Cambridge, MA: Harvard University Press, 1959), 11.

King Roger's marital history is then briefly reviewed here. His first wife, called *Albidia* by Pietro and variations of *Alberia* by other Latin sources, was a Castilian princess whose name is usually translated into English as *Elvira*. Pietro's words and the accompanying miniature suggest that Elvira's children predeceased her and that she was buried with them. Actually, at least three sons survived her death in 1135, and one of these, William I, also survived his father and reigned after him. Of course, when Pietro wrote, ca. 1195–1196, all of Elvira's sons had long been dead. The illustration shows the queen lying on her bier, with two other bodies beside her. Both are smaller than she is, and one is significantly smaller than the other, suggesting a young child. Siragusa and others speculate that one of these might be Elvira's daughter (not given a name in any known source), who, according to Romuald of Salerno's *Chronicon*, died around the same time she did (231). Kölzer's commentary (38) suggests that the other, who seems a smaller child, might be her son Henry, who apparently died in childhood.

In saying that Sibylla, sister of the duke of Burgundy, died of a miscarriage, Pietro reports more about her and the marriage than any other surviving source, and some modern writers contend that she actually had a surviving daughter. Here, the account of her childless death prepares the way for King Roger's last marriage, to Beatrix of Rethel, who would bear his true heir. Text and miniature together suggest that Constance was born posthumously, after King Roger's death on 26 February 1154.

In calling Pope Lucius III a matchmaker (*pronuba*) for the nuptials between Constance and Henry, Pietro makes another claim which many deny , but he may nevertheless be correct (see Introduction C.9). Years later, in 1191, Celestine III anointed Constance as empress, on the same occasion when he crowned Henry VI. Pietro clearly means to suggest papal benediction in general for the Roman Empire and for Henry VI in particular. The reality was more complex.

(S 3–6; KS 37)

96r *Facts of Roger II's life. Birth of Constance. Henry VI and Constance married. Their departure for Germany.* Illustrates lines 1–34, on fol. 95v.

. . . .

Dux Roggerius.	1	Duke Roger
Idem dux ungitur in regem a papa Calixto.	2	The same duke is anointed king by Pope Calixtus.
Idem rex accepit Albidiam.	3	The same king took Albidia [as wife].
Hic sepelitur Albidia cum filiis.	4	Here Albidia is entombed with her children.
Idem rex Rogerius duxit secundo Sibiliam in uxorem.	5	The same king Roger took Sibylla as his second wife.
Hic sepelitur Sebilia aborciens.	6	Here Sibylla is entombed, miscarrying.
Rex Rogerius terciam duxit uxorem nomine Beatricem.	7	King Roger took a third wife named Beatrice.
Regina Beatrix genuit Constantiam.	8	Queen Beatrice gave birth to Constance.
Hic sepelitur rex cum uxore.	9	Here the king is buried with his wife.
Regina Constantia — Rex Henricus	10	Queen Constance, King Henry
Dum rex et regina in Alemannam irent papa Lucius benedixit eis.	11	When the king and queen went to Germany, Pope Lucius blessed them.

Commentary and Notes [96r]: The first three rows of pictures (from top down) show King Roger's story. He gains his dukedom and crown, is anointed, marries one wife on each level, and dies. The last two levels show Constance's story (overlapping somewhat with Roger's). In Row 3, on the right, she appears as an infant, suckled at her mother's breast, while her father lies in his tomb. In Row 4, she marries Henry VI and departs for Germany, blessed by Pope Lucius.

The implications of these pictures are rich in interpretive possibilities. As Kölzer points out, in the "Bildkommentar" for this page, the orb, which is a symbol of kingly power, represented as a globe marked with a cross, appears repeatedly, apparently the subject of a sort of running gag. First Roger holds it, when, after being anointed king, he rides to meet Elvira. The orb is in his right hand, while in his left he holds a green palm branch, which he hands to Alberia as she sits waiting for him. However, in the next row, on the left, we see Alberia lying in her tomb beside two of her children. On the right, King Roger rides to meet his second bride. Again he holds the orb in his right hand and a palm branch in his left. Sibylla, also mounted, rides to meet him. Their horses' heads come close together, but their hands do not touch. Then, on the right, Sibylla in turn lies in her tomb, alone. (Her burial place is drawn more elaborately than Elvira's, with a bell tower in the foreground and a crenellated wall with towers in the background. Kölzer believes that this represents the royal palace, since the bell tower is not unlike the one represented for the Royal Palace elsewhere in the miniatures, for example, fols. 97r, 98r, and 124r. However, the bell towers represented at Monte Cassino, fol. 108r, and Salerno, fol. 116r, do not look much different. Siragusa, who knew that Sibylla was buried at the abbey of La Cava near Salerno, believed that the miniature represented that abbey.)

On the third level, left, under cap. 3, Roger rides to meet one more bride. He carries neither palm branch nor orb. Beatrice, riding toward him, carries the orb, holding it high over her horse's head, perhaps offering it to Roger, who holds up his right hand with the index finger extended. Kölzer suggests in his commentary that Beatrice's possession of the orb means that she is destined, as line 14 declares, to bear a child "Through whom the honor of the Roman world would increase." On the right, Beatrice suckles her newborn child (represented as wearing a crown) while Roger lies in his tomb.

On the fourth level, the adult Constance faces Henry, both standing. Henry holds a scepter in his left hand, the orb in his right. Constance holds out a large circlet in her right hand. Perhaps, as Rota suggests in the notes to his edition (7), it represents a wedding ring (the drawings are not always to scale), or perhaps it represents the crown of her realm. On the right, Constance and her husband appear on horseback, prepared to go to Germany, while Pope Lucius blesses them. This did not happen, as Kölzer points out, because Pope Lucius died before the wedding took place, and his successor, hostile to the Hohenstaufen family, did not attend. In any case, the young couple did not go to Germany immediately after their marriage, but remained for some years in Northern Italy, in their role as king and queen of Lombardy (see Introduction). However, the idea of the papal benediction is clearly important to Pietro.

(S 119–120; KS 38)

96v Particula II: Obitus W[illelmi] secundi formosi regis Sicilie.

Post obitum, formose, tuum, que sceptra gubernet   35
    Et regat ex proprio sanguine prole cares,   36
Nec facis heredem, nec qui succedat adoptas;   37
    Ex intestato debita solvis humo.   38
Quis novit secreta tue purissima mentis?   39
    Quod tua mens loquitur mundus et ipse taces.   40
Certus eras certe quoniam iustissimus heres   41
    Expugnaturus regna parentis erat,   42
Nam satis est iurasse semel, te prole carente,   43
    Quod tuus in genero sceptra teneret avus.   44

    Iurat cum multis Archimatheus idem.   45
Post miseros morbos, post regis triste necesse,   46
    Nocte sub oscura sole latente pluit.   47
Postquam dimisit rex, res pulcherrima, mundum,   48
    Inglomerant sese prelia, preda, fames;   49
Furta, lues, pestes, lites, periuria, cedes,   50
    Infelix regnum diripuere sibi.   51
Sol hominum moritur, superi patiuntur eclipsim,   52
    Anglica Sicilidem luna flet orba diem;   53
Solis ad occasum commotus eclipticat orbis,   54
    Di flent, astra dolent, flet mare, plorat humus.   55

Commentary and Notes [96v]: Here Pietro begins with an apostrophe or address to William II, the handsome and beloved king who died childless and without testament. No living person knows what his thoughts were at the end. But, Pietro adds, whatever William's secrets may have been, the identity of his legitimate heir was not one of them. The king had required his nobles and officials to swear oaths to acknowledge Constance and her husband as William's successor if he should die childless. Specifically, "the Arch-Matthew," who is to be the chief architect of Tancred's elevation to the kingship, swore this oath with all the rest.

    After stating this, Pietro paints a picture of the city in mourning for their good king, who is likened to a sun whose setting has left the world in darkness,

Section 2: The Death of William II the Handsome, King of Sicily.

Beautiful one, you lack offspring of your own blood,
    After your death, to hold the scepter and reign,
Nor do you create an heir or adopt one to succeed you;
    Without testament you pay your dues to the earth.
Who knows the most absolute mysteries of your mind?
    The world now speaks of your intent and you yourself are silent.
On that account, you made sure of that most rightful heir
    Who was to subdue your father's realms.
For it was sworn once — which was enough — that if you had no progeny,
    Your grandfather would retain his scepter through his son-in-law.

    The Arch-Matthew, with many others, swore that very thing.
After the lamentable illness, after the king's sorrowful mortal end
    The sun hides under the dark of night and rain falls.
After the king, that being of beauty, abandoned the world,
    Battles, plunder and famine gather together;
Thefts, plagues, pestilences, contentions, perjuries, and bloodshed
    Snatch the unhappy realm from itself.
The sun of men dies; the supernal powers endure eclipse;
    The English moon, bereft, weeps for the Sicilian day.
The sphere of the world, moved at the setting of the sun, lies in darkness,
    Gods weep, stars mourn, the sea weeps, the earth laments.

mourned in the reflected light of the "English moon," that is, his widowed queen,
Joanna Plantagenet, daughter of Henry II of England. These scenes build upon
his noble conception of kingship and put Constance's closest kinsman in a favor-
able light.

(S 7–8; KS 41)

44–45 (blank space). S: "A blank space follows verse 44, the size of about four
verses, but the presence of the pentameter leads one to suppose that an uneven number of
lines is missing." De Rosa likewise observes that 3–5 lines must be missing here.

97r *Illness and death of William II. The population and the magnates of Palermo weep.*
Illustrates ll. 35–55, fol. 96v.

. . . .

Achim medicus	1	Achim the physician.
Rex W[illelmus] egrotans	2	King William suffering illness
Astrologus.	3	The astrologer.
Planctus eiusdem regis defuncti.	4	Mourning for the same king, dead.
Cappella regia.	5	The Royal Chapel.
Populus Panormi.	6	The people of Palermo
Comites et barones.	7	Counts and barons.
Domini Curie.	8	The lords of the court.

Commentary and Notes [97r]: Towers and a campanile at the top of the drawing indicate the royal palace of Palermo. Below that, under several arches of a colonnade, the scenes of William II's last illness unfold. From left to right there appear: (cap. 1) a turbaned physician, holding a beaker for urine (Kölzer, "Bildkommentar," 42), (cap. 2) William, on his sickbed, fanned by a servant, (cap. 3) an astrologer, holding an astrolabe in the left hand and book (no doubt of astrology) in his right. Near the Royal Chapel (cap. 5) William's widowed queen, indicated by her crowned head, mourns her dead husband, attended by courtiers. Her situation will cause her brother, Richard I, to entangled himself in the affairs of Sicily to the detriment of Henry VI; see verses 1047–1088 and fol. 129r. At the bottom of the page, three more groups of people appear, from left to right, mourning the king: the people of Palermo (cap. 6), counts and barons (cap. 7), and "the lords of the court," that is, the council of royal ministers called *familiares* in official documents (cap. 8).

(S 121; KS 42)

97v Particula III: Lamentatio et luctus Panormi.

Hactenus urbs felix, populo dotata trilingui,   56
  Corde ruit, fluitat pectore, mente cadit;   57
Ore, manu, lacrimis clamant, clamoribus instant   58
  Cum pueris iuvenes, cum iuniore senes;   59
Dives, inops, servus, liber, pius, impius, omnes   60
  Exequias equo pondere regis agunt;   61
Cum viduis caste plorant, cum virgine nupte.   62
  Quid moror in lacrimis? Nil nisi questus erat.   63
Qui iacet in cunis, medio qui robore fretus,   64
  Et quibus est baculus tercia forma pedum,   65
Per loca, per vicos, per celsa palacia plorant.   66
  Desiccat lacrimas nona peracta dies.   67
Tunc pater antistes fuit hec affatus ad omnes,   68
  Nec potuit lacrimans plurima verba loqui: 69
"Hactenus herrantes correximus, hactenus atros   70
  "Mens erat a stabulis pellere nostra lupos;   71
"Hactenus ad caulas nullo cogente redibant   72
  "Vespere lacte graves opilionis oves;   73
"Hactenus unguiferos bos herrans nulla leones,   74
  "Rostriferas aquilas nulla timebat avis;   75
"Hactenus ibat ovans solus per opaca viator;   76
  "Hactenus insidiis nec locus ullus erat;   77
"Hactenus in speculo poterat se quisque videre,   78
  "Quod mors infregit bustaque noctis habent;   79
"Hactenus ardebant miseri candelabra regni;   80
  "Ipsa sub oscura flamma cinescit humo.   81
"Mittite quod properet Phebi soror et Iovis uxor,   82
  "Imperii cornu iungat utrumque sui."   83

Commentary and Notes [97v]: Building on the favorable picture of William II and
his reign, Pietro describes the universal mourning for the good king. The arch-
bishop Walter speaks in loving and mournful tones about the deceased king (his
former pupil, see biographical sketch), who was a mirror of admirable conduct.
Then he urges that Constance come quickly to take possession of her hereditary
realm. Constance's husband, Henry VI, is mentioned as "Jove," the chief Roman
god, because he is, or soon will be, the emperor. This conventional Latin trope

Section 3: Mourning and Lament in Palermo.

The city, fortunate until now, her people learned in three tongues,
  Collapses in heart, wavers in breast, is prostrate in mind;
With words, with hands, with tears they cry out and rush together crying,
  The boys with the youths, the young with the old;
Rich, poor, slave, free, pious, impious, all
  Perform the funeral rites of the king with equal heaviness.
Widows weep with the celibate, brides with virgins.
  But why do I linger over tears? There was no one who did not lament.
Those who lie in cradles, those who rely on middle-aged strength,
  The aged, who go about with walking sticks;
They all lament throughout neighborhoods, the streets and in lofty palaces.
  Tears dry up when nine days are over.
Then the father-bishop said these things to everyone,
  (Though he could not, for weeping, speak many words):
"Until now, we have corrected the erring;
  "Our care was to drive savage wolves from our abodes;
"Until now, with no one driving them, the sheep, heavy with milk
  "Would return in the evening to the folds of the shepherd.
"Until now, no wandering ox has feared the clawed lions,
  "And no bird the beaked eagles.
"Until now, the solitary traveler would go about exulting, even in dark places,
  "Nor was there, until now, any place for ambushes.
"Until now, everyone could see himself in that mirror
  Which now death has broken and the tombs of the night possess.
"Until now the lamps of this pitiful realm were shining;
  "Now that flame turns to ashes under the dark earth.
"Send word that Phoebus' sister, who is Jove's wife,
  "Should hasten to join both horns of her empire."

survives from the times when the pagan Roman emperors (starting with Julius Caesar) were deified or declared gods after their deaths. This convention is used extensively in Ovid's *Metamorphoses* and Lucan's *De bello civili*, two of Pietro's models shown on fol. 95r. Walter likens William himself to Phoebus, the handsome and admirable sun-god. He suggests that Constance is William's sister, through this is probably figurative.

(S 9–10; KS 45)

98r *Mourning in the streets of Palermo because of the death of William II.* Illustrates ll. 56–83 on fol. 97v.

· · · ·

Viridarium Genoard.	1	The Royal Garden of Januardo.
Civitas Panormi lugens super occasu speciosi.	2	The city of Palermo mourning over the death of the dazzling one.
Cappella regia.	3	Royal Chapel.
Ideisini.	4	Ideisini.
Cassarum.	5	The Cassaro.
Calza.	6	Calza.
Scerarchadium.	7	Scerarchadium.
Castrum Maris.	8	Castle of the Sea.
Portus Panormi.	9	Port of Palermo.

Commentary and Notes [98r]: Siragusa (122, note 1) writes, "As the preceding illustration represented the mourning for the death of William II inside the royal palace, this one represents [the mourning] in the neighborhoods of Palermo." The pictures suggests that "the population from the most distant places flowed into the Palatine Chapel (cap. 3), where the funeral was celebrated, [and] where, probably, Thomas, the archbishop of Reggio, read his elegy" of which Siragusa quotes some excerpts. Also depicted are the famous royal garden or menagerie (cap. 1), perhaps named from "the Arabic 'Gennet-ol-Ardh,' for 'terrestrial paradise'" (Siragusa 122, note 2), the ancient main street or "Cassero" (cap. 5), also called the *via Marmorea* (Siragusa 122, note 6). The name *Scerarchadium* (cap. 6) comes from the Arabic *šari al-qadi*, meaning "Street of the Judge," as Theo Kölzer explains in the commentary associated with this illustration in the the the Kölzer and Stähli edition (36). Presumably the Saracens' own judge, for their internal affairs, officiated there. The harbor, *Portus Panormi* (cap. 9) is shown by wavy lines, the artist's stylized indication for water, under which fish (disproportionately large) appear. Kölzer's commentary (46) points out that the chain which encloses the harbor is also represented.

(S 122–23; KS 46)

98v Particula IIII: Adversa et diversa petentium voluntas.

Post lacrimas, post exequias, post triste sepulchrum,   84
    Scismatis exoritur semen in urbe ducum.   85
In sua versa manus precordia sanguinis hausit   86
    Urbs tantum, quantum nemo referre potest.   87
Postquam sacrilego fuit urbs saturata cruore,   88
    A propria modicum cede quieta fuit.   89
Quisque sibi petit in regem quem norat amicum;   90
    Hic se maiorem querit, et ille parem;   91
Hic consanguineum querit, petit ille sodalem;   92
    Hic humilem laudat, laudat et ille ferum;   93
Quisque sibi regem petit hunc, legit hunc, petit illum;   94
    Non erat in voto mens Pharisea pari.   95
Tancredum petit hic, comitem petit ille Rogerum;   96
    Quod petit hic negat hic; quod negat hic petit hic.   97
Ambo duces equitum, rationis uterque magister,   98
    Hic dator, ille tenax; hic brevis, ille gigas.   99
Intus at interea vicecancellarius ardet;   100
    Ut sibi Tancredum gens petat unus agit.   101
Hoc negat antistes, qui gualterizatur ubique,   102
    Votaque Mathei curia tota negat.   103
Ille suis ceptis magis ac magis instat iniquis,   104
    In votis animam dans nichil esse suam.   105
Vi, prece, promissis trahit in sua vota rebelles,   106
    Tendens multimodis retia plena dolis.   107
Pollicitis humiles, prece magnos, munere faustos   108
    Vincit, et antistes simplicitate ruit.   109

Commentary and Notes [98v]: Pietro tells of the chaos that was to result in Tancred's elevation to the kingship. Walter the archbishop works to smooth the way for Constance and Henry, but in Palermo there is a disloyal attitude, or rather, a "Pharisaical mind" *(mens Pharisea)*. Pietro likens political loyalty to religious faith, applying this epithet of all who are not firmly committed to the legitimate heir. Within the city, two parties have gathered around two candidates for kingship:

Section 4: The Different and Conflicting Will of Those Seeking [a King].

After the tears, after the funeral rites, after the sad burial,
  The seeds of schism sprouted in the city of the dukes.
The city, its hand turned against its own breast, drank of so much blood
  That no one could tell it all.
After the city was drenched with sacrilegious gore,
  There came a little pause from civil slaughter.
Each one sought for himself as king someone he knew for a friend.
  This one sought a superior, that one an equal.
This one asked a blood relation, that one sought a comrade.
  This one praised a lowly man, that one a warlike man.
Each sought a king for himself, this man or that man;
  The Pharisaical mind was not united in its choice.
This one seeks Tancred, that one seeks Count Roger;
  What one seeks another denies, and what one denies another seeks.
Both men are commanders of knights, both masters of jurisprudence.
  One is generous, the other a miser; one is puny, the other huge.
But meanwhile, the vice-chancellor burns within himself;
  All on his own, he works to make the people as a whole choose Tancred.
The archbishop works against this, Walterizing everywhere;
  And thus the whole court denies Matthew's wishes.
But he presses on more and more in his evil undertakings.
  All the while pretending that his soul is not in what he wishes,
He draws rebels into his choices by power, prayers, and promises,
  Casting nets full of many kinds of deceit. With promises
He wins over the humble, with prayers the great, with gifts the prosperous;
  The bishop goes to ruin in his simplicity.

Tancred, Count of Lecce, and Richard, Count of Andria. Both men had enjoyed distinguished careers during the reign of William II, as military commanders and justiciars. Pietro does not say whether either one actually wishes to be king. But Matthew has decided, and he works in secret, persuading different people in different ways, until popular support for Tancred is too strong to be denied.

(S 11–12; KS 49)

99r *The populace and knights of the realm proclaim, respectively, Tancred and the Count of Andria as candidates for the throne of Sicily.* Illustrates ll. 84–109 on fol. 98v. This corresponds to Illustration 4 of the Engel edition and 3 of the Del Re edition.

· · · ·

Comes Tancredus.	1	Count Tancred.
Comes Rogerius.	2	Count Roger.
Vulgus petit Tancredum.	3	The common people entreat Tancred.
Milites comitem Rogerium.	4	The knights [entreat] Count Roger.

Commentary and Notes [99r]: The two popular candidates for kingship appear at the top, their supporters below. Seated on a folding stool to the right, Count Roger of Andria looks much larger than Tancred, who stands in the background on the left. The captions clarify what the verses left unsaid: wealth and class divide the two groups. The populace, carrying axes and daggers, favors Tancred, while the knights, carrying swords, favor Roger. Siragusa (123, note 3) writes: "Here Tancred, as elsewhere, is represented as dwarfish and deformed. His face in this miniature is completely daubed over with paint, so that it is not possible to distinguish his features." Kölzer ("Bildkommentar," 51) also observes that Tancred's face is shown in profile, implying devaluation in the Middle Ages. Here and also on 101r and 102r, Tancred's face was originally drawn with a "three-fourths" presentation, but changed later to the less sympathetic profile view, and in this case "soot-ink" was also added to darken the face, according to Fuchs, Mrusek, and Oltrogge, "Die Entstehung," 278. See Introduction A.2.

(S 123; KS 50)

99v Particula V: Suasio vicecancellarii dissuadentis ad presulem Panormi.

Sol erat occiduus, faciente crepuscula Phebo,	110
Venit Scariothis flens ubi presul erat.	111
Sic ait: "Alme pater, lux regni, gloria cleri,	112
"Utile consilium, pastor et urbis honor,	113
"Pacis iter, rationis amor, constantia veri,	114
"Respice consiliis regna relicta tuis;	115
"Consule ne pereant; vestro succurre roseto,	116
"Ne Nothus aut Boreas, ne gravis urat yemps.	117
"Elige quis regnet. Quis erit? Constancia regnet;	118
"Sic lex exposcit, sic sua iura volunt.	119
"Disce prius mores Augusti, disce furorem:	120
"Teutonicam rabiem quis tolerare potest?	121
"Parce tuis canis; pueri tibi more licebit	122
"Discere barbaricos barbarizare sonos?	123
"Ad solium regni comitem gerit Andria dignum,	124
"Set ius et mores et sua facta negant.	125
"Absit ut incestus regum mechetur in aula,	126
"Absit ut era ducum spargat aperta manus,	127
"Absit ut eveniens uxor de rege queratur,	128
"Absit ut alterius vindicet acta reus.	129
"Aptus ad hoc Tancredus erit, de germine iusto,	130
"Quem gens, quem populus, quem petit omnis homo,	131
"Quamvis fama, quamvis persona repugnet,	132
"Naturam redimat gracia, crimen honor.	133
Qui quanto duce patre superbiat, hic quoque tanto,	134
"Ex merito matris mitior esse potest.	135
"Non habet, ut timeas, dubium brevis unda profundum;	136
"Quo vis defertur remige parva ratis."	137
Talibus almipatris Matheus adulterat archam	138
Et legit ex tacito presulis ore fidem.	139

Section 5: The Dissenting Vice-chancellor's Persuasive Address to the Archbishop of Palermo.

The sun was sinking, Phoebus giving a little twilight,
    When Iscariot came weeping to where the archbishop was.
Thus he spoke: "Kind Father, light of the kingdom, glory of the clergy,
    "Beneficial counsel, shepherd and honor of the city,
"Road of peace, love of reason, constancy of truth,
    "Provide for the widowed realms through your counsels,
"Give counsel so that they do not perish; bring help to your rose garden
    "Lest Boreas or Notus or the heavy winter storms should scorch it.
"Choose who shall reign. Who will it be? Let Constance reign;
    "So the law expounds, so her rights would have it.
"But first study the ways of Augustus and consider his violence;
    "Who can endure Teutonic fury?
"Spare your gray hairs! Is it right that you should study, like a
    "Schoolboy, to make those barbaric noises barbarically?
"Andria offers a Count worthy of the royal seat,
    "But laws, morals, and his deeds stand against it.
"God forbid that a lewd man should wanton in the halls of the kings!
    "Let not an open hand squander the bronze coins of the dukes!
"God forbid that some wife should come away from the king with accusations,
    "And let not one guilty man punish the deeds of another.
"But Tancred will be quite suitable for this matter. He is of noble stock,
    "The nation, the people and every man entreats him.
"However much his reputation, however his person creates repugnance,
    "Grace redeems nature, and honor crime.
"However much he may take pride in his father's ducal status,
    "He has just as much reason to be meek, because of his mother's worth.
"You need not fear a small wave, for it has no murky depths,
    "And a little boat is borne where you wish by the rowers."
With such sayings, Matthew debases the treasury of the kind father,
    And reads a promise in the prelate's silent face.

Commentary and Notes [99v]: Now, when he has brought about a united popular demand for Tancred as king, Matthew approaches the archbishop Walter with a crafty and passionate appeal for support. First he flatters Walter with many epithets that emphasize the latter's goodness and concern for the kingdom's welfare. Then he concedes that Henry VI is William II's legitimate successor, and that, according to the laws and the sworn oaths, he should inherit. Only after that does he deplore Henry's "Teutonic fury" and his "barbaric" German language, which all the Sicilian courtiers (including gray-haired Walter) will have to learn if Henry becomes king. Matthew dismisses Roger of Andria because of his prodigality and because there are scandalous rumors about his morals. Finally, he proposes Tancred, an ideal mixture of royal blood and humble origin.

In lines 136–137, with metaphors about small boats and shallow waves, he suggests that Tancred will be weak and docile enough for his advisors to control him, as Del Re (413) and Rota (24) point out in their respective editions. With these arguments, Matthew successfully wins over the archbishop, at least to the extent of gaining his silent acquiescence.

The chronicler Falcandus, who apparently shared Matthew's abhorrence of the German tongue, also shared Pietro's hatred of Matthew himself, who was long a *familiaris* during the reign of William II. Interestingly, he states that Matthew had great skill as a flatterer and that "he would smile most greatly on those whom he hated" (*eis maxime quos oderat arridebat*) (*La Historia*, 84; see also *History of the Tyrants*, trans. Loud and Wiedemann, 133).

(S 13–14; KS 53)

100r *Matthew of Ajello attempts to induce Walter the* Protofamiliaris *to support Tancred.*
Illustrates lines 110–139 on fol. 99v.

. . . .

Sole inclinato bigamus sacerdos ivit ad domum Panormitani archiepiscopi.	1	At sunset, the bigamous priest went to the house of the archbishop of Palermo.
Bigamus sacerdos dierans ortatur pro Tancredo.	2	The bigamous priest, taking an oath, exhorts in Tancred's favor.
Gualterius famosus presul.	3	Walter, the famous prelate.

Commentary and Notes [100r]: The top of the page shows the zodiac (cap. 1), that is, the circular track of the sun, moon, and stars around the spherical earth. The sun is shown slightly below the horizon in the right-hand side, with the moon slightly above it in the left, showing that it is after sunset. Eight stars shine, six at the top and two below. The personified sun seems to be spitting a stream of water (or fire?) from his mouth and trailing a lock of hair behind.

Below this representation of the celestial clock, Matthew and his companions set out. Matthew, in the center, wears the tall hat that marks him as a "lord of the court." He rides a mule, while four messengers go before him on foot and three tonsured clerics ride behind on horses. At the bottom of the page, Matthew is again in the center, standing before the mitered archbishop Walter, his hand on the Bible, pleading on Tancred's behalf (cap. 2). However, Kölzer's commentary (54) implies that the archbishop, at his request, is absolving him of his oath of obedience to Constance. Behind him, outside the door, an attendant groom holds his mule. Cap. 2 describes Matthew as a bigamous priest, and this is not the last time he will do so. However, as far as scholars have learned, Matthew was not a priest, nor was he a bigamist in the modern sense of the word. He married twice, but did not have two wives living at one time.

(S 123–24; KS 54)

100v   Particula VI: Epistola ad Tancredum.

Protinus accepta bigamus notat ista papiro;   140
    Hec in nocturnis verba fuere notis: 141
"Hanc tibi Matheus mitto, Tancrede, salutem.   142
    "Quam cito ni venias, qui ferat alter erit.   143
"Rumpe moras, venias comitatus utraque   144
    "Prole, recepturus regia sceptra veni;   145
"Rumpe moras, postpone fidem, dimitte maritam.   146
    "Ipse tibi scribo, qui tibi regna dabo;   147
"Per me regnabis, per me tibi regna dabuntur;   148
    "Fac cito quod venias, nam mora sepe nocet;   149
"Inceptis desiste tuis, irascimur illis,   150
    "Nam, sicut debes, non sapienter agis.   151
"Cui facis heredi regnum iurare vel urbes?   152
    "Quem legis heredem, cui tua regna paras?   153
"Absenti domino magnas inducitis urbes   154
    "Ut iurent: aliis das quod habere potes.   155
"Nec te, si qua fides, nec te periuria tardent;   156
    "Gloria regnandi cuncta licere facit.   157
"Andronicus, si forte suo iuravit Alexi,   158
    "Ipse cruentato sceptra nepote tulit.   159
"Heredem regni fidei maculare pudorem   160
    "Non puduit profugum sub Manuele senem.   161
"Unum natorum, si phas foret atque liceret,   162
    Debueras dure subdere sponte neci.   163
"Ipse ego, triste pedes quotiens sinthoma perurit,   164
    "Non hominum dubito sanguinis esse reus."   165

Commentary and Notes [100v]: Now confident that Archbishop Walter will not inter-
fere, Matthew writes summoning Tancred. His tone is very different from the
one he used with Walter previously. Here he portrays himself as a powerful,
strong-willed, ruthless, crafty, and unscrupulous man who takes the Byzantine
emperor Andronicus Comnenus as a role model (see *Oxford Dictionary of Byzan-
tium*, 1:64, 94). Proudly, he claims that he bathes in human blood to alleviate his
gout. According to him, no scruple of any kind should stand in the way of "the

Section 6: Letter to Tancred.

At once that bigamist took up paper and wrote;
    By night he set down these words:
"Matthew sends this greeting to you, Tancred.
    "Unless you come with the utmost speed, another will come to carry it away.
"Cut short all delays; you must come accompanied by both
    "Sons. Come to receive the royal scepter.
"Cut short delays, put promises behind you, dismiss your wife.
    "I myself write this to you, I who will give you the realms.
    "Through me you shall reign; through me the realms will be given to you.
    "Make haste to come, for delay often causes harm.
"Abandon your undertakings; we grow angry at them:
    "For you are not acting wisely, the way you should.
"To what heir do you cause the kingdom or the cities to swear oaths?
    "What heir do you choose, for whom you prepare your realms?
"You cause the great cities to swear loyalty
    "To an absent lord. You give to others what you might possess yourself.
"No, do not let the thought of perjuries delay you, if you have faith in anything;
    "The glory of ruling makes all things permissible.
"If Andronicus, perhaps, swore anything to his Alexius,
    "Still, he took the scepter himself from his murdered nephew.
"As heir to the kingdom, he did not scruple to violate the honor of his oath,
    "That old man who was a fugitive under Manuel.
"If it were divine will and lawful,
    "You should willingly put one of [your] children to a cruel death.
"I myself, whenever my feet burn with harsh symptoms,
    "Do not hesitate to be guilty of human blood."

glory of ruling." Another side to his cleverness, however, is his demand that Matthew bring along "*utraque prole*" (lines 145–146) literally, "both offspring," meaning Tancred's two sons, Roger and William, who are later shown in Tancred's coronation procession, 102r. It is important for Tancred to show the Sicilians that he has sons who can succeed him, and, in case the people are taken aback by Tancred's dwarfish appearance, that they are fairly handsome.

(S 15–16; KS 57)

101r *Greek, Saracen, and Latin notaries. Messengers from Matthew of Ajello to Tancred.*
Illustrates ll. 166–199 on fol. 101v.

• • • •

Notarii Greci	1	Greek notaries.
Notarii Saraceni	2	Saracen notaries.
Notarii Latini	3	Latin notaries.
Bigamus nocte scribens Tancredo	4	The bigamist writing to Tancred by night.
Cursor bigami. Cursor bigami. Cursor bigami.	5	Bigamist's runner. Bigamist's runner. Bigamist's runner.
Tancredus recipit litteras bigami.	6	Tancred receives the bigamist's letter.

Commentary and Notes [101r]: This picture shows three groups of notaries, identified by captions: (1) Greek, (2) Saracen, and (3) Latin. Siragusa (9, n. 1) observes that three languages were used in the chancery of the Norman kings (Latin, Greek, and Arabic), and sometimes two languages appear together in the same document, sometimes all three (see Additional Notes). It is night (cap. 4) as Matthew writes; darkness is also indicated by a burning candle (Kölzer, "Bildkommentar," 58). In the lower half of the drawing, messengers or runners (cap. 5) travel and deliver Matthew's letter to Tancred, whose face is shown in profile as in the illustrations on 99r, 102r, and 121r.

(S 124; KS 58)

101v Particula VII: Spuriosa unctio regni.

Nec mora; perlectis que miserat ille figuris,	166
Consuluit mentis triste cubile sue.	167
Stare pudet, properare timet, cor fluctuat intus;	168
Ut puer ascensum territus optat equi,	169
Et timet et gaudet, luit et ludit, modo sursum	170
Aspirat, modo se colligit inque manus;	171
Corporis exigui memori sub mente pudorem	172
Colligit, et quatitur sicut arundo, comes.	173
Tandem Siciliam gemina cum prole petentis	174
Obprobrium patris natus uterque tegit.	175
Fabarie cum prole comes descendit avite,	176
Illinc a multis plurima doctus abit.	177
Primo mane subit, vestem ferruginis instar	178
Induit; hic habitus signa doloris habet.	179
Heu heu quanta die periuria fecit in illa,	180
Qua comes infelix unctus in urbe fuit!	181
O nova pompa doli, species nova fraudis inique,	182
Non dubitas nano tradere regna tuo?	183
Ecce vetus monstrum, nature crimen, aborsum,	184
Ecce coronatur simia, turpis homo.	185
Huc ades, Allecto; tristis proclamet Herinis,	186
Exclament Satiri: "Semivir ecce venit."	187
Ne cadat obprobrium, Lachesis sua fila moretur,	188
Ludibrium mundi perpetuate dies.	189
Quam bene conveniunt redimito cimbala mimo!	190
Ne quemquam lateat, erea plectra sonant,	191
Et quibus auditum sors aut natura negavit,	192
Ut videant, alto simia fertur equo.	193
Altera mellifluens paradisus, dulce Panormum,	194
Quam male compensas dampna priora tibi!	195
Quam male Scariothis redimit tua festa Matheus,	196
Qui titulos cauta polluit arte tuos!	197
Pro Iove semivirum, magno pro Cesare nanum	198
Suscipis in sceptrum!	199

Commentary and Notes [101v]: There are touches of sympathy in Pietro's treatment of Tancred, as he reads over Matthew's letter in a state of indecision. However, once he makes up his mind and goes to receive his crown at Palermo, mockery and

Section 7: The Fraudulent Royal Anointing.

Nor was there delay. Having read over the letters the other man had sent,
    [Tancred] took counsel with the sad lurking-place of his mind.
He was ashamed to stay, afraid to hasten; his heart wavered within him.
    Like a terrified boy who seeks to mount a horse,
He fears and rejoices, mourns and exults, now aspires upward,
    Now shrinks and draws in his hands.
Thought of his meager body brings shame to the Count's mind,
    And he shakes like a reed.
But finally he seeks Sicily accompanied by double offspring, and
    The two boys cover the reproach of the father.
At ancient Favara the count descends,
    And he departs from that place having learned much from many.
First thing next morning, he puts on clothes as dark as rusted iron;
    He wears these garments which betoken mourning.
Alas, alas, how many perjuries he performed on that day,
    When the unhappy count was anointed in the city!
O new ceremony of deceit, new face of wicked fraud,
    Do you not fear to give realms to your dwarf?
Behold the old monster, crime of nature, untimely birth;
    Behold, the ape is crowned, repulsive man.
Come, Allecto; let the grim Fury proclaim it,
    Let the Satyrs cry out, "Behold, the half-man comes!"
Lest the disgrace should abate, let Lachesis delay her thread,
    Perpetuate the day which is the scorn of the world.
How fitting is the clash of cymbals for a crowned mime!
    Lest it should be hidden from anyone, let the bronze plectra resound,
And so that people may see (if fate or nature has denied them power
    of hearing) the ape borne up on a high horse.
Sweet Palermo, second Paradise, flowing with honey,
    What an ill recompense this is for your earlier loss!
How badly this Iscariot, Matthew, crowns your festival.
    He has befouled your honors with his hidden arts.
Instead of Jove a half-man, instead of great Caesar a dwarf
    You receive as sceptered ruler!

invective take over. The coronation is as ridiculous as it is wrong. Pietro dwells on
Tancred's physical ugliness as much as on the moral ugliness of what he does.

(S 17–18; KS 61)

102r *King Tancred's triumphal entry into Palermo.* Illustrates verses 166–199 on fol. 101v.

· · · ·

Quando Tancredus usurpavit sibi regni coronam.	1	When Tancred usurped for himself the royal crown.
Isti sunt filii Tancredi.	2	These are the sons of Tancred.
Bigamus Sacerdos.	3	The twice-married priest.
Triumphus spurii Regis.	4	Triumph of the false king.

Commentary and Notes [102r]: Notice the visual gags—for example, the fact that Matthew, not Tancred, carries the orb, which is the symbol of royal power. Kölzer's commentary (62) suggests that the birds "on Tancred's head, on his horse and on [his royal] standard" are intended to make the procession seem farcical. It is tempting to see them as birds of ill omen, but they do not seem to be crows or ravens. They have crested heads and are a tan color like the cloaks Matthew and Tancred wear.

Cap. 2 mentions but does not name Tancred's two sons, but from other sources we know that the elder is Roger, soon to be proclaimed co-ruler with his father, and the younger is William.

Matthew (cap. 3), again called a "bigamous" or "twice-married" priest, rides a mule. Kölzer's commentary states that his choice of mount is a poor reflection on him, but perhaps it merely shows that he is neither young nor of the knightly class.

After this follows a parade of musicians and armed men. Siragusa (124–25, n. 3) writes: "In Tancred's triumphal procession, a band of turban-wearing musicians and armed men take part; these may represent Moslems." He calls attention to Richard of San Germano's account of Tancred's relations with the Saracens: "Tancred . . . forced five Saracen minor kings (*regulos*), who from fear of Christians had taken refuge in the mountains, to return, though unwilling, to Palermo" (*Chronica Priora*, ed. Gaudenzi, 64).

(S 124–25; KS 62)

102v   Particula VIII: Casus anathematizati et derisio nascentis.

Debuit illa dies multa pice nigrior esse,	200
Qua miser adscendit quo ruiturus erat.	201
Illa dies pereat, nec commemoretur in anno,	202
In qua Tancredus regia sceptra tulit;	203
Illa dies pereat, semper noctescat abysso,	204
In qua Tancredus preredimitus abit!	205
O nimis infelix memorabilis unctio regni!	206
Unxit abortivum que manus ausa virum!	207
Embrion infelix et detestabile monstrum,	208
Quam magis alta petis, tam gravior lues;	209
Corpore te geminas, brevis athome, semper in uno,	210
Nam puer a tergo vivis, ab ore senex.	211

Hoc ego dum dubia meditarer mente profundum:	212
Que res nature dimidiasset opus,	213
Egregius doctor et vir pietatis amicus	214
Explicuit causas talibus Urso michi:	215
"Ut puer incipiat, opus est ut uterque resudet,	216
"Ex quo perfectus nascitur orbe puer.	217
"Non in Tancredo sementat uterque parentum,	218
"Et si sementent, non bene conveniunt;	219
"Dux alter de stirpe ducum, de stegmate regum,	220
"Altera de media stirpe creata fuit.	221
"Naturam natura fugit; fornacis aborret	222
"Gemma luem, nec humus nobilitate coit.	223
"Evomit humorem tam vilis texta virilem;	224
"Concipitur solo semine matris homo.	225
"Quantum materies potuit pauperrima matris	226
"Contulit, et modicum materiavit opus.	227
"Hunc habuisse patrem credamus nomine, non re;	228
"Rem trahit a matre dimidiatus homo.	229
"Qui purgata solo bene culto semina mandant,	230
"In lolium versos sepe queruntur agros.	231
"Sepius infelix conceptum vacca iuvencum	232
"Monstriferumque pecus mollis abortit ovis."	233

Section 8: The Downfall of the Accursed One and His Ridiculous Birth.

That day must have been much blacker than pitch, on which that wretch
    Ascended to the place from where he'd fall.
Perish the day, may it never be remembered in the year,
    In which Tancred assumed the royal scepter;
Perish the day, may it always remain in the abyss of night,
    On which Tancred departed crowned before all.
O royal anointing of most unhappy memory!
    What hand dared to anoint the aborted man?
Unlucky embryo and detestable monster,
    The more you seek the heights, the greater the plague you are.
You double yourself in a single body, little atom;
    Always you live as a boy in back, an old man in your face.
¶
When I was contemplating this profound mystery with a doubtful mind,
    Wondering what operation of nature had halved this work,
Urso, a famous doctor and a friend of piety,
    Explained it to me this way.
"For a child to come into being, both parents must sweat fluid,
    "Forming a droplet from which a complete child is born.
"But in Tancred's case, both parents did not sow seed;
    "Or if they seeded, their seed did not combine well,
"Since the duke on the one hand came of ducal seed, the royal shoot,
    "And the other, the woman, was sprung of modest stock.
"Nature fled nature; the forge-hardened gem abhorred the weak liquid
    "Nor did the earth combine with nobility.
"The vile container cast forth so virile a fluid,
    "And so a man was conceived solely from the mother's seed.
"The impoverished material from the mother did all it could
    "And gave form to a modest work.
"Let us believe that this man has a father in name, not in fact;
    "The half-man derives this condition from his mother.
"Those who rightly command that only purified seed be sown
    "Often complain that fields turn to weeds and darnel.
"Quite often the unhappy cow aborts a monstrous bullock it has conceived,
    "And the gentle sheep aborts misshapen offspring."

Commentary and Notes [102v]: Pietro continues to denounce the coronation and every-one involved with it. Curiously, in line 207, he asks a rhetorical question which is hard to answer: "What hand dared to anoint the aborted man?" Ordinarily the archbishop of Palermo would perform the ceremony, but Archbishop Wal-ter clearly preferred Henry and Constance, even though Matthew, as we learned above, gained his silent acquiescence (line 139). Did Walter of Palermo actually crown Tancred? None of the contemporary chronicles makes a clear statement. Though Walter did not live long after this, Clementi states that he was alive at least until June 1190 ("An Administrative Document of 1190 from Apulia," 62, note 2). His health may not have been good, however, which might have furnished him with an excuse to avoid personal participation. Perhaps his ultimate successor, Bartholomew, had already been assigned to assist him in his duties. See Additional Notes on line 207.

After line 212, Pietro moves on to invective against Tancred personally. Not content to observe that Tancred's parents were unmarried, Pietro sets about to prove that Tancred was not really Duke Roger's son at all. He does this not by alleging that Tancred's mother was unfaithful, but by putting into the mouth of a certain learned physician, Urso, the theory that Tancred is a freak of nature, formed in this fashion because the seminal fluid shed by the king's son could not combine with that of his lowborn mistress. Curiously, a speech within the work of Pietro's near-contemporary, Falcandus, also expresses the idea that unions between nobles and commoners might produce undesirable offspring: the Calabrian nobleman who attempts to dissuade Matthew Bonello from marrying Maio's daughter also suggests that this lowborn bride will bear him children of double nature, *"generis biformitate"* (*La Historia*, ed. Siragusa, 34); Loud and Wiedemann's translation "ambiguous descent" (89) does not, perhaps, convey that same image clearly. Scholars come to Tancred's defense by pointing out that Tancred's mother was a noblewoman, the daughter of Count Achard of Lecce.

(S 19–21; KS 65)

103r *Caricatures alluding to Tancred's future fall and his deformity.* Illustrates verses 200–33 on fol. 102v.

• • • •

Fortuna Tancredi	1	Tancred's fortune
Tancredus facie senex statura puellus.	2	Tancred, an old man in face, a little boy in stature.
Querenti mihi causam de modicitate corporis Tancredi quod aborsum fuerit eius corpus, magister Urso aborcientem ovem ducit in exemplum.	3	When I inquire about the cause for the smallness of Tancred's body, Master Urso brings up the example of a miscarrying ewe to explain how his body was aborted.
Hec viso abortivo stupet.	4	This woman stares amazed, having seen the aborted one.
Hec ostendit Tancredulum	5	This woman displays little Tancred.
Mater Tancredi	6	Tancred's mother.

Commentary and Notes [103r]: As Siragusa points out (125, note 3) this page contains the story of Tancred's life from a hostile point of view, but as such it must be read from the bottom up. On the top left, a splendidly caparisoned horse stands proudly over the diminutive crowned figure of Tancred, who apparently has fallen off to his death or serious injury. Cap. 1, "Tancred's fortune" indicates that this represents Tancred's ultimate failure allegorically, perhaps taking up the image in lines 169–170 about the hesitant boy and the horse. To the right, the diminutive Tancred is shown with two faces, one of a child and one of a bearded man. Cap. 2 clarifies the meaning; his size makes Tancred look like a child from behind, but in his face he is a grown man.

In the second row, the famous doctor Urso appears, addressing the poet, who is represented as a very attentive and respectful youth, perhaps Urso's student. To their right, a sheep appears in the act of miscarrying—an example Urso has used (cap. 3) to illustrate his point. At the bottom of the page, Tancred's mother (cap. 6) appears in bed, after giving birth to her son. A midwife shows the little swaddled child to an attendant who stares in horror.

(S 125; KS 66)

103v Particula VIIII: Abortivi fallax iniquitas proscribit ascriptos.

Ridiculum, natura, tuum res simia turpis,	234
Regnat abortivi corporis instar homo!	235
Qua ratione sibi sacra convenit unctio regni,	236
Quem negat heredem non bene nupta parens?	237
Que vis, que probitas potuit, que fama, quis ensis	238
Maiestativum promeruisse decus?	239
Non sua semper amans, quotiens qui nil dedit illi,	240
Seu dedit et petit, non minus hostis erat;	241
Moribus et vita pauper, nec fama repugnat,	242
Et modicas vires et breve corpus habet.	243
Ingenii vitemus opes et recia mentis,	244
In quibus egregios scimus obisse viros.	245

¶
Cum foret ille tuus falso comes, Andria, captus,	246
Condoluit magnis rebus obesse fidem,	247
Quem periura fides, quem pacis fedus inique	248
Fallit, et oscuro carcere clausus obit.	249
Quam male credis aque trepidantia vela quiete,	250
Quas hodie Zepherus, cras aget Eurus aquas!	251
Heu ubi tanta iacet saturate copia mense,	252
Que numeri nulla lege coacta fuit!	253
Heu ubi tanta iacet maturi forma gigantis,	254
Iusticie rector!	255
Prodigus in dando, vix vix retributa recepit,	256
Prevenit meritum semper aperta manus.	257
Hunc aliosque viros fallax intoxicat anguis,	258
In quibus apparet Cesaris esse fides.	259

Commentary and Notes [103v]: After the bitterly satirical account of Tancred's elevation, Pietro paints him broadly as a corrupt, deceitful, unjust, and murderous king who destroys many others. Most of all, the poet focuses on Roger of Andria, mentioned earlier as Tancred's rival for kingship, supported by the nobles but rejected by Matthew. Here, however, Count Roger is loyal to Henry VI's party. The poet gives no details about his capture or death, but only alludes to Tancred's treachery and false promises, and to Roger's justice and generosity. According to Richard of San

Section 9: The False Iniquity of the Aborted One Outlaws Those Who Are Enrolled.

Nature, your laughing-stock is reigning now, that foul ape-thing,
    That man in the likeness of an aborted corpse!
By what reason does the holy unction of the realm belong to him,
    Whose claim is denied by a mother not properly wed?
What powers, what justice, what fame, what sword
    Could proclaim him worthy of majesty?
Always loving what is not his own, he was many times an enemy
    To those who gave nothing, and no less to those who gave and asked favors
        in return.
He is poor in morals and in life (nor does Fame refute the charge),
    And he has little strength and a short body.
Let us pass over the wealth of snares he weaves in his mind,
    Into which we know famous men have fallen.

¶

When, O Andria, your count was treacherously captured,
    He mourned because huge matters obstructed loyalty.
He himself, deceived by a perjured promise and an unjust pledge of peace,
    Died shut up in a dark prison.
How wrong you are to trust the trembling sail in quiet waters,
    For where Zephyr is today, tomorrow Eurus will drive the waters.
Alas, where now is the table spread with such plenty
    That it could not be expressed in any kind of numbers?
Alas, here lies, before his time, a giant man
    Upright in justice.
Prodigal in giving, hardly, hardly did he receive a fair return;
    The open hand always excels his reward.
The false serpent poisoned him and other men,
    In whom loyalty to Caesar appeared.

Germano's *Chronica* (65), Roger was besieged at the fortress of Ascoli [Satriano] by
Count Richard of Acerra, Tancred's brother-in-law. The latter, unable to take the
stronghold, invited Roger to a parley, captured him treacherously ("*proditorie cepit*")
and "condemned him to a wretched death (*miserabili morte dampnavit*)," some time
in 1190, "probably autumn" as Jamison suggests in *Admiral Eugenius* (319; Appen-
dix I). For comments on the title and on line 253, see Additional Notes.

(S 22–23; KS 69)

104r *The Count of Andria in prison.* Illustrates ll. 234–259 on fol. 103v.

· · · ·

Simia factus Rex.		1	The ape made king.
Castrum		2	Castle . . . .
Comes Rogerius Andrie		3	Count Roger of Andria

Commentary and Notes [104r]: Tancred, at the top (Cap. 1), has captured his rival. Once more he is drawn hunched and deformed, but now he wears a crown with pendants. Cap. 2 indicates a castle of which the name has been erased; see Additional Notes. Roger, below (Cap. 3), still of giant form and placid demeanor, is fettered and standing in front of his folding stool instead of sitting on it. As Kölzer "Bildkommentar," (70) says a servant lowers to Count Roger, by means of a rope, what might be a pot of water and "a bread-ring" of the sort that appears in the illustration on fol. 125r. The scantiness of the rations and the ungracious manner of serving them stand in ironic contrast to Roger's open-handedness and his generous hospitality, described in lines 252–253; yet more important, however, is the statement in line 258 that Roger was poisoned.

Despite some elements of realism, these illustrations are, like the others, not intended to picture physical reality precisely. Kölzer's commentary mentions that there is no support beneath Tancred's feet, so that he is "free-swimming as it were" (70). The Count's location is also unclear; he would seem to be in a dungeon, but is shown in front of a wall, as if he were outside the castle. A surface which looks like a strip of castle wall in the middle of the drawing becomes, at the bottom, a pole to which the ends of Roger's fetters are attached with a ring.

(S 125; KS 70)

104v [Particula] X: Imperialis unctio.

Serta recepturus cum Cesar venit in Urbem,	260
Exultat pompis inclita Roma novis.	261
Ad Petri devenit eques venerabile templum,	262
Quo pater antistes preredimitus erat.	263
Balsama, thus, aloe, miristica, cinnama, nardus	264
Regibus assuetus, ambra modestus odor,	265
Per vicos, per tecta fragrant redolentque per urbem;	266
Thuris aromatici spirat ubique rogus;	267
Vestit odora viam mirtus sociata dianthis;	268
Luxuriant croceis lilia iuncta rosis.	269
Prima domus templi bisso vestitur et ostro,	270
Stellificat tedis cerea flamma suis;	271
At domus interior, ubi mensa coruscat et Agnus,	272
Purpurat aurato res operosa loco.	273
A vice, Petre, tua pius introducitur heros,	274
Inclitus altaris sistitur ante gradus.	275

¶

Primo papa manus sacrat ambas crismate sacro,	276
Ut testamentum victor utrumque gerat;	277
Brachia sanctificans, scapulas et pectus inungens:	278
"In Christum Domini te Deus unxit," ait.	279
Post hec imperii correptum tradidit ensem,	280
Quem Petrus abscissa iussus ab aure tulit,	281
Ensis utrimque potens, templi defensor et orbis,	282
Hinc regit Ecclesiam, corrigit inde solum;	283
Iura potestatis, pondus pietatis et equi	284
Signat in augusta tradita virga manu;	285
Anulus Ecclesie, regnorum nobilis arra,	286
Offertur digitis, Octaviane, tuis;	287
Quam geris aurate, Cesar, diadema thiare,	288
Signat te apostolicas participare vices.	289
Post hec cantatis ad castra revertitur ymnis,	290
Mandat in Apuliam quisque quod ire paret.	291

Commentary and Notes [104v]: Henry's coronation, in contrast to Tancred's, is a ceremony full of solemn grandeur and sacred meaning. In mentioning of the high priest's slave whose ear Peter cut off, Pietro suggests that the pope, as Peter's

[Section] 10: The Imperial Anointing.

When Caesar comes to the City to receive the crown,
    Famous Rome exults in new pomps.
The horseman comes to the venerable temple of Peter,
    Where the father-bishop had been crowned before.
Balsam, frankincense, aloes, nutmeg, cinnamon, nard
    Customary for kings, amber of mild odor,
Perfume the streets and houses and spread their scent through the city.
    The smoke of aromatic frankincense spirals everywhere;
The road is clothed with sweet-smelling myrtle along with pinks;
    The lily flourishes next to the saffron-colored roses.
The first house of the temple is adorned in fine linen and purple,
    The fiery wax candles shine like stars in their pine-wood holders. However,
The interior house, where the table sparkles and also the Lamb,
    A work of much skillful labor, glows with purple in the golden place.
There, by your office, Peter, the pious hero is led in,
    Resplendent, and placed before the steps of the altar.
¶
First the pope consecrated both hands with blessed chrism,
    So that the conqueror could wield both testaments.
Sanctifying his arms, shoulders and breast [the pope] anointed him.
    "God anoints you as his Christ," he said.
After this he handed over the drawn sword of the Empire,
    Which Peter, being commanded, withdrew from the severed ear.
This sword is doubly powerful, defender of the Church and the World,
    For here it rules the Church, and there corrects the earth.
The power of law, the weight of piety and equity,
    Are signified in the rod given into the august hand.
The ring of the Church, the noble pledge of realms,
    Is placed on your fingers, Octavian.
That you bear the golden triple diadem, Caesar,
    Signifies that you participate in the Apostolic role.
After this, hymns being sung, [the emperor] returned to camp,
    And commanded that each [of his followers] prepare to go into Apulia.

vicar, should not bear the sword, but that the emperor should do so on his behalf. Line 29 also states that the emperor enjoys part of the Apostle's authority. Ideally, pope and emperor should act in harmony.

                              (S 24–25, KS 73)

105r *The Imperial Coronation of Henry VI at Rome.* This illustrates ll. 260–291 on fol. 104v.

· · · ·

Quando imperator Henricus venit Romam et a Celestino papa coronatus est.	1	When Henry the emperor comes to Rome and is crowned by Pope Celestine.	
ROMA.	2	ROME.	
Imperator.	3	The Emperor.	
Imperator — Papa Celestinus.	4	The Emperor — Pope Celestine.	
Ecclesia Beati Petri.	5	The Church of Saint Peter.	
Primo manus unguntur — Crisma.	6	First, the hands are anointed — Chrism.	
Secundo brachia.	7	Second, the arms.	
Tercio hensem papa [tradit?]	8	Third, the pope [hands over?] the sword.	
Quarta virgam.	9	Fourth, the rod.	
Quinta anulum	10	Fifth, the ring.	
Ultimo mitram	11	Last, the miter.	

Commentary and Notes [105r]: In five rows of illustrations, Pietro represents the imperial coronation in several stages, thus showing the importance he attached to this event, which happened, according to Kölzer's commentary (74), on Easter Monday, 15 April 1191. In the top row and on the sides, towers representing the city of Rome are shown. Below, Henry rides, preceded by a banner, crowned and carrying the orb. In the middle of the next row, he and Pope Celestine face one another and the ceremony proceeds. See notes for this section and the accompanying text.

(S 126; KS 74)

105v Particula XI: Regni Legates.

Suscipit interea legatos scripta ferentes,   292
    Quos proceres regni, quos docuere duces.   293

Primus magnanimus scripsit comes illi Rogerus;   294
    Scripserat infelix semivir ipse comes;   295

Scripsit Consanus patrio comes ore venustus;   296
    Scripsit Molisius inclitus ille comes;   297

Scripsit Tricarici comes et comes ille Gravini;   298
    Scripsit cum triplici prole Philippus idem;   299

Et gemini fratres magni scripsere Lupini;   300
    Scripsit et antistes hoc Capuanus idem;   301

Scripsit et antistes dominorum gemma Panormi;   302
    Scriperat et presul Bartholomeus idem;   303

Scripsit cum multis pius archilevita Salerni,   304
    Cuius pura fides purior igne manet.   305

Commentary and Notes [105v]: This list of those who wrote inviting Henry VI to claim Sicily is now thematically significant because Henry is about to take them up on it. But the first man named, Count Roger of Andria (294), is already dead. In addition, the poet indicates that two others, "the unhappy half-man" Tancred (295) and "the prelate Bartholomew" (303), have already changed their allegiance. Both "had written" (*scripserat*) to Henry, in contrast to the rest, who simply "wrote" (*scripsit*). Tancred is singled out for obvious reasons, but what of Bartholomew? The poet will not mention him again, and history does not remember him as an ardent Tancredine. He was, however, Walter's successor as archbishop of Palermo. Perhaps he performed the coronation. See his biographical sketch and Additional Notes on line 207.

    The others mentioned are probably Richard of Caleno, count of Carinola and Conza (296); Roger, count of Molise (297); Roger, count of Tricarico (298);

Section 11: Legates of the Realm.

In the meantime, he received envoys bearing writings,
    Whom the great men and leaders of the realm had instructed.

First wrote the great-souled Count Roger;
    (Before, that unhappy half-man himself, Count [Tancred], had written.)

The Count of Conza, with charming paternal bearing, wrote;
    The famous Count of Molise wrote.

The Count of Tricarico wrote, as did the Count of Gravina.
    Philip with his three sons wrote in the same vein.

And the great twin brothers, the Lupins, wrote,
    And the archbishop of Capua wrote the same.

Also the bishop wrote, the jewel of the lords of Palermo,
    (Before, the prelate Bartholomew also had written).

Amongst others the pious archdeacon of Salerno wrote,
    Whose pure faith remained purer than fire.

Tancred de Saya, count of Gravina (298); Philip, Count of Balvano (299); Hugh and Jordan Lupin (300); Matthew, archbishop of Capua (301); Walter, archbishop of Palermo (302); and Aldrisio, archdeacon of Salerno (304–305). Judging in part from the territorial bases of these magnates (mostly counts and bishops), Chalandon (*Histoire*, 2:430–31) explains that Tancred's opposition and Henry's support was centered in Apulia and Terra Laboris, the northern parts of the Sicilian kingdom, nearest Rome and the imperial lands in Northern Italy.

(S 26–28; KS 77)

Siragusa, in his textual notes (26), points out that the spaces between the couplets are in the manuscript.

106r *Runners from Sicily to the emperor. Runners from Germany.* Illustrates ll. 292–305 on fol. 105v.

· · · ·

Cursores regni missi ad serenissimum imperatorem H[enricum].

1. Runners from the kingdom sent to the most serene emperor, H[enry].

Cursores Alamannie.

2. Runners from Germany.

Commentary and Notes [106r]: This illustration shows the exchange of messengers between Henry VI and the Sicilian kingdom, which has been going on since William II's death. On the upper level, four messengers, dressed alternately in green and tan, bearing letters and carrying bags strapped to their backs, climb to where Henry sits on his throne, crowned and holding a scepter. Henry reaches out to receive the letters. On the lower level, five messengers, with walking sticks and packs, dressed alternately in green and orange, bear messages from Henry to Sicily. Kölzer's commentary (78) points out that Henry's court had already decided on a military expedition by Christmas of 1189, although at that time the Hohenstaufens were busy with Barbarossa's crusade. In May 1190, Henry Testa went to the Kingdom of Sicily with a small army. According to Jamison (*Admiral Eugenius*, 81), he had "occupied a good part of Abruzzo and eastern Apulia" with the help of Count Roger and the other nobles and clergy who had professed loyalty. Hence the messengers had plenty to talk about.

(S 127; KS 78)

106v　Particula XII: Primus imperatoris ingressus in regnum Sicilie.

En movet imperium mundi fortissimus heres	306
Et venit armata nobilitate ducum.	307
Non patitur falso laniari principe regnum	308
Quod sibi per patrios iura dedere gradus;	309
Hoc avus, hoc proavus quandoque dedere tributis,	310
Que pater a Siculis regibus ipse tulit.	311
Si numerare velis genitos a Cesare magno,	312
In medio Carolus fulminat orbe tuus;	313
Nec minor est Fredericus eo qui duxit ab illo	314
Et genus, et sceptrum, nomen et esse tuum.	315
Cuncta sibi, quecunque vides, servire coegit;	316
Vicit in hoc Carulos fortior hasta suos.	317
Quantum laudis habet mundus, quantumve triumphi,	318
Fama minus titulis asserit esse suis.	319
¶	
In modicum reputans tandem pro viribus orbem,	320
In Domino voluit spe meliore frui.	321
Alter in hoc Moyses, aliam populosus Egyptum	322
Deserit, ut redimat regna domumque Dei;	323
Iam sua vota videns inter sua gaudia, Christo	324
Migrat et eternis militat albus equis.	325
Plena potestatis fastidit ymago triumphos,	326
Est satis ex omni parte videre suum;	327
Ex hoc, ex aliis verus dinosceris heres,	328
Nam tua Pipinis gloria maior erit.	329
Augustos imitare tuos, defende tuum ius,	330
Coniugis et magni iura tuere patris.	331
Tam tua quam soceri limes conterminet unus,	332
Nam ius consortis in tua iura cadit.	333

Commentary and Notes [106v]: Here Pietro sets forth the justification for Henry's conquest of Sicily. He asserts that Sicily had always been a possession of the Holy Roman Empire, and that Sicilian kings paid tribute to the emperors, though, as Del Re (444, note 10) points out, history does not record this. Pietro praises

Section 12: The Emperor's First Advance into the Kingdom of Sicily.

Behold now! That most powerful heir sets in motion the empire of the world;
    He comes with the armed nobility of the dukes,
And does not suffer a false prince to tear apart the kingdom
    Which the laws made his through ancestral rank.
Yes, his grandfather and his great-grandfather gave this to him,
    Through the tributes which his father himself took from Sicilian kings.
[Henry], if you wish to number those born from Great Caesar,
    Your Charles hurls lightning in the midst of the world.
Nor is Frederick less than he, since he draws from him
    Both family and scepter; his name and being are yours.
He compels everything, all you see, to serve him.
    In this matter his stronger spear defeats his Carolingian forebears.
However much praise the world has, and however much triumph,
    Fame declares it less than the glory he has earned.
¶
At last, esteeming this world too small for his powers,
    [Frederick] wished to enjoy a better hope in the Lord.
Thus, as a second Moses, he departed from another populous Egypt,
    To redeem the realms and the house of God.
Now he sees his wishes among his joys, for he departed to Christ,
    Where [clothed in] white, he fights in the eternal cavalry.
This ancestral spirit full of power disdains showy triumphs;
    It is enough [for him] to see from every side what is his own.
Through this and from other things you are revealed as the true heir,
    For your glory will be greater than Pepin's.
To emulate your august ancestors, defend your right,
    Protect the rights of your consort and your great father.
Your borders and those of your father-in-law are the same,
    For the rights of your consort fall within your rights.

Henry's predecessors, dwelling mostly on the legendary Charlemagne (see Introduction C.6) and his father Frederick Barbarossa. Charlemagne is glorious, but the Hohenstaufen will exceed him.

(S 29; KS 81)

107r *Frederick I, the Emperor, starts on the crusade. His death. The entrance of Henry VI into the kingdom of Sicily.* Illustrates ll. 306–333 fol. 106v.

· · · ·

Fredericus fortissimus imperator
cum innumera procerum
multitudine domum Domini
redempturus accelerat.
Anima Frederici imperatoris.

Fredericus imperator in flumine
defunctus.
Quando serenissimus imperator
Henricus regnum Sicilie pius
ac misericors intravit.

1. Frederick. the mighty emperor,
with an innumerable multitude
of champions, hastens to redeem
the house of the Lord.
2. The soul of the emperor Frederick.

3. Frederick the emperor, dead in the
river.
4. When the most serene emperor
Henry entered the kingdom of
Sicily, pious and merciful.

Commentary and Notes [107r]: The first two rows of this illustration celebrate Frederick Barbarossa. In the first, crowned and wearing the sign of the cross on his shoulder, he departs on his crusade, leading an army represented by seven horsemen (Cap. 1). Below, Frederick appears in the river, drowned, with an expression halfway between serene and suffering; above, his soul appears as a swaddled infant, lifted into heaven by an angel. In the original manuscript this illustration was painted over; see Introduction A.2.

On the lower level, Henry enters Italy to take up the government of his kingdom (Cap. 4). Glorification of Henry's father replaces arguments about Henry's claims to the throne of Sicily.

107v Particula XIII: Castrorum inclinatur proceritas

Castra movens Cesar, Montis volat arva Casini   334
    In quo Rofridus cura fidelis erat.   335
Cum grege, cum populo fecit quod debuit abbas;   336
    Sola refrenavit Cesaris arma fides.   337

Quando capta est per vim Rocca de Archis.

Subditur imperio nota vi gloria castri   338
    Quo dux a misero rege Burellus erat,   339
Exemplum cuius quam plurima castra sequuntur;   340
    Archis enim princeps nomen et esse gerit,   341
Quam castigato natura creavit acervo,   342
    Hostes non recipit, saxa nec arma timet.   343

Quando Capuanus antistes gaudens Augustum recepit.

I, Capuane pater, nec te consulta morentur;   344
    Armos quadrupedis calcar utrumque cavet.   345
Quem tua spectabant suspiria, vota petebant,   346
    Ecce venit dominus quem tua vota petunt.   347

Assigna populos aquilis victricibus, orna   348
    Menia, quod doleas ne furor ensis agat.   349
Postpositura fidem tua gens, sanctissime presul,   350
    Suscipit ancipiti corde salutis opem.   351

Section 13: The Highest of the Castles is yielded.

Moving his camp, Caesar flies to the fields of Monte Cassino,
    Where Roffredo, faithful in his care, remained.
With his flock and with the people, the abbot did what he should.
    His faith alone checked the arms of Caesar.

When Rocca D'Arce was taken by force.

The glory of the castle is subjected to the empire by famous force,
    Where Burello was the commander for the wretched king.
Many castles follow that example;
    Archis indeed bears the name and exercises the character of "Prince."
Nature made it from a tightly compressed mound;
    It receives no enemies, and fears neither stones nor weapons.

When the archbishop of Capua received Augustus, rejoicing.

Go, Capuan father, and let no counsels delay you.
    Strike both spurs into the flanks of your four-footed mount.
He whom you hoped for with sighs and sought with vows, behold!
    Your lord comes, whom your vows seek.

Give your people to the victorious eagles, adorn the walls [with banners]
    Lest the fury of the sword should strike to grieve you.
Your people, most holy bishop, will give faith less than its due regard;
    They receive this saving work with a double heart.

Commentary and Notes [107v]: Pietro now follows Henry's military campaign. First, the abbey of Monte Cassino and neighboring towns immediately pledged loyalty to the emperor, removing the need for force. Monte Cassino is the ancient monastery originally established by Saint Benedict in 529. It is also strategically located on "a high hill," as Norwich puts it in *Kingdom in the Sun* (42–44), and dominates the territory around it. It had been a crucial frontier fortress in previous conflicts. Text and miniature here suggest that the abbot's choice to support the emperor essentially delivered the whole region to Henry at this time. Though true in a fashion, this was also an oversimplification, as Siragusa (30, n. 1) and Kölzer's commentary (86) both point out. Abbot Roffredo actually took no part in these events. He was, or claimed to be, seriously ill when Henry arrived, and permitted his deacon, Adenulf (also called Atenulf), to perform his office. Roffredo had initially opposed Tancred's succession, but was eventually pressured to offer him his oath of allegiance. He had strong motives, both practical and moral, to avoid swift and sudden violation of the oath. Also the device of allowing Adenulf to act for him could serve to protect the Abbey; should Tancred regain control of the area, he could claim that Adenulf had acted within his instructions, during his illness, and Adenulf could hide. Should Henry remain in control, Roffredo could simply endorse the deacon's actions. In actuality, Roffredo proved an important and loyal supporter of the emperor later in the conflict, although this may have had something to do with hostages he was obliged to give.

Rocca D'Arce (337–338) is a strategic border town near Monte Cassino. The name could be translated as "Castle of the Fortress," "Rock of the Citadel," or perhaps "Citadel of the Treasure Chests," but Pietro has his own thoughts about the matter (line 341). Del Re (444, n. 12) writes, "Rocca d'Arce is in Terra Laboris, and is about fourteen miles from San Germano. The castle of that territory . . . was given by Tancred into the custody of Matthew Borrello." For descriptions of the conflict, Siragusa (31, n. 2) directs readers to *Annales Ceccanenses* (p. 288) and *Annales Casinenses* (p. 314). One variant of the latter (Codices 4 and 5) states, "he takes Rocca D'Arce in a violent assault, and this brought about such boldness in his men and such diffidence in ours that they no longer contemplated resistence even in the most well fortified places; hence, defeated not so much by war as by stupor, Sorella, Atino, and Castle Coeli yielded themselves up" (*Roccam Arcis violento capit insultu. Quod factum suos in audaciam, et nostros inducit in in diffidentiam, ut iam nec loca munitissima de resistendo cogitent: unde Sorella, Atinum, castrum Coeli, non tam bello quam stupore devitae se reddunt*). The former describes an attack on a city as well as a fortress:

> On the third day before the Calends of May [the emperor] entered the kingdom in Apulia, besieged the city called Arcis, and captured it the next day, burned it along with the fort [rocca], and expelled the castellan Matthew Burrel with all the Latins. Thus, all the lands as far as Naples being brought into his power, he surrounded and besieged that city, and made war on it with many and siege engines.

After the surrender of Rocca D'Arce, the strategic city of Capua pledged loyalty, urged by its archbishop Matthew. But Pietro hints that Capua will not remain faithful. In his apostrophe to the bishop, Pietro implies that the Emperor's coming is a subject both of joy and dread.

(S 30–31; KS 85)

---

338 *nota vi.* S: *notati.* pre-S: *notani.* KS: *nota vi.* De Rosa: *nota vi* Codex: *notavi.*

347: After this line, Siragusa indicates a blank space, "for about two verses," which he also leaves blank in his edition.

108r *The Abbot of Monte Cassino in an encounter with the Emperor. The surrender of Rocca D'Arce. The Emperor accompanied to Capua by the archbishop.* This illustrates ll. 306–351 on fol. 107v.

. . . .

Quando serenissimus imperator ad Montem Casinum venit.	1. When the most serene emperor came to Monte Cassino.
Rofridus fidelissimus abbas.	2. Roffredo, the most faithful abbot.
Mons Casinus.	3. Monte Cassino.
Imperator.	4. The emperor.
Mattheus Burrellus claves castri adsignat.	5. Matthew Burrellus hands over the keys to the castle.
Rocca Archis	6. Rocca D'Arce
Imperator	7. The emperor.
Quando Capuanus ypocraticus domino imperatori obviam processit.	8. When the Capuan physician went to meet the lord emperor.
Capua.	9. Capua.

Notes and Commentary and Notes [108r]: Henry meets the archbishop of Capua for a festal entrance into the city. The emperor is followed by knights with helmets, the archbishop by other clerics. The allusion to Hippocrates in Cap. 8 (see note) implies that this clergyman is known to be learned in medicine. Perhaps it also alludes to the archbishop's wish to keep his city physically as well as politically healthy. It may also indicate Pietro's interest in medicine and those who study it. Kölzer's commentary (86) states that the emperor reached Monte Cassino in May 1191. He also suggests that the people in the foreground may be the population of nearby San Germano, since Roffredo had arranged for them to meet Henry VI and swear allegiance to him. This shows how the abbot's influence brings not merely the monastery but also much of the surrounding region under Henry's control.

(S 128; KS 86)

108v Particula XIIII: Urbs Neapolis obsessa resistit

Ut mare spumescit subito, nubescit ut aer,	352
Obsidet ut quercum multa columba brevem,	353
Sic tua, Parthenope, confinia Cesar obumbrat,	354
Et nisi pugnassent munera, victa fores.	355
Iussit ut a dextris Cesar tentoria figi,	356
Circuit in celeri menia celsus equo;	357
Sat premunitam gaudens circumspicit urbem	358
Menibus et vallo, turribus atque viris.	359

¶

Machina construitur celsis se menibus equans,	360
Porrigit ad lapides brachia longa graves.	361
Ex hac Colonii pugnant, hac parte Boemi,	362
Hac dux Spoleti menia temptat eques;	363
Ex hac turma virum plenis succinta pharetris	364
Pugnat, et hac equitum plurima tela micant.	365
Hic notat in muro sinuato cominus arcu	366
Mussantem cupidum bella videre virum;	367
Hic alium fantem convicia plura minantem	368
Colligit, et medio corrigit ore minas.	369
Unus erat qui saxa suos iactabat in hostes,	370
Vocibus insultans talia verba dabat:	371
"Iam sine cesarie, vel iam sine Cesare facti,	372
"Vix alacer de tot milibus unus erit;	373
"Noster, si qua potest, Augustus more leonis	374
"Augustum vestrum tondet et eius oves."	375
Hunc aliquis fantem, baliste cornua flectens,	376
Percutit, et summa lapsus ab arce ruit.	377

Commentary and Notes [108v]: The scene is now the siege of Naples, which Pietro calls by its ancient name, Parthenope. In this passage, he moves away from rigorous separation of good and evil, and for a time celebrates the energy and vigor of the fighters on both sides. Henry rejoices to see the well-defended city. However, Pietro does mention, to foreshadow future events, that bribery rather than honest warfare will determine the outcome of this conflict.

The duke of Spoleto (line 363) is Conrad of Urslingen (Kölzer and Stähli, *Petrus de Ebulo*, 294). The man struck with the arrow (lines 366–367) is not named in these verses, but in the accompanying illustration, Count Richard of Acerra is shown with an arrow through his cheeks and mouth. Perhaps Pietro expected readers to obtain his identity from the captions. Count Richard's wounding is described directly in lines 378–383.

Section 14: The Besieged City of Naples Resists.

As the sea suddenly foams so that the sky is clouded by it,
    And as many doves rest upon a little oak,
So Caesar overshadows your boundaries, Parthenope,
    And if bribes had not entered the fray, you would have been vanquished.
Caesar commands that the tents should be fixed on the right-hand side;
    Sublime on a swift horse he circles the walls.
He rejoices as he looks over the well-defended city,
    The walls and the palisades, towers and men.
¶
An engine is made, at equal level with the high walls;
    The long arms stretch out to the heavy stones.
From this side the Colognese fought, from this the Bohemians,
    And here the duke of Spoleto attempts the walls on horseback.
From this place a division of men girded with many quivers
    Fights, and there a division of horsemen brandishes many spears.
One man, with his bent bow, picks off from the wall, close at hand,
    A muttering man desirous of seeing the wars;
He strikes the other down as he utters threats with many insults,
    And corrects his vauntings right in the middle of his mouth.
There was a man throwing stones upon the attackers,
    And giving, in noisy mockery, words such as this:
"Now deprived of his hairy locks or his hairy Caesar,
    "Hardly one of so many thousand soldiers will show courage.
"If our Augustus can do anything, he will, in lion fashion,
    "Shear your Augustus and his sheep."
Someone, bending the horns of his ballista, struck that speaker,
    And he slid and fell down from the high tower.

There is much punning and trading of insults. *Caesaries* (372) or "hairy locks"
is clearly a pun with "Caesar"; "*Iam sine cesarie, vel iam sine Cesare*" means literally,
"Without hairy locks or without Caesar." It is not perfectly clear why the impe-
rial army is mocked for hairiness. However, Del Re (446–447, note on p. 416)
suggests that this may be an allusion to the Samson story (Judges 13–18). The
mocking speaker implies that since the German army would not fight if it lost
its Caesar, Tancred's supporters should try especially hard to kill Henry VI. The
mocking speaker also gives Tancred equal status with the emperor, calling him
"Augustus," an imperial title which Pietro usually reserves for Henry. Of course,
the mocker immediately pays with his life for this misapplication of it.

(S 32–33; KS 89)

109r   *Henry VI besieges Naples. The count of Acerra wounded.* This illustrates ll. 352–377
on fol. 108v.

. . . .

Neapolim.		1	Naples.
Comes Riccardus.		2	Count Richard.
Boemii.		3	Bohemians.
Imperator et duces.		4	Emperor and commanders.
Colonienses.		5	Colognese.

Commentary and Notes [109r]: Imperial forces battle against the defenders of Naples.
The count of Acerra appears on a high tower with an arrow through his cheeks.
In the middle row, the emperor rides to the attack, behind his standard-bearers,
but ahead of his knights. The ensign of the imperial eagle adorns his helm, his
shield, and his horse's trappings. In the lower row, knights identified by the cap-
tion as "Colognese" ride in the imperial camp. The leader bears a lion on his
shield. Siragusa (128–29, n. 4) also points out two shields on the battlements of
the castle which appear to have recognizable devices: "on one, perhaps, there is
a lion rampant, on the other a transverse band; each one is struck by an arrow."
Kölzer's commentary (90) states that this siege lasted from the end of May until
August 1191.

(S 128–29; KS 91)

109v Particula XV: Comitis percussio et Salerni exaudita peticio.

Cum comes egregius, Tancredi gloria spesque,	378
Cesaris invicti cernere castra velit,	379
Se tegit electis et menia scandit in armis,	380
Illudensque viris ars quibus arcus erat.	381
Quem quis percipiens, Liceum plicat auribus arcum,	382
Lapsaque per medias arsit arundo genas.	383
Ut fragor antique nemus ylicis implet et auras,	384
Turbine que rapido vulsa vel icta ruit,	385
Sic a strage tua, comes, omnis murmurat etas	386
Et rex ille tuus de breve fit brevior.	387
At miser antistes comitis succingitur ense,	388
Polluit oblita religione manus;	389
Pars rate tuta vagans lunatos explicat arcus,	390
Per mare quos sequitur nante Boemus equo.	391
Supplicant interea preciose nuncius urbis,	392
Exponens iuvenum pectora, vota senum,	393
Corda puellarum, mentes et gaudia matrum,	394
Et quicquid voti mens puerilis habet.	395
Sit ait archoticon: "Veniens tua nobilis uxor,	396
"Sublimis sedeat patris in urbe sui.	397
"Hic victor fera bella geras; tua nupta Salerni	398
"Gaudeat et dubiam servet in urbe fidem.	399
"Nam si bella placent, non desunt prelia longe:	400
"Hen Turris maior bella diurna movet;	401
"Est prope non longe Iufonis inutile castrum,	402
"In quo furtivi militis arma latent;	403
"Est prope dulce solum, nobis satis utile semper,	404
"Ebolus, aspirans quod petis urbis honor;	405
"Est prope Campanie castrum, specus immo latronum,	406
"Quod gravat Eboleam sepe latenter humum."	407
Hec ubi legatus fert coram principe mundi,	408
Magnanimis princeps: "Quod petis," inquit, "erit."	409
Protinus almipater Capuane sedulus urbis	410
Suscipit a domino talia iussa suo:	411
"I, bone namque pater, mentis pars maxima nostre,	412
"Facturus semper quod mea nupta velit."	413
Hec ubi legatus notat impetrata Salerni,	414
Sollempnem peragunt gaudia plena diem;	415
Exiit edictum, dominam cras esse futuram,	416
Cuius in adventum se sibi quisque parat.	417

Section 15: The Wounding of the Count, and the Petition From Salerno Heard.

When the famous count, the glory and hope of Tancred,
    Wished to see the camp of the unconquered Caesar,
He covered himself with choice armor and ascended the walls,
    Mocking at the men who were skilled with the bow.
Someone, perceiving him, bent the Lycaean bow to his ears,
    And the arrow-reed, gliding out, stung him in the midst of his cheeks.
As the crashing of an ancient holm-oak fills the forest and the air
    When it falls, whether uprooted by a fierce whirlwind or by blows,
So at your fall, Count, the whole generation murmurs,
    And that king of yours, weak already, becomes weaker still.
However, the wretched bishop girds on the sword of the count,
    And pollutes his hands, forgetting religion.
A party, roaming in a safe ship, stretches out a crescent bow,
    While the Bohemian pursues them through the sea with swimming cavalry.
Meanwhile, the ambassador of the precious city pleads,
    Putting forward the thoughts of the youths, the choices of the old men,
The hearts of the maidens, the minds and joy of the mothers,
    And whatever choices the minds of children have.
So said the Archon, "Let your noble wife come
    "And take her seat in the city of her sublime father.
"Here you, the victor, conduct fierce warfare; let your bride rejoice
    "In Salerno and preserve the doubtful faith of the city.
"For if wars are pleasing, battles are not far away;
    "Look, the Great Tower attempts battle daily,
"And not far away, in the menacing castle of Jufon,
    "The arms of bandit-knights are hidden.
"Nearby is the sweet country, always beneficial to us,
    "Of Eboli, seeking what the honor of the city requires.
"Nearby is a castle of the Campagna, a den, indeed, of robbers,
    "Which secretly oppresses Ebolean soil often."
When the legate said these things before the prince of the world,
    Thus spoke the great-souled prince: "What you ask will be."
Immediately the Capuan bishop, zealous for his city,
    Received these commands from his lord:
"Go, good father, the greatest part of our mind,
    "And always do what my bride wishes."
The legate of Salerno reported the things which had been accomplished,
    And they spent a solemn day full of joy;
The edict went forth that their lady would be there tomorrow,
    And they were all to prepare themselves for her coming.

Commentary and Notes [109v]: Pietro juxtaposes incidents from Tancredine and impe-
rial camps. Count Richard of Acerra, Tancred's brother-in-law (here described
as Tancred's most valuable follower and his great hope), looks at the battle and is
hit by an arrow. Alarmed at his fall, Nicholas, the archbishop of Salerno, then in
Naples (either because he has been driven out of Salerno, or because he naturally
gravitates to Tancred's headquarters), snatches up his sword and takes over Count
Richard's command, an action inappropriate in a priest. Meanwhile, ambassa-
dors approach the emperor, presumably accompanied by the archbishop of Capua
whom the emperor later addresses in line 410 when granting their request. They
ask that Constance be sent to Salerno, which was her father's capital in Apu-
lia, both to enjoy the location and to keep an eye on the city, whose loyalty is
suspected. The emperor agrees and particularly charges the bishop to do what
his wife wishes. The envoys return to Salerno, which receives the news with joy
and prepares a festive reception. Pietro's account stresses incautious and indecent

behavior on Tancred's side (the count's wounding, the archbishop's taking up arms), with dignified and appropriate behavior on the imperial side. As Pietro tells it, Constance's entrance into Salerno was desired by the imperial allies in Italy and was part of a serious strategy to keep and hold the loyalty of the city. On these terms, Henry agrees, with an affectionate word for the loyal Capuan bishop and special solicitude for Constance's wishes. Kölzer's commentary (94) suggests that Constance's sojourn in Salerno had something to do with her being ill and wishing to consult physicians, which seems to be implied by Godfrey of Viterbo (336, lines 85–89): "Imperatrix patitur, cepit medicinam (The empress suffered and received medicine)," although it could perhaps be figurative and ironic. Bishop Matthew of Capua is assigned the task of accompanying Constance to Salerno; as Siragusa points out (36, n. 2), this is not, apparently, because he came with the Salernitan legation but because he is especially trusted.

(S 34–36; KS 93)

110r *Medical treatment of the wound of the count of Acerra. Combat between Tancredines and Bohemians. Salernitan legation requesting that the empress enter the city. This illustrates ll. 378–419 on fol. 109v.*

• • • •

Neapolim.	1	Naples.
Quando percussus est comes Riccardus Acerrarum.	2	When Count Richard of Acerra was wounded.
Medicus.	3	Physician.
Boemii.	4	Bohemians.
Tancredini.	5	Tancredines.
Quando nuncii Salerni impetrant ab invictissimo imperatore quod illustrissimam imperatricem in Sal[ernum] venire.	6	When the spokesmen of Salerno gained their petition from the most victorious emperor that the most illustrious empress would come to Salerno.
Cioffus.	7	Cioffo.
Romoaldus.	8	Romuald.
Iohannes Princeps.	9	John Princeps.

Commentary and Notes [110r]: These illustrations show action in progress. The count (Cap. 2) is wounded, then treated by a physician (Cap. 3) and his assistants, events not described in the verses. Below, the battle rages on. The swimming "cavalry" of line 391 is shown. At the bottom, a delegation from Salerno (caps. 6–9) has an audience with Henry and Constance before their tent, to request the empress's presence in Salerno. See Additional Notes.

(S 129; KS 94)

110v Particula XVI: Augustalis ingressus in urbem.

Sol ubi sydereas ammovit crastinus umbras,	418
Urbs ruit et domine plaudit osanna sue;	419
Trinacriis pars fertur equis, qui flore fruuntur	420
Oris et etatis, pars sedet acta rotis;	421
Ipsa puellaris vittis insignis et auro	422
Occurrit cultu turba superba suo;	423
Mollis et insolitus gressus fastidit arenam,	424
Tardat arenosum litus et unda pedes;	425
Cinnama, thus, aloe, nardus, rosa, lilia, mirtus	426
Inflammant nares, aera mutat odor;	427
Tantus odor nares nardinus inebriat afflans,	428
Quod nova perfundi balsama quisque ferat.	429
Iunonem spectare suam quis tardat in urbe?	430
Cesaris in laudes cantica nemo silet.	431
Ut modulantur aves foliis in vere renatis	432
Post noctes yemis, post grave tempus aque,	433
Non aliter verno venienti plauditur ore,	434
Testantur pariter: "Luminis ecce dies."	435
Ingreditur patrias tandem Constancia sedes,	436
Que Tancridinam sentit in urbe fidem.	437
Quamplures tacita collecti voce susurrant;	438
Inter se referunt omina versa ducum;	439
Mons fugit a castro, quantum volat acta sagitta	440
Et quantum lapides mittere funda potest;	441
Hunc super ascendunt, fit machina, pugna vicissim	442
Contrahitur; variant mutua bella vices;	443
Hinc fera tela volant, fluviales inde lapillos	444
Funda iacit, lassant iactaque saxa manus.	445
Et modo tentantes mixtim prope menia pugnant,	446
Pugnando miscent tela manusque sonos.	447
Ut canis inter apros furit, e quibus eligit unum,	448
Ut rapit accipiter quam legit inter aves,	449
Non aliter nostri vellunt ex hostibus unum;	450
Commixto rapiunt ordine sepe duos.	451

Commentary and Notes [110v]: Constance enters Salerno with joyous ceremony, greeted by noblewomen adorned in their best. All the same, she is immediately aware of dissension and warfare in the city. People exchange gossip about the

Section 16: The Empress Enters the City.

When the next day's sun displaced the faded stars,
  The city runs and hails their lady with hosannas.
Some, who enjoy the flower of youth and beauty,
  Are carried by Sicilian horses; some sit, drawn by carriages.
That same maidenly throng, distinguished by garlands and gold,
  Goes to meet her, proud in its splendor.
A soft and unaccustomed step disdains the sand;
  The sandy shore and its waves hinder the feet.
Cinnamon, frankincense, aloes, nard, rose, lily, myrtle
  Excite the nostils, and the breeze changes its scent.
So much flowing perfume of nard intoxicates the nostrils,
  Because each one brings more balsam to be poured out.
Who in the city delays to look upon their Juno?
  No song was silent in the praise of Caesar.
As the birds sing in the spring when leaves are reborn,
  After the winter nights, after the season of heavy rain,
Not otherwise is her coming applauded by the voice of spring.
  Thus they declare: "Behold the day of light."
At last Constance enters her paternal seat,
  And perceives the Tancredine faith in the city.
How many people gather together and whisper with low voices!
  Among themselves they report the changed omens of the leaders.
There is a mountain, removed from the camp as far as the sped arrow flies,
  And as far as the sling can cast stones.
They climb upon this, make an engine, and battle is joined by turns;
  The chances of war favor one, then the other.
Here savage missiles fly, there the sling hurls river stones,
  And hands exhaust themselves with thrown boulders.
And now the attackers fight a mixed battle before the walls,
  In the fighting, sounds of missiles and close combat blend.
As a dog rages among boars and chooses one of them,
  As a hawk snatches the one he chooses from among the birds,
Not otherwise our men seek one from among the enemy,
  They often seize two when the ranks mingle.

progress of the war. Contending factions exchange hostilities from fortified
places in and around the city.

(S 37–38; KS 97)

---

422 *vittis*. S: *victis*. Non-S: *vittis*. Codex: (smudged, probably *victis*).

111r *Entrance of Constance into Salerno. Combat between Salernitan Tancredines and Imperialists, one force gathered in "The Great Tower" and the other on the hill "Torus."* This illustrates ll. 418–451 on fol. 110v.

· · · ·

Quando imperatrix triumphans Salernum ingreditur.	1.	When the triumphant empress enters Salerno.
Imperatrix.	2.	Empress.
Cives Salerni.	3.	Citizens of Salerno.
Nobiles mulieres.	4.	Noble women.
Turris Maior	5.	Great tower.
Torus.	6.	Torus.

Commentary and Notes [111r]: In the upper picture, the empress rides side-saddle to meet the citizens of Salerno, a group of male citizens on the left and noblewomen on the right, with a child, all carrying sprigs or shoots which Kölzer's commentary (98) describes as lilies. Expectations created by the verses are not entirely met; only the empress appears on horseback, and carriages or wheeled devices are not depicted. In the lower picture, a fierce battle rages between groups stationed in their two strongholds. An archer on the *Torus* takes aim at the *Turris Major*, while an adversary readies a stone-slinger to aim at the *Torus*. Kölzer's commentary (98) describes in some detail the weapons and engines depicted in this scene.

(S 130; KS 98)

111v   Particula XVII: Legatorum exquisicio et principis infirmitas.

Principis interea veniens legatus in urbem,	452
Eligit e multa nobilitate viros,	453
Quos ad Neapolim mittit; qui multa timentes,	454
Expediunt dubia mente laboris iter.	455
Inter quos fuit Alfanides cognomine Princeps,	456
Aldrisius, populi publica lingua sui,	457
Libraque iudicii Romoaldus; cetera turba,	458
Quid velit, auguriant, nescia causa vie.	459
Principis ut veniunt ad castra, magalia circum	460
Herrant, mirantes agmen et arma ducum;	461
Exquirunt spectare suum per castra Tonantem,	462
Nec datur accessus dux ubi magnus erat.	463
Attamen ingreditur quem gens cognominat archos;	464
Exclusis sociis, quem petit unus adit.	465
Ut videt Augustum magnis a febribus actum,	466
Lentaque purpureo menbra iacere thoro,	467
Tum color et species, tum sanguis ab ore recessit;	468
Tristis et exsanguis procidit ante thorum.	469
Ut gravis e sompno cum mater in ubere natum	470
Invenit exanimem, territa mente caret,	471
Sic ruit in gemitum lacrimabilis archilevita,	472
Certans pro tanto principe velle mori.	473
Tunc pius Augustus, quamvis grave corpus haberet,	474
Conatur tenui taliter ore loqui:	475
"Parce tuis oculis, fidissima cura Salerni,	476
"Sum bene, ne timeas, tercia febris abest.	477
"Fer sub veste manum, pulsum perpende quietum,	478
"Spes est de vita, quod mea menbra madent."	479
Plurima cum vellet, sopor est furatus ocellos,	480
Hinc rapit intuitus, surripit inde loqui.	481
Artis Ypocratice servans mandata Girardus,	482
Attente famulis ora tenere iubet.	483
Nature servabat opus studiosus amicum,	484
Nam sopor et sudor signa salutis erant.	485
Exiit ad socios tandem pius archilevita,	486
Conantur lacrime non minus ore loqui.	487
Alter in alterius iactabant lumina vultus,	488
Miscentes lacrimas mutua verba dabant.	489

Section 17: The Legation's Inquiry and the Prince's Illness.

The legate of the prince, meanwhile, coming into the city,
  Chooses men from those of great nobility,
Whom he sends to Naples; these, fearing many things,
  Hasten with doubtful mind on the labor of their journey.
Among these was that son of Alfano, known as "the Prince,"
  Aldrisio, the public voice of his people,
And Romuald their scale of judgement. The other crowd
  Takes auguries about what it means, not knowing the cause of the journey.
When they come to the camp of the Prince, circling the tents,
  They wander, admiring the troops and arms of the commanders.
Throughout the camp, they seek for a sight of their Thunderer,
  Nor is access given where the great leader was.
But yet the one whom the people call *Archon* enters;
  His companions excluded, he alone approaches the one he seeks.
Then he sees Augustus in the grip of a great fever,
  His sluggish limbs lying upon his purple couch.
Then color and beauty, then blood left his face;
  Sad and pale he threw himself down before the couch.
As a mother who, heavy with sleep, finds her child lifeless
  At her breast, and in her terror she loses courage,
So the woeful archdeacon fell to groaning,
  Protesting that he would wish to die for such a prince.
Then pious Augustus, however ill he was in body,
  Struggles with weak voice to say these words:
"Spare your eyes, well-trusted shepherd of Salerno,
  "I am well, do not be afraid; the tertian fever is gone.
"Place your hand under my clothing, feel carefully the steady pulse;
  "They expect me to live, since my limbs are sweating."
Though he wished to say much more, sleep stole over his eyes,
  Stealing away his consciousness, which in turn carried off his speech.
Girard, preserving the mandates of Hippocratic art,
  Carefully ordered the servants to restrain their speech.
That dutiful one was helping along the friendly operation of nature,
  Since sleep and sweat were signs of healing.
At last the pious archdeacon went back to his companions.
  Tears struggled to speak no less than words;
Each turned their eyes to the others,
  And they exchanged words mixed with tears.

Commentary and Notes [111v]: This is a suspenseful episode. A legate, not named but perhaps identified with the archbishop of Capua, who has a special connection to Constance's journey to Salerno, selects important men to come to Naples. They wander through the camp looking for the emperor, but when they reach his tent, they are not allowed to see him. Eventually the physician, Master Girard, brings their leader, the archdeacon Aldrisius, to the emperor's presence. The archdeacon can see for himself the reason for all the secrecy and alarm: the emperor is very ill with a fever, lying on his bed (said to be scarlet or purple in the poem but represented as green in the miniature). The consternation felt by Aldrisio is likened to a mother's reaction on finding her child lifeless at her breast. Henry speaks, however, and all his concern is for his faithful supporter; he encourages him to feel his pulse and assures him that he is on the mend after his "tertian" fever (see Additional Notes for the symptoms of malaria). The emperor, in his exhaustion, falls asleep in the middle of his speech. Girard then warns everyone to silence, not to interrupt the healing repose.

Aldrisius returns to his companions. All grieve and speak about what they have learned. Because Pietro has withheld information about these men's errand, we do not understand it well today, since we lack cultural information that the poet assumed in his audience. Theodor Toeche's *Kaiser Heinrich VI* (200), Del Re's edition (446, n. 18) and Kölzer's commentary (103) all say that Henry took hostages to guarantee his wife's safety; however, both the historical record and Pietro's narrative suggests that the men depicted were among Henry's strongest supporters. One would generally expect "hostages" to be taken from adversarial families. It is easy enough to imagine that the emperor's allies are being summoned because some major turning point in the emperor's strategy is expected; rumors of the emperor's illness may already have reached Salerno.

(S 39–40; KS 101)

112r   *The visit of the archdeacon of Salerno to the infirm emperor.* This illustrates ll. 452–489 on fol. 111v.

. . . .

Quando archidiaconus Salerni cum civibus suis Neapolim veniens invenit Augustum pacientem.	1. When the archdeacon of Salerno with his citizens coming to Naples found Augustus suffering illness.
Archidiaconus.	2. Archdeacon.
Cives Salerni e quibus solus archidiaconus a magistro Girardo introductus est ad imperatorem.	3. The citizens of Salerno from whom only the archdeacon was brought in to see the emperor by Master Girard.
Magister Girardus.	4. Master Girard.
Imperator.	5. The emperor.
Archi[diaconus]	6. Arch[deacon]

Commentary and Notes [112r]: The delegation described in the associated verses arrives at the imperial camp. In the top row, three mounted men approach the tents outside the city. In the second row, on the right, the four men stand outside the emperor's tent, and a tonsured man, apparently Girard, grips the hand (or wrist) of the leader, apparently to summon him within. On the left side, a man, perhaps a servant, draws aside the white curtain at the entrance of the tent. In the third row, again on the left, he draws the curtain further back, and the emperor is shown lying on his bed, fanned by Girard, while the archdeacon kneels before him. To mark that this is the emperor, the artist places a crown on Henry's head, although he is unlikely to have worn it under the circumstances.

(S 130–131; KS 102)

112v Particula XVIII: Exeundi prohibitio.

Cereus ille comes, sociis munitus et auro,   490
    Mandat, ut educat nullus ab urbe pedem.   491
Sic ait: "In densis latitans Philomena rubetis   492
    "Non timet adverso mitis ab ungue capi;   493
"Cum domino mundi quis enim contendere bello   494
    "Ausus erit, vel quis obviet ense pari?   495
"Si placet, o cives, meliori mente fruamur: 496
    "Pro nobis aurum pugnet et arma ferat."   497
"Si sapitis, cives, comes exeat, instet in armis;   498
    "Laus est pro domino succubuisse suo.   499
"Parcite parcendis, electis parcite vestris.   500
    "Quisque suas vires noverit, unde timet.   501
"Robore forte caret medio, quam cernitis, arbor;   502
    "Sub vacuo spirat cortice nulla fides.   503
"Pronior ad casum quanto procerior arbor,   504
    "In quam ventus agit, fulminat ipse Deus."   505
Quid Nicolaus agit, puer actu, nomine presul?   506
    Quid nisi femineas abluit ipse genas?   507
Credite pastori, pecudes, pecudes, alieno   508
    Tam male qui proprium curat ovile suum!   509
Quid facis, o Cesar? Quid frustra menia temptas?   510
    Obnebulant socios regia dona tuos,   511
Qui falso remeare rogant, ne morbus in artus   512
    Fortius insurgat, qui grave reddat iter.   513

Section 18: The Prohibition of Sorties.

The Count with the waxy-white face, well fortified with allies and gold,
    Commands that no one should set foot outside the city.
Thus he speaks: "When Philomena is hidden in thorny thickets,
    "The little creature does not fear to be seized by hostile claws.
"Who indeed will dare to contend in warfare against the lord of the world,
    "Or who could meet him with an equal sword?
"If it is pleasing, O citizens, let us profit from a better plan:
    "Let gold fight for us and bear arms."
"Citizens, do you think it wise for the count to go forth and pursue battle?
    "It is his glory to have suffered in bed for the sake of his lord.
"Be sparing of those who should be spared; spare your chosen ones,
    "For everyone knows his strength and is therefore afraid.
"The tree which you behold may perhaps lack a hard center,
    "And no faith breathes beneath the empty bark.
"The taller a tree, the more likely it is to fall,
    "When wind drives against it and God himself hurls lightning bolts."
What is Nicholas doing, childish in his actions, a prelate in name?
    What else but washing his womanish cheeks?
O flocks, flocks, committed to an alien shepherd,
    So negligent in tending his own fold!
What are you doing, O Caesar? Why do you attempt the walls in vain?
    Royal gifts befog and befuddle your allies,
So that they disloyally plead for a homeward journey, lest that disease
    Which hardly permits return, should attack their limbs more fiercely.

Commentary and Notes [112v]: This passage is confusing because apparently the speaker changes twice, without warning. However, Count Richard of Acerra is first announced as the speaker. His face still pale from his previous wounding, the archbishop Nicholas of Salerno at his side, he announces a new strategy to his supporters. The battle between the emperor and Naples, he claims, is an unequal struggle, like the fight between a little nightingale (Philomena) and some great bird of prey. But timidity serves Philomena well, and when she stays in her thicket, she will not get hurt. Similarly, the emperor, the lord of the world, is too strong for anyone to fight him directly, so everyone is to stay within the walls.

Gold will fight their battle for them. Archbishop Nicholas apparently then takes up the speech, supporting the strategy outlined by Count Richard, reminding their hearers that Count Richard has already taken a wound on King Tancred's behalf, so (by implication) neither his loyalty nor his courage can be doubted. On the other hand, it is best to make sparing use of such leaders. In line 498, he ostensibly urges the people to let the count go forth and fight: *Si sapitis, cives, comes exeat, instet in armis,* ("If you are wise, citizens, let the count go forth and pursue warfare"). This ironic exhortation is meant to make the listeners recognize the imprudence of urging the count to undertake more battles at this time. In English we might make the point clearer by adding superfluous positives, saying for example, "Yes, indeed, of course, citizens! It is truly wise for the count to go out and pursue battle at this time!" However, the idea comes across more briefly and clearly when rendered into a rhetorical question. (Pietro puts a similar locution into Constance's mouth in line 601.) Nicholas also hints that the policy they have adopted is an effective one that already, rightly, has the enemy worried. After all, things are not always as they seem, and hidden forces are at work. The imperial army may, like an impressive tree with a hollow center, be less formidable than it looks. Also, tall trees are most likely to attract lightning.

In line 506, the poet denounces Nicholas as effeminate (presumably because of his subtle and underhanded approach), a clergyman who has deserted his own flock in order to give bad advice elsewhere. This foreshadows the part that Nicholas will play in the events unfolding at Salerno.

In lines 510–513, Pietro turns to the emperor's camp and shows that the "bribe and wait" strategy is having an effect; Henry's followers are pleading for him to break the siege, using the epidemic which has struck the army as an excuse.

Difficulties in this passage stem from abrupt, unmarked shifts of viewpoint. The original Latin contains no quotation marks; however, the language makes it clear that Count Richard begins speaking in line 492, addressing the defenders of Naples. In line 500, while the defenders are still being addressed, Count Richard is mentioned in the third person, leading some to suggest that the speaker has changed. In fact, the first caption of the accompanying miniatures designates both Count Richard and Archbishop Nicholas as the ones who issue the command not to leave the city; hence, the second speaker is apparently Nicholas. The poet apparently expected readers to look at the miniature first, and read the verses to see what was said.

But in line 506, Nicholas himself is named, for the first time, in the third person, with a hostility and contempt inappropriate for Count Richard. This signifies that the poet is speaking in his own voice.

(S 41–42, KS 105)

Recedente angusto ab obsidione neapoli. Comes Ricc · Nicol psul
Salerni phibet ne pplus extra muros accepter exire.

Comes Ricc · psul Salerni

Neapoli ·

113r *Exhortation of Count Richard of Acerra and of the Archbishop Nicholas of Salerno to the Neapolitans because they are not to make sorties from the city. Neapolitan women. Illustrates verses 490–513 on fol. 112v.*

· · · ·

Recedente Augusto a obsidione Neapolim, comes Riccardus et Nicolaus presul Salerni prohibent ne populus extra muros atemptet exire.	1.	Augustus having drawn back from the siege at Naples, Count Richard and Nicholas, the archbishop of Salerno, forbid the people to attempt to go out from the walls.
Comes Riccardus.	2.	Count Richard.
Presul Salerni.	3.	Archbishop of Salerno.
Neapolim.	4.	Naples.

Commentary and Notes [113r]: In the top level, knights watch from the walls of Naples, between the towers. On the second level, Count Richard of Acerra and Archbishop Nicholas are shown, both holding swords and addressing some assembled knights. The caption indicates that they impart the command that no one from the city may go outside the walls. On the third level, four women are shown beneath a colonnade, one seated, three standing. One standing woman is bending over a child, who looks up at her, holding a (probably spent) arrow in his right hand (the shaft is badly faded). The seated woman holds a spindle. Kölzer's commentary (106) suggests that the third might be weeping or praying and the fourth may be holding a coil of thread. Apparently they are watching and waiting to learn the outcome of the battle and the strategy that the leaders have adopted. Pietro's line 508, "O flocks, flocks" *(Pecudes, pecudes)* might refer, in part, to them.

This should illustrate verses 490–513 contained on page 19 (112v) of the codex.

(S 131; KS 106)

113v [Particula XVIIII]: Imperialis ab obsidione regressus

Ut videt ere duces saturatos Cesar et aurum	514
Eructare suos, mens subit ista loqui:	515
"Qui fluvios nostros dudum siccastis Yberos,	516
"In fontes Siculos mergitis omne caput;	517
"Equor adhuc superest, licet inpotabile vobis,	518
"Nec mare, quod saturet vos, nec abyssus habet."	519
Nec mora, comperta tunc Cesar fraude suorum,	520
Arripit, a tritea febre coactus, iter.	521
O quantum pene, quantumve timoris in omnes	522
Sollicitans animos intulit illa dies!	523
Ut coadunant oves timor a pastore relictas,	524
Quas canis exclusit solus ab ore lupi,	525
Non aliter quos imperii pia gratia fovit;	526
Hic flet et ille dolet; regnat ubique metus.	527
Quid tibi tunc animi, que mens fuit, archilevita,	528
Cum recipis vetitum posse videre Iovem,	529
Et tamen evelli subito temtoria cernis?	530
Nox erat et castris nec fragor ullus erat.	531
Funes comburi, testudinis ossa cremari	532
Cernis, et auxilium Pallidis omne rui.	533
Ut quatit aura novas resecande messis aristas,	534
Ut movet equoreas Eolus asper aquas,	535
Sic, sic Alfanides patrii cognominis heres,	536
Et sine spe reditus et sine mente tremit.	537
Tunc dolor et lacrime singultibus ora fatigant,	538
Tunc mens Socratici pectoris omnis hebet.	539
Anxius ignoras quid agas? responsa referre	540
Ulla times? Labor est Itala castra sequi.	541
Quem non matris amor, nec presens gloria rerum,	542
Nec fratrum pietas, nec grave vicit iter,	543
Imperium sequitur, subit alta mente labores.	544
At Tancridini redeunt, rumoribus inplent	545
Urbem, de magno principe falsa ferunt:	546
Hic "obit!" ille, "obiit!" "calet!" hic, "frigescit!" et ille	547
Asserit; incerto fluctuat ore fides.	548

[Section 19]: The Imperial Retreat from the Siege.

When Caesar saw his commanders stuffed with base money,
    And his followers belching out gold, it entered his mind to say this:
"You who have just now dried up the Spanish rivers,
    "Now dip your whole head into Sicilian springs;
"The vast sea still remains for you, granted that it is undrinkable;
    "Neither the sea nor the abyss has what would satisfy you."
Nor was there delay, when Caesar discovered the deceit among his own;
    He took up the road, compelled by the tertian fever.
Oh, how much loss and fear did that troubling day
    Bring to every soul!
As fear drives together the sheep left by their shepherd,
    Whom a single dog saved from the jaws of the wolf;
Not otherwise they gather, who were fostered by the emperor's pious grace.
    This one weeps and that one grieves; fear reigns everywhere.
What then was in your spirit, what in your mind, archdeacon,
    When you were denied permission to see Jove,
And then suddenly you see the tents being taken down?
    It was night and in the camp there was no clamor.
You see ropes and cables consumed, the bones of the tortoise burned,
    And all the devices of Pallas crashing down.
As the wind strikes the new wheat ears and cuts them down at harvest,
    As fierce Aeolus moves over the waves of the wide sea,
Thus, thus Alfanides (heir of that paternal cognomen)
    Trembles, without hope of return and without a plan.
Then sorrow and tears vex his face with sobs,
    Then the mind in that Socratic breast becomes completely dulled.
Anxious man, do you not know what you must do? Do you fear to
    Return any answer? It is a hardship to follow the Italian camps.
He who has not been conquered by love of mother or by the glory
    Of present things, nor by pity for his brothers, nor the harsh road,
He follows the Empire and undertakes labors with a high mind.

However, the Tancredines return, they fill the city with rumors,
    Bearing false stories of the great prince.
One declares, "He's dying!"; another, "He died!" Cries one, "He burns!"
    And another, "He grows cold!" Faith wavers with uncertain voice.

Commentary and Notes [113v]: Still suffering from his tertian fever, and realizing that his followers are taking bribes from Tancred's party, which make them less than eager to capture the city, Henry abandons the siege of Naples. In line 516, there is a pun on *siccasti* and *Siculos*, since *siccus* means "dry" in Latin, and "*Siculos*" could be heard as a diminutive of that word. In general, Henry is saying that his followers are being paid twice — he exhausted his treasuries to induce them to accompany him on this expedition, and now they are taking gifts from Tancred to urge him to go away. But even that is not enough for them; they will never be satisfied.

When the emperor withdraws, his frightened Italian allies, gathering together in the wake of his departure, are likened (in an epic simile) to sheep fearing predators now that the dog has gone. The faithful Aldrisio sought and was denied an audience with the emperor just before the camp was raised without warning. Tents were removed and the siege engines destroyed. In line 532, the *testudo* or "tortoise" is a siege engine, or a structure designed to shelter soldiers while they make use of their weapons or other siege engines. Romans applied the same name to a configuration where the soldiers stood with their shields over their heads. However, soldiers would carry their shields away, and *ossa* or "bones" apparently refers to the frame of the protective structure. The Imperials are burning what they cannot take away, apparently to keep the other side from using it. Seeing this happen, Aldrisio, the "Socratic" man, temporarily loses courage (another epic simile likens his trembling to wheat shaken by the wind), but he soon resolves to follow Henry back to Germany.

Meanwhile, Tancred's partisans pour back into Salerno with news that the emperor is dead or dying. According to the Annals of Monte Cassino (*Annales Casinenses*, 315), the ailing emperor retreated to that monastery to await Constance, only to receive word that she had been captured. He then took hostages from San Germano and returned to Germany, bringing Abbot Roffredo with him. According to Richard of San Germano's *Chronica* (66), the abbot returned the following year, but left his brother Gregory in Germany as a hostage.

(S 43–44, KS 109)

547: *ille obiit.* S: *ille obit* Pre-S: *ille obiit.* KS: *ille obiit.* De Rosa: *ille obit.* Codex: *ille obit* corrected to *obiit.* Siragusa (44) attributed the correction to Bongars, the modern owner of the codex who gave the book to the Bern library; therefore he does not accept it as authoritative.

544–545: Because there is a missing pentameter here, Siragusa leaves a blank space between these lines.

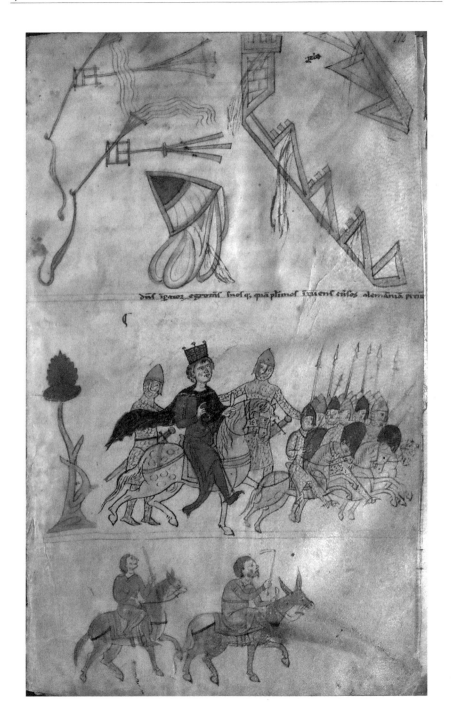

dns̄ ignoz̄ egrot̄ms̄ suosq̄; qr̄ a ptimos̄ fraient cūstos̄ alemānia pr̄ii

114r *Departure of the sick Henry VI for Germany.* Illustrates ll. 514–548 on fol. 113v.

· · · ·

Dominus imperator egrotans suosque
quam plurimos intuens eversos
Alemanniam petit.

The lord emperor, ailing, and aware
that a great many of his men are
dead, seeks Germany.

Commentary and Notes [114r]: At the top of the illustration, the abandoned impe-
rial camp appears, with siege engines and tents overturned. In the second row,
the emperor rides away, preceded by a band of knights, but with two knights
flanking him on foot, apparently to make sure that he does not fall off his horse.
Below, two men ride without armor, one on a horse, one on a donkey or mule.
They are perhaps, as Kölzer's commentary (110) suggests, the rumor-mongers
who speak in the next verses.

Siragusa points out (131, n. 4) that there should be a caption at the top of
this page to explain the first row of illustrations, but it is missing. The remaining
caption concerns the second row.

(S 131; KS 110)

114v [Particula XX]: Fidei oblita religio.

Ut rude murmur apum fumoso murmurat antro,	549
Sic novus orbanda rumor in urbe sonat.	550
Hic tres, hac septem, bis sex ibi, quattuor illic	551
Conveniunt, tenui murmure plura loqui;	552
Consilio stimulata malo, gens seva Salerni	553
Peccatum redimit crimine, fraude dolum;	554
Obsequium prestare putant periuria regi;	555
Tancredum curant pacificare sibi.	556
Ast ubi circumdant inmensa palacia regum,	557
Que Terracina nomen habere ferunt,	558
Exclamant: "Quid agis, Constancia? Stamina pensas?	559
"Fila trahis? Quid agis? An data pensa legis?	560
"Cesar abest; certe nos et te, miseranda, fefellit.	561
"Quem nimis ardebas, dic, ubi Cesar abit?	562
"Quem tociens fausto iactabas ore potentem,	563
"Dic, ubi bella gerit, qui sine crine iacet?	564
"Felix Parthenope, que nec te sola recepit!	565
"Urbs pro te, quod te viderit, ista ruet.	566
"Te vir dimisit; non vir set apostolus egit;	567
"Hostia pro nobis predaque dulcis eris."	568
In dominam iaciunt furibunde spicula lingue	569
Saxaque cum multis associata minis;	570
Quicquid funda potest, quicquid balistra vel arcus,	571
Nititur in dominam.	572
Ut cornix aquila strepitat quamplurima visa,	573
Quam fore noctivolam garrula credit avem,	574
Unguibus et rostris furit et movet aera pennis,	575
Inque modum fabri flamina versat avis,	576
Hic ferit, ille salit, saliens sequiturque cadentem,	577
Versat [in] incuso malleus ere vices,	578
Sic furit in dominam gens ancillanda potentem;	579
Vertitur in lolium triste cremanda seges.	580

[Section 20]: The Bond of Faith Forgotten.

As the harsh murmur of bees hums in the smoky grotto,
    So the new rumor noises in the city to be bereaved.
Three here, seven there, twice six somewhere, four from thence,
    They come together, and speak of many things, murmuring low.
Goaded by evil counsel, the savage people of Salerno
    Atone for a sin with a crime, a trick with deception.
They reckon that showing obedience [to Constance] is perjury towards the king,
    And busy themselves to pacify Tancred towards them.
Thus now they surround the vast palace of the kings,
    Which is said to bear the name of Terracina.
They cry, "What are you doing, Constance? Do you weigh the warp,
    "Draw the threads? What are you doing? Perhaps you gather up the measure
    you weighed out?
"Caesar is away. Surely he has deceived us and you too, wretched woman;
    "Tell us, where has Caesar gone, for whom you were too ardent,
"Whose power you boasted of, so often, with exultant words;
    "Where does he wage war now, lying without his locks?
"Happy Parthenope, who alone did not receive you!
    "This city, because it saw you, will be destroyed for you!
"Your husband has abandoned you; not your husband but the Apostle acted.
    "You will be a sacrificial offering for us, and sweet spoil."
At the lady they throw the darts of their furious tongues,
    And hurl stones along with many threats.
Whatever the sling, whatever the bow or ballista can do
    Is done against their mistress.
Thus a crow, when she sees an eagle, shrieks to as many as she can,
    Believing, the clamorous thing, that she has seen a night-flying bird;
She rages with claws and beak and stirs the air with her wings,
    And the bird whirls blasts like a blacksmith.
So [among the people], this one strikes, that one leaps, leaping to follow the
    one who falls,
    The hammer becomes the hammered metal in its turn.
Thus the people who should serve rush in rage upon their powerful mistress;
    The harvest turns to tares which, sadly, must be burned.

Commentary and Notes [114v]: Salerno once more becomes the scene of action as rumors of the emperor's hasty departure and possible death reach the city. Fearing Tancred's vengeance because they have received the emperor's representatives, the people surround Constance's palace and seek to take her prisoner. Pietro's epic similes first liken the city to a hive of angry bees stirred up by rumors, then to a flock of angry crows, stirred up by the raucous cries of one of their own, mistaking an eagle for an owl or "night-flying bird" (that is, mistaking a rightful monarch for a predator). An angry mob hurls threats and missiles at the empress.

In 559–560 *(Exclamant: "Quid agis, . . . Stamina pensas?/ Fila trahis? Quid agis? An data pensa legis?")* the Salernitans speak with double meaning, refering to simple household tasks, and to the myth of the three Fates at the same time. Both *stamen* and *filum* can be homely threads as well as threads spun by the *Parcae* or Fates. However, *stamen* also means "warp" and the expression *Fila trahis* (literally, "you draw the threads") suggests weaving or spinning. *Penso, -ere,* literally means "to weigh or pay out" but figuratively means "to measure" and "to ponder," "to repay" or "to punish." Probably Pietro expects his audience to receive the images on two levels. On the surface the crowd suggests that Constance might be about housewifely tasks appropriate to women, giving out measures of flax to spin (or perhaps cloth to weave) and getting back the measure at the end of the day. This has the ironic implication that she is, of course, doing no such thing but is interfering in their political life. On another level, they allude to the three Fates and questions about destiny which are yet uncertain. Constance's own fate may hinge on whether the emperor is alive or dead, something they do not know. The last question, *An data pensa legis*, literally, "or rather, do you gather up what has been measured out?" might be a suggestion that she is now on the receiving end of what the Fates have woven; in short, she does not have destiny under her own control. (De Rosa translates the first part of their questions, "Stai meditando sul tuo destino? (Are you meditating about your destiny?)" In line 567, the people declare that the Apostle Matthew, legendary protector and patron of Salerno, has put Constance into their power in order to protect them from Tancred's wrath.

(S 45–46, KS 113)

115r *Uprising of the Salernitans against the empress.* Illustrates ll. 549–580 on fol. 114v.

. . . .

Turris Major.	1.	Great Tower.
Teutonici.	2.	Germans.
Salernitanus populus audito recessu imperatoris in suam dominam calcaneum erexerunt.	3.	The people of Salerno, having heard of the emperor's withdrawal, lifted their heel against their mistress.
Imperatrix.	4.	The empress.
Hii gaudent.	5.	These rejoice.
Hii dolent.	6.	These mourn.

Commentary and Notes [115r]: Though the verses create the impression that Salerno has united against Constance in the wake of Henry VI's flight, the illustration gives a more complicated picture. Constance's German escort, called *Teutonici* (Cap. 2), resist their attackers by hurling stones from the palace roof. Attackers appear on two levels. Above is a knot of three who may be consulting; Kölzer's commentary (114) says that the man in the middle is perhaps being held back by the other two. On the lower level stands a crowd, some pointing their fingers and some stretching out their hands. Caps. 5 and 6, stating "these rejoice" and "these mourn," suggest that different people in the crowd have different attitudes about what is going on. Kölzer's commentary also explains that the barrel-like object beneath the palace stairs on the right is a well, and that in depicting it the artist suggests that the water-supply might be a problem.

(S 132, KS 114)

115v   [Particula] XXI: Imperialis populo resistenti loquucio

Ex hinc Teutonicus verbis respondet et armis:	581
"Ospes in ignota dimicat urbe fides!"	582
Illa tamen constans, ut erat de nomine Constans,	583
Et quia famosi Cesaris uxor erat,	584
Hostes alloquitur audacter ab ore fenestra.	585
Sic ait: "Audite quid mea verba velint.	586
"Saltim dum loquimur, compescite tela manusque;	587
"Pauca loquar, multo pondere verba tamen.	588
"Gens magne fidei, rationis summa probate,	589
"Que sim, que fuerim nostis, et inde queror;	590
"Cesar abit vel obit, vobis ut dicitur; ergo,	591
"Si placet, exul eam Cesaris orbe mei;	592
"Ad mentem revocate fidem, cohibete furorem,	593
"Nec vos seducant littera, verba, sonus;	594
"Nec quociens resonant in nube tonitrua celi,	595
"Emisso tociens fulminat igne Deus.	596
"Si presul scripsit, tamen, ut reor, irrita scripsit;	597
"Hic patrie fraudis curat et artis opus;	598
"Hic trahit in species scelerum genus omne malorum;	599
"Quod patris ora vomunt, filius haurit idem.	600
"Credite pastori profugo, qui natus ab ydra	601
"Ut coluber, nunquam degenerare potest;	602
"Est igitur virtus quandoque resistere verbis	603
"Et dare pro fidei pondere menbra neci.	604
"Si pugnare licet, superest michi miles et aurum.	605
"In propriam redeat, consulo, quisque domum.	606
"Est michi Corradus Capue, Dipoldus in Archi;	607
"Hic pars milicie, dux erit ille ducum;	608
"Darius Eboleos, ut ait michi nuncius, agros	609
"Hac cremat, hac radit ille Thetinus oves.	610
"Gens pure fidei mediis exquirit in armis	611
"Velle meum, pro me sponte parata mori,	612
"Nec sine velle meo, multo licet hoste coacta,	613
"Ad Tancridinum vult repedare scelus.	614
"Huius ad exemplum, cives, concurrite gentis,	615
"Que sit in Ebolea discite gente fides.	616
"Ebole, ni peream, memori tibi lance rependam	617
"Pectoris affectus que meruere boni."	618
Durus ad hec populus, truculentior aspide factus,	619
Acrius insurgit.	620

[Section] 21: The Speech of the Empress to the Crowd Opposing Her.

To these things, the German host responded with words and arms:
    "Faith fights as a stranger in an unknown city!"
She, however, constant, since her name meant constancy,
    And because she was the wife of famous Caesar,
Addresses her enemies boldly from the open window.
    Thus she speaks: "Hear what my words intend.
"At least while we speak, hold back your missiles and your hands.
    "I will speak few words, but they have great weight.
"O people of great faith and wisdom tested to the heights,
    "You know who I am and who I have been, and that is why I make my
    complaint to you.
"Caesar has departed or died, so it has been told you; therefore,
    "If it pleases you, let me go as an exile into my Caesar's land.
"Recall your faith to mind, restrain fury,
    "And do not be seduced by letters, words, noises.
"God does not send forth fire with lightning bolts as many times
    "As the thunder of heaven echoes in the cloud.
"Even if the archbishop wrote, I expect that he wrote nonsense;
    "That man labors to further his father's work of deceit and trickery,
"Into his sorts of crimes he draws every kind of evil.
    "Whatever his father's mouth spews out, the son drinks it all in.
"Should you indeed believe the exiled shepherd, born to the Hydra,
    "Already a serpent, whose nature could never get worse?
"Therefore, it is virtuous always to resist [such] words
    "And to offer one's limbs to death for the sake of loyalty.
"If I am allowed battle, I still have knights and gold.
    "I counsel everyone to return to his home.
"I have Conrad at Capua, Diepold at Rocca D'Arce;
    "The one will do his duty as a knight, the other lead the commanders.
"Darius, as the messenger told me, burns Ebolian fields here
    "And there shears the Theatine sheep.
"But those people of pure faith seek to do my will in the midst of warfare,
    "Willingly prepared to die for me,
"Nor do they, without my will, though hard pressed by the enemy,
    "Wish to return to the Tancredine crime.
"From the example of this people, citizens, go in haste
    "And learn about the faith that is in the people of Eboli.
"Eboli, unless I perish, I will pay back the same to you,
    "Memory measuring in heartfelt love the good things which you have deserved."
At this, the cruel people, made more ferocious than the asp,
    Attack more bitterly.

Commentary and Notes [115v]: As the angry Salernitans attack her palace, Constance, legitimate queen of the kingdom of Sicily, can rely only on her German knights, who, though strangers to the city, are faithful to her. Attempting to gain some control over the situation, she speaks to the people from the window of her palace, her tone veering between coaxing flattery and ironic denunciation. Rebuking the Salernitans' intent to take her prisoner, she reminds them of the loyalty they owe her and urges them to return peacefully to their homes. She also casts doubt on the accuracy of the reports which have spurred them to action, pointing out that the archbishop Nicholas, probable source of the information, is the son of Tancred's chief supporter, the chancellor Matthew. She likens father and son to serpents. She also reminds the people that Conrad and Diepold (mentioned here for the first time) are still under her command, at Capua and Rocca D'Arce respectively. Conrad of Lützelhard and Diepold "of Vohburg" or "of Schweinspeunt" were two of Henry VI's important commanders, and they remained behind in Italy at this time. The Italians gave Conrad the nickname Moscaincervello, meaning "fly-in-the-brain" (Siragusa, 48, n. 2) while Diepold came from a family of *ministeriales*, warriors of servile status.

In lines 609–620, Constance also commends the people of Eboli (Pietro's town), who remain loyal although they have suffered oppression from Tancred's followers. Siragusa writes (49 n. 1): "The author may have added verses 609–620 afterwards with his own hand, to make the emperor favorable toward Eboli . . ." These lines are apparently in the same hand which wrote Pietro's dedication on fol. 147v. In them, Constance declares that she will return loyal affection to Eboli for the love the people have given her, implying that, if her situation improves, they will be rewarded in other ways as well. Her speech, however, fails to change the intent of her attackers, who redouble their efforts.

(S 47–49, KS 117)

116r *The same scene as the preceding illustration. The empress speaks to the rebels.*
Illustrates ll. 581–620 on fol. 115v.

. . . .

Imperatrix alloquitur cives Salerni.

The empress speaks to the citizens of Salerno.

Commentary and Notes [116r]: The Empress speaks from the window to people, who still express their defiance with gestures, and presumably, with outcry. Her two attendants stand to the side, grieving, one with covered sleeves and the other with her cheek resting on her hand. Also in the field before the castle, attackers shoot arrows and hurl stones at the Germans guarding the palace.

116v Particula XXII: Augustalis oratio pro vindicta.

Illa genu flexo, pansis ad sidera palmis   621
  Plenaque singultu, fletibus uda suis,   622
Sic orans loquitur; clausis hinc inde fenestris,   623
  Fecerat ambiguam clausa fenestra diem: 624
"Alfa Deus, Deus O, mundi moderator et auctor,   625
  "Ex hiis vindictam, supplico, sume dolis;   626
"Alfa Deus, Deus O, liquide scrutator abyssi,   627
  "In me periuras contine, queso, manus;   628
"Alfa Deus, Deus O, stellati rector Olimpi,   629
  "Pena malignantes puniat alta viros;   630
"Alfa Deus, Deus O, iuris servator et equi,   631
  "Iam tua conflictus vindicet ira meos;   632
"Alfa Deus, Deus O, terre fundator amicte,   633
  "In me pugnantes ferrea flamma voret;   634
"Alfa Deus, Deus O, rerum Deus omnicreator,   635
  "Supplicis ancille respice, queso, preces;   636
"Iram congemines, acuas penamque, furorem   637
  "Accendas, tumidos comprime, perde feros;   638
"Contine faustosos, instantes perde feros;   639
  "Da pacem, gladios divide, scinde manus,   640
"Arma cadant, arcusque teras, balistra cremetur;   641
  "Rumpe polum, specta, collige, scribe, nota;   642
"Hos notet exilium, scribat proscriptio, plures   643
  "Obprobrium signet.   644
"Rumpe polum, transmitte virum romphea gerentem;   645
  "Eruat ancillam, dissipet ora canum.   646
"Alfa Deus, Deus O, genitor, genitura creatrix,   647
  Quod precor acceptes, Alfa Deus, Deus O."   648

Commentary and Notes [116v]: As the people of Salerno continue their attack, Constance, having closed the windows of her chamber, gives herself to prayer. She prays for *vindicta*, a word whose meaning encompasses not only vindication of her own innocence and her rights to the honors she has hitherto claimed, but also rescue from her current troubles, and the overthrow, with punishment, of those who are attacking her.

Section 22: The Empress's Prayer for Vindication.

Then with bended knee, palms spread to the stars,
    With many sobs, wet with her own tears,
She spoke and prayed thus; from then on the windows were closed,
    And the closed window made an ambiguous day.
"O God the Alpha, God the Omega, governor and author of the world,
    "I pray that you bring about deliverance from these snares;
"God the first and last, watcher of the watery abyss,
    "I beseech you to hold back these perjured hands from me;
"Divine Alpha, Divine Omega, ruler of the starry Olympus,
    "Let the evil men be punished with high punishment;
"O God the Alpha, God the Omega, preserver of law and equity,
    "Let your wrath now avenge these blows struck at me;
"God the first and last, founder of the mantled earth,
    "May your fierce flame devour those who make war against me.
"God the Alpha and Omega, God the creator of everything,
    "Consider, I beseech you, the prayers of your kneeling handmaiden.
"Let your wrath be redoubled, your punishments sharpened,
    "Your fury kindled; subdue the pride-swollen, crush the savage men,
"Restrain the envious, destroy the proud pursuers.
    "Give peace, part the swords, tear apart the struggling combatants,
"May their weapons fall down, consume their bows, may the crossbows
    be burned;
    "Open the heavens. Look out, restrain, write down, sentence them;
"Let them be sentenced to exile, let the decree of banishment be written,
    "Let many be handed over to disgrace.
"Open the heavens, send the man wielding the double-edged sword,
    "May he pluck out your handmaiden [from these troubles], and scatter the
    howling dogs.
"Divine Alpha, Divine Omega; Father, Begotten, Mother,
    "Accept my prayers, O God, the Alpha and Omega."

    Her prayer echoes the Book of Revelation, both in the repeated invocation of God as the Alpha and Omega, and in the allusion to Christ as Judge, "the man with the double-edged sword." See Additional Notes on this and also on 647–648.

(S 50–51, KS 121)

628, 639 *contine*. S: *contere*. non-S: *contine*. Codex: abbreviated expression. See note on 628, 639.

117r *The assault of the people on the palace of Terracina. The empress prays.* Illustrates ll. 620–648 on fol. 116v.

• • • •

Turris Major.	1.	Great Tower.
Teutonici.	2.	Germans.
Terracina.	3.	Terracina.
Imperatrix orans ad Dominum.	4.	The empress praying to the Lord.
Cives Salerni.	5.	Citizens of Salerno.

Commentary and Notes [117r]: The fortified Great Tower appears at the top of the illustration, flanked by three trees on each side. Below, the besieged palace of Terracina appears. German defenders, one with a shield, one with shield and spear, confront Salernitan attackers. Of these, one has a bow and arrows, while another holds, in his right hand, a sling for casting stones, and in his left, a shield. Within the royal palace, the empress prays. No attendants are shown with her. Three stars are drawn above her head. Kölzer's commentary (122) says that the stars indicate that it is night, although the poet says in the accompanying verses that she has created an "ambiguous day" by closing the window. Perhaps the stars represent at once the darkness of her current circumstances and the light of divine protection within it.

(S 132; KS 122)

117v Particula XXIII: Oratio salutaris.

"Ex oriente Deus, Augusti dirige gressus,   649
    "Ut meus hinc Cesar, te duce, sospes eat;   650
"Ex oriente Deus, conserva Cesaris actus,   651
    "Ille tuus Raphael preparet eius iter;   652
"Ex oriente Deus, Romanum protege solem,   653
    "Ut repetat patriam sospite mente suam;   654
"Ex oriente Deus, custodi super euntem,   655
    "Quo tibi pro magno munere vota feram;   656
"Ex oriente Deus, dulcem comitare maritum,   657
    "Emolli duros, saxea colla doma;   658
"Ex oriente Deus, tumidos tere, perde superbos,   659
    "Coniugis angelicum fac redeuntis iter;   660
"Ex oriente Deus, qui regnas in tribus unus,   661
    "Redde virum famule, que perit absque viro.   662
"Cui mare, cui tellus, cui celum vivit et ether,   663
    "Vir meus, inter tot dona, superstes eat.   664
"Si pereo, per eum pereo, quia Cesare vivo,   665
    "Triste nichil patiar, dummodo capta ferar."   666
¶
Proditor interea Gisualdi venit Elias,   667
    Exhonerans famulas sera podagra manus;   668
Sanguine non hominum didicit lenire dolorem,   669
    Nec sapit antidotum, seve Mathee, tuum.   670
Qui videt ut dominam, quasi Gallicus ore rotundo   671
    Fatur, et in dominam glis satur exta vomit: 672
"Heia, si qua potes, nostris virtutibus insta!   673
    "Eia, si qua potes bella movere, move!   674
"Qui cupit omne quod est, et parti cedere nescit,   675
    "Amittet totum.   676
"Sic tibi, dum velles totum quod volvitur evo,   677
    "Contigit, et regno pro breviore cadis.   678
"Est opus, ut venias merito captiva Panormum;   679
    "Sic populus, sic rex; hic petit, ille iubet."   680

Section 23: Prayer for Rescue.

"God from the East, direct the steps of Augustus,
　"That my Caesar, with you leading him, may go safely hence;
"God from the East, guard Caesar's progress;
　"May your Raphael prepare the way for him.
"God from the East, protect the Roman Sun,
　"That he may seek his homeland again with good courage.
"God from the East, guard the one who has just departed;
　"Let me bring this to you as a prayer for the greatest gift.
"God from the East, accompany my sweet spouse,
　"Soften hard hearts, tame stiff necks.
"God from the East, beat down the swollen, destroy the proud,
　"Make an angelic road for my returning husband.
"God from the East, who reigns One in Three,
　"Give back my husband to your handmaiden, who is dying without her man.
"God through whom the sea, the earth and the heavens have life,
　"May my husband still be living, [chief] among so many gifts.
"If I perish, I perish for him; because while Caesar lives,
　"I will take nothing in bitterness, even now as I am led captive."
¶
Meanwhile, the traitor, Elias of Gesualdo, comes,
　Trusting himself to servile hands because of recent gout;
He had not learned to soothe the pain with human blood,
　And did not know your remedy, cruel Matthew.
When he sees the lady, he speaks roundly like a Frenchman;
　And discharges his innards at the lady like a gorged dormouse:
"Aha! If you can do anything, stand up against our power!
　"Ah! If you can wage any war, wage it!
"Whoever wants all that is, and does not know how to relinquish part,
　"Will lose everything.
"So it befalls you: because you want everything revolving in this age,
　"You fall for the sake of a smaller realm.
"You must come, deservedly, a captive, to Palermo;
　"So say the people, so the king; the former entreat, and the latter commands."

Commentary and Notes [117v]: Constance's prayer becomes an *"Oratio salutaris."* *"Salus,"* the noun from which *salutaris* is derived, can mean "health," "salvation," and "safety." Pietro probably intends all these meanings.

The empress repeatedly asks divine comfort, guidance, and protection for her husband, whom she calls "Roman Sun" (line 653). In particular, she asks that the angel Raphael be sent to help Henry on his way (line 652). Raphael appears in the apocryphal book of Tobit where, he helps Tobit's son Tobias on a dangerous journey which reverses the bad fortune of his father and his future wife. Constance hopes for equally effective intervention.

As her prayer ends, the "traitor" Elias of Gesualdo, actually a kinsman of hers and Tancred's, suddenly arrives and tells her that she must go to Palermo as a captive.

(S 52–53, KS 125)

S. states that although there is no blank space before 667, the mark "¶" indicates a change of subject.

118r *The empress praying. Elias of Gesualdo gets the Empress in his power.* Illustrates verses 648–680 on fol. 117v.

• • • •

Terracina	1.	Terracina
Imperatrix orans.	2.	The empress praying.
Quando proditor Helias Gisualdi assecuratis Teutonicis dominam mundi cepit.	3.	When the traitor Elias of Gesualdo, having assured the safety of the Germans, captured the mistress of the world.

Commentary and Notes [118r]: Constance, in the upper half of the picture, is still kneeling at prayer amid the arches and columns of the palace. In the lower section, the aged Elias first arrives on the left, carried by two young men, because he suffers from gout. On the right hand side, he is shown again, standing on his feet and facing Constance at a parley that has been arranged. Four shield-bearing knights appear behind the empress and somewhat to her right. Constance and Elias stand some distance apart, and the location of their meeting is not shown clearly, either because the manuscript has faded or because no background was drawn in, or for both reasons.

(S 133; KS 126)

118v [Particula] XXIIII: Domine coacta descensio

At domine vultus pallescere nescius unquam,	681
In modicum pallens, lumina crispat humo.	682
Nec mora, pallor abit, proprii rediere colores,	683
Simplicibus ludunt lilia simpla rosis,	684
Ut tenuis quandoque diem denigrat amictus	685
Et subito, lapsa nube, diescit humus.	686
Pauca quidem loquitur: "Veniam, Tancrede, Panormum,	687
"Et veniam, veniam non aditura tuam."	688
Protinus obiecit: "Pactum gens annuat," inquit,	689
"Ut meus hinc salvo pectore miles eat."	690
Instanti populo placuit sententia talis,	691
Nec mens in tantis omnibus una fuit;	692
Nam Tancridini celebres nova sabbata libant,	693
Non minus inde dolent, archilevita, tui.	694
Exultant illi munus meruisse triumphi,	695
Qui titulum tante prodicionis habent.	696
Guilelmus de Pistilio, vir doctus in armis,	697
Maluit exilium quam temerare fidem.	698
Iamque parata ratis, centeno remige tuta,	699
Accelerat Zephirus, dum mare lentus agit.	700
O nova consilii species! Prudentia maior	701
Induit auratos ut nova nupta sinus;	702
Induit artiferos preciose vestis amictus,	703
Ornat et inpinguat pondere et arte comas.	704
Aurorant in veste rose, nec aromata desunt;	705
Forma teres Phebi pendet ab aure dies;	706
Pectoris in medio coeunt se cornua lune;	707
Ars lapidum vario sidere ditat opus.	708
Coniugis amplexus tanquam visura novellos,	709
Fausta venit, navem scandit et illa volat.	710

Commentary and Notes [118v]: Pietro here emphasizes Constance's courage, serenity, beauty, and prudence. At the words of Elias, she first turns slightly pale, then recovers her complexion. She resolves to go to Palermo, and delivers a punning response to Elias's moralistic accusations (see Additional Notes). There is a price for her cooperation: the Salernitans must agree to permit her knights to withdraw from the city safely. They do so. The two factions in the city have quite different feelings about what has taken place. The Tancredines exult while Archdeacon

[Section] 24: The Lady's Compelled Descent.

Now the lady's countenance, which never learned to blanch,
    Becomes somewhat pale; she turns her eyes to the earth.
But quickly the pallor goes away, and her own colors return;
    The innocent lilies frolic with the guileless roses.
So it is when a delicate cloud darkens the day,
    And suddenly, when the cloud slips away, the earth shines in daylight.
Then she speaks a few words. "I will come, Tancred, to Palermo,
    "And I do not come to beg your pardon."
Immediately she added: "Let the people accept this agreement:
    "My soldiery may depart with safe breasts."
Such a decision pleased the populace thronging near,
    Nor were they of one mind about all these things.
For the distinguished Tancredines pour out libations for the new sabbaths,
    But your party, Archdeacon, grieves no less [than the others rejoice].
Those people owning the credit for such a treacherous deed,
    Exult that their action has achieved triumph,
But William of Pistilio, a man learned in warfare,
    Preferred exile to violated faith.
And now a safe ship is prepared, with a hundred rowers,
    Gentle Zephyr gathers speed as he stirs the sea.
O new face of wisdom! Greatly prudent,
    She puts on golden vestures, like a new-wed bride.
She puts on an ingeniously decorated covering of precious robes;
    She adorns and thickens her tresses with weight and art.
Roses dawn in her robes, nor are perfumes lacking.
    The shining day, in the shape of Phoebus, hangs from her ear.
The horns of the moon come together in the midst of her breast.
    Jewels in a glimmering constellation enrich the work.
Auspiciously, as if to meet new embraces from her spouse,
    She comes, ascends the ship, and it flies off.

Aldrisio's party is downcast. With his reference to "new sabbaths" (line 693) Pietro slips in another suggestion that the Tancredine political loyalty is actually a new and false religion.

    As a ship makes ready to convey the captive empress to Sicily, Constance adorns herself splendidly. In doing this, she is not only makes a grand display, but also shows that she does not consider herself either a widow or a penitent. When the ship is ready, she enters and they depart.

(S 54–55, KS-129)

119r *The departure of the empress, prisoner, for Messina.* Illustrates verses 681–710 on. fol. 118v.

• • • •

Quando domina imperatrix a Terracina descendens, navim ascendit Messinam itura.	1. When the lady empress, descending from Terracina, ascends a ship to go to Messina.
Romanorum Imperatrix.	2. Empress of the Romans.
Helias de Gisualdo	3. Elias of Gesualdo
Imperatrix	4. Empress.
Helia	5. Elias

Commentary and Notes [119r]: The Empress surrenders herself to Elias. At the top of the page, Elias, once more supported by two attendants, stands on the left, while at the right, Constance emerges from the palace of Terracina, crowned, carrying a scepter, and flanked by two attendants.

The half-moon in the sky matches the one Constance wears on her breast. Three stars stand in a vertical line over her head. In the lower half of the drawing, she climbs, still crowned, aboard a ship with rowers, on the deck of which banners have been planted. In the waters, below the ship, fish appear, including two octopi and an eel. Pietro grants Constance, in her humiliation, all the honors of imperial rank as well as suggestions of supernatural protection.

(From this point on, headings are entirely missing from the manuscript. For the reader's convenience, the headings supplied by Rota are given here, with no further enumeration of sections until missing portions of the poem will cause Rota's numbers to be, perhaps, excessively low. See Introduction E.)

(S 133–34; KS 130)

Illustration 25, Page 26 (119r). *The departure of the empress, prisoner, for Messina.* Illustrates verses 681–710 contained on page 25 (118v) of the codex, but the lower section, representing Constance the empress on the ship on the way to Messina, could also refer to the first verses of text contained on the next page.

119v <(KS) Particula XXV: Domine adventus et loquutio ad Tancredum>
      <(Rota) Particula XXV: Domine adventus et loquucio ad Tancredum>

Et modo vela tument, modo brachia iacta resudant,	711
Attenuat ceptam remus et aura viam.	712
Suspectas, Palinure, tuas ratis effugit undas,	713
Nam nova trans vires preda fatigat aquas;	714
Iam presentit aquas dubia vertigine motas,	715
Quas vomit et subito gutture Scilla rapit;	716
Iam ratis, infide metuens vada ceca Caribdis,	717
Exercet vires remige, voce, manu;	718
Messanam veniunt, ubi rex et curia tota	719
Sperabant facilem, re perhibente, fugam.	720
A rate descendens ylari Constantia vultu,	721
Obvia Tancredo triste repensat ave.	722
Tandem suspirans Auguste frigidus inquit:	723
"Non tibi tocius sufficit orbis honor?	724
"Quid mea regna petis? Deus est, qui iudicat equum,	725
"In se sperantis vindicat acta viri.	726
"Te tua fata michi turbantem regna dedere;	727
"Hinc tuus egroto corpore Cesar abit."	728
Iulia respondit: "Quod ais, Tancrede, recordor:	729
"Ut michi retrogradum, iam tibi sidus erit.	730
"Quidquid fata volunt, stat inevitabile semper,	731
"Per varias vario curritur axe vices.	732
"Non tua regna peto, set patris iura requiro.	733
"An tu Rogerii filius? Absit. Ego	734
"Heres regis, ego matris iustissima proles	735
Lex patris et matris dat michi quicquid habes.	736
"Regna tenes tantum usurpata, set illa	737
"Vivit inexperta qui petat ense suo.	738
"Que leges, que iura tibi mea regna dederunt?	739
"Nam Lichium vobis gratia sola dedit."	740
Post hec in talamos patrios se leta recepit,	741
Italicos mores inperiosa gerens.	742

<(Rota) Section 25: The Lady's Arrival and Her Speech to Tancred.>

And now the sails swell, and now the thrust-out arms break out in sweat;
    The oar and the winds shorten the journey that has begun.
O Palinurus, a ship flees over your mistrusted waves,
    For the new prize harasses the waters beyond their powers.
Now they sense the moving waters of the fearful whirlpool,
    Which Scylla vomits and suddenly draws down her throat again;
Now the ship, fearing the blind shoals of faithless Charybdis,
    Demands the powers of the crew, by voice, by hand.
They come to Messina, where the king and the whole court
    Were hoping for easy flight, if events should call for it.
Constance, descending from the ship with a cheerful face,
    Meets Tancred and returns his gloomy greeting in kind.
At last, sighing, he speaks coldly to Augusta:
    "Was not the honor of the whole world enough for you?
"Why do you seek my realms? There is a God who judges in equity
    "And avenges the acts of men who trust in themselves.
"Your destiny gave you into my hands as you disturbed my realms,
    "And your Caesar has gone hence, sick in body."
Julia answers, "What you say, Tancred, I take to heart:
    "Your star will soon be retrograde as mine is.
"Whatever the Fates decree remains forever inevitable,
    "While it runs through various changes on [Fortune's] changing wheel.
"I do not aim at your realms, but I seek the rights of my father.
    "Are you Roger's son? Perish the thought.
"I am the heir of the king, very rightful offspring of my mother;
    "The law of my father and my mother gives me everything you have.
"Thus far you do hold the realms, though by usurpation.
    "However, he lives who seeks these untested regions with his sword.
"What laws, what oaths gave you my realms?
    "Only [King William's] gracious kindness gave you Lecce."
After saying these things, the imperious one retreated, happy,
    To the paternal bedchambers, displaying her Italian manners.

Commentary and Notes [119v]: Constance is brought on a dangerous journey through sea-roads previously traveled by Aeneas, to a confrontation with Tancred. Pietro alludes to the fate of Palinurus, Aeneas's pilot, who, in *Aeneid* 5. 835–870, is thrown overboard by personified Sleep, leaving the ship at the mercy of the waves near Naples and Salerno, the starting point of Constance's voyage, and then to Scylla and Charybdis, nearer to her destination. Scylla is a man-eating monster and Charybdis a voracious whirlpool. According to Graeco-Roman mythology, they haunt the straits of Messina, and mariners who try to avoid one of them almost inevitably fall into the power of the other. Hence, they personify the hazards of navigating in the narrow strait of Messina with its dangerous currents. The monsters are well known from Book XII of Homer's *Odyssey*, and are also mentioned prominently in Virgil's *Aeneid* 3.420–432, 553–567, where Aeneas avoids them. The Tancredine crew likewise evades these dangers, and though Pietro does not directly concede that they do anything right, the miniatures (and the contemporary chronicles) suggest that Constance is treated with courtesy and respect. At Messina she is carefully helped from the galley (whether by her own servants or by others is not clear). However, when Tancred addresses her, he echoes Elias's earlier accusation that she is suffering divine punishment for her greed and arrogance, as a disturber of his realm. When she answers, Pietro calls her "Julia" (line 729) emphasizing both her imperial rank, and perhaps the Roman stoicism inherent in the attitude she adopts. Siragusa (56, n. 2), referring to a note by Engel, points out that Augustus himself (formerly Octavian) and his wife, Livia, were adopted into the Julian family, and thus were called Julius and Julia respectively. In time, the family name became a kind of imperial title. In applying it to Constance, Pietro stresses a connection with Imperial Rome. At the same time, however, he evokes Lucan's portrayal, in *De bello civili*, of Julia, the daughter of Julius Caesar and wife of Pompey the Great. Julia's marriage to Pompey sealed the alliance between these great men, which, however, fell apart when she died (*De bello* 1.113). Her phantom appears to haunt Pompey while the war between the rivals takes shape, reproaching him for his desertion of the alliance (*De bello* 3.9–35). Constance's marriage likewise cemented an alliance between the Hohenstaufen and Hauteville dynasties, which Tancred's usurpation has disrupted.

In her speech, Constance staunchly affirms the legitimacy of her claims. Tancred's throne is only uplifted temporarily by the whimsical turnings of Fortune's wheel, while she has Fate on her side, though its workings may be slow, and Fate cannot be changed. Also, somewhat cryptically, she expresses her belief that her husband is still alive and will continue his attempts to gain the kingdom. She asserts once more that Tancred has no right to the throne of Sicily, pointing out that even his original county of Lecce was given to him only by "gracious kindness" (740). Here Del Re defends Tancred. He points out (437–438, notes on p. 219) that Tancred's maternal grandfather was Count Achard of Lecce. Thus Tancred has merely succeeded to his grandfather's rank, through his mother, whose name is not known. While this is true, "gracious kindness" did have to enter the picture at some point, since illegitimate children would not automatically inherit their parents' fiefs. Besides that, Tancred spent some years in exile because of his rebellion against William I.

When the confrontation is over, Constance cheerfully takes up residence in the palace, where Tancred apparently has chosen to lodge her.

(S 56–57; KS 133)

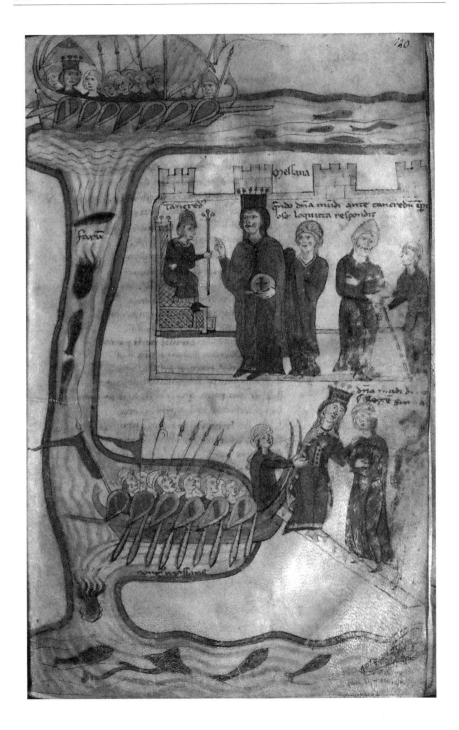

120r *The arrival of the empress at Messina.* Illustrates ll. 711–742 on fol. 118v.

. . . .

Messana	1.	Messina
Farum	2.	Faro
Tancredus	3.	Tancred
Quando domina mundi ante Tancredum imperiose locuta respondit.	4.	When the mistress of the world, standing before Tancred, answered with an imperious speech.
Portus Messane	5.	Port of Messina
[Siragusa] Domina mundi dixit: Reperite simiam	6.	(Siragusa) The mistress of the world said, "Go find the ape."
[KS] Domina mundi dixit regem simiam		

Commentary and Notes [120r]: The action of this scene follows a circular motion starting at the top of the page, where the ship appears with a sail spread (smaller than scale). Constance sits under a tent or canopy at the stern while Elias is near the bow. Fish appear under the waters. A narrow strait labeled "Farum," filled with more fish, flows curving from the top left to the bottom left of the page, into a pool labeled "Port of Messina" (Portus Messane) where Constance disembarks, helped by servants. She is met by someone whom Kölzer's commentary (134) interprets as a palace lady. Above the disembarkation scene, she is shown later, confronting Tancred, who sits on his throne, wearing a small crown and holding a scepter. Constance, however, not only stands far taller than he does, but wears a taller crown. She also holds the orb. One of her attendants stands beside her with veiled hands. Elias and another attendant are further to the right.

(S 134; KS 134)

For Cap. 6, Winkelmann and KS have *Domina mundi dixit regem Simiam* ("The mistress of the world said [that] the king [was] an ape.") Siragusa, uncertain of his reading, presented *Reperite* only with a question mark. His interpretation is potentially more dramatic: Constance, getting off the ship as a prisoner in Messina, disdainfully suggests that her captor be informed of her arrival. In the Winkelmann/ KS version, she merely utters an offhand insult outside Tancred's presence. See Additional Notes on 120r, cap. 6.

120v <(Rota) Particula XXVI: Tancredus futura cogitans lacrimatur>

Ut videt Augustam Tancredus, gaudia vultu	743
Pro populo simulans, pectore tristis erat.	744
Ingreditur thalamum, foribus post terga reductis,	745
Precipitans humili frigida membra thoro.	746
At genus incertum, sexus iniuria nostri,	747
Talia Tancredum verba dedisse ferunt:	748
"Eu michi! Quis poterit contendere Cesaris armis?	749
"Hactenus Augusti mitior ira fuit;	750
"Nec me turrite celsis in montibus urbes,	751
"Nec me defendent oppida iuncta polo.	752
"Non opus est bello, quia me fortuna reliquit;	753
"Iam vires miserum destituere senem;	754
"Mille meos equites ex augustalibus unus	755
"Vincet, et unius lancea mille fugat.	756
"Unus Rombanldus regnum michi cum tribus aufert;	757
"In Dipuldeo nomine terra tremit.	758
"Experiar superos? Si forte videbor in armis,	759
"Nostram Dipuldus non lacerabit humum?	760
"Absit ut experiar Dipuldi nomen et arma,	761
"Nec videant oculos lumina nostra suos.	762
"Est michi congnatus procera gigantis ymago,	763
"Sat probus et fortis, sed nimis arma timet.	764
"Sunt michi non pauci, quos res michi fecit amicos;	765
"Si res defuerit, denique nullus erit.	766
"Felix argentum, set eo felicius aurum,	767
"Nam ius a superis, a Iove numen emit.	768
"Eu! si forte cadet salientis vena metalli,	769
"Quis michi, quis puero causa salutis erit?	770
"Sex sumus inbelles: ego, nate, filius, uxor,	771
"Infelix pelago turba relicta sumus."	772

<(Rota) Section 26: Tancred Weeps, Thinking About the Future>

When he saw Augusta, Tancred feigned a glad face
　Before the people, but in his heart he was gloomy.
He entered his bedchamber, closing the doors behind his back,
　Throwing his cold limbs on his low couch.
Then Tancred, that man of uncertain descent, insult to our sex,
　Spoke words such as these, or so it is told:
"Alas for me! Who can contend with Caesar's armies?
　"Until now, the wrath of Augustus was rather mild.
"Nor am I defended by cities crowned with towers in the high mountains,
　"Nor towns which touch the sky.
"War is useless, since fortune deserts me;
　"Now strength forsakes the wretched old man.
"Just one of the Imperials conquers a thousand of my horsemen,
　"And the lance of one puts a thousand to flight.
"By himself Rombald, with three helping him, takes the kingdom from me,
　"And earth trembles at the name of Diepold.
"Shall I tempt the celestial powers? Oh, doubtless, if I am seen in arms,
　"Diepold will not injure our country!
"Perish the thought that I should tempt the name and arms of Diepold,
　"Or that my eyes should behold his eyes!
"I have a lofty image of a giant for a brother-in-law;
　"He is dutiful and sturdy enough, but fears arms too much.
"I have not a few supporters who are friends because of my possessions;
　"If I should lose my possessions, no one will remain in the end.
"Silver is lucky, but gold is luckier still,
　"For it buys laws from the powers above and consecration from Jove.
"Alas! if perhaps my gushing spring of precious metal should dry up,
　"What safety would remain for me, or for my boy?
"The six of us are unwarlike: myself, my daughters, my son, and my wife;
　"We are an unlucky throng abandoned in the open sea."

Commentary and Notes [120v]: This passage seems to be a late revision; the original text was erased and the verse written over in the same rough hand which wrote the poet's colophon and a few other passages. See notes on fol. 121r.

In this soliloquy, Tancred reveals his doubts and fears. An old man, father of a young son and three daughters, he sees his own followers as no match for the emperor's strong, active, and skilled fighters. The "Rombanldus" [sic] mentioned in line 757 is unknown, but Siragusa (58, n. 2) speculates that the name might be a mistake for *Bertoldus*, one of Henry VI's major commanders in this phase of the war; supporting this, he offers a citation from Richard of San Germano (*Chronica*, 66) where *Bertoldus* fights along with three associates (Conrad Lützelhard, Diepold of Schweinspeunt, and Conrad, the castellan of Sorella). These could be the three allies of "Rombanldus" to whom Tancred refers in this passage.

Tancred complains that his brother-in-law, Count Richard of Acerra, is loyal but too cautious, and that therefore his best weapon is money, gold and silver, which has helped him to buy "laws from the powers above and consecration from

Jove." This is as close as Pietro comes to discussing Tancred's success in winning the support of the papacy. Though as Pietro tells it, Tancred dismisses the thought of leading his armies in person, this is not the whole story; see Introduction C.14.

Tancred's mention of his unwarlike family shows that Pietro is telescoping events. Only one son is mentioned, although both boys, Roger and William, accompanied Tancred in his triumphal coronation procession, fol. 102r. Constance's arrival as a prisoner in Messina happened at the end of August or the first days of September in 1191, when Roger, the elder, was still living. In fact, Roger was crowned as his father's co-ruler in 1192 and married the Byzantine princess Irene either then or the next summer. He died on 24 December 1193. Pietro may have had reasons to remove a passage describing this young man's marriage and death more clearly; see Introduction A.2.

Tancred here alludes to three daughters, whom Siragusa (59, n. 2) identifies as Alberia, Constance, and Mandonia.

(S 58–59; KS 137)

121r *Tancred is sorrowful, thinking about the future. The count of Acerra sets out toward Capua.* Illustrates ll. 743–772 on fol. 120v.

· · · ·

Tancredus futura cogitans lacrimatur.	1.	Tancred, thinking about the future, weeps.
Comes Riccardus Capuam pergit.	2.	Count Richard proceeds to Capua.

Commentary and Notes [121r]: This illustration compares unfavorably in attractiveness to many of the others. The unhappy Tancred appears enthroned on the upper level. On the lower level, Count Richard of Acerra, gigantic and bland in expression, points a finger toward a crudely drawn cluster of six knights who ride ahead of him. Overall, Tancred looks dismayed and his supporters seem unimpressive and unreliable. As Kölzer and Stähli (138) and Siragusa (132, n. 2) point out, this picture was drawn over another one which had been previously erased; it is still possible to see that many armed men originally surrounded Tancred. Fuchs, Mrusek, and Oltrogge ("Die Entstehung," 278) establish that this picture was drawn by an artist whose work appears nowhere else in the codex. Kölzer suggests that this artist used other pictures in the manuscript as models. See commentary on fol. 120v.

(S 134; KS 138)

121v   <(Rota) Particula XXVII: Corradus obsessus suos alloquitur>

Urbs antiqua, suis uberrima denique campis,	773
Mater opum, felix presule, plena viris,	774
Ubere luxuriat tellus, autumnus habundat,	775
Vite maritatur populus amnis amans;	776
Ordine dispositas eadem complectitur ulmos,	777
Incola fastidit quod fluit uva merum;	778
Ter sata, ter seritur, tria dat responsa colono,	779
Ter sub sole novo semina pensat humus.	780
Urbem quam loquimur, comes obsidione coartat,	781
Que sola potuit proditione capi.	782

¶

Hanc ubi Corradus vi defensare fatigat,	783
Dicitur his verbis ammonuisse suos:	784
"Qui mecum, proceres, gelido venistis ab axe,	785
"Cernite quid populus, quid locus iste velit.	786
"Et locus et populus nostro diffidit amori,	787
"In nos astiferas cernitis esse manus;	788
"Quisque suum nudo pugnet caput ense tueri,	789
"Nec prece nec pretio gens facit ista pium.	790
"Libertas est Marte mori, servire malignum;	791
"Nobis vita mori, vivere pena datur.	792
"Hinc Augustus abest, Augustaque capta tenetur.	793
"Quid superest nobis? Restat in ense salus.	794
"Spes est nulla fuge, quia nos foris obsidet hostis,	795
"Intus adest hostis, nec domus hoste caret.	796
"Sicut aper ferus a canibus circumdatus, unco	797
"Dente furens, multos ultus, ab hoste cadit,	798
"Sic vestrum, si forte cadat, sit nullus inultus,	799
"Victorem victi penituisse iuvet."	800

¶

Exhinc ad cives ita paucis explicat ora:	801
"Vos, precor, ospitibus non temerate fidem.	802
"Augusto servate fidem; si forte, quod absit,	803
"Tancredum vestrum sanctificare placet,	804
"Nos hinc incolumes obnoxius ire rogamus;	805
"Non hic a longo venimus orbe mori.	806
"Augustus si noster abest trans climata mundi,	807
"Ipsum prolixas nostis habere manus."	808
Actenus arrecta varium bibit aure tumultum	809
Et stupet, et memor est, se superesse virum.	810

<(Rota) Section 27: Conrad, Besieged, Addresses His Men.>

The ancient city, rich indeed in its fields,
    Mother of wealth, happy in its archbishop, full of men,
Has a soil which abounds in fertility. The autumn harvest is plentiful.
    The poplar is married to the vine, loving the river;
The city is surrounded by elms set down in rows,
    And the inhabitant disdains the unwatered wine that flows from the grape.
Thrice the standing grain, thrice sown, gives threefold return to the farmer.
    Thrice beneath a new sun he measures out seed upon the soil.
The count lays siege to the city of which we speak,
    Which could be captured only by treason.
¶
While Conrad labors to defend her with strength,
    It is said that he admonished his men with these words:
"You strong men who came with me from the cold climes,
    "Discern what this people and this region mean to do.
"Both the place and the people mistrust our alliance,
    "As you see, armed bands are coming against us.
"Let each of you fight to defend your own head with a naked sword;
    "This people can be made dutiful neither by prayers nor price.
"Death in martial combat means liberty; it is an ill thing to be a slave.
    "For us, to die is life, and living is a punishment.
"Augustus is absent and Augusta is held captive.
    "What remains to us? There is still safety in the sword.
"Flight offers no hope, since the enemy awaits outside the gates,
    "And within the enemy is present, nor does the house itself lack enemies.
"As a fierce wild boar, surrounded by dogs,
    "Raging with curved tusks, falls already avenged by many deaths,
"So shall it be that not one of you, if perchance he falls, shall be unavenged;
    "Let the defeated rejoice that the victor has regretted the battle."
¶
Then he spoke a few words to the citizens, thus:
    "I pray that you not break your faith to your guests.
"Keep faith with Augustus. But if perhaps (perish the thought!)
    "It pleases you to treat your Tancred as something holy,
"Then, we do ask very humbly that you allow us to go unharmed;
    "We did not come here from distant lands to die.
"If our Augustus has gone away beyond the climates of this world,
    "You know that he has his armies spread far."
Up to this point, he drank in the changing tumult with an attentive ear,
    Greatly alarmed and yet mindful that he was still a man.

Ut cum mella volunt examina rapta tueri,   811
   Indiscreta volant, sollicitata fremunt,   812
Sic in Teutonicos urbis pene tumultuat omnis,   813
   Regem polluto nominat ore suum;   814
Non nisi Tancredum clamans se noscere regem,   815
   Preponit monstrum tam breve, stulta, Iovi.   816

Commentary and Notes [121v]: Pietro begins with a poetic description of Capua, which will be the scene of the next battle. Conrad, aware that Tancred's forces under Count Richard of Acerra are approaching, exhorts his men to fight to the bitter end, if necessary, likening their trapped army to a cornered boar who will kill many hounds before it dies. But in addressing the Capuans, he offers to withdraw

Then, as when swarms of bees wish to defend stolen honey,
    And fly about, helter-skelter, buzzing in their anger;
So does nearly the whole city cry out against the Germans,
    They call upon their king with unclean mouths;
Declaring that they recognise no king but Tancred,
    The foolish city places that puny monstrosity before Jove.

with his men if they will allow him to go safely. The citizens, determined to kill or capture the Germans, reject Conrad's overtures and shout in anger that Tancred is their king. In an epic simile, Pietro likens the rebellious people to angry bees defending stolen honey. Thus he reminds his readers that their fight is in a bad cause.

(S 60–61; KS 141)

122r *Address of Conrad of Lützelhard, besieged in Capua, to his soldiers and to the Capuans.* Illustrates ll. 773–816 on fol. 121v.

. . . .

Capua.	1. Capua.
Hic Corradus marchio obsessus a Tancredinis alloquitur suos.	2. Here Conrad the marquis, besieged by the Tancredines, addresses his men.
Hic idem Corradus alloquitur Capuanis.	3. Here the same Conrad addresses the Capuans.

Commentary and Notes [122r]: At the top of the page two large trees appear, with green foliage and green vines wrapped around them. Below, the towers of a fortified city (Capua) appear. Within the city, Conrad is shown in two adjacent pictures, addressing his men in one, and in the other addressing the Capuans. His men are represented in full armor, but Conrad wears neither hat nor helmet. His hair curls slightly around his ears, and he holds a drawn sword, upraised. When he addresses the Capuans, he wears a helmet and holds his sword with its point down. At the bottom of the drawing, outside the square representing the city walls, five clusters of wheat stalks grow. Kölzer ("Bildkommentar," 142) states that this action took place in October (1191) and that perhaps the mature wheat stalks are intended to suggest the season. Siragusa points out (135, n. 1) that two large trees wound with vines are illustrations of lines 775–776: "The autumn harvest is plentiful. / The poplar is married to the vine, loving the river."

(S 135; KS 142)

122v <(Rota) Particula XXVIII: Comitis Riccardi prodicio et Corradi dedicio>

Interea comes ante fores preludit in armis,	817
Sinones multos novit in urbe viros.	818
Hen subito patuere fores, foris obice fracto,	819
Fit civile nephas, fit populare scelus;	820
Exter ab ignoto cadit, ospes ab ospite falso;	821
Hic latus ense cavat, demetit ille caput;	822
Loricam lorica premit, furit ensis in ensem,	823
In clipeos clipei, cassis in era ruit;	824
A galeis galee famascunt, ensibus enses,	825
Tela vomunt flammas iactaque fulgur agunt;	826
Ospitis et cari telo fodit ille cerebrum;	827
Hic ferus, ille ferox; hic ferit, ille ferit;	828
Hic salit, ille salit; tenet ille, tenetur ab illo;	829
Hic levis, ille celer, aptus uterque fuge;	830
Hic caput, ille caput certat iactare periclis,	831
Opponit telis hic latus, ille latus;	832
Hii certant clipeis ludentes passibus equis,	833
Ut ludit socio sepe maritus ovis;	834
Hic ruit a muris precepsque suum trahit hostem;	835
A victo victor, victus ab hoste cadit.	836
Ut solet a capto Iovis armiger angue ligari,	837
Hic ligat, ille tenet, nexus uterque perit;	838
Non aliter qui bella gerunt in menibus altis,	839
Cum duo se miscent, sunt sibi cause necis;	840
Alter in alterius subnectens brachia dorsum,	841
Si ruit, ambo ruunt, unus et alter obit.	842
Cantet inauditum, cantet mirabile dictu	843
Nunc mea Calliope.	844
Dum comes iret eques spectatum menia circum	845
Et venisset ubi maxima turris erat,	846
Hunc vir Teutonicus summa speculatus ab arce,	847
Se dedit in comitem lapsus ad ima miser,	848
Et nisi fata virum rapuissent a strage ruentis,	849
Tunc comes elapsum triste tulisset honus.	850
Ut levis inbriferas per nubes fulgurat ether,	851
Cum sua per rimas nubila ventus arat,	852
Non secus in radiis procul armatura coruscat,	853
Nec non cristatum fulgurat omne caput.	854

<(Rota) Section 28: The Treason of Count Richard and Conrad's Surrender>

Meanwhile, the count, before the gates, prepares for battle;
    He knows many men ready to play Sinon in the city.
Ah, suddenly the gates are thrown open; the gate's barrier broken,
    Public crime and civil blasphemy unfold.
A foreigner falls by one unknown to him, a guest by a false host;
    This man pierces someone's side with his sword, another swipes off
    someone's head.
Harness crashes against harness, and sword rages against sword,
    Shield against shield; helmet rushes on bronze helmet.
Helms are dented on helms, swords on swords,
    Missiles spout forth flames and spears flash lightning.
This one pierces the brain of his guest and friend;
    This one is savage, that one fierce; he wounds and the other wounds.
One leaps, the other leaps; one holds, and the other is held by him;
    One is light, the other fast, and both are intent on flight.
This one and that one struggle to thrust their heads into perils;
    This one exposes his side to missiles, and so does that one;
These contest with their shields, prancing with balanced steps,
    As a ram often sports with a companion.
This one falls from the walls, and falling, drags his enemy with him.
    The conqueror falls by the conquered, and the conquered by his enemy,
As it often happens when the armor-bearer of Jove is bound by a serpent he has
    captured;
    He binds, the other holds on, and bound together they both fall;
Not otherwise does it fare with those who wage war on the high
    Fortifications, when two joined in combat cause their mutual death.
One seizing the other with his arms around his back,
    Throws himself down, both fall, and one and the other die.
Now she will sing unheard-of things, she will sing something wonderful,
    My Calliope.
When the count made the circuit on horseback to observe the walls,
    And came where the greatest tower was,
A German, seeing him from the highest pinnacle,
    Let himself, wretched man, fall upon the count, sliding to the depths,
And if the fates had not snatched the other from his ruin as he hurtled down,
    Then the count would have borne his fallen weight with sorrow.
As the gentle heavens shine through the mists,
    When the wind plows fissures through its rain-bearing clouds,
Just so the armor shone in rays far off,
    And every crested head gleamed.

Post procerum cedes, vitam Corradus et arma   855
    Vendicat et socios, quos superesse videt.   856
Hunc comes et socios dextra securat et ore;   857
    Non poterant proceres tot sine cede capi.   858
Ne tabo solvatur humus, quadriga laborat;   859
    Mergitur in fluidis omne cadaver aquis.   860

Commentary and Notes [122v]: Having refused Conrad's "very humble" request to be allowed a peaceful withdrawal from Capua, Count Richard induces traitors within the city to throw open the gates for his army. (In line 818 the poet alludes to Sinon, who, in Book II of Virgil's *Aeneid*, persuaded the Trojans to bring the Trojan horse into their city so that the Greek warriors hiding within the wooden image could open the city gates by night, for their companions to come in.) Having pronounced the wickedness of this strategem, Pietro turns to a heroic account of the fight. There are short vivid phrases describing common and ongoing actions (striking, wounding, leaping, falling), and longer passages describing specific but representative actions, such as the contest with shields which looks from the distance like a playful match (833–834), and a man dragging his enemy down with him to death (835–842), like an eagle (the armor-bearer of Jove)

After the slaughter of champions, Conrad bargains for his life and arms
    And the companions he sees surviving. The count offers him
And his companions assurances with right hand and mouth;
    They could not capture such champions without slaughter.
Lest the earth should dissolve into putrefaction, a four-horse chariot
    Labors; every corpse is thrown in the flowing water.

entwined with a serpent. Then Pietro marks as highly unusual and admirable (worth the special attention of the Epic Muse, Calliope) the futile attempt of a German knight to take Count Richard with him in death by leaping upon him from the highest tower (845–849). In the end, Count Richard decides he cannot afford to lose any more men. He agrees to allow Conrad and his surviving men to leave in safety, carrying their arms. The many dead bodies are collected in a cart and thrown into the river to prevent odoriferous putrefaction and resultant infection in the city. This section of the poem celebrates the courage and martial vigor of the Germans, betrayed in a city that had welcomed them, fighting against tremendous odds, and winning (after much loss) their main point: the right to depart in freedom.

(S 62–63; KS 145)

123r *Episode of the assault of Richard of Acerra on Capua. Burial of the corpses.* Illustrates ll. 817–860 on fol. 121v.

. . . .

Quando comes Riccardus
    prodiciose Capuam ingrediens
    plurimis interfectis
    marchionem et pau[cas]
    suorum reliquias assecuravit.
	1.	When Count Richard, entering
		    Capua through treachery,
		    promised security to the marquis
		    and the few of his men who
		    remained after many were killed.

Teutonicus viso comite Riccardo
    a su[mmo] usque deorsum
    sponte labitur volens se et
    [eum] perdere.
	2.	A German, having seen Count
		    Richard, falls of his own will, all
		    the way down from the top,
		    wishing to destroy himself and
		    [the count].

Tancridini.	3.	Tancredines.
Imperiales.	4.	Imperials.
Comes Riccardus.	5.	Count Richard.

Cadavera mortuorum
    proiciuntur in fluvio.
	6.	The bodies of the dead are thrown
		    into the river.

Commentary and Notes [123r]: These illustrations follow the text closely. The verses mention limbs being hacked off in the battle, and the illustration shows at least one severed hand, a foot, and two heads flying in the mêlée. The German who throws himself from the tower appears in two stages of his trajectory toward his near miss of Count Richard of Acerra, who stands among his knights, carrying a shield with a white, red-eyed lion against a green background. Count Richard himself shakes the hand (or holds the wrist) of the Marquis Conrad (mounted on a tawny horse, bearing a sword but no shield), to signify his promise to allow the safe departure of the Germans. At the bottom of the page, a man with a spear leads an ox-drawn cart. With a sort of x-ray vision, severed body parts are shown inside the cart, indicating the corpses to be thrown into the river.

(S 135–36; KS 146)

123v <(Rota) Particula XXIX: Tancredus mittit Constanciam uxori scribens ei>

Cor breve Tancredi merito diffidit, ubique   861
   Tam sibi quam mundo credit abesse fidem.   862
Nunc mare nunc terras animo scrutatur et urbes,   863
   Pectore sollicitus, nec loca fida videt.   864
Tandem consilio dubitantis pectoris usus,   865
   Curam custodis mittit ut uxor agat.   866
Accepto calamo, finitur epistola paucis;   867
   Exul quam didicit, littera greca fuit.   868

   Epistola Tancred ad uxorem.
¶
"Hoc ego Tancredus tibi mitto, Sibilia, scriptum,   869
   "Quod, postquam tacito legeris ore, crema.   870
"Tu quondam comitissa, modo regina vocaris;   871
   Tu quondam Licium, tu modo regna tenes.   872
"Quas nunc fastidis et que quandoque fuere   873
   "Divitias, memori singula mente nota: 874
"Hec est Rogerii protoregis nobilis heres,   875
   "Illius est uxor, qui quatit omne solum;   876
"Hanc ego, dulcis amor, mea prekarissima consors,   877
   "Servandum vigili pectore mitto tibi.   878
"Sis comes et custos et ei sis ospes et hostis;   879
   "Hanc nunquam sine te, si sapis, esse sinas;   880
"Una domus vobis, unum de nocte cubile,   881
   "Quam cuiquam sine te ne patiare loqui.   882
"Deliciosa duas communicet una parabsis.   883
   "Nunc maior, nunc par, nunc minor esse velis."   884
¶
Post hec, assissis sociis, Augusta Panormum   885
   Convehitur. Multi condoluere senes: 886
"Heu heu," clamantes; tacito sub pectore flebant;   887
   "Heredem regni que manus ausa tenet!   888
"Pro dolor! Ingrediens Augusta palacia patris,   889
   "Pro pudor! Insidias obsidionis habet!"   890
Ipsa tamen gaudens, tanquam vicisse resultat,   891
   Et quociens loquitur, visa superba loqui.   892
Cerree fastidit opus, fastidit amari;   893
   Fausta sedens, neutris imperiosa iubet.   894
Quo Cerrea dolet, per eam tum sepe vocatur,   895
   Mittit Tancredo talia mota suo.   896

<(Rota) Section 29: Tancred, Writing to His Wife, Sends Constance to Her.>

The stunted heart of Tancred rightly mistrusts everyone,
    He believes loyalty as absent in the world as in himself.
Now he considers the land, now the sea and now the cities
    With troubled heart, nor does he see any loyal place.
Then, taking the counsel of his doubtful breast,
    He sends word that his wife should undertake a keeper's duty.
Taking a pen in hand, he finishes a letter quickly;
    The missive was in Greek, which he had learned as an exile.

    Tancred's Letter to His Wife
¶
"I, Tancred send this writing to you, Sibylla:
    "After you have read it with silent mouth, burn it.
"You who were once a countess are now called a queen;
    "You once held Lecce and now hold the realms.
"Note and remember, in your mind, one by one, those things
    "You now disdain, which once were riches to you.
"This woman is the noble heir of Roger, the first king;
    "Her husband causes every land to tremble.
"I send her, sweet love, my very dearest consort,
    "For you to keep safely, with a watchful heart.
"Be a companion and a keeper, a hostess and hostile;
    "Never let her be anywhere without you, if you are wise.
"Be in the same house, the same bed by night;
    "Do not let her speak to anyone without you.
"One drinking vessel must convey delicacies to both of you.
    "Now be willing to be greater, now equal, now less."

After this, with assigned companions, Augusta
    Was conveyed to Palermo. Many old men mourned about it,
Crying "Alas, Alas!" and weeping silently in their hearts:
    "What hand has dared to hold the heir of the realm?
"What sorrow! Augusta going to the palace of her father —
    "For shame! will be exposed to every treachery."
She, however, sprang up rejoicing, as though she had conquered,
    And as many times as she spoke, spoke with a proud countenance.
She disdained the work of the Acerran, and disdained to be loved;
    Sitting auspiciously, the imperious one gave commands to the eunuchs.
It grieved the Acerran that she was often summoned on her account.
    Moved by such things, she sent to her Tancred.

Commentary and Notes [123v]: Tancred sends Constance as a prisoner to his wife, Sibylla, instructing her to treat the captive, simultaneously, as an honored guest and as a prisoner. Sibylla is to be (line 884) "now greater," presumably when making decisions about Constance's activities and imprisonment, "now equal" when enjoying the royal luxuries to which both are entitled, and "now less," when yielding to the empress as a woman of superior rank or when making sacrifices that hostesses make for guests. Pietro tells us that Tancred chooses this course, not because he is wise and courteous, but because he dares not trust anyone but his wife (whose political interests are the same as his own) to guard Constance properly. His letter, Pietro tells is, is written in the Greek Tancred learned during his youthful time of exile. Perhaps Pietro thinks the language appropriate for the subtlety Tancred shows here. He addresses Sibylla with great affection and reminds her of everything she owes him, while spelling out just what a delicate, burdensome, and demanding task he has set her.

Becht-Jördens and De Rosa interpret *assissis sociis* (line 885) to mean that Constance is separated from her companions at this point—presumably the two attendants who are shown leaving Terracina with her in 119r. Siragusa and the previous editors, on the other hand, interpreted this expression to mean that Constance was sent to Palermo with companions chosen by Tancred; see the note on this line.

Constance adapts serenely to her circumstances, while loyal Sicilians mourn her plight. Constance enters the palace as if she were victorious, and accepts all the hospitality she is offered at face value, disdaining "the work of the Acerran." Sibylla's duties may have included an attempt to win Constance's sympathies, a kind of political seduction. With the expression "she disdained to be loved" (*fastidit amari*) in line 893, Pietro suggest that these attempts are failures; it is unlikely that he meant to convey the idea that Constance was simply an ungrateful and impossible guest. Tancred's queen, however, finds the situation too unpleasant and decides to complain to her husband.

(S 64–65; KS 149)

124r   *The Empress brought prisoner to Palermo. Her conversation with the queen Sibylla.*
Illustrates ll. 861–896 *on fol.* 122v.

· · · ·

Cum dubitaret Tancredus tenere imperatricem apud Messanum, ipsam uxori sue custodiendam Panormum, mittet scribens ei.	1.	Because Tancred feared to hold the empress at Messina, he sent her to his wife to be guarded in Palermo, writing to her.
Cursor. Cursor.	2.	Runner. Runner.
Cives Panormi.	3.	Citizens of Palermo.
Uxor Tancredi.	4.	Wife of Tancred.
Imperatrix ingressa palacium audacter et imperiose loquitur et respondit uxori [Tancr]edi.	5.	The empress, having entered the palace boldly, imperiously speaks and answers the wife of Tancred.
Cursor adsignans licteras Tancredi uxori eius.	6.	Runner giving letters of Tancred to his wife.

Commentary and Notes [124r]: At the top of the page, a letter instructing Sibylla to take custody of Constance is being written; this is not, however, the secret letter which the verses say Tancred wrote himself but one which he dictates to a notary, or so Kölzer's commentary (151) construes the picture. Tancred, on the right-hand side, sits on his throne, crowned and holding a scepter. Less blatantly caricatured than in other drawings, he hands the finished scroll to a runner who, on the left, ax in hand, sets out for Palermo. In the middle of the page, the royal palace is represented, with its bell tower. On the bottom, left, two citizens mourn Constance's plight. Constance, with a serene expression, rides into the city wearing a crown; her attendants are not shown. On the right, Sibylla, also crowned, receives the scroll from the runner in her right hand. In her left hand she holds what Kölzer ("Bildkommentar," 151) aptly describes as "an indistinct object," shaped something like a bow but not held like a weapon.

(S 136; KS 150)

124v <(Rota) Particula XXX: Uxor Tancredi rescribit viro suo et Tancredus iterum
      rescribit ei>

Epistola uxoris ad Tancredum suum.

"Quid facis, o demens? Comitem misistis an hostem?   897
    "Ecce, quod exarsit ius patris, hostis habet.   898
"Venit ad hoc Cesar, sed ad hoc sua venit et uxor;   899
    "Victorem victum preda superba facit.   900
"Non opus est armare viros, velare carinas,   901
    "Nec proceres belli, nec numerare duces,   902
"Nec vestire sinus maculosi tegmine ferri,   903
    "Non ensare manus, non galeare caput.   904
"Protinus ut veniat, nullo discrimine vincet   905
    "Regna; per uxorem Cesar habebit opes.   906
"Quas nimis ipse doles, causis male consulis egris;   907
    "In caput a stomacho morbus habundat iners.   908
"Quam male dispensas aliis medicamina menbris,   909
    "Si caput ignoras!   910
"Si caput egrotet, valeant et cetera menbra?   911
    "Ni caput abradas, cetera menbra ruent."   912

Rescriptum Tancredi ad uxorem.
¶
Hec ub Tancredus legit, que miserat uxor,   913
    Altera rescriptum pagina tale tulit: 914
"Cara michi coniunx et casti fedus amoris,   915
    "Quam michi misisti, pagina robur habet.   916
"Vir magne fidei, mature gratia mentis   917
    "Est ibi; consilio fac, rogo, cuncta suo;   918
"Consule Matheum per quem regina vocaris;   919
    "Illi debemus quidquid uterque sumus.   920
"Trans hominem divina sapit, videt omnia longe,   921
    "Achitofel alter, pectus Ulixis habet.   922
"Hunc igitur, michi cara nimis, de more vocatum   923
    "Consule, consiliis ipsa quiesce suis."   924

\<(Rota) Section 30: Tancred's Wife Writes Back to Her Husband, and Tancred Writes to Her Again.\>

The Wife's Letter to Her Tancred

"What are you doing, madman? Did you send me a companion or an enemy?
    "Look, the enemy has her father's right, which started this fire.
"Caesar came because of this, but his wife also came;
    "The proud prize defeats the victor.
"There is no use in arming men, or fitting out ships with sails,
    "Nor counting barons and commanders in this war,
"Nor in clothing breasts with armor of stained iron,
    "Nor putting swords in hands, or helmets on the head.
"As soon as he comes, he will conquer the realms all the same;
    "Caesar will have help through his wife.
"You take bad advice about the causes of your too-grievous infirmities;
    "A sickness from the stomach overflows into an idle head;
"How badly you give medicine to the other limbs
    "If you ignore the head!
"If the head sickens, can the other limbs be well?
    "Unless you shave the head, the other limbs will be wasted."

Tancred's Reply to His Wife
¶
When Tancred read what his wife had sent,
    He sent back another message, thus:
"My dear wife and partner of chaste love,
    "The message you sent me is valid.
"Where you are, there is a man of great loyalty,
    "Thanks to a seasoned mind. Take, I ask, all his counsel;
"Consult Matthew through whom you are called queen;
    "To him we owe what we both are.
"He knows divine things, beyond human, and sees everything far off.
    "Another Achitophel, he has the heart of Ulysses.
"Therefore, consult this man, you who are so dear to me; summon him
    "According to custom, and gain peace of mind through his counsels."

Commentary and Notes [124v]: Sibylla writes to Tancred, complaining that it is dangerous to keep Constance in Palermo because her influence will help the emperor win the kingdom when he returns. To reinforce her point, she uses a medical analogy: when a body is sick in the head, all other limbs are affected, and there is no use treating them if the head is not treated. Similarly, Constance is the head of all their troubles and must be dealt with. Tancred quickly agrees, in language more polite and flowery than she has used with him, coming across as a slightly henpecked husband. He instructs Sibylla to consult Matthew the Chancellor and take his advice about this matter. His sinister compliments, likening Matthew to Achitophel and Ulysses, suggest a brief, dark future for

Constance. They also show his bad taste in counsellors. Though Ulysses, the destroyer of Troy, is a great hero to the Greeks (under the Greek name Odysseus), the Romans, with the Trojan Aeneas as their hero, admired him much less. Thus Dante places Ulysses in Hell among the False Counselors (*Inferno* 26.52–27.2). Achitophel's story is told in 2 Samuel 15:12–17:23. He stirred up strife between King David and his son, Absalom, and then killed himself when the latter failed to take his wise advice. Thus he also earns himself mention among the sowers of discord in Dante's Hell (*Inferno* 28.136–142). Absalom's rebellion failed miserably; Tancred's will not fail for the same reason since he continues to heed his Achitophel.

125r *Exchange of messages between Tancred and the queen Sibylla about the captivity of Constance.* Illustrates ll. 897–924 on fol. 124v.

．．．．

Uxor Tancredi.		1.	Tancred's wife.
Uxor Tancredi rescribit ipsi viro suo.		2.	Tancred's wife writes back to her own husband.
Tancred recipiens rescriptum uxoris sue iterum rescribit ei.		3.	Tancred, receiving the reply from his wife, writes back again.
Cursor Tancredi.		4.	Tancred's runner.
Tancredus.		5.	Tancred.
Uxor Tancredi.		6.	Wife of Tancred.

Commentary and Notes [125r]: Palace architecture and furnishings cover this page—towers, arches, and curtained recesses. On the top, Sibylla dictates a letter to a notary and hands it to a runner, who sets out; instead of an ax, he carries a staff with bread-rings, as Kölzer's commentary describes them (155), hung on it. On the next level, Tancred is shown holding Sibylla's letter in his left hand and giving a scroll to the messenger with his right. At the bottom, Sibylla receives the message. In all three pictures, a bird is depicted sitting on the ruler's crown, (twice on Sibylla's, once on Tancred's). Kölzer ("Bildkommentar," 154) interprets this, here and in the coronation scene (fol. 102r) as a form of calumny or ridicule. However, Tancred appeared without birds in 120r, 1213, and 124r. Perhaps evil omens are gathering as the usurpers contemplate harsher and possibly more treacherous treatment of Constance.

(S 136–37; KS 154)

Tav. XXXI Carta 32 (125r)

125v <(Rota) Particula XXXI: Uxor Tancredi et bigamus sacerdos>

Uxor Tancredi, vocato suo cancellario, de viro conqueritur.

Nec mora, Matheum tristis Cerrea vocavit;	925
Sic ait: "O veterum bibliotheca ducum,	926
"O regni tutela, fides purissima regum,	927
"Antidotum vite, consule, mesta queror.	928
"Sensato de rege queror, quo nescio pacto,	929
"Serpentem medio pectore gnarus alit.	930
"Ad senium properans dementior exit ab annis,	931
"Et iubet unde vivat penituisse senem.	932
Que spes regnandi, vel que michi vita superstes,	933
"Cum prope me patrio iure superba sedet?	934
"Et quotiens video, que Cesaris ore superbit,	935
"A! tociens animus deficit inde meus.	936
"Consule quid faciam; privatis consule morbis,	937
"Nam cruciant animos nocte dieque meos."	938

Responsio bigami.

Tunc ita Matheus: "Merito Sibilla vocaris,	939
"Nam procul experta mente futura vides.	940
"Regis culpa fuit, certe non inputo regi;	941
"Plurima cor nostri regis agenda gravant;	942
"Inplicitus multum dominantis sensus oberrat	943
"Et quandoque iubet quod rationis eget;	944
"Et quia castra fidem quamplurima non bene servant,	945
"Urbes spem modice credulitatis habent;	946
"Vertitur in dubium, quo sit custode tuenda;	947
"Vel quo servetur preda verenda loco."	948
Inde suos deiecit humo Matheus ocellos;	949
In cor se referens, premeditatus ait:	950
"Est locus, est, memini, mediis contentus in undis,	951
"Quem maris ex omni parte tuentur aque,	952
"Quem vis nature cumulum produxit in altum,	953
"Qui circum scopulos sub pede rupis habet;	954
"A rate remivaga scopulis munitur acutis,	955
"Hinc lapis hostiles, hinc vetat unda pedes;	956
"Qui nomen Salvator habet, quia credita salvat;	957
"Tantaque sit tanto preda tenenda loco."	958
Cerree placuit nimium quod dixerat ille;	959
Scibitur urbano pagina parva viro:	960

<(Rota) Section 31: The Wife of Tancred and the Bigamous Priest>

Tancred's wife, having summoned the chancellor, complains about her husband.

Nor was there delay; the gloomy Acerran summoned Matthew.
    Thus she spoke: "O library of the venerable dukes,
"O guardianship of the kingdom, purest faith of the kings,
    "Lifegiving antidote, counsel me! I, mournful, make my complaint.
"That very wise king! I do not know why, but I complain
    "That he knowingly fosters a serpent in the midst of his bosom.
"As he approaches old age, he becomes crazier every year,
    "And gives orders which he will regret, if only he lives long enough.
"What hope of reigning, or what life remains to me,
    "While that proud one sits near me by the right of her fathers?
"And, ah! as many times as I see her speaking proud words of Caesar,
    "So many times my courage fails me.
"Counsel me what I am to do; counsel me about my secret diseases,
    "For they torture my spirits night and day."

The Bigamist's answer.

Then Matthew spoke thus: "You are deservedly called Sibylla,
    "For in your mind you see the future far off.
"The king made a blunder, but certainly I will not blame him for it;
    "Many things that must be done weigh down the heart of our king.
"Much entangled, our master's wit wanders,
    "And now and then he orders unreasonable things.
"So because many castles do not keep good faith,
    "And cities offer little hope of trustworthiness,
"He becomes doubtful about what guard to set over the prize,
    "Or in what place in the fearful booty should be kept."
Then Matthew cast his eyes to the ground:
    Consulting his heart, he spoke after some thought:
"There is a place, I remember, confined in the midst of waves,
    "Which the waters of the sea protect on all sides,
"Which the power of nature has raised in a high mound;
    "Which has a circle of rocks at the foot of cliffs.
"High crags keep off wandering ships;
    "Hence the rocks and the waves keep away hostile feet.
"It has the name Preserver, since it preserves what is committed to it;
    "Such a place is fit to hold such booty."
The Acerran was greatly pleased with what he had said;
    A short letter was written to the man who governed the city:

"Hanc Alierne comes, munito carcere serves;   961
  "Nil super hoc regi gracius esse putes."   962
Protinus Augustam, Cerrea precipiente,   963
  Ad te, Parthenope, remus at aura vehit.   964

Commentary and Notes [125v]: Receiving Sibylla's complaint and appeal, Matthew soothes and flatters her, suggesting that she has preternatural insight like the legendary Sibyls of ancient times. (For more on Sibyls and Matthew's application of the reference, see note on line 939.) Matthew excuses Tancred's error and sets about to remedy it. After some thought, he recommends the isolated fortress of San Salvatore, near Naples. Immediately Sibylla writes to the governor of the city to send Constance there. Given the unscrupulous and murderous nature that Pietro attributes to Matthew, we would not have been surprised to hear that he

"Count Aligerno, keep this woman in the fortified prison;
  "Do not imagine that any service is more welcome to the king."
Straightaway, the Acerran being in haste, winds and oars
  brought Augusta to you, Parthenope.

had ordered Constance's murder. Perhaps we are to assume that it was not yet clear to the crafty Matthew that her death would serve Tancred (or Matthew himself) better than her continued life as a prisoner and hostage. If, however, the time came when it did, it would be easier to dispose of her if she were half-forgotten, living in an isolated prison. No other sources record that Constance was sent to prison at Naples, and Henry VI's biographer Toeche, in his *Kaiser Heinrich VI* (315–16), doubts that it happened. It is, however, hard to see why Pietro would invent the incident.

(S 68–69; KS 157)

126r   *Imprisonment of Constance at the Castle of Salvatore at Naples, through the will of Matthew of Ajello.* Illustrates ll. 925–964 on fol. 125v.

· · · ·

Scribit bigamus sacerdos ad Alierno Neapolitano ut imperatricem in castro Salvatoris ad mare bene custodiat.	1.	The bigamous priest writes to Aligerno the Neapolitan that he should guard the empress well in the castle of Salvatore at the sea.
Uxor Tancredi.	2.	Wife of Tancred.
Castrum Salvatoris ad mare.	3.	Castle of Salvatore at the sea.
Imperatrix.	4.	Empress.

Commentary and Notes [126r]: At the top of the page Matthew, sitting on a folding stool, dictates instructions concerning Constance to a notary, while Sibylla, her back to them, wearing her crown, sits musing. Below, the castle of San Salvatore is shown, on a hill, surrounded by a sea filled with fish. Constance sits there with one attendant whose hands are covered by her sleeves, in an attitude suggesting grief and sympathy.

(S 137; KS 158)

---

3.   *Castrum Salvatoris ad mare.* Kölzer ("Bildkommentar," 159) suggests that the artist had observed this castle himself.

126v <(Rota) Particula XXXII: Scelera bigami>

Sic scelus eructat, scelerum sic fumat abyssus,	965
Thuraque mortiferi sulfuris olla vomit;	966
Sic vetus exalat fumum putredinis antrum,	967
Effundit que vix texta venena capit.	968
O Sodomea lues, o Gomorrea propago,	969
Vixeris urbanis morsque ruina tuis.	970
Vas, va! peccati, veteris vetus amfora fraudis,	971
Fons odiique nephas, exciciale chaos,	972
Templum Luciferi, qui noctem Lucifer odit,	973
Qui, quanto voluit celsior esse, ruit.	974
Duxeris unde genus, gens a me nulla requirat,	975
Nam Cartago tuos dirruta misit avos;	976
Paupere lintheolo tecti venere Salernum,	977
Quorum pauperies quid nisi flere fuit?	978
Quos utinam nunquam vidissent litora nostra!	979
Ex hiis nature non quereretur opus,	980
Officium quorum, nature crimen et hostis,	981
Femineas ceca polluit arte genas.	982
Exultans odiis contraria pacis amasti,	983
Ecclesie stimulus seu rationis honus;	984
Iusticiam viduis, viso non ere, negasti,	985
Multotiens sociis causaque litis eras.	986
Primicias odii pro regno sepe litasti,	987
Unde queri poterant secula, solus eras.	988
Te sinus Ecclesie contra decreta recepit;	989
Peccati bigamum non decet ara Dei.	990
Te prece vel precio, sanctissime papa, fefellit.	991
Nescio quo pacto tanta licere viro,	992
Ut bigami scelerata manus tractaret in ara,	993
Cui Deus eterno se dedit esse parem.	994
Sepe laboranti cum nil succurrere posset,	995
Humano tepuit sanguine gutta pedum.	996
Ut Paris exussit Troiam fataliter ustam,	997
Ut Sodomos misere mersit abusa Venus,	998
Urbs ita Lernina tibi credens, false sacerdos,	999
Mortis in obprobrium per tua facta ruet.	1000
Quem, miser, extollis? Qui ius usurpat et omen,	1001
Qui male consortes precipitando ruet?	1002
Nec tu, Parthenope, quod Cesar abinde recessit,	1003
Exultes; veniet fortior atque ferus.	1004

<(Rota) Section 32: The Bigamist's Wicked Deeds>

Thus he belches out the evil deed, thus the abyss of infamy smokes,
    Thus the jar vomits incense of death-bearing sulfur.
So the old cave exhales a steam of putridity;
    And poisons pour out which an earthen jar can scarcely contain.
O plague of Sodom, O offspring of Gomorrah,
    You will have lived for the death and ruin of your city.
Ugh! Vessel of sin, ancient flask of old fraud,
    Unspeakable spring of hatred, ruinous chaos,
Temple of Lucifer, Lucifer who hates the night;
    Who hurtles lower exactly as much as he wants to mount higher.
Where did you come from? Let no one try to find the place through me,
    For demolished Carthage sent forth your forefathers.
Clothed in meager short linen, they came to Salerno
    And what could they do in their poverty but weep?
Would that our shores had never seen them!
    Then the work of nature need not have mourned on their account,
Since their trade, a crime and insult to nature,
    Is to defile feminine cheeks through dark arts.
Exulting in hatred, you loved things against the peace,
    A goad to the Church or rather a burden to right reason.
You deny justice to widows when you see no bronze coins,
    And many times you have caused quarrels among allies.
You have often offered the first fruits of hatred for the realm,
    You have often been sole cause of your generation's complaints.
The Church received you in her bosom against the laws;
    Bigamy is a sin not fitting for the altar of God.
Most holy Pope, he beguiled you by prayer or by price.
    I do not know why so much is permitted to this man,
That the accursed hands of a bigamist should draw near the altar
    Which God through eternity makes equal to himself.
Often because nothing could ease his sufferings,
    Human blood cooled down his gouty feet.
As Paris burned Troy most fatally with fire,
    As the wronged Venus wretchedly drowned the people of Sodom,
So the Lernine city, trusting you, false priest,
    Through your deeds will hurtle to a disgraceful death.
What man do you raise up, wretch, who usurps the law and auspices,
    And who wickedly destroys his comrades, by throwing them to ruin?
And do not exult, Parthenope, that Caesar has gone away;
    He shall return very strong and fierce.

Ut Iovis ad predam, quanto volat altius, ales   1005
   Descendens tanto fortius ungue ferit;   1006
Non aliter Cesar mundi descendet ab ala,   1007
   Trux veniet tandem, qui fuit ante pius.   1008

Commentary and Notes [126v]: Matthew's role in sending Constance to San Salvatore marks the high point of Matthew's wickedness; it is the last we will hear of him as a living man. Pietro denounces Matthew and his family for his base origin and predicts that they will bring about the destruction of their city. He also denounces Matthew's "bigamy" and reproaches the pope for letting him become a priest. He ends with the warning that the emperor will return, angrier than before. Kölzer's commentary (162) takes issue with this characterization of Matthew as coming from a poor family, but the evidence he cites merely shows that Matthew and his family were, by this time, quite powerful (one son an arch-

As with Jove's eagle, the higher he flies, the more violently
    His talons wound, when he descends upon the prey.
Not otherwise the world's Caesar descends on wing;
    And in the end he will come savagely, who was merciful before.

bishop, another a count). Siragusa mentions (70, n. 2) that he has found no other source confirming Pietro's claim that Matthew's family originally came from North Africa, but adds that his family certainly did not have "a title of nobility" before Matthew's son Richard was made count of Ajello.

(S 70–71; KS 161)

999: Urbs . . . Lernina . . . Siragusa writes (71 n. 4), "'Urbs Lernina' is Salerno, named by the last syllables: '[Sa]Lernina,' and perhaps with an intentional allusion to the Hydra of Lerna."

127r *Matthew of Ajello in the act of embracing his two wives. The same, as he bathes his feet in the blood of a child as a cure for podagra.* Illustrates ll. 965–1008 on fol. 126v.

• • • •

Matheus cancellarius.	1.	Matthew the chancellor.
Prima uxor — Secunda uxor.	2.	First wife — Second wife.
Quocienscumque bigamus dolorem podagricum paciebatur, interfectis pueris pedes suos in sanguine eorum mittebat.	3.	As many times as the bigamist would suffer from gout, he would have children killed and put his feet into their blood.

Commentary and Notes [127r]: At the top, Matthew embraces his two wives (Caps. 1 and 2). Beneath (Cap. 3), he dips his feet in a basin into which has drained the blood of a decapitated child, the body still held by a young servant in a knee-length tunic. The child, as Kölzer's commentary (162) points out, seems to be Moorish. It has already been pointed out (see notes on 100r) that Matthew only had one wife living at a time, and of course there is no reliable evidence that he bathed in the blood of murdered children. Apparently these illustrations summarize Matthew's character and career from Pietro's point of view. It is the last time we will see him depicted. Kölzer's commentary states that Matthew died on 21 July 1193.

(S 137; KS 162)

127v <(Rota) Particula XXXIII: Epistula Celestini et liberatio Constancie>

Temporis elapsu spacioque vagante dierum	1009
A Celestino littera missa fuit:	1010
"Hec, Tancrede, tibi mando per numina celi,	1011
"Et nisi quod iubeo feceris, hostis ero.	1012
"Unde tibi tantus furor aut dementia tanta,	1013
"In iubar illicitas solis inire manus?	1014
"Unde tibi tante superest audatia mentis?	1015
"Ausus es Experiam detinuisse diem?	1016
"Iam tumet unda maris, iam fervet et ira leonis,	1017
"Iam trepidant montes, iam mea cimba timet,	1018
"Iam fera concuciunt sine lege tonitrua mundum,	1019
"Iam polus ignescit, ethera fulgur agit.	1020
"Quam geris inclusam trans Alpes cornua fundit,	1021
"Sollicitans solem regia luna suum.	1022
"Quis tibi iura dedit? Tribuit quis vincula Petri?	1023
"Ius sine iure tenes connubiale viro.	1024
"An tibi sceptra parum regni sumsisse videtur?	1025
"Infelix, honeri cur superaddis honus?	1026
"Sepius in stragem ruit incidentis et icta	1027
"Allidens longe concutit arbor humum.	1028
"Quem gerit accintus gladiator leditur ense,	1029
"Qui prius incepit verbera, plus doluit.	1030
"Et tibi continget Saladin quod contigit olim,	1031
"Cuius Hierusalem lancea vicit humum.	1032
"Crux ubi capta fuit, qua certa redemptio nostra est,	1033
"Movit in actorem secula preda suum.	1034
"Sic in te tua preda manus converterit omnes	1035
"Et compensabit libera preda vices.	1036
"Hiis igitur lectis, tibi mitto, remitte maritam,	1037
"Ipsa suum poterit pacificare virum."	1038
Hec ubi perlegit Tancredus, ut unda movetur,	1039
Ut quatitur tumidis parvula puppis aquis.	1040
Ignorans quid agat, dominam dimittere mundi	1041
Fluctuat et contra iussa tenere timet,	1042
Ut citus inveniens nemorum diversa viarum	1043
Compita, quo tendat tramite nescit homo.	1044
Tandem consilium deliberat anxius in se:	1045
Quam tenet inclusam tristis abire iubet.	1046

<(Rota) Section 33: Letter of Celestine, and the Liberation of Constance>

Some time and a wandering space of days had gone by
 When a letter was sent by Celestine.
"This, Tancred, I send to you by the decrees of heaven,
 "And unless you do what I command, I will be your enemy.
"Whence came your madness or your frenzy,
 "To take the radiance of the sun into your law-breaking hands?
"How can you still think such rash thoughts?
 "Have you dared to imprison the Hesperian day?
"Now the waves of the sea swell, now the wrath of the lion boils,
 "Now the mountains tremble, now my little ship is fearful;
"Now wild thunders, without law, strike the world.
 "Now the vault of heaven catches fire, and lightning vexes the aether.
"She, the royal moon whom you hold in prison, pours out her powers
 "Beyond the Alps, seeking her sun.
"Who gave you these rights? Who gave you the chains of Peter?
 "You lawlessly withhold a husband's marriage rights.
"Did it seem a small thing to you to take up the scepters of the realm?
 "Unhappy man, why do you add trouble to trouble?
"Often a stricken tree, sliding a long way, falls to the ruin
 "Of the one who cut it, and crushes him to the earth.
"The girded gladiator is wounded by the sword he wields;
 "He suffers more if he began the fight.
"What will come upon you formerly came upon Saladin
 "Whose lance conquered the soil of Jerusalem.
"The cross captured there, by which our redemption is certain,
 "As booty moved all the world against the doer of the deed.
"Thus your booty turns all hands against you,
 "And liberated, that captive will lessen your plight.
"When you have read these things which I dispatch, send back the wife;
 "She will be able to pacify her husband."
Having read all this through, Tancred vacillates,
 Driven like a little boat, battered in swollen waters.
Puzzled by what to do, he shrinks from releasing the world's mistress
 But fears to hold her despite these commands.
As if, in a forest, he has suddenly come upon a crossroad where paths diverge,
 The man does not know which trail to follow.
But finally the anxious man resolves within himself:
 Gloomily he orders his prisoner to depart.

Commentary and Notes [127v]: Pope Celestine writes a letter rebuking Tancred for holding Constance captive. He describes her as "the radiance of the sun" and "the Hesperian day," whose imprisonment creates cosmic disturbances. "Hesperius" means "western." Both Sicily and Spain were described that way by poets, since both were west of Troy and Greece, the perspective of much epic poetry. (Becht-Jördens translates the word to mean "Italian.") Building on another image of light, Celestine also calls the "royal moon," desiring the company of "her sun" the emperor. Continuing to hold such a prize will bring worse consequences, like those which the famous Saladin experienced when he seized the True Cross. The True Cross reportedly was carried at the battle of Hattin in July 1187, when the armies of King Guy and the Crusader kingdom suffered a disastrous defeat at the hands of the famous Sultan Saladin. Jerusalem fell shortly afterwards. However, this victory and prize "turned the world" against Saladin and brought the Third Crusade upon him (see Introduction C.11). For all these reasons, Pope Celestine commands Tancred to release Constance, who will moderate her husband's anger. Upon receiving the pope's letter, Tancred wavers, but ultimately complies.

In this sequence, Pietro emphasizes Henry's power, the sacredness of the marital bond, and the love between the imperial couple. He also suggests that the pope's moral authority is squarely behind Henry and Constance. Nevertheless, the attentive reader will notice that the pope was never represented as denouncing Tancred as a usurper or commanding him to give up his claim to the kingdom.

In fact, Tancred had much diplomatic contact with the pope, who is generally thought to have favored his kingship. At this time, Tancred's release of Constance was one of several concessions he made to Celestine in return for the pope's official recognition of his status as king of Sicily through the Concordat of Gravina in the June of 1192, as Kölzer's commentary explains (166).

(S 72–73; KS 165)

128r *Constance is liberated through the intervention of Pope Celestine III. Her departure for Germany.* Illustrates ll. 1008–1046 on 127v.

. . . .

Quando dominus papa Celestinus misit Tancredo ut consortem Cesaris dimicteret.	1.	When the lord pope Celestine sent to Tancred that he should send away the consort of Caesar.
Cursor domini pape.	2.	Messenger of the lord pope.
Tancredus recipiens litteras apostoli[ci] dominam Romanorum et mundi liberat.	3.	Tancred, receiving the letters of the apostle, liberates the mistress of the Romans and the world.
Cursor d[omini] pape.	4.	Messenger of the lord pope.
Imperatrix.	5.	The empress.
A castro exiens Augusta versus Alemanniam pergit.	6.	Leaving the castle, Augusta goes toward Germany.
Tristis Tancredus	7.	Sad Tancred

Commentary and Notes [128r]: At the top, the mitered pope, holding his crook, hands a scroll to a messenger. In the middle, an enthroned Tancred, with a bird sitting on his crowned head, receives it. Bottom left, Constance rides away, sidesaddle, bearing a palm branch. Her attendant follows, also sidesaddle, bearing the orb. The enthroned Tancred is depicted once more, on the right, a bird still on his crowned head, facing the opposite way and looking discouraged. Explaining the remarkable fact that Constance's attendant holds the orb, Kölzer's commentary (166) states that it is some sort of mistake. On the other hand, it may represent the completeness of her triumph that she could entrust this part of the regalia to an underling. Although Pietro shows Constance riding away because of the pope's intervention, the story of her release is complicated.

(S 138; KS 166)

128v <(Rota) Particula XXXIV: Rex Anglie captus, liber absolvitur>

Cesaris ut fugeret leges, tuus, Anglia, princeps	1047
Turpis ad obsequium turpe minister erat.	1048
Quid prodest versare dapes, servire culine?	1049
Omnia que fiunt Cesar in orbe videt.	1050
Rex sub veste latens, male nam vestitus ut ospes,	1051
Captus defertur Cesaris ante pedes.	1052
Cesar cesareum vocat ad se more senatum,	1053
Conveniens regem talia questus ait:	1054
"Quis tibi posse dedit, nostrum saturate cruoris,	1055
"Nostros nocturna perdere fraude duces?	1056
"Parco tibi, iam liber eas in sanguinis haustum,	1057
"Nam tua Ierusalem dextra redemit humum.	1058
"Spectat adhuc certe reditus Trinacria vestros,	1059
"Que tibi sub falso munere preda fuit;	1060
"Nam fallis miserum sola formidine regem	1061
"Dissimulans bellum, iura sororis agens.	1062
"Te postquam vicit multo Tancredus in auro,	1063
"Ausus es in nostrum ius peribere fidem."	1064
Rex ita respondit, tollens ad sidera palmas:	1065
"A meritis," inquit, "collige digna, Deus.	1066
"O Deus omnividens, hominum qui cernis abyssum,	1067
"Qui mare, qui terras concutis, astra legis,	1068
"Quam bene respondes pacientibus ardua pro te!	1069
"Sic tuus emeruit miles ab hoste capi?"	1070
Hinc ait: "O Cesar, quod opus, quae causa, quis actus	1071
"Me nunc incusant? Rem modo causa ferat.	1072
"Sum reus? Auctor abest, nec adest; sed abesse necesse est;	1073
"Quisquis erit, vires regis et arma probet.	1074
"Salva pace tua, veniat qui pugnet, et instet	1075
"Obiectis, faciens ensis utrique fidem.	1076
"An pugnare meo solus cum Cesare veni?	1077
"Absit; in hac humili veste quis arma movet?	1078
"Et si cum domino mundi pugnare licebit,	1079
"Unde michi veniet miles et unde pedes?	1080
"O decus imperii, nec me sine iudice dampnes,	1081
"Nam tua iudicii crimine iura carent.	1082
"Me tibi committens, tuus oro mitius in me,	1083
"Quam meritum nostri postulet, ensis agat."	1084

<(Rota) Part 34: The King of England, Captured, is Allowed to Go Free.>

To flee from the laws of Caesar, your prince, England,
 Became base and performed base service.
What is the use of turning dishes, and serving in the kitchen?
 Caesar sees everything that happens in the world.
The king hidden beneath those garments, that ill-dressed stranger,
 Was captured and brought before Caesar's feet.
Caesar called the imperial senate, according to his custom,
 And facing the king, he made his complaint thus:
"What gave you the right, you who are drenched with blood of ours,
 "To destroy our commanders through ambushes by night?
"Shall I spare you? Yes, go free, even to drink blood!
 "After all, your right hand redeemed the soil of Jerusalem!
"And the three-cornered island is certainly eager to see you again,
 "After being your prey for the sake of deceitful bribes.
"For you beguiled that wretched king by terror alone,
 "Making a show of war to enforce your sister's rights.
"Then Tancred overcame you with a great deal of gold.
 "You dared let your loyalty to our right go to ruin."
The king responded thus, lifting his palms to the stars:
 "From among my merits, O God, accept what is worthy!
"O God, who sees all, who discerns the depths of men,
 "Who strikes the sea and earth and calls the stars to assemble,
"How well you respond to those suffering trials for your sake!
 "Did your knight deserve to be captured thus by an enemy?"
Then he added, "O Caesar, what work, what cause, what action
 "Do they bring against me now? At least let them make the case.
"Am I guilty? My accuser is absent, nor does he approach; but mortal
 necessity demands his absence.
 "Let someone, whoever it may be, come test my kingly strength and arms.
"Saving your peace, let a champion come to fight and press these charges,
 "So that one sword or the other will win belief.
"Now, did I come here alone to fight against my Caesar?
 "Perish the thought! Who would make war equipped as poorly as I am?
"And supposing it becomes lawful to fight with the lord of the world,
 "Where will my knights and foot soldiers come from?
"O ornament of the Empire, do not condemn me without a judge,
 "For no real case has yet been made against me.
"I commend myself to you and pray that your sword deal more kindly
 "With me than my deserving requires."

Flectitur hac humili prece, quem non mille talenta,   1085
   Nec summi potuit flectere carta patris.   1086
Imperio postquam iurans se subdidit, inquit: 1087
   "Vivat in eternum lux mea, liber eo."   1088

Commentary and Notes [128v]: The story of Richard the Lionheart relates to the situation of Joanna Plantagenet, the "English moon" (53), and Tancred's tactic of bribing away the friends and allies of Henry VI (355, 497). King Richard of England had, shortly after William II's death and Tancred's coronation, come to Sicily on his way to the crusade which he, like Barbarossa and like Philip Augustus of France, had sworn to pursue. Instead of sailing at once for the Holy Land, however, he alternated quarreling and being reconciled with his fellow crusader and with Tancred. His quarrel with Tancred concerned the lands, revenues, and honors owed to Joanna, widow of William II, by virtue of her marriage settlement. In the end, Tancred paid Richard a large sum of money to settle those claims, and Richard took Joanna away from Sicily with him. Besides this, Richard and Tancred promised each other mutual support and arranged a marriage between Arthur of Brittany, currently Richard's heir, and one of Tancred's daughters. All this was prejudicial to Henry's claims on Sicily. Henry VI's Welf antagonists were kinsmen of King Richard; see Introduction.

Because of his enmity with Philip Augustus of France, Richard tried to follow a secret route home. He suffered shipwreck near Aquileia and started across imperial lands in disguise, making for the territories of his Welf brother-in-law in Saxony. According to several sources, Richard disguised himself and performed menial tasks like cooking and serving at the table. Nevertheless, he was found out and brought to Henry VI. Henry summoned a council of the German princes, the Easter Court at Speyer in March 1193, where King Richard was permitted to appear and speak (see Gillingham, *Life and Times of Richard I*, 177–80).

Pietro, consciously using the terminology of Imperial Rome, calls the assembly a "Senate" (line 1053). As he tells it, the emperor speaks first, attacking the king with ironic words (1057–1058), implicitly thrusting aside the assumption (not directly stated) that Richard should be pardoned everything he has done simply because he is a crusader. Henry refers acidly to what Richard did not accomplish, the recovery of Jerusalem. Implied in this is a hint that he made an alliance with Saladin; hence his neglect to take Jerusalem. The poet William of Brittany, who quotes a line from the *Liber* in his own account of Richard's trial, has Henry openly accuse Richard of giving Saladin an easy peace in exchange for gifts (see Introduction). Pietro, however, emphasizes a question of murder, the implied victim being Conrad, marquis of Montferrat and king of Jerusalem.

[The emperor] was swayed by that humble prayer,
 Though the thousand talents and the Holy Father's letter could not sway him.
Later [the king] subjected himself to the emperor with an oath, saying,
 "Live eternally, my light. I go free."

Conrad, who had played a heroic part in preventing the capture of Tyre, gained the support of most crusaders and was married to the kingdom's heiress, Isabella, but Richard had refused to accept him as king, preferring his own vassal, Guy of Lusignan. Finally, as he was about to depart, he agreed to accept Conrad, but no sooner had he done so than Conrad was assassinated (28 April 1192). Apparently the deed was done by agents of the original Assassin, Rashid ed-Din Sinan of Basra, the famous "Old Man of the Mountain." But vehement rumors accused Richard I of complicity.

In the verses above, Richard denies the murder charge with great spirit and demands the right to trial by combat. He also denies the suggestion (line 1056) that he was in the process of making war on Henry when he was captured. (In William's poem, Richard denies committing "treason," and the accuser to whom he issues his challenge is, by implication, Philip Augustus himself.)

Richard is also accused of supporting Tancred (lines 1061–1064) because of the huge amount of money Tancred gave him (most of it ostensibly for Joanna's rights). On this point, he can only plead for leniency. This "humble plea," Pietro says, rather than the "thousand talents" or "the pope's letter" (lines 1085–1086), finally moves the emperor to release him. The money, of course, was paid, and the Pope wrote letters rebuking Henry VI for Richard's captivity. Pietro is saying that these things were not enough to induce the emperor to release Richard. The grateful Richard becomes Henry's vassal and departs singing his praises (February 1194). In this version of the events, Pietro affirms Henry's imperial claim to lordship over all Christian kings, and subtly defends the emperor's controversial conduct toward Richard. In William of Brittany's account, understandably different, Richard, after defending his conduct, asks Henry's pardon for mistakes he had committed and also asks Henry's pity on his homeland (*"parce patrie"*), being torn apart by the French king. He then points out that Henry, as a new monarch, is having similar troubles, and that he might need a great deal of money to establish himself, something Richard can help him with: "I will give you a thousand marks of silver, multiplied times a hundred" (*Mille dabo argenti marchas tibi centuplicates*). Richard also offers to do homage to Henry for his realm. After brief consideration, Henry responds, "Do as you have said and you shall go free" (*Sicut dixisti facias et liber abito*) (4.425).

(S 74–76; KS 169)

129r *Arrest, exculpation, and pardon of Richard the Lionhearted, returned from the crusade.* Illustrates ll 1046–1088 on fol. 128v.

• • • •

Illustris rex Anglie a Ierosolimis rediens captus presentatur Augusto.	1. The illustrious king of England, returning from Jerusalem, is presented as a captive to Augustus.
Rex Anglie de morte marcionis accusatur, quod abnegans, se ensiva manu excusaturum promittit.	2. The king of England is accused of the murder of the marquis, which denying, he promises to clear himself with a sword in his hand.
Tandem veniam petens liber absolvitur.	3. At last, seeking pardon, he is allowed to go free.

Commentary and Notes [129r]: At the top of the page, the disguised Richard is shown riding in a rustic hood and tunic with a quiver of arrows thrown over his back. Two armed knights with helmets, swords, and shields approach him on foot. On the lower level, he appears still wearing the rustic outfit, with a drawn sword. Cap. 2 indicates that he is denying the charge that he murdered the marquis, offering to prove his innocence in single combat. His crusader's cross is clearly visible on his shoulder. The emperor Henry VI faces him, enthroned, crowned, and holding a palm branch. Lower down, King Richard appears again. This time, an attendant holds the humble garments in which he was captured. Now wearing his crown, the king kisses the emperor's foot to show subjection.

(S 138; KS 171)

129v <(Rota) Particula XXXV: Quando Dipuldus aggressus est >

Interea Dipuldus ovans armenta capiscit;	1089
Virtutis sequitur gratia diva virum;	1090
Castra superba cremat, capit oppida, territat urbes	1091
Ad Tancridinam que rediere fidem.	1092
Sub pede montis adest uberrima villa Casini,	1093
Que nec pastori credere cauta fuit.	1094
Hanc ferus invadens Dipuldus ab aggere dextro,	1095
Dissipat instantes, ut leo magnus oves;	1096
Cuius ab agricolis circumdatus, a tribus horum	1097
In triplici cultro digladiatur equus;	1098
Stans pedes, ense pedes duros detruncat et armos,	1099
Se fore Dipuldum clamat et ense probat.	1100
Ut trepidant volucres Iovis in quas fulminat ales,	1101
Ut lepus algescit lapsus ab ore canis,	1102
Non aliter gens illa timet victoris ab ense,	1103
In Diopuldeo nomine victa cadit.	1104
Subditur imperio sacrati villula castri	1105
Et facit invitam dextra coacta fidem.	1106

¶

Idem post modicum paucis comitatus alumpnis,	1107
Exiit a castro, sortis agebat iter.	1108
Illo forte die propriam comes ibat in urbem,	1109
Ibat in adversum sorte latente virum.	1110
Ex hac Dipuldus, comes ex hac obvius ibat,	1111
Alter in alterius nescius ibat iter.	1112
Ventum est ad faciem, fit clamor vocis utrinque,	1113
Confractis sudibus tela reclusa micant.	1114
Hic ferit, ille ferit, cadit hic, super hunc stat et ille,	1115
Dentipotens comitem denique vicit aper.	1116
Sic Diopuldeus vir quisque suum ligat hostem	1117
Captivosque ferunt in sua castra viros.	1118

Commentary and Notes [129v]: This celebrates the heroic exploits of Diepold (first mentioned in line 607), brave, energetic, and (just now) favored by fortune. Epic

<(Rota) Section 35: When Diepold Attacked>

Meanwhile, Diepold, rejoicing, captures herds;
    Divine grace follows that man of strength;
He burns proud castles, captures towns, and terrifies cities
    Which were returning to the Tancredine faith.
At the foot of the mountain he came to the wealthy town of Cassino,
    Which was not instructed by its pastor's faith.
Diepold invades it fiercely from the ramparts with his right hand;
    He scatters those who stand against him, as a great lion scatters sheep.
He is surrounded by farmers, three of whom
    Run his horse through with triple blades.
Standing on foot, he hacks off feet and sinewy arms.
    He cries that he is Diepold and proves it with his sword.
As birds tremble when Jove's great eagle strikes like lightning,
    As a hare shivers, fallen from the jaws of the hound,
Not otherwise does that people fear the sword of the victor;
    In the name of Diepold they fall conquered.
The hamlet of the holy fortress submits to the empire,
    And, with compelled right hand, makes an unwilling pledge of faith.
¶
The same man, after a little, accompanied by a few followers
    Departed from the castle, following the path of fate.
On that day, by chance, the count was coming into his own city;
    He was going toward his adversary by the workings of hidden fate.
Diepold was coming one way, the count the other way toward him,
    Each ignorant that the other was following that road.
When they came face to face, voices clamored on both sides;
    Lances were broken, and uncovered spears gleamed.
This one wounded, that one wounded; this one fell, and that one stood over him,
    The boar, powerful in his tusks, defeated the count at last.
So each of Diepold's men bound his enemy
    And they led the captive men into their camps.

similes liken him to a lion, an eagle overcoming lesser birds, a hound seizing a hare, and a wild boar, as he gains control of the countryside.

(S 77–78; KS 173)

130r *Episode of the assault made on San Germano by Diepold of Vohberg.* Illustrates ll.
1088–1118 on fol. 129v.

• • • •

Mons Casinus	1.	Monte Cassino.

Quando Diopoldus ingrediens
  Sanctum Germanum, equum
  suum a tribus rusticis
  digladiatum ammisit et villam
  viriliter cepit.
	2.	When Diepold, entering San
		Germano, lost his horse,
		which three rustics had stabbed
		with swords, and manfully took
		the city.

Commentary and Notes [130r]: These illustrations show developing action. Diepold
enters from the right, riding a horse, which three foot soldiers attack with swords.
Further to the left, Diepold is still fighting, while the bleeding horse lies at the
bottom of the page. The boar on Diepold's helm and shield in the first picture,
and on his shield in the second picture, makes it clear that the boar is his device.
Hence, the boar seen on the lower left, biting the bird (heron or stork), is usu-
ally seen by commentators as an allegorical representation of Diepold's cause.
However, there is no consensus about what the bird represents. Since Diepold is
apparently fighting the Count of Acerra, it would be logical if the bird were his
device, but Count Richard's device, as we have seen, seems to be a lion. Siragusa
(see below) suggests that the bird stands for the Tancredine cause in general. On
the other hand, perhaps it is the ensign of the count who, according to Pietro, is
captured at this time (see notes on line 1109).

(S 139; KS 174)

130v EXPLICIT LIBER PRIMUS
INCIPIT LIBER SECUNDUS <(Rota) Particula XXXVI: Stolium et
exercitum imperator fieri iubet>

Ut pius armipotens fugat omnem letus eclipsim,	1119
Reddit et Experios in sua iussa deos.	1120
Imperat hinc puppes animosus ubique parari;	1121
Nec mora, que fiunt, vix capit unda rates.	1122
Marchio quinque minus transmisit mille carinas;	1123
Austrinus totidem miserat octo minus;	1124
Turineus centum septem minus equore classes	1125
Annumerat; Scavus non minus equor arat;	1126
Bavuarus eversat centeno remige pontum;	1127
Alsaticusque pari remige spumat aquas;	1128
Ter quater octo rates portantes agmen equorum	1129
Belgicus; et totidem linthea Saxo tulit;	1130
Mille rates ter quinque minus Pomeranicus armat;	1131
Flandicus equoreas sulcat amicus aquas;	1132
Sex decies Ligur ventis dedit ampla secundis	1133
Vela; set Olsaticus per freta longa volat.	1134
Mille viros etate pares Burgundia mittit;	1135
Mittit victrices Tuscia mille manus;	1136
Mille quidem clipeos, Iovis arma, Suevia gestat;	1137
Mille faretratos magna Boema viros;	1138
Mille coruscantes mittit Lothoringia cristas;	1139
Mittit et ignivomas Anglia mille manus;	1140
Mille Polona viros nitidis presentat in armis;	1141
Francia mille boum bellica terga tulit;	1142
Mittit silvicole Brabantia tela Diane;	1143
Balistas lectos Frisia mittit humus.	1144
Bis duodena ducum superum sol regna vocavit;	1145
Per mare, per terras numina Cesar habet.	1146
Letus in Apuliam properat, primoque Salernum	1147
Appetit, urbs merito depopulanda suo.	1148
Vulneris elapsi memor est quandoque cicatrix;	1149
Qui spuit in celum polluit ora sui.	1150

Commentary and Notes [130v]: Building up for an exciting climax in which Henry
returns and conquers where he lost the first time, Pietro reviews Henry's mighty

HERE ENDS THE FIRST BOOK.
THE SECOND BOOK BEGINS
<(Rota) Section 36: The Emperor Commands the Fleet and Army to Assemble.>

Since the pious one, mighty in arms, escapes happy from every eclipse,
    He returns, and even the Hesperian gods are within his laws.
The courageous one now commands ships to be prepared everywhere.
    Nor was there delay; when they are ready, the sea hardly contains them.
The March sent five less than a thousand keels;
    Austrians sent eight less than the same number.
The Turinese counted out a hundred less seven fleets for the sea,
    Slavonia plowed the sea no less.
Bavaria stirred up the sea with a hundred oared ships;
    As many Alsatian oarsmen foamed the waters;
Belgium sent three times four times eight ships, bearing a troop of
    Horses, and Saxony as many sails.
The Pomeranians armed a thousand ships, less fifteen.
    Friendly ships of Flanders plowed the smooth waters.
Liguria gave sixty with full sails to the favoring winds;
    And the vessels of Holstein flew a long way along the straits.
Burgundy sent a thousand likely men in the flower of their years;
    Tuscany sent a thousand victorious hands.
A thousand Swabians indeed bear shields, arms of Jove;
    Great Bohemia sends a thousand men armed with quivers.
Lotharingia sends a thousand shining crests;
    Even England sends a thousand fire-breathing warriors.
Poland presents a thousand men in shining arms;
    France sends a thousand warlike backs of oxen;
Brabant sends arrows of the forest-dwelling Diana;
    Frisia sends choice ballistas to the land.
The sun calls to the realms the twice-twelve heavenly commanders:
    Caesar has the divine will with him on land and sea.
Gladly he hastens into Apulia, and first he assails Salerno,
    The city which must be unpeopled for its reward.
There is memory of a past wound whenever there is a scar;
    Whoever spits at heaven pollutes his own face.

army and the contributions of various princes and cities. All this power is bearing
down on Salerno to punish the city for its treachery.

(S 79–81; KS 177)

131r *Emperor's army and fleet for the conquest of the kingdom of Sicily.* Illustrates ll. 1119–1150, fol. 130v.

· · · ·

Potentissimus Henricus Imperator et stolium et exercitum fieri iubet.	1.	The most powerful emperor Henry commands his fleet and army to assemble.
Marchisius senescalcus.	2.	Markward the seneschal.
Boemii.	3.	Bohemians.
Bavuerienses.	4.	Bavarians.

Commentary and Notes [131r]: The emperor, crowned and enthroned, appears at the top of the page, with ships on the left and armed men on the right. Five ships appear in a vertical column, and the occupant of the one on top, as the caption indicates, is the Seneschal Markward, who commands the fleet. Markward holds a sword in his hand and carries a shield bearing a swan or cygnet (see Siragusa's note below). On the left side is a vertical column of three groups of armed men. At the top are knights with spears, helmets, armor, and shields. The second group, Bohemians, carry bows and quivers. The third group, Bavarians, carry crossbows (ballistas). As Kölzer points out in his commentary (178), there is no attempt in either the verse or the illustration to portray Henry VI's entire army as it was, nor do the pictures interpret the words with complete literalness. For example, the Bavarians, who have crossbows in the picture, are given ships in the verses. Pietro only strives to give an impression of the power of Henry's army and the variety of forces he had under his command.

(S 139; KS 178)

131v   <(Rota) Particula XXXVII: Loquucio archilevite ad cives Salerni>

Haud procul armipotens; venit archilevita Salernum,   1151
   Cum quo, tui nomen, Guarna, Philippus erat.   1152
Sic ait: "O cives, ego sum, qui multa laborum   1153
   "Pondera portavi, multa timenda tuli;   1154
"Nunc redeo salvare meam, si creditis, urbem;   1155
   "Credite concivi, credite, vera loquor;   1156
"A domino factum est, pro vobis exul ut irem;   1157
   "Ioseph nunc vobis pacifer alter ero.   1158
"Peccastis graviter; peccatum noscite vestrum,   1159
   "Nam mens fessa sibi grande relaxat honus.   1160
"Iam prope Cesar adest, iam Cesaris arma coruscant,   1161
   "Iam vexilla micant, iam sua signa tonant;   1162
"Mittite de vestris qui dicant: Reddimus urbem;   1163
   "Subiacet imperio phisica terra tuo;   1164
"Parce tuis servis, non pena, set nece dignis;   1165
   "Que poterit nostrum pena piare scelus?   1166
"Ad veniam, credo, flectetur more Tonantis,   1167
   "Vobiscum faciens absque rigore pium.   1168
"Ut Nazarenus Deus a Patre natus in orbem   1169
   "Venit in umano tegmine factus homo,   1170
"Ipse quidem tota cum maiestate futurus   1171
   "Pro meritis iudex omne piabit opus,   1172
"Sic meus armipotens primo pius atque benignus   1173
   "Nos adiit, sed nunc ut grave fulmen adest.   1174
"Iam non multa loquar, quia iam Nuceria sentit   1175
   "Que loquor; urbs vestra mane videbit idem."   1176

Commentary and Notes [131v]: Returning from his exile in the company of Philip Guarna, the archdeacon Aldrisio warns the Salernitans of their peril at the emperor's impending attack. In lines 1157–1158, he presents himself as a second Joseph, not blaming his fellow-citizens for his misfortunes, but attributing to God's benevolent providence his sufferings on their behalf and offering to make peace between them and the emperor. This is an allusion to Genesis 45:5, where Joseph, son of Israel, refuses to blame his brothers for selling him into slavery, asserting instead that God arranged his present prosperous circumstances for the benefit of all. Henry will be inclined to mercy if they approach him before he reaches the city, admit that they have done wrong, and submit to his authority. He reminds them of their special status, as "city of physicians" (lines 1164) because

<(Rota) Section 37: Speech of the Archdeacon to the Citizens of Salerno.>

The powerful-in-armies was not far off; the archdeacon of Salerno came,
    And with him was Philip, one of your family, O Guarna.
He spoke thus: "O citizens, I have carried the burdens of
    "Many troublesome matters and undertaken many fearful things.
"Now I have come back to save my city, if you trust me.
    "Trust your fellow citizen; trust me, for I speak the truth.
"That I went into exile for you was the Lord's doing;
    "Now I will be a peacemaker for you, a second Joseph.
"You have sinned very gravely; acknowledge your sin,
    "For a weary mind confessed lessens a great weight for itself.
"Now Caesar is near, now Caesar's weapons gleam,
    "Now his banners shine, now his trumpet calls resound.
"Send messengers from among you to say, 'We give back the city;
    "The land of the physicians submits to your authority.
"'Pardon your servants, worthy not merely of punishment but of death;
    "'What penalty could expiate our wicked deed?'
"I believe he will soften and grant pardon, as is this Thunderer's custom,
    "And deal with you in mercy, not with severity.
"As the Nazarene God came from the Father and was born into the world
    "In human vesture made man,
"And will come again himself in majesty, a Judge,
    "To purge each work according to its worth,
"In the same way my armipotent one came to us,
    "Compassionate at first, and kind. But now he comes
"Like a heavy thunderbolt. From now on, I will not speak much, since Nocera
    "Already feels what I speak of. Your city will see the same tomorrow."

of their famous medical school. He likens the emperor's two expeditions to the two comings of Christ: the first time, as a humble infant and teacher, the second time as a judge and avenger. In this context, his epithet, "this Thunderer"(1167), applied to Henry VI, evokes the idea of the "deified" Roman emperors, the classical Jove or Jupiter, and the Christian God, all at the same time. Aldrisio ends with an allusion to the fate of Nocera and warns the Salernitans that they will soon face the same fate. These events apparently are taking place in the summer of 1194; according to Jamison (*Admiral Eugenius*, 114) Naples and its surrounding territories had surrendered to Henry VI in late August of that year. (Missing portions of the manuscript as well as fragmentary information about the events make it hard to assess the impact of this scene precisely.)

(S 82–83; KS 181)

xlr

The illustrations corresponding to the verses above (1151–1176) are missing from the manuscript, apparently lost before *Liber ad Honorem Augusti* was trimmed to be bound with its companions in the Bern Codex (see Introduction B.2). However, a fragment of this page apparently remains, now designated 131a in the Codex (see KS 262) and shows the beginning of a drawing of fortifications. One may speculate that the complete drawing might also have shown the Archdeacon Aldrisio, with Philip Guarna at his side, exhorting the citizens of Salerno. Perhaps they would also have shown pictures of the sack of Nocera. Since we know that Tancred was dead by this time, we may suppose that the matter could have been alluded to in this page as well.

xlv [PARTICULA XXXVIII] Lost verses, if present would be Section 38. Salerno Responds.]

(The verso of FOL. XIR presumably contained the text corresponding to the illustrations on fol. 132r below.)

This verse page, presumably the verso of (Fol. X1r) above, and the subject matter for the illustration on Fol. 132r, was apparently lost before *Liber ad Honorem Augusti* was bound with its companions in the Bern Codex. The verses should have told the outcome of Aldrisio's speech. Either the citizens rejected his words and sealed their doom, or attempted to take his advice and won some palliation. The former is more likely since the assault on the city seems to be in progress on the following illustration page, which was intended to accompany these missing verses. Contemporary sources give a grim enough account of Salerno's fate. Siragusa (81, n. 1) indicates that various sources, interpreted correctly, say that the city fell on 17 September, 1194. Among other chronicles, he quotes the account of the Annales Casinenses for that year (p. 317): "The Emperor captured Salerno by force, and in punishment for his injuries, he condemned some to the sword, some to prison, and not a few to exile, their property being confiscated and given to the army."

132r *The Emperor's assault on Salerno.* The verses illustrated by these pictures are completely missing.

Populus Salerni.	1.	People of Salerno.
Imperiale vexillum.	2.	Imperial standard.
Supellex.	3.	Household goods.
Imperator.	4.	Emperor.

Commentary and Notes [132r]: Walls and towers of a city are shown. On the left, two bearded men are in conversation, apparently about the city; Kölzer ("Bildkommentar," 182) says that one of them represents the Archdeacon Aldrisio, addressing his fellow citizens. However, the faded miniature does not clearly show either man tonsured, as Aldrisio was in fol. 112r, identified as "archdeacon" in caps. 2 and 6. In the central part of the city a cluster of women and children stand, anxious. Some of the women hold children in their arms; slightly larger children stand at the edge of the group, watching the action on the walls. Armored men with helms, swords, and shields stand on the walls. One shield-bearer holds a stone-slinger. In a sort of x-ray vision, men with bags over their shoulders containing their possessions are seen running inside the buildings in the foreground. Below, before the city walls, the crowned emperor rides with banners and armed knights. Immediately in front of Henry is a knight whose shield device is a boar; this is presumably Diepold of Schweinspeunt.

(S 140; KS 182)

132v <(Rota) Particula XXXVIII: Gesta Dipuldi>

Interea Siculis solo terrore subactis,   1177
    Dux ratis auguste Cesaris urget iter;   1178
Ut properet scribit, quia iam Trinicria victa est,   1179
    Et puppes, profugo rege, redire rogant.   1180
Iam satur a misere spoliis exercitus urbis,   1181
    Fastidit victa victor in urbe moras.   1182
Mane dato signo, tunc Calandrinus in alto   1183
    Milicie socium circuit agmen equo;   1184
Imperat ut properent; tutum est properare Panormum.   1185
    Nec mora, Teutonici iussa iubentis agunt.   1186
Est data Dipuldo renovandi cura Salerni,   1187
    Nec non totius tradita iura soli.   1188
Vir pure fidei, vir magni nominis, omnis   1189
    Milicie titulus, imperiale decus,   1190
Quem nec promissum numerosi ponderis aurum   1191
    Movit, nec potuit sollicitare timor,   1192
Hostibus in mediis, quamplurima castra subegit;   1193
    Egregius, alacer vicit in ense viros;   1194
Cuius virtutis preconia vidit Aquinum,   1195
    Quo vicit victor milia quinque virum.   1196
Vera loquar, falsumque nichil mea Musa notabit,   1197
    Nec mea Romanas fistula fallet aves.   1198
Quodam forte die veniens Dipuldus ab Archi,   1199
    Colligit in multos fulmifer arva sinus;   1200
Innumeras predatur oves, capit agmen equorum,   1201
    Agricolas multos et iuga mille boum,   1202
Que, venale genus factum vicepastor, agebat: 1203
    Heu heu, dux prede vile lupanar erat!   1204
Cum victor tandem castrum saturatus adiret,   1205
    Spectat in adversum milia quinque viros,   1206
Qui predam certare parant; stringuntur in arma,   1207
    Et tamen expositos Guido retardat equos.   1208
Tunc Dipuldus ait: "Michi sors quam sera videris!   1209
    "Hoc mens, hoc animus, hoc mea vota petunt.   1210
"Me probet esse virum contra quicunque coruscat."   1211
    Ex hinc ad socios talia verba dedit: 1212
"Nec vos aspectus numerosi terreat hostis,   1213
    "Femineos tellus parturit ista viros;   1214
"Ad speculum natos effeminat umbra quietis,   1215
    "Quos alit in teneris dulce cubile rosis.   1216

<(Rota) Section 38: The Deeds of Diepold>

Meanwhile, the Sicilians were subdued by terror alone:
  The commander of the imperial fleet urges Caesar on the way;
He writes that he should hasten, for Trinacria is conquered now,
  And since the king has fled, the ships request permission to return.
Now the army is stuffed with the plunder from the wretched city,
  And the victor scorns delays in the conquered city.
In the morning the sign is given; then Calandrinus, on a high horse,
  With a troop of allies patrolls the surrounding countryside.
He commands that they should hasten; it is safe to hasten to Palermo.
  Without delay, the Germans carry out the commands of the commander.
Diepold was given charge of rebuilding Salerno, and
  Indeed the rule of the whole region was given to him.
He is a man of pure faith, a man of great name, with every
  Honor among soldiers, an imperial ornament,
Whom the promise of a great weight of gold cannot move,
  Nor could fear trouble him.
In the midst of enemies, he subdued many castles;
  Powerful and swift, he conquered men with his sword.
Aquino saw proclamation of his courage,
  Where the victor conquered five thousand men.
I shall speak the truth; my Muse does not set down anything false,
  Nor does my pipe cheat the Roman birds.
On a certain day, by chance, Diepold went forth from Rocca D'Arce;
  The lightning-bearer harvests the fields in many hidden pockets;
Innumerable sheep are taken and he captures a herd of horses,
  Many peasants and a thousand yoked pairs of oxen,
Which a hireling tribe were driving as though they were shepherds,
  (Alas, alas, common whores had charge of the spoil!)
When at last the victor, sated, approaches his castle,
  He sees coming against him five thousand men,
Who prepare to contend for the spoil; they draw together in arms,
  And indeed Guido slows down the horses in the front.
Then Diepold says, "My fate, how late you appear!
  "My mind, my spirit, my desires seek this very thing!
"I will prove myself a man against anyone who glitters in armor."
  Thereupon he spoke these words to his companions:
"Do not be terrified at the sight of these many enemies;
  "For this land gives birth to effeminate men;
"Their dreamy reflection in the mirror make women of the boys
  "And sweet bedchambers bring them up amid tender roses.

"Hii Tancridini, sumus et nos imperiales,   1217
    "Hii pecudes, sed nos dicimur esse sues.   1218
"Sus agat in pecudes et eas et vellera portet;   1219
    "Audaces sequitur sors bona sepe viros."   1220
Hactenus innixus clipeo, commissus et aste,   1221
    Eum ferit eversos, terga ferire pudet;   1222
Mille viros flexa procer unus inebriat asta   1223
    Et ligat et tondit mille vir unus oves;   1224
Nec tracto quod neapolim devicit inhermis,   1225
    Quod loquor, expertum Terra Laboris habet.   1226

Commentary and Notes [132v]: The imperial army is urged to hasten on to Palermo, because the way is clear. The king who has fled (line 1180) is not Tancred but his young son, William III, who was crowned king some time after Tancred died, 20 February 1194. William III's age is not known, but he was clearly a minor. The *Calandrinus* who leads the army from Salerno is Henry of Kalden, one of the emperor's commanders, who may have been his tutor in his youth. The poet, having sent the imperial army on its way, mentions that Diepold has been placed in command in conquered Salerno, and reviews (lines 1187–1224) some adventures he had previously in the region of Aquino, a city between Monte Cassino and Ceprano, close to the border of the papal states. They happened, apparently, during the time when Henry VI had withdrawn to Germany and his German commanders were reduced to living off the land by plundering hostile territories. Diepold, returning to his stronghold at Rocca D'Arce after one such plundering mission, was interrupted by a certain Guido of Castelvecchio (identified in cap. 3

"They are Tancredines and we are Imperials,
  "They are sheep and we are called swine.
"Let the swine go against the sheep, and carry them off along with their wool.
  "Good fortune often follows bold men."
So saying, he relied on his shield and went to battle with his spear.
  When he struck the overthrown, he scrupled to strike at backs.
One champion with bent spear made drunk a thousand men,
  And one man bound and sheared a thousand sheep.
Nor do I discuss the way, unarmed, he subdued Naples.
  What I tell of, Terra Laboris experienced directly.

of the associated drawing), acting on behalf of the Tancredines, to deprive him of the booty. Diepold had help from some local inhabitants, apparently prostitutes who assist in driving and guarding the captive flocks and people; the poet finds rough humor in this (line 1204). Diepold bravely exhorts his men, mentioning Fortune's proverbial favoritism for daring men, perhaps an allusion to Virgil's *Aeneid* 10.283, "audentis fortuna iuvat," though there, ironically, the sentiment is uttered by Turnus, who will ultimately lose. Diepold and his men, on the other hand, outnumbered though they are, triumph once more over their enemies.

(S 84–86; KS 185)

1209 *quam*. S: *qua*. pre-S: *qua*. KS: *quam*. De Rosa: *quam*. Codex: *qua*.
  [PARTICULA XXXIX] with missing sections counted, perhaps Section 39: Diepold and Guido.

133r *The flight of Guido of Castelvecchio, who had tried to take charge of the spoil made by Diepold in his foray.* Illustrates verses 1177–1226, fol. 132v.

. . . .

Diopuldus.	1.	Diepold
Meretrices ducunt predam.	2.	Prostitutes bring the spoil..
Guido de Castello veteri volens predam eripere in fugam versus est.	3.	Guy of Castelvecchio, wishing to steal the spoil, is turned in flight.
Diopuldus.	4.	Diepold.

Commentary and Notes [133r]: At the top on the left, there is a rather blurry picture of an armed, helmeted Diepold, carrying a pennon with a banner and a shield marked with a boar. On the right, three grim and tough-looking women with clubs stand guard over two meager men who may have their hands bound. Behind them are horses, cattle, and sheep. Below the middle of the page, there are two lines of armed horsemen, one fleeing from the other. The caption "Diopuld" appears above the victorious group, and Diepold himself bears his device, the boar, not only on his shield but also on his horse's trappings, shoulder and haunches. At the bottom of the page one man, presumably from Guido's side, lies dead or wounded. Another, wounded, is falling from his horse.

(S 140; KS 186)

133v <(Rota) Particula XXXIX: Legatio Panormi>

Interea Cesar, superato Calabre toto,	1227
Venit ad insanas indubitanter aquas;	1228
Classibus expositis, furiosas transfretet undas.	1229
Post hec Messane paulo moratus, abit;	1230
Fabariam veniens, socerum miratus et illam,	1231
Delectans animos nobile laudat opus.	1232
Legati quem preveniunt ex urbe Panormi,	1233
Debita commisse verba salutis agunt;	1234
Exponunt animos populi, mentesque serenas,	1235
Affectum iuvenum, propositumque senum;	1236
Ore ferunt uno: "Tu sol, tu lumen in orbe,	1237
"Tu spectata dies qui sine nocte venis,	1238
"Tu regni tenebras armata luce fugabis,	1239
"Discutiens lites copia pacis eris,	1240
"Qui mundum sub pace ligas, qui bella coherces,	1241
"Inclita qui regum sub pede colla teris.	1242
"Quis rex, quis princeps, quis dux tua iussa recusat?	1243
"Quis valet armato Cesare bella pati?	1244
"Nam servire tibi mundo regnare videtur;	1245
"Maior in hoc magno Cesare Cesar eris.	1246
"Hen profugus nostram dimisit regulus urbem,	1247
"Radicem colubri Caltabelottus alit."	1248
Cesar ubi tante fidei legata recepit,	1249
Pace triumphali mandat in urbe frui;	1250
Protinus edictum sonat imperiale per omnes:	1251
"Ne quis presumat, unde querela venit,	1252
"Et pedes et miles caute pomeria servent,	1253
"Cesaris adventus nulla virecta gravet."	1254
Hec postquam preco clamando circuit agmen,	1255
Urbem pacifico milite Cesar adit.	1256

Commentary and Notes [133v]: Siragusa (87) notes in the margin that these events take place in October and November 1194.

The warfare is now largely over. The emperor hastens from Messina to Favara, where envoys from Palermo meet him to offer their allegiance and tell him the "little king" has fled the city and gone to Caltabellotta. They express their allegiance to Henry VI in warm and flattering terms as they look forward to a peaceful reign under a just king who makes all his subjects feel like rulers.

<(Rota) Section 39: The Legation from Palermo>

Meanwhile Caesar, having conquered all Calabria,
    Comes without trouble to the mad waters;
Having set out in the fleet, he crosses the furious waves of the strait.
    After this he leaves Messina, having lingered but briefly.
Coming to Favara, he wonders at his father-in-law and at her [Favara],
    And praised the noble work, which delights minds.
Some ambassadors from Palermo arrive before him;
    They perform the due words of greeting entrusted to them,
And explain to him the thoughts of the people, their serene intent,
    The feelings of the young and the purpose of the old.
With one voice all say, "You are the sun, you are the light in the world,
    "You are the long-awaited day who comes without night,
"You will drive away the shadows of the realm with armed light.
    "Dashing aside quarrels, you will abound in peace.
"You who bind the world together in peace and restrain war,
    "Who tread the famous necks of kings beneath your feet,
"What king, what prince, what lord can reject your rights?
    "What is the use of suffering battles when Caesar is in arms?
"For to serve you seems like ruling the world.
    "In this you will be a greater Caesar than great Caesar himself.
"See, our little king has deserted our city as a fugitive;
    "Caltabellotta fosters the root of the serpent."
When Caesar receives this embassy bearing such expressions of loyalty,
    He commands that the city should enjoy triumphant peace;
Immediately the imperial edict is proclaimed everywhere:
    "Let no one presume to do anything that might cause complaint.
"Let both knights and foot soldiers respect the sacred confines of the city;
    "Let Caesar's approach bring trouble to no green place."
After the herald makes the rounds, to proclaim this to the troops,
    Caesar approaches the city with peaceful knights.

Pleased at this news, Henry gives careful instructions to his army to approach the city in good order.

                            (S 87–88; KS 189)

[**Particula XXXX**] with missing verses perhaps Section 40: The Emperor Receives Envoys at Favara.

134r   *Castles of Sicily. The Emperor in Favara receives legates from Palermo. The sorrow of Queen Sibylla. Entrance of Henry VI into Palermo.* Illustrates verses 1226–1256, fol. 133v.

· · · ·

Catabellot.	1. Caltabellotto.
Bicarim.	2. Viccari.
Catabutur.	3. Caltavuturi.
Calatamet.	4. Calathamet.
Serenissimus imperator Henricus, Fabariam veniens, nuncios ab urbe Panormi recepit.	5. The most serene emperor Henry, coming to Favara, receives messengers from the city of Palermo.
Nuncii Panormi.	6. Messengers from Palermo.
Tristis Uxor Tancredi	7. The sad wife of Tancred.
Cum pompa nobili et triumpho glorioso Augustus ingreditur Panormum.	8. With noble pomp and glorious triumph, Augustus enters Palermo.

Commentary and Notes [134r]: Four castles, each with its name written above, appear at the top of the page. Two heads are shown peering over the battlements of Caltabellotto, apparently the young king and the mitered archbishop Nicholas of Salerno; however, Kölzer ("Bildkommentar," 192) says that these were drawn later. In the middle of the page, an enthroned Henry VI, crowned and holding a scepter, with armed knights behind his back, receives a message from kneeling envoys. On the right, Sibylla's head appears in the window of a palace, pensive, face leaning on her hand, as her crown slides off her head. At the bottom, Henry enters the city triumphantly, holding a palm branch and preceded by Saracen trumpeters on foot. Mounted knights follow him. Chalandon (*Histoire,* 2:485) observes that Caltabellotto was a very strong fortress in the province of Girgenti (Agrigento), but though the city had once been populous, it had by this time been abandoned strictly to military and defensive purposes, according to the Arab geographer Edrisi. The other castles shown are apparently crucial to the island's defense, although the precise location of "Calathamet" is disputed (Jamison, *Admiral Eugenius,* 117, n. 2).

(S 141; KS 190)

134v   <(Rota) Particula XL:Sibille questus>

Hec ubi Tancredi miseri miserabilis uxor   1257
   Respicit, ut glacies mane novella riget,   1258
Menbra cruor, calor artus, spiritus ossa reliquit,   1259
   Vix a femineis est recreata viris.   1260
At postquam sumpsit dubias in pectore vires,   1261
   In lacrimas oculos solvit amara suos;   1262
Brachia iactat humo, quos leserat ausa precari   1263
   Sanctos, nec Paulus nec Petrus audit eam;   1264
Colligit in meritum periuria multa mariti   1265
   Et cedes hominum nequicieque genus.   1266
Causatur sua gesta prius, causatur et inde   1267
   Periuri tociens impia facta viri.   1268
Sic ait: "O utinam Lichio comitissa manerem!   1269
   "Terrerent animos prelia nulla meos,   1270
"Vir michi forsan adhuc superesset et inclita proles.   1271
   "Nunc Lichium tristis orba duobus eo.   1272
"Vidisset nunquam visus Trinacria nostros!   1273
   "Nunc michi deserte dos mea tuta foret.   1274
"Quam cito falsus honor nos deserit et fugit omen!   1275
   "Ut nova furtivus bruma liquescit honor.   1276
"Ardeat in medio vicecancellarius Orco,   1277
   "Qui fuit excicii sedula causa mei.   1278
"Quantum nequicie, quantumve tirannidis ausus   1279
   "Vir meus, in penas hec tulit hora meas.   1280
"Ei michi, quid prodest quod rex tulit Anglicus aurum?   1281
   "Ei michi, quid prosunt que tibi, Roma, dedi?   1282
"Thesauros exausta meos succurre relicte,   1283
   "Auxilium perhibe, si potes, ipsa michi.   1284
"Cur tua carta virum tibi dantem dona fefellit?   1285
   "Hen tuus egrotus regnat et arma tenet.   1286
"Mortuus hen vincit, tuus eger in urbe triumphat;   1287
   Sic tua decepit littera falsa virum.   1288
"Ei michi, nec tutum est Romane credere puppi,   1289
   "Que, quas insequitur, has imitatur aquas.   1290
"Nec michi Greca nurus prodest, dulcissime fili,   1291
   "Quam, nec adhuc visa fronte, Philippus amat.   1292
"Ergo, quod est tutum, veniam summissa precabor,   1293
   "Effundens lacrimas Cesaris ante pedes.   1294
"Singultus, lacrime, gemitus, suspiria, fletus,   1295
   "Hec vir et hec proles, hec mihi frater erunt;   1296

< (Rota) Section 40: Sibylla's Complaint. >

When the wretched wife of wretched Tancred
    Gazes on these things, then as the new frost chills the morning,
So the blood left her limbs, warmth departed from her joints, and the vigor
    Left her bones. The eunuchs barely managed to revive her.
Afterward, however, she took up her doubtful strength in her breast,
    And the bitter woman washed her eyes with tears.
Her arms strike the earth; she dares to pray to the saints whom she has injured,
    But neither Paul nor Peter will hear her.
She harvests the reward for the many perjuries of her husband,
    Both the slaughter of men and the origin of his wickedness.
She first pleads an excuse for her deeds, and from there pleads excuses
    For all the impious acts of the perjured man.
Thus she speaks: "Oh, would that I had remained the countess of Lecce!
    "No battles would have terrified my spirits,
"Perhaps I would still have my husband and splendid offspring.
    "Now I go to Lecce sad and bereft of both.
"If only Trinacria had never seen our faces!
    "For now my dowry-rights would be secure to my abandoned self.
"How quickly false honor abandons us and the favorable omens flee;
    "Stolen honor melts like early snow.
"May the vice-chancellor burn in the depths of hell.
    "He was the relentless cause of my destruction.
"However much evil, however much tyranny my husband dared,
    "This hour brings it to my punishment.
"Woe is me, how does it help that the English king took gold?
    "Woe is me, what was the use of what I gave to you, Rome?
"You who have exhausted my treasures, bring me help yourself,
    "If you can, now that I am widowed.
"Why did your letter deceive my husband, who gave you gifts?
    "Behold, your sick man rules and bears arms.
"Behold, the dead conquers, and your invalid triumphs in the city;
    "Thus did your false letter deceive my husband.
"Woe is me, it is not safe to trust the Roman ship,
    "Which follows whichever way the waters flow.
"Nor, O my sweetest son, is the Greek daughter-in-law of any use to me,
    "Whom Philip loves without having yet seen her face.
"Therefore, I will do what is safe; I will surrender and pray for pardon,
    "Pouring out tears before the feet of Caesar.
"Sobs, tears, groans, sighs, weeping,
    "These will be my husband and my children and my brother;

"Pro me pugnabunt, pro me dominumque rogabunt;   1297
  "Plus facient lacrime quam mea tela michi;   1298
"Plus poterit pietas quam milia mille Quiritum;   1299
  "Plus prece quam telis Cesar habendus erit."   1300

Commentary and Notes [134v]: The focus is now on Sibylla and her situation. She faints, is revived, and prays in vain (perhaps for a miracle) to Peter and Paul. She realizes that she cannot stand up to the emperor's armies and that she is about to reap the reward for Tancred's usurpation and all the crimes that followed from it. She mourns her dead husband and son, rails on the now dead Matthew, to whom she gives the title "vice-chancellor" (1277–1278) which he bore under William II, not "chancellor," which he enjoyed under her husband. This perhaps indicates her recognition that Tancred's grants of office will be invalid from now on; also, she is recalling Matthew specifically as he was when he prevailed upon Tancred to mount the throne. Sibylla also addresses her reproaches to Rome, and pronounces on the uselessness of the English and Byzantine alliances with which she and Tancred had busied themselves.

In lines 1291–1292 (*Nec michi Greca nurus prodest . . /. . . Philippus amat*), Sibylla refers to Irene, daughter of the Byzantine Emperor Isaac Angelos and the widow of her son Roger. Irene would later marry Philip, the younger brother of Henry VI, who had recently joined the emperor's entourage. Here Sibylla suggests that Philip is already in love with his future bride without having seen her, a motif appropriate to courtly love poetry fashionable during the Middle Ages. Though undoubtedly Henry VI had political calculations in mind when he contemplated the match—either an alliance with Irene's family or territorial claims on her behalf—we need not assume that all courtly sentiments would seem

"They will fight for me, they will plead with the lord for me,
  "My tears will do more for me than my spears;
"Pity can do more than a thousand times a thousand Roman citizens.
  "Caesar will be won more easily by prayers than by spears."

hollow to the courtly audience. Undoubtedly the Hohenstaufen court was aware of the widowed Byzantine princess as they advanced on Palermo, and might already be considering a match between her and Philip. Philip, without having seen her, would have heard descriptions of her and might have been intrigued as well as moved by the loneliness of her situation. It is not impossible that he sent her a gallant message or so at this time, at his brother's instigation or with his indulgent consent. Emissaries, obviously, were coming and going between the rival camps, although Pietro does not dwell on the details.

Clearly Sibylla has been led to believe that the emperor is inclined toward compassion. Hence, she resolves to go to him and plead for pardon in her bereavement. Her portrayal at this time is potentially sympathetic, since as Pietro has told it, she was not involved in Tancred's original decision to usurp the throne. The miniatures do not caricature her as they do Tancred. Apart from supporting her husband, she has committed no particular crime, though her manner of dealing with Constance as a prisoner and her reasons for doing so could be seen as mean-spirited and churlish. Perhaps, however, bad things are foreshadowed by her shrewdness in recognizing that tears can be weapons.

(S 89–90; KS 193)

[PARTICULA XXXXI] with missing verses counted, Section 41: The Wife of Tancred Prays.

135r *Queen Sibylla praying to the apostles Peter and Paul.* Illustrates verses 1257–1300 on fol. 134v.

• • • •

Uxor Tancredi, ut videt Augustum triumphantem in urbe, orat apostolos Dei Petrum et Paulum.	1.	The wife of Tancred, when she sees Augustus triumphant in the city, prays to the apostles of God, Peter and Paul.
Sanctus Petrus.	2.	Saint Peter.
Sanctus Paulus.	3.	Saint Paul.

Commentary and Notes [135r]: Walls and towers of the palace are represented. Below, on the right, haloed images of Saint Peter and Saint Paul are standing, each with a caption above his head. Kölzer ("Bildkommentar," 194) says that the captions were added later, but the saints would presumably be recognizable without them. Saint Peter, at any rate, is holding his keys, and according to Kölzer both saints are depicted in a similar style in the Royal Chapel at Palermo, where Sibylla is understood to be praying and which the miniaturist may be copying. Sibylla is shown again on the left, standing with two attendants whose hands are covered.

(S 141; KS 195)

135v <(Rota) Particula XLI: Imperator occupat triumphans regiam>

Postquam questa sui lacrimabilis omina fati,   1301
   Ad Lichium veniam poscit itura suum,   1302
Inpetrat et supplex nato veniamque nepoti.   1303
   Inde triumphantem suscipit aula ducem;   1304
Regia letatur, tenebrarum nube fugata,   1305
   Exultans iubilos promeruisse dies.   1306
Cesar, ut accepit sceptrum regale, potenter   1307
   Multiplicat Carolis nomen et omen avis;   1308
A viciis mundat sacrata palacia regum   1309
   Et Saturninos excutit inde dolos,   1310
Et Iovis et magni tempus novat Octaviani.   1311
   Integra sub nostro pax Salomone redit,   1312
Que sub Tancredo dudum defuncta manebat,   1313
   Cesare sub nostro vivida facta viget;   1314
Cesaris invicti pax nobis exit ab armis,   1315
   Nostra stat in nudo Cesaris ense salus.   1316
Putifares omnes claves et scrinia portant;   1317
   Adsignant quasquas fiscus habebat opes;   1318
Thesauros numerant, quos vermis araneus ille   1319
   Auserat, et frustra retia nevit apris;   1320
Primus neutrorum claves escriniat omnes,   1321
   Alter apodixas explicat, alter opes;   1322
Hec quantum Calaber seu quantum debeat Afer,   1323
   Apulus aut Siculus debeat orbis habet.   1324
Miratur gazas, quas antiquissimus ardor   1325
   Sortis in incerte grande redegit honus.   1326
Divicias partitur eis, quos prelia nulla   1327
   Terruerant, bello nec renuere mori.   1328

< (Rota) Section 41: The Triumphant Emperor Occupies the Royal Palace. >

After bemoaning the portents of her lamentable fate,
    She asks pardon, meaning to return to her Lecce.
Kneeling to make her petition, she also gains pardon for her son and nephew.
    Then the palace receives the triumphant leader;
The royal residence rejoices that the murky shadows are flown,
    Exultant to be found worthy of festive days.
Caesar, in all his power, receives the royal scepter,
    And multiplies the name and authority of his Carolingian forbears;
He cleanses the sacred palace of the kings from vices,
    Casts out the deceits of Saturn,
And renews the time of Jove and great Octavian.
    Robust peace returns under our Solomon,
Which not long ago was lying dead under Tancred.
    Under our Caesar spirited deeds flourish;
The peace of unconquered Caesar comes to us from warfare;
    Our safety stands in Caesar's naked sword.
Now Potiphars carry all the keys and chests;
    They hand over all the riches the treasury has;
They count out the treasures which that spider had made ready for maggots
    When in vain he wove the net for the wild boars.
The first of the eunuchs turns all the keys;
    Another explains the receipt-box, another the treasures;
They have a complete reckoning of these things, however much Calabria
    Might owe, or Africa, or Apulia or Sicily.
He wonders at the treasures which ancient ardor
    Had collected in a great weight, when fate was doubtful.
Then he bestowed wealth on them whom no battles had terrified,
    And who did not shrink from death in war.

Commentary on [135v]: As she has resolved, Sibylla goes to Henry VI, displays her sorrow and repentance, and gains pardon for herself, her son, and her nephew. Henry then enters the royal palace and takes possession. The officials in charge of the treasury reveal their administrative methods and accounting practices to him. In lines 1319–1320, Pietro implies that Tancred had heaped up a great deal of treasure which he still intended to use for political bribery. That is, the spider (Tancred) intended the treasure as bribes for corrupt people (*vermis*, or maggots) as he struggled to defeat warlike Germans like Diepold (wild boars). The poet exults in the peace that comes after Henry's victory through arms. (See notes on l. 1317 and 1324.)

Needless to say, scholars dispute Pietro's presentation of these events. An important fact which the poet chooses not to mention is that Henry VI promised the princedom of Taranto to the young William III. Since the princedom had not previously belonged to Tancred's family or to Sibylla's, this makes Henry's agreement with Sibylla something other than a mere pardon. Such generosity on Henry's part might well demonstrate his eagerness for true reconciliation, and a concession to the fact that Pope Celestine III had, after all, recognized Tancred as king of Sicily. It might even be part of a friendly gesture toward Tancred's Byzantine allies, with whom Henry VI, as we have seen, was contemplating an alliance in the betrothal Isaac's daughter Irene to his own brother, Philip of

Swabia. Along with all this, and perhaps most important, Henry VI wished to devote every possible resource to his crusade. For this, he wanted the enthusiastic cooperation of Tancred's most able former supporters. However, not all interpret this grant in a manner favorable to the emperor.

Jamison in particular takes issue with Pietro's claim that these events constitute a "pardon" of Sibylla by Henry VI. Rather, she argues, it was a negotiated settlement in which Henry made a significant territorial grant involving the princedom of Taranto. The terms on which the princedom had been granted became the subject of much contention during Frederick II's minority. To Jamison, this grant was a treacherous ploy to induce Sibylla to abandon her still powerful position. While she held the royal palace, Henry VI could not safely take the capital, and with her son safe at Caltabellotta, while her brother commanded significant forces in Apulia, she could still have caused Henry considerable trouble. And, Jamison points out, formidable though Henry's forces might seem, they were bound only to limited terms of service, which were about to run out. Thus, initially, he not only granted princely status to William III but also apparently received some of Sibylla's supporters into his favor, for example making Admiral Margarito the Duke of Durazzo (Jamison, *Admiral Eugenius,* 119).

(S 91–92; KS 197)

[Particula XLII] With missing verses counted, perhaps Section 42: **Sibylla Pardoned; Henry Takes Possession.**

x2r

(Illustrations corresponding to verses 1301–1328 should appear here. They ought
to depict Sibylla's pleas before Henry, and should perhaps show her pardoned son and
nephew going happily away. Perhaps the captions might have alluded to the granting of
the princedom of Taranto. Henry VI might also have been shown viewing the treasures
with the eunuchs.)

x2v (**Particula XLIII**]/ Lost verses, perhaps Section 43: The Conspirators and Their Plan.)

The verses illustrated in the following picture page are missing, apparently lost before *Liber ad honorem Augusti* was trimmed to be bound with its companions in the Bern Codex (see Introduction). The verses would correspond to the illustration on fol. 136r and should have told about the origins of a conspiracy to murder Henry VI and restore William III to the throne, including details about a letter which the conspirators signed, or in which one of them (apparently the Archbishop Nicholas of Salerno, seen writing a letter in the next set of miniatures, on 136r) wrote their names.

136r *Conspiracy against Henry VI in favor of William III, son of Tancred.* (Illustrations for missing FOL. X2v, above.) Corresponds to Illustration 7 of Engel and VII of Del Re. The verses are lacking which ought to have been illustrated by the pictures on this page, and which would have furnished precious particulars about the conspirators against Henry VI.

• • • •

Regulus.	1.	The little king.
Presul Salerni.	2.	Archbishop of Salerno.
Domus in qua coniurant proditores regni.	3.	The house in which the traitors of the realm swore their oath.
Uxor Tancredi.	4.	Wife of Tancred.
Presul Salerni.	5.	Archbishop of Salerno.
Margaritus.	6.	Margarito.
Rogerius Tharthis.	7.	Roger Tharthis.
Comes Riccardus.	8.	Count Richard
Comes Rogerius.	9.	Count Roger.
Comes Riccardus de Agellis.	10.	Count Richard of Ajello.
Eugenius.	11.	Eugenius.
Comes W[ilhelmus] de Marsico	12.	Count William of Marsico
Iohannes frater presulis Salerni.	13.	John the brother of the Archbishop of Salerno.
Comes Rogerius Avilini.	14.	Count Roger of Avellino.
Alexius servus Tancredi.	15.	Alexius, slave of Tancred.

Commentary and Notes [136r]: Our ability to interpret these illustrations is hampered by the loss of the accompanying verses. On the upper half of the page, at the apex of a triangle formed by the figures, young William III (cap. 1) sits on a cushioned stool looking cheerful. Below him and to the right, Nicholas of Salerno (cap. 5), mitered, sits on a folding stool, his hands outstretched. On the left, at a level between the two, a notary writes a letter.

In the lower half of the drawing, a stylized arch supported by two columns is drawn and described with cap. 3 as the house where the traitors' oath was sworn. Below, twelve names are written in red, and beneath that is a cluster of ten figures. In the center, larger than the rest, is Sibylla, seated, holding on her lap a book marked by a cross, upon which the other figures, kneeling, are placing their hands. Presumably, they swear to be loyal to each other and to undertake various actions required by the conspiracy. Obviously, one infers from the picture, the conspirators meant to place William III back on the throne. Archbishop Nicholas had an important role, and Sibylla gave him her complete approval and support. The archbishop's two brothers are among the plotters. Some of the other names listed are known from other sources, though not otherwise mentioned in Pietro's poem.

Perhaps this low-key, straightforward account, with the mixture of names known and unknown, is more effective than hyperbolic denunciations in conveying the gravity of the situation, though these will follow.

(S 142–44; KS 198)

136v <(Rota) Particula XLII: Coniuratio proditorum >

At Deus, inpaciens fraudis scelerisque nefandi,	1329
Publicat in lucem quod tegit archa nephas;	1330
Nam nichil admittit felix fortuna sinistrum,	1331
Nec possunt quod obest prospera fata pati.	1332
Hec tria felices comitantia Cesaris actus	1333
Quam bene dispensant sors bona, fata, Deus!	1334
Conscius archani quidam secreta revelat	1335
Et docet insidias enumeratque viros;	1336
Detegit et scriptum nocturna lampade factum,	1337
Quod docet in Caypha presule posse capi.	1338
Ostupet armipotens famulos miratus iniquos,	1339
Ducit et in dubiam verba relata fidem.	1340
Postquam certa fides super hiis datur, indice scripto,	1341
Coniuratorum dissimulatur opus;	1342
Curia contrahitur, resident in iure vocati,	1343
Quisque sibi dubitans multa timenda timent.	1344
Iamque silere dato, solio redimitus ab alto,	1345
Exolvit querulo Cesar in ore moras:	1346
"Quis pro pace necem, vel quis pro munere dampnum,	1347
"Aut quis pro donis dampna meretur?" ait.	1348
"Nec Christo Cayphas fecit, nec sevius Anna,	1349
"Quam michi conscripte disposuere manus."	1350
Protinus armiferis pleno iubet ore ministris,	1351
Ut capiant quosquos littera lecta notat.	1352
Qui cito mandatis inplent pia iussa receptis,	1353
Infectos capiunt prodicione viros.	1354
Dampnatos ex lege viros clementia differt	1355
Et suffert pietas inpietatis honus;	1356
In condempnatos meritum sententia tardat,	1357
Quo datur ut vinctos Apula dampnet humus,	1358
Quam Cesar properans, ex parte licenciat agmen,	1359
Ne gravet urbanos maxima turba suos.	1360
Bavuarus et Scavus, Lonbardus, Marchio, Tuscus,	1361
In propriam redeunt Saxo, Boemus humum.	1362

<(Rota) Section 42: A Conspiracy of Traitors.>

Then God, unwilling to suffer their deceit and unspeakable wickedness,
　　Brings to light the abomination hidden in the chest.
For happy fortune allows nothing sinister,
　　Nor can the Fates, when propitious, permit obstruction.
How well these three together arrange the lucky actions of Caesar,
　　Good fortune, Fates, and God!
Someone aware of hidden things reveals the secrets,
　　Describes the ambushes and names the persons.
He even tells about the letter, written at night by lantern-light,
　　Which reveals the intent of "Archbishop Caiaphas," and how it can be seized.
The Armipotent gapes and wonders at these wicked servants,
　　He gives commands, even though he doubts the story's truth.
Afterwards, when the letter proves all these things with certainty,
　　He feigns ignorance of the work of these conspirators.
The court is summoned; they sit down and are called to judgement,
　　Each one suspecting within himself, they fear many fearful things.
Silence is imposed, and, crowned, from the high throne ,
　　Caesar ends delay with words of accusation.
"Who gives death for peace, and injury for benefits,
　　"Or who earns injury with gifts?" he says.
"Caiaphas and Annas did nothing more savage to Christ,
　　"Than those hands that wrote these letters meant for me."
Then with full voice he commands his armed attendants,
　　To seize everyone whom the letter made known as it was read aloud.
These quickly fulfill the righteous command they have received,
　　And seize the persons corrupted by treason.
Clemency turns aside strict law from those condemned;
　　Piety bears the burden of impiety.
The sentence holds back from the condemned their full punishment,
　　By which it is decreed that Apulian soil might doom the prisoners.
Going there in haste, Caesar frees part of his army,
　　So that they would not burden his city-dwellers with their great numbers.
Bavarians and Slavs, Lombards, Marchians, Tuscans,
　　Saxons and Bohemians all return to their own soil.

Commentary and Notes [136v]: News of the plot is brought to Henry, who doubts it at first, until the informer reveals the letter written at the direction of Archbishop Nicholas (mockingly called "Archbishop Caiaphas") and containing the names, probably the signatures of the conspirators. Once produced, the letter convinces Henry. He summons the court and makes his accusation with the conspirators present. All those whose names are signed (or written) in the letter are arrested.

What purpose did this secret letter serve, except to betray the conspirators and expose them to arrest? Perhaps, like the oath, it was a device to bind the conspirators together in a common cause. Or perhaps it had a more practical purpose. The conspirators did not need merely to kill Henry VI; they needed to deal with his supporters and his army. A document signed by the people who had been in control of Tancred's government until a few weeks before, and thus prov-ing that their support was really behind these actions, could be very effective in winning others to the cause and frightening enemies away. There are, of course, those who believe the letter was a fraud (see Introduction C.15).

Pietro's obscure words about the prisoners suggest that some were sentenced to punishment, to be carried out in Apulia, which Henry mercifully did not carry out at this time. The prisoners are soon sent to Germany, and some appar-ently were later blinded and mutilated, action provoked by further rebellions and conspiracies in Sicily, probably after Pietro had completed the *Liber* (see Introduction).

After the conspirators are dealt with, the emperor sends away his army.

(S 93–94; KS 201)

1330: *publicat.* pre-S: *publicat.* S: *pluplicat.* KS: *puplicat.* De Rosa: *publicat.* Codex: *pluplicat* corrected to *publicat.*

[PARTICULA XLIV] With missing verses counted, perhaps Section 44: The Con-spirators Revealed.

137r   *Denunciation of the conspiracy and imprisonment of conspirators.* Illustrates verses 1329–1362, fol. 106v. Corresponds to Illustration 8 of Engel and 8 and 9 of Del Re. Illustrates verses 1329–1362 on page 43 [106] of the codex.

· · · ·

Imperator Henricus VI.	1. Emperor Henry VI.
Monachus iste coniurationem proditorum detexit.	2. This monk revealed the traitors' conspiracy.
Isti sunt proditores.	3. These are the traitors.
Lectis litteris proditionis capiuntur proditores.	4. The treasonous letters having been read, the traitors are captured.

Commentary and Notes [137r]: In the top half of the drawing, Henry VI sits crowned, enthroned, and holding his scepter. Behind him stands an armed knight with a shield. A tonsured monk stands before him, giving information about the conspiracy (Cap. 2). On the right, the conspirators are shown gathered together in court (Cap. 3). Sibylla, the child William, and Margarito are clearly recognizable from the illustration on 136r and elsewhere. The child outside the box may be William III in an earlier stage of the proceedings; perhaps he would not ordinarily attend court councils and had to be specially summoned after the rest had gathered. The kneeling figure between the emperor and the assembled conspirators might be pleading for pardon, as Siragusa suggests, or could be providing additional information about the conspiracy. In the lower half of the page, a messenger or notary reads the crucial letter out loud, and armed men are shown on the right, holding the chains attached to a line of eight prisoners. The emperor appears again in the middle of the drawing, indicating the notary (or reader of the letter) with his right hand and the armed men with his left. Cap. 4 describes the whole dramatic sequence of events.

(S 144; KS 202)

137v <(Rota) Particula XLIII: Frederici nativitas>

Venit ab exparta nativi palma triumphi,	1363
Pernova felicis signa parentis habens.	1364
Duxerat in gemitum presentis secula vite,	1365
Quod fuerat fructus palma morata suos.	1366
Serior ad fructus tanto constantior arbor	1367
Natificat tandem, sicut oliva parens,	1368
Cumque triumphator nudis iam parceret armis,	1369
Nascitur Augusto, qui regat arma, puer.	1370
Felix namque pater, set erit felicior infans;	1371
Hic puer ex omni parte beatus erit.	1372
Nam pater ad totum victrici cuspide partes	1373
Ducet, et inperium stare quod ante dabit;	1374
Hoc speculatur Arabs et idem suspirat Egyptus,	1375
Hoc Iacob, hoc Ysaac a Daniele sapit.	1376
O votive puer, renovandi temporis etas	1377
Ex hinc Rogerius, hinc Fredericus eris,	1378
Maior habendus avis, fato meliore creatus,	1379
Qui bene vix natus cum patre vincis avos.	1380
Pax oritur tecum, quia te nascente creamur.	1381
Te nascente sumus quod pia vota petunt;	1382
Te nascente dies non celi sidera condit;	1383
Te nascente suum sidera lumen habent;	1384
Te nascente suis tellus honeratur aristis,	1385
Suspecti redimit temporis arbor opes.	1386
Luxuriant montes, pinguescit et arida tellus,	1387
Credita multiplici sorte repensat ager.	1388
Sol sine nube, puer nunquam passurus eclipsim,	1389
Regia quem peperit solis in orbe dies.	1390
Amodo non timeam suspecte tempora noctis;	1391
Per silvas, per humum, per mare tutus eo.	1392
Non aquilam volucres, modo non armenta leonem,	1393
Non metuent rapidos vellera nostra lupos.	1394
Nox ut clara dies gemino sub sole diescit,	1395
Terra suos geminos sicut Olimpus habet.	1396

<(Rota) Section 43: The Birth of Frederick>

From the one past childbearing comes the palm of natal triumph,
    Bearing newborn ensigns of his fortunate father!
It had made the people of this present generation groan,
    That the palm was delayed of her fruit.
But the later to bear fruit, the more constant the tree;
    She, like the olive tree, bears offspring at last,
So that now the triumphant one may spare the naked sword.
    A boy is born to Augustus, who shall rule over warfare.
And thus the father is fortunate, but the infant will be more fortunate.
    This child will be blessed on every side.
For the father conquers everywhere with victorious spear,
    And has caused the Empire to stand as it did in ancient times.
Arabia sees this and Egypt sighs for it;
    Jacob and Isaac know of this from Daniel.
O child of prayers, O age of renewal,
    Henceforth you shall be Roger and henceforth Frederick too.
You shall be greater than your grandfathers, made for a better fate,
    Since hardly born, you defeat your grandfathers along with your father.
Peace is born with you, because your being born causes our restoration.
    Since you are born, we become what pious vows seek;
Since you are born, the day shall not hide the stars of heaven,
    Since you are born, stars will have their light;
Since you are born, the earth is loaded down with its harvest;
    The garlanded tree shows the riches of this marvelous time.
The mountains abound in wealth, even the dry earth grows fat,
    The field pays back what is committed to it many times.
You are the sun without cloud, boy who will never suffer eclipse,
    Whom the royal day of the sun bore into the world.
Now I will not fear the seasons of doubtful night;
    Through the woods, over the soil, over the sea I go safely.
Birds will not fear the eagle, nor cattle the lion,
    Nor our wooly creatures the fierce wolves.
Night dawns as clear day under twin suns,
    The earth has its twins like Olympus.

Commentary and Notes [137v]: With joy and prognostications of future greatness, Pietro welcomes the birth of the young Frederick II of Hohenstaufen. Constance has been barren since her marriage in 1186, and although Pietro does not mention the date, she is now forty years old. The birth of his heir significantly strengthens Henry VI's political position and also gives him a good excuse to deal mildly with the conspirators, or to "spare the naked sword" (line 1369). Thus Pietro compares her to an olive tree (line 1368), a pleasant image of fruitfulness which also symbolizes peace, just as the palm represents triumph. Prophetic references multiply as Pietro mentions (line 1376) that Jacob and Isaac knew about this event from the prophet Daniel. Since the Isaac and Jacob of Genesis were born many generations before Daniel, Pietro presumably imagines a posthumous conversation in Limbo, where all three would have been together until the Harrowing of Hell, according to the ideas current in the Middle Ages. Possibly the discussion would center on Nebuchadnezzar's dream (Daniel 2), prefiguring the overthrow of three empires before the establishment of God's enduring one.

Then, in Virgilian language that recalls the classical golden age as well as the Messianic age of biblical prophecy, Pietro foretells that the child will have the best qualities of both his grandfathers, Frederick and Roger, and that his reign will be an age of peace and renewal. These themes will be expanded on in the succeeding passages.

(S 95–96; KS 205)

1364 *pernova*. Del Re, KS: *pernova*. S, De Rosa, other editions: *per nova* (two words). Codex: *per nova*

[PARTICULA XLV] With missing verses counted, perhaps Section 45

138r *The Empress, in the act of leaving for Sicily, entrusts her son to the duchess of Spoleto.* These should be illustrations of verses 1363–1396 which are read on page 44 [107] B of the codex but in those verses, which discuss the birth of Frederick II, the circumstances of the picture are not explained.)

. . . .

Imperatrix Siciliam repetens
    benedictum filium suum
    ducisse dimist.
Imperatrix.
	1.
	
	2.
		The Empress, returning to Sicily,
		    gives up her blessed son to the
		    duchess.
		Empress.

Commentary and Notes [138r]: On the top half of the page, lightly drawn or perhaps faded, three trees, perhaps palm trees, appear. The top of the page, which might have held more captions, has been cut off. In the lower half, the crowned empress, mounted on horseback, is in the center, holding in her hands her crowned infant. On the left, the duchess stands, holding out her arms for the child. Her hands are covered, perhaps by a cloth in which to wrap the baby. On the right, also on foot, are two armed men, leading the empress's horse. The empress faces away from the knights and the horse's head, toward the baby and the duchess. The two parts of the drawing convey both the joy and triumph of the birth and the sorrow at the parting between mother and child. Kölzer's commentary (206) identifies the duchess to whom she commits her son as the wife of Conrad, duke of Spoleto. Surviving sources give no detailed explanation as to why young Frederick Roger was nursed in this fashion, apart from both his parents; apparently such arrangements were not unusual in royal families and contemporaries did not think it strange. Henry VI may have thought of Spoleto as one of the more stable and settled parts of his realm, and might, especially in view of the recent conspiracy, have thought Sicily unsafe. Constance's presence and activity in governing her kingdom were, however, needed. Later, when young Frederick had been elected King of the Romans, Henry arranged for him to be brought up in Germany; Philip of Swabia was on his way to escort him there in 1197 when Henry died (Van Cleve, *Emperor Frederick II*, 24).

(S 145; KS 206).

138v <(Rota) Particula XLIV: Frederici presagia>

Res rata quam loquimur, quidam presentat Yberus	1397
Piscem, qui nato Cesare dignus erat;	1398
Quem puer accipiens, bene dispensante magistro,	1399
Dividit.	1400
Pisce tripartito, gemina sibi parte retenta,	1401
Quod superest patri mittit ab inde puer,	1402
Maxima venture signans presagia vite;	1403
Quod sibi detinuit, vesper et ortus erit!	1404
Tercia pars que missa fuit designat in armis,	1405
Tercia pars mundi quod sit habenda patri.	1406
Vive, puer, decus Ytalie, nova temporis etas,	1407
Que geminos gemina merce reducis avos;	1408
Vive, iubar solis, sol regnaturus in evum,	1409
Qui potes a cunis luce iuvare diem;	1410
Vive, Iovis proles, Romani nominis heres,	1411
Inmo reformator orbis et inperii;	1412
Vive, patris specimen, felicis gloria matris,	1413
Nasceris in plenos fertilitate dies;	1414
Vive, puer felix, felix genitura parentum,	1415
Dulcis amor superis, inclite vive puer.	1416
In media sine nube die tibi panditur yris,	1417
Omnitenens medio sol statit orbe suo.	1418
Unde venit Titan et nox ubi sidera condit,	1419
Ex yri metas sol videt esse tuas.	1420
Vive, puer, dum vesper erit, dum Lucifer ardet,	1421
Nunquam seu nusquam vespere dignus eris;	1422
Vive, puer, dum litus agit, dum nubila ventus,	1423
Ut videas natis secula plena tuis;	1424
Vive, patris virtus, dulcissima matris ymago,	1425
Vive diu, dum sol lucet et astra micant;	1426
Vive diu, Iovis et superum pulcherrime princeps;	1427
Vive diu, proavus factus ad astra voles.	1428

< (Rota) Section 44: Prophecies of Frederick. >

What we speak of is confirmed; a certain Iberian
    Presents as a gift a fish worthy of the boy Caesar.
The boy receives it, and, as his master directs him well,
    He divides it.
When the fish is divided into three parts, the boy, holding back two parts,
    Sends what remains away to his father,
Thus setting forth the greatest prognostications of life to come;
    What he held back for himself will be twilight and sunrise!
The third part, which he sent, signifies one-third of the world,
    The possession of which his father must gain through arms.
Live, boy, ornament of Italy, in whom time receives new youth,
    You who bring back both grandfathers with double richness!
Live, radiance of the sun, sun who will reign throughout the ages,
    Who can, with light from your cradle, make the day itself rejoice.
Live, offspring of Jove, heir of the Roman name,
    Reformer, indeed, of the world and the empire.
Live, image of your father, glory of your happy mother,
    You are born in the fullness of days of plenty.
Live, blessed child, happy offspring of your parents,
    Sweet darling of the supernal powers, live, illustrious boy.
In the middle of a day without clouds the rainbow is spread for you;
    The all-governing sun stands in the middle of its sphere.
Whence the Titan comes and where the night hides the stars,
    Through the rainbow, the sun sees the bounds of your domain.
Live, child, while evenings shall be, while the daystar burns,
    Never or nowhere shall you deserve a sunset;
Live, child, while the wind drives seashore and the clouds,
    So that you will see the ages filled with your children,
Live, strength of your father and image of your most sweet mother,
    Live long, while the sun shines and the stars twinkle.
Live long, fairest prince of Jove and the supernal powers;
    Live long, and when you are a great-grandfather, may you fly to the stars.

Commentary and Notes [138v]: Pietro continues happy prognostications and best wishes for the newborn child's future. He recounts a story he has heard, about a fish which an Iberian gave to the child, and which Frederick divided into three parts, keeping two for himself and sending one to his father. Such records as exist suggest that Henry saw very little of his son, who was less than three years old when his father died. Of course, dividing a fish into three pieces and sending only a third to his imperial father seems whimsical enough to be something that a child less than three years old might do. Pietro interprets this act as a highly meaningful presage of the child's future greatness. He ends by wishing the boy happiness, long life, many grandchildren, and ultimate residence among the stars.

The "Titan" of line 1419 is the Sun-god, cf. Virgil, *Aeneid* 4.119 and Ovid, *Metamorphoses* 1.10. The entire line is taken from Lucan, *De Bello Civili* 1.15, where it mentions the lands which the Romans might have conquered if Romans had not been fighting each other instead. Pietro is suggesting that the newborn child will bring healing and peaceful rule from the eastern to the western borders of the known world.

(S 97–98; KS 209)

[PARTICULA XLVI] With missing verses counted, perhaps Section 46.

x3r

The page illustrating the above verses (1397–1428) is missing. Presumably, it should contain a picture of little Frederick Roger dividing the splendid fish under the supervision of his tutor, and his imperial father Henry VI receiving, with appropriate emotion, the third part which his son granted him. Various symbolic representations of the sun, rainbows, and the dark side of the earth at night might also have been represented. Siragusa writes (98, n. 1), "After page 45 (138), because of the displacement about which I spoke in the preface, page 51 (144) must follow instead of page 46 (139)." Since this is the consensus of modern scholars, the manuscript has been rebound since his time and is now in this order.]

x3v (**Particula XLVII**] /Section 47: Court Scene)

The verses illustrated by the badly mutilated miniatures in Fol. 144r, which follows, are missing. Presumably, they contain a description of the emperor's court. Rota suggests that perhaps the birth of the imperial heir is announced here.

[**Particula XLVII**] Missing verses (3), perhaps Section 47: Court Scene

144r *A notary and the people (mutilated).*
Illustrates verses contained on the missing page after fol. 138.

• • • •

Notari[us].
Populus.
Dux — Comes — Princeps.

1. Notary.
2. People.
3. Duke — Count — Prince.

Commentary and Notes [144r]: The top half of this page, and a little more, is missing. Nevertheless, there are the remains of an upper picture as well as a lower one. The upper half probably had the emperor in the center (his feet clad in scarlet shoes). Kölzer ("Bildkommentar," 210) suggests in his commentary that the man on the right with feet somewhat lower would be the chancellor Conrad. Five mail-clad legs to the emperor's left represent his bodyguard. At the bottom of the page, the caption identifies the middle figure as a notary. He holds a scroll that says "Duke—Count—Prince" (Cap. 3), On the right hand, the "People" (cap. 2) stand, a cluster of bodies with only four faces clearly visible. Rota, in his notes on this illustration, suggests that the picture represents an announcement to the court of the birth of the imperial heir.

(S 149; KS 210)

144v <(Rota) Particula XLV: Corradi cancellarii loquucio ad proceres regni>

* * * * * * * * * * * * * * *

"Quos * * * * * * * * * * * *	1429
"Et que dictarat * * * * * * * *	1430
"Sit licet immanis commissi sarcin[a doli],	1431
"Hec augustali fit pietate minor.	1432
"Sic igitur servate fidem, ne sera cicatrix	1433
"Vulnus in antiquum rupta redire queat,	1434
"Nam meus Augustus qui lites diligit, odit,	1435
"Mites et puros more Tonantis amat,	1436
"Ne quis ob exilium, quod dudum pertulit in se,	1437
"Elatus, rediens, civibus esse velit.	1438
"Cesaris oceanum superat clementia magnum,	1439
"Et tamen illius commovet ira deos.	1440
"Si quis Tancredum nimium dilexerit olim,	1441
"Quid, nisi per vanas brachia movit aquas?	1442
"Vivit in Augusto pietas et gratia crescens	1443
"Et gladius vindex, vivit et hasta potens."	1444

Commentary and Notes [144v]: This is the other side of the page on which the frag-mented miniatures appear. The verses likewise are fragmented. Into the mouth of his patron, Conrad the Chancellor, Pietro puts a description of the ideals of Henry's reign. He means to rule justly and reconcile old enemies. In the surviv-ing portion of the speech, Conrad urges everyone to give up thoughts of revenge for past injuries, without, however, presuming on the emperor's forbearance for further wrongs. Conrad's point seems to be that those former supporters of Tancred who are willing to live peacefully should not be punished further; it

<(Rota) Section 45: Conrad the Chancellor's Speech to the Barons of the Kingdom>

* * * * * * * * * * * * * * ** * * * * * * ** * * *
"Those * * * * * * * * * * * * * * ** * * * * *
   And what he had often said * * * * * * * * * * * * * *
"Though granted that an immense pile of deceits was committed . . .
   "The mercy of Augustus regards them as small.
"Therefore, keep faith, lest the late scar
   "Should break open and make the old wound return.
"For my Augustus hates those who love quarrels.
   "He loves the gentle and pure, in the manner of the Thunderer.
"Let no one, on account of exile which he formerly endured,
   "Return and seek to lord it over the citizens.
"Caesar's clemency surpasses the great ocean,
   "And yet his wrath brings divine powers to his aid.
"If anyone loved Tancred too much in former times,
   "What did he do but weary his arms, trying to shape weak water?
"In Augustus piety lives and grace abounds,
   "But so also do the avenging sword and the mighty spear."

is punishment enough that they have wasted their energies uselessly in a cause doomed to failure.

   1431 *sarcin [a doli]*. S: *sarcin*. W: *sarcin [a doli]*. KS *sarcin [a fraudis]*. De Rosa: *sarcin [a doli]*. See note on this line.
   [PARTICULA XLVIII] With missing verses counted, perhaps Section 48: Conrad the Chancellor Admonishes the Barons.

145r *The imperial chancellor, haranguing the great men of the realm.* The composition
of this miniature represents the imperial chancellor Conrad, who speaks to
the counts and magnates of the realm, and must have illustrated verses on fol.
144v, which in the fragment that remains, contains sixteen verses, 1429–1444,
including the three mutilated ones. To judge from the other pages, there must
be about fourteen verses now missing.

· · · ·

Corradus cancellarius imperialis loquens ad proceres regni.	1.	Conrad the imperial chancellor speaking to the great men of the realm.
Comites et proceres regni.	2.	The counts and great men of the realm.

Commentary and Notes [145r]: Turreted walls and towers represent, probably, the pal-
ace at Palermo. In the middle, the chancellor Conrad (Cap. 1) sits on a thronelike
chair, while two armed knights stand behind him, on the right side of the draw-
ing. On the left side, in front of the chancellor, stand a throng of "The counts and
great men of the realm" (cap. 2). Beneath the throne an arch is represented with
bands of color.

(S 149; KS 214)

145v <(Rota) Particula XLVI: Libellus ad Augustum inscribitur>

Sol Augustorum.	1445

¶

Qui regis ad placitum victor in axe rotas,	1446
Fortunam tua dextra novam sibi condit ubique,	1447
Ducis Fortune quo tibi frena placet.	1448
Legi quos veterum servant armaria libros;	1449
Inveni titulis cuncta minora tuis;	1450
Nec Salomon, nec Alexander, nec Iulius ipse	1451
Promeruit vestri quod meruere dies.	1452
Sextus ab equivocis sexto quod scriberis evo,	1453
Signas etatis tempora plena tue,	1454
Vivat honor mundi, vivat pax plena triumphis,	1455
Vivat, et eterno nomine regnet avus,	1456
Ut videas natis plenumque nepotibus evum,	1457
Tempora zodiaci dum rota solis agit.	1458
Suscipe, queso, meum, Sol augustissime, munus,	1459
Qui mundum ditas, qui regis omne solum,	1460
Suscipe, queso, meum, lux indefecta, libellum;	1461
Ipse sui vatis vota libellus agat.	1462

Interpretatio huius nominis: Henricus.

Collige primas litteras de primis dictionibus subscritorum versuum et nomen habebis imperatoris, et de ipsis primis dictionibus eiusdem victoriam imperatoris perpendere poteris.

Hic princeps, ut habet Danielis nobile scriptum,	1463
Exaltabit avos, subigens sibi victor Egyptum.	1464
Nomen in herede patria virtute quiescet;	1465
Romani iuris duplici rogus igne calescet;	1466
Imperii formam templique reducet ad hastra.	1467
Cum non hostis erit, sua ponet cum Iove castra.	1468
Vicerit ut mundum Syon, David arce redempta,	1469
Siciliam repetens, Rome reget aurea sceptra.	1470

<(Rota) Section 46: The Book is Inscribed to Augustus>

The Sun of the Augustans
¶
    You, the victor who rules at your pleasure the wheels in their axis,
Your right hand establishes new fortune for itself everywhere,
    And you draw the reins of Fortune where you wish.
I have read the books which the old cupboards hold,
    And I find that all have earned less than your glory.
Not Solomon, not Alexander, not Julius himself
    Deserved what your days have won.
You are set down as the sixth of those with like names, in the sixth age,
    You signify the fulfilled seasons of your age.
Long live the honor of the world! Long live peace full of triumph!
    And may you also live to be a grandfather, eternal in name,
So that you shall see the age full of your children and grandchildren,
    While the wheel of the sun turns the seasons of the Zodiac.
Receive, I ask, O Sun most august, my gift,
    You who enrich the world, who rule every land.
Unfailing light, I ask that you receive my little book,
    And may it fulfill the wishes of its bard.

Interpretation of this name: Henricus.

Take the first letters of the first words of the verses written below, and you will
have the name of the emperor. And from the first words themselves, you can
understand the emperor's victory.

He shall, this prince, as the noble scripture of Daniel says,
Exalt his ancestors, this victor subjecting Egypt to himself, whose
Name shall rest in his heir through paternal virtue.
Roman law, through this sacred fire, will burn with double flame;
Imperial grace and religion he brings once more to the stars. When
Confronting no enemy, he will pitch his camp with Jove,
Victorious when Zion is cleansed, David's citadel redeemed,
Sicily he will seek again, to wield the golden scepters of Rome.

Commentary and Notes [145v]: Pietro presents his book to Henry VI and hails him as the fulfiller of the "sixth age" (line 1452). The "sixth age," according to the scheme of history which Augustine outlines in the last chapter of *The City of God* (22.30), would be the epoch between the incarnation of Christ and the defeat of the Antichrist, before the Second Coming. After the Second Coming would be the Seventh Age, where Christ would reign, until the final battle with Satan and the end of the world. This would be followed by the "eighth day," which would be, however, the beginning of new "week" in a new heaven and earth. After line 1462, Pietro offers a prose introduction to his acrostic, which he then presents (1463–1470). The first letters of these lines spell *HENRICVS*. Within them, Pietro once more predicts that Henry will restore the Roman Empire to its ancient borders, the most important labor of which will be to recover Jerusalem. Then and only then will Henry return to Sicily and rule peacefully.

S 100–1; lines 1445–1469. Siragusa takes Sol Augustorum as a heading, rather than a line. That is why his line numbers are one less than the other editions from here to the end of the poem. (KS 217)

[PARTICULA XLIX] With missing verses counted, perhaps Section 49

139r *Henry VI on his throne receives the offering of the poem by Pietro of Eboli, through the intercession of the chancellor, Conrad of Hildesheim.*

. . . .

Imperator Henricus VI.	1.	Emperor Henry VI.
Corradus cancellarius.	2.	Conrad the chancellor.
Poeta.	3.	The poet.

Commentary and Notes [139r]: Once more, towers and crenellations represent the palace. A cross is mounted on a small dome at the top of the drawing. Henry VI, crowned and sceptered, is at the center, with three armed knights behind him. The chancellor Conrad sits at his right. The poet, tonsured and robed in brown, kneels at Conrad's right, on the stairs in front of the emperor, presenting his book.

(S 145–46; KS 218)

Sirgusa observes that this miniature is Illustration 1 in Engel's edition and the frontispiece of Del Re's, and that it apparently illustrates fol. 145v (which it faces in the manuscript's current form) rather than fol. 138v, opposite to it when he examined it.

139v Incipit liber tercius ad honorem et gloriam magni imperatoris
     <(Rota) Particula XLVII: Sapientiam invocat poeta>

Desine, Calliope; satis est memorasse quod olim   1471
    Tityrus ad fagi tegmina duxit oves;   1472
Desine tu, Pean, celeberrima desine Clio;   1473
    Sit mugisse satis commemorasse Iovem;   1474
Non mea Calliopes nec Apollinis ara litabit   1475
    Carmina, que pecudum, que vorat, exta litat.   1476
¶
Te peto, te cupio, summi Sapientia Patris,   1477
    Que legis eterna mente quod orbis habet.   1478
Tu pelagi metiris aquas, metiris abissum;   1479
    Te metuunt solam, te venerantur aque.   1480
Tu patrii legis astra poli, tibi servit Olimpus,   1481
    Te sine vita perit, te sine nemo sapit;   1482
Nam quod sol hominum, Salomon, David inclita proles,   1483
    Sensit seu meruit creditur esse tuum.   1484
Tu massam discepta rudem, tu litis amice   1485
    Primicias, certo conciliata loco;   1486
Tu depinxisti fatali sidere celum,   1487
    Unde venit nosti Phebus et unde soror;   1488
Nam quod friget yemps, ver umet, torret et estas,   1489
    Siccitat autunnus, creditur esse tuum;   1490
Quod breve litus aquas refrenat turbine motas,   1491
    Quod montes, quod humum sustinet unda, tuum;   1492
Tu pudor eternus sacrasti virginis alvum,   1493
    Tu sata, tu nascens, tu genitura creans.   1494
Thesauros aperi, veniens illabere celo;   1495
    Semper es ut verax, da michi vera loqui.   1496
Tu divina loqui Petro post rete dedisti,   1497
    Ex uno per te flumina ventre fluunt;   1498
Nec minor in partes divisa, set integra constas,   1499
    Ut vis et que vis, dans tua dona tuis.   1500
Hos genus eloquii, mentes interpretis illos,   1501
    Hos virtutis opus promeruisse facis.   1502
Da michi cepta loqui, da ceptis fine potiri,   1503
    Possit ut Augusto Musa placere suo.   1504

Here begins the third book, to the honor and glory of the great emperor.
<(Rota) Section 47: The Poet Invokes Wisdom >

Cease, Calliope; you have recounted enough how in the old times
    Tityrus led his sheep under the cover of the beech tree;
Leave your songs, Pan; cease, most famous Clio;
    Let this be enough about the way Jove has bellowed.
Neither the altar of Calliope nor of Apollo, which accepts and devours
    The entrails of flocks, will receive my songs in sacrifice.
¶
I seek you, I desire you, Wisdom of the highest Father,
    You who read in your eternal mind what the world holds.
You measure the waters of the sea, you measure the abyss,
    They fear only you; the waters hold you in reverence.
You govern the stars of your father's heaven; Olympus obeys you.
    Without you, all life wastes away; without you, no one has perception.
For whatever that Sun of humanity, Solomon, famous son of David,
    Understood or deserved, it is believed to be your doing.
You overthrew wild chaos, you in friendship brought strife's
    Firstfruits to reconciliation, on firm ground;
You painted heaven with its destined configuration of stars;
    You know from whence Phoebus comes, and his sister.
For that winter chills, spring moistens, summer burns,
    And autumn dries is believed to be your doing;
That the narrow shore restrains storm-stirred waters,
    That moisture sustains mountains and earth is your doing.
You, eternal modesty, consacreted the womb of the virgin,
    From which you sprang, thus coming to birth, you creating creature.
Open your treasures, come, descend from Heaven:
    As you are always truthful, grant me the power to speak truly.
You gave Peter, when he left his fishing net, speech of divine things.
    From one womb, through you, rivers flowed.
Nor are you divided into smaller parts, but you remain complete,
    Giving your gifts to your servants, as you wish and what you wish.
You have granted to some excellence of speech,
    To some interpreting minds, and to some works of power.
Grant me the power to treat what I have taken up and bring it to its end.
    So that my Muse might please her Augustus.

Commentary and Notes [139v]: At the opening of Book 3, the poet invokes the Muse, but with a difference. He dismisses two pagan Muses by name (Calliope and Clio), and also dismisses Virgil, his epic model, with a reference to his *Eclogues* (Tityrus is a shepherd narrator of *Eclogue* 1). Instead, he appeals to a biblical and Christian Muse, whom he calls "Wisdom of the highest Father" (*summi Sapientia Patris*). Divine Wisdom is known from the Old Testament Books of

Proverbs (1:20–33) and the New Testament (Matthew 10:30 and Luke 7:35), but Pietro attributes the actions of the Holy Spirit to her as well, for example, bringing about the Virgin Mary's conception of Christ (Luke 1:34–35), and giving a variety of spiritual gifts to believers (1 Corinthians 12:4–31). The poet praises her and asks her help in bringing his poem to completion.

(S 103–4, lines 1470–1503; KS 221)

[PARTICULA L] With missing verses counted, perhaps Section 50: Invocation to Wisdom as a Muse

140r *Pietro of Eboli invokes Wisdom.* Illustrates ll. 1470–1503, on fol. 139v.

. . . .

Sapientia continens omnia.	1.	Wisdom containing all.
Mappa mundi.	2.	Map of the world.
Poeta.	3.	The poet.
Rar si ge puse — Rar se gipuse achaper	4,5.	(Old French addendum) "Seldom, if I can escape!"

Commentary and Notes [140r]: Wisdom, identified by cap. 1, holds a map of the world, labeled in cap. 2. The map is shaped like a globe, but instead of land masses and continents, five rows of buildings appear on it, above a sea into which three rivers flow. (No captions identify the rivers.) The poet, tonsured and wearing clothing of green and brown, is a diminutive figure at the bottom left of the drawing, with face and hands at the level of Wisdom's feet. He stretches out his hands toward her. Pietro envisions Wisdom as holding the world in her possession, but he is thinking of the world as inhabited by human beings in cities and towns, rather than the geographical world consisting of land masses. Of course the two concepts cannot be completely separated (hence, much unresolved discussion about the three rivers represented). Caps. 4–5 apparently belong to the jottings of a French scribe during the manuscript's sojourn in a French monastery, as Siragusa (146, n. 3) says "testing the reed" or making certain that a new quill or pen was functioning correctly. However, responding to others' attempts to interpret the saying, he states that "achaper" means to "put under a cape, hide." Kölzer's commentary (222) interprets the Old French words as an ironic response to Cap. 1's claim that Wisdom contains all things: "Seldom, if I can escape." Thus, the Old French scribe suggests that by hiding from Wisdom (presumably by being a fool), he can prevent her from containing all things.

(S 146; KS 222)

140v   <(Rota) Particula XLVIII: Pax tempore Augusti>

Fortunata dies, felix post tempora tempus,	1505
Que sextum sexto tempore cernit herum!	1506
O nimis etatis felicia tempora nostre,	1507
Propugnatorem que meruere suum!	1508
Gaudeat omnis humus, tellus sine nube diescat,	1509
Rorem spectati muneris astra pluant.	1510
Mane serena dies venit et serotinus imber,	1511
Imperium Cesar solus et unus habet.	1512
Iam redit aurati Saturnia temporis etas,	1513
Iam redeunt magni regna quieta Iovis;	1514
Sponte parit tellus, gratis honeratur aristis,	1515
Vomeris a nullo dente relata parit;	1516
Nec fecunda fimo, nec rastris indiget ullis	1517
Mater opum, pecori prospera, grata viris.	1518
Omnis olivescit Phebeis frondibus arbor,	1519
Vix arbor partus sustinet orta novos;	1520
Nec rosa, nec viole, nec lilia, gloria vallis,	1521
Marcescunt aliquo tempore nata semel.	1522
Felix nostra dies, nec ea felicior ulla,	1523
Lecior aut locuplex a Salomone fuit.	1524
Evomuit serpens virus sub fauce repostum,	1525
Aruit in vires mesta cicuta suas.	1526
Nec sonipes griphes, nec oves assueta luporum	1527
Ora timent; ut ovis stat lupus inter oves;	1528
Uno fonte bibunt, eadem pascuntur et arva	1529
Bos, leo, grus, aquila, sus, canis, ursus, aper.	1530
Non erit in nostris moveat qui bella diebus;	1531
Amodo perpetue tempora pacis erunt.	1532
Nulla manent hodie veteris vestigia fraudis,	1533
Qua Tancridinus polluit error humum,	1534
Ipsaque transibunt derisi tempora regis,	1535
Nam meus Augustus solus et unus erit;	1536
Unus amor, commune bonum, rex omnibus unus,	1537
Unus sol, unus pastor et una fides.	1538

Commentary and Notes [140v]: Once more Pietro paints an idyllic picture of the new realm, with images drawn from both classical and biblical literature. The proclamation of Saturn's reign echoes Virgil's *Eclogue* 4.6. The imagery of a fruitful land from which evil has departed, where animals are no longer carnivorous,

< (Rota) Section 48: Peace in the Time of Augustus. >

Fortunate day, happy time after the times,
  Which beholds the sixth master in the sixth age!
O exceedingly happy times of our generation,
  Who earned their champion!
Let all the land rejoice; may dawn come to earth without cloud,
  May the stars shed dew as a gift long awaited.
Serene day comes in the morning, and showers in the evening,
  Caesar alone holds the sole authority.
Now returns the golden age of Saturn,
  Now return the quiet realms of great Jove.
The earth gives birth willingly, burdened with welcome ears of grain;
  She brings forth without being touched by the teeth of plowshares,
Nor does the fertile mother of wealth, favorable to the flock and welcome to men
  Need dung or drag-hoe.
Every tree becomes green with fronds of Phoebus;
  And, hardly sprung up, each bears new fruit.
Nor do the rose, the violets, and the lily, the glory of the valley,
  Fade, no matter what time has passed, once they are born.
Happy is our day, and nor has any since Solomon
  Been brighter or richer.
The serpent has spewed out the venom hidden beneath its gullet;
  The poison of the grim hemlock has withered.
Now foals no longer fear griffins nor sheep the accustomed
  Mouths of wolves, for the wolf stands like a sheep among the sheep.
Now all drink from one spring and graze in the same pasture,
  Ox, lion, crane, eagle, pig, dog, bear and wild boar.
In our days there will be no one who wages war;
  At last the times of perpetual peace will be.
Today there remain no traces of that old deceit,
  By which the Tancredine error polluted the earth.
And the times of that ridiculous king shall disappear,
  For my Augustus shall rule, alone and solely.
There will be one love, good for all, and one king over all,
  One sun, one shepherd and one faith.

and where difficult work is no longer required echoes not only *Eclogue* 4 but also
Messianic passages such as Isaiah 11:6–9 and Amos 9:11–15.

(S 105–6, lines 1504–1537; KS 225)

[Particula LXI] With missing verses counted, perhaps Section 51: Return of the
Golden Age

tanta pax est tepe augusti cō i una fonte bibu:
ōia animalia

lions

141r *Allusive figure on the peace enjoyed under Augustus Henry VI.* Illustrates ll. 1503–1537, on fol. 140v.

• • • •

Tanta pax est tempore Augusti	1.	There is such peace in the time of
quod in uno fonte bibunt		Augustus that all animals drink at
omnia animalia.		one spring.
Fons.	2.	Spring.

Commentary and Notes [141r]: At the top of the page, a variety of flowers and plants are blooming, but any caption which may have been there to explain their meaning has been lost. Below, a spring appears with a variety of animals—cow, lion, goat, deer, boar, panther and wolf (or bear?)—gathered around it, drinking peacefully together to represent the peace of the times. Kölzer ("Bildkommentar," 226) identifies the birds as partridges. The verses would have led us to expect eagles.

(S 146; KS 226)

141v <(Rota) Particula XLIX: Teatrum imperialis palacii>

Dic, mea Musa, precor, genuit qui nobilis alvus	1539
Henricum, vel que dextra cubile dedit?	1540
Que superum nutrix dedit ubera, quis dedit artes?	1541
Quis puero tribuit scire vel arma viro?	1542
Quave domo genitus fuerit puer, aurea proles,	1543
Quis pater, unde parens, dic, mea Musa, precor.	1544
Est domus, etherei qua ludunt tempora veris;	1545
Ipse domus paries ex adamante riget.	1546
Ante domum patulo preludit sole teatrum	1547
Quo salit in medio fons, Arethusa, tuus;	1548
Ipsa quater denis innititur aula columpnis,	1549
In quibus imperii tota quiescit humus.	1550
Hic Corradus adest, iuris servator et equi,	1551
Scribens edictum, certa tributa lebens,	1552
Cancellos reserans, mundi signacula solvens,	1553
Colligit Italicas, alter Homerus, opes.	1554
Nulla fames auri, sitis illi nulla metalli;	1555
Res nova quam loquimur, mens sua numen habet.	1556
Diligit Ecclesiam, nec matrem filius odit,	1557
Dux evangelii, iuris aperta manus.	1558
Angelus in multos nec non Paracletus in omnes	1559
Mittitur, et missi fatur in ore Deus.	1560
Hic Marcualdus, cui se Neptunus ad omne	1561
Velle dedit, cui Mars se dedit esse parem.	1562
Illuc conveniunt ex omni cardine mundi	1563
Dantes Augusto plena tributa duces,	1564
Quos brevis absolvit positis apodixa tributis,	1565
Quam tua, Corrade, griphea signat avis.	1566
Hic grave pondus Arabs missi deliberat auri,	1567
Hic Melechinas exhibet Indus opes,	1568
Et decus et precium, gemmas dat Persis et aurum,	1569
Materiam superans, mittit Egyptus opus.	1570
Argentum, gemmas, auri genus, inclite Cesar,	1571
Delicias hominum, quas habet orbis, habes.	1572

<(Rota) Section 49: Theater of the Royal Palace >

Say, my Muse, I pray, what noble womb gave birth to Henry,
    Or what right hand gave him a resting place?
What immortal nurse gave him the breast; who gave him knowledge?
    Who gave understanding to the boy or arms to the man?
At what house was the boy engendered, that golden offspring?
    Say, my Muse, who was his father, whence came his mother?
There is a house where heavenly springtime is at play;
    The walls of that house are mighty with adamant.
Before the house, a theater rehearses in the open sun,
    And your fountain leaps in the midst of it, Arethusa;
The hall shines with four columns times ten,
    In which all the land of the Empire has rest.
Here Conrad comes, servant of law and equity,
    Writing the edict, collecting the established tribute,
Unlocking the chancery, opening the seals of the world.
    Another Homer, he gathers Italian wealth.
He has no hunger for gold, no thirst for any kind of metal;
    We have something strange to tell — something divine lives in his spirit.
He loves the Church, a son who does not hate his mother,
    For he is a guide to the Gospels, the open hand of the law.
He is sent as an angel to some, as a comforter to all,
    And God speaks through the mouth of the one he has sent.
Here is Markward, to whom Neptune has granted his help in all that he wills,
    Mars grants him to be his own equal.
Here they come from all corners of the world,
    The rulers, giving plentiful tribute to Augustus.
When the treasure is deposited, payment is acknowledged by a small receipt,
    Which you, Conrad, stamp with your griffin seal.
Arabia delivers a great weight of gold;
    India shows a wealth of royal coins;
Persia gives gems and gold, beautiful and precious;
    Egypt sends work surpassing the material.
Silver, jewels, crafted gold, famous Caesar,
    Delightful to men — you have what the earth holds.

Commentary and Notes [141v]: Pietro continues his idyllic portrait of the peaceful reign of Henry VI. He moves from wondering questions about Henry's origins to an idealized picture of his court, with many words of praise for the chancellor Conrad and a few for Markward.

Arethusa (lines 1548) was originally a Greek wood nymph, devoted to Artemis (or Diana), who, tired from hunting, bathed in the river Alphaeus. This river-god fell in love with her and pursued her. She called upon her divine patroness for help, and the goddess transformed her into a spring, in which form she fled into the earth, later emerging near Syracuse in Sicily. Ovid's story (*Metamorphoses* 5.579–641) leaves the impression that Arethusa has escaped her pursuer, but Virgil (*Eclogue* 10. 1 and *Aeneid* 3.363) states that Alphaeus also followed Arethusa through the earth so that their waters are now mixed. See also the Additional Notes on this line.

(S 107–8, lines 1538–1571; KS 229)

PARTICULA LXII. With missing verses counted, perhaps Section 52: The Audience Hall of the Royal Palace

142r *The "Theater of the Imperial Palace," with the fountain of Arethusa, the chancellor receiving tribute, etc.* Illustrates 1538–1571, on fol. 141v. of the codex.

· · · ·

Teatrum imperialis palacii		1.	Theater of the Imperial Palace.
			[In the upper colonnade:]
Frisia	Olsatia	Frisia	Holstein
Bavaria	Scavia	Bavaria	Slavonia
Austria	Pomerania	Austria	Pomerania
Turingia	Polonia	Thuringia	Poland
Saxonia	Westfalia	Saxony	Westphalia
Boemia	Brabancia	Bohemia	Brabant
			[In the lower colonnade]
Flandria	Suevia	Flanders	Swabia
Anglia	Liguria	England	Liguria
Belgia	Burgundia	Belgium	Burgundy
Alsatia	Marchia	Alsace	The March
Lothoringia	Lombardia	Lothoringia	Lombardy
Francia	Tuscia	France	Tuscany

Cancellarius recipiens tributa.	2.	The chancellor receiving tributes.
Arabs.	3.	From Arabia.
Indus.	4.	From India
Fons Arethuse.	5.	Spring of Arethusa

Commentary and Notes [142r]: Within a hall, "the theater" (Cap. 1; also see Additional Notes), between two lines of colonnades, Chancellor Conrad sits receiving tribute from turbaned men who kneel before him (Caps. 2–4). On the right, behind their backs, is the spring of Arethusa, with a human face, but a body of flowing water (cap. 5). Further to the right, a cloaked man, evidently Markward (Siragusa, 147–48 and n. 1) wields a sword. Siragusa points out that in 131r, Markward wore a beard. Perhaps the clean-shaven look is more appropriate for the eternal spring on display here. Also, the two miniatures apparently belong to different stages of composition; see Introduction A.2. The names of the many territories which theoretically owed obedience to the Empire are written between the columns of the two colonnades.

(S 147; KS 230)

142v <(Rota) Particula L: Domus imperialis palacii>

In talamos sex una domus partitur, et horum	1573
Prima Creatoris regia scribit opus,	1574
Illic in specie super undas diva columbe	1575
Maiestas operum pingitur ipse Deus;	1576
Altera fatiferum cataclismi pingit abyssum;	1577
Tercia fert Habrahe credulitatis iter;	1578
Quarta Faraonem submergens nudat Egyptum;	1579
Quinta domus David tempora regis habet;	1580
Sexta Fredericum divo depingit amictu,	1581
Cesarea septum prole senile latus.	1582

¶
Hic Fredericus ovans, in milibus undique fretus,	1583
Fervidus in Christo miles iturus erat.	1584

¶
Hic erat annosum multa nemus ylice septum,	1585
Non nisi per gladios silva datura vias;	1586
In nemus omne furit ferrum, nemus omne favillat,	1587
Fit via, quod dudum parte negabat iter.	1588

¶
Hic erat infide tua fallax Ungare dextra,	1589
Qualiter invito te Fredericus abit.	1590

¶
Hic Ysaac mentita fides et fictile fedus,	1591
Illic Grecorum non sine cede dolus;	1592
Hic obsessa Polis, nec non plantata per annum	1593
Vinea, cesaree quam coluere manus,	1594
Hic Conii pinguntur opes et bella ferocis,	1595
Hic Fredericiades fulminat ense procer,	1596
Hic pater arma tenet, subit illic filius urbem,	1597
Pars prior Augusto sub seniore cadit.	1598
At postquam Conii spoliis saturantur et auro,	1599
Castra movent, nec eis cura quietis erat.	1600
Proh dolor! Ad flumen ponunt temtoria Tharsis,	1601
Quo lacerat tumidas nans Fredericus aquas;	1602
Suspectas invenit aquas, qui raptus ab undis	1603
Exuit humanum, servit et ante Deum,	1604
Vivit in eternum Fredericus, lancea cuius	1605
Nunquam fraudata cuspide versa fuit.	1606

<(Rota) Section 50: Houses of the Imperial Palace>

One house is divided into six chambers, of these,
>The first records the royal work of the creator.
Here, in likeness of a dove, above the waters
>The Divine Majesty, maker of works, is pictured, God Himself.
The next depicts the depths of the fate-bearing flood;
>The third takes the road of Abraham's belief;
The fourth, drowning Pharaoh, leaves Egypt bare;
>The fifth house has the times of King David.
The sixth depicts Frederick in divine array,
>His aged side defended by Caesarian offspring.

¶
Here Frederick rejoices among thousands, supported on every side,
>He was on fire to journey as a soldier of Christ.

¶
Here was a barrier of holm-oaks in a forest full of years;
>The forest will grant no passage except through the sword.
In every grove iron rages; every grove sheds sparks,
>And road is made where, until then, passage was denied.

¶
False Hungary, here your right hand was unfaithful,
>Though Frederick crossed your lands despite you.

¶
Here Isaac's lying promise and feigned alliance showed itself,
>And there was Greek trickery, not without slaughter;
Here they besieged the Great City and Caesarian hands
>Tended vineyards planted for that year.
Here the wealth of Iconium is depicted and war with the fierce enemies,
>Here the heroic son of Frederick brandishes his sword,
Here the father holds arms, there the son subjects a city;
>The first defense falls before the elder Augustus.
And after Iconium, they are stuffed with gold and spoils;
>They move their camp without troubling to enforce quiet.
Alas, for sorrow! At the river of Tharsis they place their tents,
>Swimming here, Frederick cuts the swollen waters;
He finds the waters treacherous. Then, snatched from the waves,
>He left humanity and now serves in God's presence.
Frederick lives in eternity, the point of whose lance
>Was never turned away cheated of its object.

Commentary and Notes [142v]: Pietro describes another hall in the palace, divided into six rooms, each of which depicts an important epoch in history. Pietro's scheme, though no doubt influenced by Augustine's theory of the epochs, diverges from it somewhat; see notes. Seven lines (1574–1580) quickly move from the creation of the world to the time of King David. The rest is spent on Henry's father, Frederick Barbarossa, and the crusading expedition in which he died.

The felling of the forest described in verses 1585–1590 refers to Barbarossa's journey across Byzantine territory, where he received harassment instead of the help he had been promised by Isaac Angelus.

As lines 1594–1599 suggest, Barbarossa's bloodiest battle was against the Turks at Iconium (Konya), where, according to Choniates, he retaliated after being attacked first. Siragusa (110, n. 5) finds more details of the battle in the chronicle of Ansberto, who reports that the city fell to a coordinated strategy in which Barbarossa himself took the main fortress while his son, Frederick of Swabia, took the city itself. There was much spoil; as Ansberto writes, "Here the fury of our bellies was lessened to some extent by spoil from the enemy. Many of our men found pits filled with wheat and barley, by which the men and horses were for the most part restored. Some reported that the plunder done in that city, in gold and silver, gems and purple, was priced at ten thousand marks. For in the house of the great Melchus, the missing treasure, which unholy Saladin had sent as a dowry with his daughter, was found."

Soon after this battle, Frederick met his death on 10 June 1190 in the river Salef. This section ends with the glorified emperor watching events from heaven, as in the earlier lines 324–333.

(S 109–11 lines 1572–1605) (KS 233)

1603 *Suspectas*. S: Suspetas. Non-S: *Suspectas*. (Apparently Siragusa regards *suspetas* as a valid alternate spelling, but he offers no alternate definition.)

[Particula LXIII] With missing verses counted, perhaps Section 53

143r *Pictures adorning the six "houses" or "bedchambers" of the royal palace. Frederick I and his two sons, Henry and Philip. Frederick I, departing for the crusade, causes a Hungarian forest to be cut down.* Illustrates verses 1572–1560, on fol. 142v.

. . . .

Prima domus — Deus creans omnia.	1.	First house — God creating everything.
Secunda domus — Archa Noe.	2.	Second house — Noah's Ark.
Tercia domus — Habraham.	3.	Third House — Abraham.
Quarta domus — Moyses — Mare Rubrum.	4.	Fourth House — Moses — Red Sea.
Quinta domus — David rex.	5.	Fifth House — King David.
Sexta domus imperii — Fredericus imperator — Henricus — Philippus	6.	Sixth imperial house — Frederick the emperor, Henry, Philip.
Fredericus imperator iubet incidere nemus Ungarie.	7.	Frederick the emperor commands the forest of Hungary to be cut down.

Commentary and Notes [143r]: These illustrations purport to show six rooms, apparently with paintings which show the ages of the world from the beginning to the present time. In the top row, five of these rooms appear. In the first (cap. 1), an anthropomorphic God hovers over the waters, and various creatures look up. Noah's ark (cap. 2) is a tall building with an arched door. Three angels (cap. 3) appear to a kneeling Abraham. Moses (cap. 4) and two companions look down upon two prostrate figures, apparently drowned Egyptians.

At the far right, a crowned King David (cap. 5) sits on his throne holding his scepter. The next two levels together show the sixth house, devoted to Frederick Barbarossa and his sons. In the first of these (cap. 6) Barbarossa sits crowned and enthroned under an arch, his right hand resting on the crowned head of his son Henry while his left hand rests on the uncrowned head of Philip of Swabia. Philip (1177–1208) was originally intended for the church, but after the death of his elder brother Frederick, duke of Swabia, his plans changed. In 1195, he was made Duke of Tuscany, probably about the same time he was betrothed to Irene, daughter of Isaac Angelus. On the lower level, Frederick appears on horseback, riding before a group of knights. In front of him another group of knights is cutting down trees which bar their way.

(S 148; KS 234)

143v <(KS) Particula LI: De Septem artibus liberalibus>
      <(Rota) Particula LI: De Septem Virtutibus>

Illic diva parens, superum Sapientia mater,	1607
Uberis Henrico munera digna dabat;	1608
Ipsa ministrantes septem conventa sorores	1609
Ut puerum doceant officiosa rogat.	1610
Prima loqui recta docet; altera iurgia lingue;	1611
Tertia conditos reddit in ore sonos;	1612
Quarta, quid astra velint, cum visa coire retrorsum;	1613
Quinta docet numerum pro ratione legi;	1614
Sexta gradus in voce suos docet impare cantu;	1615
Septima metiri posse magistrat humum.	1616
Suscipit in gremio virtutum gracia mater	1617
Ore virum, iuvenem corpore, mente senem,	1618
Quem virtus dilapsa polo sic possidet omnis,	1619
Singula quod virtus asserat esse suum.	1620
Hec mores informat et usibus illa coaptat;	1621
Hec sibi preiustum vendicat, illa pium;	1622
Hec, ubi res posit, rigidum facit, illa modestum;	1623
Lex quandoque potest de pietate queri,	1624
Arma fatigarant superos, que contulit illa.	1625
Sic, sic era rigent, arma quod hoste carent,	1626
Quod Numidos, quod Sarmaticos sibi Roma subegit,	1627
Unde redit Titan nox ubi prima subit;	1628
Magnus Alexander Darium quod vicit in armis,	1629
Quod fuit imperio terra subacta suo,	1630
Et quod Pompeium Cesar patresque fugavit,	1631
Unde Tolomei crimen Egyptus habet.	1632
Nullus ei similis nisi proles, nemo secundus,	1633
Diis meus Henricus equiparandus erit.	1634
Dicitur Henricus! latet hac in voce triumphus,	1635
Quod latet in partes littera ducta parit.	1636
Certant virtutes, certatim munera prebent,	1637
Crescit in Augusto gratia plena meo,	1638
Infra quem gremium Sapientia dulce recepit;	1639
Hec os ore docet, pectore pectus alit.	1640

<(KS 237) Section 51: Concerning the Seven Liberal Arts>
<(Rota) Section 51: Concerning the Virtues>

In this place, the divine parent, Wisdom, mother of those above,
    Was giving Henry worthy gifts of her breast.
She, calling upon her seven ministering sisters,
    Dutifully entreats them to instruct the boy.
The first teaches him just speech, a second the language of contention;
    A third puts pleasant sounds in his mouth,
The fourth tells him what the stars mean, when they seem to move backwards
    to their assemblies;
    The fifth teaches him to compute numbers in his mind;
The sixth in her degree teaches him to voice unparalleled song.
    The seventh imparts the ability to measure the earth.
The gracious mother of virtues receives him into her lap,
    A man in words, a youth in body, an old man in mind,
Possessed by every virtue fallen from the sky,
    Because each virtue claimed him as her own.
One informed his manners, another taught him customs,
    One made him supremely just, another pious,
One made him stern when matters required it; another made him mild,
    So that sometimes Law can complain of his pity,
When the arms that she took up have wearied the gods.
    Thus, thus do weapons grow sluggish when there is no armed enemy.
Thus Rome subjected the Numidians and the Sarmatians to herself
    Whereby Titan returns to the place where night first arose;
Thus Great Alexander defeated Darius in arms,
    So that the earth was subjected to his command;
Thus Caesar drove out Pompey along with his senatorial supporters,
    So that Egypt endured the crime of Ptolemy.
In all of this, no one is equal to Henry except his offspring; there is no other.
    My Henry must be put on the same level as the gods.
He is called Henry! Triumph is hidden in that word;
    The separated letters reveal the meaning.
The virtues contend, and in their contention they offer gifts.
    Plentiful grace increases in my Augustus,
Whom Wisdom received sweetly into her lap,
    Her mouth taught his, her heart fostered his heart.

Commentary and Notes [143v]: In describing Henry's education among the virtues and liberal arts, Pietro also reveals his ideas about the qualities which kings need. As Del Re writes (455, n. 54) concerning line 1609, "Wisdom, the divine mother of the Heavenly beings, namely Minerva, brings together her seven sisters (namely the liberal arts) and gives the boy into their custody so that they can give him some of their milk. The first is Grammar, second Dialectic, third Eloquence [or perhaps Rhetoric], fourth Astrology, fifth Arithmetic, sixth Music, seventh Geometry. . . ." Del Re is apt in naming the Seven Liberal Arts, but Wisdom here is probably still the Divine Wisdom invoked by the poet in line 1477, though Pietro might associate her with Minerva. Law, like the Virtues, is personified as a woman or goddess in lines 1624–1625. She complains sometimes of Henry's mercy, when the gods are tired of causes for which Law has resorted to arms. (In short, Henry sometimes mitigates the harshness of the letter of the law.) For comments on the ethnic and geographical references in line 1627, see Additional Notes.

1628: *Unde redit Titan nox ubi prima subit;* Titan is the sun; see note on line 1419–1420. The point here, however, is that the sun rises, displacing the night which is already there, as, symbolically, civilization displaced chaos where Rome conquered various enemies. The cycle keeps repeating. This line is in the historical present, while the previous one and those which follow are in the perfect tense. This helps convey the idea that this phenomenon repeats itself. Line 1419 actually comes in its entirety from Lucan, *De Bello Civili* 1.15: "Unde venit Titan, et nox ubi sidera condit."

1631: *Et quod Pompeium Cesar patresque fugavit / Unde Tolomei crimen Egyptus habet.* Here *patres* refers to Romans of the senatorial class who supported Pompey, rival of Julius Caesar. After his defeat at the battle of Pharsalus, Pompey fled to Egypt and was murdered by that country's king, Ptolemy, who hoped to ingratiate himself with Caesar. The story is told by Plutarch, and also by Lucan, one of Pietro's models (see fol. 95r, cap. 2), to whom Pietro has just alluded above.

1636: *Quod latet in partes littera ducta parit.* In other words, the triumphant meaning of Henry's name is revealed in the acrostic (lines 1462–1469).

(S 112–13, lines 1606–1639)

[PARTICULA LXIV] With missing verses counted, perhaps Section 54. It describes Henry's education by Wisdom. The verses here emphasize how he is taught by the seven liberal arts, although "virtues" are mentioned in the text. The next verses, which are missing, presumably put more emphasis on his education by the virtues, which are depicted in the next set of miniatures.

x4r

The miniatures illustrating the verses 1607–1640 are missing. Presumably they would show young Henry learning some of his lessons from some of the Liberal Arts. Perhaps they would show some instances in which the Emperor displayed the qualities which he had learned. Or there might be representations from secular history to match the representations (mostly) from sacred history in fol. 143r.

x4v [**Particula LV**/ Section 55]

With missing verses counted, this might be Section 55: Henry, Tancred, and the Wheel of Fortune

---

The verses that go with the illustrations to fol. 146r are missing. This page was apparently lost before *Liber ad Honorem Augusti* was trimmed to be bound with its companions in the Bern Codex (see Introduction B. 1). Perhaps the verses would discuss the relationship between Providence and Fortune, or Virtue and Glory.

146r *Henry VI on the throne surrounded by the Virtues. Tancred struck down by the wheel of Fortune.* (Illustrates text on missing FOL. X4V.)

· · · ·

Henricus VI magnus Romanorum Imperator.

1. Henry VI, great emperor of the Romans.

Virtutes, Fortitudo, Virtutes, Justitia.

2. Virtues, Fortitude, Virtues, Justice.

Fortuna rogat Virtutes esse in consorcio earum, set repulsam passa est.

3. Fortuna asks the virtues to be in their company, but she suffers rejection.

Rota Fortune.

4. Wheel of Fortune.

Glorior elatus.

5. I am lifted in glory.

Descendo minorificatus.

6. I descend, having been made small.

Infimus axe teror — Tancredus.

7. The fallen is crushed by the wheel — Tancred.

Ru[rsus ad astra feror]

8. Again, I am lifted to the stars.

Commentary and Notes [146r]: Under an arch, Henry VI sits crowned, enthroned, and holding his scepter and orb. Seven virtues surround him, only two of them given individual names (Fortitude, with a helm, and Justice, with a book, presumably of laws). Below, Fortune speaks from her wheel, pleading in vain, as cap. 3 says, to be admitted into their fellowship. The poem about the wheel of fortune, which Siragusa (150, n. 2) suggests might be the work of Hildebert of Lavardin, was inserted by a later hand; see Additional Notes.

(S 150; KS 238)

146v <(Rota): Particula LII: Sapientia convicians Fortune>

Inclita regales crispans Sapientia vultus,	1641
Aspera Fortune talia verba dedit:	1642
"Sit tuus Andronicus saturatus cede nepotis,	1643
"Cui cruor Ytalicus potus et esca fuit;	1644
"Sit tuus Andronicus, qui crassus cede suorum	1645
"Addidit ex omni stirpe necare probos,	1646
"Cuius ad extremum, licet impar pena reatus,	1647
"Mors sua perpetuo vindice feda caret.	1648
"Sit tuus ille senex qui raptus, ut Yccarus alis,	1649
"Occidit et pelago flet sua mersa ratis;	1650
"Occidit, ut quondam series immensa gigantum,	1651
"Quis fuit imperium cura videre Iovis,	1652
"Sic et Tancredus multo, miser, ebruis auro	1653
"Occidit, in dominum dum tulit arma suum.	1654
"Si potes, Andronicum civilibus eripe telis;	1655
"Si potes, alterius regna tuere senis;	1656
"Nam meus Henricus materna sede sedebit	1657
"In qua rex Salamon sedit in orbe potens.	1658
"Talis erit sedes: ebur uxorabit in auro;	1659
"Hoc hominum sensus exuperabit opus;	1660
"Bis senos habitura gradus Henricia sedes,	1661
"Ex auro sex, sex ex adhamante gradus	1662
"Per quos fulvescent civili more leones,	1663
"Ordine suppositi, iussa sedentis agant;	1664
"Procedant de sede throni, res ardua, grifes;	1665
"Procedant aquile seu Nucerinus aper;	1666
"Procedant rigidi nostra de sede leones;	1667
"Procedat fenix, nuncia pacis avis;	1668
"A leva Neptunus aquas castiget et omne	1669
"Iuppiter a dextris corrigat ipse solum;	1670
"A leva citharam moveat Mercurius aure;	1671
"Omnividens dextra Phebus in aure legat.	1672
"Mars pre sede sedens, gladiatus territet orbem,	1673
"Cogat ad imperium sidera, fata, deus."	1674

Commentary and Notes [146v]: Wisdom rebukes Fortune, since Fortune's favorites are those like Tancred and Andronicus who enjoy temporary success as a result of their wickedness but ultimately fail and are destroyed. The success of Wisdom's pupils will be lasting, although they may suffer reverses for a while. According to Siragusa (114–15, nn. 1–2), the boar of Nocera (*nucerinus aper*) is Diepold of Schweinspeunt, whose heraldic symbol is a boar; Neptune is Markward, who has

<(Rota): Section 52: Wisdom Rails at Fortune> (S 114–115) (KS 241)

Famous Wisdom, turning her royal countenance,
    Gives these bitter words to Fortune:
"May Andronicus be yours, soaked in the blood of his nephew,
    "To whom Italian blood was drink and food;
"May gross Andronicus be yours, who added to the slaughter of his own
    "The killing of honest people of every lineage!
"At his end, the penalty for his guilt was, indeed, unparalleled,
    "And his foul death forever lacks an avenger.
"Let that old man be yours, who, snatched up like Icarus on wings,
    "Fell, and in the sea bewails his drowned boat.
"He fell, as an immense succession of giants once did,
    "Who troubled themselves to visit Jove's empire.
"So Tancred also fell, wretched man, drunk with much gold,
    "When he took up arms against his lord.
"If you are able, snatch Andronicus from the arrows of the citizens;
    "If you can, preserve the realm of that other old man;
"For my Henry will sit in the maternal seat,
    "On which King Solomon sat, powerful over all the world.
"Such shall be this seat: Ivory will be married to gold,
    "This work will amaze the senses of men;
"Henry's throne will have twice six steps leading up to it,
    "Six in gold and six in adamant,
"On which tawny lions shall comport themselves courteously.
    "Order being established, let them fulfill the commands of the seated One;
Let gryfons proceed from the seat of the throne, the steep way.
    "Let eagles proceed, or perhaps the boar of Nocera.
"Let stern lions proceed from our seat,
    "Let the phoenix proceed, the avian emissary of peace;
"At the left, let Neptune restrain the waters,
    "And on the right let Jupiter himself govern the whole land.
"At the left, let Mercury stir the air with his lyre;
    "At the right, let all-seeing Phoebus receive it in his ear.
"Let Mars, sitting before his seat, girded with a sword, terrify the earth,
    "Let him compel to the Empire's dominion the stars, the fates, and the gods."

acted as a naval commander, and Mars is Henry of Kalden or *Henricus Calandrinus*. See Additional Notes.

(S 114–15) (KS 241)

[PARTICULA LXVI] With missing verses counted, perhaps Section 56

147r *Henry VI on the throne flanked by Markward of Anweiler and the chancellor Conrad,*
   etc. Illustrates the verses 1640–1673 contained on page 53 (146v) of the codex.

. . . .

Fortuna.	1.	Fortune.
Sapientia convicens Fortuna.	2.	Wisdom condemning Fortune.
Marchisius senescalcus.	3.	Markward the seneschal. .
Henricus imperator.	4.	Emperor Henry.
Corradus cancellarius.	5.	Conrad the Chancellor.
Tancredus.	6.	Tancred.
Andronicus.	7.	Andronicus.
Sedes Sapientie.	8.	The seat of Wisdom.
Henricus Calandrinus.	9.	Henry of Kalden.

Commentary and Notes [147r]: Again enthroned and crowned, Henry is surrounded by his officials. Six steps are on each side of the throne, a lion on each one. Crowned Wisdom appears above his head. Markward the seneschal is at his right, and Conrad the chancellor at his left. On the top right of the drawing, Fortune stands with her wheel, in which Tancred is entangled. The face of an old man represents Andronicus, who was similarly destroyed. Faintly drawn, there are severed hands and mutilated bodies, perhaps victims of Andronicus, or perhaps representations of his own grisly murder. Before the throne stands Henry of Kalden, the emperor's marshal.

(S 150–51; KS 242)

147v

Ego magister Petrus de Ebulo, servus imperatoris et fidelis, hunc librum ad honorem Augusti composui. Fac mecum, Domine, signum in bonum, ut videant me Tancridini et confundantur. In aliquo beneficio michi provideat Dominus meus et Deus meus, qui est et erit benedictus in secula. Amen. Amen, amen, amen.

Commentary and Notes [147v]: Pietro here alludes to Psalm 86:17, which reads (RSV), "Show me a sign of thy favor, that those who hate me may see and be put to shame, because thou, lord, hast helped and comforted me." Siragusa also points out (116, n. 3) that Henry VI did confer property on Pietro, apparently a mill at Albiscenda (*Molendinum de Albiscenda*). Further, he describes words by other hands written on this page: "This whole caption, which is on the last page of the *Carmi*, very worn with use, appears faded, and as I said, retraced by a later

[Pietro's postscript. It is not illustrated.]

I, Master Pietro of Eboli, servant of the Emperor and faithful, wrote this book in honor of Augustus. Give me, Lord, a sign of your favor, so that the Tancredines may see me and be confounded. May my Lord and my God provide me with some reward, he who is and will be blessed throughout the ages. Amen. Amen, amen, amen.

hand to which can be attributed the completion of the words "imperatoris" and "secula." Above this are found the two following verses written in the large characters of the time and repeated two other times, the first time in characters of the end of the twelfth century or the beginning of the thirteenth century , the third later, but not by much: *Anno quinque minus numeratis mille ducentis Caesar Regna capit, et sua Nupta parit* (In the year five years before the year 1200, Caesar received his realm and his bride gave birth).

(S 116; KS 245)

Additional Notes

Fol. 95r
Illustration 1: *Virgil, Lucan, Ovid.*
(S 119)(KS 34)

At the bottom of this page, the words *Celestinorum Senonensium* appear. They were added later to indicate ownership of the book by the Cloister of the Celestines of Sens in Burgundy

Fol. 95v
Section 1: Here begins the first section, about the first king of Sicily.
(S 3–4)(KS 37)

1: *Roggerius . . . Guiscardi . . . propago.* Or "Guiscard's famous kinsman." Though *propago*, when applied to human beings, generally means "offspring," it can also mean "slip" or "shoot" when applied to plants. Pietro might have meant that Roger II was Guiscard's political offspring, as Norman ruler of southern Italy, or (as the commentary states) he might have accepted the legends which make Roger II a direct descendant of Robert Guiscard.

3: *Altius aspirat.* Here Pietro moves from the past to the "historical present"; that is, though the action is in the past, the verb tense is in the present for greater vividness, to cause the reader to see it as unfolding action. While English speakers also use this device sometimes, writers of formal English rarely do. Pietro, however, uses it quite often, and I represent it in the translation more often than is, perhaps, pleasant for the reader. However, I cannot always translate this device and still retain coherence, so I often translate according to the meaning.

5: *barbaries.* This word can mean "barbarian," and "foreign," but Pietro probably meant King Roger's North African conquests. Loud and Wiedemann, in their notes to *The History of the Tyrants of Sicily*, state that King Roger's enemies here were Berbers (78, n. 41). The anonymous Cistercian author of *Chronica S. Mariae De Ferraria*, in *Ignoti Monachi Cisterciensis S. Mariae De Ferraria Chronica et Ryccardi de Sancto Germano Chronica Priora*, ed. Augustus Gaudenzi (Naples: Giannini, 1888), 27, speaks of the inhabitants of these lands as "tripolitani de

Barbaria." Houben, *Roger II*, 92, describes the region mentioned in the chronicle as "Tripoli in Barbary."

9: *Albidia.* Sirgusa (4, n. 3) reports that Roger's first wife is assigned a variety of names in the sources, including *Alberia, Albyria, Elvira,* and *Geloira.* In their respective indexes, Chalandon calls her *Elvire* and Norwich *Elvira.* Kölzer ("Bildkommentar," 38) points out that Roger was not yet king when he married this Castilian princess. No precise date for the marriage is known, but the number and apparent ages of the sons born of the union narrow the range of possibilities; see biographical sketch for *Elvira.*

20: *De Constantini nomine nomen habens.* Pietro draws an association between Constance and Constantine in order to emphasize Henry VI's ambition to revive the empire of Constantine. Romuald of Salerno also gives an account of King Roger's family in his *Chronicon* and mentions Constance's name with allegorical intent; in his narrative, the name signifies the virtue of *constancy* which King Roger learns in his old age, after having been excessively proud in the prime of his life. Our poet, Pietro, is not himself blind to the association between Constance and *constancy*; see line 583. However, Romuald's account obscures the fact that Constance was born posthumously, since he wishes to imply that Roger named her in order to express the moral lesson he had learned. Unlike the other references to Romuald's chroncle in this apparatus, the excerpt below is not, except for one alteration which I note, from Garufi's edition but from *Cronica di Romualdo Guarna*, ed. G. Del Re, in *Cronisti e Scrittori Sincroni della Dominazione Normanna nel Regno di Puglia e Sicilia*, (Naples, 1845), 1:15–16. This is because Del Re's text is more accessible, although Garufi's is enriched by much scholarship. (In Garufi's edition, *Chronicon Romualdi II Archiepiscopi Salernitani*, ed. C. A. Garufi, RIS 7.1 [Città di Castello: Lapi, 1909–1935], this passage appears on pp. 230–1.)

---

[1] tot ("so many") is from Garufi's edition; Del Re has *tres* ("three").

Sed quia (ut ait Scriptura) *quem diligit Dominus, corrigit, et flagellat omnem filium, quem recipit*, postquam Deus omnipotens Regem Rogerium multis prosperis successibus extulit, et exaltavit, ne succedentia prospera animum ejus plus justo elevarent, eum quarumdam adversitatum flagellis paterni miseratione corripuit. Nam primo Albyria illustris Regina uxor ejus, ex qua tot[1] filios habuerat, mortua est, et filia ejus.

Post haec Tarentinus Princeps et Anfusus Capuanorum Princeps, et Henricus mortui sunt. Novissime autem Rogerius Dux Apuliae, primogenitus ejus, mortuus est Anno Dominicae Incarnationis MCXLIX Ind. XII, vir quidem speciosus, et miles strenuus, pius, benignus, misericors, et a suo populo multum dilectus. Rex autem Rogerius tot flagellis afflictus, constanti animo pii patris flagella sustinuit, et sic se medium inter prospera et adversa exhibuit, ut nec eum prospera plus justo erigerent, nec adversa penitus inclinarent. Nam licet multiplici dolorum stimulo pungeretur in animo, foris tamen consolatoriam speciem, et doloris temperantiam praetendebat in vultu, et in sua consolatione Regno suo consolationem tribuit, et inimicis suis insultandi materiam denegavit.

Because (as the Scripture says) *whom God loves, he corrects, and he chastises every son whom he receives*, it pleased the omnipotent God, in his paternal compassion, after he had raised up and exalted King Roger with many fortunate achievements, to strike him with the lashes of some adversities, lest the resultant prosperity should elevate his spirit more than was right. For first his wife, the illustrious Queen Alberia, by whom he had so many sons, died, and her daughter with her.

After this, the Prince of Taranto and Alphonso the Prince of Capua, and Henry died. Then most recently, Roger, Duke of Apulia, his firstborn, died in the year of the Lord's incarnation 1149, 12th indiction, a very handsome man and a vigorous knight, pious, benign, merciful, and much beloved by his people. King Roger, much afflicted by these blows, sustained the punishment of the merciful father with a constant spirit and thus he showed himself to be moderate in prosperous and adverse circumstances, neither raised up more than was right in his success nor deeply cast down by troubles. For, granted that many spurs of sorrow pricked his spirit, in public he put forward a consoling face, and a countenance of tempered sorrow. Thus, in his consolation, he gave consolation to his realm and denied his enemies material for attack.

Et quia solum Guilielmum Capuanorum Principem habebat superstitem, veritus ne eumdem conditione humanae fragilitas amitteret, Sibiliam sororem Ducis Burgundiae duxit uxorem, quae non multo post Salerni mortua est, et apud Caveam est sepulta. Tertio Beatricem filiam Comitis de Reteste in uxorem accepit, de qua filiam habuit, quem Constantiam appellavit. Biennio autem antequam moretur, Guilielmum filium suum Capuanorum Principem in Regem Siciliae fecit inungi, et secum jussit pariter conregnare . . .

And because surviving he [now] had only [his son] William, the Prince of Capua, and he feared that the fragility of the human condition might take him also, he took to wife Sibylla, sister of the duke of Burgundy. She died in Salerno not much later and was buried at La Cava. Then, for his third wife, he took Beatrice the daughter of the Count of [Rethel] as his wife, by whom he had a daughter, whom he called Constance. And two years before he died, he had his son William anointed as King of Sicily, commanding that he should be a co-ruler with him.

Perhaps, of course, Roger and his third queen decided on a name before the child was born. It is true that "Constance" was a rather common name among French princesses at the time. *Constantine* does not appear in a known prince of the Norman house, except for the widely reported story that Frederick II, the son of Constance and Henry, bore the name "Constantine" before he was baptized with the names *Frederick* and *Roger*; for example, see Van Cleve, *Emperor Frederick II*, 20, and his references, especially to *Annales Stadenses*, ed. G. H. Pertz, MGH 16 (Stuttgart, 1859), 271–379, here 353.

Was Constance, then, born posthumously? This matter seems to have interested only Pietro and another poet, Godfrey of Viterbo, *Pantheon*, ed. L. A. Muratori, RIS 7 (Milan: Societatis Palatinae, 1725), 351–473, here 462:

Filius ipsius Henricus, ad alta levatur,
Rite coronatur, uxoris honore beatur,
    Fit Regis Siculi filia sponsa sibi.
Sponsa fuit speciosa nimis, Constantia dicta,
Postuma, post patrem materno ventre relicta,
    Iamque tricennalis tempore virgo fuit.

His [Frederick Barbarossa's] son Henry was raised to the heights, crowned king with fitting ceremony, made blessèd with the honor of his wife:
    The daughter of the king of Sicily became his bride. His bride was more than dazzling, named Constance, born posthumously from her mother's womb after her father's death.
    By now, she had been a virgin for a term of thirty years.

It is hard to imagine why a poet would invent this story.

21: *Traditur Augusto.* . . . "Augustus" was one of Henry VI's official titles as emperor of the Romans. Pietro applies it to him throughout the poem, along with related titles such as "Caesar."

29: *Luceat in sanctis unus, celestiat alter,* Peter is playing with the names *Lucius* and *Celestine,* taking the first to mean "light" and the second to mean "celestial" or "heavenly."

34: *paritas numeri displicet ipsa Deo.* An obscure phrase. Besides "coupling," *paritas* can also mean "evenness," as in "even numbers." Roger's even-numbered marriage did not turn out well, since Sibylla died of a miscarriage. Obviously, his first and third marriages were more fruitful. Perhaps in this verse Pietro shows signs of Byzantine influence, since Greek Christianity took a harsher view than Latin Christianity of repeated marriages (even when previous spouses were dead). They were particularly severe upon any marriage beyond the third. (I am indebted to Leonard Lipschutz and Diana Wright for this information.) Cf. Jenkins, *Byzantium: The Imperial Centuries,* esp. 216–19; also "Tetragamy of Leo VI," in *The Oxford Dictionary of Byzantium,* ed. Alexander P. Kazhdan (New York: Oxford University Press, 1991), 3: 2027.

Fol. 96v
Section 2: The Death of William II the Handsome, King of Sicily.
(S 7–8)(KS 37)

40: *Quod tua mens* . . . I conjecture that Pietro meant his reader to supply the sense of some common verb, such as *habuit,* which would yield the meaning "what your mind contained" or "what your intention was." This is a difficult line, and the different translations render it variously.

40-41: . . . *loquitur mundus et ipse taces. / Certus eras certe quoniam* . . . This passage is confusing and has given interpreters much trouble. My translation is loose, but conveys the idea that William anticipated the situation described in the previous verses—that he would die some day, and people could only guess his thoughts—and therefore (*quoniam*) he took the trouble to declare his successor. There need be no contradiction with the previous lines, which state that William "adopted" no successor. Since the usual dynastic mode of inheritance already made Constance the heiress, William merely saw to it that this, and the fact that Constance's husband had been chosen with succession in mind, was openly acknowledged and confirmed. Others interpret the passage variously. Siragusa (7, n. 4), writes: "For the sense, it seems to me necessary to change '*quoniam*' to '*quominus*' or '*quod nunquam*' or something similar, but neither the abbreviations in the codex, nor the meter, even if the poet does not always respect it, permits me to do this . . ." The general sense of his translation is that William had made certain that his rightful heir would not be obliged to take the kingdom by force (or he thought he had done so). All these interpretations attempt to answer questions obviously posed by the context: oaths or no oaths, why did this good and responsible king not write a formal testament confirming his choice of successor and thus lessening the chance for civil war? Possible answers include: (1) death took William by surprise; (2) William made verbal statements about the succession and thought that was enough; (3) William had second thoughts about Henry VI's succession, but realized that nothing he said at this time would prevent Henry VI from attacking the kingdom; and (4) he still favored Henry VI, but realized that nothing he could do would ensure a peaceful succession.

45: *Iurat cum multis Archimatheus.* Though the verb is in the historical present, my translation puts it in the past for clarity. "Arch-Matthew" is Pietro's name for the Matthew the Chief Notary, vice-chancellor under William II and later chancellor under Tancred. He is often called Matthew "of Ajello" because one of his sons was later made count of Ajello. By calling him "Arch-Matthew," Pietro marks him as a great man, on analogy with *archangel, archbishop,* and *archenemy.* In his chronicle, Richard of San Germano (63) names him as one of William II's two most influential advisors, the other being Walter, the archbishop of Palermo.

44-45: (blank space). Del Re (442, n. 2) observes that two pentameters here, without a complementary hexameter, indicate that something is missing, probably "the names of several others who offered the same oath."

54: *eclipticat.* De Rosa lists this word in his glossary as one which Pietro uses with a non-standard meaning. He offers the definition *oscurarsi* (to darken oneself). My translation reflects this.

Fol. 97r
Illustration 3: *Illness and death of William II. The population and the magnates of Palermo weep.*
(S 121)(KS 42)

Cap. 1: *Achim medicus.* Siragusa (121 n. 2), writes, "*Achim* is apparently a transliteration of the Arabic '*hakim*,' which signifies 'learned,' and [also] 'physician' in common usage, the same meaning the Italian word *dottore* [doctor] eventually acquired." (The English word "doctor" also has the same ambiguity.) Thus, Siragusa suggests, *medicus* in the caption might simply be translation of the Arabic *Achim.* On the other hand, he cites "Professor Nallino" for the information that sometimes, "though very rarely," *Achim* could be a proper name. In that case, the caption would be translated "Achim the Physician," as I have rendered it. Kölzer ("Bildkommentar," 42) also says that *Achim* means "physician," but transliterates the Arabic as *hakim* in accordance with current usage.

8: *Domini Curie.* Siragusa (121, n. 4) writes: "The four figures of 'The Lords of the Court' are wearing mantles and have their heads covered by certain large *berrettoni* which, in these miniatures, ecclesiastic dignitaries customarily wear, as can be seen in the illustrations on Fols. 100r, 102r and 126r. Perhaps for this reason W[inkelmann] believes that these four men are probably bishops." Actually, in the miniatures which Siragusa points out, it is never clear that this particular kind of headgear is worn by anyone other than the court *familiares.* In two of them, Matthew himself is the only wearer.

Fol. 97v
Section 3: Mourning and Lament in Palermo.
(S 9–10)(KS 45).

55: *Hactenus urbs felix, populo dotata trilingui.* Literally, the city is "gifted" or "endowed" with "a trilingual people": Karla Mallette, *The Kingdom of Sicily: 1100–1250* (Philadelphia: University of Pennsylvania Press, 2005), 161.

65: *medio qui robore fretus . . . pedum.* Or more literally "Those who lie in cradles, those who lean upon middle strength, / And those who use a staff as kind of third foot."

68: *pater antistes.* By "father-bishop," Pietro first alludes to Walter, archbishop of Palermo. Later, in line 102, his name, Walter, is implied in a punning reference. In 100r, caption 3, he is clearly named *Gualterius famosus presul* (Walter, the famous prelate). However, Siragusa (9–10, n. 3), while allowing that the speaker is "probably" Walter, holds out the possibility that it could be "archbishop Thomas of Reggio (1177–1194)," who read an elegy about William II "to the people and the magnates of the court in Palermo." Copies of that elegy were preserved in Palermo, and Siragusa quotes some lines, noting thematic similarities with Pietro's verses. Be that as it may, the speaker here is not merely reciting an elegy but also introducing himself as one who was intimately involved in the reign of William II, now ended ("correximus," line 70), and leading up to a recommendation, most appropriate for someone still responsible for carrying out the business of government, that Constance be urged to hurry and claim her kingdom. It is unlikely that Pietro intended the reader to understand any speaker other than Walter.

76: *ovans solus per opaca viator.* Or more literally, "exulting in the dark places."

78-79: *Hactenus in speculo poterat se quisque videre, . . . noctis habent.* This suggests not only that William was an example of good conduct, but also that it was pleasant and flattering for people to see themselves in him.

82: *Phebi soror.* Siragusa states (10, n. 1), "I do not believe that the poet wished to call William I, whose sister Constance was, 'Phoebus.'" Indeed, William I, whom Pietro never mentions, is known to history as "William the Bad" (see Introduction C.7). Therefore, Siragusa suspects that the reference is to William II, "who, represented as handsome and good, could be likened to Phoebus" and adds, "one might suspect that he [Pietro], as often happened in the middle ages, believed that Constance was the sister of William II." However, Pietro the poet describes King Roger as William's grandfather ("avus," line 44) and thus clearly understands the familial connection between William and Constance. He might have considered it appropriate to refer to them figuratively as brother and sister, since they were about the same age and probably grew up together.

82: *et Iovis uxor.* Pietro repeated refers to Henry VI as the Roman god Jove (198, 529, 816, 1411, etc.), and gives him Jove's attributes. Jove's wife is Juno, and Pietro directly refers to Constance as Juno (430).

Fol. 98r
Illustration 4: *Mourning in the streets of Palermo because of the death of William II.*
(S 122–23)(KS 50)

1: *Viridarium Genoard.* Siragusa (122, n. 2) states that this "Royal Garden," known as "Genoard," "Januardo," and "Gilolardo," may derive its name from "the Arabic 'Gennet-ol-Ardh,' terrestrial paradise," information for which he cites Michele Amari, *Storia dei Musulmani di Sicilia* [*History of the Moslems in Sicily*], 3 vols. (Florence, 1854–1868), 3:554–79. It was "on the road which leads from Palermo to Monreale."

3: *Cappella regia.* Siragusa writes (122, n. 4): "The Royal Chapel, which is now called the Palatine Chapel, was described by Hugo Falcandus in his *Epistola*," (*La Historia*, 180; *History of the Tyrants*, trans. Loud and Wiedemann, 259–60). For a modern study, see William Tronzo, *The Cultures of His Kingdom: Roger II and the Cappella Palatina in Palermo* (Princeton: Princeton University Press, 1997).

4: *Ideisini.* Siragusa (122, n. 5) writes: "In the name Ideisini, we should no doubt recognize the district which draws its name from the spring 'Ain-Scindi,' 'Ain-isindi,' 'Denisinni,' or 'Dennisinni' . . . which to this day preserves the name 'Dennisyndi' or 'Denisinni.'" He cites Amari, *Storia dei Musulmani di Sicilia*, 2:33, 3:554–55, and 3:870.

5: *Cassarum.* Siragusa (122, note 6) writes, "'Cassaro' (Arabic 'Qasr') is the name of a neighborhood or quarter and the principal road which traverses it, which is also called the via Marmorea . . . ."

6: *Calza.* Here Siragusa has *Alza*, Kölzer *Calza*; the latter agrees with the fac-simile. Siragusa (122–23, n. 7) writes: "'Alza' is the inexact transcription of 'Kalsa,' 'Kalesa,' 'Halisah,' etc. The name Kalsa still endures and is also popularly given ('Gausa') to a square and the whole district near the sea, populated largely by families of fishermen. During the middle ages, that name was given to a portion of the city that was distinct, like the Cassaro, and to a fortress." For more information, he cites the Italian version of Ibn-Hawqual from Michele Amari, *Biblioteca Arabo-Sicula*, 2 vols. (Turin and Rome, 1880–1881), 1:12–13, n. 3. Kölzer says ("Bildkommentar," 46) that the fortress near the Calza dates from the tenth century. Perhaps the tower at the lower left represents the fortress; it is not drawn to scale.

7: *Scerarchadium.* Siragusa (123, n. 1) writes: "'Scerarchadium,' neighborhood of Palermo, corresponds largely to what today is called 'the Cape.' The name found in the Latin documents is 'Seralcadi' and 'Serarcadi.'" Many men in this part of the picture wear turbans. Kölzer ("Bildkommentar," 46) states that the name comes from the Arabic *šari' al-qadi* meaning "Street of the Judge." Presumably the Saracens' own judge, for their internal affairs, officiated there.

8: *Castrum Maris.* Siragusa (123, n. 2) points out that Hugo Falcandus gives a description of the Old Palace in his *Epistola ad Petrum (Letter to Peter)* (*La Historia*, 177; *History of the Tyrants*, 258–59.)

Fol. 98v
Section 4: The Different and Conflicting Will of Those Seeking [a King].
(S 11–12)(KS 49)

95: *mens Pharisea.* Translators differ in their renderings of this phrase. Pietro does not use this term again, so we have only this passage from which to draw our interpretations, plus our speculations about Pietro's understanding of the Phari-sees in the gospel accounts. De Rosa takes *mens Pharisea* to refer specifically to Matthew and translates it "l'animo farisaico di Matteo" (the Pharisaical mind of Matthew). In context, he seems to mean that Matthew's choice, already fixed on Tancred, was unlike the fluctuating loyalties of the other parties. However, the captions on the corresponding miniatures indicate that two fairly well-defined groups have by now coalesced around each of the two major candidates. I think that Pietro's "Pharisaical mind" encompasses both groups. They are alike in their indifference to the true king but incompatible in their choice of an alternative. It takes Matthew's machinations to bring them together. Thus, in the next sec-tion, Pietro gives Matthew a worse title than Pharisee, that of Judas Iscariot, the ultimate traitor (ll. 111 and 196). Siragusa likewise interprets *mens Pharisea* as a reference to all "the partisans of the aspirants to the throne" (11, n. 1).

98: *rationis uterque magister.* According to Jamison (*Admiral Eugenius*, 80), Tancred and Roger had both been master justiciars (officials responsible for administering justice) and constables (officials responsible for commanding royal knights). Probably *rationis* in this context refers to their expertise in interpreting the law. Rocco, Becht-Jördens, and De Rosa all translate it in that light.

100: *Intus at interea vicecancellarius.* Matthew bore the title "vice-chancellor" throughout the latter part of William II's reign, and it will be applied to him again in the heading of Section 5, and in line 1277. There was no actual chancellor at this time, because the previous chancellor, Stephen du Perche, had been expelled from Sicily in the midst of such serious turmoil (A.D. 1168) that the king subsequently preferred not to give any minister that title (Jamison, *Admiral Eugenius*, 48, 94). Still, the chancellor's work had to be done, hence "vice-chancellor."

102: *gualterizatur ubique.* "Walterizing everywhere" — Clearly, this a play on the name of the archbishop, Walter. This means, Siragusa writes (12, n. 2), "without doubt, . . . he made himself felt everywhere, and imposed his views."

Fol. 99v
Section 5: The Dissenting Vice-chancellor's Persuasive Address to the Archbishop of Palermo.
(S 13–14)(KS 53)

117: *Ne Nothus aut Boreas* . . . . Notus and Boreas are the South and North winds, respectively.

123: *Discere barbaricos barbarizare sonos?* Del Re writes (*De Tumulti*, 443 and n. 7), "Here the poet hints that the German language was then called 'barbaric' by the Italians, and those who spoke it [were called] 'barbarians.' Engel takes offense and says that the word should rather have been applied to us [Italians] because we have strayed far from the speech of our ancestors. The learned critic is correct, but what was the cause of that? For the rest, if the Latin language was being snuffed out among us, another was rising which would call herself a rival and imitator of her mother." (Del Re here implies that invasions of Germanic barbarians were what caused the decline of Latin; he also defends the honor of the modern Italian language.) Pietro's contemporary, Falcandus, suggests that Sicilian children were terrified by the sound of the German language (*La Historia*, 171; *History of the Tyrants of Sicily*, 253).

132: . . . *persona repugnet.* Originally, *natura* was written in place of *persona*, but it was corrected in what Siragusa believes is the poet's hand; hence he accepts *persona*, which he says in his textual notes (14) "is justified by the repetition of *natura* in the following verse, and by the greater clarity which [the correction] gives to the thought." De Rosa follows him, but Becht-Jördens, producing the text for the Kölzer and Stähli edition, took the original reading of the manuscript, without determining the claims of the revision-hand here ("Der Dichter und sein Text," 291–92). Rota and previous editions also have *natura* here.

138: *almipatris Matheus adulterat archam*: Rocco points out (Del Re edition 443, n. 5) that this means "Matthew attempted to adulterate the treasury, that is the heart, of Walter."

Fol. 100v
Section 6: Letter to Tancred.
(S 15–16)(KS 57)

140: *Protinus accepta bigamus notat ista papiro*: the word for *paper* also means *papyrus*. Papyrus was grown in Sicily and paper made from it was used for charters. See Vera von Falkenhausen, "The Greek Presence in Norman Sicily," in *The Society of Norman Italy*, ed. Loud and Metcalfe, 252–86, here 268–69.

143: *"Quam cito ni venias, qui ferat alter erit."* Matthew subtly threatens to withdraw his offer (and presumably give it to someone else) if Tancred does not act quickly.

144: *Rumpe moras, venias comitatus utraque.* Siragusa, in his textual notes (15), points out that this line, written in the margin in the poet's hand, lacks a metrical foot. He suggests that perhaps it was meant to be completed by the repetition of *venias* ["you must come"]. In his n. 2 on this page, he also points that *rumpe moras*, repeated again in l. 146, echoes Vergil's *Aeneid* 4.569 and 9.13; also Ovid's *Metamorphoses* 15.583, and Lucan's *De bello civili* 2.125.

150: *Inceptis desiste tuis, irascimur illis.* Apparently, by *inceptis* (undertakings) Matthew refers to the process which Tancred, as a loyal count and as justiciar, has already begun, of requiring cities and subjects under his jurisdiction to swear loyalty to Henry VI and Constance.

Fol. 101r
Illustration 7: *Greek, Saracen, and Latin notaries. Messengers from Matthew of Ajello to Tancred.*
(S 124)(KS 58)

1-3: *Notarii Greci. . . . Latini.* Although scribes skilled in each language are shown, Kölzer's commentary (58) points out that the proportions are probably misleading, because during the reign of William II, Latin had come to dominate the chancery, even if bilingualism was still useful. Houben associates the decline with the loss of Roger II's African empire (*Roger II*, 113); for a detailed account of the status of Arabic as an administrative language in Sicily under the Norman kings and Frederick II of Hohenstaufen, see Alex Metcalfe, *Muslims and Christians in Norman Sicily: Arabic-Speakers and the End of Islam* (New York: RoutledgeCurzon, 2002), 22–114. However, Jeremy Johns, *Arabic Administration in Norman Sicily* (New York: Cambridge University Press, 2002), esp. 207–11, shows that in Pietro's time, for certain purposes (especially record-keeping about land) Arabic remained important and even enjoyed a resurgence at the Sicilian court, as did Greek. Jamison (*Admiral Eugenius*, 105) demonstrates that Greek influence increased under Tancred, who was to make an alliance with Isaac Angelus and receive one of his daughters as a bride for his eldest son.

Fol. 101v
Section 7: The Fraudulent Royal Anointing.
(S 17–18)(KS 61)

171: *modo se colligit inque manus.* Or perhaps "draws back to hide behind his hands." Cf. Virgil, *Aeneid* 12.491): *se colligit in arma,* which Lewis and Short render "covered himself or concealed himself behind his shield" ("colligo," def. B, *A New Latin Dictionary*). Both Rocco and De Rosa interpret this passage to mean "hides among the people." Rocco has *"si raccoglie fra la gente,"* De Rosa, *"si nasconde fra la gente."* Becht-Jördens apparently takes *"se colligit"* to mean that Tancred recovers his senses. These alternate readings involve possible idiomatic usages for "se colligit" and "manus."

176: *Fabarie.* Siragusa (*Liber* 17, n. 3) writes: "In Sicily there were and are several places called Favara. Here the royal castle called Favara or Sweet Sea (*Mare dolce*), at the port of Palermo, is meant." He cites Amari, *Storia dei Musulmani,* 2:330.

188: *Lachesis sua fila moretur.* Lachesis is one of the three Fates, who spin human destinies. While Clotho begins the thread of life, Lachesis pulls it out and Atropos cuts it off. See H. David Brumble, *Classical Myths and Legends in the Middle Ages and Renaissance* (Westport, CT: Greenwood Press, 1998), 119. In this case, Lachesis, who determines the length of the thread, is being asked to make it longer.

191: *Ne quemquam lateat, erea plectra sonant. . .* Rocco writes (Del Re 443–44, n. 7), "bronze plectra are bells." Rota, in his edition (32), contradicts this and says that the *plectra* are the bronze rods with which the musicians in the miniatures strike the cymbals.

196: *Quam male Scariothis.* Judas Iscariot, who betrayed Christ.

Fol. 102r
Illustration 8: *King Tancred's triumphal entry into Palermo.*
(S 124–25)(KS 62)

1: *Comes Tancredus.* The illustrator for Engel's 1746 edition interpreted the redrawing of Tancred's face (see Introduction A 2) as vandalism, not as the intent of the original poet. Therefore, in his miniature of the coronation procession (see 102r, cap. 1, p. 20) he presented Tancred's face in original three-quarter perspective. The photocopy below is from the Del Re edition of 1868. The crested birds may be hoopoes; see Charles John Cornish et al, *The Living Animals of the World: Birds, Fishes, Reptiles, Insects* (New York: Dodd, Mead and Co.) 1902, 506.

Fol. 102v
Section 8: The Downfall of the Accursed One and His Ridiculous Birth.
(S 19–21)(KS 65)

200-211: *Debuit illa dies* . . . . */Illa dies pereat, nec commemoretur in anno / Illa dies pereat.* . . . Cf. Job 3:1–7.

200: . . . *multa pice nigrior esse.* Literally, "blacker than much pitch." Rocco and De Rosa translate the line in that spirit, while Becht-Jördens changes *multa* to *multo*, to justify reading it as an adverb. Either way, the expression must be hyperbolic; we must either imagine something blacker than pitch, or that the blackness is increased by the quantity.

207: *Unxit abortivum que manus ausa virum!* As the *Liber* shows, Walter, archbishop of Palermo, originally supported the succession of Henry VI and Constance. No source clearly states that he crowned Tancred, although he lived until June 1190 (Errico Cuozzo, "Ruggiero," 152, n. 85). The account in Richard of San Germano's chronicle (64) has been interpreted, by Siragusa (17, n. 3) to mean that Matthew performed the coronation himself. Of course, the chronicler's brisk report that "through that chancellor [Matthew], he [Tancred] was crowned king" (*per ipsum chancellarium coronatus in regem*) might merely mean that Matthew arranged the coronation. However, Dione Clementi, "The Circumstances of Count Tancred's Accession to the Kingdom of Sicily, the Duchy of Apulia and the Principality of Capua," in *Melanges Antonio Marongius* (Palermo, 1967), 57–80, here 62–63, suggests that Pietro actually means that Matthew performed the crowning. If he did, that would provide some motivation for Pietro's repeated statements, otherwise merely puzzling, that Matthew is a priest.

However, kings really should be crowned by bishops, and Matthew's son Nicholas was the archbishop of Salerno. He would be an ideal choice if the archbishop of Palermo were dead, unwilling, or unwell. William II himself had been anointed king by the archbishop of Salerno in 1166, as this archbishop, Romuald of Salerno, himself explains in his chronicle, *Chronicon Romualdi II Archiepiscopi Salernitani*, ed. C. A. Garufi, RIS 7.1, ed. L.A. Muratori, new edition (Città di Castello [1909–1935]), 254). If Nicholas performed the ceremony at his father's request, it is somewhat surprising that Pietro does not denounce him for it. If, however, the culprit is Bartholomew, brother and ultimate successor of Walter, Pietro may have reason to swallow his wrath and even delete some lines. See commentary on Section 11 and Bartholomew's biographical sketch.

Clementi ("Circumstances," 59) states the coronation happened on 18 January, explaining that most of the chronicles also suggest a date in January, except *Chronica S. Mariae De Ferraria*, which gives 8 December 1189 as the date. Instead, Clementi suggests, that was the date of Tancred's election, and the coronation followed as late as it did because Archbishop Walter objected. However, Archbishop Walter would have yielded to the papacy; he may even have been instructed to cooperate, "to countenance or even officiate at the ceremony" ("Circumstances," 63). That would explain why the *Annales Cassinenses* report, for 1190, that Tancred was crowned "with the consent of the curia" (*de assensu et favore curie romane*) even though the pope did not officially acknowledge Tancred until June 1192 ("Circumstances," 60).

209: *tam gravior lues.* Perhaps "the more punishment you will suffer," if *lues* is read as a verb *(luo –ere*, "to expiate"). Rocco, Becht-Jördens, and De Rosa all interpret the word that way. It is, however, also a 3rd declension fem. noun which can mean "plague" or "disease." Either translation makes sense; like all medieval writers, Pietro assumes that good is rewarded and evil is punished in the end. However, he does not emphasize proportional punishments for every evil deed; his greatest villains (Matthew of Ajello and Tancred) are not shown meeting their ends. In his last sections, he emphasizes the emperor's clemency and the forgetting of past wrong (see, for example, ll. 1429–1444). In this line, I think he meant to emphasize the wrong that Tancred was doing, but he did not mean to emphasize that proportional punishment was inevitable, since repentance on one side and compassion on the other make that less than certain.

216-219: *Ut puer incipiat, opus est ut uterque resudet / Non in Tancredo sementat uterque parentum, / Et si sementent, non bene conveniunt.* Urso clearly states that both mother and father must contribute a "seed" for the conception of a child, but in Tancred's case, the mother's "seed" rejected that of his father, resulting in a dwarfish offspring formed only from the mother. The account shows that Urso at any rate clearly follows the "two-seed" theory of Galen, rather than than the Aristotelian view, in which the only the father's seed produced the embryo, using material from the mother (see Kathleen Crowther-Heyck,"'Be Fruitful and Multiply': Genesis and Generation in Reformation Germany," *Renaissance Quarterly* 55 [2002]: 904–35, here 913 and n. 4). Influential though Aristotle was (see Jenny M. Jochens, "The Politics of Reproduction: Medieval Norwegian Kingship," *American Historical Review*, 92 [1987]: 327–49, here 327–28), it is not surprising that a physician would prefer Galen on such questions. This passage may show Pietro's medical knowledge (see Introduction A), though the two-seed theory could be spread by other means; for example, the poet Lucretius taught that both mother and father contributed seeds: Titus Carus Lucretius, *De Rerum Natura*, tr. W. H. D. Rouse, Loeb Classical Library, 3rd ed. (Cambridge, MA: Harvard University Press, 1947), 4: 1207–1232.

222-223: *. . .fornacis aborret / Gemma luem. . .* Siragusa (20–21, n. 2) observes that the meaning of this phrase is unclear, and mentions several alternatives, none of which completely satisfies him. "I think it improbable," he writes "that the poet employed a strange metaphor and called fire 'fornacis lues' [liquid of the furnace], wishing to say that the gem abhors the fire which changes and wastes it . . . ." He mentions comments by the scholar Huber, that "*luem*" was a mistake for "*lucem*" (light). Siragusa does not believe this, but will not completely resolve to discard Huber's other explanation, that "*lues*" might be "*limus*" (mire) and "*lues fornacis*" could be "mire [or slag?] of the furnace." However, "*gemma*" has a number of meanings, including "jewel," "bud," and "artifacts made with jewels"; likewise, "*lues*," as a noun, has several meanings including "disease," "plague" and also "liquid." Hence, I took "*gemma*" to mean some splendid artifact made in a forge, and naturally incompatible with shapeless liquid. Rocco has "la gemma abhorret la lue della fornace" (the gem abhorrs the plague of the furnace) and De Rosa has "la gemma abhorret la fango della fornace" (the gem abhors the mire of the furnace). Becht-Jördens has "vor des Ofens Schlacke schreckt der Edelstein zurück" (the jewel shrinks from the slag of the furnace).

231: *In lolium versos sepe queruntur agros.* Darnel (*lolium*), is obviously less desirable than grains such as wheat and barley which farmers plant deliberately. There is an allusion here to Matthew 13:24–30; see also notes on line 580.

232-233: *iuvencum / Monstriferumque pecus mollis abortit ovis.* Or "The unhappy cow aborts a monstrous bullock it has conceived, the gentle sheep [aborts monstrous] livestock." *Pecus* can be used of cattle, sheep, pigs, and other animals. The point, probably, is that a "monstrous" conception might not be a recognizable as a sheep, even though it is clearly the offspring of a ewe.

Fol. 103r
Illustration 9: *Caricatures alluding to Tancred's future fall and his deformity.*
(S 125)(KS 66)

The drawings for Engel's first edition, published in 1746, make the picture outlines sharper on fol. 103r, particularly of the two-faced Tancred (cap. 2) and the miscarrying ewe (cap. 3). The photocopy on the opposite page is from the Del Re edition of 1868.

6: Kölzer (67) points out that both the midwife and the attendant have covered their hands with their sleeves, in this case as a gesture of mourning or horror at the sight of this freakish child, although it is sometimes understood "as an attempt at hygiene," and as part of "Byzantine Court ceremonial, whereby one does not approach one's master with bare, unclean hands." Other illustrations in which it appears and where it could be variously interpreted are those on fols. 110r, 116r, 119r, 120r, 126r, 135r, 138r, and 142r.

Fol. 103v
Section 9: The False Iniquity of the Aborted One Outlaws Those Who Are Enrolled.
(S 22–23)(KS 69)

The meaning of the title *"Particula VIIII: Abortivi fallax iniquitas proscribit ascriptos,"* literally "The false iniquity of the aborted one proscribes the enrolled," is a little mysterious. Most of the confusion comes from questions about what "enrolled" group is being proscribed (outlawed). Becht-Jördens interprets this to mean that injustice (*Ungerechtigkeit*) punishes its own adherents (*ihre Angehörigen*), while De Rosa takes it that Tancred drives the rightful owners from their fiefs (*scaccia dai feudi i legittimi possessori*). Either interpretation could fit the context. The narrative goes on to describe the death of Roger of Andria. Since, as Pietro tells it, he had apparently made an agreement with Tancred when he was captured, he might be considered Tancred's most recent adherent. On the other hand, he could also be regarded as the rightful holder of a title, persecuted by Tancred. Since the *Liber* mentions Roger of Andria as one of several men, loyal to "Caesar," whom Tancred destroyed, I suspect the "enrolled" may be the group which originally agreed to support Henry VI, whose members wrote letters to him, as recounted in ll. 292–305.

238: *quis ensis.* De Rosa translates this "what military valor [*quale valore militare*]?"

fortuna tancdi

tancred' facie senex statura puellus

Queretr in causam 8 indicitate corpis tancdi. qd aborsun fuerit et corp' nag urso aborciere
ous ducit in exeplu.

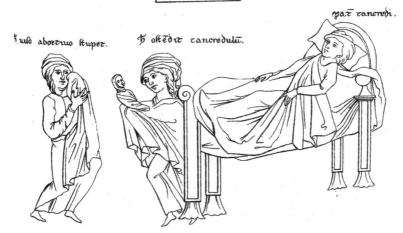

mat tancredi.

s uiso abortruo stupet. th ostedit tancredulu.

240-241: *quotiens qui nil dedit illi, / Seu dedit et petit, non minus hostis erat.* Clearly these lines suggest that Tancred demands bribes and dislikes giving anything in return for them, but Rota (39), in his notes on these lines, suggests that there is a reference to Tancred's relationship to the previous kings, first to William I, who gave him no office but kept him confined to the palace, and then William II, who made him Count of Lecce but also accepted his service in important military matters, including expeditions to Egypt and in Byzantine territory.

251: *Quas hodie Zepherus, cras aget Eurus aquas.* Or, "Where the west wind blows today, the east wind will blow tomorrow." Zephyr and Eurus are the west and east winds, respectively.

253: *Que numeri nulla lege coacta fuit!* Literally, "which could not be compelled by any law of numbers." In my text, I put what I thought was Pietro's meaning.

Fol. 104r
Illustration 10: *The Count of Andria in prison.*
(S 125)(KS 70)

2: *Castrum* . . . Siragusa states in his textual notes (125), "The name of the castle is completely erased." He adds (125, n. 4) that Hauptmann ("Die Illustrationen zu Peter von Ebulos" in *Jahrbuch der K. K. heraldishcen Gesellschaft*: *Adler,* Neue Folge 7 [1897]: 55–65, here 57), believed that this castle belonged to the captive Roger.

Fol. 104v
[Section] 10: The Imperial Anointing.
(S 24–25)(KS 73)

262: *Ad Petri devenit eques venerabile templum.* That is, Saint Peter's Church at Rome.

263: *pater antistes preredimitus erat.* Pope Celestine III was consecrated as pope only the day before he crowned the emperor. However, De Rosa's translation, Rocco's, and Becht-Jördens's all say Pietro's words mean that the pope was already waiting at the cathedral in his regalia before Henry's arrival.

264: *miristica.* The species name for the nutmeg tree is *myristica fragrans.*

277: *Ut testamentum victor utrumque gerat.* Apparently Pietro sees Henry's two hands as standing for the Old and New Testaments.

279: *"In Christum Domini te Deus unxit," ait.* This line has been interpreted variously. Becht-Jördens renders it "Zum Gesalbten des Herrn salbt Dich Gott" (God anoints you as the Lord's anointed) (a biblical expression, e.g. 1 Samuel 24:6). This might suggest that the newly anointed ruler will usurp Christ's place, something which the pope may actually have feared where Henry VI was concerned. De Rosa's translation avoids this: "Iddio ti unge nel nome di Cristo Signore" (God anoints you in the name of the Lord Christ)." My approach is similar to De Rosa's here. Whatever the translation, medieval kings and emperers were thought to stand in Christ's place and mystically share some Christlike attributes; see Ernst Kantorowicz, *The King's Two Bodies* (Princeton: Princeton University Press, 1957).

281: *Quem Petrus abscissa iussus ab aure tulit.* Pietro alludes to gospel accounts where Peter, attempting to prevent Christ's arrest, struck and cut off the ear of a member of the arresting force, the servant of the high priest, but was commanded by Christ to put away his sword (Matthew 26:51–52, John 18:10–11).

287: *Offertur digitis, Octaviane, tuis.* Octavian is another name of Augustus Caesar, which Pietro applies to Henry VI.

289: *Signat te apostolicas participare vices.* Siragusa (25, n. 1) writes, "The particulars of this imperial anointing (verses 276–289) illustrated by [fol. 105r] should be compared with the *Coronatio Romana Henrici VI* [Roman Coronation of Henry VI], attributed to Cencio Camerario [*MGH: Leges*, 2, ed. G. H. Pertz, 187–93 (Hannover: Hahn, 1886).] . . . According to *Coronatio* . . . it was necessary to confer the anointing first and then successively the ring, the sword, the crown and finally the scepter. For the crown, the poet substitutes the 'diadema aurate thiare' [the triple golden diadem], because Henry, being king of Sicily, is therefore apostolic legate," and the tiara symbolizes his Apostolic role.

But another tradition gave the Holy Roman Emperor a special status as "Christ's deputy" (Jordan, *Henry the Lion*, 8). For a review of the sacral character of medieval kingship in general, see Kantorowicz, *The King's Two Bodies*.

Fol. 105r
Illustration 11: *The Imperial Coronation of Henry VI at Rome.*
(S 126)(KS 74)

1: *Quando imperator Henricus.* Kölzer (74) reports that the pictures seem based more on an account of the German royal coronation than on the imperial Roman coronation. The implication is that Pietro did not witness the ceremony and was reconstructing it according to written records, or perhaps from verbal accounts of others relying on records.

3: *Imperator.* Siragusa (126, n. 1) writes: "Hauptmann [*Die Illustrationen zu Peter von Ebulos*, p. 57] describes the oriflamme which precedes the Emperor, in which the outlines are seen of a cross the color of orange-red."

8: *Tercio hensem papa [tradit?]* Siragusa points out in his textual notes that this caption is much faded and almost unreadable. In note 2 (126) Siragusa adds that the third row of pictures seems to represent a ceremony in a document reproduced in *MGH: Leges, 2, 187–93: Ordo qualiter rex Teutonicus Romam ad suscipiendam coronam imperiii venire debeat, ibique per manum pontificis in imperatorem coronari* (The ceremony whereby the German king must go to Rome to be crowned emperor by the pontiff's hand). The emperor was to receive the sword from the pope's hand, brandish it and then sheathe it. The pope was then to gird it on him.

Fol. 105v
Section 11: Legates of the Realm.
(S 26–28)(KS 77)

294: *Primus magnanimus scripsit comes illi Rogerus.* Roger of Andria had been Tancred's rival for the kingship; see verses 96–98 and the notes on them. As Siragusa points out (26, n. 1), Richard of San Germano's chronicle (64) confirms Pietro's account here and specifically records that Roger of Andria wrote to Henry on William's death: "He wrote as quickly as possible to Henry the King of the Germans that he should come or send . . . to receive the kingdom of Sicily" (*Hic . . . misitque quamcito ad Henricum Alemannie regem quod veniret vel mitteret . . . regnum Sicilie . . . recepturus*).

295: *Scripserat infelix semivir ipse comes.* According to Siragusa and Kölzer, no other known sources specifically say that Tancred wrote urging Henry to claim the throne. Siragusa (26, n. 2) does point out some that specifically state that he was among those who swore to acknowledge Henry and Constance as the rightful rulers should William die childless. These include *Annales Casinenses* (314) and *Gesta Henrici II et Richardi* (now known to be by Roger of Hoveden), 129. If Tancred wrote urging Henry to come to Sicily, he presumably did so very early, while he was still requiring cities and towns to swear allegiance to Henry, as the *Liber* says (ll. 150–156). This perhaps explains Pietro's use of the past perfect here, when he uses the simple past for the others.

302-303: *Scripsit et antistes dominorum gemma Panormi; / . . . et presul Bartholomeus idem.* These are Walter, archbishop of Palermo, and his brother Bartholomew, who was then, as Siragusa points out (28, n. 1), bishop of Agrigento (also called Girgenti), but who "succeeded his brother as archbishop of Palermo in 1194." Chalandon (*Histoire*, 2:428) is of the opinion that Bartholomew became archbishop of Palermo much sooner after his brother's death, perhaps by 11 April 1191, when his successor as bishop of Agrigento was consecrated.

Fol. 106v
Section 12: The Emperor's First Advance into the Kingdom of Sicily.
(S 29)(KS 81)

306: *En movet . . .fortissimus heres.* Rota, Siragusa, and De Rosa have *heres* [heir] in their text for this line; Becht-Jördens has *heros* [hero]. The latter sounds more epic, but in the facsimile, the word looks like *heres*.

309: *Quod sibi per patrios iura dedere gradus.* More literally, "which the laws gave to him through ancestral rank."

310-311: *Hoc avus . . . . . . dedere tributis, /. . .. tulit.* 312: *Si numerare velis.* The apostrophe to Henry VI begins here, although at first it could be taken as an address to the reader. By line 315, Pietro is clearly addressing Barbarossa's son.

313: *In medio Carolus.* The reference is to Charles the Great or Charlemagne (742–814, r. 800–814), the first to hold the office that came to be called "Holy Roman Emperor." He was crowned by Pope Leo III in 800.

314: *Nec minor est Fredericus eo.* Henry's father, Frederick I Barbarossa (reigned 1152–1190). Pietro will soon mention his recent death.

317: *Vicit in hoc Carulos fortior hasta suos.* Or more literally, "In this he conquers his Charleses . . ." The Carolingian dynasty took its name from Charlemagne, *Carolus Magnus* in Latin. Pietro asserts that Henry VI is not only Charlemagne's legitimate successor, but also his superior.

326: In classical usage, *imago* usually means "image," or even "phantasm," although in Virgil, *Aeneid* 4.464, it clearly means "spirit" or "shade." Also the word could refer to "an ancestral image of a distinguished Roman (usually . . . made of wax, and . . . carried in funeral processions)" (Lewis and Short, *Harper's Latin Dictionary* s.v. "imago"). Falcandus refers to such *ymagines* in his prologue (*La Historia*, 4), so the practice was known in the twelfth century. Loud and Wiedemann, in their translation of Falcandus, *The History of the Tyrants of Sicily*, 56, render the word as "masks."

330: *Augustos imitare tuos.* Literally, "to imitate your Augustuses," that is, to imitate these great emperors who have been described.

Fol. 107r

Illustration 13: *Frederick I, the Emperor, starts on the crusade. His death. The entrance of Henry VI into the kingdom of Sicily.*
(S 127–28)(KS 82)

Here Siragusa (127–28) comments, "The subject of these figures and the captions that explain them do not stand in a proper relationship with verses 305–333 on . . . (106v) of the codex. Only the last refers, not to the verses, but to the title which is placed above them: The Emperor's First Advance into the Kingdom of Sicily. After this follows, not an account of the 'first advance' but a sort of hymn to Henry VI's ancestors in the empire, especially to Charlemagne and Frederick I."

Fol. 107v

Section 13: The Highest of the Castles is yielded.
(S 30–1)(KS 85)

341: *Archis enim princeps nomen et esse gerit.* This difficult passage has given translators trouble. Becht-Jördens puts quotation marks around *princeps* ['prince'], so that it will be taken as a synonym for *Archis*, thus making Rocca d'Arce the Prince of Fortresses, an interpretation also followed in my translation. Without the quotation marks, *princeps* could easily apply to Henry VI, the prince responsible for the action here. Del Re (444–45, n. 12) offers interpretations in this light: ". . . to retain the meaning of Mr. Rocco's translation, the last verse could also be explained thus: 'since the prince bears the name and character of a fortress.' Therefore [the verse] would indicate the strength of [Henry's] spirit. Instead of that, I think that the poet was making a play on words, which alludes to the meaning of the Greek *arche*: 'principate, empire, command.' Hence, 'the prince takes control of the name and substance of the empire,' and all the rest must subject themselves to him."

345: *Armos quadrupedis calcar utrumque cavet.* Rocco, in Del Re's edition of Pietro's work, writes (445, n. 13), "'*calcar utrumque*' [both spurs] means the temporal power and the sanction of spiritual power which the bishop of Capua must set in motion."

Fol. 108r

Illustration 14: *The Abbot of Monte Cassino in an encounter with the Emperor. The surrender of Rocca D'Arce. The Emperor accompanied to Capua by the archbishop.*
(S 128)(KS 86)

8: *Quando Capuanus ypocraticus domino imperatori obviam processit.* Literally, "When the Hippocratic Capuan came to meet the lord emperor." This epithet identifies the archbishop as a disciple of Hippocrates, that is, a physician or medical student (Kölzer, "Bildkommentar," 86).

Fol. 108v
Section 14: The Besieged City of Naples Resists.
(S 32–33)(KS 89)

354: *Sic tua, Parthenope, confinia Cesar obumbrat.* *Parthenope* is an ancient poetic name for Naples, and Pietro once more applies the title "Caesar" to the emperor. Siragusa (32, n. 1) recommends Arnold of Lübeck's account of this siege (bk. 5, chap. 6): "devastating all the land, cutting down vineyards and olive-yards, they surrounded the city with a great siege" (*devastans omnem terram, succidens vineta eorum et oliveta, obsidione maxima vallavit civitatem*).

360: *Machina construitur celsis se menibus equans.* Siragusa (32–33, n. 3) points out that "the martial machine" mentioned in line 360 "at equal level with the high walls" is duly shown in the related miniatures "in the upper section of . . . 109r . . ." He quotes *Annales Ceccanensis* (288): "And with many and various machines, he made war on her [Naples]" (*Et multis et diversis machinis eam [Neapolim] debellavit*).

362: *Ex hac Colonii pugnant, hac parte Boemi.* The Colognese and the Bohemians are components of Henry VI's army.

375: *"Noster . . . Augustus . . . Augustum vestrum tondet."* As Siragusa observes (33, n. 1), another allusion to making war and shearing sheep will appear in verses 1217–1224.

Fol. 109r
Illustration 15: *Henry VI besieges Naples. The count of Acerra wounded.*
(S 128)(KS 90)

2-5: *Comes Riccardus . . . Imperator et duces.* Siragusa writes (128–29, n. 4): "Hauptmann p. 57–58, describes, from the heraldic point of view, these two shields, the standards shown on the second and third sections of the page, and the ensign painted on the helms, on the shields and on the harness of the horsemen in those two levels."

Fol. 109v
Section 15: The Wounding of the Count, and the Petition From Salerno Heard.
(S 34–36)(KS 93)

382-383: *Quem liceum . . . arcum. . . arundo genas.* Perhaps *liceum* comes from *Lycaeus*, which Lewis and Short describe as "a mountain in Arcadia, (now Dhiaforti) where Jupiter and Pan are worshiped," and for which they give references from a variety of well-known classical and late classical authors (none relating specifically to archery). In that case, Pietro would be attributing a poetic kind of excellence to the archer, and perhaps indicating a Greek style of bow or shooting. The word could also be the inconsistently spelled adjective for Tancred's county, "Lecce" (*Licium* 872, *Lichio* 1269, *Lichium* 1272, 1302), but it is unclear why someone from Tancred's own county would be shooting arrows at his most important supporter. Niermayer lists a word "licia, lice, licum," meaning "palisade," which does not exactly fit the context, but interpreted poetically, it could mean something vaguely like "warlike" or "martial." I translate the word as an adjective meaning "from Lycaeus," the mountain in Arcadia.

391: *Per mare quos sequitur nante Boemus equo.* Literally, "The Bohemian pursues them through the sea with swimming horse."

392: *preciose . . . urbis.* In context it emerges that Salerno is meant.

396: *Sic ait archoticon . . .* Siragusa states that *archoticon* is given for "archon," that is "one of the aristocrats," and refers the reader to verse 464, where a form of the word is used again. The "archon" is the leader of their legation, a man called '*Iohannes Princeps.*'

401: *Turris maior.* Siragusa (35, n. 2) notes that the "Turris maior" (Great Tower) of Salerno is described by William of Apulia, ed. G. H. Pertz, MGH 9 (Hannover: Hahn, 1851), 239–98, here 274:

> . . . [Conscendit] turrim, quae facta cacumine montis
> Praeminet urbanis, natura cuius et arte
> Est gravis accessus, non hac munitior arce
> Omnibus Italiae regionibus ulla videtur
>
> [He mounted] the tower, which, made at the summit of a mountain,
> Looks down over the city; by nature and skill
> It is difficult of access; no fortress better fortified
> Is seen in all the regions of Italy. (3. 446–450)

413: "*Facturus semper quod mea nupta velit. . .*" Siragusa (36, n. 2) writes: "From what the poet says in verses 392–417, and from the corresponding miniature [fol. 110r], it appears that the archbishop of Capua . . . was not part of the Salernitan legation, but from verses 410 to 413 there is no doubt that he is found in the camp near the emperor. It also seems that with the words '*pars maxima mentis,*' from Henry VI, he is given the duty of accompanying the Empress to Salerno."

414: *Hec ubi legatus. . . .* Siragusa (36, n. 3): "Illustration 16, [fol. 110r, caps. 7–9] completes the information about this legation of the citizens of Salerno, giving the names of the three envoys: Cioffo, Romualdo, and Giovanni [Johannes] Principe. . ."

Fol. 110r
Illustration 16: *Medical treatment of the wound of the count of Acerra.* . . . .
(S 129)(KS 94)

7, 8, 9: *Cioffus, Romoaldus, Iohannes Princeps.* For a review of the scant literary and documentary information about these men, see biographical sketches.

Fol. 110v
Section 16: The Empress Enters the City.
(S 37–38)(KS 97)

418: *sydereas* . . . .*umbras.* Or "shades of stars."

420-421: *qui flore fruuntur / Oris et etatis.* More literally, "who enjoy the flower of age and face."

421: *pars sedet acta rotis.* Or "drawn by wheels." Clearly some kind of wheeled vehicle is meant.

422: *Ipsa . . . vittis.* Classical *vittae* were bands, fillets, or chaplets, and the word is often associated with religious ceremonies. Since Pietro refers to Constance as Juno further down (line 430), he may mean to suggest that *vittae* are meant to honor one whose status on earth is equivalent to Juno's; in short, there is a solemn purpose in this display of beauty and wealth. However, Elisabeth Crowfoot and Sonia Hawkes, "Early Ango-Saxon Gold Braids," *Medieval Archaeology* 11 (1967): 42–86, here 61, show that the term *vitta* was used for a particular kind of ornamental gold band worn upon the brow of princesses and other ladies of high rank, at least in the "Merovingian and Carolingian periods." The miniatures do not clearly show that the Salernitan ladies are wearing this sort of band, but they also do not display the wheeled vehicles apparently mentioned in the verse. Pietro's meaning must therefore remain somewhat uncertain. For *vittis,* Rocco (413, line 45) has *"le bende* [headbands]"; Becht-Jördens has *"Hauben* [hoods, bonnets],*"* while De Rosa has *"nastri* [ribbons]." I chose "garlands" because the word suggests beauty as well as ceremony, and in English it alliterates with gold; also, the ladies and the child accompanying them are apparently carrying flowers, though not wearing them on their heads.

430: *Iunonem spectare.* Here Pietro specifically refers to Constance as Juno, appropriate because her husband, Henry, is customarily likened to Jove. See note on line 82.

434: *verno . . . ore:* or "vernal mouths."

436: *Ingreditur patrias . . . Constancia sedes.* Or, "Constance entered her father's capital." Salerno was the capital of the Duchy of Apulia, which King Roger II,

Constance's father, held. Siragusa states (38, n. 1): "Concerning the particulars of this sedition in Salerno and of the battle between the two parties, which is described in verses 438–451 and illustrated in the miniature . . . I do not know if there is any further testimony. According to the miniature, it seems that one party has fortified itself in the '*Turris Maior* [Great Tower]' and their opposition is gathered in the high place called '*Torus* [Mound].'"

Fol. 111r
Illustration 17: *Entrance of Constance into Salerno. Combat between Salernitan Tancredines and Imperialists, one force gathered in "The Great Tower" and the other on the hill "Torus."*
(S 130)(KS 98)

1: *Quando imperatrix* . . . Siragusa writes (130, n. 1): "Hauptmann, p. 58, discourses about the standards which are near the empress, and believes that the one on the left is the empress's own, or else that of the person who accompanied her to Salerno; however, the two standards appear planted in the earth, and in any case, the one who could be the bearer looks like a '*cives* [citizen]' of Salerno who has come outside the city to meet the empress. The same author speaks elsewhere of three shields which are attached to the battlements of the '*Turris Maior*.'" Kölzer (98) states that the empress and the Salernitans both have their banners, but the illustration gives only a general idea of the shapes of the banners, not a detailed rendering of their appearance.

6: *Torus.* Siragusa writes (130–31, n. 3): "The south side of the hills which faced the '*Turris Maior*' are called '*Tuoro*' even today . . . . Colloquially this part of the height [*altura*] is called *Mazzo della Signora* [the Lady's Bundle]."

Fol. 111v
Section 17: The Legation's Inquiry and the Prince's Illness.
(S 39–40)(KS 101)

456: *Inter quos fuit Alfanides cognomine Princeps, Aldrisius.* Pietro's discussion of Aldrisio's ancestry is confusing, but perhaps less confusing than that of the scholars who have tried to clarify the matter. Kölzer (102) states that he is part of the *Princeps* family, which was connected to the *Guarna* family (of the famous archbishop Romuald, the chronicler, who died in 1181 or 1182). Siragusa (28, n. 1) states that he is the son of Alfano. Elsewhere, Siragusa (39, n. 2) writes as if *Alfanidi* were the family surname. However, *Afanides* can also be perceived as a Greek patronymic meaning "son of Alfano" (see note on line 1596). That could, of course, be the actual origin of a family surname. But *cognomen* can also mean "nickname," and it is not clear just what Pietro means by the word here. He may only wish to associate Aldrisio and the name "Alfano," a famous one in Salerno, and the archdeacon may well have been related in more than one way to several people who bore it. According to Generoso Crisci, *Salerno Sacra*, 46–48, Bishop Alfano I, who was consecrated in 1058 and died in 1085, was a poet and scholar with a reputation for medical knowledge. He supervised the construction of Salerno's great cathedral (financed by Robert Guiscard), and played host to the exiled Pope Gregory VI, who died and was buried in the city. Alfano I was immediately succeeded by Alfano II, who, Crisci says, was bishop from about 1085–1121 (*Salerno Sacra*, 73). These men were apparently related to each other, and their family no doubt continued to flourish in Salerno, producing now and then, other members named "Alfano," one of whom might have been Aldrisio's father.

462: *Exquirunt spectare suum . . . tonantem.* In Roman mythology, the thunderbolt is Jove's special weapon; thus, by "Thunderer," Pietro means Jove, which in turn means Henry VI. See notes on line 82.

464: Siragusa (39, n. 3), writes: "'Archos' is an abbreviation for 'archonticon'; see line 396. That the poem speaks here of Aldrisio the archdeacon is clarified in . . . Illustration 18 [Fol. 112r, cap. 2]."

473: *Certans.* Siragusa (162) lists "certare" as one of the words which Pietro uses with an unusual meaning, signifying "to declare, protest, assure" instead of "to fight, strive or contest," the classical meaning of the verb. Niermeyer gives as a possible definition, "to assure, to convince."

477: *tercia febris.* The "tertian" fever of malaria occurs in a cycle of three days, with the count starting the day of the occurrence (thus, in modern parlance, we would say "every other day"). Malarial fever with this period of recurrance is commonly caused by the *plasmodium vivax* protozoan; other strains of the protozoan have different periods.

Fol. 112r
Illustration 18: *The visit of the archdeacon of Salerno to the infirm emperor.*
(S 130–31)(KS 102)

4: *Magister Girardus.* Kölzer (102) observes that this man is tonsured as a cleric.

Fol. 112v
Section 18: The Prohibition of Sorties.
(S 41–42)(KS 105)

490: *Cereus ille comes.* The poet means Count Richard of Acerra, but with a play on words. As Siragusa points out (41, n. 1), Pietro uses the epithet "Cerrea," derived from "Cerreus" to mean something like "the Acerran woman"—that is, Sibylla of Acerra, Richard's sister and Tancred's queen (ll. 893, 895, 959, 963).

Hence, he might use "Cerreus" to mean "the Acerran count," or Richard, Count of Acerra. But with one "r" left out, the word means "waxen" or "waxy." Siragusa suggests that by this Pietro means "to indicate the count's pallor, because he is still suffering from the wound of which the last verse spoke . . . ."

492: *Philomena.* Philomena, like Philomela, is a name for the nightingale.

Fol. 113r
Illustration 19: *Exhortation of Count Richard of Acerra and of the Archbishop Nicholas of Salerno to the Neapolitans because they are not to make sorties from the city . . . .*
(S 131)(KS 106)

1: *Recedente Augusto.* Siragusa writes (131, n. 3): "This caption is above the second section. Over the first there may perhaps have been one which is now lacking, probably because it was taken away in the rebinding of the book, just like the title of Section XVIII, which should be read on the verso of this page. . . . On the shield of the first warrior, as on those of the two at the opposite ends of the upper section, is the design of a lion rampant, the ensign, as it seems, of the Count of Acerra."

Fol. 113v
[Section 19]: The Imperial Retreat from the Siege.
(S 43–44)(KS 109)

516: . . *Yberos.* Siragusa (43, n. 1) writes, "Engel, p. 47, note t, explains the sense of this verse, recalling that the rivers of Iberia contain golden sands and could be taken as symbols of wealth. Winkelmann, note 50, accepts this explanation implicitly and writes '*fluvios auriferos=thesauros nostros*' [rivers bearing gold=our treasures]. So far the poetic conceit is clear: 'You who have exhausted our springs of gold, now lay your hands on the riches of Sicily.'"

528: . . . *archilevita.* Pietro addresses Aldrisio.

533: *auxilium Pallidis.* Devices of Pallas are siege engines, as Siragusa explains (44, n. 1). Pallas Athena, goddess of war as well as wisdom, is an appropriate patroness for such instruments. Siragusa cites several sources to establish that "Pallidis" is a known variant for "Palladis," not an error in need of correction.

535: . . . *Eolus asper aquas.* Aeolus is the Graeco-Roman god of the winds.

536: *Sic sic Alfanides patrii cognominis heres.* "Alfanides" could be a poetic patronymic, Greek in form, meaning "son of Alfano." Here, however, Pietro draws attention deliberately to his use of this form. Perhaps this is partly to emphasize

Aldrisio's possession of Alfano's great qualities and partly to emphasize this poem's epic qualities. See notes on ll. 456 and 1596.

540-541: . . . *Responsa referre / Ulla times?* "Do you fear to / Return any answer?" Here Pietro has addressed Aldrisio directly, and I think when he asks whether Aldrisio fears to return an answer, he means an answer to the question Pietro has just asked.

547: *Hic . . ."Frigescit!"* These lines obviously tell of an excited exchange of conflicting opinions among the Salernitans about the emperor's condition. (For the last expression, we might say in English, "He's assuming room temperature.") It is possible that Pietro sees each assertion (*obit, calet,* etc.) as an abbreviation for a longer discussion and argument, but in translation, the exchange comes through best as direct quotation. However, Rocco, Rota, Siragusa, and De Rosa do not put these words into quotation marks; Becht-Jördens does, and I follow his suggestion.

Fol. 114r
Illustration 20: *Departure of the sick Henry VI for Germany.*
(S 131–32)(KS 110)

Kölzer (110) explains that the splotches on the upper level of the picture were added later and could represent blood-spatter or perhaps fire, since Pietro has suggested in line 532 that the siege engines were burned. The color is not visible, of course, in the black-and-white illustrations.

Fol. 114v
[Section 20]: The Bond of Faith Forgotten.
(S 45–46)(KS 113)

564: *Dic, ubi bella gerit, qui sine crine iacet?* Evidently this refers back to previous lines about shearing Augustus and his sheep (372–375). Perhaps it is likewise, as Del Re believes (446–47, n. 21), an allusion to the story of Samson in Judges 16. Samson loses his strength when his locks of hair are cut off.

565: *Parthenope.* An ancient poetic name for Naples. See line 354.

567: *Apostolus.* Del Re (447, n. 21) and Siragusa (46) both point out that the Apostle Matthew is Salerno's legendary patron. According to an old tradition, the bones of the Apostle Matthew were translated from his grave in Ethiopia to Paestum, a Greek settlement in Italy (see F. G. Holweck, *A Biographical Dictionary of the Saints* [London, 1924], 824). Later they were brought to Salerno, according to Crisci (*Salerno Sacra,* 43–44).

578: *Versat [in] incuso.* Siragusa placed *in* within square brackets, because, as he explains in his textual notes (46), he added it to fill out the meter. The line is hard to read because it is partly erased and then written over. Previous editions had *inverso* instead of *incuso,* as does Becht-Jördens; De Rosa, however, takes Siragusa's reading.

580: *Vertitur in lolium triste cremanda seges.* Or perhaps "the standing grain is turned to darnel." Here Pietro again alludes to Matthew 13:24–30, the parable where a man sows good seed, only to find that, as the Latin Vulgate puts it, *zizania*—"darnel" or "tares"—are growing among the wheat, because an enemy has planted it while he slept. He instructs his servants not to pull out the young tares, because that could also damage the young wheat; rather, they must wait until harvest, when the tares can be separated from the wheat and burned. The attack on the empress, Pietro suggests, shows that a depressingly large portion of the Salernitan "harvest" is destined for burning.

Fol. 115r
Illustration 21: *Uprising of the Salernitans against the empress.*
(S 132)(KS 114)

1: Kölzer (114) points out that the two heads and the dog in the Turris Major were added by a later hand, as were the disembodied (or severed) fists in the open field below.

5: *Hii gaudent.* This caption is placed near the largest mass of finger-pointers in the crowd, so perhaps these are the ones who rejoice at Henry VI's departure and Constance's plight; however, some finger-pointers are near the other caption. The gloating and menacing words spoken in the verses seem more appropriate to the finger-pointers.

Fol. 115v
[Section] 21: The Speech of the Empress to the Crowd Opposing Her.
(S 47–48)(KS 117)

581: ... *Teutonicus.* Although this word is clearly singular, I translate it as "German host" because Pietro refers collectively to all the German defenders of the castle.

582: *Ospes...fides!* Siragusa puts this line into quotation marks, taking it to be a direct quotation from the Germans. I follow him, but suspect that the sentiment in 582 belongs more properly to the poet, conscious that the Salernitans' legitimate queen is being attacked by her own people, with only foreigners to protect her. For the Germans, to defend their empress and themselves from attack should merely be the obvious thing to do. I take it that the "words" with which the Germans respond are shouts of defiance or of reproach, not directly quoted by the poet. Del Re, Becht-Jördens, and De Rosa also have no quotation marks here. Rota, however, encloses the line in quotation marks, but renders "Ospes" as "O spes." In his interpretation, the Germans express the hope [*spes*] that "faith" in the city may yet fight for them; that is, presumably, if they hold out, allies among the Salernitans will come to help them.

582: *. . . ignota . . . urbe.* The codex has *ignota . . . orbe,* as does Becht-Jördens. Siragusa explains his emendation (47, n. 1) thus: "The evident error of the codex, '*ignota . . . orbe*' must be corrected either to '*ignoto orbe* [unknown world]' or '*ignota urbe* [unknown city].'"

In short, the problem is that while *orbis* is masculine, the adjective *ignota,* modifying it, is feminine. However, translation of the two readings need not be very different, since "*orbis*" can, among other things, mean "region." However, Siragusa's emendation seems logical, and *urbs* makes the reading more vivid, so I follow him.

587: *Saltim dum loquimur.* Here Constance switches from first person singular to first person plural or the "royal plural." This change is reflected in the translation. However, she quickly returns to the first person singular, trying to balance her dignity against her need to address the people clearly.

592: "*Si placet, exul eam Cesaris orbe mei.* Or "Let me go as an exile into my Caesar's world." Siragusa suggests this meaning in his textual notes, but I think it is more natural for Constance to plan a return to her husband's realms. The editions previous to Siragusa, as well as Becht-Jördens and De Rosa, have the reading *orba,* which would produce the meaning, "Let me go as an exile, bereft of my Caesar." Siragusa points out that *orbe* is in the codex, and that when Pietro uses *orba* is in the sense of "bereaved," he associates it with the ablative, as in lines 10 and 1272, not with the genitive, as here.

595-596: "*Nec quociens . . . . igne deus.*" Literally, "Nor as many times as the thunderings of Heaven echo in the cloud does God cause lightning to strike with emitted fire."

597: "*Si presul scripsi . . . . irrita scripsit. . .*" Literally, "If the archbishop wrote, nevertheless, I suppose that he wrote vain things." The archbishop of Salerno is Nicholas, son of Matthew, who raised Tancred to the throne and, as Siragusa points out (48, n. 1), is now his chancellor.

601: *Credite pastori profugo, qui natus ab ydra.* Literally, "Believe the fugitive shepherd, who is born from the Hydra." (I take these words to be ironic, but have rendered the translation as a rhetorical question to make the contextual meaning clearer. I translated a similar locution in line 498 the same way.) To slay "the Hydra of Lerna," a many-headed serpent which grew back two heads for each one its attackers cut off, was the second labor given to the hero Hercules, who burned the stumps to prevent the heads from growing back. Some medieval writers saw the Hydra as a symbol of "sin or passions" (Brumble, *Classical Myths*, 156, 173–74).

602: *Ut coluber nunquam degenerare potest.* Literally, "like a serpent he can never degenerate." *Degenerare* means to become worse than the parent stock; if the parent stock is the worst possible kind of creature, then degeneration is impossible. Clearly this is the case with Matthew the chancellor, the father of the archbishop.

604: *Et dare pro fidei pondere menbra neci.* Literally, "And to offer limbs to death for the weight of faith."

609-610: *Darius Eboleos . . . / . . . Thetinus oves. . .* Scholars know nothing of this episode, but they have found the name "Darius" in various documents. Siragusa suggests (48–49, n. 4) that *Thetinus* might be Theate; notes to the Kölzer and Stähli edition (p. 296) say that it could be Chieti or Teano. It seems that Darius, one of Tancred's commanders, wrought havoc both in Eboli and at "Thetinus," wherever it is. Constance may be refering to the information she heard from the legate in ll. 401–407.

Fol. 116r
Illustration 22: *The same scene as the preceding illustration. The empress speaks to the rebels.*
(S 132)(KS 118)

Siragusa writes (132, n. 1): "The general lines of this composition are the same as those of Illustrations 21, page 22 (115r) and 24 (117r). Here '*Turris Major*' is lacking its caption, which seems to have been removed by the cutting of the page."

Fol. 116v
Section 22: The Empress's Prayer for Vindication.
(S 50–51)(KS 121)

624: *Fecerat ambiguam clausa fenestra diem.* In closing the windows, Constance has darkened the room, so that it is no longer clearly day.

625: *Alfa Deus, Deus O.* This is a somewhat abbreviated form of "God alpha, God omega." It clearly echoes Revelation 1:8, "*Ego sum alpha et omega, principium et finis, dicit Dominus Deus: qui est, et qui erat, et qui venturus est, omnipotens.*" (RSV: "'I am the Alpha and the Omega,' says the Lord God, who is and who was, and who is to come, the Almighty.") (As Siragusa points out, 51, n. 1, the epithet "Alpha and Omega"is also repeated in Revelations 21:6 and 22:13.) Pietro renders the Greek Omega, "Ω" phonetically, another sign that he is familiar with that language. In her prayer, Constance repeats *Alfa Deus, Deus O* a total of eight times, every other line between 625 and 639 and once each in 648–649. While *"Alfa Deus, Deus O"* is perfectly suited to Pietro's meter and preferred patterns of euphony, the same is not true of any possible English translation. My translation, therefore, offers several variations, in the hope that these different shades of meaning, when combined, may make up for some of the intensity lost when the pattern of exact repetition is abandoned.

628: *In me periuras contine.* Siragusa reads *"contere"* (crush) here instead of *"contine"* (restrain) and also in line 639; it is a question of spelling out an abbreviated word, the same one in both places. I use *contine*, as do all editions besides Siragusa, including Becht-Jördens and De Rosa. The sense fits better with my interpretation. Siragusa felt that Constance would have wanted stronger action taken with "perjured hands," but I think "restraining" is exactly what she wants, and fits well with Pietro's themes.

633:. . . *terre*. . .*amicte*. . . Perhaps this means "cloudy" or "misty" earth. See line 695.

639: *Contine faustosos* . . . De Rosa places *faustosos* in his glossary as a word which Pietro uses with meanings not recorded elsewhere, defining it as *"chi gode della sventure altrui* [One who rejoices at the misfortunes of others]."

645: *Rumpe polum, transmitte virum romphea gerentem.* As Siragusa (51, n. 2) points out, this is an allusion to Revelation 2:12: *"Haec dicit qui habet rompheam utraque parte acutam."* (RSV: "The words of him who has the sharp two-edged sword.") The allusion encompasses Revelation 1:16–18, where the bearer of the sword is revealed as the risen Christ. Obviously Constance is calling on the highest of all authorities to help her.

646: *dissipet ora canum.* Literally "scatter the impudent noise of the dogs."

647-648: *O, genitor, genitura creatrix.* Literally "Father, [and] begotten creator." Obviously, *creatrix* is feminine in gender, and would ordinarily be taken as a noun, meaning "female creator" or "mother." Here, however, it is apparently to be perceived as an adjective modifying "genitura" which is grammatically feminine but logically of variable gender. Curiously, Pietro uses a weaker expression in describing Wisdom ("Sapientia"), in line 1476, as *genitura creans* [creating creature]. To attribute motherly qualities to God and specifically to Christ, though unusual in the medieval period, would not be obscure to learned readers and was more common during the twelfth century than it became later. Caroline Walker Bynum, in *Jesus as Mother: Studies in the Spirituality of the High Middle*

Ages (Berkeley and Los Angeles: University of California Press, 1982), 111, states that such references seem to have enjoyed a "flowering" in the twelfth century.

De Rosa paraphrases to make the meaning clearer, "*Padre e Figlio creatore* [Father and creator son]."

Fol. 117v
Section 23: Prayer for Rescue.
(S 52–53)(KS 125)

649: *Ex oriente Deus.* This phrase is repeated seven times. Admittedly, its meaning is rather obscure. Siragusa (53, n. 3) states that "'*Ex oriente Deus*' could be a reminiscence of scripture, Isaiah 41:2: '*Quis suscitavit ab oriente iustum?* [Who will bring the just man from the east?]'" Perhaps there is also an allusion to Revelation 7:2, "*Et vidi alterum angelum ascendentem ab ortu solis, habentem signum Dei vivi*" (RSV: "I saw another angel ascend from the rising of the sun, with the seal of the living God"). Since this angel holds back the destruction mandated by the opening of the sixth seal until the foreheads of the servants of God have been marked with the divine seal, it may fit the context of the empress's prayers for her husband's protection.

653: *Romanum protege solem.* Pietro tends to call monarchs "the sun" and their consorts "the moon." See line 52–53, where William II is "the sun of men" and his consort Joanna is "the English moon." See also ll. 1021–1022, where Constance is "the royal moon."

671: *Qui videt ut dominam.* The accompanying miniature shows a face-to-face meeting between Elias and Constance, but Pietro gives no details on how this was arranged or with what expectations.

671: *quasi Gallicus ore rotundo.* Literally, "as a Frenchman with a round mouth." Commentators disagree about the meaning of this expression, which Del Re (447, n. 25) interprets to mean "with arrogance and boasting." De Rosa translates it as "*dal linguaggio forbito* [with polished words]."

Fol. 118r
Illustration 24: *The empress praying. Elias of Gesualdo gets the Empress in his power.*
(S 133)(KS 126)

3: *Quando proditor Helias Gisualdi* . . . Siragusa (133, n. 1) points out that Elias is portrayed as an aged man, and that this harmonizes with what can be inferred from the dates on the documents where he appears as a witness, the earliest of which is from the abbey of Cava in 1141, about sixty years before this incident.

Fol. 118v
[Section] 24: The Lady's Compelled Descent
(S 54–55)(KS 129)

681: *At domine vultus* . . . Pietro rather consistently refers to Constance as *"domina,"* that is, "lady" or "mistress." I translate this as "lady" when his emphasis is on her exalted status, and as "mistress" when he alludes to her specific right to command obedience from those with whom she is dealing.

687-688: *"Veniam, Tancrede, Panormum / Et veniam, veniam non aditura tuam."* Another pun; in the first two instances, "veniam" is a future tense verb, meaning "I will come" but the third time it is a feminine noun in the accusative, meaning "pardon" or "leniency."

690: *Ut meus hinc salvo pectore miles eat. "Miles"* here means "soldiery" or "army" collectively.

704: *Ornat et inpinguat.* The word in the Codex is *impiguat,* and that is the reading in Del Re, Becht-Jördens, and De Rosa. Engel, Winkelmann, and Siragusa have *inpinguat,* which they justify because Pietro seems to have coined the word based on *pinguis,* "fat" or "rich." As Siragusa explains in his textual notes on p. 55, these early editors think that Constance thickened or enriched her hair, perhaps with fragrant oils, as Engel suggests. Siragusa himself, however, believes (55, n. 1), "The Empress-prisoner made the volume of her hair fatter, not with perfumed unguents but with the abundance and heaviness of ornaments." Becht-Jördens and De Rosa apply the same meaning to the word, although they retain the spelling from the Codex. Niermeyer, *Mediae Latinitatis Lexicon Minus,* gives *impinguare* with this definition, but offers no references.

706: *Forma teres Phebi pendet ab aure dies.* Or "The elegant form of Phoebus, the day, hangs from her ear." Becht-Jördens renders this, "vom Ohr hängt herab die runde Form der Sonne, leuchtend wie der Tag" (The round form of the sun, shining like the day, hangs from her ear). De Rosa has "le pendono dalle orecchie splendide gemme simili al sole," (from her ears hang splendid gems like the sun).

708: *Ars lapidum vario sidere ditat opus.* Or, "A work of art formed by [precious stones], in a varied constellation, enriches the work."

Fol. 119r
Illustration 25: *The departure of the empress, prisoner, for Messina.*
(S 133–34)(KS 130)

2: *Romanorum Imperatrix.* Siragusa writes (133, n. 2): "In this figure, the hair of the Empress is adorned with two strands of gems, and I believe verse 704 alludes to it . . . : 'She adorns and thickens her tresses with weight and art.' The ornament in the form of a half moon which rests on the bosom of Constance relates evidently to verse 707: 'The horns of the moon come together in the midst of her breast.'"

Cap. 5, interpreted by Siragusa as *"Helia,"* another reference to Elias of Gesualdo, is disputed; Siragusa writes (134, n. 1): "The name '[He]lia', from a later hand, was perhaps written by one who wished to point out among the crowd of sailors the characteristic cap [*berretto*] which Elias de Gesualdo wears in these miniatures." Kölzer (130) reads this caption only as "Lia." Elias is not visible near the word, but Elias does appear again in the next miniature, when Constance meets Tancred at Messina. This implies that he was on the ship.

Kölzer (130) points out that other sources credit Admiral Margarito with the task of conveying of the Empress Constance to Sicily. Margarito will appear in the miniatures on 136r and 137r.

Fol. 119v
<(Rota) Section 25: The Lady's Arrival and Her Speech to Tancred.>
(S 56–57)(KS 133)

713-718: . . . *tuas ratis* . . . / . . . *manu.* Apparently *ratis* (boat) is the subject of *effugit, fatigat,* and *exercet.* However, the reader will understand that the actions of the crew sailing the ship are meant.

723: *frigidus.* De Rosa states in his glossary (234) that Pietro uses this word with a specialized meaning of *timidus.* This is not reflected in my translation. Certainly it is possible that Pietro sees Tancred as timid in this situation, but nothing happens in the scene that the usual meaning of *frigidus* (cold, cool) will not cover.

734: *Absit.* Literally this means, "Let it not be so." A flat denial might seem more logical if Constance is denying that Tancred is a son of King Roger II, her most obvious meaning. As it is, she implies that the very thought that Tancred might be King Roger's son is repugnant, hence my translation. It is unlikely that Pietro means that she is about to advance arguments similar to those of Urso in ll. 216–233 (see the notes and commentary there).

742: *Italicos mores inperiosa gerens.* For this De Rosa has, *"ostentando regalement i suoi italici costumi"* (royally displaying her Italian customs).

Fol. 120r
Illustration 26: *The arrival of the empress at Messina.*
(S 134)(KS 134)

6: *Domina mundi dixit: Reperite simiam.* Kölzer and Stähli, in company with Winkelmann, read *regem* here rather than *reperite,* and declare ("Bildkommentar,"

134) that it is "unequivocal" (*eindeutig*). Siragusa states (134, textual note on line 13): "The reading '*Reperite*' [meet, discover] is very uncertain. It would have been preferable to read 'requerite' [seek out] but it does not seem doubtful to me that a 'p' follows the 're.'" Referring to Winkelmann, he knowingly rejected the *regem* reading. The word in the facsimile is indeed rather smudged.

Fol. 120v
<(Rota) Section 26: Tancred Weeps, Thinking About the Future>
(S 58–59)(KS 137)

752: "*Nec me defendent oppida iuncta polo.*" Literally, "Nor do towns joined to the [celestial north] pole defend me."

757: *Unus Rombanldus* [sic] *regnum michi cum tribus aufert.* Siragusa (58, n. 2) speculates that 'Rombanldus' might be a mistake for *Bertoldus*, one of Henry VI's major commanders in this phase of the war; see biographical sketch for Berthold of Künsberg. Rota, on the other hand, cites Bignoni that a certain "Rambaldo di Vaquerias" in the following of the Marquis of Monferrat is intended.

759-760: "*Experiar superos . . . humum.*" Literally, "Shall I tempt the powers above? Perhaps if I am seen in arms . . ." I take these rhetorical questions to be ironic, and to make the translation clearer, I render *forte* as "doubtless," rather than "perhaps."

758: "*In Dipuldeo*": Diepold "of Vohburg" or "of Schweinspeunt," first mentioned in line 607.

769: "*Eu! Si forte cadet salientis vena metalli*" Literally, "If my gushing spring of metal should fall . . ."

771: "*Sex sumus, inbelles . . .*" Here Siragusa (59, n. 2), sees an allusion to Ovid, *Heroides*, 1.97–98. There, Penelope is describing how helpless she is facing the many suitors in the absence of Odysseus: "*Tres sumus inbelles numero, sine viribus uxor / Laertesque senex Telemachusque puer*" (Three in number, we are unwarlike: a wife without power, Laertes an old man, and Telamachus a boy). The reference, if it was meant to be recognized, underscores the condition of Tancred's family, which does not contain a man of military age. Tancred's son Roger has disappeared from the action without explanation. However, Pietro knew as he finished his poem that a match between Roger's widow Irene and Henry VI's brother, Philip of Swabia, was being planned; see notes on lines 1291–1292. Perhaps the suppressed verses on this page contained some uncomplimentary allusions to Roger, the wedding, and his death, and also to Isaac Angelus and the Greek alliance; perhaps the accompanying miniature likewise alluded to Roger and the wedding. It is otherwise difficult to understand why Tancred's son is allowed to die and the Byzantine alliance to pass without comment, although Pietro elsewhere shows himself quite willing to denounce Isaac Angelus (see ll. 1591–1594).

Fol. 121r
Illustration 27: *Tancred is sorrowful, thinking about the future. The count of Acerra sets out toward Capua.*
(S 134)(KS 138)

1: *Tancred futura cogitans:* Siragusa points out (132, n. 2) out that the upper picture is drawn over as erasure, and suggests that the original drawing, with many armed men, was intended to illustrate verses that Pietro later chose to "suppress." He may have based this theory partly on the fact that the text on previous page (fol. 121v), which this picture illustrates, was erased and the verses were written over in the "revision hand" often regarded as the poet's own (see Introduction A.2). Also, as Stähli's article ("Eine Handschrift," 250) shows, fol. 121 is bound with fol. 123 to make an artificial double page in the fourth quaternion of the codex. (Ordinarily, each quaternion would consist of two double pages, and commonly the double pages would be cut naturally in the parchment. However, in several cases in this codex, individual pages are joined, sometimes with a fold, sometimes with stitches, to make double pages. This could have happened if Pietro had wished to rearrange his poem or even discard a page; on the other hand, as Stähli points out, parchment was expensive, and the scriptorium would sew pages together for usable double-pages, rather than discard them.)

Fol. 121v
<(Rota) Section 27: Conrad, Besieged, Addresses His Men.>
(S 60–61)(KS 141)

790: *"Nec prece nec pretio gens facit ista pium."* Literally, "This tribe will not do works of piety either through prayer or price." The word *pius* can have varied meanings; De Rosa takes it to mean *"gesti magnanimi* [magnanimous deeds]." Becht-Jördens has *"etwas Frommes* [anything pious]."

804: *Tancredum vestrum sanctificare.* Literally, "sanctify your Tancred," or "make your Tancred holy."

805: *Nos hinc . . . obnoxius.* As Siragusa states (61) in his textual notes, *obnoxius* is clearly the word in the codex, but previous editors emended it. He writes, "Engel proposes to read it as *'innoxios [harmless']* , Winkelmann *'obnixius* [struggling].'" The problem with *obnoxius*, as Siragusa explains (61, n. 1), is that it does not exist as an adverb, the form it clearly takes in this passage. However, he proposes, "the meaning of *'obnoxie'* or *'obnoxii'* (submissively, humbly) could supply the sense. Perhaps the author wished to coin a comparative of *'obnoxie'* to render the irony more evident." The meaning would thus by "very submissively" or "very humbly." Becht-Jördens has *obnixius* in this passage, and apparently interprets it to mean "very earnestly."

810: *Et stupet, et memor est, se superesse virum*. Literally, "Both amazed and mindful that he survived as a man." Pietro seeks to convey the frightening nature of the situation and Conrad's resolve to keep up his courage, without precisely saying that he is afraid.

Fol. 122r
Illustration 28: *Address of Conrad of Lützelhard, besieged in Capua, to his soldiers and to the Capuans.*
(S 135)(KS 143)

2: *Hic Corradus marchio . . .* Conrad of Lützelhard. Kölzer (142) states that Conrad had been named *marchio* (Margrave or Marquis) of the March of Ancona in 1177, and would be made *marchio* of Tuscany in 1192.

Fol. 122v
<(Rota) Section 28: The Treason of Count Richard and Conrad's Surrender>
(S 62–63)(KS 145)

824: *In clipeos clipei, cassis in era ruit*. Literally, "Shield [presses] shield, helmet falls on base metal."

825: *. . . famascunt*. De Rosa's glossary (233) defines *famascere* as *rimanere contuso* (to remain dented). Siragusa (*Liber*, 62, textual notes) discusses this reading at some length, with a similar conclusion: "[T]he editions correct this to *flammescunt*, a correction which does not seem necessary because a word *famascere*, '*essere ammaccato, contuso*' ['to be bruised, contused'] . . . might perhaps already exist in the twelfth century or have been made up by Pietro." Apparently the word is related to *famex –icis*, "a bruise, contusion." Becht-Jördens has *fumascunt*. He translates this as "*speien Rausch*" (spew smoke). The word in the facsimile is clearly *famascunt*.

829: *Hic salit, ille salit*. Siragusa (62, n. 3) writes: "Winkelmann, note 94, warns that Bongars, who once owned the manuscript, wrote in the *marginalia* of the codex, trying to correct the second *ferit* [*strikes* or *wounds*] of verse 828 to *ruit* [*destroys*] and the second *salit* [*leaps*] in 829 to *cadit* [*falls*] There is no reason to do it, and also it would produce a sense different from that of the author." Stähli ("Petrus," 266) asserts that Bongars made no markings on the manuscript of Pietro's *Liber*, only on the companion texts with which it was once bound; she acknowledges, however, that it has been "repeatedly asserted" (*immer wieder behauptet*) that he did.

834: *Ut ... maritus ovis.* Literally, "as the husband of a ewe ..."

835-842: *Hic ruit ... alter obit.* This might be an extended account of a single incident.

837: *Ut solet a capto Iovis armiger angue ligari ...* Siragusa (63, n. 1), points out verbal echoes of Virgil's *Aeneid* 9.564, Ovid's *Metamorphoses* 15.386, and Ermoldus Nigellus's *Carmina* 1.507. The armor-bearer of Jove is the eagle.

Fol. 123r
Illustration 29: *Episode of the assault of Richard of Acerra on Capua. Burial of the corpses.*
(S 135–36)(K 146)

1-2: ... *pau[cas] ...su[mmo]* ... Siragusa writes (135, n. 2): "This page was cut off on the lateral external margin, where several letters, indicated in parenthesis, were cut off from the words."

2: *Teutonicus viso comite Riccardo ...* Siragusa writes (135, n. 3): "About this episode, see note to verse 850. Hauptmann elucidates the little ensigns [*bandieruoli*] on the lances of the knights who meet in encounters, and the shield held by one warrior in the tower who extends a hand toward of the count of Acerra, a shield in which we recognize a white lion against a green background."

6: *Cadavera mortuorum proiciuntur in fluvio.* As Kölzer (146) notes, the river into which the bodies are thrown is the Volturno, in Capua.

Fol. 123v
<(Rota) Section 29: Tancred, Writing to His Wife, Sends Constance to Her.>
(S 64–65)(KS 149)

876: "*Illius est uxor, qui quatit omne solum ...*" Literally, "She is the wife of him who shakes every land."

877:.... *mea prekarissima consors ...* Siragusa, in his textual notes (64), points out that the abbreviated expression, *prekma* with a bar over the "m," which he interprets as *prekarissima* (very dear), was interpreted as *prebeatissima* (very blessed) by Winkelmann, who, he says, took the "k" for a "b." Becht-Jördens also has the latter reading, but De Rosa follows Siragusa.

885: *Post hec, assissis sociis.* .... Siragusa (65, n. 1), writes, "'*assidere*' also has the significance of '*assignare*' and of '*definito numero quosdam eligere* [to choose a definite number]." He adds, "[I]t seems to me probable that the poet wished to use this word (in which he seems to redouble the second 's' by influence of the first) because Constance, as a prisoner, could not be left at liberty to choose her keepers, who therefore had to be assigned by the partisans of Tancred." This certainly makes sense. Becht-Jördens, however, in his article ("Der Dichter und sein Text," 287) takes *"assissis"* to mean *"abscissis"* and translates the phrase to mean "torn from her companions": "Dannach wurden die Gefährten von der Kaiserin getrennt. . ." De Rosa interprets the word similarly. Siragusa, in his textual notes on this passage, states that Engel, Gravier, and Del Re have *ascitis* and Winkelmann has *asscitis*, a word which (in both spellings) would also tend to mean "approved" or "assigned." Similarly, Rota has *adscitis*. For the Becht-Jördens and De Rosa interpretation to be correct, we must assume that Constance was allowed to bring companions with her from Salerno, but they were taken from her when she was sent from Messina to Palermo. It is far from clear that this happens. The verse never says what companions accompany Constance from Salerno when she surrenders, but the miniatures on 119r show her leaving Terracina with two attendants. No attendants are shown with Constance as she enters Palermo (fol. 124r) to meet Sibylla, but no guards are shown either, which is hardly realistic. Later, in her solitary imprisonment at Naples, and in her journey north, she is shown with one attendant (126r and 128r), though it is hard to say whether the same woman has been with her all along. Because of the uncertainty, and because Siragusa's interpretation of the situation seems more probable, I follow Siragusa's reading here.

890: *"Pro pudor! Insidias obsidionis habet!"* Perhaps more literally, "Oh shame! She is beset by ambushes of the besiegers."

893: *Cerree*. . . .Siragusa (65, n. 2), writes: "Queen Sibylla, wife of Tancred, was, as is known, the sister of Count Richard of Acerra. The poet calls her 'Cerrea' several times, and calls her brother 'Cerreus'; see verse 490, and the related notes, 895, 925, 959, and 953."

893: *Cerree fastidit opus*. . . Del Re (448, n. 32) writes, "Engel interprets the *fastidit opus* [Constance's disdain for the 'work' of 'the Acerran woman'] variously. Now he explains it as the official responsibility that came from Tancred, having commanded Sibylla to hold her [Constance] captive; now as the authoritative manner which Sibylla assumed while Constance was in her presence; sometimes for the looks [Sibylla] was always casting around her so that she could watch [Constance's] actions attentively. Far from rejecting these interpretations, we believe that all these operations are contained in that word [*opus*]."

893: *fastidit amari*. Siragusa (65, n. 3) points out an echo of Ovid's *Remedia Amoris*, line 305.

894: *neutris*. . . . Siragusa (65, n. 4), writes: "The *'neutri* [neuters]' are the eunuchs who, as is known, worked in several capacities at the court of the kingdom of Sicily in the middle ages . . . ."

Fol. 124v
<(Rota) Section 30: Tancred's Wife Writes Back to Her Husband, and Tancred Writes to Her Again.>
(S 66)(KS 153)

912: *Ni caput abradas, cetera menbra [sic] ruent. Abrado- are* can mean "shave" or it can mean something more sinister, such as "scrape off," "erase," or "cut off." I chose "shave" because Sibylla's analogy makes Tancred into a patient who needs a cure. One would not try to cure a patient by scraping off or removing his head. However, the ambiguity might be intentional, since behind the image of Tancred the patient, Sibylla has evoked another image, that of Tancred's political opposition, a body of which Constance is the head. In that case, cutting off the "head" would supposedly rob the "body" of all its strength. Del Re (448–49, n. 33) explains that Sibylla is making that suggestion very subtly; Tancred only needs to change the *ni* in this line to a *si*, and it becomes, "If you cut off the head, the other limbs will go to ruin." Sibylla is, of course, too clever to put such a thing in writing. Rota, on the other hand, in his notes on those lines, suggests that Sibylla means something quite different; the illness in the "head" is Constance's presence in the capital, Palermo; shaving the head means sending her elsewhere.

913: *Hec ubi Tancredus legit. . .* Del Re (449, n. 34), writes, "Tancred cannot make up his mind about Sibylla's suggestions, and instead advises her to consult the oracle of Matthew the chancellor, whom he says is another Achitophel (for his faith and devotion) and has the heart of Ulysses (for his cleverness and prudence)."

919: *Consule Matheum per quem regina vocaris.* Tancred reminds Sibylla that he owes Matthew his elevation to the kingship (and that is why she is queen).

Fol. 125r
Illustration 31: *Exchange of messages between Tancred and the queen Sibylla about the captivity of Constance.*
(S 136–37)(KS 154)

2: *Uxor Tancredi rescribit ipsi viro suo.* Kölzer (155) states that the notary shown here is a layman, presumably revealed by his manner of dress.

Fol. 125v
<(Rota) Section 31: The Wife of Tancred and the Bigamous Priest>
(S 68–69)(KS 157)

926: *Sic ait: "O veterum bibliotheca ducum."* With this rather odd phrase, Sibylla compliments Matthew as a repository of old knowledge at the service of rulers. The word *dux* or "duke" is here more or less a synonym for "princes," "rulers," or "nobles," perhaps recalling a time, not so long before, when the land where Pietro lived was under the authority of the Dukes of Apulia, of Robert Guiscard's lineage, and these did not answer to a sovereign lord in any meaningful way. The word is used similarly in ll. 85, 127, and 220. Rota in his edition (129) suggests that this is an allusion to Matthew's reputation, described by the chronicler Falcandus, for knowing the tax and land records of the kingdom of Sicily by heart. According to Falcandus, these records were lost or destroyed during the coup against King William I in 1161. Matthew the Notary, who had been imprisoned as a protégé of the disgraced admiral Maio, was released so that he could rewrite the records from memory (see Falcandus, *La Historia*, 69; or the translation by Loud and Wiedemann, 121).

929: *Sensato de rege queror. . .* Literally, "I complain of the sensible king." I take *sensato* to be ironic, and my translation reflects this.

931: *Ad senium properans dementior exit ab annis.* Literally, "As he hastens toward old age, he departs from the years [in a] more demented [state]."

932: *Et iubet, unde vivat penituisse senem.* Literally, perhaps, "And he gives orders which—may he live to have regretted [them] as an old man." This passage has caused considerable trouble to editors and translators. Becht-Jördens has *iuvat* for *vivat*, which could change the translation to "[he] gives orders of which it would be good for the old man to have repented." In my translation, Sibylla is expressing a wish that Tancred may live to regret his decision, but she suggests that it is so dangerous that he may not survive it.

939: *Tunc ita Matheus: "Merito Sibilla vocaris . . ."* The name "Sibylla," often spelled "Sibyl" in English, seems to have been popular in the twelfth century. In classical times, it was a title for a prophetic priestess, sometimes associated with an oracle or shrine. In Book 6 of the *Aeneid*, one such Sibyl leads Aeneas through the underworld. Dante alludes to Virgil's Sibyl of Cumae in *Paradiso* 33.66, likening his brief vision of God to her prophecies scattered on the leaves, as told in the *Aeneid* 3.445–452. His emphasis, corresponding to Virgil's, is on the delicate and tenuous nature of the insights generally gained from the Sibyl. Augustine of Hippo discusses the Sibyls at some length in *The City of God* (18.23) and records the translation of an acrostic poem, attributed to one of them (either Virgil's Cumaean Sibyl, or another, called the Erythraean Sibyl). This may have been a model for Pietro's acrostic (ll. 1463–1470). Verses supposedly by the Erythraean Sybil were known during the Middle Ages, and the Admiral Eugenius depicted in Pietro's poem (fol. 136r, cap. 11) is thought to have translated them from Greek to Latin (see Jamison, *Admiral Eugenius*, esp. 21, n. 3). According to *The Oxford Dictionary of Byzantium* ("Sibylline Oracles," 3:1890–1891), the complete Greek text of this collection "14 books of differing dates (2nd C. BC–AD 7th century)" survives only in a late manuscript, dated somewhere between the fourteenth and sixteenth centuries. The "main goal" of the collection is "apologetic, to demonstrate that the Sibyl, the renowned pagan prophetess, was an independent witness to the truth of the Christian faith." Boccaccio, also drawing on this tradition in his *Famous Women*, trans. Virginia Brown (Cambridge, MA: The I Tatti Renaissance Library, 2003), 42–43, gives the biography of a Sibyl called Erythraea or Hierophile, and reports that God imparted to her, in the time of King Priam of Troy, the mysteries of Christ's incarnation as well as the fortunes of the Roman Empire. Cf. Brumble, *Classical Myths*, 309–11.

In short, Matthew is telling Queen Sibylla that she is divinely inspired. She probably recognizes this for the flowery compliment that it is.

947: *Vertitur in dubium, quo sit custode tuenda.* Literally, "He is turned to doubt about the guard by which she should be watched."

957: *Qui nomen Salvator habet . . .* "Salvator" means "Savior" of course. According to Siragusa, (69, n. 2) the island where Constance is sent had a chapel on it before the castle was built there, and was thus called "*Sancti Salvatoris insula*" (Island of the Holy Savior). Matthew intends a play on words; the castle keeps or preserves (from harm, theft, and escape) important treasures or prisoners entrusted to it. This castle is now called the Castel dell' Ovo.

961: *Hanc, Alierne comes. . .* Siragusa writes (69, n. 2): "Winkelmann, note 110, identifies this Aligerno with 'Alygernus Cotronis de Neapoli,'" mentioned by Richard of San Germano's chronicle (66).

Fol. 126v
⟨(Rota) Section 32: The Bigamist's Wicked Deeds⟩
(S 70–71)(KS 161)

970: *Vixeris urbanis morsque ruina tuis.* Literally, "You will have lived for the death and ruin of the inhabitants of your city."

975: *Duxeris unde genus, gens a me nulla requirat.* Literally, "From whence you draw your origin, let no tribe seek from me." In other words, he is saying, no one should ask him for directions to the place, since, as he is about to explain, it doesn't exist any more.

976: *Nam Cartago . . . dirruta . . .* Carthage, in North Africa, near modern Tunis. Books I and IV of Virgil's *Aeneid* take place there. Dido, lover and bitter enemy of Aeneas, was its legendary founder. Historically it was the enemy of Rome, which eventually destroyed it. Perhaps that is why Pietro thinks that it is a suitable place for Matthew's family to come from, although we cannot be certain he was not drawing on some actual story or legend which has not come down to us independently.

980: . . . . *non quereretur opus.* This reading is in Siragusa's edition, in those that preceeded him, and in the Codex. However, Rota, Becht-Jördens and De Rosa all read *quererentur* [third person plural] instead of *quereretur* [third person singular]. If the reading is *quererentur*, the subject is *litora*, "shores" from the line above. Thus, the personified shores of Italy have blamed the work of nature for everything that Matthew and his family have done. This makes sense, although one may wonder why the shores, natural themselves, would blame Nature for something that is clearly not her fault. To be sure, the older reading makes one wonder why Nature's work would not mourn unnatural deeds wherever they happened. The obvious solution is that Pietro wishes Matthew's forbears had not made it alive to any shore at all.

983: *Exultans odiis contraria pacis amasti.* Now Pietro addresses Matthew directly.

988: *Unde queri poterant secula, solus eras.* Literally, "Hence you alone were the one through whom all the world could complain."

998: *Ut Sodomos misere mersit abusa Venus.* The reference is to the destruction of Sodom, Genesis 19, which Pietro, in line with the traditional understanding of his culture, interprets as a punishment for sodomy, or "abuse of Venus." It is not altogether clear whether he accuses Matthew of this conduct as well, but clearly he does wish to besmirch him with the sinister reference.

Fol. 127v
<(Rota) Section 33: Letter of Celestine, and the Liberation of Constance>
(S 72–73)(KS 165)

1010: *A Celestino littera.* Siragusa (72, n. 1) cites several chronicles which discuss Constance's release, and states that Egidius, Cardinal-deacon of Saint Nicholas-in-Chains at Tulliano, in Anagni, was sent to Palermo around this time, perhaps bearing a letter whose contents Pietro imagines.

1015: *"Unde tibi tante superest audatia mentis?"* Literally, "How is it that the audacity for such a thought remains in you?"

1016: . . . .*Experiam*—for "Hesperian."

1023: . . . . *Tribuit quis vincula Petri?* De Rosa translates this, "*Chi ti ha consegnato le chiavi di Pietro?* [Who gave you the keys of Peter?]" apparently taking it as an allusion to Saint Peter's, (that is, the pope's), power to bind and loose.

1012:. . . . . *cur superaddis honus?* Literally, "why do you add more weight?" or "why increase your burden?" The pope points out that Tancred's capture of Constance will provoke more warfare from Henry VI, but also implies that his actions are wrong; hence the morally weighted word "guilt" seemed appropriate.

1034: *Movit in actorem secula preda suum.* Siragusa (73, n. 1) cites the chronicle of Jacques de Vitry about the loss of the cross at the battle of Hattin.

1034-1036: *"Movit . . . preda . . . preda . . . libera preda vices."* Though the same word, "praeda" is used three times here, clarity in the translation required it to be rendered "captive" rather than "booty" the third time.

1039: . . .*Tancredus, ut unda movetur*: Literally, "Tancred was moved as a wave is."

Fol. 128r
Illustration 34: *Constance is liberated through the intervention of Pope Celestine III. Her departure for Germany.*
(S 138)(KS 166)

7: *Tristis Tancredus.* In his textual notes, Siragusa writes that "Tristis Tancredus" is only a guess for a caption which is partly cut off and very hard to read.

Fol. 128v
<(Rota) Part 34: The King of England, Captured, is Allowed to Go Free.>
(S 74–76)(KS 169)

1057-1058: *"Parco tibi . . . . humum."* I take these to be ironic statements, but translate them as a mixture of rhetorical questions and ironic assertions. Henry is suggesting reasons why he should not immediately yield to Richard's claim, as a crusader, to be given complete indemnity. To set a murderer free would be in effect to send him on to commit more murders.

1059: *Spectat adhuc certe reditus Trinacria vestros.* Literally: "Certainly Trinacria even now awaits your return." *Trinacria* is an ancient name for Sicily, of classical Greek origin, alluding to the three-cornered shape of the island.

1072: . . . *Rem modo causa ferat.* Or, "At least let the case be opened." Perhaps more literally, "If only the lawsuit would get to the point."

1073: *Sum reus? Auctor abest, nec adest, sed abesse necesse est.* This passage presents some difficulties, but Siragusa (75–76, n. 4), plausibly suggests the following interpretation: Richard's missing accuser is the Marquis Conrad, who cannot come because he is dead. Therefore, if someone is to prove Richard guilty of treason, someone else must face Richard on his behalf in a trial by single combat. For William of Brittany's version of Richard's challenge, see Introduction B.2.

1082: *Nam tua iudicii crimine iura carent.* A difficult phrase; my translation reflects what I think is the king's most likely meaning. Since *iura* could mean "rights" or "legal processes," and *iudicium* could mean "judgement" or "legal investigation," the phrase could mean, "For your legal process still lacks proof of guilt," or (in contrast) "Your rights do not include criminal jurisdiction over me." Richard has already offered, however, to face an accuser in trial by combat, so he is not resting his defense on Henry's lack of jurisdiction. It makes sense for him to complain that Henry accuses him on the basis of rumor and gossip, without any formal investigation. It also follows naturally from the opening lines of his speech, 1071–1072.

1084: *"Quam meritum nostri postulet, ensis agat."* Richard mostly refers to himself with the first person singular, but in this line, he switches to the royal plural, no doubt to balance the more humble tone of his plea for leniency. I made no attempt to render this into English.

1085-1086: *Flectitur . . . non mille talenta / Nec summi . . . carta patris.* Richard left German captivity in February 1194. Although this is unmentioned in the poem, Tancred died shortly afterwards, and Tancred's eldest son, Roger, had died shortly before. These matters are probably dealt with in the missing portions of the poem.

Fol. 129r
Illustration 35: *Arrest, exculpation, and pardon of Richard the Lion-hearted, returned from the crusade.*
(S 138)(KS 170)

2: *Rex Anglie . . . se ensiva . . .* Siragusa's list of "unregistered words" includes *"ensiva"* (162) and the meaning he gives for it is *"armato di spada* [armed with a sword]."

Fol. 129v
<(Rota) Section 35: When Diepold Attacked>
(S 77–78)(KS 173)

1093; 1105: *villa Casini; sacrati villula castri.* Pietro conveys the idea that Cassino is an agrarian district forming part of the territory or estate of Monte Cassino, the monastery.

1094: *Que nec pastori credere cauta fuit.* Cassino, though supposedly dependent on the monastery of Monte Cassino, to which it is a neighbor, diverged from its allegiance to the emperor. Siragusa (77, n. 1) writes, "Cassino and other places in Campania were brought into submission by the combined powers of Diepold of

Vohburg and Adenolf [Atenulf], the deacon of Monte Cassino. Compare Richard of San Germano p. 66, and the *Annales Casinenses*, p. 288. . . ."

1109: *Illo forte die propriam comes ibat in urbem.* The scholars do not name this count, whose disassociated ensign appears in the miniature. However, Siragusa tentatively dates these actions to 1192, and Jamison (*Admiral Eugenius*, 112) mentions that by 1194, Count Richard of Carinola and Conza had been Diepold's captive for two years. Perhaps he is the one.

Fol. 130r
Illustration 36: *Episode of the assault made on San Germano by Diepold of Vohberg.*
(S 139)(KS 174)

2: *Quando Diopoldus.* . . Siragusa (139, n. 1) writes: "I do not know whether this episode is narrated by others. In the lower part of the page, there appears a wild boar, which seizes by the neck a bird that appears to be a heron. W[inkelmann], p. 78, suspects that this is the ensign of the count of Acerra; hence the figure or group symbolically represents the victory of the count Diepold, the attacker, against Richard of Acerra, defender of San Germano, an illustration, as it seems, of verse 1116. . . . I have, however, noted in the *Bulletino* that in three other places in these miniatures, the ensign of the Count of Acerra appears to be a lion rampant or something similar, but not a bird. . . . If this were certain, one could think of the heron as the standing for the royal crown of Tancred and believe that the aforesaid picture represented the victory of Diepold over the Tancredines in general and not over the count of Acerra in particular."

2: . . . *Diopoldus.* . . Kölzer (174) identifies the Diepold of these illustrations as "Diepold von Schweinspeunt (dead by 1221)." Van Cleve (*Frederick II,* 137) makes it clear that he is the same man as Diepold of Vohburg.

Fol. 130v
HERE ENDS THE FIRST BOOK. THE SECOND BOOK BEGINS
<(Rota) Section 36: The Emperor commands the fleet and army to assemble.>
(S 79–81)(KS 177)

1119: *Ut pius armipotens.* . . . Siragusa (79) notes in the margin that these actions take place in April, 1194.

1123: *Marchio quinque* . . . . A "March" is a territory in a border region; the nobleman who ruled over a "March" would be a marquis or margraf, just as the nobleman who governed a county would be a count. Since several "Marches" existed among the territories over which Henry had jurisdiction, Siragusa (79, n. 1) reports uncertainty about which is meant here. He writes, "This could mean a German March, but upon examining the directory of lands dependent on the

Empire on page 49 (fol. 142r) . . . . where 'March' is set down after 'Lombardy' and 'Tuscany,' one might think it meant an Italian March. Cf. l. 1361. And since in this enumeration it appears that the poet does not indicate the regions in each case but follows a certain geographical criterion, the 'March' closest to 'Austrinus' could perhaps be the Trevisian or Venetian March."

1126: *Annumerat; Scavus non minus.* Siragusa writes (81, n. 2), "If one suspects . . . that the reading is 'Scanus,' one would think of 'Scania,' as the southern part of Scandinavia was called; but in the miniature of . . . fol. 142r, the country is written down as 'Scavia' . . .. So it is question of Slavonia, which in medieval sources was called 'Sclavia' or 'Slavia' and which an Italian of the South might name 'Scavia.' Cf. l. 1361."

1134: *Olsaticus.* Literally, "the Holsteinian," meaning "the prince of Holstein" or perhaps "the contingent from Holstein."

1140: *Mittit et ignivomas Anglia mille manus* . . . Literally, "Even England sends a thousand fire-spewing armed troops." Apparently Pietro regards the English fighters as especially fiery.

1145: *Bis duodena ducum superum sol regna vocavit* . . . Since Henry VI is the "Roman Sun," his twenty-four commanders shine with reflected glory as heavenly powers. Siragusa (80–81, n. 4), writes: "In l. 1135, it is said that '*bis duodena ducum . . . regna* [twice twelve commanders . . . . into the realms]' were summoned, and in the previously mentioned miniature, there is a kind of directory notation of twenty-four countries shown as dependent on the empire, of which all except two, Westphalia and Lombardy, according to these verses, had come together with their arms on this Italian expedition. To be sure, I don't know whether this enumeration is given in other sources. But it does not seem doubtful to me that it is greatly exaggerated. . . . And it also must be observed that several of the countries which are said to have sent ships, not having ports on the sea, could not have furnished them directly. . . ."

Fol. 131r
Illustration 37: *Army and fleet of the emperor for the conquest of the kingdom of Sicily.*
(S 139)(KS 178)

2: *Marciscius Senescalcus.* Siragusa (139, n. 2) writes, "'Marciscius' or 'Markualdus senescalcus' ('Markward of Anweiler') is not mentioned in the verses illustrating this figure. Pietro of Eboli names him only once, in verses 1560–1561. . . Here he is represented as a commander of the fleet, and carries a shield with an ensign that Hauptmann, p. 58, believes to be a swan, but it seems to me to be a cygnet instead This ensign is seen more clearly on the shield of Markward in . . . fol. 147r . . ."

Fol. 131v
<(Rota) Section 37: Speech of the Archdeacon to the Citizens of Salerno.>
(S 82–83)(KS 181)

1151: . . . *armipotens*. . . translated both as "powerful-in-armies" and "armipotent one," this epithet refers to the Emperor Henry VI.

1152: *tui nomen*. Literally, "your name." This is the reading in the codex, but editors have proposed "cui nomen" ["whose name"]. Siragusa (82, n. 1) writes,

> The reading *"cui,"* proposed by Engel, by Del Re and by [R. P. Pannenborg. *Literarisches Centralblatt für Deutschland*, 242–44, n. 8,], gives an acceptable meaning, but simply a narrative one, *"cum quo erat [is] cui nomen* [with him was the one whose name was Philip Guarna]," etc. The reading of the codex, "tui," followed by the editions, gives us a high-sounding circumlocution, appropriate to the famous Guarna family, partisans of the emperor. The poet here apparently wishes to say, emphatically: "The Archdeacon came to Salerno and with him was Philip, one of your people, O Guarna."

Becht-Jördens has *cui* here but De Rosa retains *tui*.

1162: *"Iam vexilla micant, iam sua signa tonant."* Literally, "Now the banners shine, now his signals resound." Presumably the signals are trumpet calls.

176: . . . *Nuceria*. Jamison (*Admiral Eugenius*, 115, n. 1) states that "Nocera was a city belonging to Richard of Acerra's county of the Principato." Toeche, in *Kaiser Heinrich VI*, 335, reports that Nocera was destroyed at this time, in September 1194, but this line from Pietro seems to be his only source for that information.

Siragusa writes (83, n. 3), "After this page 38 (131) there is certainly a leaf missing, not two, however, as Engel believed . . . Bongars wrote in the lower margin, 'There must be an omission in this place because the city of Salerno was taken.' There is a remnant of the missing page on which it is impossible to divine the picture which would be found on the front side; but it must have represented the archdeacon of Salerno and Philip Guarna speaking to the besieged Salernitans, according to verses 1151–1176 of page 38 (131v). The missing part of the text must have contained the fall of Salerno and perhaps the death of Tancred." If Stähli ("Petrus," 266) is correct that Bongars made no markings on the manuscript of Pietro's *Liber*, the *marginalia* of which Siragusa speaks must have been made by somebody else.

Fol. 132r
Illustration 38: *The Emperor's assault on Salerno.*
(S 140)(KS 182)

3: *Supellex.* This word is loosely translated as "furniture" but would apply to utensils, pots, pans, jewelry, blankets and garments, and perhaps stores of food. Presumably the men with the bags over their shoulders are trying to get their movable possessions to a safe place.

Fol. 132v
<(Rota) Section 38: The Deeds of Diepold>
(S 84–86)(KS 185)

1198: *Nec mea Romanas fistula fallet aves.* Pietro means that he will do his duty as a poet and sing the praises of those who deserve it, in this case the Roman emperor's brave knights (with the imperial eagle on their banners).

1203: *Que, venale genus, factum vicepastor, agebat.* Literally, "Which a hireling tribe turned vice-pastor was driving." Prostitutes were apparently driving the herds and prisoners for Diepold.

1204: *Heu heu, dux prede vile lupanar erat.* Literally, "Alas, alas, the conductor of spoil was a vile brothel!" I put the line in parenthesis in my translation because I think it is somewhat ironic; Pietro imagines the Tancredines crying "alas, alas," but he himself is rather gleeful.

1207: *stringuntur in arma. . .* Apparently, this means that the two groups of warriors drew together for a battle.

1208: *expositos . . . equos.* De Rosa glosses this as "horses gathered in the first rank" *(Cavalli schierati in prima fila)*. Evidently, as the two bands drew closer, Guido commanded the horses in the front rank to slow down. Guido, as the captions make clear, is Diepold's challenger.

1222: *Dum ferit eversos, terga ferire pudet.* This means, presumably, that he did not strike at those who were running away.

Fol. 133r
Illustration 39: *The flight of Guido of Castelvecchio, who had tried to take charge of the spoil made by Diepold in his foray.*
(S 140)(KS 186)

2: *Meretrices ducunt predam.* Siragusa (140, n. 2) writes: "Cf. l. 1204 and the corresponding note. Here the miniature shows human beings, cattle, sheep and horses [being treated as] as spoil. The circumstances are clarified by Richard of

San Germano [*Chronica*], p. 66. *'Qui [Dyopoldus] cum Conrado castellano Sorelle societate contracta, equitant in terra Suessa, oves et boves, necnon et miseros homines, capiunt* [Here Diepold, having entered into an alliance with Conrad the castellan of Sorella, rides horseback into the land of Suessa, and seizes sheep and cattle and some wretched people]' . . . ."

3: *Guido de Castello veteri* . . . . Siragusa (140, n. 3) writes: ". . . Among the documents of the abbey of Cava, I found at a. 1188 [abbreviation "a." meaning "year"] one Ruggiero di Castelvetere son of Giacomo di Castelvetere, but I did not succeed in finding our Guido."

4: *Diopuldus.* Kölzer (186) states that Diepold is striking one of the fleeing knights from behind. That seems contradict the statement in line 1222, that he was ashamed [*pudet*] to strike those who were fleeing.

Fol. 133v
<(Rota) Section 39: The Legation from Palermo>
(S 87–88)(KS 189)

1243: *"Quis rex, quis princeps, quis dux."* Literally, "What king, what prince, what duke?" Although "duke" was sometimes a title of nobility, Pietro commonly uses it to mean "commander," so here I translated it more generally as "lord."

1247: *Hen profugus . . . regulus . . .* The citizens of Palermo call William III *regulus* or "little king" because he is only a child, but they may also mean to imply that as a king rather than an emperor, he is subject to Henry VI in any case.

1253: *"Et pedes et miles caute pomeria servent . . ."* Rota, Siragusa, and De Rosa read *pomeria* here, clearly the reading of the codex, though an obscure word referring to a clear space on both sides of the city walls, indicating the city boundaries. Del Re and Becht-Jördens have *pomaria,* meaning *"orchards."* However, the emperor orders the preservation of "green things" (*virecta*) in the next line, and it makes sense that he would give warnings about urban space as well. Siragusa writes in his edition (88, n. 3), ". . . I think the sense is this: the foot soldiers and horsemen must respect the sacred confines of the city ('pomeria'); the coming of Caesar does not disturb any of the countryside."

Fol. 134r
Illustration 40: *Castles of Sicily. The Emperor in Favara receives legates from Palermo. The sorrow of Queen Sibylla. Entrance of Henry VI into Palermo.*
(S 141)(KS 190)

4: *Calatamet.* Siragusa (141, n. 4) writes, "The fourth [castle named in the captions on this page], *Calatamet,* is certainly the castle of *Kala't-el-Hamma,* near

Segesta, which is transcribed *Calathammet* in a Latin document of 1100, cited by Amari, *Storia di Musulmani di Sicilia*, 3:782 and 3:811, and in *Biblioteca Arabo-Sicula*, 1.80, note 2."

8: *Cum pompa nobili et triumpho glorioso Augustus ingreditur Panormum*. Kölzer (192) states that Henry VI made this triumphal entrance on 20 November 1194.

Fol. 134v
<(Rota) Section 40: Sibylla's Complaint.>
(S 89–90)(KS 193)

1260: *Vix a femineis est recreata viris*. Literally, "She was revived with difficulty by effeminate men." Although this could be another variation on the frequently repeated trope that Tancredine soldiers are womanish when compared to the Germans, my translation probably renders the meaning Pietro intended.

1267: *Causatur sua gesta prius, causatur et inde*. Presumably, Sibylla is making excuses either to herself or to Saint Paul and Saint Peter.

1271: *Vir michi forsan adhuc superesset et inclita proles*. As far as we know, the only child Sibylla has lost since Tancred took the throne is her eldest son Roger, who died some time in 1193. Here she implies that Roger and Tancred died because Tancred usurped the throne. No such connection is clear from the record, but little is known of the circumstances of their deaths.

1275: . . . *fugit omen!*" Siragusa (89–90, textual notes and n. 1) writes that the editions have "*omnis*" instead of "*omen*." He writes, "The codex has '*om*' with an abbreviation identical to the one on the word 'omen' in line 1308. There is therefore no reason to read '*omnis*' as all the editors as far as W[inkelmann] have done. . . . The author often gives ['*omen*'] the significance of '*fortuna*' (cf. l. 1001). [Thus the verse means], 'How quickly ephemeral greatness . . . abandons us and fortune vanishes!'" Becht-Jördens has *omnis*; De Rosa *omen*.

1286: *"Hen tuus egrotus regnat et arma tenet."* Here Sibylla apparently attributes to Rome the false information that Henry VI was sick or dying, suggesting that this emboldened her husband to take actions against Constance which he otherwise would not have done. But Constance had, when attacked at Salerno, suggested that Nicholas, Matthew's son, was responsible (ll. 597–598). These possibilities are not, of course, mutually exclusive.

Fol. 135r
Illustration 41: *Queen Sibylla praying to the apostles Peter and Paul.*
(S 141)(KS 194)

1: *Uxor Tancredi.* Siragusa (140, n. 6) writes: "It seems that in the first section of this page there was a picture which has been rubbed off."

Fol. 135v
<(Rota) Section 41: The Triumphant Emperor Occupies the Royal Palace.>
(S 91–92)(KS 197)

1303: *Inpetrat et supplex nato veniamque nepoti.* In classical Latin, *nepos* generally means "grandchild," but presumably no grandchildren had been born to Sibylla at this time. The word could well have its medieval meaning, "nephew"; thus Jamison assumes that Sibylla's brother's son, "the young Roger of Acerra" is meant (*Admiral Eugenius*, 120).

1308: *Multiplicat Carolis nomen et omen avis . . .* Literally, "Multiplied the name and omen for his ancestral Charleses." This is a reference to Henry VI's Carolingian forebears.

1317: *Putifares omnes claves et scrinia portant.* Here Pietro alludes to Potiphar, Pharaoh's captain who was Joseph's first master (Genesis 39). The emperor is dealing with eunuchs of Arab or African origin who have charge of the treasury. De Rosa translates *putefares* as "i tesorieri," Becht-Jördens as "Alle Schatzmeister," both meaning roughly "the treasurers."

1324: *Apulus aut Siculus debeat orbis . . .* In this context, *orbis* apparently means something like "overall reckoning" or perhaps "list"; as Kölzer and Stähli explain ("Erläuterungen zum Text," 295), where they suggest that the word implies the use of a world map, seen in 140r, a small version of which the chancellor Conrad holds in his hand on 147r.

Fol. 136r
Illustration 42: *Conspiracy against Henry VI in favor of William III, son of Tancred.*
(S 142–44)(KS 198)

1-2: Kölzer (198) states that these captions were added later, and that the notary is writing the letter at the archbishop's dictation in the presence of William III. However, no background is drawn in, and these illustrations sometimes aim to convey a symbolic reality rather than a physical one. The illustration may only mean that the archbishop's letter involves the young William.

6: *Margaritus.* Jamison believes that Margarito is the figure "in the forefront" of this drawing, on the queen's right, "plainly to be recognized by his pirate's beard" (*Admiral Eugenius*, 123).

7: *Rogerius Tharthis.* Siragusa (142–43, n. 4) suggests that this might be a certain Roger of Tarsia who appears in a document from 1183; Jamison (*Admiral Eugenius*, 123 and n. 1) suggests that he may be Roger of Theatis (Chieti in Italian), an identification which Kölzer (198) also suggests.

8: *Comes Riccardus.* Siragusa (143, n. 1) observes that it is unclear which "Count Richard" is meant here, given that Count Richard of Ajello, brother of Archbishop Nicholas, is clearly listed below. He suggests that Pietro may have believed, erroneously, that Count Richard of Acerra, brother of Queen Sibylla, was among the conspirators. Kölzer (198) suggests that he may be "Count Richard of Carinola and Conza." According to Jamison (*Admiral Eugenius*, 112), this count's lands had already been given to another, which could explain why his county is not listed with his name and title.

9: *Comes Rogerius.* Since Count Roger of Avellino is clearly listed below, this "Count Roger" must be someone else. Siragusa (143, n. 2), reviews fragmented accounts and then proposes Count Roger of Molise, "who, after being made prisoner by the count of Acerra, followed the party of Tancred." Jamison (*Admiral Eugenius*, 123) and Kölzer (198) also suggest Roger, the son of Count Richard of Acerra.

12: *Comes W[ilhelmus] de Marsico.* Siragusa (144, n. 1) writes, "Count William of Marsico . . . was son of Sylvester, to whom belonged the houses where the little church of Saint Cataldo was, and which had belonged to the Great Admiral of William I, Maio of Bari. See my *Regno di Guglielmo I in Sicilia*, [The Reign of William I in Sicily] I, 145 and 172."

13: *Iohannes frater presulis Salerni.* The caption indicates that this is yet another son of Matthew the chancellor, and brother of Nicholas the archbishop; however, Siragusa (144, n. 2) says that no other sources mention him. The author of *The Deeds of Innocent III* mentions brothers of Archbishop Nicholas in the plural but does not give their names (18; chap. 28).

15: *Alexius servus Tancredi.* Kölzer (198) identifies this man as Tancred's great chamberlain. According to Jamison (*Admiral Eugenius*, 99), this man had served in Tancred's household since at least 1181. During Tancred's reign, his wife, whose name has not been preserved, served as the queen's chamberlain. Jamison thinks that in Fol. 136r, he might be "the little man with round cropped head and marked irregular features" (*Admiral Eugenius*, 123).

Fol. 136v
<(Rota) Section 42: A Conspiracy of Traitors.>
(S 93–94)(KS 197)

1330: . . . *quod tegit archa* . . . This might be a figurative expression, or Pietro might mean that the letter produced by the informer was hidden in a chest. Notice that *archani* [secret] in 1335 is a play on *archa* [chest].

1336: *Et docet insidias enumeratque viros.* Though "viros" is certainly masculine, I translate it as "persons" in this section because Sibylla is clearly represented as being among the conspirators.

1338: *Quod docet in Caypha presule posse capi.* My translation presumes that the informer told the emperor how to get hold of the letter without giving Archbishop Nicholas a chance to hide it. The translation causes difficulties. If "Caypha" were the accusative, the phrase might mean, "[the letter] teaches how Caiphas can be captured in the archbishop." Becht-Jördens and Rocco (Del Re 432) interpret the passage that way. De Rosa's translation implies that the informer (presumably bringing the letter with him) had some way to prove that Nicholas the archbishop was really the author.

1349: *Nec Christo Cayphas fecit nec sevius Anna.* Caiaphas was the High Priest who ordered the arrest of Christ, and Annas was his father-in-law and advisor, as explained in John 18: 13–14. Perhaps the missing verses would reveal why Caiaphas is a particularly apt characterization for Nicholas; perhaps, like his counterpart, he was of "the counsel that it was expedient that one man should die for the people" (John 17:14).

1352: *Ut capiant quosquos littera lecta notat.* Literally, "To seize everyone inscribed in the letter read." The language Pietro uses, *conscripte* (1350) and *notat* (1352), suggests, without precisely stating, that the conspirators, or some of them, may have signed the letter. That might explain why Henry found it such convincing evidence of their guilt.

Fol. 137r
Illustration 43: *Denunciation of the conspiracy and imprisonment of conspirators.*
(S 144)(KS 202)

3: *Isti sunt proditores.* Siragusa (144, n. 5) writes: "In a sort of dock, the bearded figure who is first on the left is the same who was seen on the previous page at the right of the queen Sibylla. I believe is it supposed to represent Margarito the admiral, according to that caption. There is also the figure of a woman who is, I believe, the queen, similar in the lines of her face and the arrangement of her hair to Sibylla as shown on the previous page. At her right is a boy, perhaps William

III; however, I have not succeeded in guessing whether he is also represented by the child who stands outside the dock, and looks in on it with an expression of wonder or fear."

Fol. 137v
<(Rota) Section 43: The Birth of Frederick>
(S 95–96)(KS 205)

1363: . . . *ab exparta* . . . Here the codex has an abbreviated word which has been a source of confusion and dispute. In the first edition of Samuel Engel, it was printed as "*experta*." Siragusa (95, n. 1) writes: "The word *experta* . . . in this place renders the concept somewhat obscure. [In Engel's edition] there is an annotation, (p. 139, note d), '*Ad Friderici II Henrici atque Constancie filii nativitatem haec sunt referenda* [These things should be related to the birth of Frederick II, son of Henry and also of Constance].' Rocco in the Del Re edition (433) translates, '*Dalle cose già conte vien palma di natalizio trionfo* [From the things already recounted, the palm of natal triumph comes].' But according to the editions, the '*experta*' here is definitely Constance, whose delay in producing her son is, in the second couplet, signified by the image, '*quod fuerat fructus palma morata suos* [because the palm had delayed her fruit].' Huber suggests, '*ab experta, forte* [perhaps means] *ab Experia*.'" *Experia* is a variant of *Hesperia*, or "Italy."

With this reading, the "palm of natal triumph" comes from Italy, which makes sense. On the other hand, this emendation assumes an outright error in the text, because the word in the facsimile clearly has a "t" rather than an "i" after the crossed "p" which marks an abbreviation.

Siragusa has a better solution. His note continues, "All obscurity vanishes with the reading *exparta*, participle of a verb not in common use, *expario*, but used by Varro, *De Re Rustica* II, Ch. 5, and registered by Forcellini and by Du Cange, with the meaning 'unburdened' [*sgravata*]."

This, in the context of a birth, means to be delivered of a child. For M. Terentius Varro (*De Re Rustica* 2.5.7) the word means "beyond bearing," in the sense of being too old to produce offspring; Varro is warning potential buyers to consider the fecundity of female livestock. In the context, either the late classical meaning or the Medieval Latin would suit this passage well, and it would be better still if the expression ambiguously evoked both meanings— "past bearing" in the sense of just having been through the birthing process, and "past bearing" in the sense of being beyond the age of childbearing. Constance was forty years old when she gave birth to her only child. She had otherwise been barren since her marriage in 1186, so her contemporaries had largely ceased to hope (or fear) that she would produce offspring. Thus, Pietro writes *exparta* in ironic mockery of those who thought Constance beyond childbearing, but with the same word he celebrates Constance's successful delivery.

Becht-Jördens and De Rosa both have "ab Experia" (from Hesperia) here. Whatever the reading, "the palm" in line 1163 apparently refers to the child, while it refers to the mother in 1366. Throughout the work, as we have seen, palm branches appear as a sign of festival and triumph. See 96r, 128r, 129r, and 134r.

1364: . . . *parentis* . . . This word can mean either "mother" or "father," but the mention of "ensigns" sounded martial and more appropriate to the father.

1369: *Cumque triumphator nudis iam parceret armis* . . . more literally, "So that the triumphant one might spare naked weapons."

1392-1394: *Non aquilam volucres* . . . *rapidos vellera nostra lupos.* This is clearly an allusion to Isaiah 11:7 and 65.25, prophecies of a peaceful kingdom.

1396: *Terra suos geminos* . . . Pietro has referred to Henry as the Roman Sun (line 663), and is now suggesting that his son and heir, Frederick, will be also be a sun. They will be twin suns illuminating the earth at the same time because Henry will seek to have his heir made king of the Romans as soon as possible, in order to ensure the succession; see note on line 120. In fact, Henry began working on this project immediately after Frederick's birth, negotiating with the German princes to elect his son and with the pope to anoint him.

1396: . . . *sicut Olimpus habet.* By the Twins of Olympus, Pietro probably means the constellation Gemini, or the Twins, the bright stars Castor and Pollux, who are (in Greek mythology) twin brothers of Helen and Clytemnestra, and very devoted to each other.

Fol. 138v
<(Rota) Section 44: Prophecies of Frederick.>
(S 97–98)(KS 209)

1404: *vesper et ortus erit!* Rocco, Becht-Jördens, and De Rosa all translate this passage to mean "east and west." The Latin does, however, refer directly to sunset and sunrise. Perhaps Pietro reverses what seems the logical order because the sun must set on Henry's old warlike era before it can rise on Frederick Roger's new era of peace and plenty. Since sunset and sunrise are the opposite ends of the day, Rota finds the implication that young Frederick kept the two ends of the fish (head and tail), sending the middle to his father.

1407: . . . *nova temporis etas* . . . perhaps literally, "renewed youth of time." *Etas* (classical *aetas*) has a many shades of meaning; it can mean a stage in life (from childhood to old age) or it can mean youth itself. De Rosa translates this phrase as "*iniziatore di un'epoca nuova* [initiator of a new epoch]."

1417: *panditur Yris.* Iris is a Roman goddess, and also stands for the rainbow. In this case, the rainbow is clearly meant.

Fol. 144v
<(Rota) Section 45: Conrad the Chancellor's Speech to the Barons of the Kingdom.>
(S 99)(KS 213)

1431: *Sit licet immanis commissi sarcin[a dolis]* . . . Various attempts have been made by various editors to complete this line, because the lower portions of some letters are visible where the page is torn. All agree to complete *sarcin* as *sarcina* but the remaining emendations vary. Siragusa, in his textual notes (99), approved Winkelmann's reading *doli* (tricks) but said it was not completely certain. He reports that Huber suggested *reatus* (guilty man). KS has *fraudis* (tricks or deceits). De Rosa also has *doli*.

1440: *Et tamen illius commovet ira deos.* Literally, "And yet his wrath moves the gods."

1441-1442: *Si quis Tancredum nimium dilexerit olim, / Quid, nisi per vanas brachia movit aquas?* Or, "If anyone treasured Tancred too much in former times, for what did he move his arms but empty waters?"

Fol. 145v
<(Rota) Section 46: The Book is Inscribed to Augustus>
(S 100–1)(KS 217)

1452: . . . *sexto quod scriberis evo.* Augustine's system, though widely accepted, was not the first Christian account of the seven ages or epochs of world history, the "cosmic week" as McGinn, *The Calabrian Abbot*, 57, calls it in his discussion of the contemporary prophetic writings of Joachim of Fiore. McGinn assigns this honor to the *Epistle of Barnabas*, of about 135 A.D., and also points out that the idea was many times reworked with variations and elaborations; thus, "Tertullian's contemporary Hippolytus of Rome tinkered with the doctrine . . . to show that Christ had come not at the end of the sixth age but in its middle . . ." (58–59). Pietro may also be alluding to what McGinn calls "the myth of the Last World Emperor" which had appeared "by the seventh century" (66) as the result of the positive role the Roman Empire was seen, after the reign of Constantine, to play in the spread of Christianity. This victorious emperor would establish a reign "either an image of or a replacement for the thousand-year kingdom of the Apocalypse," but would resign his power, leading to the final confrontation with "the Antichrist and his minions" (107). Though not adopted by the famous Joachim of Flora, this idea was still popular in the twelfth century (112). Pietro, however, does not suggest that either Henry VI or his son Frederick will or should give up their empire. Cf. notes on ll. 1573–1606.

1462-1469: Here is a more literal translation of the whole passage: "This prince, as the noble writing of Daniel states, will exalt his grandfathers, subjecting Egypt to himself as victor. His name finds rest in his heir, through paternal virtue. The sacred fire of Roman law will kindle with double flame. He will return imperial beauty and religion to the stars. When there is no enemy, he will pitch his camps with Jove. When he has conquered the world and redeemed Sion, the citadel of David, he will seek Sicily again and rule with the golden scepters of Rome."

In the Latin, not only do the first letters of each line spell HENRICVS, but the first words of each line also form a meaningful statement: *Hic exaltabit nomen romani imperii cum vicerit siciliam* (he will exalt the name of the Roman empire when he has conquered Sicily).

1465: . . . *rogus* . . . Literally "pyre," but Pietro did not mean that Roman law would be burned away as in a funeral.

Fol. 139r
Illustration 45: *Henry VI on his throne receives the offering of the poem by Pietro of Eboli, through the intercession of the chancellor, Conrad of Hildesheim.*
(S 145)(KS 219)

1: *Imperator Henricus VI.* Siragusa (145, n. 3) writes: "This miniature . . . is the most splendid in composition and for richness in color, [but is] today very worn and faded."

3: *Poeta.* Siragusa (146, n. 2) writes: "It should be noted that as much here as in the following page, the '*Poeta*' is drawn in ecclesiastical habit and tonsured . . ."

Fol. 139v
Here begins the third book, to the honor and glory of the great emperor. . . . .
<(Rota) Section 47: The Poet Invokes Wisdom>
(S 103-4)(KS 221)

1485-1486: *Tu massam discepta rudem, tu litis amice / Primicias certo conciliata loco* . . . De Rosa interprets these lines to mean that Wisdom "settled the strife among the primal elements" at the creation of the world. I suspect that *litis . . . Primicias* [strife's firstfruits] refers to human conflict, perhaps Cain's murder of Abel in Genesis 4 and its consequences.

1488: *Unde venit nosti Phebus et unde soror.* Phoebus and his sister; that is, the sun and moon.

1494: *Tu sata, tu nascens, tu genitura creans.* Literally, "You begotten, you being born, you creating creature." To be a "creating creature" seems more properly to apply to Christ than to the Holy Spirit (see notes on line 647), but "sata," being feminine, clearly refers back to *Sapientia*, who is likened to or perhaps identified with the Holy Spirit. Pietro may be thinking of the Nicene Creed, in which the Spirit "proceeds" from the Son as well as the Father. Dante struggles to convey similar ideas in *Paradiso* 33.115–120.

Fol. 140v
<(Rota) Section 48: Peace in the Time of Augustus.>
(S 105–6) (KS 225)

1511: . . . *serotinus* . . . This means "evening" in medieval Latin instead of "late," as in classical Latin.

1519: . . . *olivescit* . . . This is registered in De Rosa's glossary as "oliviscere=verdiggiare" (become green).

1520: . . . *partus sustinet* . . . *novos* . . . Or perhaps "bears new shoots." I follow Becht-Jördens and De Rosa in interpreting *partus* as "fruit."

1525: *Evomuit serpens virus sub fauce repostum.* In other words, having spewed out its venom, the serpent is no longer poisonous.

1526: *Aruit in vires mesta cicuta suas.* Literally, "The grim hemlock withers in its powers."

1533: *veteris vestigia fraudis.* This echoes Virgil, *Eclogue* 4. 13, 4.31.

1536: *Nam meus Augustus solus et unus erit;* Literally, "My Augustus will be alone and sole." However, the sense is that he will be the sole ruler.

1538: *una fides.* This might be translated "one loyalty," but that would obscure the association between "faith" and "loyalty" which is made throughout the work.

Fol. 141r
Illustration 47: *Allusive picture about the peace enjoyed under Henry VI, Augustus.*
(S 146)(KS 227)

1: *Tanta pax est tempore Augusti.* Siragusa (146, n. 4) writes, "It is not improbable that at the top of this page there was another caption, afterwards removed by rebinding."

2: *Fons.* Kölzer (226) states that this caption is by a later hand.

Fol. 141v
<(Rota) Section 49: Theater of the Royal Palace>
(S 107–8)(KS 229)

1548: *Quo salit in medio fons, Arethusa, tuus.* Pietro's near contemporary, Hugo Falcandus, mentions the story of Arethusa (with Virgil's slant) twice, once in his chronicle (*La Historia*, 164; *History of the Tyrants*, 217) and once in his associated *Epistola ad Petrum* [Letter to Peter], which many scholars regard as a separate work (*La Historia*, 176; *History of the Tyrants*, 257–58). In the last-mentioned passage, Falcandus suggests that Arethusa inspired poets at their work: "you who were accustomed to give rhythm to the songs of the poets" *(que poetarum solebas carmina modulari)*. This could explain why Pietro moves Arethusa from Syracuse to the palace at Palermo. On the other hand, there might have been a fountain within the royal palace which the Norman kings chose to call Arethusa. See notes on 142r below.

1551: *Hic Corradus adest, iuris servator et equi . . .* As Siragusa writes (107, n. 4), this is Conrad of Querfurt, the emperor's chancellor, "later bishop of Hildesheim."

1556: *mens sua numen habet. . . .* This phrase cannot be translated literally; some approaches might be, "His mind has an oracle," or "his spirit has the divine will." Perhaps "God is with his spirit" would do as well, but that would duplicate some of what Pietro says below.

1559-1560: *Angelus in multos necnon Paracletus in omnes / Mittitur, et missi fatur in ore Deus.* Perhaps literally, "He is sent as an angel to some, and as the Holy Spirit to all, and God speaks through the mouth of the one he has sent." Rocco (Del Re edition 436) has *"Si Manda a molti un Angeli, il Paracleto a tutti; ma Iddio Padre è nella bocca di questo messo"* (An Angel is sent to some, the Holy Spirit to all, but God speaks through the mouth of this messenger).

1566: *Quam tua, Corrade, griphea signat avis.* Perhaps literally, "Which, Conrad, your griffin-bird marks with a seal." "Griphea" is apparently an adjective formed from *gryps, gryphus* ("griffin").

1568: *Melechinas . . . opes.* Obviously, this has something to do with wealth, but the word *melechinas* is obscure. Siragusa capitalizes it like a proper name and provides no notes. Rocco, Becht-Jördens, and De Rosa all interpret the phrase in which it occurs to mean something like "royal wealth." Niermeyer's dictionary has *"melequinus,"* defined as a word from Arabic meaning "coin." Perhaps it is related to the Arabic word for "king" *(malik).*

1571: *auri genus.* Literally, "offspring of gold," this apparently means all things made from gold.

Fol. 142r
Illustration 48: *The "Theatre of the Imperial Palace,".* . . . .
(S 147)(KS 231)

1: *Teatrum imperialis palacii.* Siragusa (147–48, n. 1) writes: "Concerning the *ensemble* of the representation, discounting the circumstance that the 'Fons Arethuse' [Spring of Arethusa] stands in the middle here, it does not seem improbable to me that [the picture] it is intended to signify the famous *'aula regia que palatio subest* [royal hall which is near the palace]' of Falcandus, *Epistola* [in *La Historia*], p. 182." In Loud and Wiedemann's translation, *History of the Tyrants of Sicily,* this "Royal Hall" is mentioned on p. 260. Siragusa also refers to an account by the Arab traveler Ibn Gubayr [Ibn Jubayr] in Michele Amari's *Biblioteca Arabo-Sicula* (1:157); the traveler states that "The atrium is flanked by porticoes and the hall takes all the length of it." See also Broadhurst's translation, *The Travels of Ibn Jubayr,* 347. Kölzer (230) suggests that the twenty-four columns actually shown in the picture might recall the twenty-four elders in Revelation 4:4.

5: *Fons Arathuse.* Kölzer (230) points out that the spring of Arethusa is actually at Syracuse, and the chancellor Conrad had specifically mentioned this fact in a letter to "the provost of Hildesheim." However, some Norman-Sicilian palaces did contain fountains; see Norwich's account of the Zisa in *The Kingdom in the Sun* (239–42), for example. Adalgisa De Simone, *Splendori e Misteri di Sicilia in un' opera di Ibn Qalaqis* (Messina: Rubbetino, 1996), 20, suggests that Pietro's "Arathusa" may be the same as the fountain in the Royal Palace at Palermo, celebrated in the Arabic poem which she translates.

Fol. 142v
<(Rota) Section 50: Houses of the Imperial Palace>
(S 109–11)(KS 233)

1573-1580: In these verses (and the "houses" they describe) Pietro reviews the first five ages of the world, before the sixth. There is some overlap with Augustine's scheme, as given in *The City of God* 22.30, and but also considerable divergence. Augustine's ages are: (1) from Adam to the Flood; (2) after the flood until Abraham; (3) after Abraham, to David; (4) after David to the Exile; (5) from the Exile to the Incarnation; and (6) from the Incarnation to the Second Coming (that is, the "present age"). Thus, it takes Augustine only three epochs to reach David, because (following scriptural genealogies) he allows ten generations per "age." Only in the sixth "age" does Augustine suspend that requirement, due to Christ's declaration that the time would not be known.

Since Pietro takes five ages to reach David, he is clearly following some other scheme. Because his concern is with an earthly monarch, it is easy to see why the time of exile would not interest him. He may also see the incarnation of Christ already suggested in the coming of King David.

1577: *cataclismi . . . abyssum . . .* Literally, "abyss of the cataclysm."

1582: *Cesarea septum prole senile latus.* The sense of the verse, I think, is that these sons are a defense and support for their father and his empire.

1590: *Qualiter invito te Fredericus abit.* Literally, "In the way that Frederick departed against your will." The implication is that they attempted to prevent him from reaching the Holy Land.

1593-1594: *Hic obsessa Polis necnon plantata per annum / vinea . . .* Here Siragusa (109, textual notes) writes : "Above *polis* in the codex, there is written, perhaps by the hand of the poet, *i(idest) Constantinopolim* [that is, Constantinople]."

1596: *Hic Fredericiades . . .* This is a disputed reading. The codex has *Frederici ades*, which scholars find hard to interpret. Still, the first editions printed the word as it was. Then Rocco corrected it to *Frederici ales* (Frederick's eagle) and was followed by Winkelmann, Rota, and Becht-Jördens. Siragusa adopted *Fredericiades*, which keeps the letters in the manuscript but closes an extra space. De Rosa follows him. Siragusa (110, n. 2) points out that *Fredericiades* is a patronymic, meaning "son of Frederick" and "obviously refers to Frederick the duke of Swabia, son of the emperor and his companion on this expedition, as also appears in the following verses." Though the patronymic is a Greek form, it is used in Latin works such as Virgil's *Aeneid*, including the passage on Palinurus (*Aeneid* 5.843) to which Pietro has already alluded (l. 713). Also, Pietro seems conscious that "Alfanides," an epithet he applies to the archdeacon Aldrisius, is a patronymic (ll. 456, 536). Siragusa goes on to explain the younger Frederick's role in the battle. He refers to *Epistola de morte Friderici imperatoris* (*Letter about the death of the Emperor Frederick*), ed. G. H. Pertz, MGH 20 (Hanover: Hahn, 1868), 494–96, which tells how "the duke of Swabia was wounded, with an upper tooth being knocked out completely and half of a lower tooth" (*dux Swewiae vulneratus est uno superiori dente penitus excusso et medietate inferioris*) (495).

1597: Siragusa (110, n. 4): "Iconium was taken by Frederick, duke of Swabia, at the order of his father Frederick Barbarossa."

1598: Siragusa (110, n. 5): "The '*pars prior*' [first part] which '*cadit sub Augusto seniore*' [fell under the elder Augustus], namely Barbarossa, is meant, apparently, to signify the '*castrum*' [fortress] of Iconium which, after the victory of Duke Frederick, was, according to the testimony of Ansbertus, . . . conquered by the emperor." In other words, Duke Frederick first conquered the city, and Frederick Barbarossa took the fortress or stronghold.

Fol. 143r
Illustration 49: *Pictures adorning the six "houses" or "bedchambers" of the royal palace. . .*
(S 148)(KS 234)

Kölzer (234) suggests that the six houses represented here stand for the six ages.

5: *Quinta domus — David rex.* Siragusa (148, n. 1) writes, "The figures in the upper section of this page, which W[inkelmann] thought the best of all, is perhaps a reproduction of mosaics or frescoes in the imperial palace, since they seem to me to have a mystic inspiration and a mode of composition quite different from the usual [in this work]. . . ."

Fol. 143v
<(KS 237) Section 51: Concerning the Seven Liberal Arts>
<(Rota) Section 51: Concerning the Virtues>[1]
(S 112–13)(KS 247)

1626: *Sic, sic era rigent, arma quod hoste carent. . .* Literally, "Thus, thus do bronzes stiffen when arms lack an enemy." Rocco and Becht-Jördens apparently take this to mean that arms (in a figurative sense, that is, "armies" or "warlike powers") become stronger under these conditions. De Rosa takes it to mean that weapons rust. According to Lewis and Short, *rigeo* means "to harden," but can mean "to freeze," and hence carries secondary implications of coldness and sluggishness. Hence my translation.

1633: *Nullus ei similis nisi proles, nemo secundus.* Literally, "no one is like him except his offspring, there is no second."

1636: *Quod latet in partes littera ducta parit.* In other words, the triumphant meaning of Henry's name is revealed in the acrostic (ll. 1462–1469).

---

[1] Rota's heading differs from that of KS here because when Rota prepared his edition, the manuscript pages were out of order, and Rota decided that the verses on 143v corresponded to the illustrations on 146r, which show Henry VI surrounded by Virtues. The verses on 143v do indeed mention Virtues, although the focus is more on education and the Liberal Arts. But, as Stähli explains ("Eine Handschrift," 248), in 1935 the manuscript at Bern was rebound by Johann Lindt in what is now thought to be its correct order. The illustrations corresponding to 143v are known to be missing, as are the verses corresponding to 146r (see Introduction B. 3). Becht-Jördens invented a different section heading for KS, identifying the theme as Henry's relationship with the Liberal Arts. The poet himself no longer supplies section numbers or headings for this part of the poem; see Introduction A.2.

Fol. 146r

Illustration 52: *Henry VI on the throne surrounded by the Virtues. Tancred struck down by the wheel of Fortune.*
(S 150)(KS 238)

4-8: *Rota Fortune . . . Ru*[*rsus ad astra feror*]: Kölzer (238) says that the verses about the wheel of fortune were added by a later (14th-century) hand. Siragusa (150, textual notes and n. 2) explains that these lines were added later, apparently by a hand of a French style (*di tipo francese*) and not later than the thirteenth century (*non posteriore al sec. XIII*). He adds that the captions on the *Rota Fortune* are hard to read, but he believes they are part of a poem of unknown authorship which he has seen in several manuscripts after selections by Hildebert of Lavardin, and which may be by that poet. He has reconstructed the faint captions with help from these verses, which he sets down as follows: *Glorior elatus, descendo mortificatus / Ah! miser, axe teror, laetus ad astra feror! / Ut rota, sic homines; movet hos immobilis ordo / Exaltans humiles, magnanimosques premens.* (Puffed up, I boast; mortified, I descend / Alas, wretched me, I am trampled by the chariot, [then], happy, I am borne to the stars. As with the wheel, so with men; / The unchangeable order of things guides them, / lifting up the humble and oppressing those of proud spirit.)

7: Tancredus. Siragusa (151, textual note), writes: "'Tancredus' is of a later hand, also different from those who wrote the captions on the wheel of fortune, and it does not seem doubtful to me that it is the same that wrote the names of '*Paulus*' and '*Petrus*' on page 42 (135r) and '*Regulus* [Little King]' and '*Presul Salerni* [Archbishop of Salerno]' on page 43 (136r). That name is written twice, the second upon the first, in black and in a different hand, less old." Kölzer ("Bildkommentar," 238) also says that this caption also was added after the manuscript was produced.

Fol. 146v

<(Rota): Section 52: Wisdom Rails at Fortune>
(S 114–15)(KS 241)

1656: "*Si potes, alterius regna tuere senis . . .*" The other old man" is Tancred, of course.

1663: . . . *fulvescent* . . . Another coined word, obviously from *fulvus –a –um*, "reddish-yellow," or "tawny." De Rosa offers this translation in his glossary.

1666: . . . *Nucerinus* . . . Siragusa states (114–15, n. 2): "The 'nucerinus aper [boar of Nocera]' is certainly the boar which is the heraldic symbol of Count Diepold." See ll. 607 and 1116 and Fol. 130r.

1669: . . . *Neptunus* . . . Siragusa (115, n. 1): "Comparing this verse with verse 1560 and with the miniature of page 54 (147r), Illustration 13, one understands that 'Neptunus' is 'Marchisius senescalus' or rather Marcwald of Anweiler."

1673: *Mars* . . . Siragusa (115, n. 2): "Observing the miniature corresponding to these verses . . . it appears evident that Mars is, according to the poet, 'Henricus Calandrinus'; that is Henry of Kalindin or of Kalentin, or von Kalden. See verse 1183."

1674: Siragusa (115, 3): "At the foot of page 53 (146v) once more '*Celestinorum Senonsensium* [*the Celestines of Sens*]' appears."

Biographical Sketches

§**Ajello.** See Matthew of Ajello, Nicholas of Ajello, and Richard of Ajello.

§**Alberia**, fl. 1191–1216. Also called Albidia, Albiria, Elvira, etc. Daughter of King Tancred and his consort Sibylla. Countess of Brienne, then of Tricarico, then of Tuscany.

Though not specifically named in the *Liber*, Alberia is the eldest (*primogenitam*)[1] of Tancred's three daughters, to whom he alludes in l. 771: "The six of us are unwarlike: myself, my daughters, my son, my wife" (*Sex sumus inbelles: ego, nate, filius, uxor*). Siragusa[2] names Tancred's three daughters as Alberia, Constance, and Mandonia. Alberia, however, is best known to history. Her birth date is unrecorded, but the terms of 1191 alliance between Tancred and Richard I, agreeing to a marriage between Richard's heir Arthur of Brittany and a daughter of Tancred, presumably the eldest, states that the daughter is not yet "of marriageable age" (*ad nubiles annos*).[3]

In 1195, after the unmasking of the 1194 conspiracy against Henry VI, Alberia was brought as a prisoner to Germany along with her mother and sisters. They were confined in the "the convent of Hohenburg or Mont S. Odile," which was "an Alsatian house of canonesses in the heart of the Vosges, famous at this time for its literary and artistic work."[4] Some months after Henry's death, she was freed along with her mother and sisters. Subsequently, in "about the middle of 1199"[5] or "in the Spring of 1200,"[6] she married a French nobleman, Walter of Brienne, whose brother John would become titular king of Jerusalem after marrying its heiress.[7] Walter appealed to Pope Innocent III, now guardian for the boy-king of Sicily, Frederick II, to restore Alberia's inheritance to her; that is, to grant her the county of Lecce and the princedom of Taranto, which Henry VI had, in 1194, promised to Alberia's brother William, now dead (see *Liber*, ll. 1301–1304, and Commentary). Innocent III agreed, after demanding oaths

---

[1] *Gesta Innocenti III*, 18; *Deeds of Pope Innocent III*, 21; chap. 22.
[2] *Liber ad Honorem Augusti*, 59 and n. 2.
[3] Roger of Hoveden, *Gesta Heinrici II et Richardi I*, 119.
[4] Jamison, *Admiral Eugenius*, 125.
[5] Jamison, *Admiral Eugenius*, 164.
[6] Van Cleve, *Markward*, 143.
[7] Van Cleve, *Emperor Frederick II*, 43.

and guarantees that Walter would not attack the rights of his ward. He wanted Walter's help in driving out Henry VI's remaining German followers and establishing order in the kingdom; however, the Sicilian council of regency, directly responsible for the government, refused to accept the pope's choice in that matter and even collaborated with the Germans against him (see Introduction, C.17). On 14 June 1205, Walter died of his wounds after a battle with Diepold (q.v.) of Vohburg or Schweinspeunt.[8] Alberia then remarried, and the anonymous author of *The Deeds of Innocent* recounts that her new husband, James, Count of Tricarico, "put off consummation of the marriage because she was pregnant."[9] The son she bore, "named Walter after his father," became Count of Joppa, and married a daughter of the king of Cyprus. By James she had two children, Simon and Adalita.[10] Thomas Tuscus, who relates much legendary material (see Commentary on *Liber* ll. 1–39), but who may have good information about matters closer to him in time and geography, relates that after Alberia was widowed yet again, Pope Honorius III arranged a marriage between her and Tigrino, Count Palatine of Tuscany, and gave the couple the counties of Lecce and Montescaglioso (which had belonged to Tancred's family). Honorius III was pope from 1216–1227, still on good terms with Frederick II, who must, if the story is true, have consented to the arrangement. This is not completely implausible, since in 1225 Frederick did, with the encouragement of Honorius, marry Yolanda, daughter of John of Brienne (and thus Alberia's niece). Honorius may well have tried to reconcile the families at this time. However, Frederick was soon quarreling with his father-in-law over the right to the title "king of Jerusalem," and stories spread that he treated his new bride most unkindly. True or false, these stories suggest no lasting reconciliation between Tancredines and Hohenstaufens.

§**Aldrisius** (or Aldrisio) **Alfanides**, archdeacon of Salerno, fl. 1191–1194.

Evidently an influential member of the party favoring the emperor at Salerno, Aldrisio, called "the public voice of his people" *(populi publica lingua sui)* (l. 457), first appears as one of the delegates chosen to go to the emperor's camp at Naples, just before it breaks up. He alone is admitted to speak with the seriously ailing emperor (ll. 464–486; fol. 112r). When a short time later he discovers that the imperial camp has broken up abruptly and left, he resolves to follow the emperor to Germany (l. 544). Later, in the summer and fall of 1194, he returns "like a second peacemaking Joseph" *(Ioseph . . . pacifer alter)* (1158) to warn his fellow citizens of their peril at the emperor's second approach and to urge them to seek reconciliation before he reaches them. Presumably his advice is not taken, since

---

[8] Van Cleve, *Emperor Frederick II*, 50.

[9] 50; chap. 38.

[10] Thomas Tuscus, *Gesta imperatorum et pontificum*, ed. Ernesto Ehrenfeuchter, MGH 22 (Hanover: Hahn, 1872), 490–528, here 499. Also, Giovanni Villani's *Chronicle* (bk. 4, chaps. 19–20) gives much the same account of Alberia's family.

the city is sacked, although a lacuna in the manuscript leaves some doubts here (see the Commentary on these lines). There seems to be no further information about Aldrisio's fate. Cuozzo reports[11] that he belongs to the "Principe" family, that is, the family of John Princeps (q.v.).

§**Alfanides**. See Aldrisio Alfanides.

§**Alexius** II Comnenus or Komnenos, ca. 1168–1183. Boy-emperor of Constantinople, r. 1180–1183.

Alexius is mentioned by name (l. 158) as a victim of Andronicus (q.v.). In l. 1643, there is an allusion to him as the murdered "nephew" of Andronicus. Although his kinship with Andronicus was more distant than that (see Genealogical Table 3), the term is fitting for a young person killed by a kinsman of an older generation. His dismembered body is perhaps implied among those depicted on fol. 147r.

Alexius was the only son of the emperor Manuel (q.v.) and his second empress, Xena (formerly Maria of Antioch, a descendant of Robert Guiscard). He was perhaps born 14 September 1169.[12] According to Niketas Choniates, he "had barely reached puberty" when his father died in 1180, and thereafter his education was sadly neglected.[13] His mother, surrounded by adoring courtiers, controlled the government, and her policies did not inspire confidence in the people of Constantinople. This gave Alexius's much older cousin, Andronicus, an opportunity to present himself as a reformer. He accused the empress Xena of treason and had her first imprisoned, then executed, supposedly compelling the young emperor to sign the order.[14] Then he ordered the murder of the young emperor, which took place 24 September 1183.[15] Subsequently several pretenders would impersonate him (see Introduction, C.10).

§**Aligerno** of Cottone, count, fl. 1191–1194?

Aligerno (l. 961) is the commander at Naples into whose custody the empress Constance is sent when she is to be imprisoned in the infamous fortress of San Salvatore, later called the Castel dell' Ovo. The *Liber* makes no further mention of him.

---

[11] Errico Cuozzo, ed., *Catalogus Baronum Commentario* (Rome: Istituto Storico Italiano per il Medio Evo, 1984), index, under "Aldrisio."

[12] Brand, *Byzantium Confronts*, 14. However, Magoulias is uncertain and, in editorial notes to Niketas Choniates, *O City of Byzantium*, 96, conjectures a birth date in 1168 or 1169.

[13] *O City of Byzantium*, 127.

[14] Niketas Choniates, *O City of Byzantium*, 147–49. Brand's interpretation is that young Alexius signed only a general decree condemning traitors to death, but Andronicus stretched its purpose and used it to order Xena's execution (*Byzantium Confronts*, 46–47; chap. 3).

[15] Magoulias, editorial notes in Niketas Choniates, *O City of Byzantium*, 152.

Aligerno, or Alierno, of Cottone has been identified by one scholar as Tancred's *compalatius* or Count Palatine of Naples. As Henry VI advanced into Italy for the second time in 1194, this official apparently switched sides, along with his brother Leo, and handed over his own son to Henry as hostage for his good faith. The princedom of Sorrento was his reward.[16]

§**Anacletus II**, antipope, r. 1130–1138.

Anacletus is not mentioned in the *Liber*, but perhaps he should have been. In ll. 3–4 Pietro states that Roger, then duke of Apulia, was anointed king at the orders of Pope Calixtus II (*delegante Calisto*), but it was actually Anacletus, the antipope, who gave that permission.

Christened Pietro or Peter Pierleone, Anacletus was a member of the Pierleoni family, of Jewish origin, which had achieved power and prominence at Rome. The family had kept up a friendly exchange of letters and messengers with Norman Sicily since the time of the Great Count Roger.[17] The future Anacletus was educated at Paris, and after returning to Rome was eventually made Cardinal-Priest of Santa Maria in Trastevere, by Calixtus II.[18] Still later, as Honorius II, successor of Calixtus, lay dying in 1130, two parties of cardinals vied for power to determine the next election. They engaged in intricate negotiations over the manner and place of the next papal election, but despite all agreements, the eleven cardinals belonging to the powerful Frangipane family excluded their rivals from the deathbed, and when Honorius died, they acted immediately to elect his successor without announcing the news to anyone else. Their candidate became Innocent II. The other twenty-nine cardinals did not accept the *fait accompli*.[19] They met to elect Peter Pierleone, whom they proclaimed the legitimate pope and elevated as Anacletus II. Anacletus II was well received by the Roman populace, and Roger II, at the time Great Count of Sicily and Duke of Apulia, offered his oath of fealty, pleased at the choice. But Innocent II fled to France, where Bernard of Clairvaux, who was "practically an uncrowned king in the West,"[20] took up his cause.

Meanwhile Roger II, after negotiations with Anacletus, summoned a great assembly of nobles and churchmen at Salerno, and as Chalandon reconstructs the story,[21] these notables, after appropriate pressures and subtle suggestions from their ambitious overlord, urged him to take the title of king. Acting then

---

[16] Jamison, *Admiral Eugenius*, 100, 101, 112.

[17] Josef Deér, *Dynastic Porphyry Tombs of the Norman Period*, tr. G. A. Gillhoff (Cambridge, MA: Harvard University Press, 1959), 121.

[18] Chalandon, *Histoire de la Domination Normande*, 2:4. See also Houben, *Roger II*, 51–53.

[19] Chalandon, *Histoire*, 2:5–6.

[20] Jordan, *Henry the Lion*, 10.

[21] Chalandon, *Histoire*, 2:2–9.

on their advice, he returned to Palermo and was crowned and anointed on 25 December 1130.[22]

Eventually, Innocent II gained the support of the kings of France and England, as well as of the German Emperor Lothar. Roger II, however, remained loyal to Anacletus II, who was able to maintain his position in Rome until he died in 1138. Roger continued to collaborate with other members of the Pierleone family, to their mutual advantage, even after the death of Anacletus. They might well have supplied him with the porphyry used in the famous tombs of the dynasty.[23]

§Andronicus I Comnenus or Andronikos I Komnenos, ca. 1120–1185. Byzantine emperor, r. 1183–1185.

Andronicus is mentioned twice in the *Liber*, both times as an evil role model for Tancred. The first time, Matthew of Ajello, with ill intentions, recommends him (ll. 158–165), while the second time Wisdom condemns him along with Tancred (1643–1648). On fol. 147r, Andronicus's disembodied (perhaps severed?) head appears at the side, next to the image of Tancred, overthrown and entangled in Fortune's Wheel.

Andronicus's murderous reign in Constantinople significantly affected history (see Introduction, C.10). Among primary sources, this man's long career is described in considerable detail by Niketas Choniates, John Kinnamos, and Eustathius of Thessaloniki. He was perhaps born in 1120,[24] making him, apparently, a little older than Manuel I, who was, like him, a grandson of Alexius I Comnenus (see Genealogical Table 3). Andronicus served in Byzantine armies while in his twenties, under the emperor John I Comnenus, according to Niketas Choniates,[25] but under Manuel in 1153, he was accused of a treacherous conspiracy with the Hungarians and was imprisoned at Constantinople. Niketas adds, however, that Manuel's conscience troubled him over his treatment of his cousin, because he feared he might have judged him guilty through prejudice rather than judicious weighing of the evidence. Andronicus had once aroused Manuel's ire by saucily defending one of his own incestuous liaisons by attributing, with regrettable accuracy, worse behavior to the emperor himself.[26] The captive made daring and imaginative escapes from his dungeon, described in some detail both by Niketas and by John Kinnamos.[27] Though Andronicus was recaptured, Manuel was, according to Niketas, somewhat shamed by the scandal, and

---

[22] Chalandon, *Histoire*, 2:2–9.

[23] Deér, *Dynastic Porphyry Tombs*, 122–23.

[24] Brand, *Byzantium Confronts*, 277.

[25] *O City of Byzantium*, 30; pt 2, bk. 1.

[26] Niketas Choniates, *O City of Byzantium*, 58–60, Pt. 2, bk. 3.

[27] Niketas Choniates, *O City of Byzantium*, 73; pt. 2, bk. 4. John Kinnamos, *Deeds of John and Manuel Comnenus*, 175–77: bk. 5, chap. 10–11.

chose to patch up a reconciliation with him, trusting him once more in warfare against the Hungarians and making him governor of Cilicia in 1166. However, Andronicus's taste for incestuous liaisons overwhelmed him again. He seduced and abandoned Philippa of Antioch, sister of Manuel's second empress Xena-Marie,[28] and then fled to Palestine, absconding with tax monies to pay his expenses.[29] At Acre, he met and fell in love with Theodora, daughter of his cousin Isaac and widow of Baldwin III of Jerusalem. To avoid further imprisonment, he fled with her, and the lovers were sheltered by various Moslem potentates, until they settled down under the protection of "a Turkish emir, Saltuch," from whose lands Andronicus "raided Byzantine territory."[30] Nevertheless, as Manuel anticipated his own death and tried to smooth over possible dangers for his son, he once more sought reconciliation with his wayward and widely admired cousin. Through Theodora, he persuaded Andronicus to ask for pardon,[31] which Manuel, after exacting oaths of loyalty from him, granted. Andronicus was "made governor of Pontus," where he settled in July 1180.[32] However, "to ensure his good behavior, his three legitimate children, Manuel, John, and Maria, were kept at Constantinople."[33]

After Manuel's death, however, Andronicus learned that there was dissension in the capital under the government of the widowed empress, Xena, who ruled for her minor son. He approached Constantinople to impose his own solution, instigating a massacre of Latins (mostly communities of Genoan and Pisan merchants) by the angry populace.[34] In the *Liber*, Wisdom alludes to the special role of Andronicus here, calling him the man "To whom Italian blood was drink and food" (*Cui cruor Ytalicus potus et esca fuit*) (l. 1644). The massacre helped to establish Andronicus's authority and set the tone for his exercise of it. He took over the government and was proclaimed regent for young Alexius II. From this position of authority, he removed the Empress Xena from the palace and soon executed her. Then, after arranging to have himself crowned co-emperor, he ordered the death of the now superfluous Alexius.[35] Supposedly most of the youth's

---

[28] Niketas Choniates, *O City of Byzantium*, 75–80. "Xena" or "Xene" is a transliteration of the name this empress adopted upon her marriage to Manuel. Maria (Latin) or Marie (French) was her name as a princess of Antioch before her marriage.

[29] John Kinnamos, *Deeds of John and Manuel Comnenus*, 188; bk. 6, chap. 1.

[30] Brand, *Byzantium Confronts*, 17.

[31] Niketas Choniates, *O City of Byzantium*, 128; pt. 3.

[32] Magoulias, in editorial notes on Niketas Choniates, *O City of Byzantium*, 129.

[33] Brand, *Byzantium Confronts*, 28.

[34] Charles Brand, "The Byzantines and Saladin, 1185–1192," *Speculum* 37 (1962): 167–81, here 168.

[35] Niketas Choniates, *O City of Byzantium*, 152.

body was thrown into the sea, but his head was preserved.[36] Niketas also reports the rumor that Alexius's elder-half sister, Maria Porphyrogenita, and her husband met their deaths through poison. In any case, neither was heard from again.[37]

There followed a reign of terror. Rebellion centered for a while on the city of Nicaea, where the Angeli family, and others, had fled. In one episode, Andronicus famously bound Euphrosyne, mother of Isaac Angelus, to a "battering ram . . . and moved the engines of war up to the walls."[38] The Nicaeans managed to rescue her. Niketas also records that he captured and blinded Theodore, one of Isaac's brothers, and bound him to a pack ass which was set wandering.[39] Although the Turks rescued the youth and treated him kindly, his career as a rebel was ended. There were many other hangings, blindings, and impalings. When the champion of the rebellion, Theodore Kantakouzenos, died in battle, the Nicaeans lost heart. Isaac Angelus became their leader, and instead of continuing warfare, he negotiated a peace, with the help of the archbishop of the city. Despite the humble terms of their submission, Andronicus, after first seeming moved, exiled many of those within, imprisoned many more and "[a]s for the Turks, he impaled them in a circle around the city."[40] Isaac Angelus, however, he apparently regarded as no threat, so he treated him kindly and sent him back unharmed to the capital. He was, however, like the rest of the surviving nobles, made to take "an oath of loyalty" in which he acknowledged that he would be punished not only for treason he committed himself but also for offenses committed by his relations.[41]

Meanwhile, many Greeks fled to the West, especially to Sicily, where William II of Sicily soon planned action (see Introduction, C.10). William's fleet and army met quick success and captured Epidamnos (also called Durazzo or

---

[36] Brand, *Byzantium Confronts*, 54. Niketas Choniates reports that Andronicus had the head of young Alexius II severed and put in a place called *Katebate* in the Magoulias translation. Brand calls the place *Kalabates* (*Byzantium Confronts*, 49). The chronicler does not state precisely what this action meant. Perhaps Andronicus wished to assure himself, and to have the proof, that Manuel's heir was actually dead. If so, the device did not prevent several pretenders from claiming to be Alexius II later on; see Introduction, C.10. Niketas Choniates does not mention that anyone was interested, later, in locating the head and giving it proper burial.

[37] Niketas Choniates, *O City of Byzantium*, 145.

[38] Niketas Choniates, *O City of Byzantium*, 156–57.

[39] Niketas Choniates, *O City of Byzantium*, 160.

[40] Niketas Choniates, *O City of Byzantium*, 158.

[41] Niketas Choniates does not explain this oath in detail, but Brand deduces its use from the chronicler's scattered mentions of it. These tactics would explain why, in the wake of Andronicus's bungled attempt to arrest Isaac Angelus, not only the fugitive himself but all his relations took refuge in the Hagia Sophia.

Dyrachium) "without a blow" on 24 June 1185.[42] They took Thessaloniki on 24 August 1185.[43] The Sicilian victories increased the dismay in the capital, and Andronicus grew yet more alarmed, redoubling impalements and blindings and resorting to oracles and augury in his efforts to foresee and avoid future disasters. One diviner produced a vague clue which Andronicus's inner circle took as an indication that a man named Isaac would overthrow their emperor.[44] Andronicus at first suspected the "Isaac Comnenus" who had established himself at Cyprus, the grandson of Manuel I's brother Isaac (see Genealogical Table 3), but a favorite persuaded him that Isaac Angelus could be the man. Therefore, he sent one of his henchmen, a man called Hagiochristopherites, to arrest and perhaps execute (or blind) Isaac, just in case. But when Hagiochristopherites attempted to carry out these orders, Isaac Angelus resisted, killed him, and fled to the great Hagia Sophia for protection. Here he was soon joined by his noble relatives, who also anticipated punishment for his deed. An angry and sympathetic populace flocked to them and proclaimed Isaac as emperor.

This time, Andronicus was unable to rally the people on his behalf. He tried to flee but was captured and executed a few days later in grisly fashion.[45] The *Liber* says of him, "And his foul death forever lacks an avenger" *(Mors sua perpetuo vindice feda caret)* (l. 1648). In the aftermath of Andronicus's overthrow, his legitimate sons John and Manuel were blinded, and John soon died.[46] However, two grandsons, sons of Manuel, fled and became rulers of Trebizond; the descendants of one of them, David, ruled for many generations.[47]

§**Anweiler**, Markward of. See Markwald or Markward of Anweiler.

§**Bartholomew**, bishop of Girgenti (Agrigento); archbishop of Palermo. fl. 1171–1199.

Bartholomew is mentioned only once in the *Liber* (l. 303), as a *presul* or bishop who "had written" *(scripserat)* to Henry VI inviting him to claim his crown in Sicily. The same passage lists several others who "wrote" *(scripsit)* to Henry with the same message, but the pluperfect tense shared by Bartholomew and Tancred suggests that only those two have shifted their allegiance by the time the newly crowned emperor proposes to visit his realm (see commentary on 105v). Since Bartholomew succeeded his brother Walter (q.v.) as archbiship of Palermo,[48] he

---

[42] Niketas Choniates, *O City of Byzantium*, 129, and the editorial notes of Magoulias.

[43] Brand, *Byzantium Confronts*, 165.

[44] Niketas Choniates, *O City of Byzantium*, 188–89.

[45] Niketas Choniates, *O City of Byzantium*, 192–94.

[46] Niketas Choniates, *O City of Byzantium*, 196–97.

[47] Niketas Choniates, *O city of Byzantium*, 350–51; Runciman, *History of the Crusades*, 3:126.

[48] Siragusa, editorial notes, *Liber ad Honorem Augusti*, 28 and n. 1.

might, in that capacity, have crowned Tancred as king of Sicily. Since he evidently had his differences with Tancred, crowning him is the greatest favor he is likely to have done him to earn Pietro's notice.

Bartholomew first appears in documents as the bishop of Girgenti (Agrigento), and as a royal *familiaris* in 1171.[49] The bishop's name is subscribed to the document describing Joanna Plantagenet's dowry, as set down by Roger of Hoveden.[50] At the end of William II's reign, Bartholomew had been sent by the king on a mission to Constantinople, but Tancred recalled him so that he could become archbishop of Palermo.[51] Evidently, however, Tancred was displeased with him, because he subsequently reduced the money paid by the treasury to the church of Palermo from 29,900 taris to 11,000. However, he got those revenues back later when he was restored to the status of *familiaris* by Queen Sibylla after Tancred's death.[52] No doubt Bartholomew had some hand in negotiating the peaceful transfer of the kingdom from Tancred's widow to Henry VI in late 1194. He may well have crowned Henry VI as king of Sicily.[53] The empress Constance named him as one of the council of *familiares* to oversee the government during her son's minority; however, he did not long survive her, dying a short time after September 1199.[54]

§**Beatrix,** or Beatrice of Rethel, ca. 1136–1185. Third queen of Roger II of Sicily, mother of the Empress Constance.

Beatrice is eulogized in the *Liber* as Constance's mother (ll. 15–20), and depicted suckling her newborn child on fol. 96r. She was the daughter of Count Gunther of Rethel and Countess Beatrice of Namur, and was one of three sisters and three brothers.[55] She married Roger II (q.v.) on 19 September 1151.[56] Scholars do not record any political calculations connected with the match. Romuald makes it clear that Roger was anxious to have more legitimate children after so many of his sons by Elvira had died;[57] thus it is reasonable to assume that she was, when married, of appropriate age for childbearing and not much beyond it. Frederick II, Beatrice's grandson, in the thirteenth century, implied that fifteen

---

[49] Chalandon, *Histoire*, 2:349.

[50] *Gesta*, 94.

[51] Chalandon, *Histoire*, 2:476–77. He cites Paesano, *Memorie per servire alla storia della Chiesa Salernitana* (Salerno, 1846–1852), 2:224.

[52] Jamison, *Admiral Eugenius*, 103.

[53] Jamison, *Admiral Eugenius*, 117 and n. 2.

[54] Van Cleve, *Markward*, 126.

[55] *Chronica Albrici Monachi Trium Fontium,* ed. P. Scheffer-Boichorst, in MGH 23, ed. G. H. Pertz (Hanover: Hahn, 1866), 852.

[56] Van Cleve, *Emperor Frederick II*, 18.

[57] See excerpt in note on l. 20.

years of age was about right, and there is no reason to assume that this opinion was uncommon.[58] Hence the conjectural birth date given above.

After Roger's death in February 1154, Beatrice bore their daughter. Apparently, she did not remarry, and according to the *Necrologia Palermitana*, she herself died on 31 March 1185,[59] a few months after her daughter's marriage had been arranged but before the latter set out on her wedding journey. Beatrice evidently was buried in the Chapel of Mary Magdalene at the Cathedral of Palermo, where the grave of Roger's first queen, Elvira, also was located. However, when a new cathedral was built, the chapel was supposedly moved, along with the graves. Though the chapel that replaced it "still stands in the courtyard of the Carabinieri Barracks of S. Giacomo," it is "unfortunately without any trace of the dynastic graves."[60]

§**Berthold** of Künsberg or Königsberg. Imperial legate and count, fl. 1184–1193.

Berthold is not specifically mentioned in the *Liber*, but Siragusa suggests that l. 757, in which Tancred laments about a "Rombanldus" [*sic*] who "By himself . . . with three helping him, takes the kingdom from me" (*Unus . . . regnum michi cum tribus aufert*), may be a mistaken or miscopied reference to this man. Berthold was sent into Italy after Henry VI abandoned the siege of Naples, to direct Henry's military forces there. He was, for a time, quite successful, and it is thus remarkable that Pietro seems not to mention him and mentions the unknown "Rombanldus" instead.

Berthold appears in the historical record as early as 1184,[61] when, after the death of Archbishop Christian of Mainz, Pope Lucius III asked the Emperor Frederick Barbarossa to send another imperial legate to support him in controlling disorders in Italy. Berthold was appointed for the task. Pope Lucius dismissed Berthold before he went to Verona in the autumn of that year.[62] Later, when young Henry VI ruled in Italy as king of Lombardy, Berthold apparently served him. In 1186, he was sent to deal with troubles in Tuscany, and in June

---

[58] Frederick II of Hohenstaufen, *Liber Augustalis or Constitutiones of Melfi, Promulgated by the Emperor Frederick II for the Kingdom of Sicily in 1231*, trans. James M. Powell (Syracuse: Syracuse University Press, 1971), 119–20; bk. 3, Title XXVI (7). This is a passage revised by Frederick II himself. He states that "our excellency" will take on the wardship of the orphaned daughters of counts, barons, or knights, and will arrange appropriate marriages for them "when they arrive at marriageable age (when they turn fifteen)."

[59] Garufi, ed., p. 213 n. 4 on of his edition of *Chronicon Romualdi II Archiepiscopi Salernitani*.

[60] Deér, *Dynastic Porphyry Tombs*, 3, and notes.

[61] Toeche, *Kaiser Heinrich VI*, 11.

[62] *Annales Casineses*, 313; cod. 4,5.

1187, he returned to Germany, perhaps to consult with the emperor, Frederick Barbarossa.[63]

Berthold apparently accompanied Barbarossa on his crusade, and was among the envoys Frederick sent to Constantinople to negotiate the Treaty of Adrianople.[64] However, he returned to Germany at some point after the death of Frederick I. In the wake of Henry's withdrawal from the siege of Naples, Berthold was sent into the Norman kingdom in late 1192 or early 1193. He directed the war effort and resisted Tancred's incursions as best he could.[65] At first he made his base in Tuscany, while he sent Abbot Roffredo of Monte Cassino ahead, along with soldiers he supplied.[66] Roffredo (q.v.) then intervened in the journey of the Empress Constance (q.v.) from Tancred's prison to the pope.

Later, in November, Berthold entered the kingdom of Sicily, attacked Molise, and took fortresses, including Venafro. The Tancredines were disheartened, and Henry's supporters among the Apulian nobles, including Count William of Caserta, came to help the Germans. Berthold then decided to marry the widow of William's father, the deceased Count Robert of Caserta, and handed over command to Diepold of Schweinspeunt (q.v.) so that he could celebrate the wedding.[67] Then, as Richard of San Germano tells it, Tancred came to Apulia early

---

[63] Toeche, *Kaiser Heinrich VI*, 62, 84.

[64] Brand, *Byzantium Confronts*, 185.

[65] Jamison, *Admiral Eugenius*, 85.

[66] *Annales Casinenses*, 316.

[67] Toeche, *Kaiser Heinrich VI*, 321. Though there is general agreement that Berthold married a noblewoman of the Sicilian kingdom at this time, there is some confusion about her identity. Toeche and Cuozzo both say that she was the sister of Berard Gentilis, count of Loreto. Toeche makes it clear that he regards her not only as the widow of Count Roger, who had died in 1183 according to Cuozzo (*Catalogus Baronum Commentario*, 275–79; par 964), but as the mother of Count Roger's children, including the current count of Caserta, William, and also of Count Roger of Tricarico, who had, in 1160 been involved in the conspiracy against Maio, according to Romuald of Salerno (*Chronicon Romualdi II Archiepiscopi Salernitani,* ed. Garufi, 244). In 1168 Roger had acted as one of the judges of Richard of Mandra (Falcandus, *La Historia,* 131, 140; *History of the Tyrants,* trans. Loud and Wiedemann, 182, 193). The mother of this nobleman could no longer have been a young woman in 1193.

The only wife whom Cuozzo lists for Count Robert of Caserta is Agnes, who died in 1179. Perhaps Count Robert married again, or perhaps Toeche confuses Count Robert with a relation or a man with a similar name. Cuozzo seems unaware of any relationship between Berthold's bride and Roger of Caserta, but states that a sister of *Berardus Gentilis,* (her name unknown), married Berthold "Teutonicus . . . Imperatoris Legatus" (*Catalogus Baronum Commentario* 358; par. 1192), in "1195 circa." For this information, he cites the *Chronica monasterii S. Bartholomaei Carpineto,* in Ferdinando Ughelli, *Italia Sacra, sive de episcopis Italiae et insularum adiacentium rebusque ab iis praeclare gestis . . . .* (2nd ed., Venice, 1717–1722), vol. 10, col. 380. He also cites a manuscript, the *Corografia* of Antinori, vol. 33, p. 812. Since Berthold died in 1193, the date Cuozzo gives must be

in 1193 to face Berthold, and made his camp on Monte Fusculo. Berthold, eager to fight him, camped at "Batticanum." However, as Tancred's forces grew ever stronger with supporters who flocked to him, the gallant king realized that there was no honor in battle with Berthold, a mere count (*honor sibi non eret cum Bertoldo congredi*). Berthold, on the other hand, realized that battle would be imprudent, so they mutually withdrew from one another. Berthold returned to Molise, to besiege the fortress of Monte Rodone (*montis Rodonis*), and there he was killed by a stone cast from a siege engine. [68]

§**Burrel**, Matthew. See **Matthew** Burrel or Borell.

§**Calandrinus**. See **Henry** of Kalden.

§**Calixtus** II, Pope, r. 1119–1124.

Calixtus is mentioned in the *Liber* (l. 3) and in fol. 96r (cap. 2) as the pope who granted Roger II the royal title, but this is not true. However, Romuald of Salerno[69] also names Calixtus as the pope who authorized Roger's coronation, so the misinformation probably was not Pietro's invention. The Norman kings and their supporters did not want to call the legitimacy of their title into question.

However, it was actually the antipope Anacletus (q.v.) who first granted Roger his kingly title. Ultimately, Roger made peace with Innocent II in the treaty of Mignano (see Introduction, C.6), and it was convenient for both parties to date permission for Roger's coronation to a previous legitimate pope. To be sure, Honorius II (r. 1124–1130), whose death immediately preceded the disputed election of 1130, would have been the most obvious choice, and he is the one named in papal documents for the treaty of Mignano; see Introduction C.6. Calixtus II might be preferred because he was more famous than his successor, or because an earlier pope would endow Roger's kingship with the authority of greater age.

According to Hampe, Calixtus, formerly Guido of Vienne, "came from a Burgundian noble family and was related to almost all the ruling houses of Europe, including the Salians." [70] Hence, though "strong-willed," he took a conciliatory approach in the quarrels between emperors and popes, which led to the Concordat of Worms with Henry V in 1122. Perhaps the Norman-Sicilian writ-

---

of the record rather than the wedding. Toeche likewise cites in Ughelli (1:461) a document of Berthold's, dated May 1193. Kölzer also mentions this marriage ("Die Staufer im Süden," 25), but provides no references and lists the widowed bride as the daughter, not the sister, of Count Berard. This involves a genuine disagreement with both Toeche and Cuozzo, since both describe the bride as the sister of *Berardus Gentilis*, and according to Cuozzo (index to his *Catalogus Baronum Commentario*), the latter's father is "Rogerius de Celano."

[68]   Richard of San Germano, *Chronica,* 67.

[69]   *Chronicon,* 218.

[70]   Hampe, *Germany Under the Salian and Hohenstaufen Emperors,* 114, 116.

ers thought it plausible that he might have made a similar agreement with their king.

§**Celestine III**, Pope, or Hyacinthus Bobo, 1105–1198; r. 1191–1198.

Celestine III is mentioned in the *Liber* as the pope who anointed Constance (ll. 23–24), crowned Henry VI (fol. 105r, caps. 1 and 4), and wrote a letter commanding Tancred to release Constance after she was captured by Tancred (ll. 1010–1046; fol. 128r, cap. 1).

According to Bernard McGinn, this pope, originally Hyacinthus Bobo, was born about 1105 and had a long and varied career in the papal curia before he became supreme pontiff himself. In 1140, at the Council of Sens, "he supported Peter Abelard and Arnold of Brescia (much to the chagrin of Bernard of Clairvaux)."[71] In 1158 he was sent by Pope Hadrian to calm the angry Frederick Barbarossa over the use of the word *beneficium* in one of his letters, the famous Besançon quarrel.[72] Rainald von Dassel had interpreted the word as "fief," implying that Pope Hadrian meant to say that the emperor held the empire from the pope as from a feudal overlord. To make matters worse, Cardinal Roland (the future Pope Alexander III) had implied in his answer that this was obviously true. Cardinal Hyacinth was later sent to explain that by *beneficium*, Pope Hadrian had only meant "good deed" and had not meant to claim the rights of a feudal lord.

During his papacy, Celestine's strategy toward emperors and kings was complex rather than compliant. When he was elected on 30 March, he found Henry VI the Hohenstaufen already in the neighborhood of Rome and in possession of an agreement by Clement III, Celestine's predecessor, to confer the imperial crown on him. Backing out would have been difficult, and the emperor-elect wanted no delay. Thus, Cardinal Octavian crowned the new pope on 13 April so that the latter could crown Henry VI the next very day, 14 April.[73] Circumstances may have swept him along; neverthess, Bernard McGinn sees Celestine III not as "a vacillating old man," as do some scholars, but as one who employed "clever Fabian tactics" to gain his ends.[74] He is thought to have favored Tancred as king of Sicily, or at least to have preferred that the Norman kingdom not be incorporated into the Holy Roman Empire. However, when Henry entered the kingdom of Sicily despite "the pope forbidding and gainsaying it" (*papa prohibente et contradicente*),[75] Celestine did not excommunicate him. But a few months later, when Henry had been forced to withdraw from the siege of Naples and

---

[71] McGinn, *The Calabrian Abbot*, 14.

[72] Rahewin, Otto of Freising's continuator, *Deeds of Frederick Barbarossa*, bk. 3, chaps. 8–9; 21–23.

[73] Toeche, *Kaiser Heinrich VI*, 186–87.

[74] McGinn, *The Calabrian Abbot*, 14.

[75] Richard of San Germano, *Chronica*, 65.

the Empress Constance had been handed over to Tancred, he saw his chance. Then, "[i]n June 1192 he recognized Tancred as legitimate ruler of Sicily in return for his agreeing to cede the traditional liberties and immunities of the Sicilian Church."[76] However, as the *Liber* and other contemporary sources show, Celestine balanced this concession to Tancred with an intervention that resulted in the liberation of Constance. See the biographical sketch for **Constance of Hauteville**.

§**Charlemagne**, or Charles the Great, western emperor. 742–814; r. 800–814.

Charlemagne is mentioned in the *Liber* (l. 313) as a model both for Frederick Barbarossa and for Henry VI, but with the implication that the Hohenstaufens will excel the Carolingians. Already the center of a heroic cycle of legends in the twelfth century, Charlemagne had become king over his father's domains in 769,[77] and later, he was the first western emperor to be crowned by the pope, an event which happened in 800 (see Introduction, C.1). Though his dynasty was later set aside for a new succession of emperors, beginning with Otto I in 962, these never gained the same mythological stature. When the Salian dynasty succeeded the Ottonians, its second emperor, Henry III, claimed descent from Charlemagne through his mother Gisela.[78] Hence, the Hohenstaufens could consider themselves heirs to Charlemagne's lineage as well as his office. Frederick Barbarossa arranged for Charlemagne to be canonized by the antipope Paschal in 1165.[79] Later, Frederick II likewise honored Charlemagne as a saint, as he prepared for his crusade.[80]

§**Cioffus**. fl. 1191. Salernitan citizen, supporter of Henry VI.

Cioffus or Cioffo appears on fol. 110r, cap. 7, as a member of the Salernitan delegation sent to Henry VI to persuade Constance to come to Salerno during the siege of Naples.

Although there were several men with this name in the Salerno area at this time,[81] the reference here is probably to "Cioffus Ruffus" who is related to two other Salernitans mentioned in the *Liber*, as Cuozzo explains.[82] Cioffus Ruf-

---

[76] McGinn, *The Calabrian Abbot*, 15.

[77] Otto of Freising, *The Two Cities* 351; bk. 5, chap. 26 (see next note).

[78] *The Two Cities: A Chronicle of Universal History of the Year 1146 A.D by Otto, Bishop of Freising*, trans. Charles Christopher Mierow (New York: Columbia University Press, 1928), bk 6, chap. 28.

[79] Munz, *Frederick Barbarossa*, 242. Also Marcel Pacaut, *Frederick Barbarossa*, trans. A. J. Pomeranz (New York: Scribner, 1970), 119.

[80] Deér, *Dynastic Porphyry Tombs*, 18.

[81] Siragusa, *Liber ad honorem Augusti*, 129, n. 3.

[82] Errico Cuozzo, "Ruggiero, conte d'Andria: Ricerche sulla nozione di regalità al tramonto della monarchia normanna," *Archivio storico per le provincie napoletane*, 99 (1981): 129–68, here 152, n. 85. For the findings he summarizes here, Cuozzo cites Di-

fus was the son of Malfridus Rubeus, brother of the chamberlain Marius Ruffus. Their sister Dofa was, by her husband Lucas Guarna, the mother of Philip Guarna (q.v.) and of a daughter who married William of Pistilio (q.v.). Cioffio's wife was named Theodora. [83]

§**Conrad** of Lützelhard, fl. 1168–1197. German commander under Frederick Barbarossa and Henry VI. Also called *Moscaincervello* ("fly-in-the-brain").

Conrad plays an important part in the *Liber*, between Henry VI's raising of the siege of Naples in August 1191 and his second invasion in 1194. The empress herself, under attack at Salerno, first names him as a commander stationed in Capua upon whose help she can still call (l. 607). Later, Conrad's desperate defense of Capua is dramatized in fols. 122r and 123r and the facing verses. Despite the terrible odds, he eventually wins the right to depart freely from the city with his surviving men.

Conrad's service with the Hohenstaufen emperors can be traced back several decades, since he followed Frederick Barbarossa into Italy during the time of that emperor's third and least influential antipope, styled Calixtus III (1168–1178). [84] At this time, the emperor enfeoffed Conrad with the march of Ancona (for which he is apparently called "the Marquis" in cap. 2 on fol. 122r) and the princedom of Ravenna. The Italians called him *Moscaincervello* or *Musca in cerebro* ("fly-in-the-brain"), because "most of the time he seemed like a demented man" (*plerumque quasi demens videretur*). [85]

The *Liber* says little of Conrad after his departure from Capua, but other sources tell how he carried on the emperor's battles in his absence. He and Berthold of Künsberg besieged a Tancredine stronghold at Monte Rodone, [86] but Berthold was killed, struck by a stone. Though many then deserted, those who remained chose Conrad as commander. They took the fortress and put the defenders to death. Nevertheless the momentum of the imperial forces slackened at this time, no doubt needing further reinforcement and direction from Henry VI. [87]

After Henry's victory in 1194, when Archbishop Nicholas, Queen Sibylla, and their families were arrested, Conrad was given charge of the prisoners. [88] The

---

one Clementi, "An Administrative Document of 1190 from Apulia," *Papers of the British School at Rome* 24 (1956): 170–82.

[83] Cuozzo, *Catalogus Baronum commentario*, 152; entry 517* [*sic*].

[84] *Burchardi et Cuonradum Urspergensium Chronicon*, ed. O. Abel and L. Weiland, in MGH 23, ed. G. H. Pertz (Hanover: 1866), 356.

[85] *Burchardi et Cuonradum Urspergensium Chronicon*, 356.

This distinctive cognomen is also mentioned in the *Annales Ceccanenses* (289), and *The Deeds of Pope Innocent* III (12; chap. 9), where Powell translates it as "Fly-brain."

[86] Toeche, *Kaiser Heinrich VI*, 322.

[87] Kölzer, "Die Staufer im Süden," 25.

[88] Jamison, *Admiral Eugenius*, 124.

emperor rewarded him for his loyalty by creating him count of Molise, but to take possession of his lands, he had to dispossess the previous incumbent, Count Roger of Molise (q.v.), a Tancredine loyalist. Faced with a siege, Roger negotiated a surrender and was allowed to depart freely.[89] But before the end of 1197, Conrad (*Muscancervello*) was dead, and the emperor had given the county of Molise to Markward (q.v.).[90]

§**Conrad** of Urslingen, duke of Spoleto, fl. 1177–1202.

This Conrad was a German commander in the service of Frederick Barbarossa and Henry VI. Although he is mentioned only once, among Henry's commanders fighting the siege of Naples, and then only by his dukedom rather than his name (1. 363), he is perhaps more important to the *Liber* than at first appears. His consort, the duchess to whom the Empress Constance hands over her newborn son in fol. 138r, is also not named in the surviving portions of the manuscript, and it is only from other sources[98] that we know her to be his consort. Her name, however, has not come down to us.

Though Conrad's family is often classed with *ministeriales*, it was actually among the "*Edelfreier*, . . . what might in later ages be called landed gentry who owned their own land in freehold but did not belong to the nobility."[91] However, Conrad's father may have married a relation of the Zährigen family, thus achieving a connection with the higher nobility.[92] As early as 1177, the future duke became Barbarossa's "legate" to the duchy of Spoleto under the name of "Conrad the Swabian."[93] By 1187, he apparently held the titles and offices of duke of Spoleto and count of Assisi.[94] Clearly, he would have had frequent communication with Henry VI and Constance after their wedding in 1186, when they were left as king and queen of (Northern) Italy, while Barbarossa returned to Germany. In 1191, after Henry's disastrous withdrawal from the siege of Naples, Conrad remained in control of these territories adjacent to Rome and did much to help the emperor's efforts in the kingdom of Sicily. For example, as Henry left Monte Cassino to withdraw to Germany, he may have left some hostages from the abbey of Monte Cassino in Conrad's charge (instead of bringing them all to Germany).[95] When, in 1192, Constance had just been liberated, in theory at any rate, from Tancred's prison, and was being conducted toward Rome by cardinals sent for that purpose, Abbot Roffredo of Monte Cassino came to speak with

---

[89] Jamison, *Admiral Eugenius*, 152.

[90] Richard of San Germano, *Chronica*, 68.

[91] Mary Taylor Simeti, *Travels with a Medieval Queen* (New York: Farrar, Straus and Giroux, 2001), 230.

[92] Klaus Schubring, *Die Herzoge von Urslingen* (Stuttgart: W. Kohlhammer Verlag, 1974), 40.

[93] Schubring, *Die Herzoge von Urslingen*, 29.

[94] Toeche, *Kaiser Heinrich VI*, 63.

[95] Toeche, *Kaiser Heinrich VI*, 202.

her to such effect that she left the cardinals' escort and instead went to Spoleto, presumably under Conrad's protection.[96] During her last weeks of pregnancy, Constance also lived in the territory Conrad controlled. Then she entrusted her newborn son to his consort. When Henry returned to Germany in 1195, Conrad was made "vicar of the realm."[97]

After the death of Henry VI, Constance sent to Conrad's duchess, who was nursing (*nutriebat*) her son, and asked that he be brought to her in Palermo.[98] The duchess gave the child into the hands of the two counts Constance had sent on this errand.[99] Meanwhile, the new pope, Innocent III, was determined to gain control over the territory which Conrad held, and though Conrad made tempting offers (co-operation, financial support, and his sons as hostages), Innocent III decided against him. Conrad returned to Germany, while Innocent III put the duchy into the charge of a cardinal.[100]

Like all Hohenstaufen supporters, Conrad of Urslingen became caught up in the struggle for the succession to the Western Roman Empire (see Introduction, C.16). After the death of Constance in 1198, and, in 1202, of Markward of Anweiler (q.v.), Conrad of Urslingen was named by Philip of Swabia, now the Hohenstaufen claimant to the imperial throne, as the guardian of his now orphaned nephew, eight-year-old Frederick, the king of Sicily.[101] Probably Conrad was chosen because he and his consort had looked after the boy from his infancy. To execute this responsibility, Conrad would need to undertake a military expedition, since the child was then in the hands of a certain German freelancer, William of Capperone, who had seized control of the royal palace in the midst of the chaos that engulfed the kingdom. Evidently Conrad set out on this errand, but died that same year without accomplishing it.[102]

The origin of Conrad's duchess, Frederick's foster mother, is not known. One author writes, "[i]t is thought the Conrad had married into the local nobility. Most probably his wife was a daughter of the Antignano family of Foligno, to whom Henry VI awarded a large fief in 1197, possibly in gratitude for the care they bestowed upon his son."[103] Unfortunately, this writer lists no sources for this theory. Schubring takes into account the alliances in which the Urslingen family was involved and the names their children bear (Henry, Conrad, Berthold, Rainald), and on that basis suggests that the duchess was from an offshoot (*Seitenz-*

---

[96] *Annales Cassinenses*, 316.
[97] Jamison, *Admiral Eugenius*, 147.
[98] *Gesta Innocentii III*, 16; *Deeds of Pope Innocent III*, 19; chap. 21.
[99] Richard of San Germano, *Chronica*, 68.
[100] *Deeds of Pope Innocent III*, 10–12; chap. 10.
[101] Van Cleve, *Emperor Frederick II*, 49.
[102] Schubring, *Die Herzoge von Urslingen*, 44.
[103] Simeti, *Travels with a Medieval Queen*, 230–31.

weiges) of the family of the count of Burgundy.[104] The couple also had a daughter whose son, Eberhard, held imperial offices under Frederick II in Tuscany around 1220.[105]

§**Conrad** of Montferrat, ca.1146–1192. Marquis of Montferrat, king of Jerusalem. Kinsman of Henry VI.

Though his name is not specifically mentioned in the *Liber*, there is an important allusion to Conrad (l. 1055) as a kinsman of Henry VI, supposedly killed by the connivance of the English king, Richard I. The Lionheart defends himself against this charge and others before Henry's "imperial senate."

Conrad's family held a crucial position in Northern Italy and played an important role in Byzantine politics as well as in the Holy Land. Conrad himself had a dramatic career, ending as king of Jerusalem, second husband to the kingdom's heiress Isabella. In this role he was assassinated, apparently by agents of the original "assassin" cult of the Old Man of the Mountain. The story of his murder is told vividly by a number of secondary scholars[106] drawing on various sources. Many chroniclers report that King Richard's enemies accused him of being complicit in this murder. These included Roger of Hoveden and Radulfus de Coggeshale, Arnold of Lübeck, and the anonymous author of the *Itinerarium*.[107]

In the *Liber*, when Henry mentions his kinship with the murdered man, he uses poetic emotion rather than legal precision, saying (l. 1055) that Richard is "drenched with our blood" (*nostrum saturate cruoris*). Other chronicles describe the relationship variously; Roger of Hoveden says that Conrad is the emperor's *consanguineus* or kinsman by blood, while Radulfus states only that Conrad was the emperor's man (*hominis sui*).[108] Hoveden is correct; Conrad was related to Henry VI on both his mother's and his father's side.[109] Both were descended from Agnes the Salian, daughter of Emperor Henry IV. (Leopold of Austria, Richard's immediate captor, was also descended from Agnes; see Genealogical Table 2.) In addition, Henry VI and Conrad were both descended from Count William of Burgundy, grandfather of Barbarossa's empress Beatrix. (Conrad's grandmother Gisela was a daughter of William I of Burgundy, who was the great-grandfather of Beatrix, Barbarossa's consort and Henry's mother.)

---

[104] *Die Herzoge von Urslingen*, 39.

[105] Schubring, *Die Herzoge von Urslingen*, 38.

[106] For example, Runciman, *History of the Crusades*, 3:65; also Amy Kelly, *Eleanor of Aquitaine and the Four Kings* (Cambridge, MA: Harvard University Press, 1950), 280.

[107] Hoveden, *Chronica*, 158; Radulfus Abbas de Coggeshale, *Historia Anglicana*, MGH 27 (Hanover: Hahn, 1885), 350; Arnold of Lübeck, *Chronica Slavorum*, bk. 5, chap. 16. *Itinerarium*, 305–7; Bk. 5, chap. 27.

[108] Hoveden, *Chronica*, 158; Radulfus, *Historia Anglicana*, 350.

[109] Assmann, "Friedrich Barbarossas Kinder," 463.

Conrad was born about 1146.[110] His important adventures began around 1179, in the wake of a falling out between his father the Marquis William and Frederick Barbarossa, arising because the peace of Venice (see Introduction, C.8), was not altogether advantageous to the marquis.[111] The Emperor Manuel instigated Marquis William against Barbarossa, promising his daughter Maria Porphyrogenita to one of his sons and other rewards besides, if William would "strike a blow in Italy against Frederick's power."[112] Executing this family decision, Conrad attacked and took prisoner Barbarossa's chancellor in Italy, Archbishop Christian of Mainz. Marquis William then sent his younger son Rainier to Constantinople as the bridegroom, and Conrad also went to claim a share in the rewards, leaving their brother Boniface in charge of the prisoner. Manuel, pleased with these actions, celebrated the marriage between his daughter and Rainier. But Manuel soon died, and Boniface of Montferrat allowed the archbishop to be ransomed. Maria Porphyrogenita and her bridegroom fell victim to the bloody reign of Andronicus (q.v.). However, when the new emperor Isaac Angelus was raised to the throne, he re-established contact with the Montferrato family. In 1187, Conrad arrived in Constantinople and speedily married Isaac's sister Theodora. Isaac immediately needed his help against a talented and energetic general, Branas, who tried to supplant Isaac. When, with the support of Conrad and his Latin allies, Isaac had been induced to take a firm stand and defeat his enemies, Conrad felt that he was hated because of the death of Branas.[113] Also, he heard ominous news from the Holy Land, where his father was living, because about this time the disastrous battle of Hattin took place and Saladin was soon capturing all the significant Crusader fortresses up to the coast. So Conrad abandoned Theodora and her brother and sailed toward Acre, only to turn back when he found the city already in the hands of the Moslems. He arrived at Tyre to find that city in the process of surrendering to Saladin but before it was formally handed over. His arrival heartened the defenders to new resistance. Thus, because of him, by the time European monarchs were ready to sail on their crusade, there was still a port where they could land.[114]

The kingdom of Jerusalem was desperate. Queen Sibylla and her children were dead. The titular king, Guy of Lusignan, was captive along with most other important men who had survived Hattin. The kingdom's heiress, Sibylla's younger half-sister Isabella, already had a husband, Humphrey of Toron, but the surviving barons did not think him fit for kingship, and he fled rather than dispute the point. The barons instead resolved to give Isabella in marriage to Conrad and

---

[110] J.S C. Riley-Smith, "Corrado," *Dizionario Biografico degli Italiani* 29 (1983): 381.

[111] Brand, *Byzantium Confronts*, 18.

[112] Brand, *Byzantium Confronts*, 19.

[113] Brand, *Byzantium Confronts*, 80–84.

[114] Runciman, *History of the Crusades*, 2:471–72.

make him their king. The marriage was celebrated,[115] but not everyone accepted this solution. Richard, king of England, was the leader of the opposing party. He preferred Guy de Lusignan, who was his own vassal.

However, in 1192, when Richard knew he must return home to face the attacks made on his lands by Philip Augustus with the complicity of his own brother Prince John, he realized that he must unite the barons of the crusader kingdom around one ruler. Perceiving that everyone else rejected Guy, he finally consented to recognize Conrad. Conrad rejoiced when he was informed of this decision, but almost immediately afterwards, on 29 April 1192, he was murdered.[116] His widow, Isabella, due to pressure from the barons, remarried without delay, this time taking as her bridegroom Henry of Champagne, a grandson of Eleanor of Aquitaine through Marie of Champagne. She bore Conrad a posthumous daughter, Marie, who became the kingdom's heiress (see Genealogical Table 5).

§**Conrad of Querfurt**, bishop of Hildesheim and (later) Würtz, chancellor of Henry VI, fl. 1184–1202.

Chancellor Conrad was apparently Pietro's patron by the time the *Liber* was produced, and appears in the dedication miniature, fol. 139r, presenting the poet (who has his book in hand) to the emperor. He also figures prominently in the last two books of the *Liber*, giving a speech, for example, exhorting loyal conduct and the forgetting of past wrongs (ll. 1429–1444), and executing important government activities with despatch (ll. 1551–1559). He is of course portrayed in the associated miniatures (fols. 142r, 145r), and in another where he is not specifically mentioned in the related verses (fol. 147r). He may have become Pietro's patron after the first part of the work was substantially complete, and his influence may have been responsible for the retrospective alterations (see Introduction, A.2).

Conrad of Querfurt studied at the cathedral school of Hildesheim and then went for further study at Paris, perhaps at the same time the future archbishop Thomas of Canterbury and Pope Innocent III were there.[117] On returning to his native land, he became chaplain to Barbarossa and tutor to his son Henry. Thus, when Pietro praises Henry's education at the end of Book III, he is also implicitly praising Conrad.

In 1184, by which time he had already been elected as bishop of Lübeck, Conrad accompanied Barbarossa to the Council of Verona,[118] where negotiations with Pope Lucius III were conducted over, among other things, the marriage between Constance and Henry VI. He seems to have continued in Henry's service, and when the latter completed his conquest of Sicily, Conrad became his

---

[115] Runciman, *History of the Crusades*, 3:30–33.
[116] Runciman, *History of the Crusades*, 3:21; 3:49; 3:63.
[117] Toeche, *Kaiser Heinrich VI*, 27–28.
[118] Toeche, *Kaiser Heinrich VI*, 35.

chancellor in Sicily.[119] He followed Henry to Germany again in 1195, and was probably elected bishop of Hildesheim during the Diet of Worms.[120] On this journey, too, he may have gone to Trifels to persuade Emir Eugenius (q.v.), at that time a prisoner, to come to Sicily and help with his administration.[121] In 1196, on his way back to Italy, he wrote a letter to "the provost of his German cathedral [of Hildesheim], describing his journey."[122] Among other things, he mentions Palinurus, the helmsman of Aeneas who fell overboard, to which Pietro also alludes in the *Liber* (713). He also mentions the baths of Puteoli and their curative powers, explaining that they were founded by Virgil.[123] This clearly shows a common interest with Pietro, later author of *De Balneis*, and suggests that they were acquainted by this time.

As Henry prepared for his great crusade, Conrad the Chancellor was active in his government. He was the chief ambassador sent to the usurper Alexius in 1195[124]; in his activities as chancellor, Conrad was "charged especially with obtaining necessary supplies and ships for a crusading expedition."[125] On 1 September 1197, a few weeks before the emperor's death, Conrad departed with the crusading army for the Holy Land,[126] but this project was cut short by news of Henry's death. Conrad then became caught up in the civil war over the imperial succession. He remained chancellor for Philip of Swabia, and on this account became subject to pressures from Pope Innocent III, who intervened on a wide variety of pretexts in order to support Otto the Welf's attempt to gain the empire. Eventually, Innocent III excommunicated Conrad for accepting election to a second bishopric of Würzburg, despite his claims that Pope Celestine had given him permission to do so. Conrad traveled to Rome and humbled himself before the pope, after which Innocent eventually removed the excommunication and permitted him to be elected to the second bishopric.[127] Evidently, during this meeting or in associated communications, Pope Innocent persuaded Conrad to switch sides and work for Otto the Welf, at first while still officially serving as chancellor to Philip of Swabia. After September 1201, however, Conrad showed

---

[119] Jamison, *Admiral Eugenius*, 121–22.

[120] Jamison, *Admiral Eugenius*, 147.

[121] Jamison, *Admiral Eugenius*, 148.

[122] Jamison, *Admiral Eugenius*, 149. Jamison's source is Arnold of Lübeck, *Chronica Slavorum*, bk. 5, chap. 19.

[123] Kauffman, *The Baths of Pozzuoli*, 5.

[124] Or so Brand suggests (*Byzantium Confronts*, 191–92). This, however, is based on a statement by Niketas Choniates that one emissary "with bushy eyebrows" (*O City of Byzantium*, 261) had been a tutor to Henry VI, which could apply to other men mentioned in the *Liber*, including Henry of Kalden (q.v.).

[125] Van Cleve, *Emperor Frederick II*, 22.

[126] Jamison, *Admiral Eugenius*, 160.

[127] *Deeds of Pope Innocent III*, 59–61; chap. 44.

open enmity to Philip and fortified Würzburg against him.[128] Philip of Swabia gathered forces to attack, but on 6 December 1202, before they arrived, Conrad was murdered by two *ministeriales* with whom he was involved in an ongoing dispute.[129] Philip of Swabia did not attempt to hunt down the killers, who were nephews of his marshal, Henry of Kalden (q.v.), but allowed a cross to be set up marking the place of his death, with the Latin verses,

> Here I fall to the ground, since I am unwilling to pardon wickedness.
> May the wounds struck treacherously give me habitation in the heavens.

> *Hic procumbo solo, sceleri dum parcere nolo,*
> *Vulnera facta dolo dent habitare polo.*[130]

§**Constance** of Hauteville, 1154–1198. Holy Roman Empress and Queen of Sicily.

One of the major figures in the *Liber*, Constance was the daughter of King Roger and his third wife, Beatrice of Rethel (ll. 15–20 and Commentary and Genealogical Table 1). No full-length biography on her has been published.[131] She is best known from the early chapters of biographies about her famous son, Frederick II of Hohenstaufen, and from the passage in Dante's *Paradiso* (3.109–120), where her story is told.

This story—that she had been a nun and was forcibly removed from her convent to marry Henry VI of Hohenstaufen—has been unmasked as legendary, but it nevertheless relates to known facts about her upon which Pietro merely touches. The surviving written versions of the legend directly contradict the few verifiable facts of Constance's life and so cannot be trusted. For example, Giovanni Villani, the Florentine historian, makes Constance the daughter, not of King Roger but of Roger's son, William I. Boccaccio[132] makes her the daughter of William II. Furthermore, Boccaccio and Villani both recount that Constance lived as a nun until she was more than fifty years old, at which point the pope, unhappy with the policies of Tancred, who had seized the throne after William II's death, urged and pressured her to assert her claims and marry Henry of Hohenstaufen. As the story says, she complied (with different motives and emotions in the different versions), and then, to everyone's surprise, conceived a child

---

[128] Otto of St. Blaise, *Chronici ab Ottone Frisingensi Conscripti Continuatio: Auctore, Uti Videtur, Ottone S. Blasii Monacho*, ed. Rogerius Wilmans, in MGH SS 20 (Stuttgart: Hahn, 1868), 327; chap. 42.

[129] Winkelmann, *Philipp von Schwaben*, 1:265–69.

[130] Arnold of Lübeck, *Chronica Slavorum*, bk. 7, chap. 2.

[131] However, Mary Taylor Simeti has written a book, *Travels with a Medieval Queen*, paralleling modern reflections with meditations on Constance's life and times.

[132] Giovanni Villani, *Selections from the Chronicle*, 90; bk. 4. Giovanni Boccaccio, *Famous Women*, tr. Virginia Brown (Cambridge, MA: The I Tatti Renaissance Library, 2003), 221.

at her advanced age. To silence skeptics who believed that her pregnancy was feigned, she invited (or her husband invited, on her behalf) all the women of the kingdom to witness the birth, if they wished to. So Frederick II was born.

In fact, Constance was about thirty-two years old when she married Henry, king of the Romans, and about forty when she bore their child. Though this is sufficiently within the years of childbearing to avoid the miraculous, it was still a relatively late first marriage for a princess in those days (compare Joanna Plantagenet, q.v.). No clear explanation for the delay emerges from contemporary sources, but the uncertainties of Sicilian politics and her awkward closeness to the throne might have been reasons enough. When William II's younger brother Henry died in 1172, she became, at the age of eighteen, the presumptive heiress.

Of those sources who accurately report Constance's lineage, Pietro is the only one who declares that a pope (specifically Lucius III) desired the match (l. 22). This has been much denied and contested, but see Introduction, C.9.

Constance's near contemporaries do not report that she had become a nun. What started the rumor, then? A "much later" but apparently strong tradition passed down by Angello Manrique in the "Cistercian Annals" even specifies the Convent of San Salvatore in Palermo.[133] Since in those times it was the rule rather than the exception for royal families to support and sometimes retreat to monasteries and convents, scholars such as Ernst Kantorowicz[134] have tried to bridge the gap between legend and documents by suggesting that "[t]he fact that the princess actually spent long periods in various nunneries in Palermo may well have strengthened" the famous legend. This is plausible enough, and the increasing age of a princess who spent a great deal of time visiting convents might naturally lead to the expectation she would become a nun. Nevertheless, Richard of San Germano flatly states that Constance was living at the royal palace in Palermo when William II arranged her marriage.[135]

In the *Liber*, Constance under attack (ll. 549–742) acts as a spirited woman, aware of the importance of her position and also of her relative helplessness, but she demonstrates the virtue of "constancy" which her name celebrates, trusting that Providence will vindicate her. Such a woman would not have spent her life idly up until the time of her marriage, and probably her own interest, or lack of interest, in marriage had some bearing on her ultimate fate. Precisely what calculations, motives, promises, or persuasions led her to cooperate with these proceedings, we do not know. In the *Liber*, this question does not arise; the high value which Pietro places on the Roman Empire precludes any response other than enthusiasm from the princess sought as Caesar's bride, even if she is the

---

[133] Van Cleve, *Emperor Frederick II*, 15.

[134] Kantorowicz, *Frederick the Second*, 5.

[135] *Chronica*, 64.

kingdom's heiress. Constance's age goes unmentioned, along with the fact that she is about eleven years older than her bridegroom.

Constance's betrothal was announced 28 October 1184 at Augsburg. In August 1185, William accompanied Constance to Salerno on her way to join her future husband. Chronicles report that Frederick Barbarossa, who was then governing the imperial lands in northern and central Italy, bestirred himself to see about his daughter-in-law's welcome and reception while his son the bridegroom was preoccupied with state business on the other side of the Alps. [136] From here on, the events of Constance's life coincide with those discussed in the *Liber* and reviewed in the Introduction, C.11–16. Indeed, we see more of Constance in Pietro's work than we do anywhere else. His facts are sometimes doubted, but as he was very likely an eyewitness to her activities in Salerno and perhaps to her brief captivity in Naples, his testimony cannot be lightly dismissed.

Many things are disputed about the way in which Constance was taken prisoner and then released. As Pietro tells the story, imperial partisans among the Salernitans petitioned the emperor that she might come to reside in their city, to honor it, and thus to retain its loyalty. Scholars, not finding this a sufficient explanation, suggest that she was ill and wished to consult the city's famous physicians. While this seems plausible, the only suggestion of it in the contemporary sources is in the verses of Pietro's fellow poet, Godfrey of Viterbo, which may be in part figurative or ironic. On the other hand, they could also suggest that Constance's infertility was successfully cured during her stay in the city. The jingling half-rhymes of my translation here may suggest an ironic meaning more than a literal translation would:

> The empress suffers, and receives such medicine!
> Salernitan fools arrest their queen.
> Aboard ship they send her, compelled willy nilly;
> Conveyed to Palermo, her ruin made ready.
> Celestine by heavenly justice is called;
> He hears, greatly moved, of the wicked deed.
> Let Apulia, Sicily, and Calabria be glad,
> "At once, send her back," the king he bade.
> The empress conceived and bore a son;
> Apulia and the Principate are his own.
> He shall be Caesar, so the prophets tell,
> Possessing empire, kingdom, and sole rule. [137]

---

[136] Chalandon, *Histoire*, 2:386–87.

[137] A more literal translation of these verses would be: "The empress suffers, received medicine / Stupid Salernitans capture the queen / compelled unwilling they send her on a ship/conducted to Palermo, they prepare ruin. / Celestine is summoned by heavenly law; / he hears of such an evil deed, greatly troubled. / Let Apulia, Sicily, and Calabria rejoice; / he commands the Sicilian king to release her very swiftly. / The empress conceives and

Imperatrix patitur, cepit medicinam;
Salernitani stulti capiunt reginam,
Coacta velle nolle mittunt in carinam;
Ad Panormum ducitur; preparant ruinam.
A celo Celestinus iure nominatur,
Audit tale facinus, valde conturbatur.
Apulus et Siculus, Calaber letatur;
Iubet regi Siculo, citius reddatur.
Concipit et peperit imperatrix natum;
Tenet nunc Apuliam, habet Principatum,
Est futurus cesar, sic est vaticinatum,
Habebit imperium, regnum, monarchatum.
(ll. 85–89)[138]

Many sources report Pope Celestine's involvement in Constance's release, but his precise intent in doing so is seldom explored. Scholars assume that the papacy was on Tancred's side throughout the conflict, because the popes objected to a union between Sicily and the Holy Roman Empire (see Introduction C.9. 12, 16–17). Evidently Celestine (q.v.) wanted to balance favors to Tancred (by recognizing him as king of Sicily) with favors to Henry VI (by getting his captive empress released). However, historians tell a dramatic story in which Constance, not actually free but being sent as a prisoner to the pope by Tancred, escapes because a group of imperial soldiers accidently blunder into the way of her papal escort.[139] To the extent that this account is based on history, it is apparently drawn from this short passage in the *Annales Casinenses,* for the year 1192:

> The emperor sent Count Berthold with an army into Italy, and with him sent back the above-mentioned abbot (Roffredo of Monte Cassino); but while Berthold lingered in Tuscany, he granted soldiers to the abbot, who, going with them to Ceperano, spoke with the aforesaid empress, who was now sent back from the king; cardinals were conducting her for that purpose, sent by the pope, who expected to treat with her at Rome about the concord. But the same Augusta avoided entering the City, and passed over the Tiber to be received into the environs of Spoleto.

> *Imperator Bertoldum comitem cum exercitu mittit in Italiam, et cum eo remittit supradictum abbatem (Roffredum); sed Bertoldus in Tuscia demorans, milites*

---

bears a son. / He now holds Apulia and the Principate, and shall be Caesar, such is the prophecy. / He will have empire, kingdom, and monarchy."

[138] *Gesta Heinrici VI*, ed. G. H. Pertz, MGH 22 (Hanover: Hahn, 1872), 334–38, here 336.

[139] The idea seems to have been put forward first by Chalandon in his *Histoire* (2:467), and was taken up by Norwich in *Kingdom in the Sun* (379). Simeti's account in *Travels with a Medieval Queen* seems to follow, though with more imaginative and sensuous details (182; chap. 7).

abbati concedit, cum quibus rediens Ceperani adloquitur supradictam impera-
tricem iam a rege remissam, ducentibus eam cardinalibus adhoc missis a papa, qui
putabat Romae cum ea de concordia tractare. Sed eadem augusta Urbis declinat
ingressum, et per Tiburim in partes Spoletis recipitur. [140]

The rest of the story of her return journey is told in *Chronica Regia Coloniensis* (Royal Colognese Chronicle): [141] "Constance the empress, returning from regions of Apulia, was conducted back to the emperor by Otto, illustrious prefect of the Romans" (*Constantia imperatrix de partibus Apuliae rediens, per Ottonem illustris-simum Romanorum prefectum imperatori reducitur*).

In other words, the modern accounts read an element of force into the story, no doubt correctly, though that is precisely what the sources leave undefined. Constance, being escorted by cardinals from Tancred's custody toward Rome, does not, of course, actually have much choice about where she is going. Abbot Roffredo's appearance evidently gives her new options. That she was allowed to speak with him suggests, indeed, that she was not being treated like a prisoner, but perhaps his soldierly escort had something to do with that. However, the annals of Monte Cassino do not tell us whether the abbot had been sent expressly to speak with her or whether he came on his own initiative after learning of her journey. Nor do we know the substance of their conversation. We are not even told whether it was Abbot Roffredo, or at least some of his soldiers, who escorted Constance until Prefect Otto took up the task, though it seems a good conjecture. [142]

Pietro of Eboli makes no mention of the stories, later legendary, that Constance invited witnesses to the birth of her child. Customs were such that a royal birth would hardly have been unwitnessed, and it would not have been surprising if the empress took more care than usual to have others besides her most intimate attendants present. She apparently set out from Germany with her husband early that year, but remained at a convent near Milan for some months during her pregnancy. Then, on the news of Henry's successful conquest, she began a slow journey toward Sicily. At some point, however, she decided to stay at Jesi in

---

[140] *Annales Casinenses*, 316.

[141] *Chronica Regia Coloniensis*, ed. Georg Waitz, *Scriptores rerum Germanicarum in usum scholarum separatim editi* 18 (Hanover: Hahn, 1880), 156.

[142] Other chroniclers tell the story differently. Richard of San Germano has Tancred magnanimously release Constance on his own initiative, without papal intervention, and send her back to her husband with gifts (*Chronica*, 65). *Annales Ceccanenses*, 292, state that she actually went to Rome, and then the pope sent her back to her husband. The *Annales Casinenses* have the merit of seeming to combine elements of most of the stories, besides having been written close to the scene of the event and by an author institutionally related to one of the participants, Abbot Roffredo.

the March of Ancona, where her son was actually born on 26 December 1194.[143] Shortly after his birth, he was committed to the care of the duchess of Spoleto while Constance herself joined her husband at Bari.[144]

Pietro portrays Constance as loyal and devoted to her husband. History treats her differently, and the difference centers around two matters. One is the second, later conspiracy against Henry's life, in which she is rumored to have been involved (along with the pope), and the other involves the policies she adopted during her thirteen months of sole rule, after Henry's death (see Introduction, C.15–16).

That there was some tension and some quarreling between Henry and Constance is amply attested by the sources. One chronicle, for example, apparently treats the last conspiracy against Henry as a reaction to rumors that he had killed the empress:

> 1197. The emperor subjected the whole kingdom to a special tax. He also oppressed and afflicted many and drove them into exile. He caused a cantor of the cathedral of Palermo with others of the nobility to be burned before him and a certain deacon with others thrown into the sea.

> When the empress reproached him for this, it is said that he, moved with rage, wished to run his sword through her, but she was liberated by Markward the Marquis. When the Sicilians heard about this, the Latins and Greeks as much as the Saracens all rebelled against the emperor. But when the army was gathered, and it was heard the empress lived, the populace fell silent and all submitted to the emperor.

> *MCXCVIJ Imperator totum regnum exactioni subiecit et multos opprimit et affligit et exulare cogit. Cantorem ecclesie panormitane cum aliis nobilibus coram se igne cremari et quemdam decanum cum aliis in mari iactari fecit.*

> *Unde imperatrix redarguens eum, dicitur quot ira commotus voluit eam gladio perimere, sed liberatur a Marcualdo marchione. Quod audientes Siculi, tam latini quam greci et sarraceni, rebellati sunt omnes contra imperatorem. Sed congregato exercito et audito quod imperatrix viveret, populus conticuit, et subiecerunt se cuncti imperatori.*[145]

This "Unknown Cistercian" chronicler apparently knows nothing about an enormous conspiracy among Sicilian nobles who had already chosen one of their

---

[143] Richard of San Germano, *Chronica,* 65. See also the biographical sketch for Conrad of Urslingen.

[144] Kölzer, "Autor," 12.

[145] *Chronica S. Mariae De Ferraria,* 32.

number to marry Constance and become the next king. Though so learned a scholar as Toeche expresses the belief that Constance actually had a hand in this,[146] he apparently arrives at that opinion by trying harder to understand the emperor than the empress. Constance might well have been bitterly disappointed at Henry's approach to governing Sicily, yet she must have known that if he died, she and her infant son would face the backlash against all that he had done. Marriage to a pretender would provide very uncertain refuge for her son, and she was unlikely to bear more children.

Toeche recounts, and may have popularized (at least in its current form), the story that Henry VI punished Constance by forcing her to watch the execution of the rebels.[147] For this, he draws on the account of the *Annales Marbacenses*, which affirms that the empress was guilty and implies that, by her husband's orders, she was present at the executions.[148] However, the *Annales* are not so clear on whether the emperor's intent was to punish Constance. The account runs:

> For with the empress present and watching, he [the emperor] commanded that a crown be fixed with iron nails to the head of the [would-be] king. [Also he commanded] others to be burned with fire and some drowned in the sea. From this the greatest hatred was excited against him, not only among the natives but among others who afterwards learned of these things.

> *Nam regem, presente imperatrice et vidente, coronam clavis ferreis capiti eius affigi iussit et alios igni cremari, quosdam in mare mergi iussit. Proinde maximam adversum se invidiam tam ab incolis quam ab aliis qui post hec perceperunt excitavit.*[149]

The chronicler's focus here is on the suffering of the victims, not on that of the empress. Perhaps he thought that the pretender's wretched death was made yet more miserable by the gaze of the queen whom he had hoped to marry. Henry, on the other hand, may have wanted Constance's presence at the executions simply in order to emphasize that everything was being done with the consent of the legitimate and hereditary queen of Sicily.

Certainly Constance was not banished from Henry's court in the wake of the conspiracy. She was left able to assume control after Henry's death. Accord-

---

[146] Toeche, *Kaiser Heinrich VI*, 453–57; also 582–83.

[147] *Kaiser Heinrich VI*, 583.

[148] In their biographies of Frederick II, Kantorowicz (11) and Van Cleve (24) both mention this incident, as does Simeti, *Travels with a Medieval Queen*, 280.

[149] *Annales Marbacenses, Qui Dicuntur Cronica Hohenburgensis cum continuatione et additamentis Neoburgensibus*, ed. Hermann Bloch, in *Scriptores rerum Germanicarum in usum scholarum separatim editi* 9 (Hanover: Hahn, 1907), 69–70.

ing to Innocent III's anonmyous biographer, she was with him when he died.[150] Her efforts to obtain recognition for her infant son are discussed in the Introduction, C.16.

In her last months, Constance also gave her husband a splendid burial in Palermo, presumably in the coffin where she herself now lies.[151] Where she herself was originally buried, we do not know, but years later her son would bring from Cefalu the two superior coffins which had been made at the command of his grandfather King Roger and then kept there for political reasons. He used them for his father and himself, and apparently promoted his mother, at that time, from some less worthy coffin into the one she had prepared for her husband.

Some scholars[152] tell that Constance's last months were troubled by difficulties in arranging an honorable burial for her excommunicated husband. If so, this was merely one more threat to her son's future. This story is, however, based mostly on Roger of Hoveden's claim that when German princes elected Richard Lionheart of England as their emperor, he declined specifically on the excuse that supporters of the Hohenstaufen still hated him, since "the emperor's corpse had been exhumed because of him" (*corpus imperatoris propter eum inhumatum erat*).[153] Roger of Hoveden also reports that the pope agreed to be guardian for young Frederick II only after Constance swore on the sacrament that he was really her legitimate son by Henry. This story, found nowhere else, flatters Richard Lionheart; it puts the empress in a humiliating position while giving the English king pious reasons to abandon his ambitions against Sicily, once the pope has taken her under his protection. The account of Henry's exhumation likewise puts the dead Hohenstaufen in a bad light and justifies Richard's kinsman, Otto the Welf, in his continued struggle for the empire (see Introduction, C.13).

But was Henry VI excommunicated? Not during his lifetime; even Eduard Winkelmann, accepting a version of this story, points out that the continuous correspondance between Henry VI and Celestine III excludes this possibility. Winkelmann suggests that Celestine might perhaps have claimed, retroactively, that a general excommunication, aimed at those who captured crusaders and held them for ransom, had applied to him.[154] Certainly Henry was exhumed when

---

[150] *The Deeds of Innocent III*, 19; chap. 20.

[151] That is what Deér determined in *Dynastic Porphyry Tombs of the Norman Period*, 84.

[152] For example, Deér in *Dynastic Porphyry Tombs*, 83. Also Csendes, *Heinrich VI*, 193.

[153] *Chronica*, 177.

[154] Winkelmann, *Philipp von Schwaben*, 1:488–90. Richard also claimed that Henry, on his deathbed, had sent an envoy to England offering to pay back the ransom money, perhaps in exchange for land. Winkelmann plausibly suggests that Richard's motive was not only to increase the disrepute in which the Hohenstaufen party was held, but also to prepare for a claim to Hohenstaufen lands in Germany, for the sake of his nephew Otto.

his body, first buried in Messina, was later moved to Palermo. However, Deér's account shows that a number of royal graves were moved during this period, including those of William II's father, mother, and brothers, who were first buried in Palermo and later transferred to Monreale.[155] This was done merely to give them more splendid tombs. The same might have been the case with Henry VI.

Constance died 28 November 1198, three days after writing her testament, in which she gave orders for herself to be buried in the cathedral at Palermo with her father and husband.[156]

§**Constance**, daughter of Tancred and his consort Sibylla. fl. 1193–1200.

Constance is not specifically named by Pietro, but she is alluded to among Tancred's three daughters in l. 771. She married Pietro Ziani, a doge of Venice.[157]

§**Darius**, fl. 1161–1193. Minor palace official and Tancredine partisan.

Nothing certain is known about this person, whom the Empress Constance mentions as an oppressor of the loyal town of Eboli near Salerno (l. 609). There is a possible reference to him, in a document from July 1193, in the abbey of Cava, near Salerno, which lists Tancred as the reigning king and his son Roger as his co-ruler in the first year of his reign. Also a certain "Darius, privy counselor, palatine chamberlain of the king and master of the royal duana of the barons" (*Darius regis privatus palatinus camerarius et magister regie duane baronum*) is mentioned.[158] The word *duana* comes from the Arabic *diwan*, and in the Norman kingdom it was "an office of record and verification."[159] It is possible but not inevitable that the "Darius" with these bureaucratic responsibilities might have had military duties too. A "Darius," perhaps the same one, held a fief at Auletta near Salerno with sixteen "villeins" or serfs, his name appearing in documents (written in Greek) from 1178–1181. He might also be the same *Darius hostiarius*[160]

---

[155] Deér, *Dynastic Porphyry Tombs*, 3–4.

[156] Deér, *Dynastic Porphyry Tombs*, 16; Winkelmann, Philipp, 1:124.

[157] Siragusa, *Liber ad honorem*, 59, n. 2; Tuscus, *Gesta*, 499. Neither source gives a date for this event or mentions any children.

[158] Siragusa, *Liber ad honorem*, 48, n. 4, cites Winkelmann's edition (n. 71) for this document, found in "arca 43, no. 83." Jamison, *Admiral Eugenius*, describes the same document (324, n. 7).

[159] Jamison, *Admiral Eugenius*, 40; Johns, *Arabic Adminstration in Norman Sicily*, 14: "an administrative or government office," where records are kept or business conducted in Arabic.

[160] Jamison suggests the identification in *Admiral Eugenius*, 324, n. 7. See also Cuozzo, *Catalogus Baronum Commentario*, 175–76; par. 661. There is no clear and simple way to render *hostiarius* or *ostiarus* into English; in this context, Loud and Wiedemann translate the work as "usher," one of the meanings given in Niermeyer, *Mediae Latinitatis Lexicon Minus*, which also suggests "porter" and "household officer" (s. v. "ostiarius"). In Falcandus, *La Historia*, the *hostiarii* perform a variety of functions, sometimes acting as guards and sometimes carrying messages or commands. Examples are 46, 98, 130, 135,

who, according to the chronicler Falcandus, was commonly thought to have shot the arrow that fatally wounded William I's son Roger in 1161.[161]

§**Diepold** of Vohburg, fl. 1191–1220. Also called Diepold of Schweinspeunt.

Originally from a family of German *ministeriales*, warriors of servile status,[162] known for their effectiveness and loyalty, he first served the Hohenstaufen emperors, but later became a freebooter, wreaking havoc upon the kingdom of Sicily. Finally, he joined the Teutonic Knights.

In the *Liber* (l. 607) Diepold is first mentioned in Constance's speech to the attacking Salernitans, as a commander upon whom she can still rely, stationed at the secure fortress of Rocca D'Arce. Later Tancred (ll. 758–762) mentions him as someone he fears to encounter in battle. Pietro celebrates Diepold's action in capturing prisoners and booty in San Germano, near Monte Cassino, using Rocca D'Arce as a base (ll. 1089–1118 and fol. 130r). Salerno, once captured, is put into the hands of Diepold, who perhaps has become "justiciar of Terra Laboris."[163] The *Liber* retrospectively inserts another adventure in which Diepold and his men defeat a Tancredine commander, Guido of Castelvechio, whose followers greatly outnumber them (ll. 1187–1226 and fol. 133r). Once more, at the end, he is alluded to as the "boar of Nocera" (*Nucerinus aper*) (l. 1666).

Diepold was descended from Bavarian *ministeriales*.[164] Little apparently is known of his early life, apart from what Pietro tells. Later, after the close of the events in the *Liber*, Diepold captured Tancred's brother-in-law, Count Richard of Acerra, and received his county of Acerra as a reward.[165] After Henry's death, he became one of many Germans who declined to leave the kingdom of Sicily despite the orders of the Empress Constance, and who helped, through their struggles against the pope and his agents, to reduce the kingdom to near anarchy. Diepold, however, became reconciled to Pope Innocent (in 1206) and helped arrange for the young king, Frederick II, to be taken from the custody of a certain William of Capparone, and given "into the hands of the legate, Cardinal Gerhard, and the chancellor."[166] However, later, after Philip of Swabia's death, when Otto the Welf, after being crowned emperor, broke his promises to Innocent III that he would not invade the kingdom of Sicily, Diepold again switched sides

---

138, 151, 155, 157. Loud and Wiedemann render the word variously in these respective contexts: 99 "prison warders, 147 "sentries," 181 "usher," 186 "guards," 189 "guards," 204 "usher," 208 "usher," and 210 "sentries."

[161] *La Historia*, 62; *History of the Tyrants*, trans. Loud and Wiedemann, 114 and n. 90.

[162] Christoph von Reisinger, *Tankred von Lecce: Normannischer König von Sizilien 1190–1194* (Köln: Böhlau Verlag, 1992), 155 and n. 648.

[163] Chalandon, *Histoire*, 2:483.

[164] Kölzer, "Bildkommentar," 175.

[165] Richard of San Germano, *Chronica*, 68.

[166] Van Cleve, *Emperor Frederick II*, 53–54.

and joined Otto, who granted him the duchy of Spoleto as a reward,[167] although Innocent had taken much trouble to remove that fief from imperial control. Otto's defeat was also Diepold's defeat.[168] However, Diepold attempted to claim the duchy of Spoleto again, for which Frederick II had him "arrested and held captive by his son-in-law, James of San Severino."[169] Later, about 1220, "probably in recognition of Di[e]pold's former services to Emperor Henry VI," Frederick II finally released him in exchange for "the castles of Cajazzo and Alife in the valley of the Volturno" which his brother, Siegfried, held, and it seems he was allowed to join the crusading order of the Teuonic Knights to expiate his many crimes.[170] He was dead by 1221.[171]

§**Elias** of Gesualdo, fl. 1141–1192. Norman baron connected to the Hauteville family.

Elias abruptly appears in l. 667 and informs Constance, as she prays during the Salernitans' assault on her palace of Terracina, that she must go to Tancred as a prisoner. The associated miniatures show him negotiating with her, and later accompanying her on her voyage into captivity at Messina (fols. 118r, 119r, 120r). After this, he disappears from the story.

He is portrayed as an old man afflicted with gout, needing to lean on servants for support, and documents confirm his long life, since his name appears on donations to the abbey of Cava near Salerno in 1141, 1145, and 1152. He made the first two with his father William, and the third with his mother Alberada.[172] This Alberada was a daughter of Count Geoffrey of Lecce, Tancred's maternal uncle.[173] William was an illegitimate son of Roger Borsa, Robert Guiscard's son by Segelgaita (see Genealogical Table 1). Documents of 1183 and 1186 mention Elias as both royal constable and justiciar. In 1187, he appears in a document giving a vineyard to an adherent in return for good service, together with his son Roger, now styled "Lord of Gesualdo" (*Signore di Gesualdo*). This indicates, perhaps, that Elias was by then delegating many of his feudal responsibilities to

---

[167] Van Cleve, *Emperor Frederick II*, 136; Richard of San Germano, *Chronica*, 76.

[168] Van Cleve, *Emperor Frederick II*, states that "Dipold" showed up at the court of Frederick II in Germany, and "he appears to have been tolerated at the court, where, on 14 February 1213, he witnessed a document, under his original German title as Margrave of Vohburg" (137). In note 2 on that page, Van Cleve adds, "He was still at the court of Frederick in the latter part of March 1213 . . . and probably as late as April of that year . . ." Siragusa (*Liber ad honorem*, 48, n. 3) states that "Dipoldus," according to Winkelmann, note 70, was not the margrave but the vassal of the margrave of Vohburg. Perhaps the margrave of the same name has confused the records.

[169] Van Cleve, *Emperor Frederick II*, 137 and n. 2.

[170] Van Cleve, *Emperor Frederick II*, 137; *Chronica Albrici*, 879.

[171] Kölzer, "Personenverzeichnis," 297.

[172] Siragusa, *Liber ad honorem*, 133, n. 1.

[173] Cuozzo, *Catalogus Baronum Commentario,* 193–94, par. 707.

his sons. In 1189, he made a will specifying that he would be buried in the monastery of Monte Vergine della Montagna, where his first wife, Diomeda, already lay. She apparently died after 1188, at which time she had made a donation along with her son Roger. Elias later took a second wife, Gueriera. Then he died, May 1207, and his sons Roger and Robert carried out his will, burying him as he had specified. Roger had evidently gained the favor of Henry VI, who made him count of Gesualdo.[174]

§**Elvira,** also called Alberia, Albidia, and Geloira,[175] ca. 1101–1135. First consort of Roger II.

In the *Liber*, Elvira is mentioned as King Roger's first wife (l. 9), who bore him many children and then died. The miniatures show her marrying him and then lying in her grave with two children beside her (fol. 96r).

Few facts are known about her and her marriage. She was the daughter of Alfonso VI of Castile and of his wife Elisabeth. Scholars conclude that she married Roger "before 1118"; how long before cannot be said with certainty.[176] Since William I, who seems to have been the fourth son of the marriage, was apparently born ca. 1120,[177] a marriage date of about 1116 for Elvira would not be unreasonable. The conjectural birth date given above is based on the assumption that Elvira married at the age of fifteen. She died 6 February 1135,[178] reportedly causing her husband great grief. She had, according to Romuald of Salerno, five sons and a daughter. The daughter, reports the chronicler, died about the same time she did. The birth order of Elvira's sons is not quite clear, but Duke Roger was the eldest. The others were named Alphonso, Tancred, Henry, and William. Only the last survived his father. Henry apparently died as a child. Apart from mention of his death, the only record of him is a document in Greek granting land near Vicari in Sicily to a certain Adeline who had been his wet nurse.[179]

Although all Elvira's children were dead by the time the action of the *Liber* begins, most of them had survived her. Perhaps, however, the two shown lying

---

[174] Cuozzo, *Catalogus Baronum Commentario*, 193–94, par. 707.

[175] Siragusa, *Liber ad honorem*, 3–4, n. 3.

[176] Chalandon, *Histoire*, 2:105, passes on the speculative date from Alessandro Di Meo, *Annali Critico-Diplomatico del Regno di Napoli della Mezzana Età.*, 12 vols. (Naples, 1795–1819), 10:155–56. However, he is not pleased with his evidence. Houben, *Roger II*, 35, gives 1117 as the probable date.

[177] Romuald of Salerno, *Chronicon*, 253–54, states that King William died at forty-six years of age, in 1166.

[178] Chalandon, *Histoire*, 2:42, n. 1, cites, for this information, the *Necrologium Salernitanum*, ed. Eduard Winkelmann, in *Forschungen zur deutsche Geschichte*, vol. 28 (1828), 474.

[179] *Chronicon Romualdi II Archiepiscopi Salernitani*, ed. Garufi, 230–31, and n. 3; Johns, *Arabic Administration*, 101–2, 121–23.

beside her in the tomb represent her unnamed daughter and the child Henry, who may have predeceased her.[180]

§**Eugenius**, Admiral, ca. 1130–1203.[181]

A Greek (and Latin) official in the Norman kingdom of Sicily during the reigns of William I, William II, Tancred, Henry VI, and Frederick II, Eugenius is depicted fol. 136r, cap. 11, taking the conspiratorial oath with Archbishop Nicholas, the former queen Sibylla, and others. Evelyn Jamison identifies him as "the figure kneeling in the front row directly opposite Margaritus. With his thin pointed face and long aquiline nose, this man has great individuality, clearly differentiated from the rest."[182] The verses accompanying these illustrations, which might have defined his role more precisely, are lost.

Besides being a royal official, Eugenius is also the author of poems in Greek and some translations from Greek into Latin. The theory has been put forward[183] that he is the true author of the works attributed to the chronicler "Hugo Falcandus," although it has not been widely accepted.[184] I myself have argued that the author of these works was actually Hugues Foucaud, abbot of Saint Denis from 1186–1197, an identity indeed first proposed by a Benedictine monk in 1770.[185]

Eugenius began his career at the court of William I, to whom he addresses a panegyric in Greek.[186] He continued under the administration of William II, but his importance grew under Tancred. He may have traveled to Constantinople and worked to arrange the marriage between Tancred's son Roger and Irene Angelina.[187] In 1195, he was brought to Germany with the other accused conspirators[188] but was soon released at the wishes of Conrad of Hildesheim,[189] under whose supervision he worked once more for the administration of the kingdom. After the death of Henry VI, Eugenius served the Empress Constance, and when she died, his career continued under the Sicilian council of *familiares* ruling in the name of the child Frederick II.[190]

---

[180] Kölzer, "Bildkommentar," 38, suggests this interpretation.

[181] Jamison, *Admiral Eugenius*, 5.

[182] Jamison, *Admiral Eugenius*, 123.

[183] Jamison, *Admiral Eugenius*, 177–272.

[184] Loud and Wiedemann, in their introduction to *History of the Tyrants of Sicily*, 32–40, fail to endorse it.

[185] Gwenyth Hood, "Falcandus and Fulcaudus, *Epistola ad Petrum, Liber de Regno Sicilie*: Literary Form and Author's Identity," *Studi Medievali*, 3rd ser. 40 (1999): 1–41, here 5–6.

[186] Jamison, *Admiral Eugenius*, 61–63.

[187] Jamison, *Admiral Eugenius*, 102.

[188] Jamison, *Admiral Eugenius*, 122–45; chap. 6.

[189] Jamison, *Admiral Eugenius*, 146–74; chap. 6.

[190] Jamison hopes that he may have had some role in educating the young king (*Admiral Eugenius*, 306–7).

§**Frederick I Barbarossa**, ca. 1124–1190. Holy Roman Emperor, r. 1152–1190.

As the father of Henry VI of Hohenstaufen, Frederick Barbarossa is mentioned repeatedly in the *Liber.* In l. 315, his son Henry is called upon to imitate his example. Later (1378), the poet claims that Henry's newborn son will be like both his grandfathers, Frederick and Roger. Lines 1378–1606 celebrate Barbarossa's last cruasde and death on the way to the Holy Land, and he is depicted in fols. 107r and fol. 143r.

Frederick Barbarossa's birth date is uncertain,[191] although he appears in many contemporary chronicles, including the famous one begun by his uncle, Otto of Freising, and completed by a continuator, Rahewin.[192] He is also the subject of several modern biographies.[193]

The son of Duke Frederick of Swabia and Judith, a member of the rival Welf family (see Genealogical Table 2), Frederick was not the obvious heir to the throne and did not have a royal education. When he was born, depending on what date it was, either his great-uncle, Henry V the Salian, who died in 1125, or else Lothar of Supplingburg, the ancestor of the rival Welf family, was emperor. When Lothar died in 1137, Frederick's uncle Conrad III was elected king of the Romans. As a youth, Frederick accompanied Conrad on the second crusade, a disastrous expedition which made him averse to further crusades.

When Conrad of Hohenstaufen knew that he was dying, he designated his nephew Frederick as his heir because his own surviving son was a minor and could not effectively head the empire, given the threat of significant resistance by the rival Welf family. Also, since Frederick was himself related to the Welfs because of his mother Judith, it was hoped that he could unite the two families, as Otto of Freising asserts in his biography, *Deeds of Frederick Barbarossa.*[194] On Conrad's death, Frederick was duly elected, and Otto recounts how he went to Italy and received his imperial coronation (18 June 1155) at the hands of Pope Hadrian IV.[195] His marriage in 1147 to Adela of Vohburg, by whom he had no children, was dissolved ostensibly on the grounds of consanguinity.[196] Soon he married Beatrix, "heiress of Upper Burgundy,"[197] by whom he had many

---

[191] Baaken, "Die Altersfolge," 47, estimates some time between 1124 and 1130, while Hampe, *Germany Under the Salian and Hohenstaufen Emperors*, 153, says that he was born "1125 or 1126."

[192] *The Deeds of Frederick Barbarossa*, trans. C.C. Mierow (New York: Columbia University Press, 1953).

[193] Those by Munz and Pacaut are available in English translation (see bibliography).

[194] Otto of Freising, *Deeds*, bk. 2, chap. 2. See also *Deeds*, trans. Mierow, 49 n.2.

[195] Otto of Freising, *Deeds*, bk. 2, chap 23.

[196] Baaken, "Die Altersfolge," 47.

[197] Hampe, *Germany Under the Salian and Hohenstaufen Emperors*, 159.

children, including three who appear in Pietro's *Liber*: Henry VI, Frederick of Swabia, and Philip of Swabia.

Frederick's aim to regain the glories of the Roman Empire started him on a collision course with the papacy, the Italian cities, the kingdom of Sicily, and the Byzantine Empire. He died attempting to cross the river Seleph or Salef[198] on the way to the Holy Land on 10 June 1190.[199]

§**Frederick** II of Hohenstaufen, 1194–1250. Holy Roman Emperor, king of Sicily, king of Jerusalem.

In the *Liber*, the birth of Frederick II represents the success of Henry's long struggle, and the promise of a glorious future. This is celebrated in verses (ll. 1363–1428) and in the miniature on fol. 138r. Words and pictures make use of imagery from biblical prophecy and classical mythology, especially Virgil's *Eclogue* 4. Also an incident from his childhood in which he divides a fish which has been presented to him (ll. 1397–1428) is seen to presage a glorious and peaceful future. Little Frederick directs the fish to be divided into three parts, sending one part to his father and keeping the other two for himself. (Unfortunately, the accompanying miniature is missing.) Among other wonderful things, Pietro takes this to imply that the child will improve upon his already superlative father.

However, though Frederick had a longer life than did his father, and his later reputation is indeed more glorious, he did not enjoy the peace that Pietro foresaw for him. Still, testifying to his interest in peaceful civilization and justifying Pietro's esteem to some extent, there remain his book of Sicilian laws, *Liber Augustalis*, and his book on falconry, *De Arte Venandi cum Avibus*.[200] Some of his life is briefly sketched in the Introduction, C.15–19.

Since hatred is the other side of adulation, perhaps it is inevitable that someone who is greeted as a Messianic figure by his friends would be seen as an antichrist by enemies. So it is no great surprise that Frederick appears in Dante's *Inferno* (4.119–102) among the heretics.

Many biographies on Frederick II are available in English.[201] The one that best captures the clash between adoration and execration surrounding him is Ernst

---

[198] Munz, *Frederick Barbarossa*, 395; Kölzer, "Bildkommentar," 83.

[199] *Historia de expeditione Frederici imperatoris* (also called Ansbertus). In *Quellen zur Geschichte des Kreuzzuges Friedrichs I.*, ed. A. Chroust, 1–115. Also in MGH, Scriptores rerum Germanicarum 5 (Berlin: Wiedmann, 1928), 91–92.

[200] The work has been translated into English by Casey A. Wood and H. Marjorie Fyfe as *The Art of Falconry, by Frederick II of Hohenstaufen* (Stanford: Stanford University Press, 1943). According to David Abulafia (*Frederick II*, 452, notes on chap. 8), a facsimile edition of the surviving Vatican manuscript (Vatican MS Palatine Latin 1071) has been published, edited by C.A. Willemsen (Graz: Akademische Druck- u. Verlagsaustalt, 1969).

[201] Among other biographies, that of Thomas Curtis Van Cleve, often cited in this work, is impressive for its detailed research and clear documentation. Also worth men-

Kantorowicz's *Frederick the Second*.[202] Kantorowicz, writing while Nazi influence rose in Germany before World War II, transferred the apocalyptic imagery of the twelfth and thirteenth centuries into a Nietzschean context, portraying Frederick II as a "superman" who must destroy in order to create, though he is reluctant to play that role.[203] This approach allows sympathetic portrayal of the emperor while also acknowledging validity in the fear and hatred of his enemies.

Since Kantorowicz, scholars have sought to distance themselves from the quasi-apocalyptic excitement surrounding Frederick II, and thus to ignore Pietro da Eboli as well, except as a conveyer of fact. David Abulafia, in his effort to deflate the enthusiasm (positive and negative) which still surrounds the figure of this emperor, suggests that Frederick II as an individual had aims and abilities which were merely typical for the medieval period, and that "the interest of Frederick's reign lies in his adversaries as much as in himself."[204]

Frederick died 13 December 1250,[205] and his tomb is in Palermo, with that of his father, mother, and grandfather.

§**Frederick of Swabia**, 1167–1191. Duke of Swabia.

Apparently the third son of Frederick Barbarossa and Beatrice of Burgundy, Frederick of Swabia is mentioned once in the *Liber* as the youth who accompanied Barbarossa on his crusade and fought the Turks at Iconium. Pietro gives him the heroic patronymic *Fredericiades* (1. 1596); see Commentary on this line.

Barbarossa's third son was first called "Konrad," and then given the name Frederick after the eldest son of that name had died.[206] Destined at an early age for the dukedom of Swabia, in 1184 he was knighted at a great festival during Pentecost, at the same time that his elder brother Henry became, effectively, their father's co-ruler.[207]

In 1189, the younger Frederick accompanied his father on his crusade and played a valiant part in the battle at Iconium (modern Konya): "the duke of Swabia was wounded, with an upper tooth being knocked out completely and half of a lower tooth" (*dux Swewiae vulneratus est uno superiori dente penitus excusso et medietate inferioris*).[208] After his father's tragic drowning, the young duke took

---

tioning here is that of Georgina Masson, *Frederick II* (London: Secker and Warbeck, 1957), who pays more attention to Frederick's personal life, his relationships with his consorts, and the circumstances of his marriage to Bianca Lancia, mother of the King Manfred who would succeed him in Italy (213). Other recent English-speaking biographers prefer to omit this interesting material.

[202] Trans. E. O. Lorimer (New York: Richard R. Smith, 1931).
[203] Kantorowicz, *Frederick the Second*, 603.
[204] Abulafia, *Frederick II*, 439.
[205] Jamison, *Admiral Eugenius*, 407.
[206] Baaken, "Die Altersfolge," 47. Jordan, *Henry the Lion*, 155.
[207] Toeche, *Kaiser Heinrich VI*, 31.
[208] *Epistola de morte Friderici imperatoris*, 495.

over command of the army. There were many deaths and desertions before the survivers reached Antioch, where they buried the emperor's body.[209] Frederick of Swabia died at the siege of Acre, 20 January 1191.[210]

§**Girardus** or Gerard, fl. 1191–1201. Physician attending Henry VI during his illness (*Liber* l. 482).

Nothing certain is known about this person, but scholars have found relevant documents:

> A "*Girardus miles et medicus*" [Girard, knight and physician] is found subscribed in two documents of the abbey of La Cava, of 1176, and of June 1184 . . . and a '*magister Girardus Salernitanus*' . . . , according to the evidence of the biography of Innocent III[211] . . . , was among the prisoners on the imperial side made by Walter of Brienne in the battle near Barletta in 1201. According to a letter of Innocent III . . . Master Girardo with John Principe . . . violently occupied the archiepiscopal seat of Salerno during the captivity of the Archbishop in Germany, after the discovery of the true or supposed conspiracy against the emperor.[212]

There is no independent evidence that this Master Girard attended the emperor at the siege. Kölzer suggests that Girard might be an error, and that Pietro might really mean " the imperial household physician, Berard, the archdeacon of Ascoli Piceno" who appears on imperial documents at various times between 1186 and the emperor's death.[213]

§**Guido** of Castelvecchio, fl. 1192.

Guido is named and depicted as the supporter of Tancred who attempted to cut off Diepold of Schweinspeunt before he returned to Rocca D'Arce from one of his plundering expeditions, to take his booty from him (l. 1208; fol. 133r).

No exact match for this person has been found in documents and sources. Siragusa claims that "among the documents of the abbey of Cava, I found at 1188 one *Ruggiero di Castelvetere* son of *Giacomo di Castelvetere*, but I did not succeed in finding our Guido."[214] According to another view,[215] which Siragusa mentions but does not endorse, Guido was the same person as the royal official (*logothete*)

---

[209] Runciman, *History*, 2:17.

[210] Runciman, *History*, 2:32.

[211] *Gesta Innocenti III*, 49; *Deeds of Pope Innocent III*, 46, chap. 34. Powell translates the name as "Gerard."

[212] Siragusa, *Liber ad honorem*, 40, n. 1.

[213] Kölzer, "Bildkommentar," 102.

[214] *Liber ad honorem*, 40, n. 3.

[215] Toeche, *Kaiser Heinrich VI*, 320, n. 1.

mentioned by Richard of San Germano as having encountered Diepold around this time:

> The aforesaid Diepold joins battle in Aquino with a certain logothete of the king [Tancred], whom he defeated and who fled the field of battle, [leaving] many of his men captured and many drowned in the lake. This same Diepold's forces then increase.

> *Dictus Dyopuldus apud Quinum cum quodam regis logotheta confreditur, quem campestri bello fugatum devicit, multis ex suis captis, multis in lacu summersis, et tunc vires acrescunt ipsi Dyopuldo.* [216]

§**Henry VI** (Heinrich VI) of Hohenstaufen, 1165–1197. Holy Roman Emperor, r. 1191–1197. Son of Frederick Barbarossa (q. v.) and father of Frederick II of Hohenstaufen (q. v.).

Henry VI is one of the main characters in the *Liber*; he is mentioned on the first page of verses and depicted in the associated miniature. The work is dedicated to him (139r), and he also appears on the last page.

Histories treat his reign with various degrees of detail, and biographies of his son, Frederick II, usually deal with him at some length. [217]

Henry was the second son of Frederick Barbarossa and his empress, Beatrice of Burgundy; however, his fragile elder brother soon died. [218] His father arranged his election as King of the Romans in 1169 when he was four years old. The youth was carefully instructed, and had as tutors several men who remained in his entourage later. These included his chaplain, Godfrey of Viterbo, the poet; his chancellor, Conrad of Querfurt, who became the patron of Pietro da Eboli; his marshal, Henry of Kalden; and his seneschal, Markward of Anweiler. [219] Frederick Barbarossa evidently chose to make his son an active participant in government as soon as possible. Thus, when the Peace of Venice was negotiated in 1177 (see Introduction, C.8), twelve-year-old Henry came to Italy with his mother, the Empress Beatrice. They resided at the castle of Gaiba, and according to the custom of the time, the bishop of Verdun swore on Henry's behalf that he would keep the treaty. [220] In 1184, Henry and his younger brother Frederick were knighted in a magnificent ceremony at Mainz. [221] Later the same year, he was formally betrothed to Constance (q.v.), heiress of Norman Sicily. The splen-

---

[216] Richard of San Germano, *Chronica*, 66.

[217] There is currently no full-length biography of Emperor Henry VI in English, but German biographies include those by Theodor Toeche and Peter Csendes.

[218] Assmann, "Friedrich Barbarossas Kinder," 459.

[219] Toeche, *Kaiser Heinrich VI*, 27; c.f. Van Cleve, *Markward*, 16.

[220] Romuald of Salerno, *Chronicon*, 292. See also Chalandon, *Histoire*, 2:383, and Toeche, *Kaiser Heinrich VI*, 29.

[221] Munz, *Frederick Barbarossa*, 360; chap. 8.

did wedding ceremony took place 27 January 1186, and at the same time, Henry VI was crowned king of Lombardy. This was no empty honor, since Frederick Barbarossa then returned to Germany, leaving Henry to govern northern Italy in his absence, with his new queen at his side. From then on, Henry's life becomes the history recounted in the *Liber* and the commentaries on it. Some additional details are included in the Introduction, C.8–15. He died at Messina, 26 September 1197.[222]

§**Henry of Kalden** or **Calandrinus**. fl. 1186–1208. German *ministerialis* and commander.

Calandrinus is mentioned in the *Liber* (l. 1183), as the commander who gives the word that it is safe to advance to Sicily after Salerno is taken in the fall of 1194. He is also depicted on 147r (cap. 9) in a symbolic picture where he is apparently associated with the god Mars.

Henry of Kalden or Kalindin came from a family of *ministeriales* serving the Hohenstaufen. He drew his name from a city in Nordgau, and belonged to the Papenheim family.[223] He may have served as one of Henry VI's tutors, instructing him in knightly arts during his youth. In 1186, he appears with the young King Henry in Italy as his marshal.[224] Later, perhaps, he was sent as an envoy to Constantinople: he may be the man with "bushy eyebrows" to whom Niketas Choniates refers, "remarkable for having been given the responsibility for the king's education as a child," who made threatening speeches to Emperor Alexius III and demanded compensation for past injuries to the kingdom of Sicily along with cooperation for a future crusade.[225]

In the spring of 1197, Henry of Kalden stood by the emperor during the second conspiracy (see Introduction, C.15). In the September of that year, like Conrad of Hildesheim, he departed with the crusading army, but returned to Germany when he learned of the emperor's death.[226] Later he became Philip of Swabia's marshal. When Philip was murdered 1208, he tracked down and slew the killer. After tossing the head into the Danube,[227] he threw earth over the torso in the open field, where years later it was found for honorable burial.[228]

---

[222] Assmann, "Friedrich Barbarossas Kinder," 459.

[223] Toeche, *Kaiser Heinrich VI*, 27.

[224] Toeche, *Kaiser Heinrich VI*, 59.

[225] *O City of Byzantium*, 261.

[226] Winkelmann, *Philipp von Schwaben*, 1:60.

[227] Van Cleve, *Emperor Frederick II*, 68; *Annales Marbacenses*, 78.

[228] Winkelmann, *Philipp von Schwaben*, 1:477.

§Hugh (II) Lupin, fl. 1175–1197. Count of Conversano and Catanzaro. See **Lupin brothers,** Hugh (II) and Jordan.

§Irene Angela or Irene Angelina, ca.1178–27 August 1208.

Irene is alluded to only once, rather vaguely, in the surviving portions of the *Liber,* in the speech of Tancred's widow Sibylla, as she expresses alarm at Henry VI's inexorable advance on Palermo:

> Nor, sweetest son, is my Greek daughter-in-law of any use to me,
> Whom Philip loves without having yet seen her face."

> *"Nec michi Greca nurus prodest, dulcissime fili,*
>   *Quam, nec adhuc visa fronte, Philippus amat."*
> (ll. 1291–1292)

Evidently Pietro knew that Tancred's deceased eldest son Roger had married a daughter of the Byzantine emperor. He also seems to know that there is some talk of a match between this princess and the emperor's brother, Philip of Swabia. His awareness of this may even have been the motive for some clumsy revisions in the manuscript of the *Liber* (see Commentary and notes on fols 120v and 121r). Perhaps Tancred's son Roger is spared direct invective because of his connection with Irene. Young Roger, though never mentioned by name, is shown riding with his younger brother in his father's coronation procession (fol. 102r). As a matter of history, though Pietro does not recount it, Tancred's great moment of triumph occurred after Constance was handed over to him as a prisoner in 1191. When he released her at the pope's demand, he received in return (unmentioned by Pietro) recognition by the pope as king of Sicily. Very likely, these events influenced the Byzantine emperor to agree to the alliance with Tancred and to send his daughter over the sea as a bride for young Roger, who was then crowned as Tancred's co-ruler. It is surprising that our pro-imperial poet let all of this pass without comment. However, in the hastily revised verses on fol. 124v (see notes on that page), Tancred speaks as though he has only one son, who is still a boy (ll. 770–772). Roger's death has been passed over, though Sibylla alludes to a lost son in her speech:

> Thus she speaks: "Oh, would that I had remained the countess of Lecce!
> No battles would have terrified my spirits,
> Perhaps I would still have my husband and splendid offspring.
> Now I go to Lecce sad and bereft of both."

> *Sic ait: "O utinam Lichio comitissa manerem!*
>   *Terrerent animos prelia nulla meos,*
> *Vir michi forsan adhuc superesset et inclita proles.*
>   *Nunc Lichium tristis orba duobus eo."*
> (1269–1272)

Perhaps our poet, aware that Roger's widow had been proposed as a match for Philip of Swabia (q.v.), decided to remove a viciously satirical account of the bride's first wedding and her bridegroom.

Irene was a daughter of Isaac Angelus (q.v.), Emperor of Constantinople, and his first wife, whose name is not known to history and who was already dead, according to Niketas Choniates,[229] in 1185, when Isaac was proclaimed emperor by a crowd at the Hagia Sophia. Her date of birth is uncertain.[230] The precise date of Irene's marriage to Tancred's son Roger is also disputed; perhaps as early as 1192[231] or "between May and July 1193."[232] One chronicle states that she was not yet nubile.[233] In any case, she became a widow when her bridegroom died in December 1193. Henry VI's triumph seemed assured when Tancred also died in February the following year.

Pietro's cryptic words suggest that there was talk of a love affair between Philip and Irene, even before Henry VI reached Palermo in his march and before Sibylla made her peace with him. Certainly Henry's court must have known about the Byzantine princess at Sibylla's court. She might well have been discussed by envoys and messengers. It is not impossible that Philip sent some gallant messages to her, most likely prompted or encouraged by his brother the emperor. Sibylla might have been aware of this as she negotiated her peace with Henry VI, a matter which was more complicated than a simple plea for pardon as Pietro represents it.

Irene's marriage with Philip was solemnized 27 May 1197 at Gunzenle near Augsburg. She took the name "Maria" at this time. It is probably partly because of this expressed allegiance to the Queen of Heaven that the German minstrel Walther von der Vogelweide celebrated her in a much-quoted verse as "a rose without a thorn, a dove devoid of gall."[234]

Why the two-year wait before the marriage? Perhaps the ceremony was put off because of the volatile situation; after all, in 1195, just a few months after Henry gained control of Sicily, Irene's father was deposed and blinded by his own

---

[229] Magoulias, editorial notes on Niketas Choniates, *O City of Byzantium*, 231.

[230] Though of an aristocratic family, kin to the emperors, Irene's father Isaac Angelus was not in the usual line of succession, nor was he the eldest brother in his (initially) large family (see Genealogical Table 3). Hence there is no reason to assume an extremely youthful marriage; that he wed at the age of twenty or so, in about 1175, seems a fair conjecture. This would give the three known children of his first marriage about a decade to be born before his accession to the throne.

[231] Brand, *Byzantium Confronts*, 190.

[232] Jamison, *Admiral Eugenius*, 97. This author places the wedding at Brindisi and chooses both time and place from an examination of Tancred's itinerary, not from any surviving documents or accounts of the festivities.

[233] *Continuationes Weingartenses*, 479.

[234] Toeche, *Kaiser Heinrich VI*, 479; verse quoted from Van Cleve, *Emperor Frederick II*, 26–27.

brother. The value of such a marriage in such circumstances was unclear. Would it become an alliance with Irene's wronged father and siblings, and would her husband—and by extension, his brother the emperor—become their protectors and rescuers? Or did Henry mean to put his brother Philip on the Byzantine throne, in the right of his consort Irene? Mere knowledge of Irene's presence in Henry's court may have restrained Isaac's usurping brother from acting upon any murderous impulses he might have had toward his young nephews, since their deaths would only leave Irene the obvious inheritor of their claims. Whatever his reasons, chroniclers report that Henry did arrange the match.[235]

After Henry VI died and Philip of Swabia accepted election as King of the Romans, Irene-Maria's brother Alexius escaped from their usurping uncle (also named Alexius) and found refuge in Philip's court. In 1203, with Philip's help and through alliance with the advancing armies of the fourth crusade, he did briefly regain Constantinople and help his blinded father back to the throne. But old Isaac Angelus soon died, and young Alexius, hated in Constantinople because of the promises he had made to the crusaders, was tricked and murdered by his uncle's son-in-law, who briefly ruled after him as Alexius V.[236] Then Constantinople, sacked by the crusading army, fell for a time under the control of Latin emperors who did not draw their claims from Irene's family.

According to one chronicler,[237] it was Irene who persuaded Philip to permit Tancred's widow, Sibylla, and her daughters to leave their genteel imprisonment at the convent in Hohenburg and go into exile, where they were able to trouble Sicily during Frederick II's minority. If this is true, Irene-Maria proved more useful as a daughter-in-law than Sibylla said in the *Liber*, l. 1291. To be sure, we know that Innocent III also busied himself on behalf of Tancred's family, and the anonymous author of his *Deeds* states that the family "escaped with difficulty as a result of the Apostolic mandate," without quite explaining how that happened.[238]

Irene's life came to a sad end in 1208 when her husband was treacherously murdered as the result, apparently, of a personal quarrel with Otto of Wittels-

---

[235] For example, Otto of St. Blaise, *Chronici ab Ottone Frisingensi Conscripti Continuatio*, 328; Ch. 43: "the Emperor Henry . . . betrothed to his brother Philip the daughter of the blind king, [previously] betrothed to the son of Tancred, whom he found at Palermo" (*ceci regis filiam filio Tancredi . . . desponsatam imperator Heinricus apud Palermum repertam Philippo fratri suo deponsaverat*).

[236] Brand, *Byzantium Confronts*, 250–51.

[237] Thomas Tuscus, *Gesta imperatorum et pontificum*, 499. Tuscus, to be sure, is a doubtful source; among his many errors, he states that the princess was the daughter of the emperor Manuel (q.v.), not Isaac; however, he does know that she was successively the wife of Tancred's son Roger and Henry's brother, Philip of Swabia.

[238] *Deeds*, trans. Powell, 29; chap. 25.

bach. Irene was pregnant at the time, and her shock and grief induced a miscarriage, during which she died on 27 August 1208.[239]

§**Isaac Angelus**, ca. 1156–1203. Byzantine emperor.[240]

Pietro refers to "Isaac's lying promise and feigned alliance" (ll. 1591–1593) in the context of Barbarossa's difficult passage through his Byzantine territory on his way to the Holy Land in 1189–1190 (see Commentary). Isaac is not depicted in the miniatures, and his alliance with Tancred, sealed by the marriage of Isaac's daughter to Tancred's elder son, is only vaguely alluded to in the surviving portions of the manuscript. Some material may have been removed out of tactful consideration for Irene Angelina (q.v.), since Pietro seemed aware of a possible match between her and Henry VI's brother.

Isaac was born in relative obscurity as a younger son of Byzantine noble, related to the reigning Comnenus dynasty but not close to the throne. When, after the death of Manuel I (q.v.), Andronicus seized control of the government, took charge of the young Alexius, and imprisoned the empress Marie-Xena, many nobles rebelled. His evil intentions were clear by that time, particularly when he incited mob violence against "the judges of the *velum*, the principal judicial body of the empire," who attempted to prevent the empress's arrest.[241] Men of the Angelus family were chief among the rebels, and several were blinded for their opposition. Isaac himself, however, later returned to Constantinople as the result of a treaty. But when the increasingly paranoid Andronicus ordered his arrest in 1185, he resisted and sought refuge at the Hagia Sophia, where a sympathetic crowd soon proclaimed him emperor. (See the biographical sketch of Andronicus, above, for a fuller account of these events.)

Niketas Choniates says that Isaac "was not yet forty years old when dethroned," which happened in 1195; this would give him a birth date in 1155. Thus he was about thirty years old when he became emperor. By then, he already had a son (the future Alexius IV) and two daughters by a deceased wife whose name is not known to history.[242]

Immediately on accession, he had to face a Sicilian invasion (see Introduction, C.10). He also had to deal with attacks from other quarters. In an effort to strengthen his position, he made an alliance with King Bela of Hungary, marrying the latter's daughter, who was "not ten years old."[243]

Isaac received at his court **Conrad of Montferrat** (q.v), giving him his sister Theodora in marriage. However, Conrad soon deserted Isaac and Theodora, in

---

[239] Van Cleve, *Frederick II*, 68–69; see also *Annales Marbacenses*, 79.

[240] "Isaac II Angelus," in *Oxford Dictionary of Byzantium*, 2:1012.

[241] Brand, *Byzantium Confronts*, 46.

[242] Niketas Choniates, *O City of Byzantium*, 231, 246; in this edition see also the comments of Magoulias, 396, n. 1969.

[243] Niketas Choniates, *O City of Byzantium*, 203.

order to help the beleaguered crusader kingdom. He actively spread word that Isaac Angelus was treacherously in league with Saladin.

There was some truth in this story. Isaac had been sheltered during his exile (under Andronicus) by Saladin, and when he reached the throne, his brother Alexius, the only Angelus brother still alive and unblinded, was living at Saladin's court. Isaac sent for him, but when Alexius set out for Constantinople, he was seized and imprisoned at Acre because "rumor of the Byzantine-Muslim alliance had already reached the crusader states."[244] When Saladin captured Acre, he sent Alexius home, and Isaac congratulated the sultan on his victory. The two soon concluded an alliance, which Andronicus had proposed earlier, aimed at the western crusaders. However, the only "detailed account" for the "sojourn" of Isaac and Alexius with Saladin, for Andronicus's proposed alliance with him, and for Isaac's later entrance into it[245] is found in a letter inserted into the chronicle of *Magnus Presbyterius Reicherspergensis.*[246] The chronicler does not say who sent this letter. One conjecture is that it probably came from "Conrad [of Montferrat] or his circle." [247]

Isaac's machinations against Frederick Barbarossa (q.v.) were thus the result of a very specific promise made to Saladin that he would "oppose any [crusading] army which tried to pass through his dominions."[248]

Isaac Angelus sent his daughter Irene (q.v.) to be the consort of Tancred's son Roger (q.v).

In March 1195, Isaac decided to lead his armies against the Vlachs, who had made repeated incursions on Byzantine territory. While he was on this campaign, his brother Alexius, who accompanied him, staged a coup against him, captured him, blinded him, and had himself proclaimed Emperor Alexius III.[249] Isaac's son, also named Alexius, eventually escaped from prison, and with help from his sister Irene, sought support from the forces of the Fourth Crusade. When the crusaders encircled the city, Isaac's treacherous brother fled, and the people of Constantinople removed the blinded emperor from prison and placed him on the throne, to avoid further hostilities from the Latins.[250] Isaac thus was briefly restored to power in the middle of July 1203 as a co-ruler with his son, Alexius IV. He was eager to get revenge on those who had dethroned and blinded him and also resented the fact that his son was now perceived as the real

---

[244] Brand, "Byzantines and Saladin," 169.

[245] Brand, "Byzantines and Saladin," 168–69, nn. 2–5.

[246] Magnus Presbyterius Reicherspergensis, *Chronica collecta a Magno Presbytero*, in MGH 17, ed. G. H. Pertz (Hanover: Hahn, 1861), 511–12.

[247] Brand, "Byzantines and Saladin," 191.

[248] Brand, "Byzantines and Saladin," 173.

[249] Niketas Choniates, *O City of Byzantium*, 245–50.

[250] Magoulias, editorial comments in Niketas Choniates, *O City of Byzantium*, 301.

emperor.[251] Meanwhile, the Latins put much pressure on the younger Alexius to fulfill the extravagant promises he had made in return for their help. The angry people of the capital demanded yet another emperor, even seizing and proclaiming an unwilling man, not closely connected to the Angelus or Comnenus family, who did not live long. Weary and disillusioned, Isaac Angelus died in January 1204.[252] His son was dethroned and murdered by yet another Alexius, son-in-law of his usurping uncle (see Genealogical Table 3). The crusaders sacked the city and set up a Latin emperor in Constantinople.[253]

§James, count of Tricarico, fl. 1188–1209?

The Count of Tricarico is mentioned (1. 298) as one of those nobles who invited Henry VI to claim his rightful crown in Sicily. He does not appear again, and Pietro doubtless means us to presume his loyalty throughout. Who was he? In 1189, when William II died, both Roger of Tricarico (q.v.), count from at least 1160, and his son James (q.v.), who succeeded him, were alive. Siragusa[254] and Cuozzo[255] both assume that Roger was the count meant by Pietro. On the other hand, for 1188, the previous year, the *Annals of Ceccano* describe James, who was marrying Mabilia, the daughter of the count Landulf of Ceccano, as "Count of Tricarico."[256] It could be a mistake or it could mean that Roger had handed over many comital duties to his adult son. Roger apparently died in Acre with the remnants of Frederick Barbarossa's crusade. It is possible he joined with Barbarossa's armies at some time before William II's death, leaving his son behind to manage his Sicilian possessions. If so, James would have been the count of Tricarico who wrote to Henry VI.

If so, no documents describe his activities during the time covered by the *Liber*. On 10 January 1197, however, he was in the favor of Henry VI, witnessing a document at Barletta.[257] In 1200, during Pope Innocent's regency, he appears with his son by Mabilia, Robert Benedict, who has been made count of Montescaglioso, making a donation to the monastery of S. Michele at Montescaglioso.[258]

---

[251] Niketas Choniates, *O City of Byzantium*, 304–5.

[252] Niketas Choniates, *O City of Byzantium*, 308.

[253] Runciman, *History of the Crusades*, 3:120–25. There is some doubt about where Isaac's death fits into the sequence of events. Runciman puts the death of Isaac after the coup against his son, saying that "he died of grief and judicious ill-treatment" (3:121). Brand says, "Isaac Angelus, already extremely ill, apparently died naturally about this time" (*Byzantium Confronts*, 251). Niketas Choniates says only that Isaac "lay breathing his last," as Alexius faced the coup (308). He does not mention when the last breath ceased.

[254] *Liber*, 27, nn. 1 and 2.

[255] Cuozzor, *Catalogus Baronum Commentario*, 32–33; par. 100.

[256] *Annales Ceccanenses*, 288.

[257] Jamison, *Admiral Eugenius*, 156.

[258] Cuozzo, *Catalogus Baronum Commentario*, 33; par. 100.

Richard of San Germano's chronicle tells that in 1204, when Walter of Brienne was besiged at Terracina in Salerno by the German freebooters, Diepold of Schweinspeunt and his allies, James of Tricario along with Richard of Chieti (*Theate*) came to his rescue and drove the Germans away.[259] When Walter of Brienne died in 1204, James, who was apparently a widower by then himself, married his widow, Tancred's daughter Alberia, and according to Thomas Tuscus, had two children by her, Simon and Adalita, before he died himself.[260]

§**Joan, or Joanna** Plantagenet, 1165–1199. Consort of William II of Sicily (q.v.), and sister of Richard I of England (q. v.).

Though her name is not given, Joanna is mentioned (*Liber*, l. 53) as "the English moon" (*Anglica Luna*) and depicted mourning over her deceased husband in the miniature on fol. 97r. Later, Pietro alludes to the quarrels that Richard undertook on her behalf because Tancred imprisoned her and did not assign her the dower lands provided in her marriage treaty (*Liber*, l. 1062). However, Pietro gives no details about the quarrel and its outcome.

Joanna was born in October 1165 in Angers,[261] the daughter of Eleanor of Aquitaine and Henry II of England. Though negotiations for her marriage with William of Sicily may actually have begun when she was quite young, they did not become serious and practical until 1176.[262] She arrived in Sicily the following year and was given a most gratifying welcome:

> In the same year, before the purification of the Blessed Mary, Joanna, daughter of the aforesaid king of England, who had been sent to marry King William of Sicily, came to Palermo with bishop Giles of York and the other envoys of the king of England her father, who were conducting her. And when she and her retinue entered Palermo by night, the whole city greeted them, and there were such and so many lighted lanterns that the city might almost seem to be burning. The rays of the stars could by no means compare to the great splendor of such lights. Then the king's daughter, upon a royal horse, illustrius in royal robes, was brought to a certain palace, so that she could more pleasantly await the day of her espousal and coronation. And so, a few days having passed, the previously mentioned daughter of the king of England was espoused by King William of Sicily and solemnly crowned at Palermo in the royal chapel in the presence of archbishop Giles of York and the other envoys of the king of England, both clerics and laymen, who had been sent with her, and many archbishops, bishops, counts and barons of the kingdom of the king of Sicily. She was therefore crowned the Sunday before the beginning of Septuagesima, namely the Ides of February, and

---

[259] Richard of San Germano, *Chronica*, 71.
[260] Tuscus, *Gesta*, 499.
[261] Kelly, *Eleanor of Aquitaine*, 103.
[262] Kelly, *Eleanor of Aquitaine*, 132–90.

honorably endowed with the county of Monte Sant'Angelo and the city of
Siponti and the city of Vesti and many other places and castles.

*Eodem anno ante purificationem beate Marie Iohanna, filia predicti regis Angli-
ae, que missa fuerat maritanda regi Willelmo Sicilie, Panormum venit cum Egid-
io Ebroisensi episcopo et aliis nunciis regis Anglie patris sui, qui eam conducebant;
et cum ipsa et sui civitatem Panormi de nocte intrassent, tota civitas eis aplaus-
it, et tot et tanta accensa sunt luminaria, ut civitas penitus crederetur comburi,
et stellarum radii pre fulgore tantorum luminum nullatenus possent comparare.
Ducta est ergo predicta filia regis Anglie super equum regium, vestibus regali-
bus insignita, in quoddam palatium, ut ibidem desponsationis et coronationis
sue diem gratius posset expectare. Paucis itaque elapsis diebus, prenominata regis
Anglie filia desponsata fuit regi Willelmo Sicilie et sollemniter coronata Panormi
in capella regia coram Egidio Ebroisensi episcopo et aliis nunciis regis Anglie, tam
clericis quam laicis, quos cum ea miserat, et coram multis archiepiscopis et episco-
pis, comitibus, et baronibus regni regis Sicilie. Desponsata itaque et coronata fuit
die dominica ante ingressum septuagesime, scilicet Idus Februarii, et dotata hon-
orifice de comitatu Sancti Angeli et civitate Simponti et civitate Veste et pluribus
aliis tam castellis quam locis.*[263]

Sicilian chroniclers seemed pleased with the English marriage; even the short
Chronica S. Mariae de Ferraria alludes to it in its brief summary of William's nota-
ble points.[264] In the absence of any evidence to the contrary, Joanna is assumed to
have been happy in her marriage, but Richard of San Germano[265] mentions that
God, granting so many other benefits to William, had made his consort barren
(*conclusit enim uterum consortis illius, ut non pareret vel conciperet filium*). This must
eventually have become a source of anxiety and sorrow to her.

On William's death, she was apparently denied some of her dower rights and
also imprisoned by Tancred, though chroniclers are vague about exactly what
happened and why; Hoveden simply says that Joanna remained under Tancred's
control (*remansit in custodia regis Thancredi*).[266] It is commonly assumed that she
did not favor Tancred's succession and supported Constance, who had been Wil-
liam's choice. A few months later, her brother Richard arrived in Sicily on the
way to the crusade. Richard first quarreled with Tancred, but afterwards made
peace with him and accepted a large payment of money in place of Joanna's dower
rights. He brought her with him on his crusade, where, it seems, the money was
mostly spent.[267]

Joanna traveled separately from her brother as he sailed back to England;
thus she escaped the shipwreck which sent the Lionheart crossing the emperor's

---

[263] Roger of Hoveden, *Gesta*, 93.

[264] *Chronica S. Mariae de Ferraria*, 31.

[265] *Chronica*, 63.

[266] Richard of San Germano, *Chronica*, 150.

[267] Kelly, *Eleanor of Aquitaine*, 355.

realms in disguise. She married Count Raymond of Toulouse and bore him a son in 1197. Later, pregnant with her second child, and driven from her husband's lands by treacherous and rebellious barons, she came to Fontevrault at Rouen and insisted on being received as a nun; there she died "September 1199, aged thirty-four." Her son Raymond, born in 1197 in Beaucaire, was her husband's heir. She is buried at Fontevrault near her mother, her father, and her brother Richard. [268]

§**John Princeps** (Johannes Princeps, Giovanni Principe), fl. 1191–1198.

John Princeps was a citizen of Salerno, a man of distinguished family, and, in the *Liber*, a supporter of Constance and Henry VI. He is named in a caption on fol. 110r as part of the delegation from Salerno which petitions the emperor at the camp before Naples (ll. 396–407), asking that his consort, Constance, might come to Salerno to guard the city from Tancredine influences. He is otherwise not mentioned in the surviving text. He seems to share his surname, Princeps, with the archdeacon Aldrisio (q.v.), apparently a kinsman. During part of the time when the archbishop Nicholas (q.v.) was a prisoner in Germany, he controlled the ecclesiastical affairs of Salerno, and was "Elect" (archbishop-elect) of Salerno in the years 1195–1196.[269] He still retained some control after the death of Henry VI, as attested by a letter from April 1198[270] in which Pope Innocent III complains that the possessions of the church in Salerno are being held by "John Princeps and Master Gerard, who, while the archbishop in question is detained in chains, have tried to invade the place through laymen's power" (*Ioannem Principem et magistrum Gerardum, qui, memorato archiepiscopo detento in vinculis, locum eius invadere per laicalem potentiam attentarunt*). Apparently a party among the clerics at Salerno wished to put him in place of Nicholas of Ajello, but Innocent III clearly concedes no validity to his claims.

§**John (Ioannes or Johannes) of Ajello,** fl. 1194. Son of Matthew of Ajello, brother of Archbishop Nicholas of Salerno, and of Richard, count of Ajello.

Identified as "the brother of the archbishop Nicholas," John appears on fol. 136r, cap. 13, swearing the conspiratorial oath along with his two brothers, the former Queen Sibylla, and the rest. Nothing further is known of him. Innocent III's anonymous biographer mentions that Henry VI had the brothers (in the plural) of Archbishop Nicholas blinded,[271] but no sources other than Pietro give the third brother a name or assign a particular role to him.

§**Jordan Lupin,** fl. 1175–1197. Count of Bovino.

See **Lupin brothers,** Hugh (II) and Jordan.

---

[268] Kelly, *Eleanor of Aquitaine*, 354–55, and 404, n. 25 to chap. 31.

[269] Kölzer, "Bildkommentar," 95, 297.

[270] Siragusa, *Liber ad honorem*, 129–30, n. 5; PL 214, col. 55.

[271] *The Deeds of Innocent III*, 18; chap. 18.

§Lucius III, Pope, r. 1181–1185.[272]

The *Liber* (ll. 22–24) states that Pope Lucius III had been "a matchmaker" (*pronuba*) for the marriage between Henry VI and Constance. On fol. 96r, he is said to bless the couple as they depart for Germany (cap. 12). The first claim has been doubted but may be true, while the second is impossible, since Lucius died before the wedding (see Introduction, C.9).

Lucius's name was originally Ubaldo Allucingol. He had been made cardinal-bishop of Ostia by Pope Alexander III and was elected pope on the latter's death, "with great dispatch to avoid the possibility of a schism."[273] Lucius tended to be conciliatory toward secular monarchs. Besides, ominous events in the Holy Land caused him to focus much attention on organizing a crusade. At a conference in Verona in 1184, he discussed this with Frederick Barbarossa, along with many other issues, while Barbarossa negotiated the match between his son Henry VI and Constance of Hauteville, paternal aunt of William II.[274] The couple's betrothal was sworn in Augsburg, 19 October 1184. Lucius died, 25 November 1185,[275] after **Constance** had reached her father-in-law's realms, but a few weeks before the marriage.

§Lupin brothers, Hugh (II) and Jordan, fl. 1175–1197. Noblemen of Calabrian origin, kinsmen of the empress.

The "great twin brothers, . . . the Lupins" (*gemini fratres magni . . . Lupini*) are mentioned (l. 300) among those who, after William II's death, invited Henry VI to claim Sicily as his rightful kingdom. They are not mentioned again. Pietro apparently wishes them to be understood as loyalists to the cause of Henry and Constance, but they seem to have switched sides.

Hugh and his brother Jordan were sons of Hugh (I) Lupin and Clementia, the countess of Catanzaro. Their mother, a descendant of an elder half-brother of the Great Count Roger and thus a blood relation of the empress,[276] was the heiress of Catanzaro in Calabria. Perhaps instigated by her mother and her maternal uncles, she, in her youth, rebelled against King William I. For this, her uncles were executed in 1162, while she and her mother were brought as prisoners to Palermo. Apparently she was among those freed by the queen-mother, Margaret, during William II's minority. Later, she married Hugh Lupin, a kinsman of the queen, or at least of the queen's favored kinsman, Stephen du Perche. In 1168,

---

[272] Walsh, *Illustrated History*, 252.
[273] McGinn, *The Calabrian Abbot*, 10.
[274] Chalandon, *Histoire*, 2:385.
[275] Siragusa, *Liber ad honorem*, 5, n. 5.
[276] Jamison, *Admiral Eugenius*, 158–59; see Genealogical Table 1.

when the government was seized by a coalition hostile to Stephen, Hugh was spared exile because the victors did not think him very dangerous.[277]

Documents show that members of this family continued in royal service, although it is not always possible to distinguish the father Hugh from his son of the same name.[278]

Quite possibly Pietro uses the word "twin" figuratively when speaking of the brothers, simply meaning "two," since he also states that Tancred reaches Sicily

---

[277] Falcandus, *La Historia*, 35, 75–77, 162–63; *History of the Tyrants*, trans. Loud and Wiedemann, 90, 126–27, 215 and n. 272. Although for the convenience of English-speaking readers I provide citations to the Loud and Wiedemann translation, in this case my summary and its implications about Hugh (I) Lupin clash with those of Loud and Wiedemann. Falcandus writes (*La Historia*, 162–63):

> *(C)ogitabant etiam curie magnates Hugonem comitem Catacensem, quia cancellarii consanguineus erat, expellere. Sed quia nullius consilii audacie homo erat ut vel occulte paraturus insidias, vel ex precipiti magnum ausurus aliquid timeretur, maluerunt ei parcere, sperantes eo ipso posse regine indignationem aliquatenus mitigari.*

> The magnates of the Curia also considered expelling Hugh, the count of Catanzaro, because he was a blood relation of the chancellor. But since he [Count Hugh] was not a man of bold purpose, the sort who either would secretly prepare ambushes or, from headlong impulse, dare to do any great thing to make himself feared, they chose instead to spare him, hoping that by this in itself they might soften the Queen's indignation to some extent.

Loud and Wiedemann apparently take *"nullius consilii audacie homo"* (which I read literally as "a man of no counsel of audacity") to mean something like "a man of recklessness, of no counsel." Thus their translation reads "a stupid and violent man" (*History of the Tyrants*, 215).

[278] In some of these documents, where "Hugh Lupin" appears alone, the elder Hugh, the father, is likely meant. However, when Hugh and Jordan appear together, the reference is probably to the sons. Siragusa, *Liber ad honorem*, 27, n. 4, writes, "Hugh is a witness in a documento of 15 August 1176 (cf Garufi, *Catal[ogo] del tabulario di S. M[aria] la Nuova in Monreale*, p. 11). . . . Hugh and Jordan are found together in a document of 1183 and in another of 1189 (Garufi, *Documenti inediti dell' epoca Normanna*, p. 191 and p. 216). In the first document, Hugh calls himself '*domini regis privatus* [privy councilor of the lord king]', in the second, '*Lupinus domini regis senescalcus*, [Lupin the seneschal of the lord king].'" Siragusa also points the reader to no. 418 in the collection published by Karl Friedrich Stumpf-Brentano, in *Acta imperii adhuc inedita* (Vol. 3 of *Die Reichskanzler vornehmlich des X., XI., und XII. Jahrhunderts*, Innsbruck, 1865–1881), 584–85. In this documented, dated 11 January 1195, Henry VI and Constance confirm the privileges of William II's foundation at Monreale. Hugh and Jordan Lupin are both witnesses, along with Bartholomew, archbishop of Palermo, Boniface, marquis of Montferrat, Conrad (Urslingen), duke of Spoleto, and Henry of Kalden, among others.

For a translation of the 1183 document, see Johns, *Arabic Administration*, 321 (Private 20).

literally "with twin offspring" (*gemina cum prole*) (l. 172), when the miniatures (fol. 102r, cap. 2) clearly show that these boys are of different ages. (Therefore my translation reads "with double offspring.") Still, the birthdates of the Lupin brothers are not known, though Hugh (II), named after his father, is presumably the elder. He is in fact the one who succeeded to the county of Catanzaro in 1195, presumably on the death of his father. [279]

By that time, Henry VI had gained his victory, and the brothers were in his favor. Previously though, at Tancred's accession, in 1189–1190, the elder Hugh still lived and neither of his sons had a title, although Hugh apparently had already held the office of seneschal under William II. Tancred, looking for loyal and youthful support, gave them counties in Apulian territory, Conversano to Hugh and Bovino to Jordan. The new counts served Tancred for a time, but "both went over to Henry VI at some unknown date after the summer of 1192 and are found frequently at his court in the winter and summer of 1194–1195, attesting imperial diplomas."[280] On "10 January 1197" another Lupin, "Herricus or Henricus," appears, and "attests an imperial document as count of Conversano," possibly the son of Hugh II, who, having succeeded his father as count of Catanzaro, passed his newer county to his eldest son.[281]

But there is no more clear record of these Lupins as living people, merely of the disposition of their property. Jamison believes they were caught up in the conspiracy of 1197, and were perhaps its leaders. In 1197 or 1198 Hugh's county, Conversano, was given to Berardus Gentilis, count of Loreto.[282] Jordan's county, Bovino, "disappears altogether" from the record, and in 1201 a house which had once belonged to Jordan was granted to someone else. Quite possibly Jordan Lupin is the same person as the "Jordan of Sicily" (*Jordanus de Sicilia*) mentioned in the *Annales Stadenses*, who, because he aimed at the throne, was executed by having "a crown . . . nailed to his head." [283] Though the victim's name is not widely reported, the gruesome punishment for the pretender is mentioned by many other chronicles.[284] See also the biographical sketch for **Constance** of Hauteville, above.

§**Mandonia** or **Medania**, fl. 1193–1200. Daughter of Tancred and his consort Sibylla.

Pietro does not name any of Tancred's daughters, but Tancred alludes to the three of them in l. 771: "The six of us are unwarlike: myself, my daughters, my

---

[279] Jamison, *Admiral Eugenius,* 158.

[280] Jamison, *Admiral Eugenius,* 159.

[281] Jamison, *Admiral Eugenius,* 159.

[282] Cuozzo, *Catalogus Baronum Commentario,* 358; par. 1192.

[283] Jamison, *Admiral Eugenius,* 158–59. *Annales Stadenses,* MGH SS 16 (Hanover: Hahn, 1859), 271–379, here 352.

[284] Including Niketas Choniates, *O City of Byzantium,* 262. Also *Annales Marbacenses,* 69–70.

son, my wife" (*Sex sumus inbelles: ego, nate, filius, uxor*). The other two sisters are Alberia (the eldest) and Constance.

Sources give contradictory information about Mandonia. One[285] says that she did not marry, while another states that she became the wife of Giovanni Sforza of Sanseverino and Avezzano.[286]

§**Manuel I Comnenus**, ca. 1123[287]–1180; Byzantine emperor, r. 1143–1180.

Manuel is mentioned once in the *Liber* (l. 161) as the emperor under whom **Andronicus I Comnenus** (q.v.) endured a long exile.

Manuel had been the youngest of the four sons of the Emperor John II, of whom the eldest, Alexius, had already been associated with his father in the imperium when he died suddenly in 1142. The second brother, Andronicus, died soon afterwards. Then, according to a story told quite similarly by Kinnamos and Niketas Choniates at the openings of their chronicles, the Emperor John II himself, fatally wounded in a boar-hunt in April 1143, decided to pass over his third son, Isaac, and designate his youngest son, Manuel, as his heir. Thus Manuel succeeded to the throne, but not without some quick maneuvering to exclude his elder brother.

Manuel was an energetic ruler who, among other things, made vigorous efforts to re-establish Byzantine power in the west, both against the Norman kingdom of Sicily and against the German emperor, posing sometimes as the defender of the pope (see Introduction, C.8). His two marriages involved connections with each of these powers in turn. Manuel's first wife, Bertha of Sulzbach, was the sister-in-law of Conrad III of Hohenstaufen. Upon her marriage, she took the name Irene. Her daughter by Manuel, Maria Porphyrogenita, was for some time the sole heiress of the empire. However, his second wife, Princess Marie of Antioch, renamed Xena after her marriage, bore a son, Alexius, in 1169.[288]

In the marriages of his children, Manuel also sealed alliances with the west, although his conduct toward William of Sicily departs strangely from that pattern. In 1172, a marriage was definitely arranged between Maria Porphyrogenita and the youthful William, but for unknown reasons, Manuel changed his mind and simply did not send his daughter to Sicily during the time agreed. This so embittered the chronicler Romuald of Salerno that he attributes Manuel's disastrous defeat at Myriocephalum, at the hands of the sultan of Iconium in 1176, to divine punishment for this perfidious behavior.[289] Manuel's last days were consumed with anxieties about the magnitude of that catastrophe and with worries

---

[285] Tuscus, *Gesta*, 499.

[286] Siragusa, *Liber ad honorem*, 59, n. 2, citing Rocco Pirri, *Chronologia Regum Siciliae* (Palermo, 1643), 72.

[287] This conjectural date of birth is supplied by Brand, *Byzantium Confronts*, 277.

[288] Brand, *Byzantium Confronts*, 14.

[289] *Chronicon*, 261; 267–68.

about the future.[290] Still, he did what he could to smooth the way for his young son, through alliances and diplomatic activity. He arranged a marriage between Maria Porphyrogenita and Rainier of Montferrat, a brother of the Marquis **Conrad** (q.v.) who was later king of Jerusalem. He brought Agnes, a daughter of the French king, Louis VII, to Constantinople to marry his son Alexius. He sought reconciliation with his exiled cousin Andronicus and collected pledges for help from various rulers, in exchange for unknown promises and concessions.[291] Unfortunately, this was not enough (see **Alexius** II and **Andronicus**).

§**Margarito** of Brindisi, Admiral, fl. 1186–1198.

Margarito is depicted in fol. 136r, cap. 6, swearing the conspiratorial oath with Archbishop Nicholas and Sibylla, the former queen. The associated versepage, which might have described his part in the plot, is missing. He is not otherwise mentioned in the surviving portions of the *Liber*, although it is clear from other sources that he played an important part in the events.

Niketas Choniates calls him "Megareites," and describes him as "the most formidable pirate on the high seas at that time,"[292] that is, in the late 1180s, after William II's invasion of Byzantine territory in 1185. Margarito came to the aid of the Isaac Comnenus who had declared himself emperor in Cyprus and allied himself to **William** II of Sicily (q.v.) while **Andronicus** (q.v.) was in control of Byzantium. When Isaac Angelus, new to the throne, attacked the new Cypriot ruler, William II protected him through Margarito. In the last years of William II of Sicily, as preparations for the third crusade were underway, Margarito was made Count of Malta and had charge of the fleet.[293] It was his responsibility to keep the sea free of Turks and pirates and to gaurantee safe passage for the crusading armies to Palestine. He performed this task very effectively.

From Tancred, after he took the throne, Margarito received charge of the Sicilian navies. His activities in the bay of Naples prevented Henry VI from fully blockading the city.[294] According to several chroniclers,[295] he is the one who conveyed Constance, the captive empress, from Salerno to Messina in 1191. Sicardo da Cremona, for example, writes in his chronicle that "a certain pirate named Margaritus, capturing Augusta, and bringing her as far as the royal city, that is, Palermo, guarded her with most worthy honor" (*sed Augustam quidam pyrata nomine Margaritus aput Salernum capiens eam regalem ad urbem, Panormum scilicet, usque deducans, honestate dignissima conservavit*).[296]

---

[290] Runciman, *History of the Crusades*, 2:413–14.

[291] Brand, *Byzantium Confronts*, 14–30.

[292] *O City of Byzantium*, 204.

[293] Toeche, *Kaiser Heinrich VI*, 197.

[294] Toeche, *Kaiser Heinrich VI*, 98.

[295] Siragusa, *Liber ad honorem*, 133, n. 1.

[296] Sicardus Cremonensis Episcopus, *Cronica*, ed. Oswald Holder-Egger, MGH 21 (Hanover: Hahn, 1905), 22–188, here 173–74.

During Henry VI's second campaign, illness evidently kept Margarito from making effective resistance.[297] Then Henry, making peace with Tancred's widow, also made Margarito the Duke of Durazzo, apparently intending to use his military skills in an eastern campaign.[298] However, a number of sources, not merely the *Liber*, report that he was among those accused of conspiring against the emperor.[299] Also, several report that he was blinded in prison.[300] After the emperor's death, he was released and came to Rome.[301] His further activities are uncertain. Roger of Hoveden[302] reports that he subsequently visited King Philip Augustus in France to discuss strategies for conquering Constantinople, but was murdered by one of his own servants after he returned to Rome.

§**Markwald** or Markward of of Anweiler or Annweiler, fl. 1185–1201. German *ministerialis* and nobleman, seneschal to Henry VI.

Markwald, called *Marchisius* in the text of the *Liber*, is depicted on fol. 131r (cap. 2), with the impressive forces which Henry VI musters for his second and successful invasion of Sicily in 1194. Later, in l. 1561, he is named *Marcualdus* in an idealized roster of Henry's officials, attending to the business of the Sicilian kingdom after conquest, and cap. 3 once more identifies him in the accompanying miniature (fol. 147r). His activities are also discussed in the Introduction, C. 15–17.

The town, Anweiler, from which Markwald draws his name, is near "the imperial castle of Trifels." He came from a family of *ministeriales*, and became *dapifer* or seneschal to Henry VI some time after the young king was knighted in 1184. There is documentary evidence of his presence from 1185 on.[303]

Markwald accompanied Barbarossa on his crusade, and was among the envoys he sent to Constantinople to negotiate the Treaty of Adrianople.[304] After Barbarossa's death, he returned to Henry's service. As the commander of Henry's naval forces, it was his particular task to see that the cities of Pisa and Genoa both delivered what they promised, and that their fleets, once assembled, fought the enemy instead of one another.[305] After the conquest in 1194, as a reward for

---

[297] Jamison, *Admiral Eugenius*, 114.

[298] Jamison, *Admiral Eugenius*, 119.

[299] Jamison, *Admiral Eugenius*, 155.

[300] Including Otto of St. Blaise in his *Continuatio* (chap. 39) and Roger of Hoveden, *Chronica*, 181–82.

[301] Jamison, *Admiral Eugenius*, 164.

[302] Chronica, 181–82. Given the active life reported of him after his release, Chalandon, *Histoire*, 2:491, expresses some doubt that he could really have been blinded.

[303] Van Cleve, *Markward*, 20–22. Van Cleve was unable to establish a birth date for Markwald.

[304] Brand, *Byzantium Confronts*, 185.

[305] Reisinger, *Tankred von Lecce*, 180.

his great service, Markwald was given his freedom and made margrave of Ancona, duke of Ravenna, and count of Romagna.[306]

During the last, dangerous conspiracy in 1197, it was to Markwald (and Henry of Kalden, q.v.) that Henry turned. They induced Messina to "shut the gates" on the conspirators, and with the help of armies gathered for the crusade, they put down the rebellion.[307] Markward was with the emperor when he died and received from him a document which later became controversial, since it was captured after a battle near Monreale in June 1200.[308] Though described by the pope's biographer as the emperor's testament,[309] Van Cleve explains that it consisted, rather, of Henry's instructions about the way his successors should negotiate with the pope.[310] Henry could not, however, control the actions of the German princes after his death. There was a disputed election, and his brother, Philip of Swabia, became the claimant for the Hohenstaufen cause. Meanwhile, Constance dismissed Markward and the other Germans from her government. Markward, who acknowledged Philip of Swabia as his king "as early as 28 August 1198,"[311] obeyed her orders to leave the kingdom during her lifetime, but returned after her death and attempted to follow Henry's instructions and those of Philip of Swabia. Van Cleve, at least, takes his word that he did this in good faith, though Innocent III and his biographer continually assert that Markward was merely out for himself, that he spread stories that young Frederick II was "not the son of either the emperor or the empress, but a substitute,"[312] and that he wished to become king of Sicily himself. His actions and the pope's attempts to counter them kept Sicily in a state of upheaval. Markward reached the height of his power when he successfully seized the royal palace and the boy-king in the fall of 1202.[313] He died a few months later, while undergoing surgery for kidney stones.[314]

§**Matthew**, fl. 1191–1199, archbishop of Capua.

The archbishop is first mentioned in l. 301 as one of those who wrote inviting Henry VI to claim his crown. Later (ll. 344–351) he persuades his city, Capua, to receive the emperor, and is depicted on the miniature (fol. 108r) with the caption identifying him as "Capuan physician" (*Capuanus ypocraticus*). In ll. 412–417, he is apparently given the responsibility to accompany the empress Constance to

---

[306] Schubring, *Die Herzoge von Urslingen*, 33.

[307] Csendes, *Heinrich VI*, 190.

[308] *Deeds of Innocent III*, 34 and n. 53; chap. 27.

[309] *"testamentum imperatoris"; Gesta Innocent III*, 34 (chap. 27).

[310] *Emperor*, 38; *Markward*, 67.

[311] Van Cleve, *Emperor Frederick II*, 38.

[312] *Deeds of Pope Innocent III*, 25; chap. 23. *Gesta Innocent III* 22, "suppositus partus."

[313] Van Cleve, *Emperor Frederick II*, 49.

[314] *Deeds of Pope Innocent III*, 34 and n. 52; 46–47 (chap. 35).

Salerno and see that all goes well. His activities in the subsequent exchange of messages and envoys can be assumed, but the poem does not give details.

After the death of Constance, Matthew was one of the council of *familiares* governing the kingdom during her son's minority. He died some time after April and before September of 1199.[315]

§**Matthew** of Ajello, fl. 1161–1193. Royal official in the kingdom of Sicily; Tancred's chancellor.

Matthew is mentioned and depicted numerous times in the *Liber*. As Pietro tells it, he decided to make Tancred king and saw that it was done, even persuading Walter, Constance's chief supporter, to go along (ll. 100–165; fols. 100r, 101r, 102r). Afterwards he was Tancred's most important advisor, whom Tancred recommended to his consort Sibylla for the delicate problem of dealing with the captive empress (ll. 913–964; fol. 126r). Matthew bathes in the blood of murdered children (fol. 127r) in order to soothe his gout and urges Tancred to be equally ruthless in pursuing his ends (ll. 142–165).

According to the chronicler Romuald of Salerno, Matthew was brought up in the royal palace (presumably under King Roger, since Romuald alludes to events in 1167, when Matthew was clearly an adult): "the aforesaid Matthew was a wise and discreet man, and he had been brought up in the royal palace from boyhood, and he was of proven fidelity in royal business" (*praedictus Matthaeus homo erat sapiens et discretus, et in aula regia a puero enutritus, et in agendis regiis probatae fidelitatis inventus*).[316] The most vivid chronicler of this period, Hugo Falcandus, gives a different view of him. According to Falcandus, Matthew was a supporter and pupil of Admiral Maio (the overall villain of Falcandus's work) and learned craftiness from him. Hence, he was imprisoned in the wake of Admiral Maio's murder in 1160, but a few months later, after **William** I (q. v.) survived the coup against him, he was removed from prison because he was thought to be the only man who could reconstitute from memory the records which had been destroyed in the sack of the palace.[317] Queen **Sibylla** (q.v.) may have this in mind when she addresses Matthew as "ancient library of the dukes" (*veterum bibliotheca ducum*); see commentary on l. 926.

Matthew continued to wield powerful influence during the rest of William I's reign, and William II's as well. Falcandus states, "Matthew the notary, who could do much in the Curia, tried to imitate the ways and customs of the admiral,

---

[315] Van Cleve, *Markward*, 126.

[316] *Chronicon*, 257. See also Loud and Wiedemann's translation of an excerpt from *Chronicon sive Annales*, years 1153–1169, in *History of the Tyrants*, 219–43, here 242.

[317] *La Historia*, 42–44, 69; *History of the Tyrants*, 99, 121. See also Johns, *Arabic Administration*, 177, 220, 310 (*Diwani* 35). An Arabic document suggests that Matthew may already have been restored to the government by February, shortly before before the coup attempt in March.

showing himself affable to all, and he would smile most upon those whom he hated" (*Matheus ergo notarius, cum iam plurimum posset in curia, disposuerat admirati ritus et consuetudines imitari, omnibusque se prebens affabilem, eis maxime quos oderat arridebat*).[318] In the *Liber*, he shows the same capacity to ingratiate himself, at least where Walter the archbishop and Queen Sibylla are concerned, but does take a more bracing tone with Tancred.

Falcandus adds that, knowing that he could not be "the great admiral" as Maio was, he hoped instead to be chancellor. However, during William II's reign he was allowed only to be vice-chancellor (*vicecancellarius*), the title with which he signs, for example, the document describing Joanna Plantagenet's dowry.[319] According to Richard of San Germano's chronicle, Matthew became, along with Walter of Palermo, one of William II's two most important advisors, but although the two pretended to mutual friendship, they secretly hated each other. Hence Walter's support for the Hohenstaufen marriage and succession, and Matthew's opposition to it.[320]

After William's death, Matthew engineered Tancred's succession and became his chancellor. His son **Richard** (q.v.) then became count of Ajello, providing a surname which has traditionally been applied retrospectively to the whole family. Matthew died 21 July 1193.[321]

Pietro abusively calls Matthew a "bigamous priest" in cap. 2 on 100r; he also calls him a "bigamist" several times (ll. 140, 938–939, 990, and 993, and fols. 100r, 101r, 102r, 126r, 127r). In fact, there are no records that he was a priest, although he adopted a religious affiliation later in his life and "put on the ecclesiastical habit as a 'converso' ('oblatus') in the Basilian monastery of Messina."[322] Though he married twice, his first wife died before he married the second.[323] However, see note on l. 34.

§**Matthew Burrel** or Borell, fl. 1191. Castellan (for Tancred) of Rocca D'Arce.

Matthew Burrel is identified by a caption as the man handing over the keys of Rocca D'Arce to Henry VI on fol. 108r, an event that happened just before

---

[318] *La Historia*, 83; *History of the Tyrants*, trans. Loud and Wiedemann, 133.

[319] As set down in Roger of Hoveden's *Gesta*, 94.

[320] *Chronica*, 63.

[321] Jamison, *Admiral Eugenius*, 94.

[322] Siragusa, *Liber ad honorem*, 137, n. 3, referring to "documents of the *Tabulario* of Messina" as cited by Pirri, *Sicilia Sacra* (2:980) 3rd ed. 2 vols. (Palermo, 1733).

[323] Siragusa, *Liber ad honorem*, 137, n. 3. Siragusa writes: "Matthew of Ajello had, indeed, two wives. The first, 'Sica,' was already dead in 1171, and the second, 'Giuditta,' died on 25 June 1180, as I now show from the *Liber Confratrum ecclesie Salerno*, page 31 B, col 4a. See the documents of March and May of 1171, and, in Garufi, *Documenti inediti dell'epoca Normanna*, pp. 129 and 137. In his partisan hatred, the poet translates two legitimate marriages into bigamy, and bigamy itself, here as elsewhere in the poem, he makes simultaneous with the improper status of priest."

the beginning of May in 1191. Little more is known about this man or about his later career. Siragusa writes,[324]

> The well-known Burello family was one of the most considerable in the kingdom of Sicily. Another Matthew, perhaps a forebear of the defender of Rocca d'Arce, signed a document of 1113;[325] a Mario, *vir eloquentissimus* ["a most eloquent man"] took a notable part in the sedition which disturbed the reign of William I.[326]

The Borell family, orginally from the Abruzzi, branched out "south-westwards from their ancestral lands in the upper Sangro valley."[327]

§**Molise**, count of. See Roger, count of Molise.

§**Nicholas of Ajello**, 1162[328] –1121. archbishop of Salerno, r. 1182–1121.

Nicholas of Ajello was the archbishop of Salerno from 1182 until about 1221. Nicholas was the son of **Matthew** of Ajello (q.v.). No doubt his father's prominent position as the vice-chancellor of King William II helped him obtain his position as archbishop of Salerno in 1182, after the death of the famous Romuald II of Salerno, the chronicler. When, after William II's death in 1189, Matthew become one of Tancred's most important supporters, Nicholas gave him crucial backing, although he was thwarted within the diocese by the archdeacon Aldrisio (q.v.) who took the part of Henry VI and Constance. Nicholas's brother **Richard** (q.v.) was made count of Ajello by a grateful King Tancred. He and his brother were both made *familiares* of King Tancred,[329] a title given to the king's closest and most important counselors. Nicholas took a leading part in Tancred's political and military actions against Henry, but apparently was not able to keep his city, Salerno, from initially going over to Henry VI and inviting Constance to reside within it. He remained at Naples during the siege of 1191. In ll. 387–389, Pietro states that when **Richard**, count of Acerra (q. v.), Tancred's

---

[324] *Liber ad honorem*, 31, n. 1.

[325] Siragusa, *Liber ad honorem*, 31, n. 1. Here Siragusa refers to a document in Garufi, *Documenti inediti*, 7–11.

[326] Siragusa, *Liber ad honorem*, 31, n. 1. Here Siragusa refers the reader to his edition of Falcandus (*La Historia*, 29, 78, 80). The equivalent passages appear in Loud and Wiedemann's translation, *History of the Tyrants of Sicily*, 83, 129, and 131, where this person is called Mario Borell.

[327] Loud, *Age of Robert Guiscard*, 77.

[328] No record of his birth is given, but if we conjecture that he was at least twenty years old when be became archbishop of Salerno, 1162 would be a reasonable guess. Accessible sources do not record which of Matthew's wives was the mother of Nicholas, but if the above conjectural birth date is correct, she must have been Mathew's first wife, Sica, known to have been dead by 1171; see biographical sketch for **Matthew of Ajello**, above. See also Kölzer, "Bildkommentar," 162.

[329] Jamison, *Admiral Eugenius*, 94.

brother-in-law, was wounded, Nicholas girded on his sword and took over military command. Pietro clearly implies that this was an impious deed.[330] Perhaps partly due to the damaged state of the *Liber*, Nicholas drops from sight until after Tancred's death, Henry VI's victory, and Sibylla's surrender and pardon. Then he suddenly becomes the major organizing figure in the conspiracy against the emperor's life. Surviving sources do nothing to clarify what was happening at this time. Accounts are contradictory,[331] but some documents indicate that Nicholas avoided capture when Salerno fell (September 1194) and rejoined Queen Sibylla.[332] Pietro's assumption, thus, is apparently that Nicholas was reconciled to Henry VI along with Sibylla, and then, as an expression of his basically treacherous and opportunistic nature, organized the conspiracy, for which the poet calls him "Archbishop Caiaphas" (*Caypha Presul*) (l. 1338).

With Sibylla, her family, and the other prisoners, he was sent to Germany around May 1194.[333] Pope Celestine III tried in vain to persuade the emperor to release him; and after Henry's death in 1197, Innocent III, through a delicate maneuver, successfully induced Philip of Swabia to do so, by permitting German bishops, in return for the release of Nicholas, to absolve Philip of a sentence of excommunication he had incurred during the previous reign (see Introduction, C.15). This way, Innocent did not have to become personally reconciled with Philip. The release of Nicholas did not, however, result in his re-instatement, and Innocent III was still trying unsuccessfully to bring this about when the Empress Constance died.[334] The archbishop was free in 1199, but did not succeed

---

[330] However, Siragusa, *Liber ad honorem*, 34–35, n. 2, while pointing out that Pietro is the only source to mention this incident, also summarizes a scholarly controversy which seems to resolve the matter in the archbishop's favor: "Concerning the circumstance that Nicholas had girded on the sword during the siege of Naples . . . . Paesano (*Mem. della chiesa Salernitana* 2:244) debates whether in such cases an ecclesiastic may make use of arms, and concludes that the deed attributed to the archbishop Nicholas was licit and legitimate."

[331] Crisci, *Salerno Sacra*, 79, states that Nicholas and his brothers were made prisoner 17 September 1194 (when Salerno fell), and cites documents which state that they were already in Germany as prisoners when the conspiracy took place in December 1194.

[332] Jamison, *Admiral Eugenius*, 117–18, n.4: "Nicholas was certainly in Palermo in October, because the diplomas of William and Sybilla that month are given under the hands of two archbishops, Bartolomeo of Palermo and Nicholas of Salerno." Here Jamison also points out that fol. 134r of the *Liber*, illustrating verses which claim that the "little king" has taken refuge at Caltabellota, shows "the two heads, one mitered, the other a child's, looking out from the battlements" of the fortress. Though aware that these are probably "a later addition" to the drawing, she says, "if so, they obviously recall a tradition."

[333] Jamison, *Admiral Eugenius*, 124.

[334] *Deeds of Pope Innocent III*, 20–21; chap. 22.

in regaining possession of his archbishopric until 1205. [335] Since Nicholas owed so much to Innocent III, he might have been expected to adhere loyally to the latter's policies in the future, but this apparently did not happen. A document of 1212 shows him supporting Otto of Brunswick's claims on the Kingdom of Sicily, [336] an allegiance never approved by the pope, since Innocent's policy was to keep the "Holy Roman Empire" and the Norman kingdom of Sicily under separate monarchs. That was chiefly why Innocent had backed Otto for the imperial crown instead of his young ward Frederick, whose claims, initially widely recognized in Germany and supported by his uncle Philip, Innocent consistently denied (see Introduction, C.17). On the other hand, he firmly supported young Frederick as king of Sicily, and when Otto invaded the realm, Innocent changed his position on his ward's rights to the empire and encouraged a new election. It seems that Nicholas ultimately went along with this, and by 1216 he had apparently made his peace with the Hohenstaufen. In that year the empress, Frederick II's first consort, Constance of Aragon, along with with her son Henry (then about five years old), granted to Archbishop Nicholas claims on some of the revenues of Eboli, at the request of his brother Richard. [337] After Frederick II returned from Germany, he confirmed the archbishopric's privileges. [338] That apparently ended Nicholas's struggles against the Hohenstaufen, at least as a living man. After his death, admittedly, the see of Salerno was vacant around five years, [339] apparently because he had chosen his own successor, and Frederick II was not inclined to trust his judgement. [340]

Nicholas died 10 February, in 1221 or 1222. [341]

---

[335] Mario Del Treppo, "Aiello, Nicolò d'," *Dizionario Biografico degli Italiani,* 1 (1960), 518–19.

[336] Del Treppo, "Aiello, Nicolò d'," 518–19.

[337] Siragusa (*Liber,* 143, n. 3) refers to this document, by which, in 1216, Constance of Aragon with her son Henry grants to the Archbishop Nicholas the tithes on the "platearum et plancarum terre Eboli" [the tolls and {vineyard produce?} of the territory of Eboli] on the pleading of Nicholas the archbishop, as well as his brother. His source is Eduard Winkelmann, *Acta imperii inedita saeculi XIII: Urkunden und Briefe zur Geschichte des Kaiserreichs und des Königreichs Sicilien in den Jahren 1198–1273* (Innsbruck 1880–1885) 376.

[338] Huillard-Bréholles, *Historia Diplomatica,* 2:111.

[339] Crisci, *Salerno Sacra,* 78–80.

[340] Kantorowicz, *Emperor Frederick the Second,* 145.

[341] According to Crisci, *Salerno Sacra,* 78–80, the *Liber Confratrum* of the Cathedral at Salerno says that he died 10 February 1221. Kölzer, "Personenverzeichnis," 297, gives him a death date of 1222, perhaps because, as the Crisci account explains, another document says that "he lived in his episcopacy around 40 years" *(vixit in pontificatu annos 40 circa)* which would produce a date of death in 1222.

§**Philip**, count of Balvano, fl. 1175–1197.

In *Liber* l. 299, "Philip," not otherwise described, writes along with three sons to invite Henry VI to claim the crown of Sicily. He has been plausibly identified as Count Philip of Balvano. The count and his three sons (Roger, Thomas, and Simon) were the only supporters Count **Roger** of Andria (q.v.) had left in the fall of 1190, after Henry VI's commander, Henry Testa, had withdrawn. This is attested by a document drawn up for Roger of Andria at Ascoli Satriano, presumably in the "autumn" of 1190, and signed by Roger himself, by his son Richard, and by the three sons of Count Philip mentioned above, among others.[342]

When Richard, count of Conza and Carinola, was arrested with the conspirators of 1194, Henry VI conferred the county of Conza upon Philip, allowing Philip's eldest son Roger to receive the county of Balvano during his lifetime, a title by which he is described in a document of 18 October 1196, where he is also called "an imperial justiciar."[343]

Philip first appears on the record in 1155, when he comes to court in place of his uncle Gilbert, who was apparently ailing (he died the following year), to give an account of the feudal obligations he owed.[344] By 1174, he has four sons—the three named above, and another, Geoffrey. In 1183, he acts as a royal constable and justiciar, along with Elias of Gesualdo (q.v.), in settling quarrels over a disputed property. In 1197, he is still involved in administering his own property, but by 1199 he is dead.[345]

§**Philip Guarna**, fl. 1184–1195. Salernitan supporter of Henry VI.

Philip Guarna appears in l. 1152, accompanying Archdeacon Aldrisio on his mission to save Salerno from destruction by begging pardon from Henry VI. The next page of miniatures, missing from the manuscript, probably depicted this Philip with Aldrisio, and the missing verses on the opposite side of that page presumably would have explained the outcome of their attempt, perhaps even assigning Philip a larger role. Philip's father was Lucas Guarna, castellan at Mandra, which belonged to Count Robert of Caserta, royal justiciar, according to *Catalogus Baronum.*[346]

Lucas, his father, was justiciar in the the principate of Salerno from 1171–1189.[347] Philip, with his father Lucas Guarna, witnessed a document in 1184 in which William of San Severino confirmed a donation to the abbey of Cava.[348] His mother's name was Dofa, and his full sister (her name not given in

---

[342] Jamison, *Admiral Eugenius,* 82; 319–21; Appendix 1.

[343] Jamison, *Admiral Eugenius,* 321, n. 2.

[344] Cuozzo, *Catalogus Baronum Commentario,* 118; par. 433.

[345] Cuozzo, *Catalogus Baronum Commentario,* 190–91; par. 702.

[346] Toeche, *Heinrich VI,* 147, n. 1; *Catalogus baronum Neapolitano in regno versantium,* in *Cronisti e Scrittori Sincroni della Dominazione Normanna,* par. 579.

[347] Cuozzo, *Catalogus Baronum Comentario,* 151, par. 517*[*sic*].

[348] Cuozzo, *Catalogus Baronum Comentario,* 122, par. 438.

the sources) was the wife of William of Pistillio (q.v.). In some documents dated from 1179 and 1195, Philip appears as knight (*miles*), and in 1195, he was made count of Marsico or at least administrator of the county.[349] See below, William, count of Marsico.

§**Philip of Swabia**, 1177–1208.[350] Brother of Henry VI; German king (King of the Romans), reign (contested) 1198–1208.

Philip is mentioned in the *Liber* (l. 1292) as being in love with the Byzantine princess, widow of Tancred's son Roger (see Irene Angelina), although he has not yet seen her. He is also shown among the miniatures on fol. 143r, in a sort of family portrait, depicting Frederick Barbarossa with his two sons, Henry and Philip. This suggests his importance in Henry's reign, though his role is not yet defined.

The youngest son of Frederick Barbarossa and Beatrix of Burgundy, Philip was born about February or March 1177 and was originally intended for the church. Perhaps he was given the name "Philip" because Philip of Weinsburg, archbishop of Cologne, was his godfather and may have overseen his education.[351] In his youth he was elected to the bishopric of Wirzburg.[352] However, after the death of his elder brother, Frederick of Swabia (q.v.), plans apparently changed. Philip was made duke of Tuscany in 1195, and of Swabia in 1196.[353] On 28 May 1197, at Gunzenle near Augsburg, he married Irene Angelina,[354] widow of Tancred's son Roger and daughter of Isaac Angelus (q. v.) who was by then deposed and blinded.

At the death of Henry VI, he had been summoned to central Italy to escort the young Frederick II to Germany, where the child would be brought up as German king and future emperor. But with the news of the emperor's death, disorders broke out in Italy which prevented him from reaching Frederick, and the child was brought to Palermo instead, where his mother Constance renounced his imperial claims on his behalf. For a while Philip attempted to represent the rights of his young nephew, "to assume the guardianship in accordance with German law, which recognized this as a right and duty of the nearest agnate," but when it became clear that the Welf faction (see Introduction, C.17) was gaining strength and could not be defeated by an absent child, he allowed himself to be elected as emperor on 8 March 1198. Philip was crowned for the first time in Magdeburg on Christmas Day in 1199, but as the Welf opposition argued that

---

[349] Cuozzo, *Catalogus Baronum Commentario*, 151, par. 517[*sic*]*; see also Jamison, *Admiral Eugenius*, 155 and n. 3.

[350] Assmann, "Friedrich Barbarossas Kinder," 459.

[351] Assmann, "Friedrich Barbarossas Kinder," 465.

[352] Toeche, *Kaiser Heinrich VI*, 425.

[353] Hampe, *Germany Under the Salian and Hohenstaufen Emperors*, 238.

[354] Van Cleve, *Emperor Frederick II*, 26–27, 51–53.

this was not appropriate, he was crowned again at Aachen in 1205 on "the Day of Epiphany." Nevertheless, Philip attempted to remain Frederick's guardian, trying, among other things, to arrange a marriage between the young king and Maria, daughter of the duke of Brabant, in 1204. This, of course, angered the pope. [355]

Despite Pope Innocent's support for Otto the Welf (he ultimately weighed in with an excommunication against Philip and his supporters), Philip prevailed in his struggle, and it seems that he and Pope Innocent were on the point of making peace with an agreement that included a marriage between one of Philip's daughters and a nephew of the pope. [356] But suddenly, the Count Palatine Otto of Wittelsbach, an old friend now become an enemy, sought Philip's presence at his palace, took a sword as if in play, stabbed him fatally in the neck, and fled. [357] Otto was apparently embittered because Philip had rejected his suit for the hand of one of his daughters.

Philip was first buried in the cathedral at Bamberg, [358] but Frederick II later transferred his tomb "to the burial church of the Salians at Speyer." [359]

§**Richard I**, king of England (known as the Lionheart), 1157–1199; r. 1189–1199. [360]

In the *Liber*, Richard is first mentioned on fol. 128v (ll. 1047–1088), and is pictured only on fol. 129r. There the part he has been playing in the story is revealed very briefly and somewhat cryptically. Richard is specifically accused of extorting money from Tancred by threats, supposedly in pursuit of his sister's dower rights, and of killing a kinsman of Henry VI, presumably **Conrad of Montferrat** (q. v.). He defends himself against the charges and is permitted to go free. Later, English soldiers are seen in Henry's army as it starts out for Sicily (l. 1140).

William of Brittany, chaplain of King Philip Augustus of France and author of a poem about him, the *Philipis*, borrowed one of Pietro's lines describing Richard's defense before Henry VI, thus stirring up discussion about his familiarity with the *Liber ad honorem Augusti* (see Introduction, B.2).

In July 1189, Richard succeeded his father as king of England. Like Frederick Barbarossa, he had pledged himself for a crusade, and he coordinated his plans with Philip Augustus of France, who was, in theory, his overlord for exten-

---

[355] Van Cleve, *Emperor Frederick II*, 29.
[356] Hampe, *Germany Under the Salian and Hohenstaufen Emperors*, 242.
[357] *Annales Marbacenses*, 78.
[358] Winkelmann, *Philipp von Schwaben*, 1:465–68.
[359] Deér, *Dynastic Porphyry Tombs*, 18.
[360] Richard the Lionheart is well known in history and legend. Gillingham's scholarly biography is helpful, and Kelly, *Eleanor of Aquitaine and the Four Kings*, also reviews his story in considerable detail where it involves his interactions with Henry VI and the Sicilian kingdom.

sive territories in France. Both, accepting the generous offer of William II of Sicily, planned to go by sea-routes, setting out from Sicily together.[361] By the time both reached Messina in September 1190, William II was dead, and Tancred had been proclaimed king. Richard first quarreled with Tancred, investigating rumors that his sister Joanna (q.v.), widow of the late King William, was being denied her proper rights and that Tancred had imprisoned her. He also demanded a legacy that the dying William II had supposedly made on behalf of Richard's father. In response, Tancred released Joanna and gave her a large sum of money, a million tarens (*decies centena mila terruncios*), in place of her lands; likewise, he satisfied Richard with money in place of the legacy. The two also made an alliance, and Tancred promised one of his daughters to Richard's nephew and heir, Arthur of Brittany. King Richard made Pope Clement III the arbiter of any conflicts that might arise about this match, and wrote a letter to the pontiff informing him of this.[362]

Philip Augustus was none too pleased to witness these procedings and was still less pleased when, in February 1191, Richard's mother Eleanor of Aquitaine arrived, bringing with her the Navarrese princess, Berengaria, as a bride for Richard. This displaced Alais, the sister of Philip Augustus, to whom Richard had theoretically been affianced in childhood. King Richard explained that he was unwilling to marry Alais "because my father had knowledge of her and fathered a son from her" (*quia pater meus cognovit eam, generans ex ea filium*).[363] Philip Augustus demanded the return of her sister and her dowry, which included some crucial borderland territories. Richard agreed, but postponed the whole matter until after the crusade.[364]

In April, Richard departed on the crusade, bringing Joanna and Berengaria with him. Of all the western crusaders on this expedition, he was the most successful. Barbarossa, after all, had died on the way, and his son Frederick of Swabia, leading the demoralized Germans, also died in early 1191, before Richard had yet set out. Philip Augustus arrived before Richard did, but soon departed, claiming illness.[365] Richard stayed and fought with considerable success, at least at first. On the voyage, he conquered Cyprus from the Byzantine tyrant who claimed it and paused there to marry his bride Berengaria.[366] Acre fell to the crusaders soon after he actually arrived in the Holy Land, and then his forces took Arsuf, Jaffa, and Askalon, which Saladin abandoned at his approach.[367] But his choices and policies may have created disunity and hindered the success of others

---

[361] Chalandon, *Histoire*, 2:435.

[362] Roger of Hovenden, *Gesta*, 118–20.

[363] Roger of Hovenden, *Gesta*, 126.

[364] Kelly, *Eleanor of Aquitaine and the Four Kings*, 261.

[365] Kelly, *Eleanor of Aquitaine and the Four Kings*, 273–74.

[366] Runciman, *History of the Crusades*, 3:43–46.

[367] Runciman, *History of the Crusades*, 3:54–59.

in the enterprise, and thus the enterprise itself. For example, he supported the claim of Guy of Lusignan, his vassal, for kingship of Jerusalem, although most of the barons of the crusader kingdom mistrusted Guy as incompetent, blaming him for the disastrous battle at the Horns of Hattin[368] (see Introduction, C.10). The dissension this caused made cooperation difficult.

Meanwhile, both Philip Augustus of France and his own brother, Prince John, were making common cause against him in his own lands. Realizing that he must return, he asked the barons of Outremer to choose their own king and was suprised that they all chose **Conrad** of Montferrat (q.v.).[369] He gave his consent, but almost immediately afterward, Conrad was assassinated (28 April 1192). Agents of the famous "Old Man of the Mountain," the original Assassin, Rashid ed-Din Sinan of Basra, are thought to have done the deed, resentful that Conrad had captured a ship which belonged to them. However, among the westerners, some believed that Richard had arranged it.[370]

Richard now realized that he could not stay long enough to take Jerusalem, and therefore, to leave behind him as stable a situation as possible, he made a three-year treaty with Saladin. However, he was obliged to abandon his conquest in Askalon, which he had fortified so carefully. Ill and under great pressure when he made this difficult decision,[371] he was nevertheless, if William of Brittany is to be believed, accused by Henry VI of being taken in by Saladin's gifts (see Introduction, B.2). In the *Liber* (l. 1058), Henry VI hints that he has not done his duty as a crusader.

Richard then set sail for home, choosing a roundabout way because of warnings that Philip Augustus and Henry VI were watching the seacoasts for him. He suffered shipwreck in the Adriatic[372] and tried to sneak across Henry's realms to the lands where his nephews were rebelling against the emperor. Accounts vary; in Roger of Hoveden's, Richard and several companions lingered for four days at one place, spending too much money, and when they received a friendly warning that they might have attracted too much attention, Richard fled on horseback with only one companion. Riding day and night, the two came close to Vienna and took lodging at an inn. While Richard slept, his companion went to buy food but was recognized by a soldier (*serviente*) of the Duke of Austria. Captured and brought to the duke, Richard's servant was unable to deny his identity. He led his captors to the house where his king still lay sleeping so that they could seize him.[373] Otto of St. Blaise says in his *Continuatio* that King Richard was found in the act of roasting meat, at which sight the people of the city laughed in

[368] Runciman, *History of the Crusades*, 3:21; 3:49.
[369] Runciman, *History of the Crusades*, 3:64.
[370] Runciman, *History of the Crusades*, 3:64–65.
[371] Runciman, *History of the Crusades*, 3:71–73.
[372] Kelly, *Eleanor of Aquitaine and the Four Kings*, 301.
[373] Roger of Hoveden, *Chronica*, 158.

derision.[374] The line which William of Brittany and Pietro share (*Philipis* 4.343; *Liber ad honorem* 1049)[375] seems to refer to some such story.

In any case, Duke Leopold of Austria had a special grudge against Richard because the latter had insulted him and the remnant of Barbarossa's German crusaders after his arrival at Acre.[376] Of course, the darker accusations concerning Conrad of Montferrat pursued the Lionheart too,[377] to the extent that the Old Man of the Mountain may have been moved or bribed to send a letter to Leopold of Austria, claiming credit for the murder and exonerating the English king.[378]

For Henry VI, to whom Richard was soon handed over, the Lionheart was a valuable prisoner but also an embarrassing one. Although his hostile actions against Henry were obvious enough, Richard was, after all, a king and a crusader. Harsh dealings with him could further complicate Henry's already delicate situation. Hence, Richard's spirited manner of answering the accusations against him helped to narrow Henry's options. Execution clearly was out of the question, and secret murder would cause too much suspicion and outrage. A long or indefinite imprisonment, until Richard had given appropriate satisfaction for his past offenses, was the best that could be done. In the end, Richard agreed to pay a huge ransom, to betroth his nephew Arthur to a daughter of the duke of Austria (instead of Tancred's daughter), and to reconcile his Welf relations to Henry. A runaway marriage between Richard's nephew, Henry of Brunswick, and Agnes of Hohenstaufen, Henry's cousin, may have helped bring about the resolution[379] (see Introduction, C.13). So with the promised political realignment, Richard paid part of his ransom, did homage to Henry VI for England, and was allowed to leave on 4 February 1194.[380] Pietro mentions that an English contingent was among the ships sent against Tancred during the second invasion: "England even sent a thousand fire-spewing troops" *(Mittit et ignivomas Anglia mille manus)* (l. 1140).

After Henry's sudden death, Richard backed his Welf nephews for the Holy Roman Empire, rejecting an offer of the crown for himself, on the grounds that he dared not go to Germany for fear of falling into the hands of Henry's allies, who would naturally hate him because, he claimed, "the emperor's corpse had

---

[374] *Gesta*, 324; chap. 38.

[375] *Quid prodest versare dapes, servire culine?* ("What was the use of turning dishes and serving in the kitchen?")

[376] Gillingham, *The Life and Times of Richard I*, 115–17.

[377] For example, *Chronica Regia Coloniensis*, 155–56, states that Richard was arrested "on account of the death of the Marquis Conrad and many deeds not well done at Acre" *(ob mortem Cunradi marchionis et multa apud Acram non bene gesta)*.

[378] *The Chronicle of the Third Crusade: Itinerarium Peregrinorum et Gesta Regis Ricardi*, trans. Helen Nicholson (Burlington, VT: Ashgate, 1997), 384–85.

[379] Csendes, *Heinrich VI*, 422.

[380] Gillingham, *The Life and Times of Richard I*, 188.

been unburied because of him" (*corpus imperatoris propter eum inhumatum erat*).[381] The idea that Henry VI had been excommunicated because of his detention of Richard might be an error or deliberate propaganda (see the biographical sketch of **Constance** of Hauteville). However, Richard's support for the imperial ambitions of his Welf nephews was real enough. Since Henry of Brunswick, the elder, was absent on crusade, Richard encouraged the younger brother Otto.

Richard died, however, on 6 April 1199, and thereby "deprived [his nephew Otto] of his chief support."[382] As the story is frequently told, the Lionheart attacked a vassal, Count Aymar of Limoges, who had supposedly discovered a treasure on his land and was willing to give up only half. As the king of England stormed the castle of Châlus, he was struck by an arrow and soon died from that wound.[383]

§**Richard** of Ajello, ca. 1170[384]–1220. Son of Matthew of Ajello, brother of archbishop Nicholas of Salerno, count of Ajello.

Richard of Ajello is mentioned only in cap. 10 on fol. 136r, swearing the conspiratorial oath along with his brothers, including the archbishop Nicholas. The verses accompanying this illustration are missing. Perhaps they would have said more about his role.

His activities in history are more apparent than those of many others who appear in the *Liber.* He was a son of Matthew of Ajello by his first wife Sica.[385] After his father helped Tancred to the throne and thus became his chancellor, Richard was made count of Ajello, Ajello being "one of the new counties created by Tancred as a means of establishing his officials in strategic positions."[386]

During Tancred's reign, Richard was a *familiaris* or royal minister, and helped with the difficult and volatile negotiations with King Richard of England, when he came to Messina. He also helped negotiate the Concordat of Gravina between Tancred and the pope, through which Tancred gained recognition as king of Sicily.[387] He may have been among the defenders of Salerno during Henry's

---

[381] Roger of Hoveden, *Chronica,* 177

[382] Hampe, *Germany Under the Salian and Hohenstaufen Emperors,* 240.

[383] Kelly, *Eleanor of Aquitaine and the Four Kings,* 341–44.

[384] This conjectural birthdate is based on the assumption that, given the complex and sophisticated activity with which Richard, count of Ajello, is charged when he first appears on the record, he cannot have been much younger than twenty in 1190, when his recorded career began.

[385] R. Manselli, "Aiello, Riccardo d'," *Dizionario Biografico degli Italiani,* 1 (1960), 519.

[386] Jamison, *Admiral Eugenius,* 94, n. 1. Because the county's name is far more distinctive than "Matthew" or any other name associated with this family, it has traditionally become a sort of family cognomen, even denoting the family in years before Richard received the title, and before he was born.

[387] Jamison, *Admiral Eugenius,* 93–94.

second assault in 1194, but if so he avoided capture and made his way to Palermo to join Queen Sibylla in her last attempts to defend the kingdom.[388] Pietro's account suggests that he was included in the initial peace with Sibylla but later conspired against Henry and was sent to Germany with the other prisoners. According to Innocent III's anonymous biographer, Henry VI had the archbishop's brothers blinded in captivity,[389] which would include Richard. Otto of St. Blaise states that a certain very learned Count Richard (*comite Richardo litteris apprime erudito*) among the prisoners had been blinded at the emperor's orders, quite possibly a reference to Richard.[390]

Richard was released after the death of Henry VI, but continued to have quarrels with the royal government, since a house he had owned was given away in 1205. At this time, it is true, the government in Sicily was controlled by William of Capparone, a German freebooter appointed neither by the pope nor by Philip of Swabia.[391] In 1216, he was apparently in the favor of the empress Constance of Aragon, Frederick II's first consort, who held the regency for Sicily while her husband established himself on the imperial throne. She granted him and his brother the Archbishop **Nicholas** of Salerno (q. v.) claims to revenues from Eboli. In 1220, Richard attended Frederick II's imperial coronation at Rome. Afterwards, Frederick confirmed his right to the county of Ajello, granted him originally by Tancred. However, he was obliged to surrender the associated castle.[392]

§**Richard** of Aquino, or Medania-Aquino, ca. 1168?–1196 or 1197. Count of Acerra. Later Count of the Principate. Brother of Sibylla, Tancred's consort.

Count Richard was Tancred's chief political and military supporter in the mainland territories. In *Liber ad Honorem Augusti*, he is depicted on the miniatures of fols. 109r, 110r, 113r, 121r, and 123r, and mentioned in ll. 378–387, 490–497, 763–764, 781–782, 817–860, and perhaps by implication in l. 1296. That his ultimate fate is not mentioned in the surviving portions of the poem, when he played such an active role in the early parts of it, is one of the puzzles of the work.

Richard's date of birth is uncertain. His father is said to be Count Roger of Aquino, mentioned as count from 1134–1167,[393] his mother Caecilia of

---

[388] Jamison, *Admiral Eugenius*, 115–96.

[389] *Deeds of Innocent III*, 18; chap. 18.

[390] Otto of St. Blaise, *Continuatio*, chap. 39. Also Jamison, *Admiral Eugenius*, 155, n. 3, suggests this, observing that Richard had sometimes acted as chancellor for Tancred in his father's absence, and this showed that he was a man with notable learning.

[391] Van Cleve, *Emperor Frederick II*, 49.

[392] R. Manselli, "Aiello, Riccardo d'," *Dizionario Biografico degli Italiani*, 1 (1960), 520.

[393] Chalandon, *Histoire*, 2:428.

Medania.[394] As Richard was presumably an adult in 1185, when he was sent as a military commander with William II's invasion of Byzantine territory, it is reasonable to suppose that he was not born much later than 1168, probably earlier. He was apparently hanged at Capua, by the orders of Henry VI, but different accounts lead to different dates for his death. One scholar, after weighing the confusing evidence, decides on December 1196 (just before the Christmas court at Capua).[395] However, Richard of San Germano, the chronicler who gives the most detailed account, places only his capture in 1196, with his execution following in 1197.

As an individual, Richard first appears on the historical record in 1185, among the land forces advancing on Constantinople when Tancred, the future king, was the commander of the naval forces. The Sicilian armies had been sent to attack the Emperor Andronicus (q. v.), who had murdered the child-emperor Alexius and helped instigate a massacre of the Latins in Constantinople at the same time. Support for Andronicus tottered in Byzantine territory, and the Sicilian invasion met much success, capturing Durazzo and Thessaloniki. Then the people of Constantinople deposed the tyrant and set up Isaac Angelus (q. v.) in his place. The Sicilian invaders soon found themselves confronting an army under Alexios Branas, sent by the new government. The Byzantine forces attacked the Sicilians by surprise while a truce was in force, overcame them, and killed many, taking many prisoners, including Richard of Acerra. *Annales Ceccanensis* relate that the emperor Isaac was so ashamed of the manner in which the prisoners were taken that he let them go free. Niketas Choniates, on the other hand, records that Isaac had both Richard of Acerra and his fellow commander Baldwin blinded. Nothing further is known of Baldwin, but it seems that Richard can hardly have been blinded at this time, given his later career. [396]

In describing the Sicilian invasion, Niketas Choniates mentions that Count Richard is Tancred's brother-in-law, which could indicate that the relationship already existed then, and thus the wedding had taken place before 1185. But we cannot rely on this inference; Niketas clearly wrote in retrospect, conscious of the fact that Tancred later became king. At some point, Count Richard of Acerra gained his release from Byzantine captivity and returned home.[397]

---

[394] Reisinger, *Tankred von Lecce*, 12.

[395] Jamison, *Admiral Eugenius,* 153.

[396] Niketas Choniates, *O City of Byzantium*, 199–200; also *Annales Ceccanenses*, 287. Perhaps it is relevant that the *Oxford Dictionary of Byzantium*, under "Blinding" (1:297–98), reports that several different processes were used in blinding, and that "the degree of blindness achieved could be of varying severity, so that some generals continued to command armies after the operation."

[397] If Jamison, *Admiral Eugenius*, 123, is correct, the *nepos* (nephew or grandson) for whom Sibylla gains Henry's pardon in *Liber* 1303 is Richard's son, Roger, but no consort is named for Richard in the *Liber* or in any source which I have yet found.

When Tancred was declared king early in 1190, his brother-in-law inevitably became his right-hand man. Chronicles report that it was Count Richard who successfully overcame Count Richard of Andria, and that he did to Count Roger what the Greeks had done to him: he made use of an arranged parley and captured his antagonist by treachery.

> Indeed the said count of Andria, remaining in Apulia, having strengthened the fortress of Saint Agatha which he held, retreated to hold Asculo against the king. The said Count of the Acerrans hemmed him in with a siege placed all around him, and when he could not bend him by prayers or promises, he invited him to a parley on a certain day, captured him treacherously, and condemned him to a wretched death.

> *Dictus vero Andrie comes in Apulia remanens, firmata rocca Sancte Agathe quam tunc ipse tenebat, de suis confisus viribus, se in Asculo recipit contra regem. Quem dictus Acerrarum comes intus circumposita obsidione coartans, cum flectere illum precibus et promissis non posset, vocatum ipsum ad colloquium quadam die, proditorie cepit et miserabili morte dampnavit.*[398]

Perhaps preferring to limit charges of treachery to Tancred, Pietro' leaves Count Richard out of this story (ll. 246–259). Fol. 104r pictures the unhappy Count Roger as a captive of the misshapen king, who is perhaps supervising the administration of poison as he watches food being lowered to his prisoner by a rope.

In the *Liber*, Richard becomes prominent as the defender of Naples against Henry VI's attack, along with Nicholas of Ajello (q.v.), the archbishop of Salerno. Looking out over the walls to view the besieging forces, he is wounded in the cheek by an arrow (ll. 378–383), and then given medical treatment (fols. 109r, 110r). No other source mentions this incident.

Subsequently, Richard decides to fight the emperor's army with bribes instead of warfare, and communicates this decision to the assembled knights of Naples (ll. 490–497).[399] Apparently, in Pietro's view, this scheme works, since the emperor attributes his failure to take Naples to the fact that his allies have been bought off (ll. 514–519). However, the verses admit that the epidemic that strikes the army is also partly responsible for the decision to raise the siege.

When the emperor retreats across the Alps and Constance is captured, Count Richard is given the task of attacking Henry's lieutenants in Italy, notably Conrad Lützelhard (q.v.), called Moscaincervello, at Capua. Richard is shown heading toward Capua in 121r, in the unique miniature executed by the artist

---

[398] Richard of San Germano, *Chronica*, 65 (note for the year 1190).

[399] That Richard of Acerra was responsible for giving bribes is a charge echoed in codices 4 and 5 of *Annales Cassinenses*, 314, though recorded for 1190 and thus not dated as a response to the siege of Naples.

whose work appears nowhere else in the *Liber*.[400] On the opposite page (120v), the original verses were completely erased and new contents written over them. In the new verses, Tancred reflects that his brother-in-law is a gigantic man and loyal enough, but too reluctant to join battle with his enemies (ll. 763–764). Richard's subsequent attack on Capua seems sufficiently successful, and he is a striking figure in 123r, bearing a shield with the device of a lion rampant. The glory of the victory is perhaps undercut by Pietro's account that Richard gains entrance to the city through treachery.

Also, Count Richard is unwilling to carry on the siege to its bitter end, the capture or extermination of all the Germans. Instead, he finally negotiates a surrender and permits Conrad a safe departure with his few surviving followers (ll. 855–860). While Pietro does not complain about this, some rhyming verses[401] inserted into the *Annales Ceccanenses* do mourn Count Richard's negligence in letting any Germans escape. Though this poem is generally hostile to Henry VI, Richard of Acerra gains little glory from it. (Walter of Brienne, who later married Tancred's daughter Alberia, is actually the hero of the piece.) Interestingly enough, the verses echo Pietro in claiming that Richard was excessively slow in defending Tancred's beleaguered realm. Likewise, they echo Pietro's suggestion that he took the city with craft rather than valor. Some relevant verses run:

> Indeed his heart was small, but his stature very high,
> Fair in aspect; yet to vision, snakelike, he was shy,
> He shunned the clash of battle, when weapons make debate;
> Riccardo was his name, and he went to war too late. . . .
> To Capua he came, unwarlike, and won it through deceit;
> He meant to send them all to death in battle, as was meet,
> The river, uncommanded, bore dead and dying[402] away,
> Carrion heavy on the cart, snatched from dogs at play.
> Then with Capua's castle he made unwarlike peace,
> And granted Conrad Flybrain safe conduct and release.

---

[400] Fuchs, Mrusek, and Oltrogge, "Die Entstehung der Handschrift," 251.

[401] These verses are attributed to the deacon of Monte Cassino and a certain John the Monk. However, Giuseppe Del Re, in his edition with a different title, *Chronicon Fossae Novae*, in *Cronisti e Scrittori Sincroni della Dominazione Normanna nel Regno di Puglia e Sicilia*, ed. idem (Naples, 1845), 492–556, here 535, n. 32, justly points out that since the Archdeacon Atenulf is an accomplice with Conrad in the deeds that are being lamented, he is probably not the author of the verses, despite what the manuscript says. Del Re suspects that the anonymous chronicler wrote the poem himself.

[402] Although the Latin text here follows the Del Re edition, for this translation I take the sense of the word *morientibus* ("dying") from the Waitz edition, instead of *monentibus* ("those who had been warned") from Del Re. Either way, these verses apparently describe the scene in *Liber* ll. 859–60, depicted on fol. 123r.

I'll say no more; their evil tribe came back to do much ill;
Two of them, pestilent Germans, remain to harm us still.[403]

Corde quidem parvus fuit hic, sed corpore magnus,
Pulcer in aspectu, viso velud angue receptus,
Et fugit in bello vel ferrum cingere ferro,
Nomine Riccardus, nimis ad certamina tardus. . . .
Hic Capuam venit, hancque dolo non marte recepit:
De quibus invenit, nullum plus vivere quaerit.
Dantur et aquaeductus monentibus his sine iussu
Quod plaustro ponunt, canis est et fluminis onus.
Et de castello Capuae fit pax sine bello:
Liberet ut dictus Corradus se dedit ipsum.
Nil modo plus dicam, rediit gens pestis iniqua
Ad mala multorum remanent duo Teutonicorum.[404]

After his prominent role in the taking of Capua, Richard of Acerra does not appear again in the *Liber*, though we would expect him to be concerned with the final assault on Salerno and Henry's advance toward Palermo. When the distressed widow, Sibylla, mentions that tears will be her offspring, husband, and brother (ll. 1295–1296), the reader would naturally wonder what her living brother is doing. Since he was involved with the defense of Salerno, one might guess that he was destroyed in that city's overthrow, where missing pages would explain why the surviving verses do not mention it. Contemporary chronicles and poems are often confused in their reporting of events, but some do record Richard's death in a sequence that suggests that he was captured and executed during the operations surrounding Henry's storming and destruction of Salerno.

---

[403] Unlike Pietro throughout most of the *Liber*, this anonymous poet poet makes use of a rhyme scheme. Though the pattern is internal, within each line of this poem, rhymed verse of some sort captures the effect better than blank verse or plain prose. A more literal translation of the words might run like this:

Indeed his heart was small, but his body great,
Handsome to see, but avoiding vision, like a snake;
He fled from war and the clash of iron with iron,
Riccardo by name, extremely late to battles. . . .
He came to Capua and acquired it through fraud, not warfare,
Seeking that all he found there should live no longer,
So borne by the water, without command, those who are dying
Are laid in the cart, the possession of the dog, the burden of the river.
And from the castle of Capua he made peace without battle:
He permits the said Conrad to surrender to him.
I will say no more now; the evil pestilent tribe returned,
Two of the Germans remain for the harm of many.

[404] *Chronicon Fossae Novae*, 519; *Annales Ceccanenses*, 289.

One passage comes from Otto of St. Blaise's *Continuatio*.[405] Otto states that the count was captured by Diepold and hanged at Capua, head down, because the emperor was "worthily made ferocious against him because of outrage at the capture of the empress" (*digna indignatione pro capta imperatrice in eum efferatus*). In Otto's account, the fall of Salerno soon follows, and he gives the date as 1193, a year too early even for Henry's conquest, thus showing that (as with many other chronicles) he is writing retrospectively and piecing together imprecise information as best he can. The same is likely to be true of Godfrey of Viterbo, who in his *Gesta Heinrici VI* writes:

> He placed on the gibbet the Count of Acerra,
> Slew some by the sword, divided some with the saw,
> Deprived some of their eyes; all the land was silent,
> Every city feared; there was no war at all.

> *Ponit in patibulo comitem de Cerra*
> *Quosdam cedit gladio, quosdam secat serra*
> *Quosdam privat lumine; silet omnis terra*
> *Timet omnis civitas; non est ulla guerra*.[406]

However, Richard was still alive and at large in Apulia as Henry VI advanced on Sicily after the sack of Salerno in the spring of 1194. He fled or held back from challenging the emperor's mighty army, and Henry did not take the time to deal with him as he moved toward Palermo. This agrees with what Pietro and the *Annales Ceccanenses* say about the count's cautious nature. Sibylla's words about her brother (ll. 1295–1296) might be an acknowledgement that (alive or not) he has been ineffective in defending her.[407] It is the chronicle of Richard of San Germano which seems to have the most detailed and best-informed account of Richard of Acerra's capture and execution:

> ... 1196 At this time the said Richard, Count of Acerra, wishing to leave the kingdom secretly, having abandoned the fortified places in Campania and Brianza[408] which he was holding, was betrayed by a certain white [Cistercian] monk to whom he had trusted himself. Captured by the aforementioned Diepold, he was sent to prison, to be handed over to Caesar.

---

[405] 324, chap. 39. Rota, in his edition (150, note on l. 1147), refers to Otto here, and dates Richard's death to this time.

[406] Godfrey of Viterbo, *Gesta Heinrici*, 337; ll. 133–136.

[407] According to Jamison, it is the continued threat posed by Richard of Acerra that necessitates Henry VI's reputed treachery against Sibylla; the emperor needs to escape from the excessively generous terms which he dishonestly offered Tancred's widow in order to lure her, with her children, from her stronghold at Caltabellota (*Admiral Eugenius*, 121). However, see Introduction C.15.

[408] Jamison, *Admiral Eugenius*, 153, provides the identification for this place.

... 1197 When the emperor himself returned from Germany, Diepold the castellan of Rocca D'Arce handed over the aforesaid Count of Acerra to him at Capua, as he presided over a general court. [The emperor] ordered him [Count Richard] first to be dragged by a horse through the squares of Capua and finally to be hung alive with his head downward. When he was still alive after two days, a certain clown of the emperor's, called Bag, in accordance with the emperor's pleasure, tied a stone of no light weight around his [Richard's] neck and foully compelled him to breathe his last. Then the emperor imposed a general tax on the whole kingdom. Then Diepold himself was made Count of Acerra by the emperor.

1196 ... Eo tempore dictus Riccardus Acerrarum comes regnum exire occulte volens et a facie fugere imperatoris, relictis Campania et Burgentia munitionibus quas tenebat, proditus a quodam albo monacho cui se dediderat, captus a iam dicto Dyopuldo est et custodie traditus carcerali, cesari assignandus. ...

1197 ... Imperator ipse de Alamannia rediens, assignatum sibi a Dyopuldo rocce Arcis castellano dictum Acerrarum comitem cum aput Capuam regeret curiam generalem, trahi primum ab equo per plateas Capue, et demum verso deorsum capite vivum suspendi iubet. Quem viventem post biduum quidam imperatoris ystrio Teutonicus cognomines Follis, ut ipsi imperatori placeret, ligato ad guttur eius non parvo lapidis pondere, ipsum turpiter exalare coegit. Tunc imperator ipse generalem toti regno collectam imponit. Tunc ipse Dyopoldus per imperatorem comes factus est Acerrarum.[409]

Did Pietro know about this grisly execution when he finished his poem? It seems unlikely. The poem's conclusion does not prepare its readers for a series of executions. If Pietro had known these were to happen, and if that did not completely ruin his poetic mood, we might expect him to defend these harsh actions and to heighten the villainy of the destined victims. As noted above, other sources make the count of Acerra responsible for the death of Count Roger of Andria, for whom Pietro expresses admiration and sympathy; yet the poet blames the murder entirely on Tancred, and Count Richard is not even mentioned in that connection. It is likely, then, that Pietro did not anticipate Count Richard's fate when he finished *Liber ad honorem Augusti*.

§**Richard** of Caleno, fl. 1190–1194. Count of Carinola and Conza.

The Count of Conza is mentioned in the *Liber* l. 296 as one who invited Henry VI to come claim his kingdom; he is not mentioned again under that title. Scholars have suggested that he is perhaps to be identified with the "Count Richard," otherwise undescribed, who appears among the conspirators in fol. 136r (cap. 8).

---

[409] *Chronica*, 68.

He was apparently count of Conza at least as far back as 1185, son of a count Jonard or Jonathan.[410]

This Count Richard of Conza and Carinola was at first the leader of the pro-Henry party in Terra di Lavoro.[411] Like Count Roger of Andria, he co-operated with Henry's commanders in their early efforts to bring the kingdom under Henry's control. But after Tancred's brother-in-law began to succeed in his military advances, Richard of Conza evidently changed sides, as Jamison explains; then Tancred made him leader of his own forces in Terra di Lavoro.[412] However, by 1193 Count Richard was a captive of the imperial party, in the hands of Diepold of Schweinspeunt.[413] Perhaps he is the unnamed "count" captured by Diepold in the fierce battle described by ll. 1089–1118 and the accompanying miniature (fol. 130r).

As a captive, Richard could give Tancred no further aid, and Henry VI had other uses for his lands. Jamison states that in 1194 the emperor awarded the county of Carinola to Leo Cottone, whose strategic change of sides at this time gave his army easy entrance into the region around Naples.[414]

Still, the *Annales Ceccanenses* report that Henry sent his prisoner, Richard, as an envoy to negotiate with the grieving and frightened Sibylla, believing that this choice of messagers would help reassure and win her over.[415] Perhaps, then, after the peace was made, Richard was set at liberty, only to become involved in the conspiracy against Henry. His disgraced and landless state might explain why he is listed as a count without the county being named.

There seems to be no record of Richard after this event.[416]

§Robert Guiscard. ca. 1015–1085. Norman adventurer, later duke of Apulia.

Robert Guiscard is mentioned at the opening of the *Liber* (l. 1) as the predecessor or ancestor of Roger, the first king of Sicily. As stated in the commentary, Pietro's use of the word *propago* (offspring) might be figurative, or he might actually be acquainted with legendary accounts like those recounted by Tuscus and

---

[410] Siragusa, *Liber ad honorem*, 26, n. 3, citing "a document of the monastery of Montevergine (*Arch. di Stato di Napoli, I, 22*)," states that the Count of Conza in 1185 was Richard, "son of the former Jonard" (*filius quondam Ionardi*), a name which Siragusa thinks may be a mistake for Jonathan, because that was the name of the Count of Conza during the reign of William II, according to Falcandus (*La Historia*, 29 and 78; *History of the Tyrants*, trans. Loud and Wiedemann, 83 and n. 50; 129). See also the *Catalogus Baronum*, 589.

[411] Jamison, *Admiral Eugenius*, 80–81.

[412] Jamison, *Admiral Eugenius*, 87.

[413] Jamison, *Admiral Eugenius*, 110–12.

[414] Jamison, *Admiral Eugenius*, 112, and see **Aligerno** of Cottone, above.

[415] *Annales Ceccanenses*, 290; Jamison, *Admiral Eugenius*, 119.

[416] Jamison thinks it likely that he was executed (*Admiral Eugenius*, 155 and n. 3).

Villani that Roger of Sicily was one of Robert Guiscard's sons (see Introduction C.2, and Commentery on ll. 1–34).

A historical figure of major importance, Robert Guiscard appears in many histories, and there are some detailed accounts in English, including the very readable *The Other Norman Conquest* by John Julius Norwich.[417] He and his son Bohemund are also major figures in the *Alexiad* of Anna Comnena.

Robert Guiscard was remembered in Italy as a "crusader," who won Sicily from the Moslems, for which Dante places him among the Warrior Saints in the Sphere of Mars (*Paradiso* 18.43–51).

In history, he was the eldest son of the second marriage of the Norman vavassor Tancred of Hauteville, who had five sons by his first wife Muriella, six sons by Fressende, his second wife, and some daughters besides.[418] Since Tancred's land was not enough to support them, the elder sons came to Italy and served its Lombard rulers as mercenaries. They gained territorial power in reward for their services, through alliances, and by conquest. Eventually Robert Guiscard, with his brother Roger as a partner, gained control of most of southern Italy, with Robert becoming Duke of Apulia and Roger the Great Count of Sicily (see Introduction, C.2–3). The "Roger II" who became king of Sicily was Guiscard's nephew.

§**Roffredo,** also called *Roffredus de Insula*, fl. 1188–1210, abbot of Monte Cassino.

Abbot Roffredo, in *Liber* 334–337, is said to have done his duty by the emperor and by his own flock. He appears in the accompanying miniature, fol. 108r, with a caption describing him as "Roffredo, the most faithful abbot" (*Rofridus fidelissimus abbas*). Monte Cassino, the abbey, was in a strategic location and owed allegiance to the empire; hence, the abbot's faithfulness, in Pietro's conception, does honor to himself and to the emperor. However, in history, his behavior was somewhat more ambiguous, as Siragusa notes:

> The abbot Roffredo "de Insula" . . . wavered dexterously between the parties of Henry VI and Tancred. In 1191, the year to which this information refers, the men of Cassino swore faith to Henry VI through the work of the deacon [Adenulf] of the abbey, because "the abbot, being ill, could not be engaged in such things" (*abbas egrotans non poterat in talibus occupari*).[419]

---

[417] *The Other Norman Conquest of Sicily in the 11ᵗʰ Century* (New York: Harper, 1967).
[418] Chalandon, *Histoire*, 1:82.
[419] Siragusa, *Liber ad honorem*, 30, n. 1.

Roffredo became abbot of Monte Cassino in 1188,[420] and was made a cardinal later that year.[421] When William II died, Roffredo arranged an alliance among the counts and barons in the region, presumably[422] because of the violence which had broken out in Palermo, where there was civil war among Christians and Saracens and the latter fled to the mountains. Presumably, like most of the nobles of Apulia, Roffredo at first opposed Tancred's elevation, but when Tancred's brother-in-law, Count Richard of Acerra, succeeded in getting control of the region, he was eventually induced to take the oath of loyalty to him.[423] To solidify the abbey's support, Tancred then granted it the castles of Rocca d'Evandro and Rocca Guglielma.[424] Hence, when Henry VI appeared, Abbot Roffredo no doubt wished to avoid direct violation of his oath. Pleading illness, he permitted the deacon Adenolf to swear loyalty to the emperor and arrange for the people of the region to do so.

It was to Monte Cassino that the emperor returned during the crisis after his abandonment of the siege of Naples. From there he tried to send for Constance while he planned his next actions.[425] When he learned that Constance had been taken prisoner, Henry caused the abbot of Monte Cassino to swear allegiance to him once more and then took him with him to Germany, presumably as a hostage. Monte Cassino, under the direction of the deacon Adenolf, thus remained loyal to the emperor during his absence. When the abbot returned in 1193, he left his brother Gregory, presumably in Germany, as a hostage.[426] Roffredo also had a crucial meeting with the empress Constance (q. v.), as she was being conducted from Tancred's custody to see the pope, inducing her to refuse the invitation to Rome.[427] Meanwhile, when Henry invaded the second time, he again came by way of Monte Cassino and sent the abbot ahead to make peace and arrange terms of surrender for those who were willing to swear allegiance to him.[428]

After the death of Constance, Markward entered the kingdom of Sicily and sought to gain Roffredo's cooperation for the Hohenstaufen imperial cause. But Roffredo, who had already acknowledged Innocent III's regency (*ballium*), refused.[429] The angry Markward devasted the territory around Monte Cassino, but Roffredo stood firm.

---

[420] *Annales Casinenses*, 131.

[421] Chalandon, *Histoire*, 2:452.

[422] As one version of the *Annales Casinenses* makes clear: 314; cod. 4, 5.

[423] Richard of San Germano specifically records that he did so (*Chronica*, 65).

[424] Jamison, *Admiral Eugenius*, 93.

[425] Toeche, *Kaiser Heinrich VI*, 202.

[426] Richard of San Germano, *Chronica*, 66.

[427] *Annales Casinenses*, 315–16.

[428] Chalandon, *Histoire*, 2:483. Richard of San Germano, *Chronica*, 328.

[429] Richard of San Germano, *Chronica*, 69.

Roffredo died in May 1209 or 1210.[430]

§**Roger II**, 1095–1154. Great Count, then king of Sicily.

Roger II's story is told in the opening verses of the *Liber* (1–34) and depicted in the accompanying miniature on fol. 96r, with emphasis on his three marriages and the birth of his daughter Constance. Afterwards, he is mentioned or alluded to several times when Constance's legitimacy and the dignity of her dynasty are issues: ll. 44, 332–333, 734–736, 875, 1378.

A figure of considerable historical importance, Roger II is treated in a variety of historical works.[431]

Roger was the second son of Roger, the Great Count of Sicily, and his third wife, Adelaide of Savona, and was born 22 December 1095.[432] His father died in June 1101 and was succeeded by his eldest son, Simon, who died in 1105, at which time ten-year-old Roger became count.[433] His mother acted as regent during his minority, which probably ended in the spring of 1112 when he was knighted at Palermo.[434] The following year, his mother sailed to the Holy Land as a wealthy bride for King Baldwin I of Jerusalem,[435] an adventure which ended badly, with her repudiation after her dowry was spent.[436] However, her departure and her death in 1118, shortly after her unhappy return to Sicily,[437] clearly left her son free to follow his own counsel.

In 1127 on the death of William, son of Roger Borsa, son of Robert Guiscard (see Genealogical Table 1), Count Roger claimed the dukedom of Apulia. Having obtained control of these immense territories, he sought the royal title, gaining approval from his nobles and the pope. However, since the pope who gave permission was Anacletus II (q.v.), the beneficiary of a double election who ultimately lost the papacy in the court of public opinion, Roger was obliged to defend the claim with much warfare and diplomacy (see Introduction, C.6)

---

[430] *Annales Casinenses*, 319, and Kölzer and Stähli, "Personenverzeichnis," 297.

[431] In English, two readable books by John Julius Norwich deal extensively with his career: *The Normans in the South* and *The Kingdom in the Sun*. More recently, a scholarly biography has appeared in translation from the German: Hubert Houben, *Roger II of Sicily*, trans. Graham A. Loud and Diane Milburn (New York: Cambridge University Press, 2002).

[432] The date of his birth can only be counted backwards from Romuald of Salerno's account of his age at death: fifty-eight years, five months and two days (*Chronicon* 236). Chalandon relies on this account (*Histoire*, 1:352), as does Houben (*Roger II*, 31).

[433] Chalandon, *Histoire*, 1:358.

[434] Chalandon, *Histoire*, 1:359.

[435] Chalandon, *Histoire*, 1:362.

[436] Runciman, *History of the Crusades*, 2:102–105.

[437] Chalandon, *Histoire*, 1:363.

before he made a tenuous peace with the papacy and empire. Roger died on 27 February 1154.[438]

§**Roger III**, d. 1193. Tancred's eldest son, nominally his co-ruler from 1192–1193.

Roger is not named in the surviving portions of the *Liber*, but there are a number of allusions to him. Matthew of Ajello, instructing Tancred to come to Palermo to obtain the kingship, makes it clear he has two sons, whom he is to bring (ll. 145–146), and he obeys (l. 175); both are depicted riding in his coronation procession on fol. 102r, identified by cap. 2, "these are sons of Tancred" (*Isti sunt filii Tancredi*). Later, Tancred speaks as though he has only one son, who is still a boy (ll. 770–772). The widowed Sibylla mentions being bereft (*orba*) of a son as well as of her husband (ll. 1269–1272), and addresses the absent son in an apostrophe (ll. 1291–1292), indicating that through him she now has a useless Greek daughter-in-law (**Irene** Angelina, q.v.). It is possible that some references to young Roger were removed deliberately out of tactful concern for Irene, who would later marry Philip of Swabia.

Roger was the eldest son of Tancred and Sibylla, but his birth date is not known. Pietro implies that his existence, and that of his younger brother, increased Tancred's eligibility for the kingship in the eyes of the populace, which had just witnessed the death of their beloved but childless William II. Roger was made duke of Apulia in 1191 and crowned co-ruler with his father in July or August 1192, perhaps with the pope's permission.[439] He may have married Irene at that time.[440]

Little else is known of Roger. Apparently he did not take part in any of his father's military campaigns. He died 24 December 1193.[441]

§**Roger** of Acerra, fl. 1194–1197. Nephew of Queen Sibylla, son of Count Richard of Acerra.

The *Liber* (l. 1303) mentions a *nepos* (nephew or grandson; the Latin word can mean either) of Queen Sibylla, whom Henry VI, when he has gained virtual possession of Palermo, agrees to pardon along with the widowed queen herself.

---

[438] Romuald of Salerno gives the day, but incorrectly lists the year as 1152, an error which his editors correct. See *Chronicon Romualdi II*, 236, and Garufi's note 4 on that page; see also Loud and Wiedemann's translation of this passage in *History of the Tyrants*, 221, and n. 8.

[439] Chalandon, *Histoire*, 2:448; 2:446.

[440] Jamison asserts that the wedding was later, "between May and July 1193" (*Admiral Eugenius*, 97). To be sure, negotiations for this match would take time, and Tancred's position would be stronger after his agreement with the pope.

[441] Siragusa, *Liber*, 59, n. 21; he cites *Necrologium Liciense* (the Necrology of Lecce) in *Reisefrüchte aus Italien*, ed. Eduard Winkelmann, in *Forschungen zur deutsche Geschichte*, vol. 28 (1828), 476.

This *nepos* is not named, and nothing further is said of him in the surviving vers-es, but scholars speculate that he might also be among the conspirators, listed as "Count Roger" in fol. 136r, cap. 9, but without his county being specified.[442]

Evidence for this Roger's existence, name, activities, and title as "count" are very scarce, but when all is reviewed, he does seem the best possibility for this identification.

First of all, our poet does mention the *nepos* whose pardon Sibylla initially gained from Henry, and it probably does mean a nephew, since we do not know of any grandchildren Sibylla had at this time. Also, a son of Sibylla's brother and chief supporter, Count Richard of Acerra, would clearly both need and deserve her mediation. But since Sibylla subsequently became involved in a conspiracy, we would expect her nephew to help her, or at least to be accused of doing so, if sufficiently mature to be of use. Moreover, the *Continuationes Weingartenses*, in describing the execution of Count Richard of Acerra in 1196 or 1197, specifically mention that this man's son is a prisoner "in the Rhine region" (*in confinia Reni*) along with "Tancred's small son" (*parvulo filio Dancredi*).[443] If this Roger was called "count" during his father's lifetime, Tancred must have conferred a new county on him, a logical step if Roger were old enough to help with military and administrative tasks. That would also explain why cap. 9 mentions no specific county. While Henry VI would not have confirmed Tancred's grant, the poet, in the reconciling mood with which he closes the work, would still allow him comital rank as a courtesy.

No known source confirms that Richard of Acerra's son was named Roger. His birthdate and the name of his mother seem unavailable. His subsequent fate remains unilluminated by the sources I have consulted.

§Roger, count of Andria, fl. 1154–1190.

Roger, count of Andria, initially appears in the *Liber* as Tancred's rival for the kingship after the death of William II (ll. 96–99, fol. 99r). After Tancred becomes king, however, he is a loyal follower of Henry VI. Tancred treacher-ously kills him under conditions not clearly described, but poison is suggested (ll. 124–129, 246–259, 294; fol. 104r).

When Matthew of Ajello reviews the respective qualifications of Tancred and Roger of Andria for the kingship, he implies that Roger is something of a womanizer; while sources do not give details on this point, they also do not name any wife for Roger.[444] On the other hand, he did have a son, called Robert of Calagio.

---

[442] Jamison , *Admiral Eugenius*, 123. Kölzer, "Bildkommentar," 198.

[443] *Continuationes,* 479; also Jamison, *Admiral Eugenius*, 155.

[444] Not even Errico Cuozzo, in his index to the *Catalogus Baronum Commentario*, seems to have this information.

By the time William II died, Roger of Andria had been prominent in the Sicilian kingdom for more than two decades. Marking his high prestige, Romuald of Salerno, his fellow envoy at the Peace of Venice in 1176, stated in a speech to Frederick Barbarossa that Count Roger was "sprung of royal blood" (*de sanguine regio ortum*).[445] Scholars have therefore struggled to trace his royal descent, which would also explain why he is considered for kingship in the *Liber*.

However, after a careful inquiry, Errico Cuozzo explains[446] that he can find no evidence either of Hauteville descent or descent from the family of a former Count Richard of Andria who had fallen in battle against the attacking Byzantine forces in 1155 or 1156.[447] Some had made that identification, at least tentatively. After all, this Roger first appears in Falcandus as "Roger, the son of Richard,"[448] which, in absence of clear alternatives, suggests such a relationship.[449] But Cuozzo's article establishes that this Roger was the son of quite a different Richard, the baron of a territory called "*Vico et Contra et Flumara*" (134).[450] In the male line, Roger was descended from a family with the cognomen *de Ollia*, derived from their Norman place of origin, Oully-le-Tesson.[451]

Roger could possibly have a connection to some more illustrious dynasty through his mother Sabasta or his father's mother, Maria, since no details are given about their ancestry.[452]

Back in 1122, when Roger's grandfather, Richard, was no baron but only the castellan of Vico, or Trevico, in Avellino, he was killed by rebellious peasants (*villani*). Then, as the chronicler Falco of Benevento says, his feudal overlord, William of Apulia (grandson of Robert Guiscard), gathered an army to take "an unheard-of revenge" (*inauditem . . . ultionem*), even hanging two priests who were involved.[453] This Richard's son, Richard the father of Roger, served the Hautevilles loyally and was probably at the council of nobles who elected Roger II to

---

[445] *Chronicon*, 290.

[446] Cuozzo, "Ruggiero, conte d'Andria."

[447] John Kinnamos, *Deeds of John and Manuel Comnenus*, trans. Charles M. Brand (New York: Columbia University Press, 1976), bk. 4, chap. 4.

[448] Falcandus. *La Historia*, 17, 162–63; *History of the Tyrants*, 69.

[449] For Chalandon, a study of Count Roger's seal was crucial in establishing that he was the son of the previous Count Richard of Andria (*Histoire*, 2:208), and he cites a study by "Promis, *Notizie di una bolla in piombe del secolo XII*, in *Atti della reale academia della scienze di Torino*, Vol. IV, 670."

[450] Cuozzo's new information is based partly on unpublished documents, some from the suppressed monastery of S. Pietro, now preserved in the Museo Sannio at Benevento, and some from the archives of Monte Vergine.

[451] Cuozzo, "Ruggiero," 120–30.

[452] Cuozzo, "Ruggiero," 133.

[453] Qtd. in Cuozzo, "Ruggiero," 131.

the kingship in 1130. In 1142, he received the barony to which his son succeeded at an unknown date.[454]

In 1155, Roger is old enough to cause trouble and become involved in a conspiracy along with Count Geoffrey of Montescaglioси (Tancred's uncle) against William I's Great Admiral Maio. William I settled this matter by giving the rebellious nobles permission to depart freely into exile, but Count Geoffrey, who lingered too long, was soon arrested and blinded. Evidently Roger avoided this fate, perhaps by departing punctually.[455]

"Roger son of Richard" reappears in 1166 and becomes count of Alba, when the regent Margaret, acting for her young son William II, who has just succeeded to the throne, creates eight counts the first year of his reign.[456]

In 1166, the county of Andria was conferred on a young kinsman of Queen Margaret, Bertram, the son of her ambitious and overbearing cousin, Gilbert of Gravina. By 1168, Gilbert's machinations had so gravely offended a coalition of Sicilian nobles, officials, and ethnic populations (Greek and Saracen) that they joined forces to expel him and his confederates (mostly French kinsmen of the queen and their followers) and seize the government. Roger, count of Alba, was sent, among others, to enforce their sentence of confiscation and exile on Gilbert and Bertram, father and son;[457] the strategic county of Andria, especially significant for guarding against invasions from the sea, was apparently the reward for his success, but he gave up Alba in order to obtain it.[458]

As a further sign of the trust the king reposed in him, Roger was appointed both constable and justiciar, to which Pietro alludes in the *Liber*.

In 1176, Barbarossa's armies under Archbishop Christian of Mainz encroached on the Norman kingdom, and Count Roger was sent, along with Count Tancred, his later rival, to drive them off. The Sicilians were defeated in their encounter with the archbishop at Carsoli, but Barbarossa himself soon suffered a still more devastating defeat at the battle of Legnano, which ultimately proved more important.[459] Later, in July 1177, Count Roger was sent with Archbishop Romuald of Salerno to negotiate the Peace of Venice. These negotiations

---

[454] Cuozzo, "Ruggiero," 132–34.

[455] So Cuozzo speculates in "Ruggiero," 140–41. The story is told by Falcandus, *La Historia*, 17, 162–63; *History of the Tyrants*, 69.

[456] *La Historia*, 101, 108; *History of the Tyrants*, 149, 157. Falcandus does not say which county "Roger son of Richard" received, but Cuozzo, "Ruggiero," 143–45, determines that it was Alba, since some documents show that Roger, baron of "*Vico et Contra et Flumara*," also held the county of Andria, while others show that at some point the famous Roger, count of Andria, had been count of Alba.

[457] Falcandus, *La Historia*, 162.

[458] Cuozzo, "Ruggiero," 143. See also Loud and Wiedemann, *History of the Tyrants*, 214–15, n. 271.

[459] Chalandon, *Histoire*, 2:375–76; *Annales Casinenses*, 312.

were not without their tense moments, for example when the Venetians seemed inclined to admit Frederick Barbarossa to their city along with his army, which would have given him overwhelming power, destroying the validity of any agreements reached at the time. Romuald and Count Roger (who thus demonstrated his naval responsibilities) offered to remove the pope in Sicilian ships, at which point the Venetians, fearful of losing their rights to Sicilian trade, decided to exclude Barbarossa after all.[460] The negotiations proceeded and were successful.

Clearly this was a high point in Roger's career. After the death of William II, he wrote urging Henry VI to claim the crown as quickly as possible (*concito*).[461] But Henry, preoccupied with his father's crusade and other troubles (see Introduction, C.11–13), could only send subordinates, who were not able to overcome Tancred's brother-in-law, Richard of Acerra, even with Roger's help. Therefore, Roger took refuge in the fortress of Saint Agatha, where Count Richard soon besieged him. But when Tancred's brother-in-law could not take the castle directly, he resorted to trickery, inviting him to a parley (*vocatum ipsum ad colloquium*), seized him treacherously (*proditorie cepit*) and in some fashioned killed him or "condemned him to a wretched death" (*miserabili morte dampnavit*).[462] The account in the *Liber* suggests that he was poisoned in prison.

After his death, his son, Robert of Calagio, held the fortress of Saint Agatha in Apulia. In 1193, however, Tancred captured the fortress and took Robert prisoner.[463] Though it is often assumed that he was killed, Cuozzo's documents indicate that he in fact survived, and even held the barony "*De Vico et Contra et Flumara*," which he handed down to his son "Riccardus Benedictus filius Riccardi"[464] when he died in 1227. The strategic county of Andria, however, was no longer in the family.

§**Roger**, count of Avellino, fl. 1185–1194.

Roger, Count of Avellino, is listed in cap. 14 as one of the conspirators depicted on fol. 136r.

Roger of Castelvetere, lord of Taurasi, was already count of Avellino in 1191. Previously, he had an extensive military career, and had accompanied William II's 1185 invasion of Byzantine territory, where the future king Tancred, as commander of the naval forces, may have observed his abilities.[465] From his portrayal in the *Liber*, we must presume that he served Tancred and then Sibylla, and was arrested for involvement in the conspiracy of 1194. Ansbertus[466] also

---

[460] Chalandon, *Histoire*, 2:381–82.
[461] Richard of San Germano, *Chronica*, 65.
[462] Richard of San Germano, *Chronica*, 65.
[463] Richard of San Germano, *Chronica*, 66.
[464] Cuozzo, "Ruggero," 137–38.
[465] Jamison, *Admiral Eugenius*, 89.
[466] [Ansbertus], *Historia de expeditione Friderici*, 110.

lists a "Comes Avellinus Rugerius" among the conspirators. By 1196, Roger was apparently dead, since "his widow, Perrona, who described herself as *olim comitissa Avellini* [formerly countess of Avellino], . . . made a donation in January 1196, together with her son Matthew of Castelvetere, Lord of Taurasi, to Monte Vergine."[467]

§**Roger,** count of Chieti, fl. 1193–1212.

Perhaps he is the "Roger Thartis" listed in cap. 7, fol. 136r.[468] Chieti in Latin is spelled *Theatis* or *Theathis*—it actually means "the city of Thetis," that is, of the mother of Achilles, as the chancellor Conrad of Querfurt (q.v.) explains in a contemporary letter.

Thus "the scribe's error" could reasonably change it to *Tharthis*.[469] Roger was initially made castellan of Chieti as part of Tancred's policy of relying on such officers instead of hereditary counts, since the latter (especially in Apulia) leaned toward the emperor's party. Presumably, having proved his worth, he was made count.[470] In 1193 he was "the valiant defender of Vairano,"[471] when Count Berthold, Conrad "*Muscincervello*," and Diepold of Schweinspeunt attacked "*Roggerius de Theate*" at the castle of "*Vayranum*" but were unable to capture it.[472] His movements from then on are uncertain. Perhaps he returned to Queen Sibylla in Palermo while Henry advanced on Sicily.[473] If Roger was among the conspirators, he survived imprisonment, since Eugenius (q.v.), who also was released, later subscribed to a document conferring "the county of Civitate" on him in 1199.[474] He died in 1212.[475]

§**Roger,** count of Molise, fl. 1190–1197.

The count of Molise is listed (l. 297) as one who wrote inviting Henry VI to claim the Sicilian throne. Some speculate that he might be the "Count Roger" depicted in fol. 136r, cap. 9, for whom no county is mentioned.[476] If this is the case, Pietro must be error, since although Roger of Molise apparently changed sides and became a loyal follower of Tancred, he was still at large in Apulia in December 1194 and was therefore not among the conspirators or prisoners.

Count Roger of Molise may be a son of the Richard of Mandra who was created count of Molise during the minority of William II of Sicily, by the regent

---

[467] Jamison, *Admiral Eugenius*, 89, n. 2.

[468] Kölzer, "Bildkommentar," 198; Jamison, *Admiral Eugenius*, 123, n. 1.

[469] Jamison, *Admiral Eugenius*, 143, n. 1; 149.

[470] Jamison, *Admiral Eugenius*, 87, 395.

[471] Jamison, *Admiral Eugenius*, 123.

[472] Richard of San Germano, *Chronica*, 66–67.

[473] Jamison, *Admiral Eugenius*, 116.

[474] Jamison, *Admiral Eugenius*, 164.

[475] Kölzer, "Personenverzeichnis," 297.

[476] Siragusa, *Liber ad honorem*, 143, and Kölzer, "Personenverzeichnis," 198.

Queen Margaret.[477] Neither the date of Roger's birth nor of his succession is known, but sources show that since at least 1187, Roger was the name of the Count of Molise.[478] Roger first adhered to Henry VI's party, but after the raising of the siege of Naples, he faced the retaliatory military campaign of Tancred's brother-in-law, Richard of Acerra, and was captured. Evidently he then changed sides and did not welcome Henry's second invasion or join his conquest. His county of Molise was therefore awarded to Conrad of Lützelhard, who in 1196, making good his claim, besieged Count Roger at Rocca Mandolfi, one of his strongholds.[479] Roger negotiated a surrender which allowed him to leave the kingdom freely with his men, and subsequently[480] "in the course of time, he died" (*processu temporis mortuus est*).

§**Roger**, count of Tricarico, fl. 1160–1192.

The Count of Tricarico is mentioned, l. 298, as one who invited Henry VI to claim his rightful crown in Sicily. His name is not given. It is therefore uncertain whether Pietro means Roger, who died on the third crusade at Acre,[481] or his son James (q. v.) who succeeded him, perhaps during his life. Both were members of the San Severino family, which was "ancient and powerful" and was "still playing an important part in the politics of southern Italy in the fourteenth century."[482]

Roger's mother was the sister of Count Berard of Laureto.[483] Sources do not establish a date of birth for him, but chronicles mention his activities as early as 1160 and 1168.[484] Roger and his son James were both living early in 1188,[485] as was Roger's consort Roazia;[486] however, one chronicle[487] mentions the marriage of James in 1188, describing him as the "Count of Tricarico." This might be an error, or could indicate that Roger had given up his county to James, possibly in anticipation of the crusade.

---

[477] Falandus, *La Historia*, 161–62; *History of the Tyrants*, 214.

[478] Siragusa, *Liber ad honorem*, 26, n. 4.

[479] Jamison, *Admiral Eugenius*, 152.

[480] Richard of San Germano, *Chronica*, 68.

[481] Cuozzo, *Catalogus Baronum Commentario*, 32–33.

[482] Jamison, *Admiral Eugenius*, 364 and n. 4.

[483] Toeche, *Kaiser Heinrich VI*, 321.

[484] Romuald, *Chronica*, 228, and Falcandus, *History of the Tyrants*, 182 and n. 206.

[485] Siragusa, *Liber ad honorem*, 27, nn. 1 and 2, cites "two documents of the Abbey of Cava, one of September 1187, the other of 1188, cited by (Di Meo, *Annali Critico-Diplomatico del Regno di Napoli della Mezzana* , vol. 11), 15 and 19" to show that Roger and James are father and son, both living.

[486] Toeche, *Kaiser Heinrich VI*, 146; bk. 1, chap. 3.

[487] *Annales Ceccanenses*, 288.

§**Roger,** duke of Apulia (ca. 1118[488]–1148). Son of Roger II, father of Tancred.

Not specifically named in the *Liber*, the father of Tancred is mentioned as a duke (l. 134), or as a descendant of the dukes (l. 220). Duke Roger was the eldest son of King Roger, but the date of his birth is unknown. The chronicler Falcandus attests that Roger was a promising youth much beloved by his father and his subjects as well.[489] Made knight in 1135,[490] he participated in his father's government and in his military activities from his youth. At some point, Duke Roger had a liaison with a daughter of Count Achard of Lecce whose name is unknown; she bore him two children, William and Tancred.[491] Around 1140 Duke Roger married Elisabeth, daughter of Count Theobald of Champagne,[492] but the marriage was childless. The circumstances of Roger's death are not recorded.[493]

§**Roger** of Tarsia, fl. 1183.

Perhaps to be identified with **Roger Tharthis,** listed in cap. 7 on fol. 136r. See also **Roger** of Chieti.

In a document of 1183, Roger and his wife Maria renounce a claim on the territory of Bisacquino, which they concede belongs to the royal demesne. They agree that a fine will be paid should they or their descendants ever claim it. Maria had inherited the lands of her father, Robert de Malconvenant, and the dispute over the territory apparently came with it. The document was attested by William II's vice-chancellor **Matthew** of Ajello (q.v.). Documents reveal nothing further about this Roger.[494]

§**Rombanldus,** fl. 1191–1192

In *Liber* l. 757, Tancred laments about a "Rombanldus" who "By himself. . . with three helping him, takes the kingdom from me (*Unus . . . regnum michi cum tribus aufert*)." This person is otherwise not known to history. See **Berthold** of Künsberg.

---

[488] Chalandon, in his *Histoire*, passes on the speculative date of 1118, from the scholar Di Meo, *Annali Critico-Diplomatico del Regno*, 10:155–56, who reportedly stated, but without citing specific documents, that Elvira's eldest son died at the age of thirty in 1148. Similarly, citing documents which sometimes contradict each other, Chalandon settles on 2 May 1148 as the date of Roger's death (2:105).

[489] *La Historia*, 6; *History of the Tyrants*, 59.

[490] Houben, *Roger II*, 36.

[491] Chalandon, *Histoire*, 2:425; Falcandus, *La Historia*, 23; *History of the Tyrants*, 76.

[492] Chalandon, *Histoire*, 2:106. Houben, *Roger II*, 88.

[493] Norwich, *Kingdom*, 148, speculates that "he fell in some skirmish on the northern frontiers of his dukedom."

[494] Siragusa proposes the identity in *Liber ad honorem*, 142–43, n. 4, where he also points out that "the cleric Ansbertus" lists a "de Tarsia" among the conspirators, although his first name is "Tancredus" rather than "Rogerius." For a summary of the 1183 document, see Johns, *Arabic Administration*, 321 (Private 20).

§Romuald, fl. 1191. Salernitan citizen, supporter of Henry VI and Constance.

Romuald is depicted on fol. 110r (cap. 8) as a member of the delegation which invites the empress Constance to Salerno, and again in 112r, when a similar group travels on a secret mission to the emperor's camp at Naples, just before the siege is abandoned. The verses associated with the latter picture describe him as Salerno's "scale of judgement" (*Libraque iudicii*) (l. 458). He may belong to the Guarna family, which also produced the famous bishop and chronicler Romuald II of Salerno, and is probably related by blood as well as by political allegiance to the other Salernitans in these two delegations.[495] Precise information is not known, however.

§Saladin, ca. 1136[496]–1193 (Malik al-Nāzir Salāh al-Din Abu'l Muzaffar Yūsuf ibn Ayyūb).[497] Sultan of Egypt and Damascus, antagonist of the Latin crusader state.

Saladin's campaigns in the Holy Land greatly reduced the Latin crusader state, evoking the Third Crusade and inspiring the alliance between **Frederick Barbarossa** and **William II** of Sicily (qq.v.). This brought about the marriage between **Henry VI** of Hohenstaufen and **Constance of Hauteville** (qq.v.) and set the stage for the conquest of Sicily. Saladin is directly mentioned in *Liber* l. 1031, when **Pope Celestine**, in a letter to **Tancred** (qq.v.), compares the abduction of the empress Constance to Saladin's capture of the True Cross, suggesting that it will rebound against Tancred in the same way (see Commentary on that passage; see also the Introduction, C. 9–11).

Grandson of a Kurdish tribesman named Shadi, governor of Tikrit under the Seljuks, Saladin (called Yusuf) was born the day his father, Ayyub, was sent into exile with his brother Shirkuh because the latter had murdered a scribe. Under Zengi, atabeg of Mosul, Ayyub was given command of the fortifications at Baalbek, and there his sons grew up.[498] After Zengi's death in 1146, Ayyub and Shirkuh served his son Nur al-Din. Shirkuh, probably with Saladin among his followers, was sent to Egypt in 1164 to reinstate a deposed vizier of the Fatamid caliph in Cairo. Rather than pay his debts to Shirkuh, the vizier, Shawar, summoned Amalric, king of Jerusalem, to his help. After a series of advances and retreats, sieges and skirmishes, Shirkuh deposed Shawar and became the new vizier of Egypt, while the Fatimid caliph insisted on Shawar's execution. By some accounts, the killing was done by Saladin himself, who was in any case chosen vizier himself on the death of Shirkuh. As vizier he became chief ruler of Egypt

---

[495] Siragusa, *Liber ad honorem*, 129, n. 4; Kölzer, "Bildkommentar," 95. Kölzer mentions the odd fact that he wears a turban.

[496] Malcolm Cameron Lyons and D. E. P. Jackson, *Saladin: The Politics of Holy War* (New York, Cambridge University Press, 1983), 2.

[497] *Chronicle of the Third Crusade*, 406 (index).

[498] A. R. Azzam, *Saladin* (New York: Pearson, 2009), 27–28.

when he switched the allegience of the Cairo and Fustat mosques to the Abbasid caliph at Baghdad and refused to allow the Fatimid caliph's son to suceed him when he died.[499] Wooing followers with gifts, displays of power, and calculated acts of both ruthlessness and magnanimity, Saladin later won control of Syria after Nur al-Din had died, leaving his territories to be divided among a minor son and quarreling nephews.[500] As sultan of Egypt and Damascus, Saladin fought against the Latin kingdom. The victory at Hattin and the conquest of Jerusalem in 1187 marked the apex of his triumph (see Introduction C.10).[501] Though recognizing him as their chief adversary, some Latin chroniclers remember him with gratitude for his mercy and magnanimity to many individual crusaders and their families.[502] Probably because of this, Dante places in him in Limbo among the virtuous pagans (*Inferno* 4.127) rather than further down, say, in the eighth circle, with Mohammed and Ali (*Inferno* 28.22–63). Similar acts of generosity won him the friendship of the Byzantine emperor **Isaac Angelus** (q.v.), causing the latter to intrigue against Frederick Barbarossa.

For the rest of his career, Saladin struggled to hold his conquests, with mixed success. He retained Jerusalem, but the Third Crusade won back the port city of Acre and adjacent territories, notably under the leadership of **Conrad of Montferrat** and **Richard Lionheart** (qq.v.).

When Saladin died, his territories were divided among his brothers and some quarreling sons.

§**Sibylla,** consort of Roger II, king of Sicily. ca. 1134[503]–1151.

Sibylla, mentioned ll. 1–2 and depicted fol. 96r, cap. 6, is Roger's second queen, who died of a miscarriage. Pietro is the only source who states unambiguously that Sibylla died without giving birth to live offspring, and some dispute this.[504]

---

[499] Azzam, *Saladin*, 55–91. Lyons and Jackson, *Saladin*, 6–47.

[500] Azzam, *Saladin*, 98–119. Lyons and Jackson, *Saladin*, 81–110.

[501] Lyons and Jackson, *Saladin*, 284.

[502] Azzam, *Saladin*, 3.

[503] The estimated birth date above is based on my conjecture that she would have been about fifteen years old at the time of her marriage, since the main reason for the marriage was the production of heirs.

[504] Cuozzo, *Catalogus Baronum Commentario*, 328–30, speculates that a certain Adelicia (the name is variously spelled), daughter of King Roger, who married a certain Count Joscelin or Gozzolino of Loreto, was probably Sibylla's daughter, an assertion which Loud and Wiedemann repeat: *History of the Tyrants*, 157, n. 162. However, the document on which Cuozzo bases his interpretation is reproduced in part by Vincenzo Bindi, *Monumenti Storici ed Artistici degli Abruzzii* (Naples, 1889), 586. Bindi cites v. 1069 of Archivio di Stato di Napoli, fols. 14 and 16, in which the count's wife is said to be a "daughter of the former King Roger, of glorious memory" (*filie quondam Regis Rogerii gloriose memorie*). No mention is made of her mother. This is not inconsistent with ille-

Sibylla, whom Roger married in 1149, was a sister of Duke Hugh II of Burgundy. She died in 1151 and was buried at the abbey of La Cava near Salerno.[505] Siragusa reports that an entry in the Necrology of Salerno (*Necrologium Salernitanum*) in the *Liber confratrum ecclesiae Salernitanae* states, "Lady Sibylla, illustrious queen, was laid to rest in the year 1150 of the Lord's incarnation" (*Depositio domine Sibylle illustris regine anno domine incarnationis MCL*). Also a twelfth century urn in the portico of the church of the Abbey of Cava has an inscription "in modern characters" which says, "King Roger of Sicily gives the plowed land of Sicily to this rocky fortress; his wife, mournful Sibylla, gives her own ashes" (*Rex huic dat rupi Rogerius arva Siclarum, dat coniux cineres moesta Sybilla suos*). A medallion on the sarcophagus shows an effigy of Sibylla. [506]

§**Sibylla** of Acerra, consort of King Tancred. ca. 1160–1200.[507]

A significant person in the *Liber*, Sibylla is mentioned and depicted frequently. Her individual role is most prominent when Tancred sends the captive empress Constance into her keeping (ll. 869–964; fols. 123r, 124r, 125r), and when she prepares to face Henry VI's last invasion, resolves to ask for pardon, and is arrested for her involvement in a conspiracy against Henry's life (ll. 1257–1362; fols. 134r, 136r).

She was the daughter of Count Raynald of Aquino, and of Cecilia of Medania (Cuozzo, *Catalogus Baronum Comentario* 83, par. 344).[508] Her brother, Count Richard of Acerra, became Tancred's most important military supporter. The date of Sibylla's birth is not known, nor is the date of her marriage or the age of

---

gitimate birth. King Roger's illegitimate daughters were sought after as marriage prizes, as one story told by Falcandus makes clear: see Siragusa, *La Historia*, 32; *History of the Tyrants*, 87. However, Houben, *Roger II*, xxiii, lists "Adelisa" as a legitimate daughter of Roger, without specifying which queen is her mother.

[505] Chalandon, *Histoire*, 2:106; Romuald, *Chronicon*, 321.

[506] Siragusa, *Liber ad honorem*, 4–5, n. 4.

[507] It is hard to conjecture Sibylla's dates. Though she clearly has been married for some time when Tancred becomes king, sources do not seem to mention her until then. The conjectural birth date which I give her involves subtracting 15 years from the conjectured date of her marriage, which I fixed halfway between the earliest likely date for that event and the latest likely one. As explained in his biographical sketch, Tancred probably did not marry before 1169, when the exiles from William I's reign were recalled. On the other hand, if the storyline behind fol. 102r is correct, then her younger son (see sketch for William III) is six or seven in 1190. Her elder son, Roger, looks to be at least two years older, probably more. That would yield a marriage date not later than 1181. Halfway between these two dates is 1175. If Sibylla was fifteen at the time of her marriage, she would then have been born in 1160. It is impossible, however, to guess a date of death. In the sources I have seen, she is last mentioned around 1200, when Innocent III demands an oath from her that she will not attempt to take the realm of Sicily from his young ward, Frederick II.

[508] Cuozzo, *Catalogus Baronum Commentario*, 83, par. 344.

her husband. Pietro, however, implies that Tancred is much older that she is. In the *Liber*, she once refers to him as *senex* (old man) (l. 932), a word he also applies to himself (l. 754). At any rate, Tancred was old enough to be involved in an active rebellion against William I in 1161, and after that, he spent much of his youth in either detention or exile. Thus it is fair to conjecture that he did not marry until after 1169, the date by which he was reconciled to William II and had been made Count of Lecce.[509] It was probably Sibylla's first marriage, because children of an earlier marriage would likely have become conspicuous during Tancred's reign, just as Sibylla's brother did. If male, they would likely have been entrusted with important positions. If female, there would have been negotations for their hands.

Sibylla had five known children (see biographical sketches for Alberia, Constance, Mandonia, Roger III, and William III).

The *Liber* itself gives a vivid account of Sibylla's activities during Tancred's reign. After she and her family were arrested, they were taken to Germany. She and her daughters were confined to "the convent of Hohenburg or Mont S. Odile" which was "an Alsatian house of canonesses in the heart of the Vosges, famous at this time for its literary and artistic work."[510] After Henry VI's death, Sibylla was released with her daughters and went to France where she apparently arranged a marriage between her eldest daughter Alberia (q.v.) and a French count named Walter of Brienne. The date of her death is unknown.

§**Tancred** of Hauteville, ca. 1130[511]–1194. Count of Lecce, king of Sicily.

Tancred is a major figure in the *Liber*, frequently mentioned in the verse and depicted in the miniatures (96–101, fol. 99r). He first appears as one of the candidates for kingship, preferred by the common people rather than the nobles. His

---

[509] Chalandon, *Histoire*, 2:426.

[510] Jamison, *Admiral Eugenius*, 125.

[511] Estimates of Tancred's date of birth remain uncertain, since there is no clear record, and judgments of probability vary widely. Reisinger, Tancred's biographer (*Tankred von Lecce*, 11–12) relates but casts doubt on the theory of Carlo Alberto Garufi and Salvatore Tramontana, who suggest that since Duke Roger went to Lecce in 1127 or 1128, Tancred might have been conceived and born around that time. But Reisinger himself thinks this unlikely because with the birth date generally attributed to him, Duke Roger would have been at most ten years old at that time. He himself estimates that Tancred was likely to have been born somewhere between 1134 and 1138. However, Duke Roger's own birth date is also uncertain (see his biographical sketch, above). If Roger II, like his grandson Frederick, fathered a son at the age of sixteen, that son might have been fifteen in 1128. Toeche, in his *Kaiser Heinrich VI*, added a short biography of Tancred in his Third Appendix (Dritte Beilage) and puts his birth date between 1130 and 1140. Houben, *Roger II*, 88, n. 57, gives Tancred a birth date after February 1140, on the grounds that "Duke Roger only came to Apulia in April/May 39." This argument would surely prevail if there were no alternative dates and ways for Tancred's conception. However,

summons to the kingship, his coronation procession, Urso's account of his freak-ish conception and birth, and his murder of his rival, Roger of Andria, are viv-idly told (140–259; fols. 101r–104r). After that, Tancred and his supporters, the Tancredines (*Tancridini*), are mentioned frequently. He enters the action directly once more when Constance is brought to him as a captive, and he is required to release her (ll. 711–772, 861–964, 1009–1046; fols. 120r–121r, 124r–126r, 128r). Tancred then disappears from the surviving portions of the manuscript. Line 1180 may suggest that Tancred fled from Salerno as Henry approached, although historically speaking, Tancred died months before this event, which Pietro may well have recorded in one of the missing passages. He is clearly dead by l. 1247, when a delegation of citizens to Favara speaks of the "little king" who has fled to Caltabelotta; perhaps that was also meant in l. 1180.

Tancred was the son of Duke Roger of Apulia, eldest son of King Rog-er, and a mother whom Falcandus describes as "very noble" (*nobilissima*) and with whom Duke Roger had a "customary association" (*ad quam dux ipse consue-tudinem habuerat*) which produced two boys, Tancred and his handsome brother William.[512] After Tancred's time, many fanciful stories were told, giving a vari-ety of names to the lady.[513] Tancred himself clarifies the question of lineage in a donation made in May of 1190 (a few months after his coronation) to the con-vent of San Giovanni in Lecce. Here he described the abbess, Emma, as *metatera* (maternal aunt). Emma was the daughter of Count Achard II of Lecce and sister of Geoffrey II of Lecce.[514] This Geoffrey is the same person as Count Geoffrey of Montescaglioso,[515] whose rebellion against William I and consequent blind-ing, about 1156, is described by the chronicler Falcandus.[516] Geoffrey's rebellion could be the reason why Tancred and his brother William were then brought to the royal palace at Palermo and confined there at what may have been a young age. In other interpretations, Duke Roger's liaison with Count Achard's daughter could have been what soured Geoffrey's relationship with the Hauteville dynasty, and Duke Roger's sons were kept at the palace to prevent any possible attempt to claim the throne. Later stories assert that Duke Roger had indeed secretly mar-ried Tancred's mother. Two of these stories may draw upon gossip among crusad-ers who had heard it while passing through Sicily in 1190–1191. One is *Chronica*

---

the incomplete record does not permit such a conclusion. I have followed Toeche's early estimate.

[512] *Historia*, 23; *History of the Tyrants*, 76.

[513] Chalandon, *Histoire*, 2:425, mentions "*Blanche, Beatrice et Sibille*," while Siragu-sa, *Liber ad honorem*, 20, n. 2, settles tentively on *Marizia*.

[514] Chalandon, *Histoire*, 2:425 and 2:21

[515] Jamison, *Admiral Eugenius*, 183, n. 1.

[516] *Historia*, 15–18, 20–22; *History of the Tyrants*, 69. Falcandus, however, neglects to mention that Geoffrey is Tancred's uncle.

Albrici Monachi Trium Fontium (*The Chronicle of Alberic Monk of Three Springs*),[517] which describes the secret bride as "a palace handmaiden" (*ancillam palatii*) and states that Duke Roger was disinherited on this account. Roger of Hoveden, on the other hand, asserts that Duke Roger married without consulting or informing his father (*nesciente patre suo et inconsulto*) and then predeceased his father.[518] Both accounts explain how Tancred might be a legitimate son, but passed over in the succession. Hoveden's account allows more legitimacy to Tancred's claim, implying as it does that King Roger simply did not know of his son's marriage, and thus might have countenanced it had he lived. Also, despite its many errors in its account of the Hauteville dynasty,[519] it fits the facts of Duke Roger's life better than Alberic's chronicle, for the historical record makes it clear that Duke Roger was not disinherited but remained his father's right-hand man until his death in 1148.[520] Roger of Hoveden's plausible tale obviously would have helped Tancred's prestige after his coronation, and Richard I of England certainly had motives to accept it when he made an alliance with Tancred, arranging a marriage between his nephew and heir Arthur and Tancred's daughter, as Roger of Hoveden relates.[521]

Richard of San Germano, like Falcandus, describes Tancred as a natural son (*filius . . . naturalis*),[522] and most historians follow his lead. Indeed, whatever date is given to this supposed marriage, is hard to reconcile it with the known facts of the marriage between Duke Roger (q.v.) and Elisabeth of Champagne.

Falcandus relates that Tancred's brother, William, died while confined to the Royal Palace, at the age of twenty or twenty-two.[523] Tancred subsequently

---

[517] *Chronica Albrici Monachi Trium Fontium*, ed. P. Scheffer-Boichorst, in MGH 23, ed. G. H. Pertz (Hanover: Hahn, 1866), 864.

[518] *Gesta*, 129.

[519] Among other things, Roger of Hoveden here states (*Gesta*, 129) that Robert Guiscard's son and heir died without offspring; however, Robert Guiscard's heir by Segelgaita was Roger Borsa, who had offspring; see Introduction, C.5 and Genealogical Table 1. In his *Chronica*, 157, Hoveden tells much the same story but supplies the name "Tancred" for the son and heir of Robert Guiscard who died childless. Hoveden knows of only one consort for Roger II, who actually married three times.

[520] Reisinger, *Tankred von Lecce*, 66–67.

[521] *Gesta*, 119.

[522] *Chronica*, 64.

[523] *La Historia*, 51. The two versions of Falcandus's history give slightly different ages for Tancred's brother William at his death — twenty or twenty-two. In Siragusa's edition the passage reads:

Tancredum vero, sicut predictum est, intra palatii muros tenebat inclusum, cuius etiam frater Willelmus ibidem, non sine magna regis invidia, nuper obierat, adolescens utique pulcherrimus, qui, cum fere .xxii. etatis annum ageret, neminem militum viribus sibi parem reppererat. (Tancred, indeed, as previously stated, was kept shut up within the palace walls. His brother William had recently died in the same place, not without the king's great ill

became involved in the plot of Matthew Bonellus to capture King William I; in fact, the prisoners, released from their dungeons, surprised the king in his palace, imprisoned him, and proclaimed his young son Roger as king. An insurrection among the people of Palermo obliged them to release him, and afterwards they negotiated a settlement which allowed most of them to go safely into exile.[524] Tancred himself, however, avoided surrender and raised rebellion at Butera with another noble, Roger Sclavo, inciting the people in the surrounding towns to massacre the Saracen inhabitants wherever they found them. Thus,

> Then there fell a multitude of that people, hardly easy to count, and the few who experienced propitious fortune, whether because they slipped away in secret flight or because they put on the garments of Christians, fled to the southern part of Sicily, to safer towns belonging to Saracens, and now everywhere they abhor the Lombard race. Not only do they not wish to live in that part of Sicily, they will avoid all approach to it.

> *Eius tunc gentis haud facile numerabilis cecidit multitudo, paucique qui, vel fuga furtim elapsi, vel Christianorum assumentes habitum, propitiam sensere fortunam, in australem Sicilie partem, ad tutiora Sarracenorum oppida confugerunt, et usque nunc adeo Lombardorum gentem exhorrent, ut non solum eam partem Sicilie deinceps habitare noluerint, verum etiam accessum eius omnino devitent.*[525]

William I, however, besieged Butera until the nobles, fearing betrayal from the townspeople, anticipated it and handed the strongholds over to the king in return for permission to depart.[526] Pietro implies that Tancred spent his exile in Greece (l. 868).

William I died in 1166, and in 1169, at the close of another stormy insurrection described by both Romuald and Falcandus, the governing council chose

---

will. When this most beautiful youth had reached about twenty-two years of age, none of the knights could be found his equal in strength.)

   For some reason, Loud and Wiedemann (*History*, 105) translate "*obierat*" as "visited," which is linguistically defensible but does not make sense in context. After all, Falcandus has said (*La Historia*, 23; *History of the Tyrants*, trans. Loud and Wiedemann, 76) that both boys were confined to the palace; he never said that either was released. Also, William is never heard from again in Falcandus. Romuald, another contemporary chronicler, does not mention him at all; there is scant documentary evidence of his existence. Most scholars interpret the passage to mean that William died, including Reisinger, *Tankred von Lecce*, 11, and Chalandon, *Histoire*, 2:426, n. 1.

   [524] *La Historia*, 52–69; *History of the Tyrants*, trans. Loud and Wiedemann, 105–20.

   [525] Falcandus, *La Historia*, 70.

   [526] *Historia*, 74; *History of the Tyrants*, trans. Loud and Wiedemann, 124–26.

to recall many of the exiles.[527] Tancred apparently also returned about that time and was made Count of Lecce.[528]

After that, Tancred served William II loyally. He was sent on military expeditions to Egypt in 1174[529] and to Northern Italy in 1176.[530] In February 1181, he became master constable and master justiciar of Apulia and Terra Laboris.[531] Later, he was commander of the naval forces in the attack on Constantinople (see Introduction, C.10).

Shortly after the death of William II, Tancred was chosen as king by a faction of nobles, bishops, and officials strongly influenced by Matthew of Ajello, perhaps with the tacit consent of Pope Clement III.[532]

Immediately after his coronation, the Saracen chieftains rebelled (perhaps taking advantage of the weakness of the new king, or perhaps they remembered his activities at Butera, years before) and withdrew to hideouts in the mountains. According to Hoveden, after Tancred and Richard Lionheart made their alliance, these Saracen chieftains submitted and gave hostages for their good behavior.[533]

Being thus preoccupied with Saracens in the south and the arrival of the crusading kings, Richard I of England (q.v.) and Philip Augustus, and with quarrels about the dower lands of Joanna Plantagenet (q.v.), Tancred at first left defense of Apulia and the more northerly parts of the kingdom under the charge of his brother-in-law, Count Richard of Acerra, who acted, as Pietro describes it, in close coordination with the archbishop Nicholas of Salerno, son of Tancred's chancellor, Matthew. These clearly managed the defense of Salerno sufficiently well to raise the emperor's siege of Naples and bring the empress Constance to Tancred as a prize captive.

These events strengthened Tancred's position. He was then able to negotiate with Pope Celestine III for official recognition as king of Sicily, although in return he was obliged to release Constance and to surrender cherished royal rights over the Sicilian church which the Norman kings had always exercised (see Introduction, C.12–14).

---

[527] *Ignoti Monachi Cisterciensis S. Mariae de Ferraria Chronica*, in *Ignoti Monachi Cisterciensis S. Mariae de Ferraria Chronica et Ryccardi de Sancto Germano Chrionica Priora*, ed. Gaudenzi, 30.

[528] Chalandon, *Histoire*, 2:426.

[529] Chalandon, *Histoire*, 2:389. Norwich, *Kingdom*, 307. *Ignoti Monachis Chronica*, 31. *Annales Casinenses*, 312.

[530] Chalandon, *Histoire*, 2:375; *Annales Casinenses* 312.

[531] Chalandon, *Histoire*, 2:426.

[532] *Annales Casinenses*, 314. Richard of San Germano, *Chronica*, 64. *Annales Ceccanenses*, 288.

[533] Roger of Hoveden, *Chronica*, 151.

From here on, the *Liber* implies that Tancred was a weak or cowardly ruler who left his slightly less cowardly brother-in-law, Richard of Acerra, to fight his battles for him, but it seems that in fact he did cross the straits of Messina to fight Henry's remaining commanders in 1193. He seized the fortress of St. Agatha and the castle of Savignano (*Sabiniani*) and put many German captives to death. Then, despite the victory of Diepold (q.v.) at Monte Rodinis, rather dimmed by the death of Berthold, he went to Terra Laboris and besieged Caserta, withdrawing, however, when its count, William, returned. He then besieged Aversa, which surrendered to him and gave hostages. Then he approached Abbot Roffredo (q.v.) at Teano, and tried to win him over, but the latter responded neither to gifts nor threats even of penalties imposed by the pope, because he was "a man provident for the future and conscious of justice" (*vir consilii providus futurorum et iustitae conscius*). Then the king, "seized with an illness" (*aegritudine correptus*), returned to Sicily.[534] He died 20 February 1194.[535]

§**Tancred** of Saya or Say, count of Gravina.

The count of Gravina is mentioned, l. 298, as one who wrote to Henry VI, inviting him to claim the realm. Tancred of Saya had held that title since at least 1189.[536] He was a descendant of Richard of Saya or Say, to whom, in 1169, the royal court at Palermo had given the task of expelling the contemporary count of Gravina, Gilbert. Gilbert, a kinsman of young William II on his mother's side, had supported Chancellor Stephen du Perche and made himself an enemy to several powerful men who seized the government and became royal *familiares* at this time (see Introduction, C.16). After Richard of Saya successfully enforced Gilbert's banishment, he received the county of Gravina as a reward. His son Tancred inherited it, and as his descendants still held it in 1210,[537] he presumably kept the favor of Henry VI. However, he is not remembered for any great part in the action.

§**Tharthis**, Roger.

This name is listed in cap. 7 on fol. 136r. Scholars have tentatively identified him with **Roger**, count of Chieti (q.v.) or **Roger** of Tarsia (q.v.).

---

[534] *Annales Casinenses*, 317.

[535] Jamison, *Admiral Eugenius*, 101.

[536] Siragusa, *Liber ad honorem*, 27, n. 2; he relies on Ferdinando Ughelli, *Italia Sacra, sive de episcopis Italiae et insularum adiacentium rebusque ab iis praeclare gestis* . . . . 2nd ed., 10 vols. (Venice, 1717–1722), 7:118.

[537] Falcandus, *La Historia*, 162. Loud and Wiedemann, *History of the Tyrants of Sicily*, 215 n. 271. For information on Richard de Saya, Loud and Wiedemann cite W. Hagemann, "Kaiserurkunden aus Gravina," *Quellen und Forschungen aus Italienischen Archiven und Bibliotheken* 40 (1960): 196–97.

§**Tricarico**, Count of. See James, Count of Tricarico.

§**Urso** of Salerno, fl. 1189–1225. Salernitan physician.

Urso gives a speech, ll. 214–243, and is depicted in the accompanying miniature, fol. 103r. He explains how Tancred's freakish conception caused him to be born as a dwarf. The learned explanation effectively robs Tancred of any claim to royal lineage, even illegitimate.

There was indeed a physician of that name in Salerno during this period. He is mentioned by his contemporary, Egidio di Corbeil, as the author of *On Pulses and Urines (De pulsibus et urinis)*, and the maker of some medicines including "the little pills of Master Urso, excellent for whatever joint pain you please" (*pillulae magistri Ursonis ad quamlibet artheticam opportunae*) and the "syrup of Urso, against liver blockage" (*syrupus Ursonis contra oppilationem hepatis*). He may be the Master Urso who died in 1225, as recorded by the Necrology of the *Liber Confratrum* of the cathedral at Salerno.[538]

§**Walter** of Palermo, fl. 1161–1190, royal minister and archbishop of Palermo.

Walter is depicted at the beginning of the *Liber* as an elder statesman, William II's faithful friend and wise advisor, who delivers a eulogy after the king's death, recommends that Constance be summoned to rule the kingdom in accordance with previous oaths, and then, through Matthew's craftiness, is persuaded to acquiesce as Tancred is summoned and crowned king. Later, Walter is named among those who actually wrote inviting Henry VI to claim the kingdom (ll. 68–139, 302; fol. 100r).

Walter's lineage is unknown. Some histories, taking his cognomen *Offamil* or *ophamil*, which appears in some documents, as a transliteration of the English phrase "of the Mill," conclude that he is an Englishman.[539] However, scholars now believe that *Ophamil* is a corruption of *protofamiliaris*, meaning "chief *familiaris*,"[540] reflecting the reality that Walter was for many years William's most important royal minister.[541] Peter of Blois, who knew him, and was perhaps

---

[538] Siragusa, *Liber ad honorem*, 20 n. 1. He cites De Renzi, *Storia documentata della scuola medica di Salerno*, 2nd ed. (Napoli, 1857), 335–39. Siragusa adds, "A treatise with the title *Compendium magistri Ursonis de urinis* [Compendium of Master Urso concerning urines] is found in codex 1487 of the Biblioteca Angelica of Rome (V. 2, 8) of the twelfth and thirteenth centuries, and was published by [Piero] Giacosa, *Magistri Salernitani nondum editi* [Torino, 1901, pp. 283–89]. In the Necrologium of the Liber Confratrum Ecclesiae Salernitanae, page 41 A, col. 2, reads, 'Anno Domini .MCCXXV. obiit magister Urso' and it could be the Urso named by the poet."

[539] John Julius Norwich, for example, passes on this name and interpretation (*The Kingdom in the Sun*, 253).

[540] Donald Matthews, *The Norman Kingdom of Sicily* (New York: Cambridge University Press, 1992), 217.

[541] Loud and Wiedemann report that "Walter remained senior *familiaris*, whose name always appeared first in the dating clauses of royal diplomas, until the death of Wil-

not a friend, suggests that his parentage was nothing to be proud of. In one letter he suggest that Walter should, "From reverence for him who raised you from contemptible poverty, . . . perform your office with fuller humanity" (*Ob reverentiam illius qui de contemptibili paupertate vos extulit, plenioris exhibeatis humanitatis officium*).[542]

Before he became archbishop of Palermo, Walter was archdeacon of Cefalù, then the deacon of Girgenti, and then a canon of the royal chapel of Palermo.[543] He was also tutor to the sons of William I, in which capacity the chronicler Falcandus records some of his actions.

Falcandus first mentions Walter in 1161, when the royal palace was suddenly seized by prisoners released from the palace dungeons, and his pupils, the king's sons, were taken captive with the royal family. Walter made a speech declaring that William I (who had immediately offered to abdicate when seized by his enemies) was a tyrant, and urging the assembly to swear loyalty to Simon, the king's half-brother and momentary leader of the rebels. Probably Walter had to pay this price for remaining in touch with his captive pupils;[544] nevertheless, tragedy struck, for when the citizens of Palermo attacked the palace to free the king, young Roger was accidentally killed.[545] Walter, however, remained tutor to the younger boys. When palace prisoners attempted another coup later, Walter

---

liam II." See *The History of the Tyrants of* Sicily, 218 n. 282, citing Hiroshi Takayama, *The Administration of the Norman Kingdom of Sicily* (New York: E. J. Brill, 1993), 120–22.

[542] Quoted by G. B. Siragusa, *La Historia*, 58, n. 2; citing PL 209, col. 195, Epistle 66.

[543] Siragusa, in *La Historia*, 58, n. 2.

[544] Chalandon (*Histoire*, 2:278) takes Walter's action, urging people to swear obedience to Simon, a bastard son of king Roger, as a sign that the rebels have started quarreling among themselves, and that Simon is making a bid for the throne. Norwich, *Kingdom in the Sun*, 227, adopts this theory without mentioning Walter's involvement, which he, perhaps rightly, thought incredible. That Walter would have turned on his young pupils at such a time is inconsistent with his later career, since William I obviously kept him on as his sons' tutor after surviving the coup. William II, seven years old at the time of the disaster, also kept him as his most trusted advisor throughout the reign. Rather, it seems that in collecting pledges for the leader of the rebels—or perhaps for the man who had direct custody of the royal children—Walter earned his right to maintain contact with his pupils. That Simon was the current leader in the captured palace is a point suggested but somewhat obscured in Falcandus's narrative because the organizer of the plot, Matthew Bonellus, receives more emphasis, though absent from the city when the crisis erupts. See Falcandus, *La Historia*, 54–58; *History of the Tyrants*, trans. Loud and Wiedemann, 107–11.

[545] Falcandus, *La Historia*, 61–63; *History of the Tyrants*, trans. Loud and Wiedemann, 112–14.

rushed the children to safety in the bell tower, presumably of the royal chapel,[546] thus preventing them from being taken hostage once more.

After the death of William I, Walter was supplanted for a time by Peter of Blois as the young king's tutor, and Stephen du Perche, a relation of Queen Margaret, was given the chancellorship and the archbishopric of Palermo. Stephen's policies, perhaps well-intentioned but indifferent to the laws and special circumstances of the kingdom of Sicily, stirred up general revolt, and resulted in his expulsion. In order to remove all possibility of his return, the new *familiares* arranged Walter's election and confirmation as archbishop of Palermo. Falcandus, an ally of Stephen, states bitterly that Walter soon "bound the king to him with an intimacy that was rather mistrusted, to such an extent that he seemed to rule not merely the court but also the king himself" (*sibi regem eatenus suspecta satis familiaritate devinxerat ut non tam curiam quam regem ipsum regere videretur*).[547] He was consecrated archbishop in November 1169.[548]

According to Richard of San Germano, Walter strongly supported the succession of Constance and her marriage to Henry, King of the Romans, in fact being the main engineer of the match. Not very plausibly, the chronicler claims that Walter's chief motive was to get back at his rival, Matthew the vice-chancellor, for having persuaded the king to build and endow his great cathedral at Monreale, thereby diminishing the importance of the Palermitan archbishopric.[549] The date of Walter's death is unknown, but he did not long survive William II.[550] His brother Bartholomew (q.v.) succeeded him as archbishop.

---

[546] Falcandus, *La Historia*, 85; *History of the Tyrants*, trans. Loud and Wiedemann, 135.

[547] Falcandus, *La Historia*, 167; see also *History of the Tyrants*, trans. Loud and Wiedemann, 218. Loud and Wiedemann interpret this passage differently, indicating that William II's friendship (*familiaritate*) with Walter "had been in doubt" (*suspecta*) until after the latter was in secure possession of his important office. This interpretation is linguistically defensible, but I believe mine is valid and fits the context better. In "Falcandus and Fulcaudus," I argue that Falcandus is likening the unhealthy intimacy between Admiral Maio and William I to that between Archbishop Walter and William II. The chronicler thought that Walter's worst offense was persuading his king to give Constance in marriage to Henry VI. However, my interpretation assumes (as Loud and Wiedemann do not) that the *Epistola ad Petrum*, found with the *Historia* in all extant manuscripts, was intentionally connected to it by its author.

[548] Chalandon, *Histoire*, 2:349.

[549] *Chronica*, 63–64.

[550] Jamison (*Admiral Eugenius*, 232, n. 1) states, "The archbishop of Palermo is never mentioned among the Sicilian magnates who carried on negotiations with Richard of England in the autumn and winter of 1190–1191, and the inscription formerly on his tomb at Palermo proves that he died at this time."

§**William I (the Bad)**, ca. 1120[551]–1166. King of Sicily, r. 1154–1166.[552]

Not named, and perhaps pointedly ignored in the *Liber*, William I is alluded to in ll. 43–44: "For it was sworn once—which was enough—that if you [William II] had no progeny, / Your grandfather would retain his scepter through his son-in-law [Henry VI]" (*Nam satis est iurasse semel, te prole carente, / Quod tuus in genero sceptra teneret avus*). The poet knew that William was the grandson of Roger II, while Constance was his daughter. Obviously William had a father who was King Roger's son, though in absence of other evidence, readers might suppose that all Queen Elvira's sons had predeceased both mother and father, as the opening lines of the poem and the facing miniatures (fol. 96r) suggest.

William I's reign was turbulent, and he was sufficiently unpopular as to earn the epithet "the Bad" (*il Malo*), as opposed to "the Good" (*il Buono*), given to his son. Because William I's story also has its touching side, Norwich suggests that he should instead be called "William the Sad."[553] Much of his bad reputation stems from his vivid portrayal in the history of Hugo Falcandus, whose biases no doubt distort the story somewhat; deriding this tendency, Chalandon calls Falcandus a *pamphlétaire*.[554] However, even the much friendlier (and briefer) Romuald of Salerno says of William I that he was "hateful to his kingdom, and more feared than loved."[555] It is true that he had reported, similarly, of King Roger, that he was "to his subjects more terrifying than beloved, a dread and a fear to Greeks and Saracens" (*suis subditis plus terribilis quam dilectus, Grecis et Saracenis formidini et timori*).[556] Romuald may have believed that kings needed to be frightening at times, to fulfill their roles properly.

William, apparently the fourth son of Roger and his first queen, Elvira, was given the princedom of Taranto only after the death of an elder brother, Tancred, who previously had the princedom and then died on 16 March of an uncertain year between between 1138 and 1140.[557] He became prince of Capua after the

---

[551] Romuald's statement that William was forty-six years old at his death in 1166 is the only evidence which permits us to estimate his date of birth; see Garufi, ed., *Chronicon*, 253–54. Also *History of the Tyrants*, trans Loud and Wiedemann, 219–42, here 238. Houben, *Roger II*, 36, n. 10, synthesizes some of the scant data for determing age and birth order of Roger II's sons by Elvira.

[552] Calculated from date of sole rule.

[553] *Kingdom in the Sun*, 245.

[554] *Histoire*, 2:169.

[555] *History of the Tyrants*, trans. Loud and Wiedemann, 219–42, here 238. Latin: *regno suo odibilis, et plus formidini quam amori*. See Garufi, ed., *Chronicon*, 253–54.

[556] *Chronicon Romualdi II Archiepiscopi Salernitani*, ed. Garufi, 237; *History of the Tyrants*, trans. Loud and Wiedemann, 221.

[557] Chalandon, *Histoire*, 2:105. Houben, *Roger II*, 67, n. 4, states that Tancred had been prince of Bari, not Taranto, and "the principality was suppressed . . . after the death of Tancred c. 1138, while the principality of Taranto was created c. 1140 for Roger's fourth son William (see Roger II, *Diplomata*, appendix ii/3)."

death of another brother, Anfusus or Alphonso, in 1144. When his eldest brother, Roger, died in 1148, he became duke of Apulia and heir to the throne. In 1151, Roger II had him crowned co-ruler during his lifetime.[558] He became sole ruler upon his father's death three years later.

William's reign, though relatively short, was eventful. The most detailed sources are the histories of Romuald II, archbishop of Salerno, and of "Hugo Falcandus," whose identity is the subject of a long-running dispute. Since the Emperor Manuel attacked Sicily during William's years, the chronicles of Niketas Choniates and John Kinnamos also cover the reign in some detail. John Julius Norwich, in *The Kingdom in the Sun*, chaps. 9–13, supplies a highly readable account in English, derived largely from these chronicles but fleshed out with other material. Also, Loud and Wiedemann have published an English translation of the chronicle of "Hugo Falcandus," as well as most passages from Romuald which deal with William I and William II.

According to Falcandus, Roger II considered William an unpromising son and hesitated to endow him even with the princedom of Taranto.[559] Chalandon, in his *Histoire,* contradicts this statement by revealing the succession of offices which William was given after the death of each brother (as stated above), but Falcandus's point about Roger's attitude is ultimately a subjective one which documents will not prove or disprove.[560] As the chronicler tells it, William's chief vice was that, lazy or weak in his administrative interests, he preferred to leave the kingdom in the charge of strong ministers who told him that all was well and did not bother him with details. In the first part of his reign, a certain Maio of Bari, given the title of "Great Admiral," was only too eager to accept this role. However, his policies and actions caused troubles which almost led to William's deposition or death in a palace coup in 1161, which did result in the death of his eldest son, Roger (see Introduction C.7).[561] But he survived these troubles, and during the second part of his reign, William did better with a triumvirate of

---

[558] Chalandon, *Histoire*, 2:169–71.

[559] *La Historia*, 19–20; *History of the Tyrants*, trans. Loud and Wiedemann, 59.

[560] Read in isolation, Falcandus's account would suggest that up until the death of Duke Roger, his eldest brother, William had received only the princedom of Taranto, and his father had granted that reluctantly. Chalandon establishes that this is factually untrue and produces a long list of the titles that William had held much earlier in Roger II's reign. The king's reluctance to confer them on him is not elsewhere attested. However, though Falcandus may have witnessed some of the events he recounted and may have gained some authentic information from court insiders, his account is probably written in retrospect, and nothing suggests that he had consistent access to written documents. Thus, he might have received accurate information about Roger II's attitude toward his son, without having at his fingertips a detailed list of all the offices William held, and when he held them.

[561] *La Historia*, 61–62; *History of the Tyrants*, trans. Loud and Wiedemann, 112–13.

advisors dominated by the tactless but very able Richard Palmer, bishop-elect of Syracuse, who insisted on being truthful with the king.[562]

Perhaps of more significance to Pietro da Eboli were William's activities in the region near Salerno. According to Falcandus, the king nearly ordered the destruction of the city in 1162, in the wake of the conspiracies and coup of the previous year. He was persuaded to spare it only by the persistent urging of his *familiares*, including Matthew of Ajello, who convinced him to punish only those directly involved with the conspiracy. As a sacrifice, Matthew handed over an innocent Salernitan enemy of his, who was duly hanged, and this wicked deed provoked a sign from the heavens: a terrifying storm from a clear sky, and later a disaster which brought down a whole house on the wedding festivities of Matthew's niece.[563] Romuald also mentions this terrifying storm, but states that the king had threatened to destroy the city unless a sum of money were paid. In his account, the storm itself, sent by the mediation of the Apostle Matthew, patron of Salerno, is what induced the king to call off the city's destruction and also to depart from it immediately.[564] These local events, rather than those of distant Palermo, might explain William I's unpopularity in the poet's neighborhood.

§William II (the Good). ca. 1153[565]–1189. King of Sicily, r. 1166–1189.

William II, whose death brings on the succession crisis with which the story begins, is portrayed in the *Liber* as an ideal king, a model of virtue, an effective ruler who kept his kingdom peaceful and prosperous, and also a handsome man, deeply mourned by his people and his courtiers (ll. 35–83; fol. 97r, 98r).

Pietro's good opinion of William II seems shared by his contemporaries and chroniclers of the next generation. An anonymous Cistercian chronicler states that William "pious, just, handsome and kind, . . . held the kingdom of Sicily, Apulia and Terra Laboris in peace" (*pius, iustus, pulcer et benignus; pacifice regnum Siciliae, Apulie et Terre Laboris tenuit*).[566] Richard of San Germano begins his chronicle with a prologue praising William II as a king without equal, and his reign as a time of unparalleled justice, peace, prosperity, and security. He

---

[562] *La Historia*, 84; *History of the Tyrants*, trans. Loud and Wiedemann, 134.

[563] *La Historia*, 81–83; *History of the Tyrants*, trans. Loud and Wiedemann, 131–33.

[564] *Chronicon*, ed. Garufi, 251; *History of the Tyrants*, trans. Loud and Wiedemann, 236.

[565] William's birth date can only be conjectured from the statements by Romuald and Falcandus about his age on accession; the former states (254) that he was twelve years old (*natus annos duodecim*) while the latter says (89) that he "had now almost begun his fourteenth year (*iam fere .XIIII. annum etatis attigerat*). Since, as Siragusa points out (*La Historia*, 89, n. 1), to begin his fourteenth year means to complete thirteen years, and he had not quite done this, he must have been twelve years and some months old. Hence, he was probably born in 1153. See also *History of the Tyrants*, trans. Loud and Wiedemann, 138.

[566] *Chronica S. Mariae de Ferraria*, 31.

then supplies a eulogy in rhymed verse, touching on the same themes.[567] On the other hand, there are sour notes too. The anonymous Cistercian adds that William "died without heirs because of his own particular sins" (*ipse pro peccatis propriis sine herede decessit*),[568] without saying what those sins were. Falcandus, whose historical account reaches no further than William's sixteenth year or so, states, probably retrospectively, that the second William takes after his father, William the Bad. At the end,[569] he implies that Walter (q.v.), the new archbishop of Palermo, will play an evil part, similar to that of Admiral Maio, Falcandus's chief villain, in dominating the young king and leading him to unwise decisions. Richard of San Germano reports that Walter of Palermo arranged the marriage between Contance and Henry VI, which could well be what Falcandus had in mind.[570]

Modern scholars look upon William II with somewhat skeptical eyes. The praise of the chroniclers, in tandem with scarce information, creates suspicion. John Julius Norwich points out that despite his reputation for peacefulness, he sent out many military expeditions from Sicily, without ever leading them himself.[571] In 1174 he sent his fleet to Egypt to help King Amalric of Jerusalem, but the king was already dead by the time it arrived, and as Norwich explains, the operation was a disaster.[572] In 1185, William's armies under Count Tancred (q.v.) and Richard of Acerra (q.v.) invaded Byzantine territory. Contemporary Italian chronicles do not directly criticize him for this, though of course the Byzantine chroniclers, Niketas Choniates and Eustathios of Thessaloniki, deplore his actions against the eastern emperor (see Introduction, C.10). After Jerusalem fell in 1187, he was deeply involved in preparations to help with the crusade. Assessment of his character is difficult when the known facts of his life are a puzzle with many missing pieces.

His mother, Margaret of Navarre, bore William I four sons, according to Romuald. One of these, Robert, must have died young.[573] Roger, the eldest, was accidentally killed in a palace coup (see Introduction, C.7). Thus, when his father died in 1166, William II succeeded to the throne at twelve years and some months.[552] In 1172, when his younger brother Henry died of an illness,[574] his paternal aunt, **Constance** of Hauteville (q.v.), became presumptive heiress. About this time, the Byzantine emperor Manuel (q.v.) promised his daughter Maria Porphyrogenita to William II, but for unknown reasons, Manuel broke his word

---

[567] *Chronica*, 63–64.

[568] *Chronica S. Mariae de Ferraria*, 32.

[569] *La Historia*, 61–62, 167; *History of the Tyrants*, trans. Loud and Wiedemann, 112–13, 218.

[570] *Chronica*, 64. See also Hood, "Falcandus and Fulcaudus," 31–32.

[571] *Kingdom in the Sun*, 305, 354.

[572] *Kingdom in the Sun*, 389.

[573] *Chronicon*, 243; *History of the Tyrants*, trans. Loud and Wiedemann, 226, n. 24.

[574] Romuald, *Chronicon*, ed. Garufi, 261.

and did not send the princess.[575] It was not until 1177 that a bride for William, Joanna Plantagenet (q.v.), arrived in Sicily. The marriage was childless, however. In the next decade, instead of educating offspring, William was building the magnificent cathedral at Monreale as a place of burial, and transferring the bodies of his father and brothers there. Richard of San Germano explains that with this pious good work, William hoped to move Heaven to grant children to him and his consort.[576] His mother, Margaret of Navarre, was buried there after she died on 31 July 31 1183.[577]

Although Falcandus writes of William II's youth and minority, and Romuald covers the kingdom of Sicily until the Peace of Venice in 1177, no detailed account of William's last twelve years, the late seventies and the eighties, survives from contemporary chronicles.[578]

As king, William II rarely left Palermo, but he moved around more than usual during the years between 1182 and 1185, while simultaneously overseeing the campaign against Andronicus and arranging Constance's marriage to Henry, king of the Romans. He made a progress through his kingdom in Constance's company, escorting her on her wedding journey. They reached Salerno by August of 1185, at which point she crossed over the frontiers into imperial territory. In December, William was back in Messina again, and then in Palermo. Documents show no evidence that he left the city again.[579] From Palermo, in his last years, he planned extensive support for the third crusade. However, death cut all this short on 28 November 18 1189.[580] He is buried at the cathedral of Monreale, which he had founded.

§**William III**, ca. 1184–ca.1198. Son of Tancred and Sibylla; crowned king of Sicily in 1194.

Though never mentioned by name, William appears at least three times in the surviving miniatures. Several verses also allude to him. For example, when Matthew of Ajello instructs Tancred to bring "both offspring" (*utraque prole*) (l. 144) for his coronation, he actually means "both boys" (*natus uterque*) (l. 175), and Tancred obeys. The two are shown riding in the procession (fol. 102r), identified by caption 2: "these are the sons of Tancred" (*Isti sunt filii Tancredi*). William, the younger of the two, rides horseback beside his elder brother Roger, apparently

---

[575] Assmann ("Friedrich Barbarossas Kinder," 437) believes that Manuel was trying, at the same time, to arrange a marriage between his daughter and Frederick Barbarossa's son. This might explain his strange action. Perhaps, however, Manuel learned something that has eluded later generations.

[576] *Chronica*, 63.

[577] Deér, *Dynastic Porphyry Tombs*, 14–15.

[578] Norwich, in chapters 14–19 of *The Kingdom in the Sun*, gives a readable account based on what knowledge there is, but much explanation must be based on conjecture.

[579] Chalandon, *Histoire*, 2:353.

[580] Jamison, *Admiral Eugenius*, 80.

exchanging words and gestures. Later, in l. 771, a weeping Tancred mentions only one son, meaning William, since Roger has apparently died (see notes on 121r). Still later, after Tancred's own death, William is mentioned as the "little king" (*regulus*) who, Henry VI learns at Favara (l. 1247), has fled to Caltobellota. Sibylla wins pardon for him (l. 1303), but as *regulus* he is once more depicted on fol. 136r, a central figure in the conspiracy, because, although he probably knew nothing about it, the plotters meant to set him back on the throne. He also appears in the court scene on fol. 137r, sitting beside his mother, and perhaps also entering the dock to join her, though no caption marks the identity of either figure.

Neither his birth date nor his death date is known, and contradictory information is given in various places. The miniatures depicting him, as well as the story Pietro tells—that Tancred, at Matthew's direction, brought his two sons, without his wife's knowledge, to ride in the procession with him—suggests that the younger son cannot be much less than six or seven years old. The estimate of his birth date, given above, is based on these speculations.[581]

After the 1194 conspiracy, William III was brought to Germany with the other prisoners, and though at first he may have had companions, at some point he was held separately in the castle of Hohenems in Vorarlberg, modern Austria.[582] Innocent III's anonymous biographer states that his mother and sisters were released shortly after he died (*vix tandem ipso puero . . . defuncto*).[583]

Gruesome things are, however, reported about William's fate in a variety of sources. Otto of St. Blaise says that he was blinded, using language suggestive of a legal sentence: "[the emperor] commanded . . . the son of king Tancred, who was as yet a boy, to be deprived of his eyes and guarded in perpetual captivity at the castle Hohenems" (*filium Tancredi regis adhuc puerum . . . oculis privari et in castro Amiso perpetue captivitati addictum custodiri precepit*).[584] He adds a rumor that William, when he grew up, chose to be a monk: "He, when he reached a

---

[581] Simeti, *Travels*, 242, gives the boy's age as five in 1194, but she does not name her source. In Powell's translation of *The Deeds of Innocent III*, William is described as "an infant son" at Tancred's death (18; chap. 18), but the Latin text from the edition by David Gress-Wright (*Gesta*, 15) actually describes him as Tancred's "single small son" (*unicum filium parvulum*).

[582] Houben, *Roger II*, 175. Jamison, *Admiral Eugenius*, 125. As Jamison also points out (155, n. 1), some scholars assume from the account of the *Continuationes Weingartenses*, 479, that most of the prisoners were kept together, until after the execution of Count Richard of Acerra in 1196–1197; then, according to that chronicle, Henry sent instructions concerning those imprisoned in the Rhine region (*in confinia Reni*), to have some blinded and some imprisoned separately. Perhaps William III was not sent to Hohenems until this time. However, given his unique status as crowned king, he might have been kept separate from the first.

[583] *Deeds of Pope Innocent III*, 29 (chap. 25); *Gesta Innocenti*, 27.

[584] *Continuatio*, 326; chap. 41.

man's age, despairing of transitory things, sought, it is said, eternal good works, panting after heavenly things, because he could not do so with earthly matters. For removed by compulsion from the active life, he eagerly sought the contemplative life, meritoriously, I hope" (*Qui ubi ad virilem etatem pervenit, de transitoriis desperans, bonis operibus, ut fertur, eterna quesivit, celestibus inhiando, quia terrenis non potuit. Nam de activa translatus coacte contemplative studuit, utinam meritorie*). Obviously, this contradicts the *Gesta*'s account, that William died young. More gruesome still is Roger of Hoveden's story that William was not only blinded but was also castrated (*et Willelmum regem, filium Tankredi regis, excecavit et ementulavit*).[585] Innocent III's anonymous biographer mentions that some of Henry's prisoners were blinded, but does not name William among them:

> He sent them as captives into Germany, causing the brothers of the aforesaid archbishop and some others to be deprived of their eyesight; the archbishop, indeed, and the queen, her son and her daughters, [he caused] to be held in close custody.

> *[E]osque captivos in Theutoniam destinavit, faciens fratres predicti archiepiscopi aliosque nonnullos privari luminibus oculorum, archiepiscopus vero, reginam et filium eius ac filias in arcta custodia detineri.* [586]

The language implies but does not say outright that the prisoners of the highest status, namely Tancred's family and the archbishop, were spared mutilation but guarded more strictly. (Conversely, it implies that the blinded prisoners were less trouble to guard.)

Theodor Toeche made it his task, among other things, to examine all the accounts concerning William III's imprisonment and death to decide which was the most credible.[587] In the end, he concluded that Innocent III, actively involved in winning freedom for Henry VI's surviving prisoners, knew more than any other extant source, so that his actions and statements on such issues must be given the most weight. The pope wrote a letter on 26 February 1198, in which he demands the release of Sibylla, her son, and her daughters. But Innocent's

---

[585] *Chronica*, 171. Tuscus (*Gesta*, 499) reports the same atrocity, as does the much later Villani (*Chronicle*, 91; Bk. 4, chap. 20).

[586] *Gesta*, 15. The author of the *Gesta Innocenti* reports no castrations. Although the translation of the passage above is my own, Powell's translation, in *The Deeds of Pope Innocent III*, 18 (chap. 20), does not suggest a vastly different interpretation; indeed he renders *vero* as "but," implying even more strongly than I that the archbishop and Tancred's family were in a different category from the blinded prisoners. Roger of Hoveden, the chronicler, on the other hand, reports castration of other prisoners besides William, for example, Margarito. Toeche (*Kaiser Heinrich VI*, 581) points out that other sources say that Margarito was blinded, but only Roger of Hoveden says that he was castrated.

[587] *Kaiser Heinrich VI*, 581–82.

biographer, discussing his efforts to release prisoners that year, gives a detailed account of Sibylla and her daughters but mentions no effort to free the son, whom he later reports to have died.[588] Thus, Toeche concludes, Innocent had learned of William's death some time after writing the letter in February. Since the biographer makes no mention of any physical mutilations done to Tancred's son, and the author, bitterly hostile to Henry VI, has no reason to conceal such knowledge, probably they did not happen. Toeche points out Roger of Hoveden's fierce bias against Henry VI,[589] influenced by his Plantagenet perspective. After the death of Henry VI, Richard Lionheart and later his brother King John supported their nephew Otto the Welf in his struggle to gain the empire, opposing Philip of Swabia and later Frederick II. Tales that blackened the name of Henry VI and made him out to be a terrible monster would of course serve their purposes.

The story told by Otto of St. Blaise is not as easy to explain away. Van Cleve says that this Otto "managed to appear to maintain a non-partisan view, although he was unmistakably in fact a strong Staufen supporter."[590] Yet despite being a supporter of the Hohenstaufen dynasty, he still reported as a fact, not a rumor, that Henry VI had ordered the blinding of a mere boy for offenses not his own. Perhaps this shows that Otto, writing during times of civil war, judged that the danger William represented was great enough to justify very harsh measures. Perhaps in sympathy he softened the story by reporting the rumor that the youth adopted the religious life whole-heartedly. Since, in chaotic times, compassion can be seen as a weakness which invites further attack, a certain ruthlessness in rulers can be demanded and admired by their followers. Thus, a rumor to the effect that William III had been blinded might have been somewhat to Henry VI's advantage even if the thing itself was not done. Perhaps that explains why, for the Welf partisans, the blinding, which could be seen as harsh but prudent, was not enough, and castration had to be added to the list of horrors.

§**William** of Pistilio. fl. 1142–1195.

William is mentioned, l. 697, as one who chose to go into exile rather than accept the Salernitans' action against the Empress Constance. He was a relative of the Guarna family of Salerno, fighting on the imperial side.[591] Among the documents at Cava, he is described as "William of Pistillio, justiciar and constable

---

[588] *Deeds of Innocent III*, chaps. 22 and 25.

[589] Roger of Hoveden is, after all, following King Richard's career, and King Richard did his best to back his own Welf nephews (see C.13). It is not surprising that an unfavorable view of the Hohenstaufens emerges from his account. Sometimes obvious errors also appear. For example, Hoveden reports in his *Chronica* (171) that Constance was at court in December 1194, when Henry was crowned, at the same time when Henry insultingly had the bodies of Tancred and his son Roger dug up. In fact, Constance was at Jesi in the March of Ancona, waiting to give birth (see her sketch).

[590] *Emperor Frederick II*, 543.

[591] Toeche, *Kaiser Heinrich VI*, 201, n. 6.

of King William, son of Rao and son-in-law of Lucas Guarna" (*Guilelmus de Pistilio, regis Guillelmi Iusticiarius et comestabulus, filius Raonis et gener Luce Guarne*). In the *Catalogus Baronum*, he is said to hold "Castellazzo, . . . Serretella, and the fief of Richard Alfino . . . . Sylva Nigra" (*tenet Castellazzum . . . Serrentellam et feudum Riccardi Alfini . . . Sylvam Nigram*).[592]

Extant documents concerning William begin in 1142, when he confirms a donation. In 1159, he appears with a colleague as royal justiciar and in November of 1161 as royal justiciar and constable (*regalis justitiarus, et comestabulus*). In April 1195, he witnesses a document of William, count of the Principate, thus demonstrating that he has returned from exile.[593]

§**William**, Count of Marsico.

This Count William is depicted among the conspirators in fol. 136r, cap. 12. He is not mentioned in the surviving verses. Siragusa, *Liber ad Honorem*, 144, n. 1) writes: "Count William of Marsico, much noted, recurs several times in the documents. He was son of Sylvester, to whom belonged the houses where the little church of Saint Cataldo was, and which were established by the Great Admiral of William I, Maio of Bari. See my *Regno di Guglielmo I in Sicilia*, I, 145 and 172."

According to Falcandus, Count Sylvester of Marsico was a *familiaris* of William I after the death of Maio. Sylvester died around 1162 or 1163,[594] and his son William succeeded him as count in 1166 or 1167, during the first year of William II's reign, when Queen Margaret was regent.[595] The reason for the delay of several years is unclear. After William II died and it became apparent that there would be a war over the succession, Count William apparently hesitated to choose sides; in a document of May 1190 he "describes himself . . . as count of Marsico by the grace of God, without reference to any king."[596] Eventually, however, he chose Tancred and remained loyal.[597] His fate after 1194 is uncertain.[598]

---

[592] Siragusa, *Liber ad Honorem*, 54, n. 1.

[593] Cuozzo, *Catalogus Baronum Commentario*, 123 par. 440. William of the Principate, a son of Henry or Rodrigo, brother of Margaret of Navarre (consort of William I of Sicily, mother of William II), had remained loyal to Henry VI and Constance during the conflict (see Jamison, *Admiral Eugenius*, 91, n.1); hence Tancred conferred his county on his own brother-in-law, **Richard** of Aquino, q.v. He is not mentioned by Pietro da Eboli in the *Liber*.

[594] *La Historia*, 83; *History of the Tyrants*, trans. Loud and Wiedemann, 133.

[595] *La Historia*, 108; *History of the Tyrants*, trans. Loud and Wiedemann, 157.

[596] Jamison, *Admiral Eugenius*, 81.

[597] Jamison, *Admiral Eugenius*, 104.

[598] Jamison, *Admiral Eugenius*, 155 and n. 3. Jamison suspects that William was "put to death," judging from that fact that his county is "in other hands" in 1196, when Philip Guarna (q.v.) describes himself as "By the grace of God and the Emperor, lord of the county of Marsico and justiciar" (*Dei et Imperiali gratia Comitatus Marsici Dominus et Justiarius*). Since, however, Philip is not actually "count," Jamison leaves open the possibility that Philip simply had administratrative duties at this time.

Genealogical Tables

These genealogies do not give a comprehensive account of these families. Their purpose is rather to provide some context for the characters who appear in *Liber ad Honorem Augusti*, or who are mentioned in the associated commentary, introduction, or biographical sketches; much information presented here in graphic form is presented with footnotes there. Other sources are provided in footnotes.

Table 1: The Hauteville Family[1]

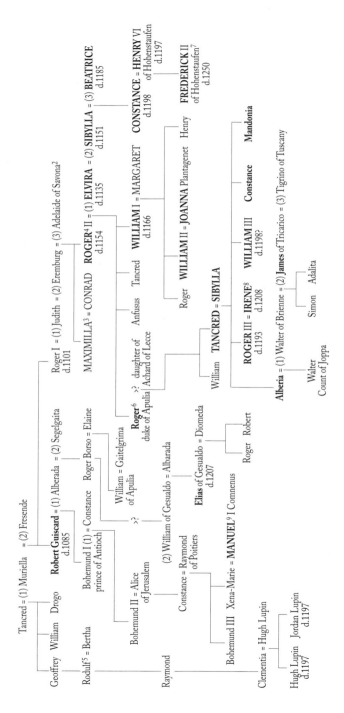

[1] Runciman supplies a detailed genealogical tree for "The Princes of Antioch and Kings Of Sicily" in *History of the Crusades* (*The Kingdom of Jerusalem and the Frankish East, 1100–1187*), "Appendix III" after p. 491.

[2] For Great Count Roger, see Introduction C.3. For his wives and children, cf Chalandon, *Histoire*, 1:350–354.

[3] See Table 2 and Introduction C.4. It is uncertain which countess bore Maximilla. Holtzmann, "Maximilla," 164, believes she was, like Roger II, a daughter of Adelaide, and thus could not have been more than five years old when she married Conrad the Salian in 1095; indeed, a contemporary chronicler describe her as being "still small" (*admodum parvula*).

[4] 1st king of Sicily

[5] 1st count of Catanzaro

[6] Duke Roger of Apulia (d. 1148) married Elisabeth, daughter of the count Theobald of Champagne, but the union was childless.

[7] Frederick II of Hohenstaufen also appears in Tables 2, 4, 5, and 6, the last being an account of his descendants.

[8] Irene, daughter of Isaac Angelus, also appears in Tables 2 and 3. Her descendants (with **PHILIP** of Swabia) appear in Table 2.

[9] Main account Table 3

Table 2: German Emperors: Salians and Hohenstaufens[10]

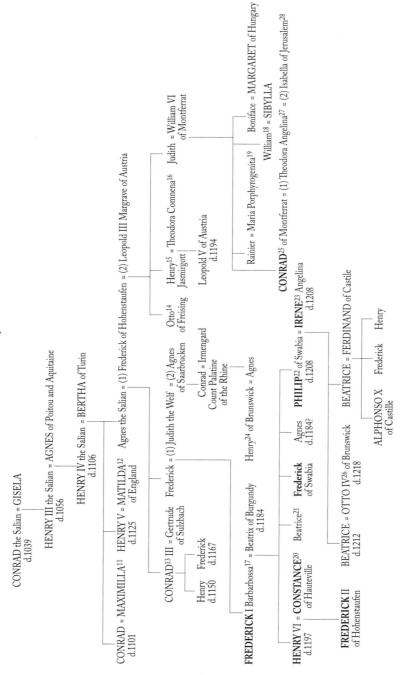

10 Much information on the Salian Dynasty comes from Hampe, *Germany Under the Salian and Hohenstaufen Emperors*, and also from Mierow's notes in his translations of Otto of Freising's two works. Detailed genealogies, provided by John Carmi Parsons, in his *Eleanor of Castile: Queen and Society in Thirteenth Century England* (New York: St. Martin's, 1995; repr. Palgrave Macmillan, 1997), 255–58, are particularly helpful in tracing descendants of Philip of Swabia and Irene Angelina.

11 Daughter of Roger I of Sicily; see Introduction C.4 and Table 1.

12 Daughter of Henry I of England; mother of Henry II through 2nd marriage to Geoffrey of Plantagenet. See Table 4.

13 1st monarch of the Hohenstaufen dynasty.

14 Author of *De Duabus Civitatibus* and *Gesta Frederici*.

15 1st Babenburg duke of Austria.

16 Granddaughter of Emperor John Comnenus through his son Andronicus.

17 Assmann, "Friedrich Barbarossas Kinder," 435–72 and Baaken, "Die Altersfolge der Söhne," 47–68 give much detailed information on the ancestry and descendants of Frederick Barbarossa, as well as of Conrad of Montferrat.

18 William and Sibylla of Jerusalem were parents of BALDWIN V. See Introduction C.9 and Table 5.

19 Daughter of MANUEL, see Table 3.

20 Daughter of ROGER II of Sicily. See Introduction C.4 and Table 1.

21 Apparently the bride offered to WILLIAM II of Sicily (Introduction C.8); estimated date of death from Assmann, "Friedrich Barbarossas Kinder," 448–50.

22 See Table 3.

23 See Tables 1 and 3.

24 Elder brother of Emperor OTTO IV of Brunswick; see Introduction C.13 and Table 4.

25 See Introduction B.2, C. 11, Table 3 and Table 5.

26 See Table 4.

27 Sister of Isaac Angelus; Table 3.

28 daughter of BALDWIN III; for descendants (with CONRAD of Montferrat), see Table 5.

Table 3: Eastern Emperors: Comneni and Angeli[29]

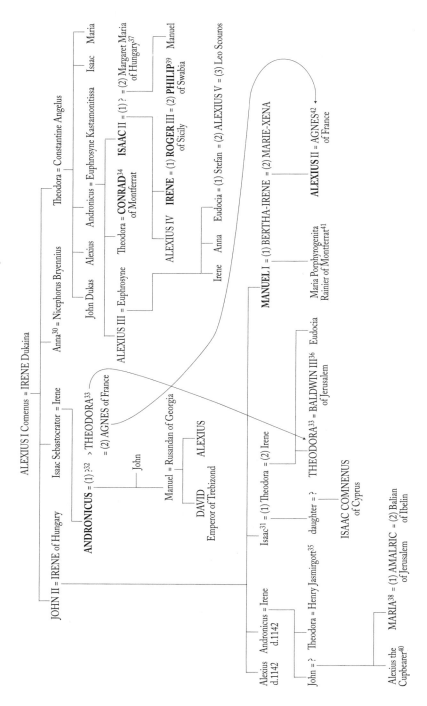

29 Genealogies for the Comneni and the Angeli famlies are provided in Brand, *Byzantium Confronts the West*, 277–78. Also in *Oxford Dictionary of Byzantium*: "Selected Genealogy of the Angelos Dynasty (1185–1204)," 1: 98, and "Genealogy of the Komnenos Family," 2: 1145.

30 Author of the *Alexiad*. A grandson of hers, named Andronicus, was blinded by the Emperor **ANDRONICUS COMNENUS** (Niketas, *O City of Byzantium*, 234).

31 The names of this Isaac's two wives and their children are found in "Genealogy of the Komnenos Family," *Oxford Dictionary of Byzantium*, 2: 1145.

32 The name of Andronicus's first wife is not known, but Brand, *Byzantium Confronts*, 277, believes her to have been a sister of George III of Georgia.

33 This Theodora became the favorite mistress of **ANDRONICUS I**. They had two children whose marriages occasioned some quarrels; cf. Niketas Choniates, *O City of Byzantium*, 145, 171, 234.

34 See Tables 2 and 5.

35 Uncle of **FREDERICK** Barbarossa; see Table 2.

36 See Table 5.

37 2nd husband Boniface of Montferrat, brother of **CONRAD**; see Table 2.

38 See Table 5.

39 See Tables 1 and 2.

40 See Introduction C. 10.

41 Brother of **CONRAD** of Montferrat; see Table 2.

42 Agnes of France was sister of Philip Augustus of France. She was sent to Constantinople as a child to marry **ALEXIUS II** and took the same of Anna. After the death of Alexius, **ANDRONICUS I** married her.

Table 4: The Royal Family of England[43] and the German Welfs[44]

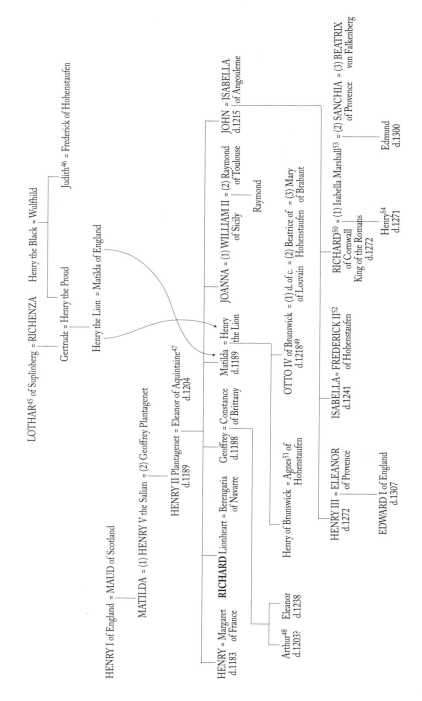

[43] Kelly, in *Eleanor of Aquitaine and the Four Kings*, gives detailed information about the Plantagenets of this time, frequently cited in the biographical sketches. T. W. E. Roche, *The King of Almayne* (London: Murray, 1966) gives most of what appears here about the next generations, with several detailed tables relating to Richard of Cornwall's family, after p. 225 in his book.

[44] Jordan, *Henry the Lion*, 256–60, has detailed information about the Welfs, including the Hohenstaufens with Welf connections.

[45] See Introduction C.5.

[46] See Table 2.

[47] ELEANOR had been married previously to LOUIS VII of France, and had borne him two daughters. The marriage was annulled ostensibly because of consanguinity.

[48] Arthur of Brittany, once betrothed to **Alberia**, had a fate even more mysterious than that of **WILLIAM III** of Hauteville. He disappeared into King John's prison, and no official account of his death survives. The date given here comes from Roche, *King of Almayne*, 225.

[49] OTTO of Brunswick's marital history here is pieced together from Kelly, *Eleanor and the Four Kings*, 336–37 (Otto was married to "the infant daughter of the duke of Louvain"), from Bradbury, *Philip Augustus*, 296 and 297) and from Van Cleve, *Emperor*, 78. His date of death comes from Van Cleve, *Emperor*, 121.

[50] RICHARD, brother of HENRY III of England, was elected as Holy Roman Emperor, but never crowned by the pope; hence, like CONRAD III of Hohenstaufen, he is called king of the Romans, not emperor.

[51] Daughter and heiress of Conrad, count palatine of the Rhine, half-brother of **FREDERICK** Barbarossa. See Introduction C.13

[52] For ISABELLA Plantagene's descendants, with **FREDERICK II**, see Table 6.

[53] Isabella, daughter of William Marshall, was the widow of Gilbert de Clare, Earl of Gloucester.

[54] Dante's *Inferno* 12.118–120 refers to Henry of Cornwall's murder at Viterbo.

Table 5: The Royal Family of Jerusalem[55]

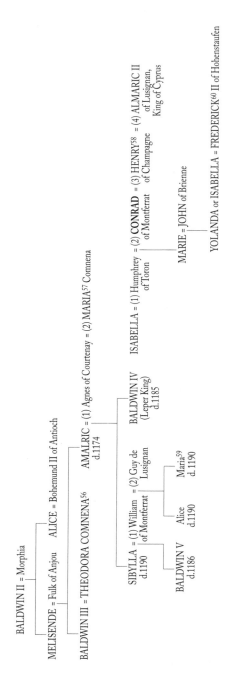

BALDWIN II = Morphia

MELISENDE = Fulk of Anjou   ALICE = Bohemund II of Antioch

BALDWIN III = THEODORA COMNENA[56]   AMALRIC = (1) Agnes of Courtenay = (2) MARIA[57] Comnena
d.1174

SIBYLLA = (1) William = (2) Guy de Lusignan   BALDWIN IV (Leper King) d.1185   ISABELLA = (1) Humphrey of Toron = (2) CONRAD of Montferrat = (3) HENRY[58] of Champagne = (4) ALMARIC II of Lusignan, King of Cyprus
d.1190   of Montferrat

BALDWIN V d.1186   Alice d.1190   Maria[59] d.1190

MARIE = JOHN of Brienne

YOLANDA or ISABELLA = FREDERICK[60] II of Hohenstaufen

---

55   Much information here is found in Runciman's genealogical table for "The Royal House of Jerusalem," in *History of the Crusades*, vol. 2 (*The Kingdom of Jerusalem and the Frankish East, 1100–1187*), "Appendix III" starting after p. 491.

56   Niece of MANUEL Comnenus, daugher of JOHN II. Subsequent mistress of Andronicus; Table 3.

57   Grand-niece of MANUEL Comnenus, granddaughter of Andronicus, son of JOHN II Comnenus; see Table 3.

58   Henry of Champagne was a grandson of Eleanor of Aquitaine by her first husband, Louis VII of France. His mother was Countess Marie of Champagne.

59   Runciman, *History of the Crusades*, 3:30 (*The Kingdom of Acre*), supplies the date of death for SIBYLLA and her two young daughters by GUY de Lusignan.

60   See Tables 1, 2, 4, and 6 (descendants).

Table 6: **FREDERICK** II of Hohenstaufen and Descendants

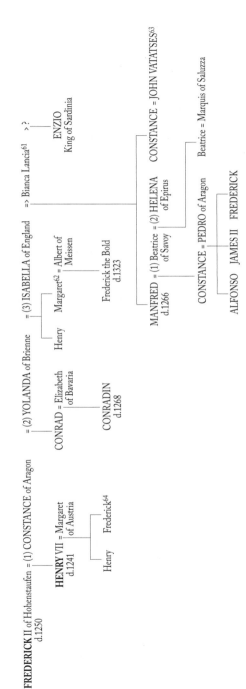

61 Frederick II's liaison with Bianca Lancia began before he married Isabella of England, but he married her before her death; see for example Masson (*Frederick II*, 213)

62 Information on Margaret, her husband, and her son is found in Steven Runciman, *The Sicilian Vespers: A History of the Mediterranean World in the Later Thirteenth Century* (New York: Cambridge University Press, 1958; repr. 2002), 295, n. 1 for p. 27.

63 Emperor of Nicaea; see Runciman, *The Sicilian Vespers*, 26.

64 For information on the sons of Henry VII by Margaret of Austria, see Eduard Winkelmann, "Heinrich VII, römanisher König," in *Allgemeine Deutsche Biographie* (ADB), Vol. 11 (Leipzig: Duncker u. Humblot, 1880), 433–39, here 438.

BIBLIOGRAPHY

Primary Sources

Acta Imperii adhuc inedita. Ed. K.F. Stumpf-Brentano. In *Die Reichskanzler vornehmlich des X., XI., und XII. Jahrhunderts*, vol. 3. Innsbruck: Wagner, 1865–1881. Available online at http://books.google.com/[1]

Acta Imperii inedita saeculi XIII: Urkunden und Briefe zur geschichte des Kaiserreichs und des Königreichs Sicilien in den Jahren 1198–1273. Ed. E. Winkelmann. Innsbruck: Wagner, 1880–1885. Available online at http://books.google.com/

Amari, Michele, ed. *Biblioteca Arabo-Sicula.* 2 vols. Turin and Rome: Ermanno Loescher, 1880–1881. Available online at http://books.google.com/

Annales Casinenses. Ed. G.H. Pertz. In MGH 19, 303–20. Hannover: Hahn, 1866. Available online at www.dmgh.de

Annales Ceccanenses. Ed. G.H. Pertz. In MGH 19, 275–302. Available online at www.dmgh.de

———. *Chronicon Fossae Novae.* Trans. S. Volpicello. In *Cronisti e Scrittori Sincroni della Dominazione Normanna nel Regno di Puglia e Sicilia*, ed. Giuseppe Del Re, 1: 491–556. Naples: Forni, 1845. Available online at http://books.google.com/

Annales Marbacenses, qui dicuntur Chronica Hohenburgensis cum continuatione et additamentis Neoburgensibus. Ed. Hermann Bloch. In MGH, *Scriptores rerum Germanicarum in usum scholarum separatim editi* 9. Hannover: Hahn, 1907. Available online at www.dmgh.de

Annales Stadtenses. Ed. G.H. Pertz. In MGH 16, 271–379. Stuttgart, 1859. Available online at www.dmgh.de

---

[1] URLs provided by Google books are too unwieldy to print; it is best to go to the main site, do an "advanced book search" (<http://books.google.com/advanced_book_search>), limit it to items with "full view," and enter appropriate search terms (author, title, date), to get the desired volume.

Anon. *The Deeds of Pope Innocent III: by an Anonymous Author.* Trans., intro., and annot. James M. Powell. Washington, DC: Catholic University of America Press, 2004.

———. "The *Gesta Innocenti III*: Text, Introduction and Commentary." Ed. D.R. Gress-Wright. Ph.D. diss., Bryn Mawr College, 1981.

[Ansbertus.] *Historia de expeditione Frederici imperatoris.* In *Quellen zur Geschichte des Kreuzzuges Friedrichs I.*, ed. A. Chroust, 1–115. MGH SRG n.F. 5. Berlin: Weidmann, 1928. Available online at www.dmgh.de

Arnold of Lübeck. *Chronica Slavorum.* Ed. G.H. Pertz. In MGH 21, 100–250. Hannover: Hahn, 1869. Available online at www.dmgh.de

Boccaccio, Giovanni. *Famous Women.* Trans. Virginia Brown. Cambridge, MA: The I Tatti Renaissance Library, 2003.

Burchardi et Cuonradi Urspergsensium *Chronicon.* Ed. O. Abel and L. Wieland. In MGH 23, 333–83. Hannover: Hahn, 1886. Available online at www.dmgh.de

Catalogus Baronum Neapolitano in regno versantium qui sub auspiciis Guilielmi cognom. Boni ad Terram Sanctam sibi vindicandam crucem susceperunt. In *Cronisti*, ed. Del Re, 1: 571–616. Available online at http://books.google.com/

Cencio Camerario. *Coronatio Romana Henrici VI imperatoris.* "Ordo qualiter rex Teutonicus Romam ad suscipiendam coronam imperii venire debeat, ibique per manum pontificis in imperatorem coronari." Ed. G.H. Pertz. In MGH Leges 2, 187–93. Hannover: Hahn, 1886. Available online at www.dmgh.de

Chronica Adonis."Ex Adonis archiepiscopi Viennensis chronico usque ad a. 859." With "Continuatio I a. 866–896" and "Continuatio II ex codice Bernensi a. 897–1031." Ed. G.H. Pertz. In MGH SS 2, 315–26. Hannover, 1829. Available online at www.dmgh.de

Chronica Albrici Monachi Trium Fontium. Ed. P. Scheffer-Boichorst. In MGH 23, 631–950. Hannover: Hahn, 1866. Available online at www.dmgh.de

Chronica Regia Coloniensis. Ed. G. Waitz. In MGH, *Scriptores . . .in usum scholarum separatim editi* 18. Hannover: Hahn, 1880. Available online at www.dmgh.de

Chronica S. Mariae de Ferraria. In *Ignoti Monachi Cisterciensis S. Mariae de Ferraria Chronica et Ryccardi de Sancto Germano Chronica Priora*, ed. A. Gaudenzi, 11–39. Naples: Giannini, 1888.

The Chronicle of the Third Crusade: Itinerarium Peregrinorum et Gesta Regis Ricardi. Trans. Helen Nicholson. Burlington, VT: Ashgate, 1997.

Chronicon Romualdi II Archiepiscopi Salernitani. Ed. C.A. Garufi. *Rerum Italicarum Scriptores* 7.1. New ed. Città di Castello: Lapi, 1909–1935.

——— (*Cronica di Romualdo Guarna*). Ed. and trans. G. Del Re. In *Cronisti*, ed. idem, 1: 1–80. [excerpt, 1122–1177.] Available online at http://books.google.com/

————. In *History of the Tyrants of Sicily*, ed, and trans. Loud and Wiedemann, 219–42.

Anna Comnena. *The Alexiad of Anna Comnena.* Trans. E.R.A. Sewter. New York: Penguin, 1969.

Continuationes Weingartenses. Ed. G.H. Pertz. In MGH 21, 473–80. Hannover: Hahn, 1869. Available online at www.dmgh.de

Epistola de morte Friderici imperatoris. Ed. G.H. Pertz. In MGH 20, 494–96. Hannover: Hahn, 1868. Available online at www.dmgh.de

Ermoldus Nigellus. *Carmina in Honorem Hludvici I.* In *Poetae Latini Carolini Aevi,* ed. E. Dümmler, 2: 1–91. MGH AA 1. Berlin: Weidmann, 1884. Available online at www.dmgh.de

Eustathios of Thessalonica. *The Capture of Thessaloniki.* Ed., annot., and comm. J.R. Melville Jones. Canberra: Australian Association for Byzantine Studies, 1988.

Falcandus, Hugo. *La Historia o Liber de regno Sicilie e la Epistola ad Petrum Panormitane Ecclesie Thesaurarium di Ugo Falcando.* Ed. G.B. Siragusa. Rome: Istituto storico italiano, 1897.

————. *The History of the Tyrants of Sicily.* Ed. and trans. Graham Loud and Thomas Wiedemann. New York: Manchester University Press, 1998.

Frederick II of Hohenstaufen. *The Art of Falconry.* Trans. C.A. Wood and H.M. Fyfe. Stanford: Stanford University Press, 1943.

————. *De arte venandi cum avibus.* Ed. C.A. Willemsen. Graz: Akademische Druck- und Verlagsanstalt, 1969.

————. *Liber Augustalis or Constitutions of Melfi, Promulgated by the Emperor Frederick II for the Kingdom of Sicily in 1231.* Trans. James M. Powell. Syracuse: Syracuse University Press, 1971.

Garufi, C.A., ed. *Documenti Inediti dell'epoca Normanna.* In *Documenti per servire alla storia di Sicilia.* Diplomatica 18. Palermo: Società siciliana di storia patria, 1899. Available online at http://books.google.com/

Giacosa, Piero, ed. *Magistri Salernitani nondum editi.* Turin: Bocca, 1898. Available online at http://books.google.com/

Godfrey of Viterbo. *Pantheon.* In *Rerum Italicarum Scriptores* 7: 351–473. Milan: Societas Palatina, 1725.

————. *Gotfredi Viterbiensis opera.* Ed. G. Waitz. In MGH 22, 1–338. Hannover: Hahn, 1872. Available online at www.dmgh.de

Huillard-Bréholles, J.L.A., ed. *Historia Diplomatica Friderici Secundi sive Constitutiones, Privilegia, Mandata, Instrumenta quae supersunt istius imperatoris et filiorum ejus.* 6 vols. Paris: Plon, 1852–1861. Repr. Turin: Bottega d'Erasmo, 1964. Vols. 5.1 and 6.1–2 available online at http://books.google.com/

Ibn Jubayr. *The Travels of Ibn Jubayr.* Trans. R.J.C. Broadhurst. London: Jonathan Cape, 1952.

John Kinnamos. *Deeds of John and Manuel Comnenus.* Trans. Charles M. Brand. New York: Columbia University Press, 1976.

Lucan. *The Civil War.* Trans. J.D. Duff. Loeb Classical Library. New York: Putnam, 1928.

Magnus presbyterus Reicherspergensis. *Chronica collecta a Magno Presbytero.* Ed. G.H. Pertz. In MGH 17, 476–523. Hannover: Hahn, 1861. Available online at www.dmgh.de

Niketas Choniates. *O City of Byzantium: Annals of Niketas Choniates.* Trans. Harry J. Magoulias. Detroit: Wayne State University Press, 1984.

Otto of Freising. *Ottonis episcopi Frisingensis Chronica sive Historia de duabus civitatibus.* Ed. A. Hofmeister. MGH SRG. Hannover and Leipzig: Hahn, 1912. Available online at www.dmgh.de

———. *The Two Cities: A Chronicle of Universal History of the Year 1146 A.D. by Otto, Bishop of Freising.* Trans. C.C. Mierow. Ed. A.P. Evans and C. Knapp. New York: Columbia University Press, 1928.

——— and Rahewin. *Gesta Frederici I imperatoris.* Ed. B. von Simson. MGH SRG. Hannover and Leipzig: Hahn, 1912. Available online at www.dmgh.de

———. *The Deeds of Frederick Barbarossa.* Trans. and annot. C.C. Mierow, with R. Emery. New York: Columbia University Press, 1953. Repr. New York: Norton, 1966.

Otto of St Blaise. *Chronici ab Ottone Frisingensi conscripti Continuatio: auctore, ut videtur, Ottone S. Blasii monacho.* Ed. R. Wilmans. In MGH 20, 302–37. Suppll. I, V, VI, XII, ed. G.H. Pertz. Stuttgart, 1868. Available online at www.dmgh.de

Ovid. *Heroides, Amores.* Trans. Grant Showerman. 2 vols. Loeb Classical Library. New York: Putnam, 1921.

———. *Metamorphoses.* Trans. Frank Justus Miller. 2 vols. Loeb Classical Library. New York: Putnam, 1916.

Peter of Eboli. *Petri d'Ebolo Carmen de Motibus Siculis et rebus inter Henricum VI Romanorum Imperatorem et Tancredum seculo XII gestis.* Ed. Samuel Engel. 1ˢᵗ ed. Basel, 1746. Ed. Joannes Gravier. 2ⁿᵈ ed. Naples, 1777. Available online at http://books.google.com/

———. *De Tumulti Avvenuti in Sicilia e de'Fatti Operati nel XII Secolo tra Arrigo VI, Imperatore de'Romani, e Tancredi: Carme di Pietro d'Eboli (Petri d'Ebulo Carmen de Motibus Siciliis, et rebus inter Henricum IV* [sic] *Romanorum Imperatorem et Tancredum seculo XII gestis).* Trans. Emmanuele Rocco. In *Cronisti,* ed. Del Re, 1: 403–56. Available online at http://books.google.com/

———. *Des Magisters Petrus de Ebulo Liber ad honorem Augusti.* Ed. E. Winkelmann. Leipzig: Duncker u. Humblot, 1874.

———. *Petri Ansolini de Ebulo De rebus Siculis carmen.* Ed. Ettore Rota. In *Rerum Italicarum Scriptores* n.s. 31.1. Città di Castello: Lapi, 1904. Available online at http://books.google.com/

————. *Liber in Honorem Augusti di Pietro da Eboli. Second il Cod. 120 della Biblioteca Civica di Berna.* Ed. G.B. Siragusa. Rome: Istituto storico italiano, 1906.

————. *Il De Balneis Puteolanis di Pietro da Eboli.* Ed. and trans. Silvia Maddalo. Vatican City: Biblioteca Apostolica Vaticana, 2003.

Radulfus Abbas de Coggeshale. *Historia Anglicana.* Ed. F. Liebermann and R. Pauli. In MGH 27, 344–68. Hannover: Hahn, 1885. Available online at www.dmgh.de

Richard of San Germano. *Ryccardi de Sancto Germano Chronica Priora.* In *Ignoti Monachi. . .*, ed. Gaudenzi, 63–155.

Roger of Hoveden. *Gesta Heinrici II et Richardi I.* Ed. G. Waitz. In MGH 27, 81–132. Hannover: Hahn, 1885. Available online at www.dmgh.de

————. Ed. Stubbs. Rolls Series 49. London, 1867.

————. *Ex Chronica.* Ed. G. Waitz. In MGH 27, 133–83. Available online at www.dmgh.de

Sicard of Cremona. *Sicardi Episcopi Cremonensis Chronica.* Ed. O. Holder-Egger. In MGH 21, 22–188. Hannover: Hahn, 1905. Available online at www.dmgh.de

Tacitus. *The Compelete Works of Tacitus.* Trans. A.J. Church and W.J. Brodribb. Ed. and intro. M. Hadas. New York: Modern Library, 1942.

Thomas Tuscus. *Gesta imperatorum et pontificum.* Ed. E. Ehrenfeuchter. In MGH 22, 490–528. Hannover: Hahn, 1872. Available online at www.dmgh.de

Venantius Fortunatus. *Venanti Fortunati presbyteri italici opera poetica.* Ed. F. Leo. MGH AA 4.1. Berlin: Weidmann, 1881. Available online at www.dmgh.de

Villani, Giovanni. *Selections from the Chronicle of Villani.* Trans. R.E. Selfe, ed. P.H. Wicksteed. London: Constable, 1906. Available online at www.Elfinspell.com/VillaniStart.html

Virgil. *Eclogues, Georgics, Aeneid. Minor Poems.* Trans. H. Rushton Fairclough. 2 vols. Loeb Classical Library. New York: Putnam, 1916–1918.

William of Apulia. *Gesta Roberti Wiscardi.* Ed. G.H. Pertz. In MGH 9, 239–98. Hannover: Hahn, 1851. Available online at www.dmgh.de

William of Brittany. *Ex Willelmus Brittonis operibus.* Ed. A. Molinier et al. In MGH 26, 295–389. Hannover: Hahn, 1882. Available online at www.dmgh.de

Secondary Works

Abulafia, David. *Frederick II.* Oxford: Oxford University Press, 1988.

Amari, Michele. *Storia dei Musulmani di Sicilia.* 3 vols. Florence: Successori le Monnier, 1854–1868. Vol. 3 available online at http://books.google.com/

Assmann, Erwin. "Friedrich Barbarossas Kinder." *Deutsches Archiv für Erforschung des Mittelalters* 33 (1977): 435–72.

Azzam, A.R. *Saladin*. New York: Pearson, 2009.

Baaken, Gerhard. "Die Altersfolge der Söhne Friedrich Barbarossas und die Königserhebung Heinrichs VI." *Deutsches Archiv für Erforschung des Mittelalters* 20 (1968): 47–68.

Becht-Jördens, Gereon, trans. and ed. *Petrus de Ebulo: Liber ad Honorem Augusti, sive de rebus Siculis. Codex 120 II der Burgerbibliothek Bern*, ed. T. Kölzer, M. Stähli et al., 33–246. Sigmaringen: Jan Thorbecke, 1994.

———. "Der Dichter und sein Text." In *Petrus de Ebulo*, ed. Kölzer et al., 287–92.

Benson, Robert L. "Political *Renovatio*: Two Models from Roman Antiquity." In *Renaissance and Renewal in the Twelfth Century*, ed. idem and Giles Constable, 339–86. Cambridge, MA: Harvard University Press, 1982.

Bignoni, Guido. *Una fonte per la storia del Regno di Sicilia*. Genoa, 1901.

Bindi, Vincenzo. *Monumenti storici ed artistici degli Abruzzi*. Naples: Giannini, 1889.

Bloch, Herbert. *Monte Cassino in the Middle Ages*. 3 vols. Cambridge, MA: Harvard University Press, 1988.

Block, Paul. *Zur Kritik des Petrus de Ebulo*. 2 vols. Prenzlau: C. Viscont'schen Buchdruckerei, 1883. Vol. 2 available online at http://books.google.com/

Bradbury, J. *Philip Augustus: King of France 1180–1223*. New York: Longman, 1998.

Brand, Charles M. "The Byzantines and Saladin, 1185–1192." *Speculum* 37 (1962): 167–81.

———. *Byzantium Confronts the West, 1180–1204*. Cambridge, MA: Harvard University Press, 1968.

Brown, Michelle P. *Illuminated Manuscripts: A Guide to Technical Terms*. Los Angeles: Getty Publications, 1994.

Brumble, H. David. *Classical Myths and Legends in the Middle Ages and Renaissance*. Westport, CT: Greenwood Press, 1998.

Bynum, Caroline Walker. *Jesus as Mother: Studies in the Spirituality of the High Middle Ages*. Berkeley: University of California Press, 1982.

Chalandon, Ferdinand. *Histoire de la Domination Normande en Italie et en Sicile*. 2 vols. Paris: Picard, 1907; repr. New York: Burt Franklin, 1960.

Clementi, Dione. "The Circumstances of Count Tancred's Accession to the Kingdon of Sicily, Duchy of Apulia, and the Principality of Capua." In *Mélanges Antonio Marongiu*, 57–80. Palermo: Università di Palermo, 1967.

Cowdrey, H.E.J. *Pope Gregory VII, 1073–1085*. New York: Oxford University Press, 1998.

Crisci, Generoso, and Angelo Campagna. *Salerno Sacra*. Salerno: Edizioni della Curia Arcivescovile, 1962.

Crowfoot, Elisabeth, and Sonia Hawkes. "Early Anglo-Saxon Gold Braids." *Medieval Archaeology* 11 (1967): 42–86.

Crowther-Heyck, Kathleen. "'Be Fruitful and Multiply': Genesis and Generation in Reformation Germany." *Renaissance Quarterly* 55 (2002): 904–35.

Csendes, Peter. *Heinrich VI.: Gestalten des Mittelalters und der Renaissance*, ed. Peter Herde. Darmstadt: Wissenschaftliche Buchgesellschaft, 1993.

Cuozzo, Errico. "Ruggiero, conte d'Andria: Ricerche sulla nozione di regalità al tramonto della monarchia normanna." *Archivio storico per le provincie napoletane* 99 (1981): 129–68.

———. *Catalogus Baronum Commentario*. Rome: Istituto storico italiano per il Medio Evo, 1984.

D'Amato, Jean Marie. "Prolegomena to a Critical Edition of the Illustrated Medieval Poem *De Balneis Terre Laboris* by Peter of Eboli (Petrus de Ebulo)." Ph.D. diss., Johns Hopkins University, 1975.

De Renzi, Salvatore. *Storia documentata della scuola medica di Salerno.* 2nd ed. Naples, 1857. Available online at http://books.google.com/

De Rosa, Francesco, ed. *Liber ad Honorem Augusti di Pietro da Eboli: secondo il Cod. 120 della Biblioteca Civica di Berna.* Cassino: F. Ciolfi, 2000.

———, intro., trans., and comm. *Pietro da Eboli: Liber ad Honorem Augusti.* Cassino: F. Ciolfi, 2001.

De Simone, Adalgisa, trans. and ed. *Splendori e Misteri di Sicilia in un'opera di Ibn Qalaqis.* Messina: Rubbetino, 1996.

Del Treppo, Mario. "Aiello, Nicolò d'." In *Dizionario biografico degli Italiani* 1: 518–19. Rome, 1960.

Deér, Josef. *Dynastic Porphyry Tombs of the Norman Period.* Trans. G.A. Gillhoff. Cambridge, MA: Harvard University Press, 1959.

von Falkenhausen, Vera. "The Greek Presence in Norman Sicily." In *The Society of Norman Italy*, ed. G. Loud and A. Metcalfe, 252–86. Leiden: Brill, 2002.

Fuchs, Robert, Ralf Mrusek, and Doris Oltrogge. "Die Entstehung der Handschrift: Materialien und Maltechnik." In *Petrus de Ebulo*, ed. Kölzer et al., 274–92.

George, H.B. *Genealogical tables Illustrative of Modern History.* 2nd ed. Oxford: Clarendon Press, 1875. Available online at http://books.google.com/

Gibbon, Edward. *The Decline and Fall of the Roman Empire*, annot. H.H. Milman. New York: Collier, 1899; new ed. intro. H. Trevor-Roper. New York: Random House, 1993.

Gillingham, John. *The Life and Times of Richard I.* London: Weidenfeld & Nicolson, 1973.

Hagemann, W. "Kaiserurkunden aus Gravina." *Quellen und Forschungen aus Italienischen Archiven und Bibliotheken* 40 (1960): 188–200.

Hampe, Karl. *Germany Under the Salian and Hohenstaufen Emperors.* Trans. and intro. R.W. Bennett. Totowa, NJ: Rowman & Littlefield, 1973.

Holweck, F.G. *A Biographical Dictionary of the Saints.* London: Herder, 1924.

Holzmann, Walter. "Maximilla Regina, soror Rogerii Regis." *Deutsches Archiv für Erforschung des Mittelalters* 19 (1964): 148–67.

Hood, Gwenyth. "Falcandus and Fulcandus, *Epistola ad Petrum, Liber de Regno Sicilie*: Literary Form and Author's Identity." *Studi Medievali*, 3rd ser., 40 (1999): 1–41.

Houben, Hubert T. *Roger II of Sicily.* Trans. Graham A, Loud and Diane Milburn. New York: Cambridge University Press, 2002.

Huillard-Bréholles, J.L.A. "Notice sur le véritable auteur du poème *De balneis Putolanis*, et sur une traduction française inédite du même poème." *Mémoires et dissertations sur les antiquités nationales et étrangères* 21 (1852): 334–53.

Jamison, Evelyn. *Admiral Eugenius of Sicily: His Life and Work and the Authorship of the Epistola ad Petrum and the Historia Hugonis Falcandi Siculi.* London: British Academy, 1957.

Jenkins, Romilly J.H. *Byzantium: The Imperial Centuries, A.D. 610–1071.* London: Weidenfeld & Sons, 1966; repr. New York: Random House, 1969.

Jochens, Jenny M. "The Politics of Reproduction: Medieval Norwegian Kingship." *American Historical Review* 92 (1987): 327–49.

Johns, Jeremy. *Arabic Administration in Norman Sicily.* New York: Cambridge University Press, 2002.

Jordan, Karl. *Henry the Lion.* Trans. P.S. Falla. Oxford: Clarendon Press,1986.

Kantorowicz, Ernst H. *Frederick the Second.* Trans. E.O. Lorimer. New York: Richard R. Smith, 1931.

———. *The King's Two Bodies.* Princeton: Princeton University Press, 1957; repr. 1997.

Kauffmann, C.M. *The Baths of Pozzuoli.* Oxford: Bruno Cassirer, 1959.

Kelly, Amy. *Eleanor of Aquitaine and the Four Kings.* Cambridge, MA: Harvard University Press, 1950.

Kelly, Thomas Forrest. *The Exultet in Southern Italy.* New York: Oxford University Press, 1996.

Kington, T.L. *The History of Frederick the Second: From Chronicles and Documents Published Within the Last Ten Years.* 2 vols. London: Macmillan, 1862. Available online at http://books.google.com/

Kölzer, Theo. "Autor und Abfassungszeit des Werkes." In *Petrus de Ebulo*, ed. idem et al., 11–13.

———. "Bildkommentar." In *Petrus de Ebulo*, ed. idem et al., 34–238 [facing pages].

———. "Die Staufer im Süden." In *Petrus de Ebulo*, ed. idem et al., 15–31.

Leger, Louis. *A History of Austro-Hungary from the Earliest Times to the Year 1889.* Trans. Mrs Birkbeck Hill. London: Rivington, 1889. Available online at http://books.google.com/

Lewis and Short. *Harper's Latin Dictionary.* New York: American Book Company, 1907.

Loud, Graham A. *The Age of Robert Guiscard.* New York: Pearson, 2000.

————. "The Papacy and the Rulers of Southern Italy." In *The Society of Norman Italy*, ed. idem and Metcalfe, 151–84.

Lyons, M.C., and D.E.P. Jackson. *Saladin: The Politics of Holy War.* New York: Cambridge University Press, 1983.

Mallette, Karla. *The Kingdom of Sicily, 1100–1250.* Philadelphia: University of Pennsylvania Press, 2005.

Manselli, R. "Aiello, Riccardo d'." In *Dizionario Biografico degli Italiani* 1: 519–20. Rome, 1960.

Martin, Janet. "Classicism and Style in Latin Literature." In *Renaissance and Renewal in the Twelfth Century*, ed. Benson and Constable, 537–68.

Masson, Georgina. *Frederick II.* London: Secker & Warburg, 1957.

Matthews, Donald. *The Norman Kingdon of Sicily.* New York: Cambridge University Press, 1992.

Metcalfe, Alex. *Muslims and Christians in Norman Sicily: Arabic-Speakers and the End of Islam.* New York: RoutledgeCurzon, 2002.

McGinn, Bernard. *The Calabrian Abbot: Joachim of Fiore in the History of Western Thought.* New York: Macmillan, 1985.

Munz, Peter. *Frederick Barbarossa: A Study in Medieval Politics.* Ithaca: Cornell University Press, 1969.

Niermeyer, J.F. *Mediae Latinitatis Lexicon Minus.* New York: Brill, 1993.

Norwich, John Julius. *The Other Conquest: The Norman Conquest of Sicily in the Eleventh Century.* New York: Harper, 1967.

————. *The Normans in the South.* London: Longman, 1967.

————. *The Kingdom in the Sun.* London: Longman, 1970.

Oxford Dictionary of Byzantium, ed. A. Kazhdan. 3 vols. New York: Oxford University Press, 1991.

Pacaut, Marcel. *Frederick Barbarossa.* Trans. A.J. Pomeranz. New York: Scribner, 1970.

Parsons, John Carmi. *Eleanor of Castile: Queen and Society in Thirteenth-Century England.* New York: St Martin's Press, 1995; repr. Palgrave Macmillan, 1997.

Peters, Edward. *The Shadow King: Rex Inutilis in Medieval Law and Literature, 751–1327.* New Haven: Yale University Press, 1970.

von Reisinger, Christoph. *Tankred von Lecce: Normannischer König von Sizilien, 1190–1194.* Cologne: Böhlau, 1992.

Riley-Smith, J.C. "Corrado." In *Dizionario Biografico degli Italiani* 29: 381–87. Rome, 1983.

Roche, T.W.E. *The King of Almayne.* London: Murray, 1966.

Runciman, Steven. *A History of the Crusades.* 3 vols. Vol. 1: *The First Crusade and the Foundation of the Kingdom of Jerusalem.* Vol. 2: *The Kingdom of Jerusalem and the Frankish East, 1100–1187.* Vol. 3: *The Kingdom of Acre.* New York: Cambridge University Press, 1951–1954.

———. *The Sicilian Vespers: A History of the Mediterranean World in the Later Thirteenth Century.* New York: Cambridge University Press, 1958; repr. 2002.

Schaff, Philip. *History of the Christian Church.* 8 vols. Available online at www.ccel.org

Schubring, Klaus. *Die Herzoge von Urslingen: Studien zu ihrer Besitz, Sozial- und Familiengeschichte mit Regesten.* Stuttgart: Kohlhammer, 1974.

Simeti, Mary Taylor. *Travels with a Medieval Queen.* New York: Farrar, Straus and Giroux, 2001.

Siragusa, G.B. *Il regno di Guglielmo I in Sicilia.* 2nd ed. Palermo: Sandron, 1929.

Stähli, Marlis. "Petrus de Ebulos 'Unvollendete' – Eine Handschrift mit Rätseln." In *Petrus de Ebulo*, ed. Kölzer et al., 247–74.

Stelten, Leo F. *Dictionary of Ecclesiastical Latin.* Peabody, MA: Hendrickson, 1995.

Takayama, Hiroshi. *The Administration of the Norman Kingdom of Sicily.* New York: Brill, 1993.

Toeche, Theodor. *Kaiser Heinrich VI.* Leipzig, 1867. Available online at http://books.google.com/

Tronzo, William. *The Cultures of his Kingdom: Roger II and the Cappella Palatina in Palermo.* Princeton: Princeton University Press, 1997.

Van Cleve, Thomas C. *Markward of Anweiler and the Sicilian Regency.* Princeton: Princeton University Press, 1937.

———. *The Emperor Frederick II of Hohenstaufen.* Oxford: Clarendon Press, 1972.

Walsh, Michael. *An Illustrated History of the Popes from Saint Peter to John Paul II.* New York: Bonanza Books, 1980.

Winkelmann, Eduard. *Philipp von Schwaben und Otto IV. von Brauschweig: Jahrbücher der deutschen Geschichte.* 2 vols. Leipzig: Duncker und Humblot, 1873–1878. Available online at http://books.google.com/

Winston, Richard. *Charlemagne: From the Hammer to the Cross.* New York: Vintage, 1954.

Wolfe, Kenneth Baxter. *Making History: The Normans and their Historians in Eleventh-Century Italy.* Philadelphia: University of Pennsylvania Press, 1995.